D1824552

Functional Perspectives on Grammar and Discourse

Studies in Language Companion Series (SLCS)

The SLCS series has been established as a companion series to *Studies in Language,* International Journal, sponsored by the Foundation "Foundations of Language".

Volume 85

Functional Perspectives on Grammar and Discourse
In honour of Angela Downing
Edited by Christopher S. Butler, Raquel Hidalgo Downing and Julia Lavid

Functional Perspectives on Grammar and Discourse

In honour of Angela Downing

Edited by

Christopher S. Butler

University of Wales, Swansea

Raquel Hidalgo Downing

Julia Lavid

Universidad Complutense, Madrid

John Benjamins Publishing Company
Amsterdam/Philadelphia

™ The paper used in this publication meets the minimum requirements
of American National Standard for Information Sciences – Permanence
of Paper for Printed Library Materials, ANSI z39.48-1984.

Library of Congress Cataloging-in-Publication Data

Functional Perspectives on Grammar and Discourse : In honour of Angela
    Downing / edited by Christopher S. Butler, Raquel Hidalgo Downing and
    Julia Lavid.
        p.   cm. (Studies in Language Companion Series, ISSN 0165–7763 ; v.
85)
        Includes bibliographical references and indexes.
        1. Grammar, Comparative and general. 2. Discourse analysis. 3.
        Functionalism (Linguistics) I. Butler, Christopher, 1945- II. Hidalgo
        Downing, Raquel. III. Lavid, Julia. IV. Downing, Angela.

        P201.F779 2007
        415--dc22   2007060661
        ISBN 978 90 272 3095 9 (Hb; alk. paper)

John Benjamins Publishing Co. · P.O. Box 36224 · 1020 ME Amsterdam · The Netherlands
John Benjamins North America · P.O. Box 27519 · Philadelphia PA 19118-0519 · USA

Table of contents

Contributors

Karin Aijmer is professor of English at Göteborg University. Among her recent publications are *Conversational routines in English. Convention and creativity* (1996) and *English discourse particles. Evidence from a corpus* (2002). She is one of the editors of *English corpus linguistics. Studies in honour of Jan Svartvik* (1991). She is the leader of the project 'Contrastive Studies in a Translation Perspective' which has the aim of carrying out cross-linguistic research on the basis of the English-Swedish Parallel Corpus. She is also responsible for the Swedish part of collecting a spoken learner corpus of advanced Swedish learners and has been involved in the collection of the Swedish component of the International Corpus of Learner English. Her research interests include text and discourse, spoken English, corpus linguistics, cross-cultural linguistics, learner English. She is currently working on a book on modal adverbs of certainty together with Anne-Marie Simon-Vandenbergen.

Bengt Altenberg is Professor (Emeritus) of English at the University of Lund, Sweden. He has written extensively on the use of English in speech and writing and is the author of *The genitive vs. the of-construction. A study of syntactic variation in 17th century English* (Lund University Press, 1982) and *Prosodic patterns in spoken English. Studies in the correlation between prosody and grammar for text-to-speech conversion* (Lund University Press, 1987). Most of his recent work has been devoted to corpus-based contrastive linguistics, comparing various aspects of English and Swedish on the basis of the English-Swedish Parallel Corpus, a bi-directional translation corpus. He has also co-edited several collections of corpus-based studies, such as *Advances in corpus linguistics. Studies in honour of Jan Svartvik* (Longman, 1991), *Languages in contrast* (Lund University Press, 1996), *Lexis in contrast* (John Benjamins, 2002) and *Advances in corpus linguistics* (Rodopi, 2004).

Enrique Bernárdez (Madrid, Spain, 1949) studied German at the Universidad Complutense, Madrid, then did postgraduate study on Dutch at the Rijksuniversiteit Groningen, The Netherlands. He has been teaching at the Universidad Complutense since 1972, since 1986 as Full Professor; he has taught English historical linguistics and Issues in Cognitive Linguistics. He has published books on general linguistics and text linguistics, and many papers on these subjects and also historical and typological language studies. He is also a translator, especially from Old and Modern Icelandic, ranging from Sagas and the Edda to such contemporary authors as Gudbergur Bergsson, Halldór Laxness and Sjón. He has been an invited professor and researcher at several universities in the UK, the US and other countries and has taught and delivered lectures at many universities in Spain and abroad.

Christopher Butler taught linguistics for 25 years in the UK, first at the University of Nottingham, then at what is now York St John University, where he held a Professorship in Linguistics. He took early retirement in order to devote more time to research and writing. He holds an Honorary Professorship in the Department for Applied Language Studies of the University of Wales, Swansea, UK, and is a member of the research group SCIMITAR (Santiago Centred International Milieu for Interactional, Typological and Acquisitional Research). He has published a number of books and more than 50 articles on a range of topics, including functional linguistics, computational and statistical techniques of language study, and corpus linguistics, especially as applied to the functionally-oriented study of English and Spanish. His latest book, *Structure and function: A guide to three major structural-functional theories* (John Benjamins, 2003) offers, in two volumes, a detailed comparison of Functional Grammar, Role and Reference Grammar and Systemic Functional Grammar.

Peter Collins is an associate-professor in Linguistics and Head of the Linguistics Department at the University of New South Wales in Sydney, Australia. He has taught linguistics at Sydney University, Macquarie University, and Rusden College in Melbourne, and served recently as Editor of the *Australian Journal of Linguistics*. His main areas of interest are grammatical theory and description, corpus linguistics, and Australian English. He was a member of the project supervised by Rodney Huddleston which produced the *Cambridge grammar of the English language* (2002). His publications include: (with Blair) *Australian English: The language of a new society* (1989); *Cleft and pseudocleft constructions in English* (1991); *English grammar* (1998); (with Lee) *The clause in English* (1999); (with Hollo) *English grammar: An introduction* (2000); (with Blair) *English in Australia* (2001) and (with Amberber) *Language universals and variation* (2002).

Kristin Davidse is Professor of English Linguistics at the University of Leuven. Her main research interest is the description of English grammar from a functional-cognitive perspective. She has published on such topics as 'ergative' and middle clauses, factive clauses, existential, attributive and identifying clauses, *it-* and *there*-clefts, and quantification and identification in the English NP.

Eirian Davies began her career working under Basil Bernstein in the Sociological Research Unit at the London University Institute of Education and then became one of the original members of the Nuffield Programme in Linguistics and English Language Teaching under Michael Halliday at University College London, contributing two papers to the first set of the Programme's publications. She has since held teaching posts at Cardiff University, and then at London University (Bedford College, subsequently Royal Holloway). Her PhD thesis (1976) was published in a revised form (1979) as, *On the semantics of syntax: Mood and condition in English* (London: Croom Helm). Her first publication was on comment adjuncts (*Transactions of the Philological Society,* 1967) and the most recent proposes a modality of telling. She has also published on topics within discourse and on legal language. She is currently (post-retirement) an Honorary Research Associate in the Department of English, Royal Holloway, University of London.

Robin Fawcett is Research Professor in Linguistics and Director of the Computational Linguistics Unit in the Centre for Language and Communication, Cardiff University. His research interests embrace linguistic theory, systemic functional linguistics in a cognitive-interactive framework, the computer modelling of language in both generation and understanding, and the description of English and other languages for these two purposes and for the analysis of texts. He has published seven books, over fifty papers in journals or as book chapters, and a similar number of research reports. Recent book publications include *Meaning and form: Systemic functional interpretations* (co-edited with M Berry, C Butler and G Huang), Ablex 1996, and *A Theory of syntax for Systemic Functional Linguistics,* Benjamins 2000. He is currently working on two major volumes: *The functional syntax handbook: Analyzing English at the level of form* and *The functional semantics handbook: Analyzing English at the level of meaning,* to be published by Equinox. He is on the Editorial Board of *Functions of Language* and is series editor for Functional Linguistics, published by Equinox.

Bruce Fraser graduated from MIT (Linguistics) in 1965 after which he served in the USAF and then became Director of the Language Research Foundation before joining the faculty of Boston University in 1971 where he is currently Professor of Linguistics and Education. His research interests lie primarily in pragmatics, where he has written extensively, most recently in the area of Discourse Markers. (Towards a theory of discourse markers. In *Approaches to discourse particles,* edited by K. Fischer. Elsevier, 2006), and the language of mediation (Pragmatic tactics in mediation. In *Studies in language: Pragmatics today* edited by P. Cap. Lang, 2005.)

T. Givón has been trying to understand language and grammar in their wider adaptive context: communicative use, neuro-cognitive processing, diachronic emergence, typological diversity, language learning and bio-cultural evolution. Among his books are: *Studies in ChiBemba and Bantu grammar* (UCLA 1972*), On understanding grammar* (Academic Press 1979), *Ute reference grammar* (Ute Press 1980), *Topic continuity in discourse* (John Benjamins 1983), *Syntax: A functional-typological introduction* (John Benjamins 1984/1990), *Mind, code and context* (Erlbaum 1989), *English grammar* (John Benjamins 1993), *Functionalism and grammar* (John Benjamins 1995), *Running through the tall grass* (a novel; Harper Collins 1997), *Syntax* (John Benjamins 2001), *Bio-linguistics* (John Benjamins 2002) and *Context as other minds* (John Benjamins 2005). He is Emeritus Distinguished Professor of Linguistics and Cognitive Science at the University of Oregon and lives near Ignacio, Colorado.

Mike Hannay is Professor of Language and ICT at the Vrije Universiteit, Amsterdam. He has mainly published in the area of Dik's Functional Grammar concerning the relation between grammar and discourse, particularly relating to the beginning of the clause and matters of clause combining. He is also interested in the application of functional linguistic insights to the teaching of advanced writing skills, and is co-author together with Lachlan Mackenzie of *Effective writing in English: A sourcebook* (Coutinho, 2002).

Laura Hidalgo Downing is a lecturer in the Department of English Studies at the Universidad Autónoma de Madrid. She is the author of the volume *Negation, text worlds and discourse. The pragmatics of fiction*, published by Ablex in 2000. She has also published in different journals in the fields of pragmatics, discourse analysis, stylistics and applications to the teaching of English as a foreign language.

Raquel Hidalgo Downing is a lecturer in linguistics in the Department of Spanish at the Universidad Complutense de Madrid. Her main areas of interest are functional grammars and pragmatics, the grammar of spoken language, conversational analysis. She is the author of the volume *La tematización en el español hablado*, published by Gredos in 2003. She has also worked and published in related areas such as contrastive linguistics and translation studies.

Michael Jordan started his career as an electrical engineer and became qualified in technical publications, marketing and corporate secretaryship before turning his hand to English language. His linguistic work concentrates on systems of continuity and meaning within and between all levels of English discourse (from morphology and complex nominal groups to paragraphs and spans), and includes details of the signalling devices used to indicate continuity and to express relational meanings. Dr. Jordan takes for granted that meaningful conclusions about language discourse can only be achieved and explained through a detailed analysis of actual language use.

Julia Lavid has recently been appointed Professor of English Philology at the Universidad Complutense, and taken up the co-editorship of the journal *Estudios Ingleses de la Universidad Complutense* – founded by Angela Downing in 1992 – in the Department of English Language and Linguistics where she has lectured for over twenty years. She was an invited research fellow at the Information Sciences Institute (ISI) of the University of Southern California (Los Angeles, USA) where she collaborated with the Natural Language Group in several projects dealing with technological applications of the contrastive and functional approach to language. During the 1990s she was the team leader of the Madrid site in several international projects funded by the Commission of the European Communities, and she has also coordinated several national projects. Together with Prof. Angela Downing, she is currently the coordinator of a research group on functional linguistics and its applications at her University. She has published extensively on a range of topics, most of them dealing with functional and contrastive linguistics (English-Spanish and other languages) and computational and corpus linguistics. She is the author of a recent book, *Lenguaje y nuevas tecnologías:*

Nuevas perspectivas, métodos y herramientas para el lingüista del siglo XXI (Ediciones Cátedra, 2005) where she offers an interdisciplinary view of the impact of new technologies on the language sciences.

J. Lachlan Mackenzie is Honorary Professor in the Faculty of Letters of the Vrije Universiteit Amsterdam (Netherlands) and works from his base in Lisbon as an Academic Consultant in Languages and Linguistics. He is a member of the international linguistics research group SCIMITAR, based in Santiago de Compostela. His work focuses on the relationship between discourse and grammar, in particular the incorporation of aspects of discourse analysis into Functional Grammar. He is also interested in exploring the implications of recent findings in studies of language production for models of grammar. He is currently, together with Kees Hengeveld, preparing a book-length presentation of recent developments in Functional Grammar, *Functional Discourse Grammar*. With Matthew Anstey, he was editor of *Crucial readings in Functional Grammar* (2005), an anthology of articles in Functional Grammar, and with María Gómez-González, of *A new architecture for Functional Grammar* (2004). He is one of the editors of the journal *Functions of Language*.

Kathleen Rymen studied Germanic Languages at The University of Leuven from 1994 till 1999. She wrote her MA-thesis on *A constructional approach to ranges: The promoted circumstance range and the cognate object range* (1999) under the supervision of Kristin Davidse. She is now working for Fortis Bank as an ESP-specialist, coordinating courses and tests for Fortis staff.

Anne-Marie Simon-Vandenbergen is Professor of English linguistics at Ghent University. She has published on various aspects of English grammar, especially modality, register variation and media discourse. Her research areas include functional linguistics and she was one of the founding editors of the journal *Functions of Language*, which she currently edits with Lachlan Mackenzie and Geoff Thompson. Her publications in this area include the co-edited volumes *Reconnecting language* (1997) and *Grammatical metaphor* (2003). She has supervised a number of research projects in contrastive linguistics, including the project which has led to the production of a *Contrastive verb valency dictionary of English, French and Dutch*. At the moment she is also co-supervisor of a new major contrastive project at Ghent University, *Meaning in between structure and the lexicon*. Her recent publications with Karin Aijmer (in *Linguistics, Journal of Pragmatics* and *Languages in Contrast*) are in the field of pragmatic markers. She is currently working on a book on modal adverbs of certainty together with Karin Aijmer.

Svilen Stanchev is Associate Professor of English Language and Linguistics at the Department of English and American Studies at the University of Veliko Turnovo, Bulgaria. He has taught at the University of Sofia and other major Bulgarian universities. His main areas of interest are Functional Grammar, syntax and semantics, and contrastive linguistics Bulgarian-English. Svilen Stanchev was awarded a Fulbright research grant at the University of California at Berkeley and taught a course in Functional Grammar at the University of Bielefeld, Germany. He has numerous publications in FG and contrastive linguistics and has given occasional lectures at the American University in Bulgaria, the University of Bielefeld and the University of Wolverhampton. In 2001 he published a book on predicate formation and transitivity in English and Bulgarian.

Andrei Stoevsky is a Senior Lecturer in the Department of English and American Studies at the University of Sofia. He teaches English morphology and syntax. His primary interests lie in the cross-linguistic examination of verbal categories, particularly in the expression of modality, temporality and aspectuality. He is also interested in the philosophy of language, pragmatics, cross-cultural influences, sociolinguistics and corpus linguistics. Some of his articles published in English include: *Tense meaning and pragmatics* (1992), *The influence of English on the Bulgarian political lexicon and problems of political lexicography* (1993), *On the use of computerized corpora of English* (1996), *Remarks on the status of the English perfect* (1999), *The perfect, perfectivity, iterativity and identity* (2000), *Nonsexist language and androcentrism* (2001), *Aspect, perception and markedness* (2001).His most recent articles, published in Bulgarian, are concerned with such pragmatic and sociolinguistic issues as terms of address, and the increased English cultural influence in Bulgaria.

Gordon Tucker is senior lecturer in the Centre for Language and Communication Research, Cardiff University, UK. After teaching systemic linguistics in an EFL context at the University of Pisa, Italy, he returned to the UK to work with Professor Robin Fawcett on a computational linguistics research project (COMMUNAL), developing and implementing a systemic functional grammar as a sentence generator, a grammar which has come to be known as the Cardiff Grammar. His research has focused primarily on lexical aspects of SFG, in an exploration of Halliday's notion of 'lexis as most delicate grammar'. His initial explorations are reported in his book, *The lexicogrammar of adjectives* (1998), published by Cassell. In his most recent work, he has sought to provide a systemic functional account of lexical expressions, phraseology and formulaic language, drawing substantially on corpus-based evidence.

Ludmila Urbanová is Associate Professor in English Language and Linguistics at the Department of English and American Studies, Faculty of Arts, Masaryk University Brno, Czech Republic. In the years 1961–1966 she studied English and German at the same university, her most influential teachers being two renowned Czech professors of English, Professor Josef Vachek and Professor Jan Firbas. After her graduation she spent 27 years at Šafárik University in Presov teaching and helping to establish a new department of English studies in East Slovakia. In 1992 she returned to her alma mater in Brno where she has been teaching linguistic theory and applied linguistics at the Pedagogical Faculty and the Faculty of Arts, doing research in the field of spoken language and fictional dialogues. Her main research interests are pragmatics, stylistics, discourse analysis and sociolinguistics.

Lieven Vandelanotte was awarded a PhD in Linguistics from the University of Leuven (Belgium) in 2005 for a dissertation entitled 'Types of speech and thought representation in English: Syntagmatic structure, deixis and expressivity, semantics'. He has published on various topics in English grammar, including prenominal adjectives, modified proper names, types of reported speech constructions, and tense in indirect speech. He is currently Lecturer in English Language and Linguistics at the University of Namur (Belgium).

Editorial introduction

Christopher S. Butler[1], Raquel Hidalgo Downing[2] and Julia Lavid[2]
University of Wales Swansea, UK[1] and Universidad Complutense de Madrid[2]

It is certainly difficult to do justice in this brief introduction to the enormous contribution of Professor Angela Downing to the advancement and promotion of functional linguistic studies, both in her home institution in Spain, and as an international scholar. As a professor of English Linguistics at the Department of English Language and Linguistics (Universidad Complutense de Madrid), she has been a pioneering figure in the introduction of functional approaches to the study of the English language and a model for many generations of Spanish linguists who followed her example.

For a period of over thirty years she has taught generations of students, becoming a key figure in the social and academic network of anglicists in Spain – a network which also had important international connections in Europe and elsewhere. Thanks to her professionalism and inspirational role, the position of professor of English Linguistics at the Universidad Complutense has acquired international prestige, stimulating local high-quality research as part of her legacy. Among her outstanding achievements at the Universidad Complutense is the foundation of the journal *Estudios Ingleses de la Universidad Complutense* (EIUC), of which she was the editor-in-chief from 1992 to 2006. At a national level she has been appointed General Editor of the journal *Atlantis*, the standard Spanish journal for Anglo-American studies.

Her scholarly output reflects a wide range of linguistic interests as a result of her independent and curious mind. Angela Downing has written on issues of English grammar and stylistics, as well as on discourse and pragmatic issues, always favouring balanced and time-tested positions and open to new linguistic ideas and developments. There is her "magnum opus", jointly written with Philip Locke, *A university course in English grammar* (Prentice-Hall International, 1992), which received The Duke of Edinburgh's Award, First Prize in the Class of Grammars and Dictionaries in 1993, and the Spanish National Research Prize awarded by the Spanish Association for English and American Studies in 1994. The influence of this textbook has been fundamental in the training of graduates in functional English grammar at Spanish Universities, especially at the Universidad Complutense. The success of this book, originally published by Prentice Hall, is evidenced by the two editions which followed, one in 2002, 10 years after the original, and a revised one in 2006, both available world-wide from Routledge.

Open to new methodologies and approaches, Angela Downing has been sensitive to corpus-based methodologies in functional studies, and to the insights provided by contrastive linguistic work, with the result of a plethora of high-quality publications which have been influential in different domains of enquiry. Thus, from semantically-oriented contributions (*get*-passives), going through her numerous publications on textually-related issues (left-dislocation, topicality, theme, information progression), and the more recent ones on interpersonal aspects (pragmatic markers), her work is well known and highly regarded in different functional linguistic circles. These include the Systemic-Functional linguistic community, the Functional Grammar community, and the so-called West Coast functionalists.

One of the main features of her personality is her capacity for work, her willingness to face challenging tasks, her self-discipline, and her ability to combine different functions and commitments. Those of us who have had the pleasure of cooperating with her in different projects, in addition, would emphasize her professionalism, and her ability to take the challenges of linguistic investigation very seriously. Those who know her best are witness to her generosity and dedication to her family, for whom she has been, in spite of her time-consuming professional activities, a loving and caring wife, mother and grandmother.

This volume is a scholarly tribute to an academic career with outstanding achievements. It is a striking reflection of the esteem in which Angela Downing is held worldwide, that friends and colleagues based in no fewer than eleven countries (Australia, Belgium, Bulgaria, Canada, the Czech Republic, the Netherlands, Portugal, Spain, Sweden, the UK and the USA) were delighted to contribute to it.

The papers in this collection are functionalist in their approach, as befits a Festschrift for a prominent proponent of functional linguistics. The main principle guiding the arrangement of the papers is Halliday's recognition of three main types of **metafunction** which language serves, and which are reflected in language patterning (see Halliday and Matthiessen 2004: 29–31). Some parts of the grammar, which Halliday terms **experiential**[1], are concerned with relationships between language and the worlds to which it refers: examples of such areas are relationships between predicates and their arguments, the linguistic encoding of various kinds of time relationship, and the resources available for referring to entities by means of simple or complex noun phrases. Other areas of the grammar are **interpersonal**, in that they are involved in the allocation of roles within the discourse and the expression of the speaker or writer's own viewpoint: here, we are dealing with areas such as speech act force, modality and attitudinal markers. Yet other parts of the grammar, those which Halliday allocates to the **textual** metafunction, serve to create a text which is cohesive within itself and coherent with respect to its environment: the concepts of theme and rheme, and the information

---

1. The experiential metafunction of language is, in Halliday's classification, part of a wider 'ideational' metafunction, which also subsumes a 'logical' subcomponent concerned with the combination of simple units into complexes.

status of entities reflected in the discourse are obvious candidates here. So are the larger-scale patterns within the discourse, including the relationships between propositions and the mechanisms for ensuring cohesion. Although the metafunctional division of the grammar proposed by Halliday is not explicitly recognized in all the papers which make up this collection, it nevertheless acts as a convenient organizing principle.

There are three papers which, while still very much concerned with a functional approach to language, are of a higher degree of generality and so do not fit easily into this classification, and we have chosen to place these at the beginning of the collection. We then come to a set of contributions which are largely oriented towards the function of language in representing the world around and within us, continuing with those which deal with textual/discoursal matters, and ending with a set of articles concerned with the expression of speech acts, modalities and attitudes. Of course, all classifications leak, and some of the papers bridge two of the functions. Where this occurs, we have endeavoured to place the paper at an interface position between others which are more easily classified. Because of the inevitable fluidity of this arrangement, we have not divided the papers into named sections.

The first of the three more general papers, by **T. Givón**, deals with grammar as the product of an adaptive evolutionary process. Givón is essentially concerned here with a cognitive account of the 'discourse context' which is the functional correlate of the grammar. Beginning with the idea that discourse context can be identified, at a deeper cognitive level, as communicative intent, Givón goes on to show how this can be recast more precisely in terms of the speaker's construction of mental models of the mind of the hearer, which are in turn concerned with assessments of the addressee's beliefs and intentions in relation to particular discourse contexts which are so frequent that they have become routinized, or grammaticalized. Givón assumes that such common discourse contexts are adaptively relevant, and much of the paper is concerned with evolution of both grammar and the 'other minds' of which the speaker needs to form models.

Christopher Butler's paper takes on the task of formulating an outline of a model of text comprehension whose grammatical component is based on a functional grammar, namely Role and Reference Grammar. Butler first describes and illustrates two important models of text comprehension: Kintsch's construction-integration model and Werth's text worlds model. Similarities and differences between these models are then discussed, and it is shown that although rather different in orientation, they are by no means incompatible. What both lack, however, is a detailed grammatical component which they can hook up to. The author discusses the properties which such a grammar should have, and then argues that Role and Reference Grammar has the required set of characteristics. A short, complete text is then examined in the light of the various parts of the model.

The third general paper, by **Andrei Stoevsky**, argues that if we are to attain true explanatory adequacy, the complexity of language, both as a system in itself and in relation to cognition and social factors, requires that we adopt an integrationist rather than a segregationist approach to language. Although the dichotomies which have dominated much of linguistic thought, such as langue/parole, synchronic/diachronic linguistics, external/internal linguistics, form/meaning still have their place, it is crucial to recognize the dialectical nature of such oppositions. Stoevsky discusses the integration of semantics, the question of linguistic autonomy, the factors contributing to language as a fast and efficient form of communication, the possibility of recognizing dynamism within a state of language, and finally the matter of degrees of explanatory adequacy with exemplification from the area of aspect.

The discussion of aspect, concerned with the internal temporal constituency of events, links Stoevsky's paper to that of **Bengt Altenberg**, who presents a detailed treatment of the expression of habitual aspect in English and Swedish. Using the English-Swedish Parallel Corpus, Altenberg first investigates the English translations of clauses using the Swedish auxiliary form *brukade*, expressing past habit. He then reverses the direction of the study, examining the translation of English *used to* into Swedish. It is shown that the choice of expressions to indicate past habit is governed by a complex array of factors, including aktionsart (state vs. activity), generic subject, temporal specification and other contextual features[2].

The paper by **Kathleen Rymen and Kristin Davidse** examines one facet of the area of transitivity, identified within Hallidayan linguistics as being concerned with the process in a clause and its attendant participants and circumstantial elements. More specifically, they subject to close scrutiny Halliday's claim that cognate complements in clauses such as *They danced the tango* and circumstantial complements in clauses such as *They climbed the stairs* represent one unified semantic role, the Range, which delimits the extent, or range, of the process. By means of a careful quantitative analysis of corpus data, Rymen and Davidse examine the two kinds of evidence which Halliday adduces for his claim: the alternations into which the constructions enter, and restrictions on the types of determiners and modifiers used. They conclude that the semantic relations of cognate and circumstantial complements to the process are rather different, and that it may be best to operate with two different categories, as is more usual in the literature on this area of the grammar.

The paper by **Enrique Bernárdez** is also concerned with the area of predicate-argument relationships. Bernárdez presents an analysis of a construction in Icelandic in which the verb *verða*, 'to become', takes an experiencer or affected argument and a

---

2.   In Halliday's classification into experiential, interpersonal and textual metafunctions of language, habitual aspect , as expressed in English by the modals *will/would* and adverbs such as *usually*, is regarded as interpersonal, forming part of the system of 'modalization' which also includes choices relating to the assessment of probability (see Halliday and Matthiessen 2004: 147). This decision appears to be motivated partly by the commonality of expression by means of modal verbs, modal adjuncts or both. However, it is by no means clear that such parallels would be found across a range of typologically diverse languages. We would contend that aspect properly belongs with tense as one facet of the coding of temporal relationships, and we therefore treat it as belonging to that part of the grammar which is concerned with the expression of our experience of the world.

lexical verb in the neuter past participle form. The meaning of this construction is similar to that of 'happen to' in English: the human experiencer is seen as not being responsible for the resulting action or process. Bernárdez situates this construction within the general area of other Icelandic constructions indicating reduced agentivity.

With **Robin Fawcett**'s paper, we move from the clause to the nominal group (Halliday's term for the noun phrase). Although the discussion ranges over choices of various functional types, it is concerned with the language/world relationship in that it deals with the selection of particular aspects of the referents of nominal groups. Fawcett presents a detailed description, in many places backed up by corpus evidence, of the semantic and functional syntactic properties of quantifying and deictic determiners, based on the concept of selection, and integrated into the 'Cardiff model' of Systemic Functional Grammar. Equally important, however, is the fact that Fawcett also discusses in some detail the methodological framework which allows him to decide which of three possible types of structure should be allocated to a given example.

Eirian Davies's contribution is also concerned with the nominal group, and presents a detailed analysis of a single example taken from a UK tabloid newspaper, with a view to establishing how far two standard accounts of the nominal group/noun phrase, Greenbaum and Quirk's *A student's grammar of the English language* and Halliday and Matthiessen's (2004) *An introduction to functional grammar* (3rd edn.), account for the premodification patterns found this example. The main difference between the two versions is Halliday's proposal that the nominal group, like the clause, shows two kinds of patterning, 'experiential' and 'logical', within the 'ideational' metafunction of the grammar. Davies argues that these two aspects of structure are not mutually independent, since the set inclusion properties of the experiential structure give rise to the features Halliday includes under logical structure.

The paper by **Lachlan Mackenzie**, on double possessive nominalizations of the type *Iraq's invasion of Kuwait*, takes us to the interface between what Halliday would regard as experiential and textual functions of language, in that such nominalizations are a way of repackaging, in the form of a noun phrase, experiential information which could have been expressed as a clause (*Iraq invaded Kuwait*). As Mackenzie demonstrates, particular types of nominalization, such as the double possessive type, are not totally equivalent to their non-nominal analogues, either semantically or syntactically. Through analysis of corpus data, Mackenzie shows that double possessive nominalizations have a range of meanings which can be linked metonymically, and that they are not freely interchangeable with full clauses, being obligatory in some contexts and expressing meanings which are not realisable in clausal form. Mackenzie's paper brings in insights from both Halliday's and Dik's functional models.

Svilen Stanchev's paper, on pronominal clitics in Bulgarian, moves us into the area of the 'textual' phenomena of Topic and Focus, analysed in terms of Dik's Functional Grammar. Stanchev shows that Bulgarian pronominal clitics have a dual function, as full pronominal forms and as grammaticalized markers pertaining to syntagmatic sequences centred on the verb. In this latter function, they are reduplicative, acting as cross-reference markers of the object. Basing his analysis on his previous work on special positions in the clause structure for pragmatically important elements, Stanchev presents an analysis of the main patterns of Topic and Focus assignment involving constructions with reduplicating clitics.

The contribution by **Mike Hannay** is also concerned with the distribution of information in the clause, now within the specific perspective of the development of writing skills in English. The paper is concerned with what, within Hallidayan linguistics, is termed multiple theme, i.e. the placing of more than one constituent in the initial, thematic area of the English clause, under the assumption that the theme extends up to and includes the first ideational element in the clause. The components of the multiple theme can be derived from the textual and interpersonal metafunctions, as well as from the ideational. For instance, Halliday and Matthiessen (2004: 81) give the example *well but then surely Jean wouldn't the best idea be to join in*, where *well, but* and *then* represent textual themes, *surely*, the vocative *Jean* and the modal *wouldn't* interpersonal themes, and *the best idea* the ideational ('topical') theme. Building on the work of Smits (2002), Hannay makes use of corpus data to identify three major patterns in written English, which he calls 'stepwise', 'focalizing' and 'grounding', and shows that Dutch learners of English, though they use all three patterns, overuse the stepwise type at the expense of the other two, when compared with native English writers. Hannay argues for the construction of example and exercise materials derived from learner corpora of English.

Michael Jordan's paper takes us into the area of the larger-scale structuring of discourse. Jordan is concerned here with interactive problem-solution structures, in which a solution proposed in order to alleviate a problem actually causes another problem for some second entity, usually but not always a second person or group of people, and more rarely the initiator of the original solution. The author discusses such structures and their associated signalling predominantly in relation to informal writing in the natural sciences, though other types of text, such as general journalism, business and politics are also discussed more briefly. Jordan suggests that interactive problem-solution structures are also central to structure and signalling in other genres, such as soap opera, sitcoms and films.

The article by **Bruce Fraser** is also concerned with the signalling of discourse relations, in this case the relations of contrast signalled by the discourse marker *instead* in English. Fraser demonstrates that two main types of relation are involved: in the 'pseudo-action' use, *instead* signals a contrastive relationship between an action which occurs and one which does not occur; while in the 'actual action' use, the relationship is between two actions which both occur. The semantic restrictions on the two types are investigated, and the author then proceeds to discuss the variant *instead of*, the relationship between *instead* and *but*, and the combination of *instead* with *and*, *but*, and *so*.

Julia Lavid's paper takes a cognitive perspective on the structuring of discourse, investigating how speakers focus their global and local attention in one type of task-oriented dialogue, those whose aim was the scheduling of an appointment. The corpus sample had already been annotated for the function of discourse segments. The analysis of global attention involves the recognition of Topic Types and Topic Shift Candidates, while the local attentional state is analysed in terms of the distribution and progression of Focal Points and the means used for their realization. Lavid points out that studies of this kind are relevant not only for the linguistic description of task-oriented conversation, but also for computational implementations in which the recognition of topics is an important task.

We now come to a group of papers which bridge the textual and interpersonal functions of language. The paper by **Raquel Hidalgo Downing and Laura Hidalgo Downing**, like that of Lavid, is concerned with topicality, this time in Spanish. These authors show that topic marking by left-dislocation in spoken Spanish serves a variety of discourse functions, not all of which are concerned with the informational status of elements in discourse. They explore the idea that topic is related not so much to 'what the utterance is about' as to the metadiscoursal function of orienting the hearer to how the utterance should be interpreted, and what may follow it. For full noun phrases, this metadiscoursal function is particularly prominent in framing and in topic reintroduction, and offers not only new information but also clues to topic sequencing. The main part of the discussion in the paper, however, concentrates on left-dislocated pronouns. Demonstrative pronouns are shown to have a textual function in processes such as closing and encapsulation, while left-dislocated first person pronouns serve an interpersonal function in introducing the speaker's own voice in the discourse.

Ludmila Urbanová's paper deals with phatic communion and small talk in the dialogues of a modern English novel. Urbanová shows that these fictional dialogues not only make use of linguistic features characteristic of authentic spontaneous conversation, such as ellipsis and loose syntactic structures, but also create new meanings which are frequently concerned with the expression of differing points of view. Small talk is seen as reflecting a broad concept of socialization, while phatic communion, which is highly context-dependent, is regarded as a more specific part of small talk.

With **Lieven Vandelanotte**'s article, we come to a final set of contributions centrally related to the interpersonal functioning of language. Through the use of corpus and web data, Vandelanotte examines what he calls 'framing' adjectives which invoke someone else's prior discourse, such as *purported*, *alleged* and *so-called*, focusing particularly on the last of these. He argues that such adjectives serve an interpersonal rather than a representational function, providing a perspectivizing overlay for units of different sizes. The author goes on to look in detail at the distribution and function of *so-called*, comparing it with adjectives of similar meaning. He shows that *so-called* is frequent, occurs across a range of registers, is not collocationally specific, and is associated with a 'dissociative' semantic prosody often directed towards the individual who designates him/herself by means of a particular term. These observations are then interpreted in terms of a process of subjectification, through which the expression loses some of its original propositional meaning and becomes a signal of a subjective meaning based on the speaker's own beliefs. Finally, Vandelanotte examines in detail the construction *Mr so-called X* in a set of examples from the internet.

Gordon Tucker's paper examines the expression of apologies using formulaic expressions with *sorry*. He points out that the grammar of such expressions is not always easy to describe in terms of a clause grammar which is intended to capture a wide range of generalizations. One solution to this problem is to see formulaic expressions as lying outside the grammar, but Tucker shows that there are many intermediate cases, in which a basically formulaic expression is elaborated in terms of resources which certainly belong to the general grammar. He goes on to examine, through the theoretical apparatus of the Cardiff version of Systemic Functional Grammar, the relationship between the form and underlying semantic/grammatical options in the area of apologizing, and to specify the formal resources called upon, in terms of the systemic networks which represent speaker choice in this area, together with functionally-motivated structures for the integrated realizations of these choices.

The article by **Anne-Marie Simon-Vandenbergen and Karin Aijmer** builds on the work of Nuyts (2001) on adjectival and adverbial realizations of modality. Using data from the British National Corpus, the authors examine two broad issues: firstly, how the constructional properties of the adjectival expressions lead to behavioural properties which are different from those of the adverbial expressions; secondly, how the adjectival realizations are used rhetorically and how their discourse function might differ from that of the adverbial expressions. Nuyts' criteria of intersubjectivity, salience, performativity and discourse strategy are all shown to be relevant, in that adjectival modalities are usually intersubjective and salient and can be descriptive, but it is also demonstrated that these factors do not always distinguish clearly between the two types of modal expression. The factor of discourse strategy proves to be important, in that adjectival and adverbial forms can be shown to be exploited rhetorically in rather different ways.

The final paper in the collection, by **Peter Collins**, is also concerned with modality in English, in this case focusing on modal and semi-modal verbs expressing prediction and volition (*will, shall, be going to/gonna, want to/wanna,* and *be about to*). Like Simon-Vandenbergen and Aijmer's article, it is based on the analysis of corpus data. Collins compares British, American and Australian data and presents quantitative analyses of both regional and stylistic variation. He shows that *want to/wanna* is not only very frequent in American English, but also that it is much more frequent in spoken than in written language. This colloquialization is seen even more strongly with *be going to/gonna*. On the other hand, *be about to* and *shall* have only low frequencies, the decline of the latter being less marked in British English than in the other two regional varieties, and in written as compared with spoken language.

From the foregoing, it will be clear that this collection of 20 papers represents an important contribution to studies of grammar, discourse and their relationships, seen primarily from a functionalist perspective. We believe that it is also a fitting tribute to a fine linguist who, through her teaching, research and publications, has been an inspiration to many generations of students and to a large number of friends and colleagues throughout the world. We join the other contributors to the book in wishing Angela a very happy – and also productive – retirement.

References

Halliday, Michael A. K. and Christian M. I. M. Matthiessen. 2004. *An introduction to functional grammar*. 3rd edn. London: Arnold.

Nuyts, Jan. 2001. *Epistemic modality, language, and conceptualization: A cognitive-pragmatic perspective*. Amsterdam: John Benjamins. [Human Cognitive Processing 5].

Smits, Aletta M. 2002. *How writers begin their sentences: the discourse functions of complex beginnings in written English.*. Utrecht: LOT. [LOT dissertation series 69].

Publications of Angela Downing

A. Books

1979   *A mosaic of Modern English: A selection of texts for advanced students*. Madrid: Sociedad General Española de Librería.

1985   *Temas y textos de C.O.U. Inglés*, + a book of exercises. Madrid: Editorial Coloquio.

1992   (with Philip Locke) *A university course in English grammar*. New York, London, Toronto, Sydney, Tokyo, Singapore: Prentice Hall International.

1998   (with José I. Albentosa and A. Jesús Moya) *Patterns in discourse and text. Ensayos de análisis del discurso en lengua inglesa*. Cuenca: Ediciones de la Universidad de Castilla-La Mancha.

2000   (with José I. Albentosa and A. Jesús Moya) *Talk and text: Studies on spoken and written discourse*. Cuenca: Ediciones de la Universidad de Castilla-La Mancha.

2002   (with Philip Locke) *A university course in English grammar* (new edition). London, New York and Toronto: Routledge.

2006   (with Philip Locke) *English grammar: A university course*. 2nd revised edition. London and New York: Routledge.

B. Articles in journals

1976   "Vacilación en el uso de los pronombres personales en inglés". *Filología Moderna* 56–58: 219–227.

1978   "La subjetivización del adverbio en el inglés". *Filología Moderna* 63–64: 213–227.

1979   "Desviación de la norma en el sistema de los pronombres relativos en inglés". *Estudios de Filología* (EFI), Anejo III. (Monografía): 1–35.

1980   "The dialects of Lancashire: some phonological features". *Atlantis* 1(2): 108–112.

1981   "Language and theme in the novels of J. Ngugi". *Atlantis* 2: 73–87.

1982   "From Quenya to the Common Speech: Linguistic diversification in J. R. Tolkien's *Lord of the Rings*. *Revista Canaria de Estudios Ingleses* 4: 23–31.

1982   "Acceptability in the English genitive noun". *Estudios de Folología* (EFI) 10: 213–228.

1983   "Strategies of verbal humour in a contemporary British novelist". *Language and Literature (LNL)* VIII, 1–3: 17–32.

1985   "The autobiography of Hamed Bin Muhamed El Murjebi, 'Tippu Tip'". *Bells* 1: 61–70.

1986   "Un tipo de relaciones sintagmáticas en inglés". *Filología Moderna* 74–76: 240–259.

1986   "Recursive premodification as a stylistic device in Iris Murdoch's *The Sea, The Sea*". *Revista Canaria de Estudios Ingleses* 10: 55–80.

1990   "The discourse function of presentative *there* in Middle English and Present-day English". *Occasional Papers in Systemic Linguistics* 4: 103–126.

1990   "Sobre el tema tópico (topical theme) en inglés". *Revista Española de Lingüística Aplicada, Anejo I: Nuevas corrientes lingüísticas. Aplicación a la descripción del inglés*, ed. by María Teresa Turell, 119–128.

1991   "La 'metáfora gramatical' de M.A.K. Halliday y su motivación funcional en el discurso". *Revista Española de Lingüística* 2(1).i: 109–123.

1991   "An alternative approach to Theme: a systemic-functional perspective". *WORD* 2(2): 119–143.

1995   "A functional grammar for students of English". Review article on T. Givón (1993) *English grammar: A function-based introduction*. Amsterdam: John Benjamins. *Functions of Language* 2(2): 229–247.

1997   "Encapsulating Discourse Topics". *Estudios Ingleses de la Unviersidad Complutense* 5: 147–168.

1998   (with JoAnne Neff, Marta Carretero, Elena Martínez-Caro and Soledad Pérez de Ayala) "Structuring and signalling topic management". *LACUS Forum* XXV: 68–91.

2001   "'Surely you knew!' *Surely* as a marker of evidentiality and stance". *Functions of Language* 8(2): 251–282.

2001   "Talking topically". *CÍRCULO* 5: 1–12.

2002   "Evaluating evaluation". Review article on *Evaluation in text. Authorial stance and the construction of discourse*, ed. by S. Hunston and G. Thompson. Oxford: Oxford University Press, 1999. Estudios Ingleses de la Universidad Complutense 10: 283–302.

2004   "Achieving coherence: Topicality, conceptualisations and action sequences in negotiating conflicting goals". *Revista Canaria de Estudios Ingleses* 49: 13–28.

forthcoming   "Discourse markers, pragmatic markers, stance markers". *Proceedings of the XXIV International AESLA Congress held at Palma de Mallorca, 10–12 March, 2005.*

C. Articles in collected volumes

1989   (with P. Locke) "Transposition and modulation processes in translation". *Estudios de filología inglesa*, ed. by Antonio León Sendra, 75–117. Córdoba: Universidad de Córdoba.

1991   "Theme within the framework of systemic functional grammar". *Estudios de filología. Homenaje a Pedro Jesús Marcos Pérez*, 27–44. Alicante: Universidad de Alicante.

1995   "Thematic layering and Focus assignment in Geoffrey Chaucer's *General Prologue to the CanterburyTales*". *Thematic development in English texts*, ed. by Mohsen Ghadessy, London: Pinter, 129–146.

1995   "Register and/or Genre?". *Current issues in genre theory*, ed. by Ignacio Vázquez-Orta and Ana Hornero, 11–27. Zaragoza: Mira.

1996   "Discourse-pragmatic distinctions of the past-in-present in English and Spanish". *Meaning and form, Systemic functional interpretations. Studies for Michael Halliday*, ed. by Margaret Berry, Christopher Butler, Robin Fawcett and Guowen Huang, 509–532. Norwood, NJ: Ablex.

1996   "The semantics of *get*-passives". *Functional descriptions: Theory in practice*, ed. by Ruqaiya Hasan, Carmel Cloran and David G. Butt, 179–205. Amsterdam and Philadelphia: John Benjamins.

1996   "Thematic progression as a functional resource in analysing texts". *Os estudios ingleses no contexto das novas tendencias*, ed. by Mª Teresa Caneda Cabrera and Javier Pérez Guerra, 23–41. Vigo: Universidad de Vigo.

1997   "The discourse-pragmatic functions of the Theme constituent in spoken European Spanish". *Discourse and pragmatics in Functional Grammar*, ed. by John H. Connolly, Roel M. Vismans, Christopher Butler and Richard A. Gatward, 137–162. Berlin and New York: Mouton de Gruyter.

1998   (with Julia Lavid) "Information processing strategies in administrative forms". *Linguistic choice across genres*, ed. by Antonia Sánchez Macarro and Ronald Carter, 99–115. Amsterdam and Philadelphia: John Benjamins.

1999   "Mismatches between English and Spanish in the use of left-dislocated constituents". *Estudios funcionales sobre léxico, sintaxis y traducción. Homenaje a Leocadio Martín Mingorance*, ed. by Silvia Molina and Mª José Feu. Cuenca, 91–104. Ediciones de la Universidad de Castilla-La Mancha.

2000   "Nominalization and Topic management in leads and headlines". *Discourse and community: Doing functional linguistics*, ed. by Eija Ventola, 354–378. Tübingen: Gunter Narr Verlag.

2002   "Topicality, coherence and interaction". *Perspectivas recientes sobre el discurso. Recent perspectives on discourse*, ed. by Ana I. Moreno and Vera Colwell, 57–82. León: Secretariado de Publicaciones de la Universidad de León.

2002   "Negotiating topic coherence through talk-in-action". *Language in function (A festschrift for Jan Firbas)*, ed. by Josef Hladký, 119–134. Amsterdam and Philadelphia: John Benjamins.

2006   "The English pragmatic marker 'surely' and its functional counterparts in Spanish". *Pragmatic markers in contrast*, ed. by Karin Aijmer and Anne-Marie Simon-Vandenbergen, 39–58. Amsterdam, Boston, Heidelberg, London, New York, Oxford, Paris, San Francisco, Singapore, Sydney and Tokyo: Elsevier.

D. Reviews

1980   Review of K. M. Petyt, *The study of dialect: An introduction to dialectology* (André Deutsch, The Language Library, 1980). *Filología Moderna* 68–70: 393–397.

1986   Review of Jennifer Coates *The semantics of the modal auxiliaries*. London: Croom Helm. *Revista Canaria de Estudios Ingleses* 12: 171–180.

1995   Review of Ronald Geluykens, *From discourse process to grammatical construction: On left dislocation in English*. Amsterdam and Philadelphia: John Benjamins, 1992. *WORD* 46(2): 269–276.

2006   Review of Douglas Robinson *Performative pragmatics*. New York and London, 2006. *Intercultural Pragmatics* 3(2): 225–237.

Grammar as an adaptive evolutionary product

T. Givón
University of Oregon

The functional correlates of grammatical constructions can be given heuristically as (i) "the discourse context within which the grammatical construction is used". They can also be given as the more cognitive-sounding (ii) "the communicative intent of the speaker using the construction". In this paper I will suggest that the cognitive-sounding definition (ii) above needs to be specified more precisely in cognitive terms, bringing it in line with more up-to-date work in cognitive neuro-science. More specifically, I will suggest that in using grammar, speakers create mental models of the knowledge (epistemic) and intention (deontic) states of their interlocutors, in a way already implicit in H. P. Grice's work. These models are created rapidly, on-line, automatically and with high specificity of the ever-shifting communicative context. The traditional pragmatic notions of "communicative context" (i) and "communicative intent" (ii) may thus be expressed more precisely in terms of so-called "Theories of Mind", i.e. the mental models socially-cooperative organisms build of the presumed mental states of their interlocutors.

1. Sociality, communication and other minds[1]

The empirical study of the functional correlates of grammar rises and falls with a certain methodology, that of observing the distribution of grammar in text, and of then seeking reliable statistical correlations between grammatical devices and *discourse contexts*. However, "discourse context" is but a methodological heuristic, a short-hand for something else, something more profound and cognitive – *communicative intent*. What I will try to do in this paper is show how the mentalistic notion "communicative intent" that is associated with the use of grammar can be recast in more precise cognitive terms as the speaker's *mental models of the mind of the hearer*.

---

1. I am indebted to Mike Posner, Don Tucker, Brian MacWhinney, David Premack, Andrew Carstairs-McCarthy, and Bernard Comrie for many helpful comments on earlier versions of the manuscript, and to Andrew Meltzoff for a timely stack of his papers. They are all, needless to say, absolved of any responsibility for the final product.

The mental models I will propose here, constructed by the speaker rapidly and subconsciously during real-time communication, pertain to the hearer's presumed states of *belief* and *intention* at specific discourse contexts. Not just any discourse context, but those contexts that are so common, so recurrent and thus presumably so adaptively relevant, that they have become conventionalized, automated or *grammaticalized*. This paper is thus, in a way, an attempt to flesh out three old programmatic observations:

- Grammar is petrified cognition (Paul 1890)
- Grammar is an automated discourse processing strategy (Givón 1979)
- Syntax is grammaticalized pragmatics (Langacker 1987)

2.   Mental models

Cognitive psychologists have long recognized three major, distinct but closely interacting systems of metal representation in the human mind/brain (Atkinson and Shiffrin 1968), given below together with their transparent communicative equivalents:

Cognitive label	Communicative equivalent
• semantic memory	the lexicon
• episodic memory	the current text
• working memory and/or attention	the current speech situation

These three systems of mental representation are known not only for their distinct cognitive-behavioral properties, but also for their specific brain locations. We will consider them in order.

2.1   Semantic ("procedural") memory

The functional properties of semantic memory and structural organization of the generic/cultural lexicon of conventionalized *types* of entities (nouns), states (adjectives) and events (verbs) have been discussed extensively in the cognitive literature (see summaries in Givón 2002, 2005). The interaction of semantic memory with episodic memory is noted below. The cortical localization of the lexical-semantic networks has been identified, albeit tentatively, as left-inferior pre-frontal cortex (Posner and Pavese 1997; Abdulaev and Posner 1997), but older sub-cortical limbic areas are also strongly implicated (Tucker 1991, 2002, Mesulam 2000). Experimental evidence strongly suggests that a single neuro-cognitive semantic network is responsible for representing both visual (pre-linguistic) and verbal (linguistic) concepts (Humphreys and Riddoch 1987, 1988, ed. 1987; Riddoch and Humphreys 1987a, 1987b; Riddoch et al. 1988). This makes perfect sense from an evolutionary perspective (Givón 2002, chs 4-5). It also parallels the cross-modal input into episodic memory (see below).

2.2   Episodic ("declarative") memory

Propositional-declarative information about *unique* events, states or individuals, or about their concatenations in longer chunks of coherent discourse, is represented in episodic memory (Kintsch and van Dijk 1978; Gernsbacher 1990; Kintsch 1982, 1994; Ericsson and Kintsch 1995). Both visual and linguistic input are represented in this system, earlier on in the sub-cortical limbic system (*hippocampus* and *amygdala;* Squire 1987; Squire and Zola-Morgan 1991; Petri and Mishkin 1994; Goodale 2000; Mesulam 2000). The limbic-based early episodic representation is the one most relevant to on-going human communication (Ericsson and Kintsch 1995); while a large capacity, the hippocampus-amygdala episodic representation is still a limited, temporary storage system. It is also an active processor where information is restructured and consolidated. For longer-term, more stable storage, episodic information must be transferred to a front-cortical area (Squire 1987; Squire and Zola-Morgan 1991).

2.3   Working memory and/or attention

Working ("short term") memory represents what is available for immediate activation by the attentional system. It thus overlaps partially with the attentional system (Schneider and Chein 2003; Posner and Fan 2004; Mesulam 2000). Working memory is a limited storage-and-processing buffer of small capacity and short duration, where material is kept temporarily activated pending further processing decisions. It has a cross-modal conscious component that interacts with the *executive attention* (Schneider and Chein 2003; Posner and Fan 2004), as well as several modality-specific non-conscious components (visual, auditory, tactile etc.; Baddeley 1986, 1992; Shallice 1988; Gathercole and Baddeley 1993; Carpenter and Just 1989; Just and Carpenter 1992; Ericsson and Kintsch 1995; Treisman 1995; Treisman and DeSchepper 1996; Treisman and Kanwisher 1998).

Material kept in the working-memory buffer must receive some type of attentional activation in order to reach longer-term episodic representation. Retrieval of information from episodic memory requires attentional re-activation, thus presumably bringing material back into some working-memory buffer. The retrieval cues may vary, depending on the type of information and the type of attentional activation that funneled the in-bound information to begin with (Treisman 1995; Treisman and Kanwisher 1998; Fernández-Duque 1999a, 1999b; Thornton and Fernández-Duque 1999).

2.4   Interaction between the three representation systems

(a) Semantic memory and episodic memory
An asymmetrical two-way relation holds between permanent semantic memory and episodic memory. First developmentally, memory traces of unique but similar

tokens of experience are presumably responsible, in collaboration with innate capacities, for the eventual construction of generic lexical concepts.

Second, in the on-line processing of unique experiences, entities, states or events are recognized as tokens of established, conventionalized generic types. Put another way, semantic memory must be co-activated with episodic memory if episodic traces of unique entities, states or events are to be meaningful.

(b) **Working memory/attention and episodic memory**

The interaction between working memory and episodic memory may be given schematically as flow chart (1):

(1)

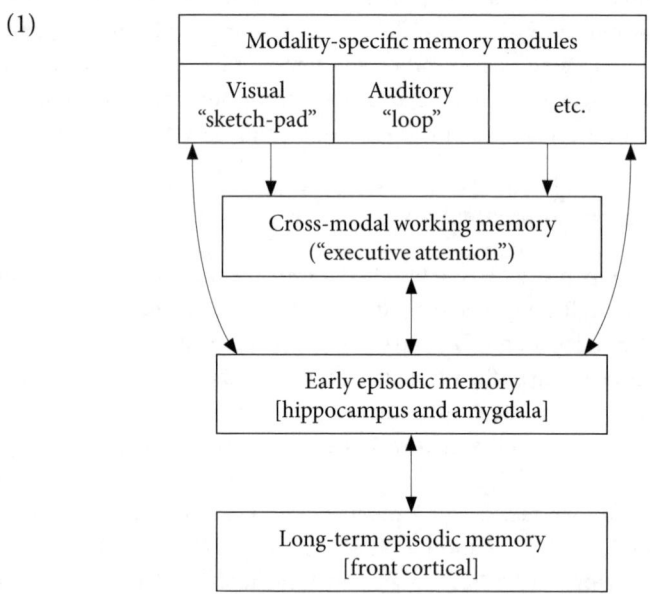

Other aspects of the interaction between working memory and episodic memory are discussed in Ericsson and Kintsch (1995).

3.   Grammar

3.1   An adaptive evolutionary perspective

Grammar is probably the latest evolutionary addition to the mechanisms that drive human communication (Givón 1979; 2002, ch.4; Lieberman 1984; Bickerton 1981, 1990; Li 2002). While the evolutionary argument remains conjectural, it is supported by a body of suggestive evidence.

Ontogenetically, children acquire the lexicon first, using pre-grammatical (pidgin) communication before acquiring grammar (Bloom 1973; Bowerman 1973; Scollon

1976; Givón 1979, 1990). Likewise, natural second language acquisition follows the same course, though most often it stops short of grammaticalization (Bickerton 1981, 1990; Bickerton and Odo 1976; Selinker 1972; Schumann 1976, 1978, 1985; Andersen 1979; Givón 1979, 1990).

A well-coded lexicon can be acquired by many non-human species (Premack 1971; Gardner and Gardner 1971; Fouts 1973; Terrace 1985; Savage-Rumbaugh et al. 1993, 1998; Savage-Rumbaugh and Lewin 1994; Pepperberg 1991, 1999; Tomasello and Call 1997; inter alia). This supports the suggestion that the neuro-cognitive structures which underlie semantic memory are old pre-human, pre-linguistic structures (Givón 2002, chapter 4). In contrast, the communicative natural use of grammar in non-human species has never been attested, nor has any success in teaching grammar to non-human species been reported (Premack 1971; Terrace 1985; Pepperberg 1991, 1999; Tomasello and Call 1997; Hauser 2000). Grammar as we know it seems a uniquely human capacity.

3.2   Grammar as structure

As a symbolic code, grammar is much more complex and abstract than the sensory-motor codes of the lexicon. At its most concrete, the primary grammatical signal involves four major coding devices:

(2) **Primary grammar-coding devices**:
- Morphology
- Intonation:
  - clause-level melodic contours
  - word-level stress or tone and melody
- Rhythmics:
  - pace or length
  - pauses
- Sequential order of words or morphemes

Some of the primary coding devices (morphology, intonation) are more concrete, involving the same sensory-motor channels that code the lexicon. But these concrete devices are integrated into a complex whole with the more abstract elements of the code (rhythmics, sequential order) that are, in all likelihood, second- or third-order constructs.

The most concrete element of the grammatical code, grammatical morphology, is a diachronic derivative of lexical words (Givón 1971, 1975, 1979; Traugott and Heine 1991; Heine et al. 1991; Hopper and Traugott 1993; Bybee et al. 1994; inter alia).

The primary grammar-coding devices in (2) are in turn used to signal yet more abstract levels of grammatical organization:

(3) **More abstract levels of the grammatical code**:
- Hierarchic constituency
- Grammatical relations (subject, object)

- Syntactic categories (noun, verb, adjective; noun phrase, verb phrase)
- Scope and relevance relations (operator-operand, noun-modifier, subject-predicate)
- Government and control relations (agreement, co-reference, finiteness)

3.3   Grammar as adaptive function

The great complexity and abstractness of grammar is due, inter alia, to the complexity of its functional interaction with many other language-processing modules. It interacts intimately with semantic memory, propositional semantics, episodic memory (discourse coherence), working memory and attention, and with Broca's area.

The functional correlates of grammar have been ill understood until fairly recently, due to an entrenched methodology of studying grammatical structures in isolation from their natural communicative context. Once grammar is studied in its natural adaptive context, the communicative functions of both constructions and morphology can be shown to be highly specific (Givón 2001). However, the systematic deployment of grammar to signal mental representation of other minds is often obscured in functionalist work. This is sometimes due to entrenched traditional terminology. In other instances, it is due to an incipient empiricist mind-cast of mistaking text distributions and textual contexts for communicative functions (Givón 1995, chapter 7).

The discourse-coherence communicative functions coded by grammar can be re-interpreted, rather transparently, as *perspective-shifting* operations (MacWhinney 1999, 2002), and those, in turn, can be further re-interpreted as systematic manipulation (in production) or anticipation (in comprehension) of the interlocutor's current states of belief and intention.

The most common discourse-pragmatic domains coded by grammar are listed in (4) (Givón 2001).

(4) **Discourse-pragmatic functions of major grammatical systems**

Structures	Functions
NP grammar	**Referential coherence**
a. Grammatical relations	referential coherence
b. Definiteness, reference	referential coherence
c. Anaphora, pronouns	referential coherence
d. Deictics	referential coherence
e. Pragmatic voice	referential coherence
f. Topicalization	referential coherence
g. Relativization	referential coherence, event grounding
h. Focus and contrast	referential coherence, grounding

VP grammar	Event coherence
i. Tense	temporal grounding of event
j. Aspect	aspectual grounding of event
k. Modality	epistemic-deontic grounding of event
l. Speech acts	epistemic-deontic grounding of event to speaker/hearer

Cross-clausal grammar	Event/chain coherence
m. Inter-clausal connectives	event grounding, chain grounding
n. Chain-initial adverbials	chain grounding
o. Presentative constructions	referential grounding, chain grounding

As can be seen in (4), some grammatical systems can function in more than one discourse-pragmatic domain. Thus, for example, relativization (4g) and contrastive focus (4h) are part of the grammar of both referential coherence and event coherence. Tense (4i), aspect (4j) and modality (4k) are used to signal both temporal-aspectual-modal grounding and event coherence. And the grammar of inter-clausal connectives (4m) integrates devices that signal both referential coherence and event-coherence, albeit often at higher hierarchic levels.

3.4   Communication without grammar

The adaptive function of grammar comes into sharper relief when one notes that humans can, in some developmental, social or neurological contexts, communicate without grammar. In such context, they use the well-coded lexicon together with some rudimentary combinatorial rules. That is, they use *pre-grammatical* pidgin communication (Bloom 1973; Bowerman 1973; Scollon 1976; Bickerton 1981, 1990; Bickerton and Odo 1976; Selinker 1972; Schumann 1976, 1978, 1985; Andersen 1979; Menn 1990; Givón 1979, 1990). In reference to one such context, early child communication (ca. 18 months of age), Bowerman (1973) observes:

> ...early child speech is "telegraphic" – that is consists of strings of content words like nouns, verbs, and adjectives, and lacks inflections, articles, conjunctions, copulas, prepositions and post-positions, and, in general, all functors or "little words" with grammatical but referential significance... (Bowerman 1973: 3-4)

In the absence of morpho-syntactic structure, the bulk of coded clues for establishing text coherence in pre-grammatical discourse, above and beyond situational inferences (Kintsch 1992), are furnished by the lexicon. But a small component of *proto-grammar* is already evident in pidgin communication. The below-generative regularities of proto-grammar are cognitively transparent (iconic) and highly universal (Haiman 1985a, 1985b; Givón 1990). Neither the lexical clues nor proto-grammar disappear in fluent grammatical communication of native adults; rather, vocabulary-cued processing remains a parallel channel alongside grammar (Kintsch 1992; Givón 1990). And the conventions of proto-grammar are integrated with the more conventional rules of grammar, a process observed in both language diachrony and language ontogeny, and may indeed recapitulate the course of language evolution (Givón 1979: chapter 5; 2002: chapter 4).

The major differences between pre-grammatical (pidgin) and grammatical communication are summed up in chart (5).

(5) **Pre-grammatical vs. grammatical communication** (Givón 1979; 1989)

Properties	Grammatical	Pre-grammatical
STRUCTURAL:		
a. Morphology	abundant	absent
b. Constructions	complex, embedded	simple, conjoined
c. Word-order	grammatical (subj/obj)	pragmatic (topic/comment)
d. Pauses:	fewer, shorter	copious, longer
FUNCTIONAL:		
e. Processing speed	fast	slow
f. Mental effort	effortless	laborious
g. Error rate	lower	higher
h. Context dependence	lower	higher
i. Processing mode	automated	attended
j. development	later	earlier
k. consciousness	sub-conscious	more conscious

The heavy dependency of pidgin communication on lexical vocabulary tallies with the fact that lexicon is acquired before grammar in both first and second language acquisition, as well as with the fact that more abstract vocabulary is the diachronic precursor of grammatical morphology in grammaticalization. Pre-grammatical children, adult pidgin speakers and agrammatic aphasics comprehend and produce coherent multi-propositional discourse, albeit at slower speeds and higher error rates than those characteristic of grammatical communication. The identification of grammar with a more automated, speeded-up language processing system has been suggested in Givón (1979, 1989), Blumstein and Milberg (1983), and Lieberman (1984).

4.   Grammar and other minds

4.1   The mental representation of context

In evolving its lexical and grammatical codes, human language had liberated itself, albeit only partially, from the tyranny of paying constantly attention to context. This partial liberation involved two separate waves of partial automation of language processing, whereby the two codes – lexical phonology and grammar – now automatically activate mental structures that represent, systematically and reliably, the most relevant, recurrent and frequently-accessed aspects of the communicative context. As a result, language production and comprehension is now faster, less error-prone, and less dependent on limited attentional resources.

Three distinct types of context are accessed repeatedly during human communication, and are thus good candidates for automation. The three correspond, rather transparently, to the three neuro-cognitive representation systems noted in section 2 above:

(6)   **Context types as cognitive representation systems**:

Context	Representation system
• The shared generic knowledge	semantic/lexical memory
• The shared speech situation	working memory/attention
• The shared current text	early episodic memory

In this section, I will begin to flesh out the claim that grammar is used systematically during on-line communication to activate mental representations of the interlocutor's current states of belief and intention. The more traditional pragmatic terminology for tapping into the mind of the interlocutor is that of *shared context*; that is, the assumption that the mental representation that is currently activated in my mind is also concurrently activated in yours. Within such a framework, the three types of contexts in (6) represent three types of *grounds* that justify the assumption of shared context during on-line communication.

In the space below we examine only a small set of examples illustrating the role of grammar in accessing the three types of mental representations in (6). For a more extensive discussion and illustration of this framework, see Givón (2005: chapters 4, 5, 6, 7). Our first demonstration involves the grammar of definite description.

4.2   Access to definite referents

In using definite grammatical cues, a speaker assumes that the referent, while not necessarily currently activated, is nonetheless mentally *accessible* to the hearer. Such accessibility may depend on at least one of the three cognitive systems which can represent the *shared context*. A definite referent is thus *grounded* to at least one of those representation systems.

4.2.1   *Grounding referents to the shared semantic lexicon*

As noted earlier, the culturally-shared generic lexicon is coextensive with semantic/ lexical memory. During on-line communication, different nodes in this representational system in the mind of the hearer are activated by the speaker's use of different lexical words. Some of these words, however, are not generic (do not represent a type), but rather have a unique referent which is *globally accessible* to all members of the relevant social unit. Part of knowing the meaning of the word is knowing that it has such a unique referent. In using such a word, a speaker needs only to mark it with a *definite* grammatical marker ("the"), which then signals to the hearer that there is no need to search further for unique reference. The automatically-activated lexical node itself will suffice.

(7)   **Globally-accessible definite referents**:

Referent	Relevant social unit
a. **The sun** came out.	all humans
b. **The president** has resigned.	a nation-state
c. They went to **the cemetery**.	a community
d. **The river** is frozen over.	a community
e. Call **the sheriff**!	a county
f. **The Gods** must be angry.	a religion
g. **Daddy** is home!	a family

The cuing of unique reference through grounding in the shared generic lexicon may also involve a mixed access system. In such a system, one referent is activated first via another type of shared context. Another referent is then activated automatically as a connected node of the first. This hybrid referential access is sometimes called *frame-based* or *script-based* (Anderson, Garrod and Sanford, 1983; Yekovich and Walker, 1986; Walker and Yekovich, 1987). Thus consider the examples in (8):

(8)   **Double-grounded "frame-based" definite referents**:
   a. My boy missed school today,
        he was late for the bus.
   b. She showed us this gorgeous house,
        but the living room was too small.
   c. She went into a restaurant
        and asked the waiter for the menu.

The word *school* in (8a) automatically activates its cluster of connected nodes ("frame"), including in this culture *bus*. The word *house* (8b) automatically activates its cluster of connected nodes, among them *living room*. The word *restaurant* automatically activates, among others, *waiter* and *menu*. The speaker uses the definite article with the expectation that those concepts are accessible, in this case also activated, in the hearer's mind.

4.2.2   *Grounding referents in the shared speech situation*

When we share the same speech situation with others, referents within that space-time grid are, at least in principle, equally accessible to all present on the scene. This entitles speakers to assume that information which is accessible to them in the immediate speech situation, via visual or auditory channels, is also accessible to others who share the same space-time grid. This is nothing but a mundane application of the old principle of *reasoning by feature association* (Givón 2002, 2005):

> Since both I and my interlocutor share the same speech situation, then if I have a mental model of entities present in that speech situation, my interlocutor must have the same mental model.

In the grammar of definite reference, a number of well-known examples exist where the assumption of unique reference depends on equal access in the current speech situation. They all fall under the general label of *deixis*. The most common ones are shown in (9):

(9) a. **Interlocutors**:
         *I am telling **you** that...*
     b. **Other referents**:
         *No, she doesn't want **this** book, she wants **that** one.*
     c. **Location**:
         *There was no room for them **there**, so they came **here** instead.*
     d. **Time**:
         *He wanted to come **then**, but I told him to wait till **now**.*

4.2.3   *Grounding referents in the shared current discourse*

By far the most common grounds for assuming that a referent is currently accessible to the interlocutor involves our assumption that the just-transacted current discourse is just as mentally accessible to our interlocutor as it is to us. That is, we assume that a mental trace of the just transacted current text exists, and is accessible, in our interlocutor's *episodic memory*.

When a referent is introduced into the discourse for the first time, the speaker assumes the existence of no such mental trace, and therefore marks the referent grammatically as *indefinite*. Subsequently, if the referent is deemed to be still accessible, various *definite* grammatical devices may be used, depending on further details of the discourse context. As a simple illustration, consider the short narrative in (10) below[2].

---

2.   For a more detailed discussion of this topic, see Givón (2001a: chapters 9, 10; 2005: chapter 5).

(10)   a. *There was **a man** standing near the bar,*
  b. *but we ignored **him** and went on across the room,*
  c. *where **another man** was playing the pinball machine.*
  d. *We sat down and ordered a beer.*
  e. ***The bar tender** took his time,*
  f. *I guess **he** was busy.*
  g. *So we just sat there waiting,*
  h. *when all of a sudden **the man standing next to the bar** got up and...*

In marking *man*, introduced for the first time in (10a), with the indefinite *a*, the speaker cued the hearer that he doesn't expect him/her to have an episodic mental trace of the referent. In coding the same referent with the anaphoric pronoun *him* in (10b), the speaker assumes that the referent is not only accessible, but is still *currently activated*.

Another referent is introduced for the first time in (10c), this time with the indefinite marker *another*. On the other hand, *the bar tender* is introduced for the first time in (10e) – but marked as *definite*. This is so because the prior discourse had activated *bar*, which then remained activated by the persistence of the narrated situation. And *bar tender* is an automatically-activated connected node of the lexical frame *bar* (see (8) above).

The continued reference with the anaphoric pronoun *he* in (10f) again indicates the assumption that the referent is both accessible and currently activated.

Finally, the man introduced first in (10ab), absent for five intervening clauses, is re-introduced in (10h). The use of a definite article suggests that the speaker assumes that this referent is still accessible to the hearer, but that the hearer's search in episodic memory is not going to be simple. Another man has been mentioned in the intervening (10c) as *playing the pinball machine*. Both referents are assumed to be still accessible, and would thus compete for the simple definite description *the man*. To differentiate between them, a *restrictive relative clause* is used, matching *standing next to the bar* in (10h) with the proposition *a man standing near the bar* in (10a). In using this grammatical cue, the speaker reveals his/her assumption that the hearer still has an episodic trace of both the referent and the proposition in (10a).

4.3   Access to epistemic and deontic states

The narrative example in (10) reveals another important feature of our presumption of access to other minds: Our mental model of the interlocutor's mind shifts constantly, from one clause to the next, during live communication. As speakers release more information, they constantly update what they assume that the hearer knows. They thus seem to possess a shifting mental model of the hearer's labile *epistemic* (knowledge) states. In this section we will show that speakers also possess, equally, a shifting mental model of the hearer's labile *deontic* (intentional) states.

The deontic (and epistemic) states we will consider here may be cued by several grammatical sub-systems, the bulk of which are discussed elsewhere (Givón 2005: chapter 6). The most conspicuous of these sub-systems, and the easiest to illustrate, is the grammar of *speech-acts*.

The study of speech-acts has traditionally centered on a set of *felicity conditions* (or *use conventions*) associated with the various speech-acts (declarative, imperative, interrogative, etc.). These conventions have had an illustrious history in post-Wittgensteinean philosophy and linguistics (Austin 1962; Searle 1970; Cole and Morgan eds 1975; *inter alia*). They are also known as *conventional implicature* (Grice 1968/1975; Levinson 2000).

As an illustration, consider the somewhat schematic but still plausible dialogue between speakers A and B in (11):

(11) A-i: *So she got up and left.*
      B-i: *You didn't stop her?*
      A-ii: *Would you?*
      B-ii: *I don't know. Where was she sitting?*
      A-iii: *Why?*
      B-iii: *Never mind, just tell me.*

In the first conversational turn (11A-i), speaker A executes a *declarative* speech-act, which involves, roughly, the presuppositions about hearer B's current mental states (in addition to the speaker's own mental states) shown in (12):

(12) a. **Speaker's belief about hearer's epistemic state:**
         • Speaker believes hearer doesn't know proposition (11A-i).
         • Speaker believes hearer believes that speaker speaks with authority about proposition (11A-i).
      b. **Speaker's belief about hearer's deontic state:**
         • Speaker believes hearer is well-disposed toward the speaker communicating to him/her proposition (11A-i).
      c. **Speaker's own epistemic state:**
         • Speaker believes he/she knows proposition (11A-i).
      d. **Speaker's own deontic state:**
         • Speaker intends to inform hearer of proposition (11A-I).

In the next turn (11B-i), B, now the speaker, executes an *interrogative* speech-act (yes/no question), which involves, roughly, the presuppositions about hearer A's current mental states (as well as the speaker's own) shown in (13):

(13) a. **Speaker's belief about hearer's epistemic state:**
         • Speaker believes hearer knows the declarative proposition underlying question (11B-i).
         • Speaker believes hearer knows speaker does not know that proposition.

    b. **Speaker's belief about hearer's deontic state:**
      • Speaker believes hearer is willing to share their knowledge of that
        proposition.
    c. **Speaker's own epistemic state:**
      • Speaker is not certain of the epistemic status of the proposition under-
        lying (11B-i).
    d. **Speaker's own deontic state:**
      • Speaker would like hearer to share their knowledge with him/her.

In turn (11Biii), lastly, speaker B executes a *manipulative* speech-act which involves, roughly, the presuppositions about hearer A's current mental states (as well as the speaker's own) shown in (14):

(14) a. **Speaker's belief about hearer's epistemic state:**
        • The hearer believes the hearer knows that the desired event (*You tell
          me*) is yet unrealized.
      b. **Speaker's belief about hearer's deontic state:**
        • Speaker believes hearer is capable of acting so as to bring about the
          desired event.
        • Speaker believes hearer is well-disposed toward acting to bring about
          the desired event.
      c. **Speaker's own epistemic state:**
        • Speaker believes the desired event (*You tell me*) is yet unrealized.
      d. **Speaker's own deontic state:**
        • Speaker would like the event (*You tell me*) to come about.

At every new turn in the conversation of (11), not only do the speaker's own belief-and-intention states change, but also his/her mental representation of the hearer's belief-and-intention states. And one would assume that a similar fast-paced adjustment also occurs in the hearer's mental model of the speaker's belief-and-intention states.

5. The selectivity of mental models

Earlier above (section 3.4) we noted that focal attention and working memory are both a highly selective entry channel into longer-term episodic representation. What is more, this selectivity makes episodic memory itself a highly selective repository of past experience, be it visual or verbal. We also noted, (section 3.4, example (10)) that grammar bears all the marks of a highly automated processing system. And one of the hallmarks of automation is decreased reliance on the conscious *executive attention* system.

Fluent speakers of human language are notoriously bad at giving a conscious account of why they have just used a particular grammatical construction. They are equally unreliable, with minor exceptions, at episodic recall of the grammatical form of just-produced discourse – once that discourse has left the short-term working-memory buffer (Barker 2004). Grammar is just like any other *skilled performance* executed by an *expert*. And as Socrates has discovered to his chagrin and eventual sorrow (and reported in both *Meno* and the *Apology)*, experts are too skilled to know how or why they do things. They just do them.

Only few grammatical sub-systems can be recalled reliably from a just-concluded discourse (Barker and Givón 2003); otherwise, the rapid, fluent deployment of grammatical form is relatively sub-conscious. One can recall it only as long as the utterance remains within the short range of the working-memory buffer (auditory loop, visual sketch-pad; Gernsbacher 1985; Gathercole and Baddely 1993). Beyond that range, grammar is not, by and large, consciously retrievable from episodic-memory (Barker and Givón, forthcoming).

The subliminal nature of grammar, ever-present but seldom recalled[3], contrasts sharply with lexical and propositional information, which speakers tend to attend to consciously, store reliably in, and retrieve consciously from, episodic memory (Kintsch and van Dijk 1978; Gernsbacher 1985; Dickinson and Givón 1997; Barker and Givón 2003; Barker 2004). By automating a processing system, one tends to bar conscious access to it. The material can still be stored in a long-term bin, but it cannot be retrieved with conscious cues (Treisman 1995; Bar and Biderman 1998).

We have noted above, albeit only sketchily, that grammatical constructions are systematically associated with speakers' explicit mental models of their interlocutors' shifting epistemic and deontic states. This is the only way the systematic communicative use of grammar can be explained. What is more, these mental models are by-and-lange sub-conscious. But why?

Two complementary explanations suggest themselves:

- **Automaticity**: The speaker's shifting mental models of their own and the hearer's shifting mental states are constructed automatically, implicitly and subconsciously. Like other information reaching episodic memory without conscious attention, these mental models are inaccessible to conscious verbal recall, even if they do have episodic traces (Treisman 1995; Treisman and Kanwisher 1998; Fernández-Duque 1999a, 1999b; inter alia).

- **Irrelevance**: Much of the information about the speaker's *and* hearer's shifting epistemic and deontic mental states is wholly irrelevant at any point in the discourse *except* during the fleeting moment of processing a particular conversational turn or clause. Storing that information in longer-term episodic memory, and making it consciously accessible at any other time, would serve no useful purpose. Indeed, it might interfere with the mental representations which are relevant at *that* – later – time.

---

3.   When Xenophon went to Delphi to consult the oracle prior to departing for his ill-fated *Anabasis*, the Pythia is reputed to have said: "Invoked or uninvoked, the God [Apollo] will be there". Grammar seems to enjoy the same measure of behind-the-scenes ubiquity.

These explanations also hold for why grammatical form itself is not stored in and re-trieved from episodic memory, at least not consciously:

- Its activation and use are automatic; and
- It is relevant only in the discourse context in which it was originally transacted.

The coherence structure of discourse is profoundly reshuffled in early episodic mem-ory (Loftus 1980; Gernsbacher 1990; Ericsson and Kintsch 1995; Dickinson and Givón 1997; Barker and Givón 2003; Barker 2004). Recalling propositions from episodic memory clad in the same grammatical garb with which they entered would be an adaptive distraction (Givón 1995: chapter 8). Grammar as a language-processing de-vice is but a means to an end, an input/output *translation code*. What is stored in the hearer's episodic memory, in addition to lexical and propositional information, is not grammatical structure itself, but what it stands for – the *coherence structure* of multi-propositional discourse (Gernsbacher 1990). To echo Wittgenstein's ladder metaphor, once grammar has been used to get us where we need to go (coherent episodic repre-sentation), it is discarded: for excellent adaptive reasons.

6.   Other minds in an evolutionary perspective

6.1   Overview

The discussion of so-called *Theories of Mind* was launched with a prescient article by Premack and Woodruff (1978) titled "Does the chimpanzee have a theory of mind?" While largely programmatic, Premack and Woodruff's article was brimming with theo-retical and methodological insights. In a concluding line which anticipates empiricist objections, Premack and Woodruff (1978) suggested, perhaps tongue in cheek:

> Moreover – and we add this with more than facetious intent – it would waste the behaviorist's time to recommend *parsimony* to the ape. The ape could only be a mentalist. Unless he is intelligent enough to be a behaviorist (1978: 526; italics added).

The evolutionary import of the 1978 article was clear from the start, be it from the cross-species or cross-developmental comparative orientation, be it from the una-bashed invocation of "naturalness" or "primitiveness" as key element in the mentalist account of inferences of other minds:

> The important point here is that assigning mental states is not a sophisticated or advanced act but a primitive one (1978: 525). [...] Having decided that behav-iorism is *unnatural* because it requires suppressing *primitive inferences*, whereas theories of mind are *natural* (1978: 526; italics added).

The intensive discussion that follows has engendered too vast a literature for me to be able to review exhaustively here. The literature may be divided, roughly and with a generous allowance for overlaps, into six more-or-less distinct bins:

(a) **Theory of mind in human adults:**
Gopnik and Wellman (1994); Whiten (ed. 1991); Dunbar (1998); Malle *et al.* (eds. 2000), Fussell and Kreutz (eds 1998); inter alia.

(b) **Children's theory of mind:**
Wellman (1990); Gopnik & Wellman (1992); Bartsch and Wellman (1995); Povinelli and de Blois (1992); Meltzoff (1999, 2002a, 2002b); inter alia.

(c) **Autistic (children's) theory of mind:**
Baron-Cohen (1995); Leslie and Frith (1988); Pener *et al.* (1989); Morton *et al.* (1991); inter alia.

(d) **Non-human primates' theory of mind:**
Povinelli & Preuss (1995); Povinelli and Eddy (1996a, 1996b, 1996c); Povinelli et al. (1990, 1992) Tomasello (1996); Tomasello and Call (1997); inter alia.

(e) **Theory of mind and the brain:**
Dunbar (1998); Baron-Cohen (2000); Morton et al. (1991); Meltzoff (2002b); inter alia

(f) **Evolution of theory of mind:**
Byrne and Whiten (eds.1988); Povinelli & Preuss (1995); Mithen (1996); Dunbar (1998); Byrne (1998); Baron-Cohen (2000); Meltzoff 2002b; Meltzoff and Prinz (eds 2002); inter alia.

In her critical review of the research that imputes theories of minds to non-human primates, Heyes (1998) chose to take Premack and Woodruff at their literal word, interpreting their closing lines as a *parsimony* argument in philosophy of science. She pointed out, I think correctly, that Occam's Razor is hardly a winning argument in science, given that all other things are seldom equal. Her loud protestations notwithstanding, Heyes' review is a spirited articulation of the traditional behaviorist rejection of mental categories. Now reluctantly conceded to humans, mental models of other minds – indeed of one's own mind – are still denied to our nearest kin. Heyes lists the behaviors that have been proposed as evidence for theories of mind in non-human primates:

- imitation
- self-recognition
- social relationships
- deception
- role-taking
- perspective-taking

Then she argues that in each case, a simpler, traditional *associationist* explanation accounts for the observed behavior[4].

---

4.   It seems to have never occurred to Heyes that her argument is a classical parsimony one, of the type she faults Premack and Woodruff (1978) for.

As many of the Heyes' peer commentators noted at the time, the criterial bar she holds up is so high that only organisms capable of *verbal articulation* of their theories of mind could possibly clear it (Gray and Russell 1998; Slaughter and Mealey 1998)[5], and perhaps not even those (Gordon 1998; Kamawar and Olson 1998).

Spirited empiricism aside, much of the Theory of Mind literature since Premack and Woodruff's clarion call has been plagued by four abiding and to my mind questionable, assumptions about mental models in general and mental models of other minds in particular. These assumptions have not always been explicit, but they nonetheless insinuate themselves into much of the discussion by *bona fide* mentalists.

(a) **Gapped evolution**: The Theory of Mind literature, including Heyes' own review, reveals a clear if sometime implicit Cartesian bias. It attempts, whether in cross-species or cross-developmental comparisons, to draw too sharp a line between species or developmental stages that have Theories of Mind, and those that don't. In the same breath, too sharp a line is drawn between mental capacities which qualify as Theory of Mind and those which don't. Whether intended or not, the discussion thus presupposes a profoundly non-Darwinian, non-gradualistic model of gapped evolution (Eldredge and Gould 1972). This model has been largely rejected by evolutionary biologists (Lande 1980, 1986).

(b) **Mega-modularity**: A natural concomitant of gapped evolution is an assumption, sometime implicit, that has bedeviled Evolutionary Psychology from the very start: that the emergence of complex new mental capacities must perforce involve the concomitant emergence of brand new brain structures or mega-modules. This assumption disregards the two most common developmental trends in evolution, including brain evolution:

- **Terminal modification**: The gradual modification of an extant module to perform, at least initially, *both* its old function and a similar-but-not-identical new function.
- **Distributiveness**: The assembly of complex new modules from pre-existing simple ones, whereby the novelty is not the structures themselves, but their coordinated, *spatio-temporally distributed* activation pattern.

(c) **(Self-) Consciousness**: The third silent partner in the discussion, invoked from the very start by the label "Theory of Mind" itself, is a strong bias toward conscious – indeed self-conscious – mental models of both one's own mind and the mind of the interlocutor. This bias again flies in the face of the vast neuro-cognitive literature which

---

5.   This is, in essence, how older children managed to clear the bar, by being able to furnish verbal accounts of their theories of minds.

documents the existence of unattended, subconscious mental models, as well as the complex interaction between attention and automaticity[6].

(d) **Categorization and mental models**: Lastly, the Theories of Mind literature has tended, on the whole, to not avail itself of what is known about human categorization, and about the three neuro-cognitive capacities which serve as the most common repositories of mental models: Semantic memory, episodic memory and working-memory-cum-attention.

My own take on the subject tends in the opposite direction from gapped evolution, mega-modularity and self-consciousness, harkening back to Premack and Woodruff's (1978) original gut instincts, that:

- The "primitive" mechanisms that license what appears to be inferences about other minds are old and well entrenched evolutionary precursors to both conscious (2nd-order) and self-conscious (3rd-order) mental representation.
- That such evolutionary precursors (or pre-adaptations) contributed to an incremental development of mental models, first of one's internal somatic states, then of one's visceral-emotional states, then of one's mind, and lastly of other minds.
- That as a result of this gradual incrementation, the neural mechanisms that support our more complex, higher-order mental models may well be distributive and multi-modular.
- And that the role of consciousness and executive attention must be examined as one component within the complex, multi-step development of these mental models.

The latter point is particularly important because grammar, the most complex and sophisticated – and most likely the most recent – evolutionary addition to the tool-kit of human representation and communication, is by and large a subconscious, automated processor of our mental models of other minds.

6.2   "Reasoning" by feature association: The wrong metaphor?

As noted elsewhere (Givón 2005: chapter 2), reasoning by feature association is an ancient, entrenched concomitant of biologically-based categorization. It is part of the adaptive motivation for the evolution of generic mental categories. But however convenient the metaphors of "reasoning" or "inference" may be as illustrative devices, they are in fact somewhat misleading, for they mis-represent the underlying neuro-

---

6.   There are some refreshing exceptions. Thus, Gordon (1998) in his commentary observes: "Heyes seems to be asking: "Do they have a theory of mental states, with law-like generalizations, inferences from behavior to mental states, and so forth, or do they have only non-mentalistic resources?" The thesis [is] that if it is a mentalistic resource then it is a theory in a full-blooded sense" (1998: 121).

cognitive mechanisms involved in this type of "reasoning". Habituated, generic mental categories do not depend on rational, conscious inferences such as (15):

(15)   **Reasoning by feature association as an abductive inference:**

Category *A* has strongly-associated features *a, b, c, d, etc.*
Individual *x* is a member of category *A*.
Individual *x* possesses feature *a*.

Therefore individual *x* must also possess features *b, c, d, etc.*

Inferences such as (15) are convenient, schematic, post-hoc rationalizations of the *end product*, but they don't describe the *process*.

In the processing of conceptual-semantic categories, the adaptive ends of schematic feature-association inference like (15) are accomplished much more efficiently by automatic activation of the prototype node-cluster, an activation that may be triggered by few or even one salient core feature. "Reasoning" by feature association is an *automated*, frequency-driven neuro-cognitive mechanism. It had served for eons of vertebrate evolution in the processing of external, somatic-internal and visceral-emotional referents. There is no reason to assume that it was not pressed into service, in a like manner, to process *mental-internal* ("cognitive") referents. That is:

(16)   If it looks like me, behaves like me, is my conspecific, then it must surely also possess my mental properties.

The only prerequisite for "inference" in (16) is that one has a mental representation of one's *own* epistemic and intentional states, and perhaps also that one is *as conscious* of one's mental state as one is of one's internal-somatic, motor states and of external perceptual input. But whether fully conscious, attended processing is implicated here remains a matter of debate.

6.3   Neurological incrementation: From old-brain to limbus to neo-cortex

The oldest area of our brain, the so-called *old brain* (hind-brain; medula and pons), is used in the current mammalian brain to represent, primarily, *internal somatic input*; that is, internal and largely sub-conscious – autonomous – bodily states (circulatory, digestive, pulmonary). In reptiles, the *fore-brain* was used to represent *external sensory* input, including *motor-sensory* input from the limbs. The proto-cortical *thalamic* and *limbic* systems (diencephalon) mediate between the old ("reptilian") brain and the cortex (telencephalon) in the current mammalian brain. The mammalian *cortex* was projected from various regions of the thalamic and limbic proto-cortex. It contains further, "more cognitive" elaboration of various older limbic systems (Martin 1985; Kelly 1985; Mesulam 2000). But almost all major cortical systems in primates still have subcortical limbic and/or thalamic components. So that the thalamic-limbic systems form the core and the cortical component the outer shell of complex, vertically-integrated, multi-modular distributive systems (Mesulam 2000; Tucker 2001). That is:

> A new theoretical model of the cortex, what might be called a "core-and-shell" model. At the limbic core of the cortex are motivational [deontic] mechanisms, centered on the hypothalamus. Forming the shell or interface with the environment are the sensory and motor neocortical networks. Memory is organized through a reentrant arbitration, creating a functional resonance between the paralimbic networks of the core and the neocortical networks of the shell (Tucker 2001: 1-2).

This pattern of inter-connectivity may be given diagrammatically (Mesulam 2000) in (17):

(17)

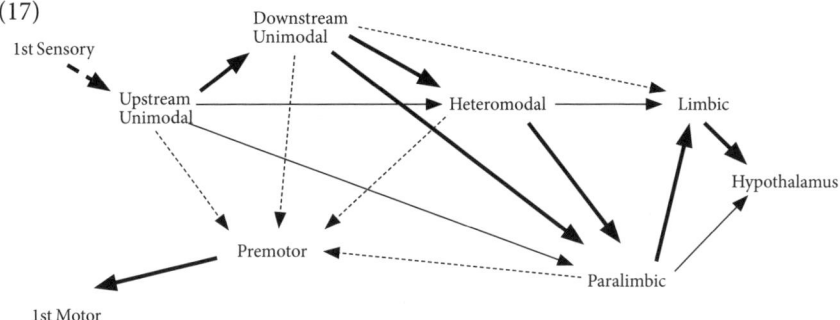

The representation of mental states of *volition/intention* (deontic) and *belief/knowledge* (epistemic) in the primate brain is still "rooted" in the *thalamic-limbic* proto-cortical core (Tucker 1991, 2001, 2002; Mesulam 2000). In addition, the proto-cortical core also has "downward" connections to the somatic-visceral representation of the old brain.

It is of course possible to dismiss thalamic-limbic representation as purely "not quite cognitive". But given the profound core-shell connectivity and distributiveness of the major memory and attention networks, such a strict dichotomy is untenable. Further, the transition from "purely perceptual" to "cognitive" representation in the primate visual cortex is gradual and multi-staged (Kaas 1989). And further, the major cognitive representation sub-systems of human language – semantic and episodic memory – are a transparent, recent evolutionary elaboration on the two "streams" of visual processing system (Givón 2002: chapter 4). And both are rooted in limbic "core" structures (Tucker 1991, 2001, 2002).

Finally, there is a body of evidence about the communicative behavior of Alex, an African grey parrot, who has not only acquired a considerable auditory/oral-coded English lexicon, including a number of abstract concepts, but also seems to distinguish between declarative, interrogative and manipulative speech acts (Pepperberg 1991, 1999). Alex was also recorded rehearsing his English phonetics at night after being chided for faulty performance earlier in the day[7]. Thus, not only does this avian have representations of intentional and belief states, but he appears to be conscious of having them, and thus perhaps even self-conscious, all of which is accomplished, largely, with a thalamic-limbic proto-cortex.

6.4   Transformations of the referent

It is perhaps useful to propose a natural step-wise evolutionary progression whereby the mechanisms of mental representation have incremented slowly and gradually, with each step relying on the application of the same neuro-cognitive equivalent of "reasoning" by feature association (15/16). The steps are as shown in (18):

(18)   **Evolutionary precursors of mental models of other minds**:
    a. External-sensory representation
    b. Motor-sensory (limbs & muscles) representation
    c. Internal-somatic ("autonomous") representation
    d. Internal visceral representation
    e. Internal emotional representation
    f. Internal deontic (cum-epistemic) representation
    g. internal epistemic representation

The arguments in support of this gradual progression are as follows.

6.4.1   *The primitive vs. less-primitive representations*
It is not clear which of the three older representation systems –*external-sensory, motor-sensory* or *internal-somatic* – precedes in evolution. In reptiles, internal-somatic representation (18.c) remains in the old brain, but both the external-sensory (18.a) and motor-sensory (18.b) representations are localized in the thalamic-limbic proto-cortex, a separation that persists in avians and mammals. Either one of these three or even all three could have been the evolutionary precursors of the more sophisticated *internal epistemic* representation (18.g). What is more, *internal deontic* representation (18.f) could have arisen gradually via internal-somatic (18.c), internal-visceral (18.d) and internal-emotional (18.e) representation.

An intriguing body of evidence suggests the existence of a natural, and perhaps phylogenetically old, association between internal motor control, internal somatic representation and external visual representation. This involves first the work of Rizzolatti and associates on the co-activation of visual *mirror neurons*, visual representation neurons that are interspersed within the primary motor cortex in both humans and non-human primates (Rizzolatti and Gentilucci 1988; Rizzolatti et al. 1996a, 1996b; Rizzolatti and Arbib 1998; Rizzolatti et al. 2000). Briefly, when a primate sees a conspecific perform motor routines, the visually-activated mirror neurons co-activate

---

7.   Irene Pepperberg (in personal communication); see also Pepperberg (1999).

relevant motor-program routines in the primary motor cortex of the viewer, this way providing for passive *imitation learning*. Conversely, when a primate performs motor routines, the relevant mirror neurons are co-activated in the primary motor cortex, so that a performer can *visualize* his/her own motor performance like an observer.

More recently, a similar association between the visual and motor-gestural systems has been identified in the *ventral visual information stream,* earlier identified (Ungerleider and Mishkin 1982) as dedicated to the processing of a spatial relations and spatial motion (Milner and Goodale 1995, 1998; Gallese *et al.* 1999).

At the very least, these findings suggest an overlapping activation mechanism between the somatic-motor and external-perceptual representation system. But since there are also strong feedback connections between the *primary motor cortex* (posterior-frontal) and the adjacent *somatic sensory* representational region (anterior-parietal), the external-sensory (18.a) and the motor-sensory (18.b) representation systems are now connected via co-activation. This three-way connectivity suggests possible neural mechanisms for *self-other analogy, imitation* (Byrne 1998; Meltzoff 2002a, 2002b) and thus perhaps, ultimately, *empathy.*

6.4.2   *From internal-somatic to visceral-emotional to deontic representation*
It is possible now to consider *internal-somatic* representation (18c), an ancient old-brain capacity, as the evolutionary precursor of *internal-visceral* representation (18d) such as hunger, pain or adrenaline arousal. And that, in turn, may be considered the evolutionary precursor of *internal-emotional* representation (18.e) such as urge, positive affect, fear or revulsion. And that, lastly, may be considered the evolutionary precursor of *internal deontic* representation proper, such as volition, rejection and, ultimately, intention.

6.4.3   *From deontic to epistemic*
One of Premack and Woodruff's (1978) more intriguing suggestions was that the representation of deontic states (volition, intention) is somehow "more primitive" than the representation of epistemic states (knowledge, belief). However intuitively appealing, this suggestion is somewhat implausible as it stands, since knowledge is already implicit in volition. To illustrate this, let us consider the volitional expression (19a), which necessarily presupposes the *realis* proposition (19b) while asserting the *irrealis* proposition (19c):

(19) a. I want to leave the room.
     b. I am in the room now.   (R; presupposed)
     c. I will be outside the room later.   (IRR; asserted)

Both the presupposition (19b) and assertion (19c) are epistemic mental states, as are the propositional referents ("verbal complements") of intentional predicates in general.

Whether the epistemic state is realized (R) or unrealized (IRR) is hardly an issue, given that both memorized and imagined information is represented in the same limbic-based (hippocampus and amygdala) episodic memory system. Whether the epistemic state is visual or verbal is not an issue either, since the limbic-based episodic memory system, originally set up as part of visual information-processing system, is the locus of *both* visual and verbal early episodic memory (Mishkin 1978, 1982; Mishkin et al. 1984; Ungerleider and Mishkin 1982; Squire 1987; Squire and Zola-Morgan 1991; Petri and Mishkin 1994). Finally, the limbic-based episodic memory system is an ancient proto-cortical system shared by all primates.

There remains a considerable residual appeal to Premack and Woodruff's conjecture about the "primitiveness" of the deontic vis-a-vis the epistemic. This may be due to the connection between intention and "primitive urges" (6.4.2. above). But even in the minuscule proto-cortex of the avian brain, a conscious attentional system seems to mediate "primitive urges", tempering them with relevant epistemic information and with, perhaps, the weighing of possible consequences and alternative actions. That is, given Alex the African grey parrot's communicative behavior. What is more, at least two of the main attentional networks in humans still contain limbic and/or thalamic sub-modules (see section 6.6.3. below).

The conjecture that deontic representation preceded epistemic representation in the evolution of mind may still be sustained, albeit in a modified form. Epistemic representation may have appeared first as an obligatory component of deontic representation (see (18) above). Only later on did it *liberate* itself from this subordinate status. Cases of such liberation are widely attested in the diachronic rise of irrealis/future epistemic modalities out of precursor deontic verbs such as "want" or "must" (Heine 1993; Hopper and Traugott 1993; Bybee et al. 1994).

Support for our revised conjecture also comes from the observation that in spontaneous non-human communication, whether by avians, canines or primates, only *manipulative* speech-acts are used; that is, speech-acts where epistemic representation is embedded in and subordinate to the deontic representation (see again section 4.3. above). In child development as well, early speech-acts are overwhelmingly manipulative; unembedded declaratives emerge only later (Carter 1974; Bates et al. 1975, 1979).

6.4.4   *From perception to cognition*
We noted above the possible "liberation" of epistemic representation from prior subordination to deontic representation. There may have been another "liberation" trend in the rise of "strictly-cognitive" representation from phylogenetically older *perceptual-cum-cognitive* representation. Thus, seeing-and-therefore-knowing what is under the *current* focus of attention may well be the evolutionary precursor of *remembering* what one doesn't see any more, or of *imagining* what one has never seen.

If this line of reasoning pans out, it may suggest that longer-term memory systems are a later evolutionary elaboration of the modality-specific working-memory-cum-attentional-activation system. The fact that to this day the latter is the gateway to the former is consonant with this evolutionary conjecture. This is so because in general, older brain systems tend to be the input gateways to new ones that evolve as their extensions. The progression, in visual information processing, from eye to thalamus to cortex (Hubel 1988) is a case in point.

6.5   The puzzle of consciousness

6.5.1   *How old is consciousness?*

I see no cogent basis for pinpointing the exact stage where *consciousness* –as distinct from *self-consciousness* – interjected itself into the representational equation. There is no compelling evidence to suggest that either avians or mammals are *not* conscious of, at the very least, the external referents (1st order framing; (18a)) of their deontic or epistemic states, at least if the referents are present here-and-now. What is more, the human working memory/attention system, including conscious executive attention, deals with information that is either strictly here-and-now (if entering through sensory channels) or strictly now (if retrieved from memory). Some neurological structure in support of conscious attention must already exist in avians, let alone mammals and primates. The capacity for consciously attending to *what* one sees, knows or wants, may be an old evolutionary adaptation.

Mishkin et al. (1984) have suggested that automatic processing is phylogenetically older than attended processing. Their arguments involve the fact that in the current primate brain, the oldest structures (old-brain) are fully automated before birth. The next oldest (thalamic-limbic systems) are not fully automated at birth, but become automated early in post-natal maturation. While the cortex, in particular its youngest frontal and pre-frontal regions, is automated last and only partially, allowing for life-long learning and skill acquisition. And last but not least, the conscious executive attention is a pre-frontal capacity.

I think there are good reasons to suspect that this argument is ill-conceived, and that to the contrary, consciousness always precedes automaticity. To begin with, in both ontogenetic maturation and life-long learning, attended processing always precede automaticity. Indeed, it is the high-frequency of *attended* processing that leads to automation (Schneider 1985; Schneider and Chein 2003). It is highly unlikely that evolution bucks these developmental trends. As elsewhere, a recapitulation scenario is more plausible. Thus, the evolutionary sequence of the automation of brain regions does not indicate that automaticity is ontogenetically older than consciousness, but only that older brain regions had shifted earlier from attended to automated processing.

To the extent, then, that a central modulating and context-scanning governing mechanism exists in any vertebrate nervous system, there is no reason to assume that it was not the *functional equivalent* of the current primate conscious executive attention.

The most compelling claim that an organism lacks the functional equivalent of a conscious executive attention would require showing that all the circuits that mediate between sensory input and action output in the organism are fully automated. One has to go far down the evolutionary ladder, far below vertebrates, to find an organism that could possibly be that primitive. Such an organism would be utterly oblivious to finer

shades of contextual variation. Its information processing system would be fully algo-
rithmic, and would depend on purely Platonic categories that are immune to variation,
learning and adaptive change. It is not clear how such a Cartesian creature – or carica-
ture – could have ever existed, let alone evolved.

6.5.2   *How old is self-consciousness?*

It is not altogether clear how old in phylogeny self-consciousness is; that is, consciousness of one's mental states (2nd-order framing). The limbic-projected primate and human neo-cortical structures that support self-representation, mediated intentionality
and the executive attention system are indeed late evolutionary elaborations. But to
this day they are part of *distributive networks* that include "core" thalamic-limbic components (Mesulam 2000; Tucker 2001; Schneider and Chein 2003; Posner and Fan
2004). At the very least, one cannot assume that self-consciousness must have arisen
in its current primate-brain location. As with consciousness, the precursor or functional equivalent of self-consciousness may have resided in pre-mammalian thalamic-
limbic structures. This is certainly consonant with the evolutionary rise of the neo-
cortical systems of visual, auditory, somatic-sensory and motor representation, all of
them later elaborations of the earlier thalamic-limbic loci.

The distributive network of executive attention is represented pictorially in (20),
following Schneider and Chein (2003). Of the five major components of the network,
only two – the Goal Processor in the *dorso-lateral prefrontal cortex* (DLPFC) and the
Attention Controller in the posterior-parietal cortex (PPC) – are neocortical. The other three are either paralimbic (the Activities Monitor in the *anterior cingulate cortex)*,
limbic (Episodic Storage in the hippocampus), or thalamic (Gating & Report Relay in
the *thalamus)*.

(20)   **Brain Locations of the Major Components of the Executive Attention Network**

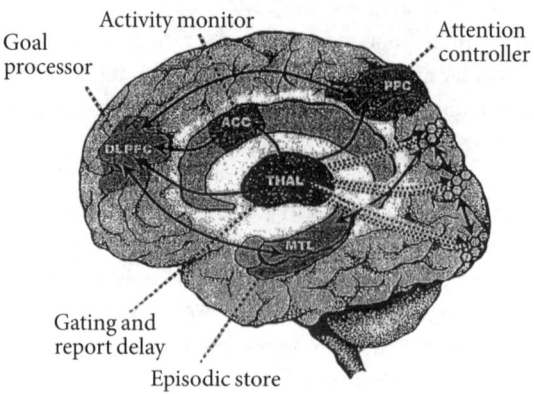

Of the two neocortical components, one – the posterior-parietal cortex (PPC) – is also the center of another attentional network, the one that controls the orientation of attention and keeps various options available in cross-modal working memory (Mesulam 2000; Posner and Fan 2004).

There is one theoretical argument that suggests that 1st-order framing – of internal-visceral, somatic-sensory and external-sensory input – is an evolutionary prerequisite for 2nd-order framing –of the output of 1st-order framing. And likewise, that 2nd-order framing (self-consciousness) is a prerequisite to 3rd-order framing – of the mind of others. But this argument does not indicate exact timing, only relative ordering.

6.5.3   *Consciousness and frames-within-frames: Russell's nightmare*

The difference between sub-conscious, conscious and self-conscious mental processes is not as easy to demonstrate as one would have thought. From a purely logical perspective, it seems a matter of hierarchy of frames akin to Russell's Theory of Types (Russell 1908; Givón 2005: chapter 1). The representation of sensory input (18a, b, c) is the 1st-order frame. Representing one's 1st-order mental representation is a 2nd-order frame. With each successive hierarchically-higher representation, another frame is added. Neat?

Alas, things get a bit messy when one adds consciousness to the equation. To begin with, consciousness does not add a frame whose scope is wider than that of sub-conscious cognition. It merely endows an erstwhile sub-conscious frame – be it 1st-order or 2nd-order – with a certain quality. No new referential domain is added.

Next, consciousness without self-consciousness – conscious 1st-order framing – would presumably involve awareness of a *sensory referent* (18a,b,c) but not of "seeing", "knowing" or "wanting" it. That is, the mental frames "want" and "see"/"know" are imbued with consciousness, but they themselves remain outside consciousness' frame. This may make perfect mathematical sense in Russell's framework, but is it cognitively feasible? What exactly would it entail to be conscious of *what* one wants or knows but not of "wanting" or "knowing" it? How can one refrain from spreading consciousness upwards automatically to one's 2nd-order and 3rd-order frames? What plausible biological mechanism could enforce Russell's injunction?

Consider next the likely referents of older primal visceral feelings such as pain, hunger, adrenalin arousal, comfort or fear. Are they external vis-a-vis the representational system, or are they, reflexively, both referent and representation? If the latter, then by being conscious of the referent, one is automatically also conscious of the relevant mental model that represents the referent. That is, one is *self-conscious.*

Further, primal-visceral mental states are cognitively intrusive and thus highly salient. Even if their referent could be somehow externalized, how can one be aware of such an intrusive referent without being aware of the equally intrusive primal visceral-awareness prompted by that referent?

It may well be, lastly, that at least in principle one cannot constrain a pragmatic framing system from automatic recursive self-extension. Once an organism has framed an "external" world, it has gained the capacity to frame its own framing mechanism.

Cognition, like Pandora's Box (or Chomsky's recursive embedding), can never be shut down once it has been opened. As a logician, Russell could legislate against any but first-order framing. Biological organisms are more likely to have some *selectional adaptive mechanisms* that constrain the proliferation of meta-frames and the attendant complexity above a certain upper bound (Chomsky 1965), but perhaps not below.

6.5.4   *Descartes' receding line of defense: Verbally-reported consciousness*

Consciousness, or the executive attention system, may be an old pre-mammalian capacity. Can self-consciousness and its presumed supporting neurological mechanisms in the pre-frontal cortex of *Homo sapiens* be a brand new capacity, developed only during the last 40,000 years in humans (cf. Baron-Cohen 2000)?

In the Theory of Mind literature, it has been taken for granted almost universally that self-consciousness – being aware of one's own mental processes – is the prerequisite for a "real" Theory of Mind (e.g. Povinelli and Preuss 1995). And further, that this is the line that separate human from pre-human cognition (or autistic from normal cognition, or early-childhood from late-childhood cognition), with a certain hedge about our nearest kin. The insistence on drawing such a sharp demarcation line seems but the last, ever retreating, line of defense of the old Cartesian brick wall between "us" and "them". But again and again, it seems, the only reason why "they" could not have a Theory of Mind is because "they" are incapable of reporting verbally.

6.6   The adaptive context of framing other minds

6.6.1   *Social cooperation*

The most important adaptive capacity a social, cooperating species may need is the ability to forecast the behavior of conspecifics; not only what they might do in general, but what they will do right now, in the present context. The cheapest and most natural adaptive mechanism a social organism may have for predicting the social intentions of its conspecifics is by extending the contextual scope of the entrenched adaptive strategy of *reasoning by feature-association*. In such an extension, the most natural null hypothesis one could entertain is that one's conspecifics have a mind roughly like one's own, with similar deontic and epistemic capacities, and further, with the same causal goal-tree mappings between such mental capacities and future action.

6.6.2   *Communicative behavior*

Purposive communication is the use of some behaviors which may have been originally non-communicative as *speech acts*; that is, as a dedicated signaling system whose purpose is to induce others to comprehend what is in one's mind. Not only to comprehend, but hopefully also to spring into relevant action. Such behavior is inconceivable without a running on-line mental model, however subconscious, of the interlocutor's rapidly-shifting intentional and epistemic states. A purely associationist account of this capacity (e.g. Bloomfield 1933) would crash on the very same grounds as Quine

(1951) and Premack and Woodruff (1978) have suggested. But, such purposive communicative behavior is an old pre-mammal capacity that is not fully automated even in avians (Ristau ed. 1991; Pepperberg 1999).

6.6.3   *Human communication*

As noted earlier above, much of past discussion of Theory of Mind has tilted, whether explicitly or implicitly, towards equating the "real" item with the human ability to report about such a theory verbally. While expressing serious reservations about the validity of this Cartesian bias, one must nonetheless acknowledge the possibility that the rise of well-coded human communication may have indeed had a profound impact on our species' ability to extend framing operations beyond their earlier bounds. Whether this extension turns out to be a matter of kind or degree is for the moment unclear and perhaps even irrelevant[8].

(a) Phonological words and semantic memory

A great number of distinct processing steps occur in rapid succession during lexical understanding, and the early ones are all subconscious and automated. The auditory (for spoken words) or visual (for written words or visual objects) stages of language processing are highly automated, and do not reach conscious semantic representation till ca. 200-250 millisec (Swinney 1979; Treisman and Kanwisher 1998; Barker and Givón 2002).

The mere fact that human language has dedicated code units, the phonological words, which automatically activate conceptual nodes in semantic memory, makes those units – and their mental referents – akin to external objects of perception. That is, phonological words are themselves available to conscious attention. Both auditory and written word-forms can be kept activated in the respective working-memory buffers for ca. 2-5 seconds, an activation that can be further extended by conscious rehearsal (Gathercole and Baddely 1993). Lexical concepts, including those with purely mental referents (*want, know*), can thus persist under the scope of conscious attention just like *external objects* of sensory perception. And this, in turn, may contribute to extend our consciousness to mental predicates, both those referring to one's own mind and those referring to other minds.

(b) Grammar and episodic memory

As noted above (but see also Givón 2005), the systematic on-line construal of mental models of the current epistemic and deontic states of the interlocutor is the central adaptive motivation for the evolution of grammar. Specific grammatical constructions are used to code (in the speaker's mind) and cue (in the hearer's mind) specific mental models of the interlocutor's current mental states. This system is highly automated and

---

8.   As noted elsewhere (Givón 2005: chapters 1, 2), the difference is logically arbitrary, depending on the construal of some relevant context. The original observation is, of course, due to Aristotle's *Metaphysics*.

sub-conscious, and by all available accounts also a relatively recent evolutionary addition (Bickerton 1981, 1990; Li 2002; Givón 1979, 2002).

The phylogenetic recency and high automaticity of human grammar does not mean, however, that the construction of mental models of the interlocutor's current (and constantly shifting) mental states is necessarily a recent, human-specific capacity. It only means that the streamlining and *automation* of this capacity is recent and human-specific.

Likewise, the high level of automaticity of human grammar does not itself indicate whether the same capacity in pre-human organisms was (or is) subconscious, conscious or self-conscious. If anything, the absence of grammar may simply suggest that the underlying capacity of constructing mental models of other mind is more conscious – thus slow and laborious – in pre-human social organisms. As noted above, attended processing by-and-large precedes, and is a prerequisite to, automation in the developmental sequence (Schneider 1985; Schneider and Chein 2003).

(c) Declarative speech-acts

Even with a well-coded lexicon, early childhood as well as non-human communication are heavily weighted toward manipulative speech-acts (Tomasello and Call 1997; Savage-Rumbaugh et al. 1993; Pepperberg 1991; Carter 1974; Bates et al. 1975, 1979). In contrast, the bulk of the grammatical machinery of human language is invested in coding declarative speech-acts (Givón 2001); and at the use-frequency level, natural human discourse is tilted heavily toward declarative speech-acts (Givón 1995: chapter 2).

The emergence of declarative speech-acts, whose communicative goal is largely epistemic, may have enhanced the liberation of epistemic mental predicates from their erstwhile subordination to deontic predicates. And the separate and more explicit representation of epistemic predicates may have, in turn, contributed towards heightened consciousness of these quintessential *mental framing* operators, first those referring to one's own mental states, and then, by extension, those referring to the mental states of others.

(d) Displaced spatio-temporal reference

Both early childhood and primate communication are weighted heavily towards here-and-now, you-and-I, and this-or-that referents that are perceptually accessible within the immediate speech situation. Mature human communication is, in contrast, heavily tilted towards spatio-temporally displaced referents, states and events. In terms of use-frequency, again, human communication is heavily weighted toward *displaced reference*. This use-frequency bias is, in turn, reflected in the fact that much of our grammatical machinery is dedicated to communicating about displaced referents, states and events (Givón 2001).

The immediate speech situation is mentally represented in the working memory/attention system. Such representation shifts from one moment to the next, and is thus temporally unstable. In contrast, displaced referents are more likely to be represented in episodic memory. Compared to working memory, episodic representation is a much more stable mental representation. And this *temporal stability* may have contributed toward the objectivization of verbally-coded referents, including mental predicates.

(e) **Multi-propositional discourse**

Early childhood and primate communication are overwhelmingly mono-proposition-al (Tomasello and Call 1997; Savage-Rumbaugh *et al.* 1993; Bloom 1973; Carter 1974; Scollon 1976; Bates *et al.* 1975, 1979). In contrast, mature human communication is, at the use-frequency level, overwhelmingly multi-propositional. This is reflected, in turn, in the fact that the bulk of the machinery of grammar is invested in coding multi-propositional – cross-clausal – coherence (Givón 2001). What is more, grammar-coded discourse coherence is primarily involved with mental models of the interlocutors' current epistemic and deontic states. The high automaticity of grammar may mean, among other things, that the evolution of grammatical communication was motivated, at least in part, by the strong adaptive pressure of having to deal with a high frequency of perspective shifting; perhaps an order-of-magnitude higher than what pre-human social species had to deal with.

7. Closure

The evolution of grammar is unlikely to have been a simple process triggered by a fortuitous mega-mutation and a single "grammar gene". Like other complex neuro-cognitive faculties, grammar arose from multiple functionally-amenable precursors ("pre-adaptations") and thus, most likely, in multiple successive steps. This is why grammar reveals, to this day, a wide *distributive network* pattern of functional and neurological connectivity. Within this network, many of the sub-modules are not specific to grammar, but rather continue to perform, in parallel, their older – pre-grammatical or pre-linguistic – cognitive functions. Such functional ambiguity is the hallmark of *evolutionary recency*, just as it is the telltale sign of recent diachronic change.

The most likely sub-modules implicated in the distributive network of grammar are shown in (21):

(21) **The Connectivity of Grammar**

Functional module	Likely neural locus
Semantic lexicon	left pre-frontal cortex
Grammatical morphology	???
Episodic memory	hippocampus and amygdala
Propositional semantics	temporal-parietal cortex (Wernicke's area)
Rhythmic-hierarchic structure	left-pre-frontal cortex (Broca's area)
Working memory	posterior-parietal cortex
Executive attention	dorso-lateral pre-frontal cortex anterior cingulate cortex (paralimbic)

Hypotheses about the exact course of the evolution of grammar, whatever that may turn out to be eventually (e.g. Givón 2002: chapter 4), must take account of both the adaptive function(s) of grammar as a complex, interactive information-processing tool, and the multiple functional-neurological connectivity of grammar as a distributive, multi-modular network. A recalcitrant Cartesian account of grammar as an evolutionary mystery involving a purely formal single module (recursiveness; cf. Hauser *et al.* 2002) is not all that plausible.

References

Abdulaev, Yalchin G. and Michael I. Posner. 1997. "Time-course of activating brain areas in generating verbal associations". *Psychological Science* 8: 56–59.

Andersen, Roger. 1979. "Expanding Schumann's pidginization hypothesis". *Language Learning* 29: 105–119.

Anderson, Anne, Simon C. Garrod and Anthony J. Sanford. 1983. "The accessibility of pronominal antecedents as a function of episodic shift in narrative text". *Quarterly Journal of Experimental Psychology* 35A: 427–440.

Atkinson, Richard C. and Richard M. Shiffrin. 1968. "Human memory: A proposed system and its control processes". *The Psychology of Learning and Motivation*, ed. by Kenneth W. Spence and Janet T. Spence, vol. 2, 89–195. New York: Academic Press.

Austin, John L. 1962. *How to do things with words*. Oxford: Oxford University Press.

Baddeley, Alan D. 1986. *Working Memory*. Oxford: Oxford University Press.

Baddeley, Alan D. 1992. "Working memory: The interface between memory and cognition". *Journal of Cognitive Neuroscience* 4(3): 281–288.

Bar, Moshe and Irving Biederman. 1998. "Subliminal visual priming". *Psychological Science* 9(6): 464–469.

Barker, Marjorie. 2004. *Effects of divided attention on verbal episodic memory*. PhD dissertation. Eugene, Oregon: University of Oregon (ms).

Barker, Marjorie and T. Givón. 2002. "On the pre-linguistic origins of language processing rates". *The evolution of language out of pre-language*, ed. by T. Givón and Bertram F. Malle, 171–214. Amsterdam: John Benjamins. [Typological Studies in Language 53].

Barker, Marjorie and T. Givón. 2003. "The representation of conversation in episodic memory: Information vs. interaction". *TR no. 03–1*, Institute of Cognitive and Decision Sciences, University of Oregon.

Barker, Marjorie and T. Givón (forthcoming) "Memory for grammar".

Baron-Cohen, Simon 1995. *Mindblindness: An essay on autism and theory of mind*. Cambridge, Mass.: MIT Press.

Baron-Cohen, Simon 2000. "The evolution of a theory of mind". *The descent of mind*, ed. by Michael Corballis and Stephen E. G. Lea (eds.), 261–277. Oxford: Oxford University Press.

Bartsch, Karen and Henry M. Wellman. 1995. *Children talk about the mind*. Oxford: Oxford University Press.

Bates, Elizabeth, Laura Benigni, Inge Bretherton, Luigia Camaioni and Virginia Volterra. 1979. *The emergence of symbols: Cognition and communication in infancy*. New York: Academic Press.

Bates, Elizabeth, Luigia Camaioni and Virginia Volterra. 1975. "The acquisition of performatives prior to speech". *Merrill-Palmer Quarterly* 21: 205–226.

Bickerton, Derek 1981. *Roots of language*. Ann Arbor, Mich.: Karoma.

Bickerton, Derek 1990. *Language and species*. Chicago: University of Chicago Press.

Bickerton, Derek and Carol Odo. 1976. *Change and variation in Hawaiian English*, vol. I: *The pidgin*, NSF Final Report (grant GS–39748). Honolulu: University of Hawaii (ms).

Bloom, Lois. 1973. *One word at a time: The use of single word utterances before syntax*. The Hague: Mouton.

Bloomfield, Leonard. 1933. *Language*. New York: Holt, Rinehart and Winston.

Blumstein, Sheila E. and William Milberg. 1983. "Automatic and controlled processing in speech/language deficits in aphasia". Paper presented at *Symposium on Automatic Speech*. Minneapolis: Academy of Aphasia.

Bowerman, Melissa. 1973. *Early syntactic development*. Cambridge: Cambridge University Press.

Bybee, Joan, William Pagliuca and Revere Perkins. 1994. *The evolution of grammar: Tense, aspect and modality in the languages of the world*. Chicago: University of Chicago Press.

Byrne, Richard W. 1998. "Learning by imitation: A hierarchic approach". *Behavior and Brain Sciences* 21: 667–721.

Byrne, Richard W. and Andrew Whiten (eds.). 1998. *Machiavelian intelligence: Social expertise and the evolution of intellect in monkeys, apes and humans*. Oxford: Oxford University Press.

Carpenter, Patricia A. and Marcel A. Just. 1989. "The role of working memory in language comprehension". *Complex information processing: The impact of Herbert Simon*, ed. by David Klahr and Kenneth Kotovsky, 39–68. Hillsdale, NJ: Erlbaum.

Carter, A. 1974. *Communication in the sensory-motor period*. PhD dissertation. Berkeley, University of California.

Chomsky, Noam. 1965. *Aspects of the theory of syntax*. Cambridge, Mass.: MIT Press.

Cole, Peter and Jerry Morgan (eds.). 1975. *Speech acts: Syntax and semantics*, Vol. 3. New York: Academic Press.

Dickinson, Connie and T. Givón. 1997. "Memory and conversation". *Conversation: Cognitive, communicative and social perspectives,* ed. by T. Givón, 91–132. Amsterdam: John Benjamins. [Typological Studies in Language 34].

Dunbar, Robin I. M. 1998. "The social brain hypothesis". *Evolutionary Anthropology* 6(5): 178–190

Eldredge, Niles and Stephen J. Gould. 1972. "Punctuated equilibria: An alternative to physical gradualism". *Models in paleobiology*, ed. by Thomas J. M. Schopf, 82–115. San Francisco: Freeman, Cooper and Co.

Ericsson, K. Anders and Walter Kintsch.1995. "Long term working memory". *Psychological Review:* 102(2): 211–245

Fernández-Duque, Diego. 1999a. "Processing of object identity, location and change in the absence of focused attention". *TR no. 99–03*, Institute of Cognitive and Decision Sciences, Eugene, University of Oregon.

Fernández-Duque, Diego. 1999b. *Automatic processing of object identity, location, and valence information*. PhD dissertation. Eugene, Or, University of Oregon (ms).

Fouts, Roger S. 1973. "Acquisition and testing of gestural signs in four young chimpanzees". *Science* 180: 178–180.

Fussell, Susan R. and Roger J. Kreuz (eds.). 1998. *Social and cognitive approaches to interpersonal communication*. Mahwah, NJ: Erlbaum.

Gallese, Vittorio, Laila Craighero, Luciano Fadiga and Leonardo Fogassi. 1999. "Perception through action". *Psyche* 5.21, http://psyche.cs.monash.edu.au/v5/psyche-5–21-gallese.html.

Gardner, Beatrix T. and R. Allen Gardner. 1971. "Two-way communication with an infant chimpanzee". *Behavior of non-human primates*, ed. by Allan Schrier and Fred Stollnitz, 117–184. New York: Academic Press.

Gathercole, Susan E. and Alan D. Baddeley. 1993. *Working memory and language*. Hillsdale, NJ: Erlbaum.

Gernsbacher, Morton A.1985. "Surface information loss in comprehension". *Cognitive Psychology* 17: 324–363.

Gernsbacher, Morton A. 1990. *Language comprehension as structure building*. Hillsdale, NJ: Erlbaum.

Gernsbacher, Morton A. (ed.). 1994. *Handbook of psycholinguistics*. New York: Academic Press.

Givón, T. 1971. "Historical syntax and synchronic morphology: An archaeologist's field trip". *Chicago Linguistics Society*: 7: 394–415. University of Chicago: Chicago Linguistics Society.

Givón, T. 1975. "Serial verbs and syntactic change: Niger-Congo". *Word order and word order change*, ed. by Charles N. Li, 47–112. Austin: University of Texas Press.

Givón, T. 1979. *On Understanding Grammar*. New York: Academic Press.

Givón, T. 1989. *Mind, code and context: Essays in pragmatics*. Hillsdale, NJ: Erlbaum.

Givón, T. 1990. "Natural language learning and organized language teaching". *Variability in second language acquisition: Proceedings of the 10th Second Language Research Forum (SLRF)*, ed. by Hartmut Burmeister and Patricia Rounds. Eugene: University of Oregon.

Givón, T. 1995. *Functionalism and grammar*. Amsterdam: John Benjamins.

Givón, T. (ed.) 1997. *Conversation: Cognitive, communicative and social perspectives*. Amsterdam: John Benjamins. [Typological Studies in Language 34].

Givón, T. 2001. *Syntax*, 2 vols. Amsterdam: John Benjamins.

Givón, T. 2002. *Bio-Linguistics*. Amsterdam: John Benjamins.

Givón, T. 2005. *Context as other minds: The pragmatics of cognition and communication*. Amsterdam: John Benjamins.

Givón, T. and Bertram F. Malle (eds.) 2002. *The evolution of language out of pre-language*. Amsterdam: John Benjamins. [Typological Studies in Language 53].

Goodale, Melvyn A. 2000. "Perception and action in the human visual system". *The new cognitive neuroscience*, ed. by Michael S. Gazzaniga, 2nd edition, 365–377. Cambridge, Mass.: MIT Press.

Gopnik, Alison and Henry M. Wellman. 1992. "Why the child's theory of mind is really a theory". *Mind and Language* 7: 145–171.

Gopnik, Alison and Henry M. Wellman.1994. "The theory theory". *Mapping the mind: Domain specificity in cognition and culture*, ed. by Lawrence A. Hirschfeld and Susan A. Gelman, 257–293. Cambridge: Cambridge University Press.

Gordon, Robert M. 1998. "The prior question: Do human primates have a theory of mind?". Peer commentary on Heyes. *Behavior and Brain Sciences*: 21(1):120–121.

Gray, Colin and Phil A. Russell. 1998. "Theory of mind in non-human primates: A question of language?" Peer commentary on Heyes. *Behavior and Brain Sciences*: 21(1): 121.

Grice, H. Paul. 1968/1975. "Logic and conversation". *Speech acts: Syntax and semantics*, vol. 3, ed. by Peter Cole and Jerry Morgan, 41–58. New York: Academic Press.

Haiman, John. 1985a. *Natural syntax*. Cambridge: Cambridge University Press.

Haiman, John (ed.). 1985b. *Iconicity in syntax*. Amsterdam: John Benjamins. [Typological Studies in Language 6].

Hauser, Mark D. 2000. *Wild minds*. New York: Henry Holt.

Hauser, Mark D., Noam Chomsky and W. Tecumseh Fitch. 2002. "The faculty of language: What it is, who has it, how did it evolve?", *Science* 298: 1569–1579.

Heine, Bernd. 1993. *Auxiliaries.* Oxford: Oxford University Press.

Heine, Bernd, Ulrike Claudi and Friederike Hünnemeyer (eds.). 1991. *Grammaticalization: A conceptual framework.* Chicago: University of Chicago Press.

Heyes, Cecilia M. 1998. "Theory of mind in non-human primates". *Behavioral and Brain Sciences* 21(1): 101–114.

Hopper, Paul and Elizabeth Traugott. 1993. *Grammaticalization.* Cambridge: Cambridge University Press.

Hubel, David 1988. *Eye, brain and vision.* New York: Scientific American Library.

Humphreys, Glyn W. and M. Jane Riddoch. 1987. "Introduction: Cognitive neuropsychology and visual object processing". *Visual object processing: A cognitive neuropsychological approach,* ed. by Glyn W. Humphreys and M. Jane Riddoch, 1–15. London: Erlbaum.

Humphreys, Glyn W. and M. Jane Riddoch (eds.) 1987. *Visual object processing: A cognitive neuropsychological approach.* London: Erlbaum.

Humphreys, Glyn W. and M. Jane Riddoch. 1988. "On the case of multiple semantic systems: A reply to Shallice". *Cognitive Neuropsychology:* 5(1): 143–150.

Just, Marcel A. and Patricia A. Carpenter. 1992. "A capacity theory of comprehension: Individual differences in working memory". *Psychological Review* 99: 122–149.

Kaas, Jon H. 1989. "Why does the brain have so many visual areas?". *Journal of Cognitive Neuroscience* 1(2): 121–135.

Kamawar, Deepthi and David R. Olson. 1998. "Theory of mind in young human primates: Does Heyes' task measure it?". Peer commentary on Heyes. *Behavioral and Brain Sciences* 21(1): 122–123.

Kelly, James P. 1985. "Anatomical basis of sensory perception and motor coordination". *Principles of neural science,* ed.by Eric R. Kandel and James H. Schwartz, 2nd edition, 222–243. New York: Elsevier.

Kintsch, Walter 1982. "Memory for text". *Text processing,* ed. by August Flammer and Walter Kintsch, 186–204. Amsterdam: North Holland.

Kintsch, Walter 1992. "How readers construct situation models for stories: The role of syntactic cues and causal inference". *From learning processes to cognitive processes. Essays in honor of William K. Estes,* vol. 2, ed. by Alice F. Healy, Stephen M. Kosslyn and Richard M. Shiffrin, 261–278. Hillsdale, NJ: Erlbaum.

Kintsch, Walter 1994. "The psychology of discourse processing". *Handbook of psycholinguistics,* ed. by Morton A. Gernsbacher, 721–739. San Diego: Academic Press.

Kintsch, Walter and Teun van Dijk. 1978. "Toward a model of text comprehension and production". *Psychological Review* 85: 363–394.

Lande, Russell. 1980. "Microevolution in relation to macroevolution". *Paleobiology:* 6(2): 233–238.

Lande, Russell 1986. "The dynamics of peak shifts and the pattern of morphological evolution". *Paleobiology* 12(4): 343–354.

Langacker, Ronald W. 1987. *Foundations of cognitive grammar.* Stanford: Stanford University Press.

Leslie, Alan M. and Uta Frith. 1988. "Autistic children's understanding of seeing, knowing and believing". *British Journal of Developmental Psychology* 6: 315–324.

Levinson, Stephen C. 2000. *Presumptive meaning.* Cambridge, Mass.: MIT Press.

Li, Charles N. (ed.). 1975. *Word order and word order change.* Austin: University of Texas Press.

Li, Charles N. 2002. "Missing links, issues and hypotheses in the evolutionary origin of language". *The evolution of language out of pre-language,* ed. by T. Givón and Bertram F. Malle, 83–106. Amsterdam: John Benjamins. [Typological Studies in Language 53].

Lieberman, P. 1984. *The biology and evolution of language*. Cambridge, Mass: Harvard University Press.

Loftus, Elizabeth F. 1980. *Eyewitness testimony*. Cambridge: Harvard University Press.

MacWhinney, Brian. 1999. "The emergence of language from embodiment". *The emergence of language*, ed. by Brian MacWhinney, 213–256. Mahwah, NJ: Erlbaum.

MacWhinney, Brian. 2002. "The gradual emergence of language". *The evolution of language out of pre-language*, ed. by T. Givón and Bertram F. Malle, 231–263. Amsterdam: John Benjamins.

Malle, Bertram, Louis J. Moses and Dare A. Baldwin (eds.). 2000. *Intentionality: A key to human understanding*. Cambridge: MIT Press.

Martin, John H. 1985. "Development as a guide to the regional anatomy of the brain". *Principles of neural science*, ed. by Eric R. Kandel and James H. Schwartz, 2nd edition, 244–258. New York: Elsevier.

Meltzoff, Andrew N. 1999. "Origins of theory of mind, cognition and communication". *Journal of Communication Disorders* 32: 251–269.

Meltzoff, Andrew N. 2002a. "Imitation as a mechanism of social cognition: Origins of empathy, theory of mind and the representation of action". *Blackwell handbook of child cognitive development*, ed. by Usha Goswami, 6–25. Oxford: Blackwell Publishers.

Meltzoff, Andrew N. 2002b. "Elements of a developmental theory of imitation". *Blackwell handbook of child cognitive development*, ed. by Usha Goswami, 19–41. Oxford: Blackwell Publishers.

Meltzoff, Andrew N. and Wolfgang Prinz (eds.). 2002. *The imitative mind: Development, evolution and brain bases*. Cambridge: Cambridge University Press.

Menn, Lise 1990. "Agrammatism in English: Two case studies". *Agrammatic aphasia* (3 vols), ed. by Lise Menn and Loraine K. Obler, 117–179. Amsterdam: John Benjamins.

Menn, Lise and Loraine K. Obler (eds.). 1990. *Agrammatic aphasia* (3 vols). Amsterdam: John Benjamins.

Mesulam, M. Marsel. 2000. *Principles of behavioral and cognitive neurology*. New York: Oxford University Press.

Milner, A. David and Melvyn A. Goodale. 1995. *The visual brain in action*, Oxford: Oxford University Press.

Milner, A. David and Melvyn A. Goodale. 1998. "The visual brain in action". *Psyche* 4(12). http://psyche.cs.monash.edu.au/v4/psyche-4-12-milner.html.

Mishkin, Mortimer. 1978. "Memory in monkeys severely impaired by combined but not by separate removal of amygdala and hippocampus". *Nature* 273 (5660): 297–299.

Mishkin, Mortimer. 1982. "A memory system in the monkey". *Philosophical Trans. R. Society of London Ser. Biol.* 298: 85–95.

Mishkin, Mortimer, Barbara Malamut and Jocelyn Bachevalier. 1984. "Memories and habits: Two neural systems". *Neurobiology of learning and memory*, ed. by Gary Lynch and James L. McGaugh, 65–77. New York: Guilford Press.

Mithen, Steven 1996. *The prehistory of mind*. London: Penguin.

Morton, John, Uta Frith and Alan M. Leslie. 1991. "The cognitive basis of a biological disorder: Autism". *Trends in Neuroscience* 14(10): 433–438.

Paul, Hermann. 1890. *Principles of the history of language*, translated by Herbert A. Strong. London: Swan, Sonnenschein and Co.

Pepperberg, Irene M. 1991. "A communicative approach to animal cognition: A study of conceptual abilities of an African Grey Parrot". *Cognitive ethology*, ed. by Carolyn A. Ristau, 153–186. Hillsdale, NJ: Erlbaum.

Pepperberg, Irene M. 1999. *The Alex studies: Cognitive and communicative abilities of grey parrots*. Cambridge, Mass: Harvard University Press.

Perner, Josef, Uta Frith, Alan M. Leslie and Susan Leekam. 1989. "Exploration of the autistic child's theory of mind: Knowledge, belief and communication". *Child Development* 60(3), 689–700.

Petri, Herbert L. and Mortimer Mishkin. 1994. "Behaviorism, cognitivism and the new psychology of memory". *American Scientist* 82: 30–37.

Posner, Michael I. and Jin Fan. 2004. "Attention as an organ system". Department of Psychology, University of Oregon (ms).

Posner, Michael I. and Oscar S. M. Marin (eds.). 1985. *Attention and performance XI*. Hillsdale, NJ: Erlbaum.

Posner, Michael I. and Antonella Pavese. 1997. "Anatomy of word and sentence meanings", paper presented at the *Colloquium on Neuroimaging of Human Brain Functions*, Michael Posner and Marcus Raichle, orgs, *Nat. Acad. of Sciences*. Irvine: CA, May 1997 (ms).

Povinelli, Daniel J. and Sandra de Blois. 1992. "Young children's understanding of knowledge formation in themselves and others". *Journal of Comparative Psychology* 106: 228–238.

Povinelli, Daniel J. and Timothy Eddy. 1996a. "What young chimpanzees know about seeing". *Monographs of the Society of Research on Child Development* 61 (3, Serial No. 247): 1–152.

Povinelli, Daniel J. and Timothy Eddy. 1996b. "Factors affecting young chimpanzees' recognition of attention". *Journal of Comparative Psychology* 110: 336–345.

Povinelli, Daniel J. and Timothy Eddy. 1996c. "Chimpanzees: Joint visual attention". *Psychological Science* 7: 129–135.

Povinelli, Daniel J., Kurt E. Nelson and Sarah T. Boysen. 1990. "Inferences about guessing and knowing by chimpanzees (Pan troglodytes)". *Journal of Comparative Psychology* 104: 203–210.

Povinelli, Daniel J, Kurt E. Nelson and Sarah T. Boysen. 1992. "Comprehension of role reversal in chimpanzees: Evidence of empathy?". *Animal Behavior* 43: 633–640.

Povinelli, Daniel J. and Todd M. Preuss. 1995. "Theory of mind: Evolutionary history of a cognitive specialization". *Trends in Neuroscience* 18(9): 418–424.

Premack, David. 1971. "Language in chimpanzee?". *Science* 172: 808–822.

Premack. David and Guy Woodruff. 1978. "Does the chimpanzee have a theory of mind?" *Behavioral and Brain Sciences* 4: 515–526.

Quine, Willard van O. 1951. "Two dogmas of empiricism". *Philosophical Review* 60: 20–43.

Riddoch, M. Jane and Glyn W. and Humphreys. 1987a. "Visual optic processing in a case of optic aphasia: A case of visual semantic agnosia". *Cognitive Neuropsychology* 4: 131–185.

Riddoch, M. Jane and Glyn W. Humphreys. 1987b. "Picture naming". *Visual object processing: A cognitive neuropsychological approach,* ed. by Glyn W. Humphreys and M. Jane Riddoch, 107–143. London: Erlbaum.

Riddoch, M. Jane, Glyn W. Humphreys, Max Coltheart and Elaine Funnell. 1988. "Semantic systems or system? Neuropsychological evidence reexamined". *Cognitive Neuropsychology* 5(1): 3–25.

Ristau, Carolyn A. (ed.) 1991. *Cognitive ethology.* Hillsdale, NJ: Erlbaum.

Rizzolatti, Giacomo and Michael A. Arbib. 1998. "Language within our grasp". *Trends in Neuroscience* 21: 188–194.

Rizzolatti, Giacomo, Luciano Fadiga, Leonardo Fogassi and Vittorio Gallese. 1996a. "Premotor cortex and the recognition of motor actions". *Cognitive Brain Research* 3: 131–141.

Rizzolatti, Giacomo, Luciano Fadiga, Massimo Matelli, Valentino Bettinardi, Eraldo Paulesu, Daniela Perani and Ferruccio Fazio. 1996b. "Localization of grasp representation in humans by PET: 1. Observation vs. execution". *Experimental Brain Research* 111: 246–252.

Rizzolatti, Giacomo, Leonardo Fogassi and Vittorio Gallese. 2000. "Cortical mechanisms subserving object grasping and action recognition: A new view on the cortical motor functions". *The new cognitive neuroscience*, ed. by Michael S. Gazzaniga, 2nd edition, 539–552. Cambridge: MIT Press.

Rizzolatti, Giscomo and Maurizio Gentilucci. 1988. "Motor and visual-motor functions of the premotor cortex". *Neurobiology of neocortex*, ed. by Pasko Rakic and Wolf Singer, 269–284. Chichester: Wiley.

Russell, Bertrand. 1908. "Mathematical logic based on a theory of types". *American Journal of Mathematics* 30: 222–262.

Russell, Bertrand. 1956. *Logic and knowledge*. London: Routledge.

Savage-Rumbaugh, E. Sue, Janine Murphy, Rose A. Sevcik, Karen E. Brakke, Shelly L. Williams and Duane M. Rumbaugh. 1993. "Language comprehension in ape and child". *Monographs of the Society for Research in Child Development* serial No. 233, Vol.58, Nos.3–4.

Savage-Rumbaugh, E. Sue and Roger Lewin. 1994. *Kanzi: The ape at the brink of the human mind*. New York: Wiley and Sons.

Savage-Rumbaugh, E. Sue, Stuart G. Shanker and Talbot J. Taylor. 1998. *Apes, language and the human mind*. Oxford: Oxford University Press.

Schneider, Walter. 1985. "Toward a model of attention and the development of automatic processing". *Attention and performance XI*, ed. by Michael I. Posner and Oscar S. M. Marin, 475–492. Hillsdale, NJ: Erlbaum.

Schneider, Walter and Jason M. Chein. 2003. "Controlled and automatic processing: Behavior, theory, and biological mechanism". *Cognitive Science* 27: 525–559.

Schumann, John. 1976. "Second language acquisition: The pidginization hypothesis". *Language Learning* 26: 391–408.

Schumann, John. 1978. *The pidginization process: A model for second language acquisition*. Rowley, Mass.: Newbury House.

Schumann, John. 1985. "Nonsyntactic speech in the Spanish-English basilang". *Second languages: A cross-linguistic perspective*, ed. by Roger W. Andersen, 355–374. Rowley, Mass.: Newbury House.

Scollon, Ron. 1976. *Conversations with a one-year old child*. Honolulu: University of Hawaii Press.

Searle, John. 1970. *Speech acts*. Cambridge: Cambridge University Press.

Selinker, Larry. 1972. "Interlanguage". *International Review of Applied Linguistics* 10: 209–231.

Shallice, Tim. 1988. *From neuropsychology to mental structure*. Cambridge: Cambridge University Press.

Slaughter, Virginia and Linda Mealey. 1998. "Seeing is not (necessarily) believing". Peer commentary on Heyes. *Behavioral and Brain Sciences* 21(1): 130.

Squire, Larry R. 1987. *Memory and brain*. Oxford: Oxford University Press.

Squire, Larry R. and Stuart Zola-Morgan. 1991. "The medial temporal lobe memory system". *Science* 253: 1380–1386.

Swinney, David A. 1979. "Lexical access during sentence comprehension: (Re)consideration of context effects". *Journal of Verbal Learning and Verbal Behavior* 18: 645–659.

Terrace, Herbert S. 1985. "In the beginning was the 'name'". *American Psychologist*: 40(9), 1011–1028.

Thornton, Ian M. and Diego Fernández-Duque. 1999. "An implicit measure of undetected change". *TR*: 99(02). Institute of Cognitive and Decision Sciences, University of Oregon.

Tomasello, Michael. 1996. "Do apes ape?" *Social learning in animals: The roots of culture*, ed. by Cecilia M. Heyes and Bennett G. Galef, 319–346. New York: Academic Press.

Tomasello, Michael and Josep Call. 1997. *Primate cognition*, Oxford and NY: Oxford University Press.

Traugott, Elizabeth C. and Bernd Heine (eds.) 1991. *Approaches to grammaticalization* (2 vols). Amsterdam: John Benjamins.

Treisman, Amme. 1995. "Object tokens, attention and visual memory". *Attneave Memorial Lecture*, Eugene, University of Oregon.

Treisman, Anne M. and Brett De Schepper. 1996. "Object tokens, attention and visual memory". *Attention and performance XVI: Information integration in perception and communication*, ed. by Toshio Inui and James McClelland, 15–46. Cambridge, Mass.: MIT Press.

Treisman, Anne M. and Nancy G. Kanwisher. 1998. "Perceiving visually presented objects: Recognition, awareness, and modularity". *Current Opinion in Neurobiology* 8: 218–226.

Tucker, Don M. 1991. "Developing emotions and cortical networks". *Developmental neuroscience. Minnesota symposium on child psychology*, vol. 24, ed. by Megan R. Gunnar and Charles A. Nelson, 75–128. Hillsdale, NJ: Erlbaum.

Tucker, Don. 2001. "Motivated anatomy: A core-and-shell model of cortico-limbic architecture". *Handbook of neuropsychology, Vol. 5: Emotional behavior and its disorders*, 2nd edn, ed. by Guido Gainotti, 125–160. Amsterdam: Elsevier.

Tucker, Don M. 2002. "Embodied meaning: An evolutionary-developmental analysis of adaptive semantics". *The evolution of language out of pre-language*, ed. by T. Givón and Bertram F. Malle, 51–82. Amsterdam: John Benjamins.

Ungerleider, Leslie G. and Mortimer Mishkin. 1982. "Two cortical visual systems". *Analysis of visual behavior*, ed. by David G. Ingle, Melvyn A. Goodale and Richard J. Q. Mansfield, 549–586. Cambridge: MIT Press.

Walker, Carol H. and Frank R. Yekovich. 1987. "Activation and use of script-based antecedents in anaphoric reference". *Journal of Memory and Language* 26: 673–691.

Wellman, Henry. 1990. *Children's theories of mind*. Cambridge, Mass: MIT Press.

Whiten, Andrew. (ed). 1991. *Natural theories of mind*. Oxford: Blackwell.

Yekovich, Frank R. and Carol H. Walker. 1986. "The activation and use of scripted knowledge in reading about routine activities". *Executive Control Processes in Reading*, ed. by Bruce K. Britton and Shawn M. Glynn, 145–176. Hillsdale, NJ: Erlbaum.

Towards a cognitive-functional model of text comprehension

Christopher S. Butler
Honorary Professor, University of Wales Swansea, UK

This paper examines two cognitively-based models of text comprehension and suggests how these might be combined, and integrated with a functional grammar in order to provide an overall model which takes us from a structured sequence of words to the understanding of the concepts conveyed. The paper first provides illustrated summaries of Kintsch's construction-integration model and Werth's text world model. Discussion of their similarities and differences suggests that they are not incompatible, but that both lack a suitable grammatical component. The paper then examines the properties which such a grammar needs to have, and demonstrates that Role and Reference Grammar is an appropriate choice. The parts of the model are then brought together in relation to a short but complete text taken from a corpus. The paper is rounded off with some concluding remarks.

1. Introduction[1,2]

The aim of this paper is to examine two cognitively-based models of text comprehension, those of Kintsch (1988, 1998) and Werth (1999), and to suggest how these might be combined, and integrated with a functional grammar in order to provide an overall model which takes us from a structured sequence of words to the understanding of the concepts conveyed.

---

1.   It is a great pleasure to dedicate this paper to Professor Angela Downing, whose work on grammar and discourse has been a constant source of inspiration to me, and whose friendship over the years I value greatly.

2.   The work reported in this paper formed part of a larger project, **BFF2002–02441,** *Análisis del discurso en lengua inglesa: aspectos cognitivos, contrastivos y de adquisición* (Analysis of discourse in English: cognitive, contrastive and acquisitional aspects), which was financed by the Spanish Ministry of Education, with further support from the Xunta de Galicia (**XUGA, grant reference PGIDIT03PXIC20403PN**). I gratefully acknowledge the support provided by these authorities.

In §2 I provide an illustrated summary of Kintsch's construction-integration model of comprehension, and §3 does the same for Werth's text world model. §4 then discusses the similarities and differences between the two approaches, suggests that they are by no means incompatible, and points out that what both lack is a grammatical component which they can hook up to in order to provide the initial stages of a full comprehension model. In §5 I examine the properties which such a grammar needs to have in order to be suitable for this task, and demonstrate that Role and Reference Grammar (Van Valin 2005, Van Valin and LaPolla 1997), is an appropriate choice. In §6 I show how the complete model can be applied to a short but complete text taken from the British National Corpus. The paper is rounded off with some concluding remarks in §7.

2.   Kintsch's construction-integration model

Van Dijk and Kintsch (1983) set out the principles of a strategic model of discourse comprehension, in which a basically bottom-up mode of operation, from words, through clauses, complex sentences, sequences of sentences, and global text structures, is complemented by feedback mechanisms from higher to lower levels. Their model distinguishes between two structures represented in episodic memory: a proposition-ally-organised **textbase**, in which propositions derived from the text, and the relationships between such propositions, are built up and stored, and a **situation model**, which is the cognitive representation of the situation reflected in the text, and may contain information derived from previous experience and from general knowledge. There is also a **control system** which regulates processing in short-term memory, acting on information concerned with the situation type, discourse type, goals of the participants and knowledge of textual macrostructures. The model is concerned not only with the building-up of propositions in the textbase and situation model, but also with the establishment of local coherence relations between sentences. Further levels of structure are also proposed: **macrostrategies** infer, from the sequence of propositions expressed by a text, a set of macropropositions, which form the textual macrostructure, and can themselves be organised into even higher-level schemas, such as the narrative schema of Setting, Complication and Resolution. Van Dijk and Kintsch (1983: 8–9) recognise three important limitations of their model: the lack of a full model of the parsing process; the incomplete, intuitive and *ad hoc* specification of the knowledge base required for discourse understanding; and the lack of any specific representation of contextual information.

Kintsch (1988) builds on the earlier work by incorporating a further layer of processing, the integration component of the model. According to this modified view, the initial process of proposition construction, using information from the text and the user's knowledge base, is not heavily constrained, but can lead to multiple interpretations, incompatibility between propositions and lack of coherence. The output of this process is structured as an associative network of relations, which can then be tightened up, in the integration phase of comprehension, but means of mechanisms which have their roots in connectionist approaches. Although it is clearly not possible to go into detail about these processes here, a little more explanation, together with some exemplification, is required in order to get an idea of how the model works. From this point on I will refer to Kintsch (1998), the more recent and detailed account of the model.

The first step in the formation of a text base from the input text is the (ongoing) construction of propositions. Kintsch (1998: 69–73) points out that there is considerable evidence for the psychological reality of propositional representations, from studies of recall experiments, reading times and priming effects. Kintsch (1998: 54, 96) recognises that an explicit parsing component is missing from the current model; in practice, what he does is to carry out a manual propositional analysis of the text. As an example of this process let us take the text in (1) below, taken from the original version of the British National Corpus (BNC), and the analysis given in Figure 1.

(1)   *The skeleton acts as an internal physical barrier and is protective; the hard bony skull protects the brain; the vertebral column protects the spinal cord; and the ribs protect the lungs and heart. The intact skin acts as a barrier between the internal and the external environment which contains many potentially harmful agents. The filtering function of lymphatic tissue enables the tonsils and adenoids to trap pathogens. The cilia in the respiratory tract hasten the exit from the body of possibly harmful foreign material. By reflex action – a mechanism of the nervous system – the threatened hand is instantly withdrawn and the threatened eye closed. The eye is further protected by the constant secretion of tears.* (BNC B14 0524–0529)

This analysis is similar to the one presented for a short text by Kintsch (1998: 62–63), though I have attempted to remedy some (though by no means all) of the problems which, from a linguist's point of view, are evident in his analysis, without doing violence to his intentions. The first column lists, in order, the text elements which are isolated by taking content words together with any preceding function words. Here, I have followed Kintsch's practice of treating prepositions as function words, and compound nominals (e.g. *respiratory tract*) as single items. The second column, in Kintsch's analysis, contains what he calls "the syntactic tags required for building propositions" (p62), but these are in fact a rather mixed bag of labels, with a clearly semantic basis: for instance, they include relationships such as specification and source, and the terms subject/object are clearly intended to reflect underlying semantic roles. I have therefore replaced the labels in this column with more clearly semantic ones. The third column contains propositions which are still being constructed and therefore incomplete: note that, with Kintsch, I indicate as yet unspecified components by referring forward to the items which will eventually complete the proposition, although clearly this cannot reflect what actually occurs in comprehension.

Entry	Relation	Representation	Resolved representation
E1 The skeleton	agent E2 & E7		
E2 acts	pred	ACT[SKELETON, E5]	ACT[SKELETON, BARRIER]
E3 as an internal	qual E5	INTERNAL[E5]	INTERNAL[BARRIER]
E4 physical	qual E5	PHYSICAL[E5]	PHYSICAL[BARRIER]
E5 barrier	role E2		
E6 and	new prop (E7)		
E7 is protective;	pred		PROTECTIVE[SKELETON]
E8 the hard	qual E10	HARD[E10]	HARD[SKULL]
E9 bony	qual E10	BONY[E10]	BONY[SKULL]
E10 skull	agent E11		
E11 protects	pred	PROTECT[SKULL,E12]	PROTECT[HARD & BONY[SKULL],BRAIN]
E12 the brain;	patient E11		
E13 the vertebral column	agent E14		
E14 protects	pred	PROTECT[COLUMN,E16]	PROTECT[COLUMN,CORD]
E15 the spinal cord	patient E14		
E16 and the ribs	agent E17		
E17 protect	pred	PROTECT[RIBS,E18 & E19]	PROTECT[RIBS,LUNGS]
E18 the lungs	patient E17		PROTECT[RIBS,HEART]
E19 and heart.	patient E17		
E20 The intact	qual E21	INTACT[E21]	INTACT[SKIN]
E21 skin	agent E22		

E22 acts	pred	ACT[INTACT[SKIN],E23]	ACT[INTACT[SKIN],BARRIER]
E23 as a barrier	role E22		
E24 between the internal	qual E26a	BETWEEN[BARRIER, INTERNAL[E26a], X_1]	
E25 and the external	qual E26b	BETWEEN[BARRIER, INTERNAL[E26a], EXTERNAL[E26b]]	BETWEEN[BARRIER, EXT[ENVIRON-MENT],INT[ENVIRONMENT]]
E26 environment =E26a & E26b	loc E23		
E27 which	ref E26 / loc E28		
E28 contains	pred	CONTAIN[ENVIRONMENT,E32]	CONTAIN[ENVIRONMENT,MANY & POTENTIAL[HARMFUL[AGENTS]]]
E29 many	quant E32	MANY[E32]	
E30 potentially	qual E31	POTENTIAL[E31]	POTENTIAL[HARMFUL]
E31 harmful	qual E32	HARMFUL[E32]	MANY & POTENTIAL[HARMFUL[AGENTS]]
E32 agents.	theme E28		
E33 The filtering	qual E34	FILTERING[E34]	FILTERING[FUNCTION]
E34 function	agent E36		HAVE[LYMPHATIC TISSUE,FILTERING [FUNCTION]]
E35 of lymphatic tissue	qual E34		
E36 enables	pred	ENABLE[FUNCTION,E37 & E38,X_2]	
E37 the tonsils	patient E36 / agent E39	ENABLE[FUNCTION,TONSILS,X_2]	
E38 and adenoids	patient E36 / agent E39	ENABLE[FUNCTION,ADENOIDS,X_2]	

E39 to trap	pred	TRAP[TONSILS & ADENOIDS,E43]	TRAP [TONSILS & ADENOIDS, PATHOGENS]
E40 pathogens.	patient E39		ENABLE[FUNCTION,[TRAP[TONSILS & ADENOIDS,PATHOGENS]]]
E41 The cilia	agent E43		IN[CILIA,TRACT]
E42 in the respiratory tract	loc E41	HASTEN[CILIA,E44]	
E43 hasten	pred		HASTEN[CILIA,EXIT]
E44 the exit	patient E43		SOURCE[BODY,EXIT]
E45 from the body	source E44		
E46 of possibly	assess E47	POSSIBLE[E47]	POSSIBLE[HARMFUL]
E47 harmful	qual E49	HARMFUL[E49]	
E48 foreign	qual E49	FOREIGN[E49]	POSSIBLE[HARMFUL &FOREIGN[MATERIAL] EXIT[MATERIAL,BODY]
E49 material.	agent E44		
E50 By reflex action	manner E56	MANNER[E56,REFLEX ACTION]	IS[REFLEX ACTION,MECHANISM]
E51 a mechanism	specification E50		HAVE[NERVOUS SYSTEM,MECHANISM]
E52 of the nervous system	qual E51		
E53 the threatened	qual E54	THREATENED[E54]	THREATENED[HAND]
E54 hand	patient E56		
E55 is instantly	qual E56	INSTANT[E56]	INSTANT[WITHDRAW[Ø,HAND]
E56 withdrawn	pred	INSTANT[WITHDRAW[X_3,HAND]	MANNER[WITHDRAW[Ø,HAND], REFLEX ACTION]]
E57 and	new prop E58-E60		

E58 the threatened	qual E59	THREATENED[E59]	THREATENED[EYE]
E59 eye	patient E60	CLOSE[X_4,EYE]	CLOSE[Ø,EYE]
E60 closed.	pred		
E62 The eye	patient E64	FURTHER[E64]	
E63 is further	qual E64	PROTECT[E66,EYE]	
E64 protected	pred	FURTHER[PROTECT[E66,EYE]	
E65 by the constant	qual E66	CONSTANT[E66]	
E66 secretion	agent E64	SECRETE[X_5,X_6]	
	]	CONSTANT[SECRETE[X_5,X_6]]	PROTECT[CONSTANT[SECRETE[Ø, TEARS]]],EYE]
		PROTECT[CONSTANT[SECRETE[X_5,X_6]]],EYE	
E67 of tears.	patient E66	]],EYE	

Figure 1. Propositional analysis of text in example 1

The fourth and final column contains propositions which can be completely specified at the relevant point in the processing of the text. A further difference between my analysis and Kintsch's is that I have tried to make rather more transparent the semantic relationships coded by prepositional phrases in the text. Clearly, I have taken numerous decisions which could well be challenged: for instance I do not wish to make any claim for the particular set of semantic labels used in the second column. The aim is merely to give an idea of the kind of analysis envisaged in Kintsch's model.

The atomic propositions derived from the text (those in the fourth column of Figure 1) are combined into complex propositions, in which a number of atomic propositions may be subordinated to a single core proposition (Kintsch 1998: 38). This is achieved by placing modifying propositions in their proper places in the overall structure. By way of exemplification, Figure 2 shows the complex propositions which could be formed from E1-E7 in our example text.

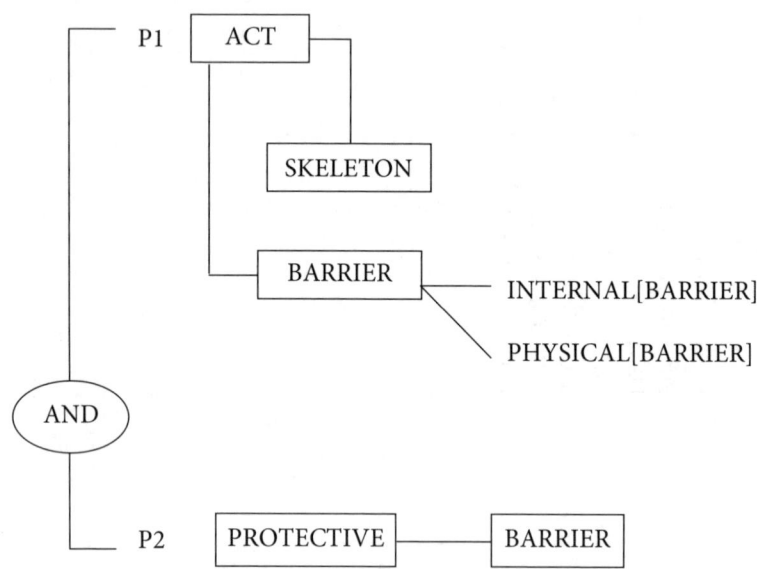

Figure 2. Complex propositions from E1-E7

Drawing on the earlier account in Van Dijk and Kintsch (1983), Kintsch (1998: 39–40) proposes three levels of relationship between (potentially complex) propositions: indirect coherence, involving the sharing of a time, place or argument, the propositions being part of the same textual episode; direct coherence, in which the type of coherence just specified is supplemented by explicit markers such as *and*, *so*, *then*, *therefore* and the like; and the subordination of one proposition to another, or to some component such as a single argument (e.g. in the case of restrictive relative clauses). For instance, in

Figure 2, there is direct coherence between P1 and P2, signalled by the connector *and*, but coherence is also achieved through the sharing of the argument BARRIER.

The analysis in terms of atomic and then complex propositions constitutes the microstructure of the textbase. There are also relationships of a higher order, which organise complex propositions into larger macropropositions, forming the global structure, or macrostructure, of the textbase (1998: 64–69). There is, Kintsch claims, strong evidence for the psychological reality of macrostructures. The operations which form macropropositions are governed by a set of what are called macrorules (Van Dijk 1980): any proposition which is not required for the interpretation of another proposition can be deleted; if each of a sequence of propositions entails a further proposition, then that more general proposition may be substituted for the sequence; and similarly a proposition which is entailed by a sequence of propositions, taken together, may be substituted for that sequence. For instance, in our example (1), the propositions in E8-E12, E13-E15 and E16-E19 present three sets of information which are exemplifications of the general statement made in E1-E7. Since the *skull*, *vertebral column* and *ribs* are all parts of the *skeleton*, and *protect-s/-ive* is repeated in each proposition, it is clear that each of the three later propositions is entailed by the combination of propositions in E1-E7, which we can therefore regard as the core, deleting the others.

As indicated by Van Dijk and Kintsch (1983) and reiterated by Kintsch (1998: 67), the formation of macrostructures depends on material available in the text itself, but also on general cultural knowledge. One example of a text-internal clue is the cohesive repetition of *protect-s/-ive* mentioned above. Another is the fact that a title, *Physical barriers and secretions* precedes the text shown in 1, pointing to a division of the text into E1-E60, which are concerned with physical barriers, and E61-E67, which deal with secretion. The general cultural knowledge needed to comprehend the text includes knowledge of the type of situation: the fact that we are concerned here with an informative text of a biological/medical nature concerned with the human body, that the writer will probably be someone not known personally to the reader, and perhaps even anonymous, and so on. As Kintsch (1998: 68) observes, language users' knowledge of the ways in which particular text types are structured is also relevant to the formation of macrostructures. For instance, narratives (in our culture, at least) have a basic structure involving setting (or exposition), complication and resolution, and this schematic structure can be used in the assignment of macropropositions. The importance of schemas (scripts, etc.) is not confined to narratives, but is evident in many everyday situations, as illustrated by Kintsch's analysis of a text evoking the grocery-shopping script (1998: 111–118).

In taking the step of forming macropropositions, then, we have begun to go beyond the information which is actually available in the text itself, to call upon the language user's knowledge of various kinds. Here, therefore, is where we start to move from the textbase into the situational model. Kintsch (1998: 104) points out that the extent to which we need to fill out the textbase by means of a situational model will differ from one text to another, but that typically, the mental representation of a text is a mixture of the two kinds of information, in varying proportions.

So far, we have been concerned with the constructive part of Kintsch's construction-integration model of comprehension. In order to understand the need for the second, integrative component, it is necessary to realise that the construction of the textbase may lead to alternative, possibly incompatible, interpretations of (part of) a text. Consider, for example, the word *acts*, which occurs twice as an intransitive verb in example (1). In this text, the appropriate meaning is the one which appears in the Collins English Dictionary as 'serve the function or purpose (of)'; however, there are also other meanings, such as 'to perform (a part or role) in a play, etc.', 'to conduct oneself or behave (as if one were)', and 'to behave in an unnatural or affected way'. Kintsch's contention (1998: 95) is that propositions with all possible meanings of a word will be formed, but that the inappropriate readings will be rapidly suppressed. As a second example, consider the sentence in (2):

(2)   *This is especially so in the case of visiting competitors.* (BNC J7B 1248)

This corresponds, potentially, to two different predications, one in which the competitors are visiting someone, the other in which they are being visited. According to the construction-integration model, both will be activated briefly. That the first of these interpretations is the correct one is shown by the context of the sentence, as shown in (3):

(3)   *Likewise, if visitors have been allowed to walk around his premises without restriction then the court will take this into account in its examination of the claim. This is especially so in the case of visiting competitors. If an employer does not prevent them availing themselves of the opportunity to learn business secrets how can he later seek to restrain an employee from using the same information.* (BNC J7B 1247–1249)

The suppression of inappropriate readings, and more generally the tightening up of the initial partially contradictory and incoherent set of propositions into a coherent structure, is achieved through the integration component of the model. In order to understand how this works, we need to say a little more about the form in which the knowledge base is claimed to be represented.

Knowledge, in the construction-integration model, is seen as an associative network, with nodes representing concepts and links between the nodes representing associations of varying strength between the concepts. In Kintsch's model (1998: 74), the nodes of a knowledge net are propositions, schematic constructs (schemas, frames, scripts) and production rules, all of which can be represented in the propositional format of predicates and arguments. The meaning of any given node is the whole set of relations, of varying strengths, which it contracts with its near and further neighbours. Kintsch points out, however, that in the processing of a particular piece of language, only those nodes which are actually active in working memory at the time form part of the meaning of nodes to which they are connected. In psychological terms, then, meaning is very flexible, being constructed on the fly, and so slightly different each time a concept is required.

We are now in a position to see, in outline, how the integration process works (Kintsch 1998: 98–103). The basic principle is that of spreading activation, a process of key importance in connectionist models. Activation spreads to any given node from all the nodes which are its neighbours, according to their strengths of connection, in a process which has been mathematically modelled. Some links will be inhibitory, with negative strength values: for instance, a proposition will inhibit another proposition with which it is contradictory. Eventually, the activation process reaches a steady state. Nodes which have numerous positive connections with other nodes will be strengthened, while nodes with few and/or negatively weighted connections will diminish in importance and may even disappear. The model postulates that as text elements are processed, the new propositions formed are immediately integrated with the existing textual representation, but that integration at the end of a sentence is of particular significance in that for all but the shortest sentences the working memory will be saturated at this point, so that the text representation must be transferred into long-term memory, only one or two propositions being retained in working memory because they appear to be relevant to further processing[3].

An important question, of course, is how we might go about constructing a knowledge base for use in testing the predictions of the construction-integration model. The method used by Kintsch and his associates involved a technique known as Latent Semantic Analysis (LSA) (see Kintsch 1998: 86–91 and the references given there, also the papers available for downloading at http://lsa.colorado.edu[4]), in which the frequencies of word forms in a collection of texts are used to create a mathematical model of the strengths of association between words, also between (words and) sentences, and between texts. As Kintsch recognises, the information so obtained is limited in that no account is taken of syntactic relationships. Nevertheless, the technique has been shown to have considerable potential for knowledge representation.

In the second part of his book, Kintsch (1998) presents detailed empirical evidence in relation to word identification, the formation of macrostructures and their role in the putting together of textbases and situation models, the role of working memory in comprehension, memory for text, learning from text, and the solving of verbally-posed problems in arithmetic, finally moving to consider action planning, problem solving, decision making, and the representation of the self, all in relation to the construction-integration model. Further work on the model and its applications can be found in Weaver, Mannes and Fletcher (1995).

---

3.   See also Rayner and Sereno (1994: 74), who state that there is evidence, from studies of eye movements during reading, that "readers attempt to integrate information from within a clause or sentence and that these additional processing demands are reflected in longer fixations occurring at the end of the clause or sentence".

4.   Accessed 15 October 2005.

Given the concept-based nature of Kintsch's model, it seems pertinent to consider whether this approach could fruitfully be integrated, as part of the process component, into a more linguistically-oriented model of language. There are, however, some issues which need to be addressed.

Firstly, the relationship between words and concepts in the Kintsch model seems to me to be rather unclear. In his discussion of concepts and the construction of meaning, Kintsch states:

> In a mental lexicon, one looks up the meaning of a word. In a knowledge net, there is nothing to look up. Meaning has to be constructed by activating nodes in the neighbourhood of a word. (Kintsch 1998: 76)

But surely the nodes in a knowledge net are not themselves words, but concepts (furthermore, propositional concepts), so that the idea of the neighbourhood of a word does not seem coherent: what we need to know is the relationship between a word and particular conceptual nodes in the network. This confusion is compounded by the LSA technique used as an approximation to knowledge nets: as outlined briefly earlier, this technique computes relationships between linguistic units (word forms, sentences, texts), and these are then taken to represent concepts. However, the relationship between the words of a language and the underlying concepts they encode is indirect, complex and culturally relative, and although this may not be of crucial importance in the context of a psychological theory of discourse comprehension, it is clearly a key issue for any linguistic theory which is concerned not only with psychological but also with sociocultural adequacy.

The idea of a network of conceptual relationships is, of course, not specific to Kintsch's model: such networks are also used both in cognitive-functional linguistics (see e.g. the Functional Procedural Grammar of Nuyts 1992, 2001) and in computational linguistics, where they go under the name of ontologies. Figure 3 shows the least detailed end of the conceptual ontology elaborated in the Mikrokosmos project (Mahesh 1996). At first sight, there seems to be some discrepancy between Kintsch's knowledge nets and an ontological network of the kind displayed in Figure 3, in that the nodes in a knowledge net represent propositional concepts, while those in the ontology represent entities, events and properties. This difference may, however, be more apparent than real. Kintsch's networks actually contain nodes referring to a wide range of concept types, from propositions themselves to complex frames, scripts and schemas; the important point is that all of these can be represented in propositional form. When we look in greater detail at the Mikrokosmos ontology, however, we find that concept definitions are presented as frame structures, and that the most important aspects of the knowledge model are the properties (relations and attributes) through which concepts are linked. These, like the nodes in Kintsch's knowledge nets, effectively build in propositional information. As an example, consider the representation for the concept ACQUIRE in the ontology (Beale, Nirenburg and Mahesh 1995: 5). The frame for this concept specifies that the concept requires an AGENT which must be HUMAN, and a

THEME which must be a non-human OBJECT. We could thus construct a partial specification in propositional terms, as in (4):

(4)   ACQUIRE(AGENT[HUMAN],THEME[OBJECT])

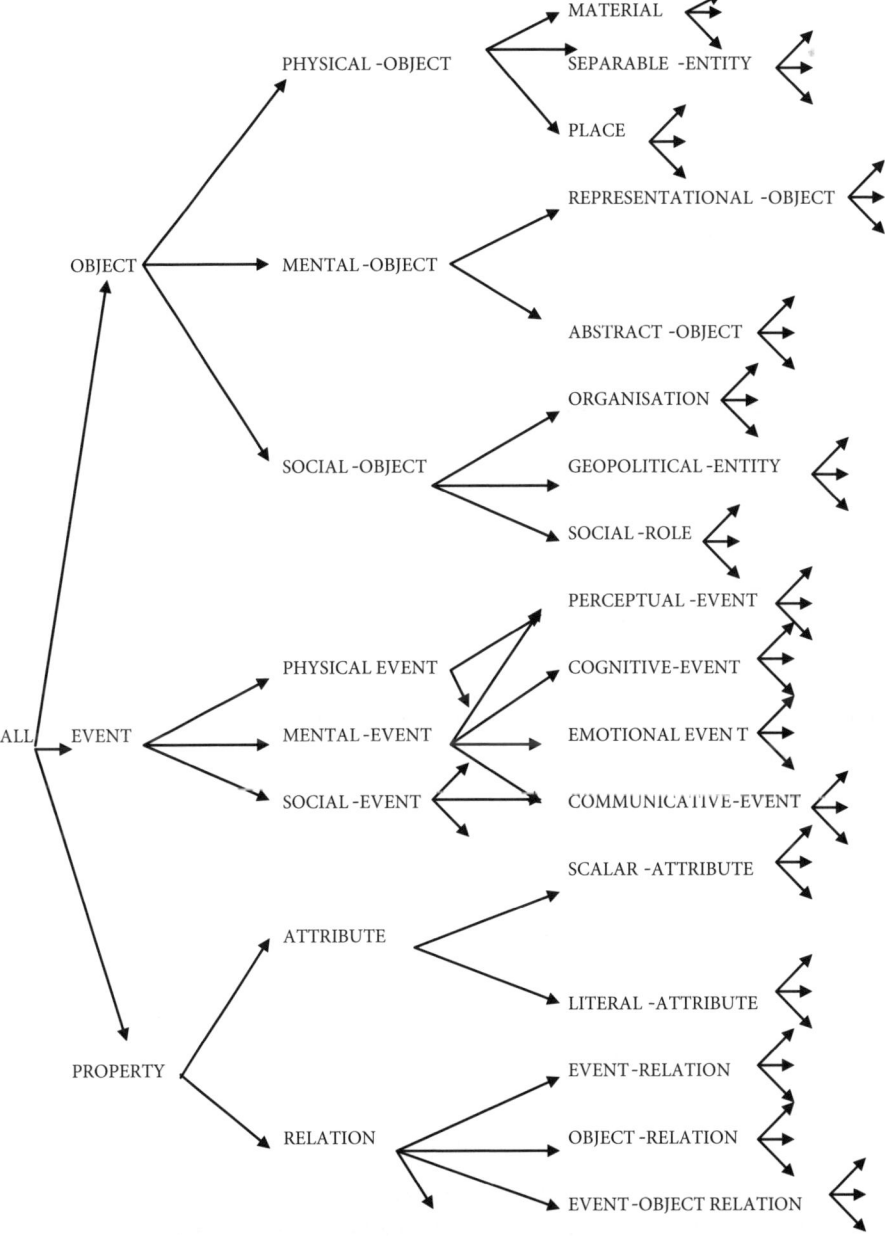

Figure 3. The highest levels in the Mikrokosmos ontology

Further slots are concerned with the basic nature of the concept (it IS-A type of TRANS-FER-POSSESSION), the PURPOSE of acquiring (specified as BID), the INSTRUMENT (HUMAN or EVENT), a PRECONDITION (in terms of OWNERSHIP), a SOURCE (specified as HUMAN) and a LOCATION (some PLACE). Certainly it would seem that it is worth exploring, in future research, the relationships between Kintsch's knowledge nets and ontologies of the kind illustrated by Mikrokosmos.

A second problem, as Kintsch himself has recognised, is that further work is needed on the provision of an adequate parsing component in the model. Kintsch (1998: 54) comments that he has had no success in taking already developed parsers as front ends to his comprehension model. What is clear is that in order to be consistent with the construction-integration model, a parser would have to be interactive, in the sense of using a variety of information sources in an integrated manner, rather than autonomous, with a separate syntactic parser running independently of semantic processing. It is also clear that the parser would have to operate on the principle that lexical activation is itself not highly sensitive to context; rather, the required lexical item is selected through a subsequent process of integration by spreading activation as described earlier.

Finally, Kintsch's work is concerned only with the comprehension of discourse, whereas in any comprehensive linguistic model we also need to address the discourse production process and its relationship with comprehension. Studies of discourse processing in production have so far lagged behind those concerned with comprehension.

3.   Werth's text world model

In Werth's Cognitive Discourse Grammar, set out in some detail in a book (Werth 1999) published a few years after his untimely death, the concept of discourse is defined as follows:

> A deliberate and joint effort on the part of a producer and recipients to build up a 'world' within which the propositions advanced are coherent and make complete sense. (1999: 51)

Werth's book is concerned primarily with the question:

> how do we make sense of complex utterances when we receive them (as hearers or readers? (1999: 7)

and with the related question:

> how do we as speakers (writers) put together a complex utterance in order to express particular concepts? (1999: 7)

The model is thus intended to address the issues of both discourse comprehension and production. As a major part of the answer to both of the above questions, Werth advances the hypothesis that we form mental constructs which he calls **discourse worlds,**

text worlds and **sub-worlds**, which are a subtype of the more general category of **situation**. A situation consists of (i) some location l_i; (ii) some time t_j; (iii) a set of entities $\{e_n\}$ such that at least one of these (p_1) must be a participant in the discourse, with the possibility of further participants (p_{2-n}) and inanimate objects (o_n); (iv) a set of functions $\{r_n\}$, such that the set of expressions mapping entities into functions holds at the specified location and time (1999: 84). This definition allows the building up of rich worlds reflecting not only the semantic and pragmatic content of any proposition currently in the focus of attention, but also the knowledge invoked by that proposition and by the preceding discourse.

Two kinds of situations are represented together in a discourse: the immediate situation or **discourse world** and the textual situation or **text world**. The discourse world is "the situational context surrounding the speech event itself" (1999: 83), and contains not only the discourse participants and the entities they can perceive, but also whatever they can work out from what they perceive, including the products of interaction with processes of remembering, imagining, and the like. The text world is "a deictic space, defined initially by the discourse itself, and specifically by the deictic and referential elements in it" (1999: 51). It is "the 'story' which is the subject of the discourse, together with all the structure necessary to understand it" (1999: 87). As Werth points out, most discourses are concerned with situations which are remote in time and space from the actual situation of discourse, though some are concerned with the discourse world itself. In both cases, Werth distinguishes the two types of world: when the discourse world itself is the topic of interaction, then the text world is that part of it which is in focus at the time. Werth notes (1999: 20) that the concept of text world has something in common with Fauconnier's (1985/1995) concept of mental spaces, Fillmore's (1985) frames, and Lakoff's (1987) idealised cognitive models. Deictic and referential items given in the discourse specify times, places, people, objects, their properties and relationships. These, in turn, can activate frames, "areas of memory which relate to areas of experience and knowledge encoded as complex conceptual structures" (1999: 51)[5].

A crucial concept in Werth's model is that of context, since it provides the link between a text and the discourse of which it is the verbal part: a discourse is a text plus its relevant context (1999: 47). Werth (1999: 78–80) distinguishes between the verbal context (i.e. what I have called the cotext) and the situational context. As he points out, many linguists have been somewhat reluctant to engage with situational context, believing that it is too vast to be handled in any principled, systematic way within linguistics. Werth's way of making it more manageable is to propose, as a major element of his model, that what counts as relevant situational context for a particular discourse is restricted by the text which that discourse produces:

---

5.   Zwaan, Langston and Graesser (1995) have also proposed that time, space and protagonists (as well as causality and intentionality) are dimensions on which readers construct representations of stories. Zwaan (1996) presents evidence from reading time studies to show that when processing narrative texts, readers build time-based models in response to temporal phrases in the text.

> The relevant situation is [...] *precisely* restricted in every case by the text which its discourse produces, and the discourse provides just enough detail to set up a text world and to activate the relevant areas of knowledge. No further details are necessary than are provided by the discourse together with information available from the frames accessed by participant knowledge. (Werth 1999: 80, emphasis in original)

An important feature of context in Werth's model is that it is not simply 'there', but is actually constructed in a process of negotiation on the part of the discourse participants (1999: 118–19). This dynamic, ethnographically-oriented approach to context has been characterised by Goodwin and Duranti as being concerned with

> ... how participants attend to, construct, and manipulate aspects of context as a constitutive feature of the activities they are engaged in (Goodwin and Duranti 1992: 9).

This means that

> Instead of viewing context as a set of variables that statically surround strips of talk, context and talk are now argued to stand in a mutually reflexive relationship to each other, with talk, and the interpretive work it generates, shaping context as much as context shapes talk. (Goodwin and Duranti 1992: 31)

This approach to context is reminiscent of that taken in Systemic Functional Linguistics, where the work of Martin, Hasan and others has adopted a dialogic perspective, according to which text and context are in a mutually dependent relationship (see the summary in Butler 2003b: 377–390 and the references given there). It would therefore be of interest to investigate the extent to which categories of contextual description derived from systemic accounts could be used to add depth of detail to Werth's more cognitively-oriented model.

The process of context construction in Werth's model leads to a set of propositions which acts as what Werth calls the Common Ground (CG), which is:

> the totality of information which the speaker(s) and hearer(s) have agreed to accept as relevant for their discourse (1999:119)

That part of the CG which constructs the text world (world-building information) is background information, while that which is contributed by the discourse itself (function-advancing information) is foreground information. The CG alters as the discourse proceeds, with addition of new information and modification and decaying of old information (1999:120).

Particularly important to the building up of the CG is the shared knowledge of the discourse participants, which Werth (1999: 96ff) divides into general and mutual types. General (or public) knowledge is that which individuals possess because they belong to particular social groupings, and is divided into cultural and linguistic subtypes. Cultural knowledge is characterised as being "partially structured, open-ended and contingent"

(1999: 97), and the structured elements of it are stored in frames. Linguistic knowledge, on the other hand, is "structured, systematic and analytical" (1999: 98). The two types of general knowledge are seen as linked in complex ways. Mutual knowledge is private knowledge which comes about, during interaction, by the incrementation of the CG as the discourse proceeds. It may be derived from the mutual perceptions of the immediate situation of the discourse, or from shared experience, that is, situations in which both/all the discourse participants have directly participated, or with which they have some specifiable connection. Cross-cutting the distinction into general and mutual knowledge is that between propositional and functional types (1999: 101–07): propositional knowledge expresses facts of a cultural, linguistic, perceptual or experiential nature; while functional knowledge is concerned with the ability to act towards some particular goal, and can again be of any of the four types outlined above. Werth (1999: 110) links this distinction to a typology of frames, distinguishing between propositional, content-oriented frames, and functional frames of the type which cognitive linguists call image schemata, based on physical and conceptual action.

The CG is also crucial to the treatment of textual coherence in Werth's model. It is proposed that a Coherence Constraint filters out all non-coherent propositions. This constraint is expressed in terms of the CG as follows:

> … for any proposition there is a Common Ground (CG) relating to the same discourse as the proposition under consideration, and this proposition bears one of the functional conditions with respect to that CG. (Werth 1999: 129)

The functional conditions concerned here are those of full or partial synonymy, antonymy, hyponymy, metonymy or metaphor. It is proposed in Werth (1984) that a mechanism of emphasis placement converts coherence into patterns of Given and New information and their realisation.

Werth also makes interesting suggestions about the shape of a semantics which would be compatible with his cognitively-based discourse model, distinguishing (1999: 157) between what he calls the modality function of language ("the situating of the information with respect to the current context") and the information function (basically consisting of what is frequently called propositional meaning). The modality function includes meanings related to probability, social deixis, and what he calls viewpoint, concerned with relationships in space and, derived from this, time[6]. These various types of meaning are, Werth contends, crucially involved in the building of text worlds.

---

6.   The distinction between modality and informational functions looks rather like the distinction between interpersonal and ideational/representational function, made in Systemic Functional Grammar (see e.g. Halliday and Matthiessen 2004) and Functional Grammar (see Hengeveld 1989), where meanings concerned with probability and with social deixis would be interpersonal in nature. However, Werth's viewpoint category, concerned with relationships in space and time, would be seen in other approaches as basically ideational/representational categories. A comparison of Werth's views with those of systemic linguists would be a particularly interesting exercise.

As a very brief and over-simplified illustration of how text worlds are built up, let us consider the short excerpt in (5) below:

(5)   *Mrs Hobden went into the kitchen, and a few minutes later she came through the doorway carrying a tray. Robert jumped to his feet, but she waved him aside and placed the tea and biscuits on a nearby table.* (BNC JYE 4520–21)

This comes very near the beginning of a chapter in a novel. There will, of course, be elements already available to the reader from the previous discourse, but I will concentrate here on just this passage, to show how the text world corresponding to the situation described in it can be created. First of all, let us examine the world-building, deictic and referential, elements of the passage, which relate to time, place and the entities mentioned (1999: 187). With regard to time, the tense locates the action in the past with respect to the time of narration, and *a few minutes later* locates the action of coming through the doorway with respect to that of going into the kitchen.

The locational elements are *the kitchen, the doorway*, and *a nearby table*[7]. The relevant entities are *Mrs Hobden, Robert* (who are characters in the text), *a tray*, and *the tea and biscuits*. These various elements are involved in a number of propositions, most of which are plot-advancing (or, to use the more general term which Werth coins to cover a range of genres rather than just narratives, function-advancing). *Mrs Hobden went into the kitchen, (Mrs Hobden) came through the doorway, Robert jumped to his feet, (Mrs Hobden) waved (Robert) aside, (Mrs Hobden) placed the tea and biscuits on a nearby table*, all represent what Werth, following the terminology of cognitive linguistics, terms paths, and all advance the sequence of the narrative action. On the other hand, *carrying a tray* offers more descriptive information. The various elements and their relationships are shown in Figure 4, in which vertical arrows represent paths, while horizontal arrows represent modifications using steady state predications, and also clause connections. In addition to the relationships explicitly signalled in the text, we must take into account those which can be inferred, including those arising from the interaction of textual elements with the reader's knowledge of appropriate schematic structures or frames. For instance, even without any previous context to guide us, we can infer that Mrs Hobden moved to and from a room in which she and Robert are both located at the beginning of the mini-text in 5. Furthermore, we can infer that the tea and biscuits are on the tray which Mrs Hobden brings from the kitchen. The mention of trays, tea and biscuits also invokes a culturally significant frame concerned with the provision of light refreshments for visitors.

---

7.   For the purposes of this exercise, I will assume that *jump to one's feet* and *wave aside* are complex predicates.

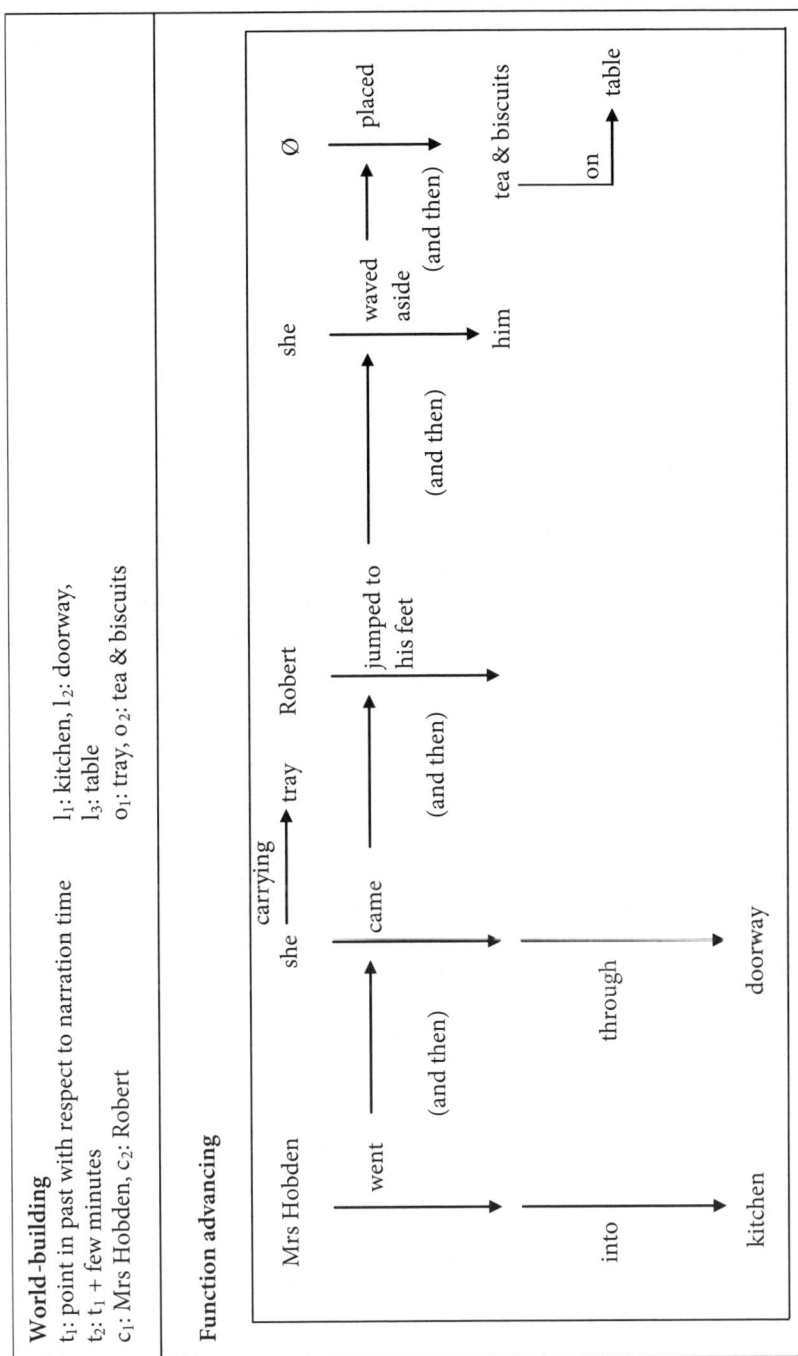

World-building
t_1: point in past with respect to narration time l_1: kitchen, l_2: doorway,
t_2: t_1 + few minutes l_3: table
c_1: Mrs Hobden, c_2: Robert o_1: tray, o_2: tea & biscuits

Function advancing

Figure 4 Representation of the text world built up from example (4)

The above brief account has by no means done justice to the richness and complexity of Werth's text worlds model: for instance, I have not talked about subworlds (Werth 1999: Chapter 8), or the techniques of revealed reference and accommodation, by means of which the presence of a referent in a text world is taken to be assumed without having been explicitly established (1999: Chapter 9). Nevertheless, I hope that I have been able to give at least a general idea of what Werth has in mind. A book-length application of Werth's model in relation to the area of negation in fictional writing can be found in Hidalgo Downing (2000).

4.   Towards a synthesis of approaches

It is obvious, from the preceding accounts, that there are major differences of orientation and aims between Kintsch's and Werth's models. Kintsch is concerned to establish a psychological theory of discourse comprehension, which explicitly models the processes of construction and integration through which we are said to come to an understanding of a discourse, and presents empirical evidence bearing on the claims made. Werth, on the other hand, is concerned with a specification of the overall mental models which we create in response to a text embedded in its situation, without presenting any detail of the psychological processing involved, or any psycholinguistic evidence.

Despite these clear differences, however, there are some interesting similarities between the two approaches. Both, in their rather different ways, stress the importance of both the text itself and its context: Kintsch's model distinguishes the textbase and the situation model, while Werth's has a parallel distinction between the information derived from the text and the situational information which is activated by the textual information. Both scholars adopt an essentially constructivist approach to discourse processes: Kintsch emphasises that meanings are not just 'there', but are constructed through activation of nodes in the knowledge net, sensitive to the context; Werth stresses that context is not something fixed and external, but is constructed as the discourse proceeds. Both models use propositional structures and although Werth does not follow Kintsch in proposing that non-propositional knowledge should be expressed propositionally, he does recognise that functional knowledge can, in principle, be converted to propositional knowledge (Werth 1999: 103). It would be useful to investigate the extent to which Kintsch's hierarchy of atomic propositions, complex propositions and macropropositions can be mapped on to the text worlds and subworlds of Werth's model. Clearly, a discourse model which uses propositional representations is an advantage in terms of specifying the relationships between discourse structures and clauses, which also encode propositional information.

It does, then, seem worthwhile for future research to explore the relationships between these models, in order to arrive at a more comprehensive picture of discourse processing which could form part of our overall model. Furthermore, it would be instructive to examine the extent to which the units and relationships proposed in various functionally-based approaches to discourse relate to the categories and relationships of Kintsch's and Werth's models. Suitable candidates for further study would include: the units of Hengeveld's Functional Discourse Grammar (Hengeveld 2004a, 2004b, 2005; Hengeveld and Mackenzie 2006, in preparation); the rank-based hierarchy of units in Sinclair and Coulthard's (1975) model of discourse; the idea units realised by intonation or punctuation groups in the proposals of Roulet (1997), Chafe (1994) and Hannay (1998); the acts and subacts of Mackenzie's (2000, 2004) Incremental Functional Grammar; the stretches of discourse connected by functional relations in Rhetorical Structure Theory (Mann and Thompson 1987, 1988); and the functional elements of Hasan's (1978, 1984, 1985/1989) generic structure potentials.

A final similarity between the Kintsch and Werth approaches which is of some consequence for our own purposes is concerned with the linkage, or lack of it, between the discourse model and an underlying theory of semantics and form. As we have seen, Kintsch's model is not linked to any specific underlying linguistic theory which could provide appropriate semantic and syntactic representations. Indeed, as Kintsch himself remarks (1998: 60), for the psychological purposes for which the model is intended, "we do not need a logically consistent system or a detailed semantics". Similarly Werth, despite recognising relationships with the cognitive linguistic work of scholars such as Lakoff, Fauconnier and Fillmore, does not provide any account of how his discourse model, or the semantics which underlies it, hook up to a more detailed specification of meanings, forms and the relationships between the two. It is to such a specification, and its links with other components of the overall model of linguistic communication, that we now turn.

5.   In search of an appropriate grammatical component

5.1   The role of the grammar in comprehension

5.1.1   *Introduction*
A survey of work in the comprehension of spoken language is available in Cutler and Clifton (1999), and a parallel survey for written language in Perfetti (1999); the following brief summary draws heavily on these two sources. I shall start from the point where a word has been recognised, either form the spoken input stream or from a written text: models of how recognition occurs, which are covered in the survey articles cited above and also in the briefer and simpler survey by Reeves, Hirsch-Pasek and Golinkoff (1998), are less relevant to our present concerns. As far as spoken language is concerned, it will suffice to say here that it is generally agreed that word recognition occurs by a process of competition between candidate words which are activated as a result of compatibility with some part of the speech signal (Cutler and Clifton 1999: 134). There are two main types of model which appear to account well for the recognition of written words: the Dual Route Model proposes that written words are identi-

fied, according to the particular circumstances, either by a direct route from graphemic information to the word representation, or by a route which is mediated through grapheme-phoneme relationships (Perfetti 1999: 173–74); the PDP (parallel distributed processing) model postulates that word recognition occurs through distributed patterns of activation during propagation across layers of units of several kinds (Perfetti 1999: 171–72).

The question which is of greatest interest here is what kinds of information the successful lexical candidate brings with it for use in subsequent stages of comprehension. In what follows, we shall look briefly at evidence for the participation of morphological, semantic and syntactic phenomena in comprehension.

5.1.2   *Morphology*

Cutler and Clifton (1999: 139–40) summarise the evidence for morphological structure in the stored forms of words, concluding that morphologically complex words in English are probably activated as the full form, though recognition of a spoken word will make available morphological information, such as marking for tense and number, which aids in the construction of higher-level units. The authors add that a model which is valid for English may not hold for languages of other morphological types. Perfetti's review of written language comprehension claims that "readers can be quite sensitive to the morphological structure of words under some circumstances" (1999: 180), though it is an open question whether words are actually decomposed into their morphemes during reading.

5.1.3   *Semantics*

Clearly, the meaning of a word, in its context, is of paramount importance for the listener or reader in deciding what part that word plays in the utterance being decoded[8]. Cutler and Clifton's (1999: 140–41) summary of evidence regarding the semantic information available on spoken word recognition suggests that all meanings of an ambiguous word are potentially available, but that all but the most contextually appropriate meanings decay rapidly, to the extent that very strongly biasing contexts can virtually suppress activation of all but the meaning which best fits the context. For written language comprehension, Perfetti (1999: 182) concludes that most of the experimental results obtained can be accommodated under the view that all meanings of an ambiguous word are indeed activated, but that the extent of activation depends on

---

8.   For an account of the neural architecture of word meanings, and support for the view that knowledge of a concept is distributed among a number of subsystems corresponding to the channels (auditory, visual, tactile, kinaesthetic, action-oriented) through which information about the concept is acquired, see Saffran and Sholl (1999).

the context of utterance, and also on the frequency of the meanings concerned[9]. Wingfield and Titone (1998: 253–57), in their discussion of experimental evidence regarding the role of context, also come to the conclusion that multiple meanings are initially activated for ambiguous words, and that context then filters out all but the meaning most appropriate to the context.

5.1.4   *Syntax*

An introductory treatment of the role of syntax in sentence processing can be found in Wingfield and Titone (1998), and a much more detailed account, angled towards neurocognitive considerations, in Hagoort, Brown and Osterhout (1999), on which much of the current section is based. There is a strong general consensus in the processing literature that syntactic processing is a central component of comprehension as well as production:

> … it is a nearly universally accepted notion in current models of the production and interpretation of multiword utterances that constraints on how words can be structurally combined in sentences are immediately taken into consideration during speaking and listening/reading. (Hagoort, Brown and Osterhout (1999: 273)

As a simple illustration of the importance of syntax, Hagoort, Brown and Osterhout point to the fact that we can parse sentences without understanding their meaning, in cases where nonsense words are embedded in a normal syntactic structure. A frequently cited example is from Lewis Carroll's poem *Jabberwocky* from *Through the Looking Glass*: when we read or hear *'Twas brillig, and the slithy toves did gyre and gimble in the wabe*, there is a lot that we can deduce about the structure: *brillig* and *slithy* are adjectives, *tove* and *wabe* nouns, *gyre* and *gimble* verbs; *slithy* is a modifier of *toves*; and so on.

There is also evidence from reading studies that reading rate decreases at clause boundaries, indicating that such boundaries are important in online processing (for a summary see Wingfield and Titone (1998: 236–37).

Although the importance of syntax in comprehension seems to be beyond doubt, the detailed operation of syntactic parsing in language comprehension is still the subject of vigorous debate, as Cutler and Clifton (1999: 142–43) point out. Perfetti's (1999: 182–86) brief summary of work on parsing during reading presents a similarly diffuse picture of the state of the art.

Hagoort, Brown and Osterhout (1999: 276–80) discuss five areas of debate about the precise nature of the parsing mechanisms. Firstly, there is the question of whether the same devices are used for parsing and for grammatical encoding during language production; the authors regard this as an open issue at present. Secondly, we need to

---

9.   The importance of frequency in comprehension is also suggested by work on Event Related Potentials (ERPs) in the brain, which demonstrates a component sensitive to the frequency of occurrence of the eliciting word in the language as a whole (see the summary in Kutas, Federmeier and Sereno (1999: 366) and the reference cited there).

know whether the same parser is used for both listening and reading; most models of comprehension assume a common parser, which is augmented with extra speech-specific information sources in listening. Thirdly, there is a debate concerning the type of working memory resource (general or dedicated) used for parsing. Fourthly, there is the question of what sources of information are used to assign a structure to a string of words during comprehension: some models propose that a structure is first built wholly on syntactic principles, and then passed to a semantic interpreter; other approaches postulate that a number of sources of information (pragmatic and semantic as well as syntactic) immediately combine to guide the formation of the structure. The authors' view is that recent evidence favours the second of these claims. Finally, there is still some debate about whether an actual syntactic structure is produced at all during comprehension: although it is generally agreed that syntactic information is used, some scholars hold that the information from various levels is integrated into a direct mapping between word-level information and an interpretation of the sentence.

Hagoort, Brown and Osterhout (1999: 280–305) go on to discuss the evidence on syntactic processing which has been accumulating in recent years from electrophysiological studies, brain imaging techniques and the effects of anatomical lesions. Lack of space precludes further discussion of this work here.

5.1.5   The components of an adequate grammar

Although there is still clearly a very long way to go in unravelling the complexities of language comprehension, the above brief review of what is known about processing provides us with some clear guidelines about what components should figure in our grammar. The model will certainly need to have separate semantic and morphosyntactic representations, together with a lexicon. The claim that semantic and discoursal information is used in the determination of syntactic structures during processing means that the various components, though separate, interact in complex ways. Finally, the fact that we are looking for a theory for incorporation into a usage-based, processing-oriented model suggests that a functional approach would be most appropriate.

At the semantic level, our grammar should deal with propositional structure and meaning. Thus, we need to account for:
- the semantics of predicates and their arguments, and of satellites/adjuncts
- the roles associated with arguments and satellites/adjuncts
- the content and structuring of meanings, such as those of tense, aspect, modality, illocution, definiteness, etc, which are realised grammatically in many languages.

The lexicon will, of course, need to play a key part in the model, especially in view of the well-documented importance of lexical selection processes in language production and comprehension. Clearly, any psychologically adequate model of the lexicon must take fully into account what is known of mechanisms of lexical storage and access. Although research in this complex area has not yet led to any definitive view, it does seem that spreading activation models of the kind proposed in Kintsch's construction-integration theory have considerable explanatory power. It is also important to bear in mind the likelihood that many multiword sequences are stored and retrieved as (partially or fully) pre-formed chunks, at least in certain processing conditions (for detailed discussion and a model of formulaic language see Wray 2002).

Finally, we need an expression component, to convert lexicalised syntactic structures, with their semantic mappings, into the final form of the utterance.

5.1.6   *Role and Reference Grammar as an appropriate grammatical component for a comprehension model*

In this section I shall demonstrate that Role and Reference Grammar, as most recently set out in Van Valin (2005) fulfils the requirements detailed above[10].

In common with other functional theories, RRG recognises the (partial) semantic motivation for syntax. However, Van Valin (1990) argues that in order to capture crucial syntactic differences between languages, a distinct level of syntax is required. The syntactic elements postulated for the clause are **core** and **periphery**[11]. The core contains the **nucleus** (housing the predicate) together with the core syntactic arguments of the predicate; the periphery contains optional adjuncts (non-arguments). In some languages, the clause has a **pre-core slot**, which is the position in which *wh* and fronted items occupy in English; some other languages have a **post-core slot** with similar functions. Outside the clause, but inside the sentence, there may be **left detached** and/or **right detached** positions, marked off from the clause itself by punctuation, or by pausing in the spoken language. Clear syntactic evidence for the distinctness of left detached elements and the pre-core slot has been adduced from several languages. The syntactic structure of the simple sentence in (6) is given in Figure 5:

(6)   *She kissed Ian warmly.* (BNC AN8 0155)

The syntactic structure given in Figure 5 is the **constituent projection** for the sentence. Associated with this are two further structures: (i) the **operator projection**, showing the values of operators for properties such as illocutionary force, tense, aspect, modality, etc., and the unit in the structure to which each is attached; and (ii) the **focus projection**, showing the domain of focus in the sentence, within the potential focus domain allowed by the language concerned. For the above example, the operator projection would show that declarative illocutionary force and past tense are associated with the unit clause, the former operator having scope over the latter. The focus projection would show, in what is perhaps the most likely reading of the sentence, that

---

10.   For further suggestions regarding the implementation of RRG in a parser, see Van Valin (2006), and for a production model incorporating RRG Butler (2007). For detailed comparison of RRG with Functional Grammar and Systemic Functional Grammar see Butler (2003a, 2003b).

11.   In the latest proposals for RRG, the clause and nucleus also have their own periphery (Van Valin 2005: 21). This will not be explored further in the present paper.

the actual focus domain is the constituent *warmly*, falling within the potential focus domain for English, which is the whole clause.

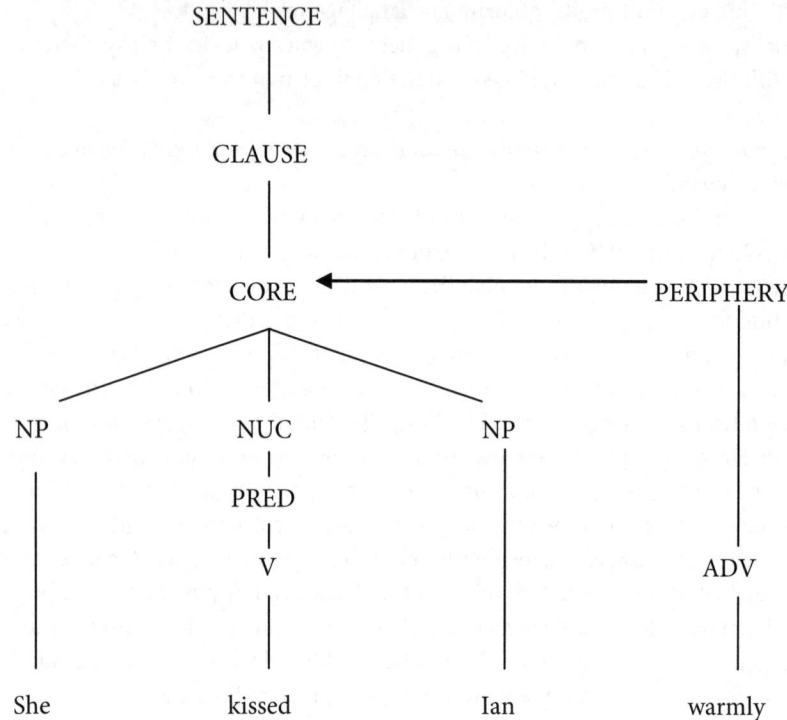

Figure 5. Syntactic structure of example (6)

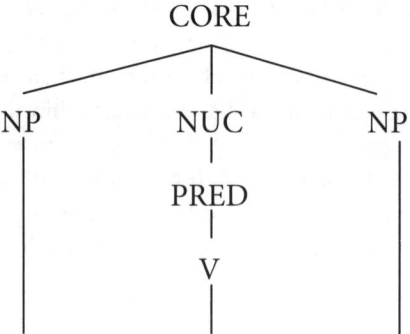

Figure 6. The core-3 template needed for the structure of example (6)

The syntactic configurations which are possible in a given language are stored as a set of **constructional templates**. In many ways these are analogous to the constructions of

Construction Grammar, with the important exception that Construction Grammar postulates that all types of information are integrated into a construction, while RRG keeps the syntactic inventory of templates separate from the lexicon. The constructional template needed for the clause in (6) is shown in Figure 6, taken from Van Valin (2005: 15).

The semantic representations of RRG are centred on the **logical structures** associated with predicates, and are stored in the lexicon. The semantic structure of example (6) is shown in (7).

(7)   **warm′** ([**do′** (3sgF, [**kiss′** (3sgF, Ian)])])

In this representation, elements with primes, such as **kiss′** or **warm′**, do not stand for the English words they resemble, but are placeholders for eventual decompositions into putatively universal semantic components. This aspect of RRG was, until recently, very under-developed, though Van Valin and Wilkins (1993) offer some amplification. Of considerable interest, therefore, is the recent work of Mairal Usón and his colleagues (Mairal Usón and Van Valin 2001; Mairal Usón and Faber 2002, 2005; Guest and Mairal Usón 2005), who propose a synthesis of RRG with the Functional Lexematic Model (FLM, see Martín Mingorance 1998, Faber and Mairal Usón 1999). The FLM in turn develops the potential of the lexicon in Functional Grammar (Dik 1997a, 1997b) by importing from Coseriu's (1981) lexematics the structuring of the lexicon in terms of lexical fields, or domains. The rich lexical structures developed in the FLM thus provide the detailed semantic decomposition which was lacking in RRG.

Logical structure configurations, such as that in (7), automatically determine what semantic roles will be associated with the arguments of the predicate. The first argument of the activity predicate **do′** (identical to the first argument of **kiss′**) is an EFFECTOR, while the second argument of the activity predicate is a PATIENT. Thematic roles can be generalised into two larger classes known as **macroroles**; Actor and Undergoer, the allocation of which is determined by the Actor-Undergoer Hierarchy (Van Valin 2005: 61) shown in Figure 7.

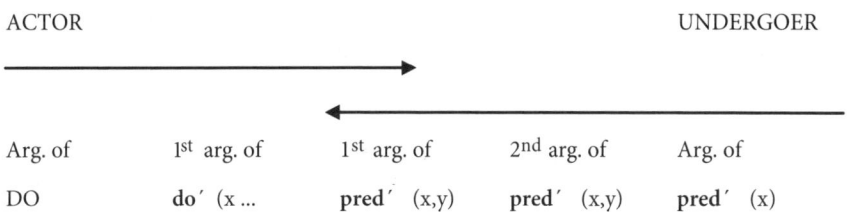

Figure 7. The RRG Actor-Undergoer Hierarchy

If there are two or more core arguments in a clause, the default is for the argument furthest to the left in the hierarchy to act as Actor, while the one furthest to the right acts as Undergoer. For example (6), then, *she*, the first argument of **do′**, is the Actor, while *Ian*, the second argument of **kiss′**, is the Undergoer.

RRG also postulates syntactic and semantic structures for noun phrases, which for the sake of simplicity are not included in the above representations.

Semantic and syntactic representations are linked by separate cross-linguistically tested linking algorithms going from semantics to syntax (needed for language production) and syntax to semantics (needed for comprehension). Details of these mapping rules for simple clauses can be found in Van Valin and LaPolla (1997: 172–178, 317–436), Van Valin (2005: Chapter 5), and a summary of the 1997 version in Butler (2003a: 143–148).

In the light of the above sketch of RRG, let us revisit the desiderata for the grammatical component of a comprehension model. We came to the conclusion that an appropriate theory must have separate semantic and morphosyntactic levels of representation, a lexicon, and of course mechanisms which relate all these components. RRG, we have seen, does indeed have distinct syntactic and semantic representations, a lexicon which is central to the theory, and sets of linking algorithms which involve all of these. Furthermore, it is interesting to note that in Mairal Usón and Faber's synthesis of RRG with the FLM, it is proposed that lexical entries should be linked to a conceptual ontology, so that each lexeme points to a particular path in that ontology. They suggest, for instance, that the Affected Object of the predicate *whittle* should be specified by means of linkage to the path terminating in the concept WOOD in the Mikrokosmos ontology (see Figure 3), as shown in (8), while the Affected Object of *mow* is specified by linkage to the path terminating in the concept GRASS as shown in (9).

(8)   ALL → OBJECT → PHYSICAL OBJECT → MATERIAL → PLANT-DERIVED SUB-
       STANCE → <u>WOOD</u>

(9)   ALL → PHYSICAL OBJECT → SEPARABLE ENTITY → ANIMATE → PLANT → <u>GRASS</u>

6. A worked example

It will be clear from the foregoing discussion that there are many important issues to be resolved regarding the compatibility of the various components in the model I have outlined, and the ways in which these components might interact. This is certainly not the place to attempt to resolve those issues: they must form the backbone of a future research program. All I can do, in conclusion, is to present a partial analysis of a single short, authentic text, attempting to show something of how the various components might work. The text I shall discuss is shown in (10).

(10)   *Max Grundig, 81, died yesterday in Baden-Baden. He opened his shop in*
       Nurenburg selling radios and producing transformers in 1930, and in 1945 he
       was allowed by the Allies to relocate his business in Furth, where it was one of
       the first to produce FM radios, then television sets — and high fidelity reel-to-
       reel tape recorders which serious musicians felt obliged to pay serious money
       for. (BNC A9B)

This is a complete text, which forms part of the British National Corpus and is taken from the obituary section of the British broadsheet newspaper *The Guardian*. The provenance of the text activates culturally embedded frames concerned with both obituaries and UK broadsheet newspapers. From the obituary frame, the reader will expect to be told
- that someone important has died
- who that someone was
- (usually) how old they were
- some important things about their lives.

The reader will also expect that the passage will consist largely, if not entirely, of statements, related to past time. From the fact that the obituary appears in a broadsheet rather than a tabloid newspaper, we might expect a fairly formal style, though this is certainly an oversimplification of the facts.

As an illustration, I shall discuss just the first sentence in relation to the retrieval of the underlying predication, starting with the orthographic words. The technique adopted is an informal one: I take each word in turn, and indicate briefly the processes which might be claimed to occur in the processing of that word in the ongoing stream, and the kinds of knowledge on which these processes draw.

Max:
Our culturally-based linguistic knowledge tells us that this may be a proper name, a forename for a male person (or conceivably a shortened form of *Maxine*, a female name), probably European/American. Since the word is not a lexical verb or an auxiliary, the parser may set up the hypothesis that the clause is going to be declarative, rather than imperative or interrogative. The parser provisionally activates an RRG core template with an initial NP slot. Note, however, that *max* can also be an abbreviation for *maximum*: according to Kintsch's spreading activation model, this meaning will be activated too, but upon integration with further information in the clause, this meaning will become deactivated.

Grundig:
The capital letter and knowledge of naming systems suggests this is a surname. Our cultural knowledge may associate the name Grundig with the well-known makers of sound equipment, since the obituary frame leads us to expect information about a person of some cultural importance. Max Grundig can be established as a character in the text, in terms of Werth's text worlds model. The proper name links to specification of human beings (and, provisionally, maleness), in the conceptual knowledge net to which descriptions of lexical items refer.

,
The comma signals, provisionally, some following expansion of *Max Grundig*.

81:
This fulfils the expectation, from the obituary frame, of being told the age of the deceased. The reader must invoke cultural knowledge of ways of expressing age: the use of years as a measure is not the only possible way. The item links to the appropriate number concept in the knowledge net.

,
The second comma delimits the additional information.

died:
This is a lexical verb, confirming the declarative status of clause through association with unmarked SV order. The parser can now specify further the core template structure involved, as one with NP + PRED. The lexeme DIE links to an appropriate path in the knowledge net, so that a logical structure expressed in terms of conceptual primitives can be formed. The appearance of this word furthermore confirms the frame-based expectation that we will be told of a death, and also the expectation of situations relating to past times.

yesterday:
Coming after an SV structure, this can be interpreted by the parser as an Adjunct, a peripheral element being added to the structure. This lexical item links to a time specification path in the knowledge net, giving additional past time information consistent with past tense of verb, again in conformity with the obituary frame.

in:
The parser will interpret this as introducing a further Adjunct, probably one of location.

Baden Baden:
The parser attaches this as the complement of the preposition *in* and adds the Adjunct to the structure. This item also confirms the locational meaning, linking to paths relating to place in the knowledge net.

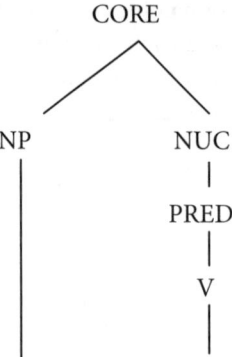

Figure 8. The core-4 template

On recognition of the full stop as an end of sentence marker, the parser can conclude that it has formed the complete structure of the sentence.

During the ongoing processing, syntactic template selection has occurred, the final result being the core-4 template proposed by Van Valin (2005: 15), as in Figure 8, instantiated and supplemented with Adjuncts as in Figure 9:

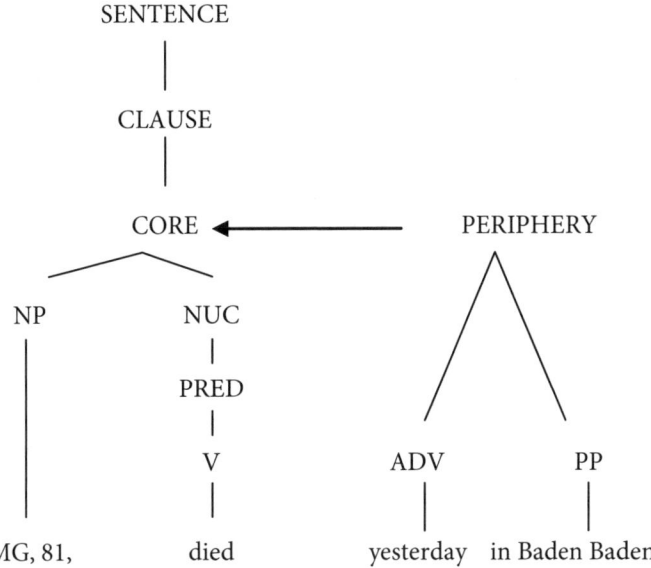

Figure 9. Final structure of example (10)

Interleaved with the syntactic processing, semantic interpretation of the structure has occurred. The predicate-argument relations of DIE, as well as the decomposition of the meaning, are retrieved from the structure of the ontological concepts on to which this item maps. The single syntactic argument is linked to the sole (Undergoer) macrorole of the predicate. The concepts to which IN and YESTERDAY are linked are also retrieved and added into the emerging propositional structure.

Similar analyses could be produced for the other sentences in the text. In Figure 10, I have shown a possible propositional rendering for the complete text, along the lines set out earlier for Figure 1. Again, there are aspects of the analysis which are certainly open to dispute, but I do not want to get bogged down in the detail of alternative semantic analyses here, as the aim is merely to indicate how the model might work. Figure 11 sets out the complex propositions of the text.

E1	Max Grundig	patient E3	
E2	81	qual E1	
E3	died	pred	DIE[M.G.]
E4	yesterday	temporal E3	YESTERDAY[DIE[M.G.]]
E5	in Baden Baden.	location E3	IN[YESTERDAY[DIE [M.G.]],BADENBADEN]
E6	He	ref E1; agent E7; (possibly) agent E10 & E13	
E7	opened	pred	OPEN[M.G.,E8]	HAVE[M.G.,SHOP]
E8	his shop	patient E7		OPEN[M.G., SHOP]
E9	in Nurenburg	loc E8 OR E7		IN[NURENBURG,SHOP] OR IN[NURENBURG,[OPEN[M.G., SHOP]]]
E10	selling	pred, qual E8	SELL[SHOP,E11]	
E11	radios	patient E10		SELL[SHOP,RADIOS]
E12	and	new proposition		
E13	producing	pred, qual E8	PRODUCE[SHOP,E14]	PRODUCE[SHOP,TRANSFORMERS]
E14	transformers	patient E13		
E15	in 1930,	temporal E7		IN[1930,[OPEN[M.G.,SHOP]]]
E16	and	new proposition		
E17	in 1945	temporal E21	IN[1945,E21]	

E18	he	ref E1		
E19	was allowed	recipient E19		
		agent E21		
E20	by the Allies	pred	ALLOW[E20,M.G.,E21]	
E21	to relocate	agent E19	ALLOW[ALLIES,M.G., E21]	
E22	his business	pred, patient E19		
		patient E21	RELOCATE[M.G., BUSINESS,E23]	RELOCATE[M.G.,BUSINESS,FURTH]
E23	in Furth,	location E21		
E24	where	loc, ref E23	IN[FURTH,E25-E44]	
E25	it	ref E22		
E26	was one of the first	agent E27		
E27	to produce	pred	ONE_OF_FIRST [BUSINESS,E27]	
		pred, qual E26	ONE_OF[BUSINESS, FIRST[BUSINESSES [PRODUCE[E29&E32&E35]]]]	
E28	FM	qual E29	FM[E29]	PRODUCE[BUSINESS[FM[RADIOS]]]
E29	radios	patient E27		
E30	then	sequence		
E31	television sets	patient E27		PRODUCE[BUSINESS[TELEVISION SETS]]]
E32	and high fidelity	qual E34	HI-FI[E34]	
E33	reel-to-reel	qual E34	REEL-TO-REEL[E34]	

E34	tape recorders	patient E27	PRODUCE[BUSINESS [HI-FI[REEL-TO-REEL [TAPE RECORDERS]]]] ONE_OF[BUSINESS,FIRST[BUSINESSES [PRODUCE[FM[RADIOS]& TELEVISION SETS & [HI-FI[REEL-TO-REEL TAPE RECORDERS]]]]]]
E35	which	ref E34 goods E40	GOODS[TAPE RECORDERS,E40]
E36	serious	qual E37	SERIOUS[E37]
E37	musicians	experiencer E38 agent E40	SERIOUS[MUSICIANS]
E38	felt	pred	FEEL[MUSICIANS,E39]
E39	obliged	sensation E38	FEEL[MUSICIANS, [OBLIGED,MUSICIANS,E40]
E40	to pay	pred, qual E39	FEEL[MUSICIANS, [OBLIGED,MUSICIANS [PAY,MUSICIANS,E42, TAPE RECORDERS]
E41	serious	qual E42	SERIOUS[E42]
E42	money	patient E40	SERIOUS[MONEY]
E43	for		FEEL[MUSICIANS,[OBLIGED, MUSICIANS[PAY,MUSICIANS, [SERIOUS[MONEY],TAPE RECORDERS]]]]

Figure 10. Propositional analysis of the text in example (10)

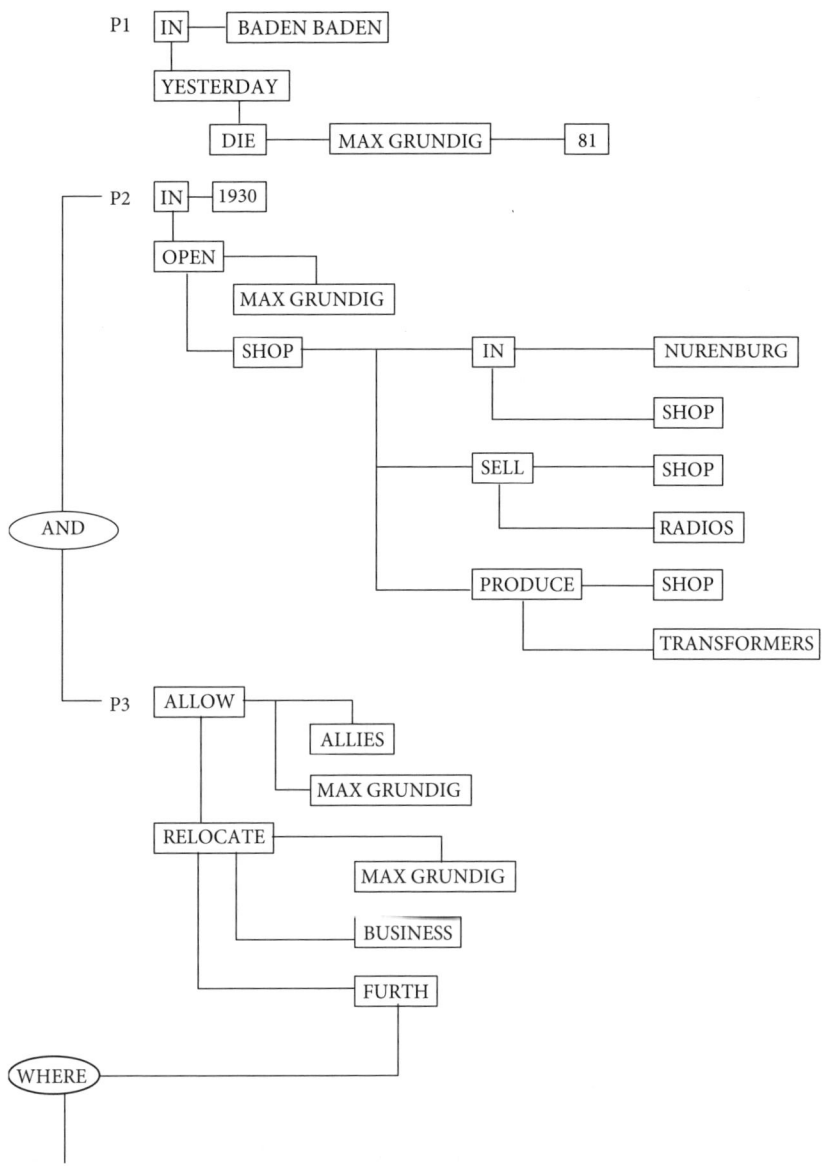

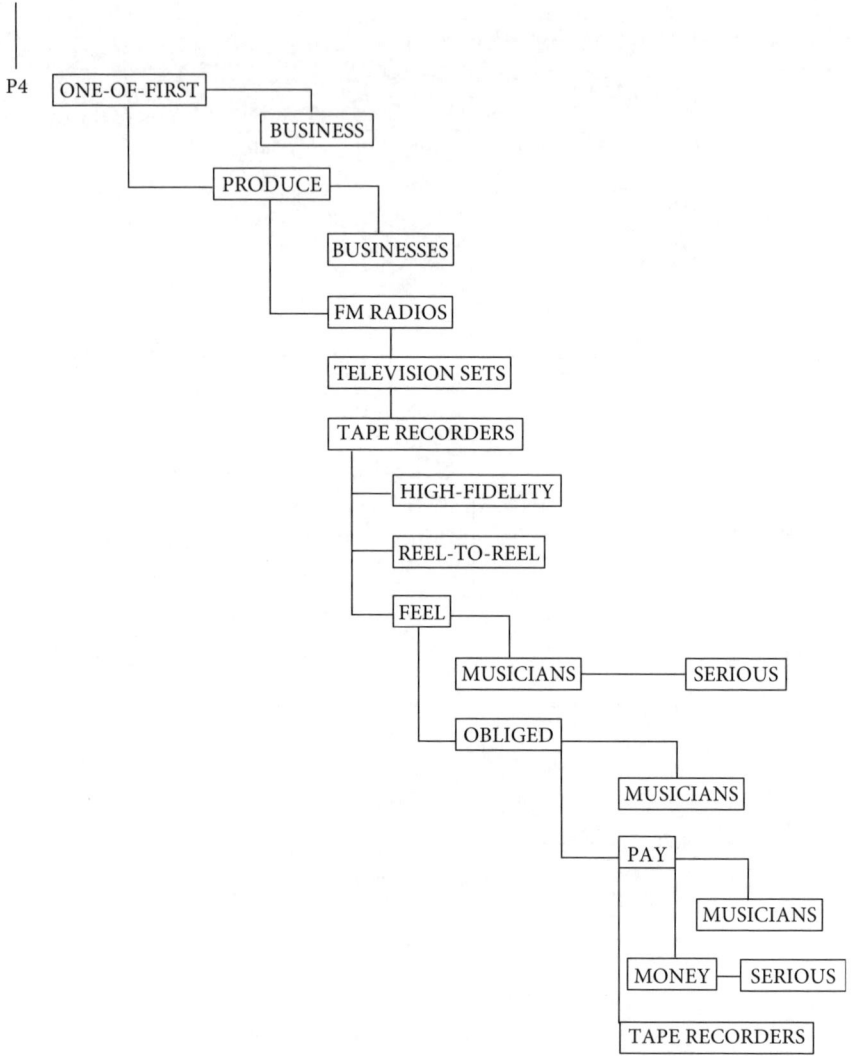

Figure 11. Complex propositions in example (10)

As successive items arrive on the input stream, the propositions formed are integrated with the cognitive model constructed so far, and at the ends of (at least some) major syntactic units, the short term memory buffer is cleared and a skeleton model is retained for further processing. The building of a coherent mental model is aided by the links between the concepts activated by items in the text: for instance, there are close conceptual links among the lexical items *shop*, *sell*, *pay*, *money*, and also *radio*, *television*, *tape recorder*; the anaphoric pronoun *he* and the determiner *his* can unambiguously be taken as referring to Max Grundig, *it* to the shop, *where* to Furth and *which* to the tape recorders.

As all this occurs, the reader builds the appropriate text worlds. As suggested in §3, embedded in the discourse world involving the writer and the readers of the obituary, we have a text world peopled by characters (Max Grundig, the Allies, musicians) and objects (the shop, transistor radios, tape recorders). We saw that location in time and space is particularly important in this text, and that deictic shifts in these parameters can be related to the creation of sub-worlds.

7. Conclusion

In this paper I have outlined and exemplified two important cognitive models of text comprehension, Kintsch's construction-integration model and Werth's text worlds model. Although these are in many ways very different, the former being rooted in cognitive psychology and the latter in textual analysis, they share some important characteristics: both stress the importance of the text itself, and of the context of text reception; both adopt a constructivist approach to discourse processes; both make use of propositional structures. Unfortunately, both also lack any explicit link to an underlying theory of semantics and form. I have attempted to remedy this situation by surveying the characteristics which the grammatical component of a theory of comprehension should have, and then showing that RRG, especially in the version enriched with lexical decomposition à la Functional Lexematic Model, is an appropriate theory for our purposes. Finally, I have sketched very briefly the workings of the complete model in relation to a single authentic text.

References

Beale, Stephen, Sergei Nirenburg and Kavi Mahesh. 1995. "Semantic analysis in the Mikrokosmos Machine Translation Project". *Proceedings of the Second Symposium on Natural Language Processing (SNLP-95)*, August 2–4, Kaser Sart University, Bangkok, Thailand.

Butler, Christopher S. 2003a. *Structure and function: A guide to three major structural-functional theories. Part 1: Approaches to the simplex clause.* Amsterdam: John Benjamins.

Butler, Christopher S. 2003b. *Structure and function: A guide to three major structural-functional theories. Part 2: From clause to discourse and beyond.* Amsterdam: John Benjamins.

Butler, Christopher S. 2007 "Notes towards an incremental implementation of the Role and Reference Grammar semantics-to-syntax mapping rules for English". *Structural-functional studies in English grammar: In honour of Lachlan Mackenzie,* ed. by Mike Hannay and Gerard J. Steen, 275–308. Amsterdam: John Benjamins.

Chafe, Wallace L. 1994. *Discourse, consciousness, and time.* Chicago: Chicago University Press.

Coseriu, Eugenio. 1981. *Lecciones de lingüística general.* (Readings in general linguistics.) Madrid: Gredos.

Cutler, Anne and Charles Clifton, Jr. 1999. "Comprehending spoken language: A blueprint of the listener". *The neurocognition of language*, ed. by Colin M. Brown and Peter Hagoort, 123–66. Oxford: Oxford University Press.

Dik, Simon C. 1997a. *The theory of Functional Grammar, Part 1: The structure of the clause*, 2nd edn, ed. by Kees Hengeveld. Berlin: Mouton de Gruyter. [Functional Grammar Series 20].

Dik, Simon C. 1997b. *The theory of Functional Grammar, Part 2: Complex and derived constructions*, ed. by Kees Hengeveld. Berlin: Mouton de Gruyter. [Functional Grammar Series 21].

Faber, Pamela and Ricardo Mairal Usón. 1999. *Constructing a lexicon of English verbs*. Berlin: Mouton de Gruyter. [Functional Grammar Series 23].

Fauconnier, Gilles. 1985/1995. *Mental Spaces*. (2nd ed. 1995). Cambridge, Mass.: MIT Press.

Fillmore, Charles. 1985. "Frames and the semantics of understanding". *Quaderni di Semantica* VI(2), 222–53.

Goodwin, Charles and Alessandro Duranti. 1992. "Rethinking context: An introduction". *Rethinking context: Language as an interactive phenomenon*, ed. by Alessandro Duranti and Charles Goodwin, 1–42. Cambridge: Cambridge University Press. [Studies in the Social and Cultural Foundations of Language 11].

Guest, Elizabeth and Ricardo Mairal Usón. 2005. "Lexical representation based on a universal semantic metalanguage". *Revista Electrónica de Lingüística Aplicada* 4: 125–173. At http://dialnet.unirioja.es/servlet/listaautores?tipo_busqueda=REVISTA&clave_busqueda=6978&inicio=21.

Hagoort, Peter, Colin M. Brown and Lee Osterhout. 1999. "The neurocognition of syntactic processing". *The neurocognition of language*, ed. by Colin M. Brown and Peter Hagoort, 273–316. Oxford: Oxford University Press.

Halliday, Michael A. K. and Christian M. I. M. Matthiessen 2004. *An introduction to functional grammar*. 3rd edn. London: Arnold.

Hannay, Mike. 1998. "The utterance as unit of description: Implications for Functional Grammar". *English as a human language: To honour Louis Goossens*, ed. by Johan van der Auwera, Frank Durieux and Ludo Lejeune, 201–11. Munich: Lincom Europa.

Hasan, Ruqaiya. 1978. "Text in the systemic-functional model". *Current trends in textlinguistics*, ed. by Wolfgang U. Dressler, 228-46. Berlin: Walter de Gruyter.

Hasan, Ruqaiya. 1984. "The nursery tale as a genre". *Nottingham Linguistic Circular*, 13: 71-102. Reprinted in *Ways of saying: Ways of meaning. Selected papers of Ruqaiya Hasan*, ed. by Carmel Cloran, David Butt and Geoffrey Williams, 1996, 51–72. London: Cassell.

Hasan, Ruqaiya. 1985/1989. "The structure of a text". *Language, context, and text: Aspects of language in a social-semiotic perspective*, Michael A. K. Halliday and Ruqaiya Hasan, 52–69. Geelong, Victoria: Deakin University Press. Republished, 1989, Oxford: Oxford University Press.

Hengeveld, Kees 1989. "Layers and operators in Functional Grammar". *Journal of Linguistics* 25(1), 127–157.

Hengeveld, Kees. 2004a. "The architecture of a Functional Discourse Grammar". *A new architecture for Functional Grammar*, ed. by J. Lachlan Mackenzie and María de los Ángeles Gómez-González, 1–21. Berlin: Mouton de Gruyter.

Hengeveld, Kees. 2004b. "Epilogue". *A new architecture for Functional Grammar*, ed. by J. Lachlan Mackenzie and María de los Ángeles Gómez-González, 365–78. Berlin: Mouton de Gruyter.

Hengeveld, Kees. 2005. "Dynamic expression in Functional Discourse Grammar". *Morphosyntactic expression in Functional Grammar*, ed. by Casper de Groot and Kees Hengeveld, 53–86. Berlin: Mouton de Gruyter. [Functional Grammar Series 27].

Hengeveld, Kees and J. Lachlan Mackenzie. 2006. "Functional Discourse Grammar". *The ency-clopedia of language and linguistics.* 2nd edn, vol. 4, ed. by Keith Brown, 668–676. Oxford: Elsevier, .

Hengeveld, Kees and J. Lachlan Mackenzie. In preparation. *Functional Discourse Grammar.* Oxford: Oxford University Press.

Hidalgo Downing, Laura. 2000. *Negation, text worlds, and discourse: The pragmatics of fiction.* Stamford, Connecticut: Ablex Publishing Corporation. [Advances in Discourse Processes Vol. LXVI].

Kintsch, Walter. 1988. "The role of knowledge in discourse comprehension: A construction-integration model". *Psychological Review* 95: 163–82.

Kintsch, Walter. 1998. *Comprehension: A paradigm for cognition.* New York: Cambridge University Press.

Kutas, Marta, Kara D. Federmeier and Martin I. Sereno. 1999. "Current approaches to mapping language in electromagnetic space". *The neurocognition of language,* ed. by Colin M. Brown and Peter Hagoort, 359–392. Oxford: Oxford University Press.

Lakoff, George. 1987. *Women, fire and dangerous things.* Chicago: Chicago University Press.

Mackenzie, J. Lachlan. 2000. "First things first: Towards an Incremental Functional Grammar". *Acta Linguistica Hafniensia* 32: 23–44.

Mackenzie, J. Lachlan. 2004. "Functional discourse grammar and language production". *A new architecture for Functional Grammar,* ed. by J. Lachlan Mackenzie and María de los Ángeles Gómez-González, 179–195. Berlin: Mouton de Gruyter.

Mahesh, Kavi. 1996. "Ontology development for machine translation: ideology and methodology". Report MCCS–96–292. Computing Research Laboratory, New Mexico State University.

Mairal Usón, Ricardo and Pamela Faber. 2002. "Functional Grammar and lexical templates". *New perspectives on argument structure in Functional Grammar,* ed. by Ricardo Mairal Usón and María J. Pérez Quintero, 39–94. Berlin: Mouton de Gruyter.

Mairal Usón, Ricardo and Pamela Faber. 2005. "Decomposing semantic decomposition: towards a semantic metalanguage in RRG." Paper presented at the International Course and Conference on Role and Reference Grammar. Taiwan, 21 June–1 July, 2005.

Mairal Usón, Ricardo and Robert D. Van Valin, Jr. 2001. "What Role and Reference Grammar can do for Functional Grammar". *Challenges and developments in Functional Grammar,* ed. by María J. Pérez Quintero, 137–66. La Laguna, Tenerife: Servicio de Publicaciones, Universidad de La Laguna. [Monographic section of *Revista Canaria de Estudios Ingleses* 42].

Mann, William C. and Sandra A. Thompson. 1987. "Rhetorical Structure Theory: a framework for the analysis of texts". *IPrA Papers in Pragmatics* 1: 79–105.

Mann, William C. and Sandra A. Thompson. 1988. "Rhetorical Structure Theory: Toward a functional theory of text organization". *Text* 8(3): 243–81.

Martín Mingorance, Leocadio. 1998. *El modelo lexemático-funcional: El legado lingüístico de Leocadio Martín Mingorance.* (The Functional Lexematic Model: The linguistic legacy of Leocadio Martín Mingorance.), ed. by Amalia Marín Rubiales. Granada: University of Granada.

Nuyts, Jan. 1992. *Aspects of a cognitive-pragmatic theory of language.* Amsterdam: John Benjamins.

Nuyts, Jan. 2001. *Epistemic modality, language, and conceptualization: A cognitive-pragmatic perspective.* Amsterdam: John Benjamins.

Perfetti, Charles A. 1999. "Comprehending written language: A blueprint for the reader". *The neurocognition of language,* ed. by Colin M. Brown and Peter Hagoort, 167–208. Oxford: Oxford University Press.

Rayner, Keith and Sara C. Sereno. 1994. "Eye movements in reading: Psycholinguistic studies". *Handbook of psycholinguistics*, ed. Morton A. Gernsbacher, 57–81. San Diego: Academic Press.

Reeves, Lauretta M., Kathy Hirsch-Pasek and Roberta Golinkoff. 1998. "Words and meaning: From primitives to complex organization". *Psycholinguistics*, ed. by Jean Berko Gleason and Nan Bernstein Ratner, 157–226. Fort Worth: Harcourt Brace College Publishers.

Roulet, Eddy. 1997. "A modular approach to discourse structures". *Pragmatics* 7(2): 125–46.

Saffran, Eleanor M. and Alexandra Sholl. 1999. "Clues to the functional and neural architecture of word meaning". *The neurocognition of language*, ed. by Colin M. Brown and Peter Hagoort, 241–272. Oxford: Oxford University Press.

Sinclair, John M. and Malcolm Coulthard. 1975. *Towards an analysis of discourse: The English used by teachers and pupils*. London: Oxford University Press.

Van Dijk, Teun A. 1980. *Macrostructures*. Hillsdale, NJ: Lawrence Erlbaum.

Van Dijk, Teun A. and Walter Kintsch. 1983. *Strategies of discourse comprehension*. New York: Academic Press.

Van Valin, Robert D., Jr. 1990. "Layered syntax in Role and Reference Grammar". (eds.) *Layers and levels of representation in language theory*, ed. by Jan Nuyts, A. Machtelt Bolkestein and Co Vet, 193–231. Amsterdam: John Benjamins. [Pragmatics and Beyond New Series 13].

Van Valin, Robert D., Jr. 2005. *Exploring the syntax-semantics interface*. Cambridge: Cambridge University Press.

Van Valin, Robert D., Jr. 2006 Semantic macroroles and language processing. *Semantic role universals and argument linking: Theoretical, typological, and psycholinguistic perspectives*, ed. by Ina Bornkessel, Matthias Schlesewsky, Bernard Comrie and Angela D. Friederici, 263–302. Berlin: Mouton de Gruyter.

Van Valin, Robert D., Jr. and Randy J. LaPolla. 1997. *Syntax: Structure, meaning and function*. Cambridge: Cambridge University Press.

Van Valin, Robert D., Jr. and David P. Wilkins. 1993. "Predicting syntactic structure from semantic representations: *Remember* in English and Mparntwe Arrernte". *Advances in Role and Reference Grammar*, ed. by Robert D. Van Valin, Jr., 499–534. Amsterdam: John Benjamins.

Weaver, Charles A., III, Suzanne Mannes and Charles R. Fletcher (eds.). 1995. *Discourse comprehension: Essays in honor of Walter Kintsch*. Hillsdale, NJ: Lawrence Erlbaum.

Werth, Paul. 1984. *Focus, coherence and emphasis*. London: Croom Helm.

Werth, Paul. 1999. *Text worlds: Representing conceptual space in discourse*. Harlow: Longman/Pearson Education Ltd. and New York: Pearson Education Ltd.

Wingfield, Arthur and Debra Titone. 1998. "Sentence processing". *Psycholinguistics*, ed. by Jean Berko Gleason and Nan Bernstein Ratner, 227–74. Fort Worth: Harcourt Brace College Publishers.

Wray, Alison. 2002. *Formulaic language and the lexicon*. Cambridge: Cambridge University Press.

Zwaan, Rolf. 1996. "Processing narrative time shifts". *Journal of Experimental Psychology: Learning, Memory, and Cognition* 22: 1196–1207.

Zwaan, Rolf, Mark Langston and Arthur Graesser. 1995. "The construction of situation models in narrative comprehension: an event-indexing model". *Psychological Science* 6: 292–297.

Towards an integrational approach in linguistics

Andrei Stoevsky
St Kliment Ohridsky University, Sofia

Integrationism has had a rather chequered history in post-Saussurean linguistics. This paper chronicles some of its manifestations and argues, to put it paradoxically, that crossing the dividing lines in the well-known dichotomies, *langue* vs. *parole*, synchrony vs. diachrony, internal linguistics vs. external linguistics, etc., does not amount to a methodological transgression. A substantial part of the discussion also bears on the issue of what counts as an adequate explanation. The aim of this study is to lend support to the view that given the complexity of language, both internally and in its relation to cognitive and social systems, truly explanatory adequacy is achievable only by applying an integrational approach.

1. Introduction

Integrationism has had a rather chequered history in post-Saussurean linguistics. On the one hand, conceptually, if not nominally, it has always been at the center of attention, because of its direct relation to the question about the scope of linguistic investigation; on the other hand, it does not seem to have received the terminological and conceptual recognition it deserves. This becomes immediately evident if we decide to scan the indexes of many major works in linguistics, as well as many specialized reference books, where integrationism is conspicuous by its absence. In the literature where integrationism is discussed, we find a certain degree of terminological immaturity manifested in the fact that three adjectives, 'integrated', 'integrative'[1] and 'integrational' are in circulation, often without much discrimination. Finally, as is common in linguistics, we find a lack of terminological consistency, in that one and the same term, 'integrational', is variously used by different authors. Lieb (1992: 128), for example, is

---

1. As far as the opposition between *integrated* and *integrative* is concerned, the problem is partly due to the fact that the past participle in English can have both active and passive meaning, though the latter is more common. Moreover, typical heads such as *theory* and *approach*, can be seen both as resultative objects and as instruments, hence the possible occurrence (see BNC) both of *integrated theory/approach*, and of *integrative theory/approach*.

keen to point out that his brand of Integrational Linguistics "shares its name only with an approach advocated by Harris". In an earlier publication (1983: 1), Lieb also insists that in his use Integrational Linguistics (further IL) is only an approach, which need not be codified into a linguistic school. Clearly, IL is not a unitary concept: each interpretation has its own theoretical and historical underpinnings. Calls for an integrated theory or an integrated approach have always been made in reaction to whatever brand of linguistic segregationism might have been dominant at a given point in time. Katz and Postal (1964) react against the segregation of syntax from semantics, which was typical for structuralism and early generativism.[2] Unlike Katz and Postal, who seem to be primarily concerned with the promotion of integration between the levels *within* linguistics, the generative semanticists (cf. Lakoff 1974: XI-1) argue for maximal expansion of linguistics, once again in response to the more restrictive aspects of Chomsky's theory. The seventies and eighties see the ever increasing prominence of pragmatics, of iconicity, of cognitivism, and generally, of a tendency to seek external explanations to linguistic problems. The drive to integrate reaches its peak in R. Harris's theory (Harris 1981, 1998a, 1998b), where linguistics loses its identity and becomes "a form of philosophy" (Harris 1998b: 25). In the last several decades the emphasis seems to have been much more on external integration, i.e., on the proper inclusion of language in some super-ordinate system, such as, for example, that of communication (Harris 1998a: 1); a professedly less reductionist line is taken by Lieb (1983: 3):

> I consider it as reductionism of an outdated type to construe linguistics as a branch of either sociology, psychology, or biology. True enough, linguistics and its branches do not stand alone. On my conception linguistics is ultimately a branch of semiotic and is related to psychology, sociology, biology, and other 'irreducible' disciplines mainly through general relations that connect semiotic with these fields.

Reductionism seems to have become unfashionable even with Chomsky (2000: 106), who expresses the hope that "a naturalistic approach to linguistic and mental aspects of the world" will lead to an "eventual unification with the 'core' natural sciences: unification, not necessarily reduction."

The chronology of integrationism is essentially the chronology of a series of attempts to overcome many of the divisions posited by Saussure in dichotomies such as langue vs. parole, synchrony vs. diachrony, arbitrariness vs. motivation, internal vs. external linguistics, social (objective) vs. individual (subjective/psychological), as well as the traditional opposition of form vs. meaning, and various subdivisions in terms of levels of analysis. Our position, like that of many integrationists, is that while it is important to acknowledge the existence of such dichotomies, failure to recognize the dia-

---

2.   One qualification should be made here: Katz and Postal see their contribution not as criticism of generative grammar, but rather as an extension designed "to bring it [generative grammar] in line with the latest developments in semantics" (1964: 1). A more critical attitude towards Chomsky's views on meaning is taken in Katz (1980).

lectical nature of the oppositions can only be detrimental to the scientific study of language. As has already been pointed out, what is also needed is a sense of historicity. It should be obvious from the following quotation that Saussure's insistence on the need for language to be studied in isolation is very much a reaction to a previous situation:

> language must, to put it correctly, be studied in itself; heretofore language has almost always been studied in connection with something else, from other viewpoints. (Saussure 1974 [1916]: 16)

In turn, many of the debates in the last forty years, including the ongoing one between Bybee (2005) and Newmeyer (2003) on the relationship between language and usage, are in response to Saussure's segregationist dictums. The linguistic debate, as we have presented it so far, seems to have swung to and fro in pendulum fashion. But does it have to be that way? The short answer is: not necessarily. There are a couple of points to be made here.

First of all, it is something of a misrepresentation to see Saussure only as a proponent of segregationism. We only need to be reminded of his understanding of the linguistic sign as a unity of signified and signifier (1974: 114), of the relationship between thought and sound being like the two sides of a sheet of paper (p.113), of his position on evolution as a "continual passage from motivation to arbitrariness and from arbitrariness to motivation" (p.134), of the importance accorded to semantics in establishing diachronic identity (p.182) and others. Some of his other statements, if followed through, may have implications that most likely were unintended at the time. Consider, for example, the statement that "language never exists apart from the social fact, for it is a semiological phenomenon" (p.77), which in the particular context is meant to emphasize the social aspect of language, yet anticipates the importance to be attached to pragmatics, deriving from the fact that the sign has significance only in relation to its interpreters. This is a point we shall return to presently.

Secondly, modern adherents to both segregationism and integrationism express some readiness to recognize the positive aspects in the position of their opponents. Thus, before pointing out that "transformational grammar has pretty much outlived its usefulness as a research strategy" Lakoff (1974: XI-2) admits that

> many of the advances made in the period of transformational grammar could not have been made had Chomsky not limited the object of his theory to something that does not exist in the real world, namely the abstract set of rules of grammar (excluding meaning and use, and production and perception mechanisms) internalized in the mind of an ideal speaker-hearer in a homogenous speech community. (Lakoff 1974: XI-1).

Similarly, in his discussion of the three models of signification Harris (1998c: 117) acknowledges the advantages of Saussure's structural model over what he calls "the surrogational model", before himself arguing in favour of an integrational model.

In some cases (cf. Croft 1995: 490) the opposition between segregationism vs. integrationism is cast in terms of another opposition, that between structuralism vs.

functionalism. The problem with such parallels is that they require numerous qualifications, due to the heterogeneity of both schools.[3] We may be reminded, for example, that structuralism has integration as one of its fundamental principles – the all too familiar principle that language is a system in which everything holds together[4]. So the dividing lines should be drawn rather in relation to two specific issues:

(1) What is the position of semantics in relation to the structural levels?
(2) Is language a self-contained object which can be studied in isolation from external influences?

2. The integration of semantics

The role attributed to semantics in structuralism and generativism has varied a lot over the years. In some extreme forms of American structuralism (descriptivism) in the early 50s the goal was to exclude semantics from linguistic description altogether. In Chomsky's standard theory, which reflected the process of encoding and decoding, semantics was some sort of rather ill-organized content existing at a basic level which by the application of some grammatical rules had to come to the surface in the form of comprehensible messages. Then, in the so called Revised theory, semantics had to be partially brought up to the surface. Whether the standard theory was abandoned hastily, as claimed by Bever, Katz and Langendoen (1976: 2), or not, is a separate issue; what is important for the present discussion is that language has a layered structure, which has evolved in a way designed to speed up decoding. The addressee does not have to wait to hear the whole string of sounds contained in a message to start chunking and analyzing possible relations; instead, s/he does so at the borders of each successive rank unit as the message progresses, and s/he confirms or revises (e.g, because of garden path phenomena) the already built hypotheses about one or another possible interpretation. This is an important consideration in support of the relative autonomy of rank units[5].

We would also like to add just a brief note about the way semantics is integrated with the other levels. Katz and Postal (1964: 1), who presumably want to argue for a

---

3.   For a discussion see, for example, Newmeyer 2000: 7-18.

4.   On the attributions of "où tout se tient" see Koerner (2004: 178-187).

5.   The relative autonomy of the rank units is also reflected in the relative autonomy of the levels of analysis. There is sufficient evidence to prove the need both for segregation and interpenetration of levels. Langendoen and Bever (1976: 251), in an attempt to save Chomsky's Standard Theory, conclude that a restriction should be introduced, according to which "no syntactic transformational rule is permitted to make use of the internal morphological structure of lexical items"; the restriction is, however, immediately relaxed, in a footnote, with reference to the separable prefixes in German and Dutch. Often lexicalization is accompanied by greater semantic rigidity, sometimes due to idiomaticity, which enhances the impermeability of the unit.

more prominent role of semantics in generative theory, are nevertheless of the opinion that of the three components, syntactic, semantic, and phonological, "the syntactic component is fundamental in the sense that the other two components both operate on its output". In other words, syntax is where all the important action takes place, the rest is just a side-show. It is remarkable how the emphasis has shifted since then, because in the dominant verbocentric view of the last several decades it is the lexical meaning of the verb that determines the argument structure of the sentence. The position taken in one of my own papers (Stoevsky 1983) is that semantics is not on a par with the grammatical and lexical levels[6], but intersects with these, because meanings can be expressed both lexically and grammatically. Harmonious relations between the levels are non-problematic, while disharmonious relations may result in hostility (an unacceptable sentence), or domination of one level over another.

3.   Autonomy vs. Integration

We turn our attention now to the second of the two divisive issues mentioned above: whether or not language is a self-contained system to be studied in isolation from external influences. Put this way, the question addresses only one aspect of the relationship between language and the extra-linguistic world, that of language as an affected participant, and not in its agentive role, which has also been studied extensively. This particular slant on language should explain why the debate often takes place under the heading of "autonomy in language" (Croft 1995) and "internalist perspective/explorations" (Chomsky 2000, Chapters 5 and 6), rather than under the label of "Integrational Linguistics". The question that is of primary concern to all theoretical linguists is, to quote from Newmeyer (2000: 96), "what counts as an acceptable explanation". It is well known that linguists fall broadly into two camps over this question – internalists and externalists. As the names suggest, the first group seek to give an explanation that is based on the interaction of the elements within language structure; the second group find such explanations insufficient and look for external motivations[7]. The position that we shall advocate is for a balanced integrational approach, which recognizes the relative autonomy of subsystems, yet takes full account of external conditioning. There is nothing very original in this position, because as Newmeyer (2003: 687) points out,

> In every other domain [apart from linguistics – A.S.] that I am aware of, *formal and functional accounts are taken as complementary, rather than contradictory*".
> (emphasis added)

---

6.   We have in mind the traditional division into lexical, grammatical and phonological.

7.   'Internalist' is yet one more term which is variously used by linguists. In its traditional structuralist use it simply means 'internal to the system'; in Chomskyan linguistics it is linked to I-language, the knowledge an individual has of his/her language.

Despite occasional calls for an integrative approach, the internalists and externalists seem to be quite entrenched in their positions, each group fighting their own corner. In a re-enactment of the debate on the pages of Saussure's *Cours*, the internalists (N. Chomsky, F. Newmeyer, N. Smith among many) are seen as advocating that linguistics should be focused on the knowledge of grammatical rules (on grammars, and not parsers – N. Smith (1999: 109)), on synchrony and the relative stability within a language state, on those aspects in the evolution of natural objects that show that the system is not necessarily becoming adapted to their functions (Chomsky 2000: 161). By contrast, externalists (T. Givon, J. Bybee, W.Pagliuca, E. Traugott, P. Hopper, W. Croft, and others)[8] focus their attention on usage, both across and within language states, and on some very obvious regularities in the evolution of languages, which call for an explanation. As might be expected from two camps largely bent on segregation, different aspects of the same phenomena are selected as evidence for radically different conclusions. Thus usage may be presented in a negative light as lacking the abstractness and crystallized form of grammar, or in a positive light, as the dynamic situation, the melting pot, in which language is exposed to various influences and is constantly being changed. Similarly, exceptions to unidirectionality in language evolution may be demonstrated as evidence disproving the validity of the whole theory, and not merely as exceptions, as claimed by Traugott (2001: 1), to what is hypothesized as a "robust tendency". One cannot but notice a certain softening of positions of internalists and externalists, but does this amount to increased awareness of the need for a truly integrational approach? Bybee (2005: 1–2), talking of converging trends in linguistic theory, gives as examples usage-based corpus linguistics and studies related to "the use of grammar in discourse". However, while corpus linguistics may have advanced a lot in the last decades due to computer technology, the corpus approach to the study of grammar is hardly anything new – we only have to think of Otto Jespersen (cf. Johansson 1992: 333). Speaking from the internalists' camp, Newmeyer proposes to "address the question of *how* syntax can be both autonomous and externally motivated". His argumentation, based on the analogy between grammar and chess, largely follows Saussure's:

> The principles of chess, like those of generative syntax, form an autonomous system. That is, the layout of the board, pieces, and possible moves make no reference to principles from outside the game itself. ... But the 'autonomy of chess' does not exclude the possibility that aspects of the system were motivated functionally. Perhaps its original developers worked out the most optimal set of moves to make chess as satisfying a pastime as possible. (Newmeyer 2000: 161; Newmeyer 2003: 687)

Saussure (1974 [1916]: 22, 88, 110) uses the chess analogy to illustrate a number of points, among them – that "what is external can be separated relatively easily from what is internal", that "a state of the set of chessmen corresponds closely to a state of

---

8.   For a more comprehensive list see Newmeyer 2001.

language", that "the respective value of the pieces depends on their position on the chessboard", and that "the system is always momentary". The analogy between chess and language seems to illustrate a few points very clearly, but is in need of elaboration beyond a certain point. The first problem is that of the identity of the pieces. For Saussure "the notion of identity blends with that of the value and *vice versa*". Thus a chess piece may be treated as a knight even when "shorn of any resemblance to a knight" (p.110). Let us suppose, however, that all pieces on the chessboard looked exactly the same, including colour, and that the two players had to rely only on the position of each piece in order to identify it. Once past the initial stage, the game will become almost impossible[9]. While such a game may look totally absurd, there are elements of this in the language game. Due to the asymmetrical relation between form and function, the interlocutors often have to resolve identity problems. Polysemy, homonymy and synonymy, if applied to chess, will mean that the manner in which a given piece can move will vary in different situations, that identical pieces will move differently, and finally, that some pieces that look different will have to follow the same pattern of movement. Given that the language game looks immeasurably more complex and confusing, and that unlike chess players the participants involved in a conversation do not have two hours to make sixty moves, but seem to communicate quickly and quite effortlessly, one is bound to ask how this could be achieved[10].

4.   Factors contributing to quick and efficient communication

There is no short answer to the question above, but an integrational approach should consider at least three major factors:
(1) the considerable degree of congruence between communication and representation;
(2) the hierarchical constituent structure of language;
(3) the principle of cooperation between the interlocutors (Grice 1975).

The first factor, congruence, is often discussed under the rubrics of psychological reality of linguistic structures, of iconicity, and of others. Congruence is certainly crucial in securing a quick interface between representation and communication. Ease of communication is largely determined by ease of recall, which, as is well known, is determined by the peculiarities of the human nervous system. As a rule, recall is facilitated by greater motivation of signs (iconic representation, polymorphemic words, metaphorical and metonymic extension of meanings). However, increased transpar-

---

9.   Chess masters, who play without looking at the chessboard, presumably can do so because they do not deviate much from some memorised schemes.

10.   We consider speech to be quick and effortless in that conversations typically progress with very few interruptions to remove misunderstandings. Newmeyer (2003: 693), on the other hand, considers human speech to be "painfully slow" when compared to the transmission rate of personal computers.

ency, such as in polymorphemic words, runs against the principle of economy[11]. Thus a mechanism that may be seen as functional in one respect may happen to be dysfunctional in another. A case in point is also metaphorical expansion, which may be seen as "natural" in that it is supported by the neural network, makes use of analogy and lessens the burden on memory by allowing a single signifier to cover a number of senses; but at the same time the polysemy resulting from metaphorical expansion is a source of ambiguity, hence a potential impediment in decoding.

The second factor accountable for quick, and *reliable*, communication is the hierarchical structure of language. Generally speaking, the identity of a language unit is established at the level which is immediately superordinate to its own[12]. As Benveniste (1971) puts it, " a unit will be recognized as distinctive at a given level if it can be identified as an 'integral part' of the unit of the next higher level ...". This type of structuring allows for early disambiguation, and constant monitoring during language processing.

The third factor, that of the Cooperative Principle as defined by Grice (1975: 41–58), is of crucial importance for the proper understanding of many linguistic facts. The Maxim of Relevance, for example, may be viewed as the social equivalent of perceptual saliency, which is responsible for assigning markedness in structural oppositions (e.g. emphasis due to inversion). The Maxim of Quality/Truthfulness has to be invoked to explain the non-witness mood in the languages that grammaticalize this distinction (e.g., Bulgarian, Georgian, Turkish and others). The Maxims of Quantity and Quality should account for the fact that past tense forms can be expected to indicate not only preteriteness but also some kind of aspectual distinction, because withholding information about the completion of an activity in the past may amount to a violation of the Cooperative principle (Stoevsky 1992). An interesting fact from a diachronic point of view is that, as Bybee (2006:188) puts it, "[p]ragmatic inference is an important mechanism of change in grammaticalization", an observation which is also made by Traugott (1989) and Carey (1990).

There are some loose ends to tie up at this point. A large part of the discussion was devoted exclusively to the question whether or not language is a self-contained system to be studied in isolation from external influences. Our own position was stated unequivocally: what is needed is a balanced integrational approach, which recognizes the relative autonomy of subsystems, yet takes full account of external conditioning.

---

11.   For Saussure (1974 [1916]: 133) the extent to which a language is arbitrary/motivated can form the basis for typological classification.

12.   There are some well-known exceptions to the rule that the identity of the units of language is established at the *immediately* superordinate level – morphemes attached to phrases rather than to words (e.g., phrasal genitives in English such as *my mother and father's photos*), stranded prepositions, garden path structures and others.

5.   Change within a language-state?

Much of the debate between formalists and functionalists is not about whether to recognize the importance of external conditioning, but rather whether it is a part of synchronic or diachronic linguistics. This becomes obvious from the following quotation:

> both Newmeyer 1998 [=Newmeyer 2000 –A.S.] and GGUU [= Newmeyer 2003 – A.S.] take pains to stress that the (synchronic) autonomy of grammar as a system is in no way incompatible with its shaping by use over historical time."
> (Newmeyer 2005: 233)

The essence of the debate then is about whether to recognize *dynamism within a language state*, and inevitably about the implications from this decision. Those who take Newmeyer's point of view will, no doubt, claim that 'synchronic dynamism' is a contradiction in terms, because dynamism by definition is historical in that it registers change over time. By contrast, a 'language state' is characterized by (relative! – A.S.) stability over time; so the task of the 'synchronic' linguist presumably is only to describe the knowledge of chess/language players about the rules of the game. It is something of a commonplace that language is learnable because of its relative stability. What should be equally obvious though, is *that there cannot be changes across language states unless there are changes within language states*. People learn languages the way they get on a slow-moving train. The question then is whether the movement of the language-train is in any way affected by its passengers. There is a group of linguists who want to convince the rest that they should be interested in the train itself and that there is no need to look out and bother about the direction of the train, because it is not moving fast anyway. There is also another, much larger group of functionalists, who nevertheless keep shouting, "It's moving, it's moving!", and insist that the movement of the train has a lot to do with various characteristics of its passengers, which is why they should be kept under constant observation. Typologists, both formalists and functionalists, argue, of course, that we need to look at many trains if our generalizations are to have any validity. Finally, all will agree that despite the aspirations of some passengers (language planners, prescriptivists), there is actually no one in the driving seat; where linguists are bound to disagree is about the vehicle itself. Many will claim that language is not a train in the first place, but rather an off-road vehicle, because there is simply no track to follow. Others, more deterministically-minded, will argue that the tracks are all there.

What is the integrationist's position? First of all, that the method of analysis must reflect the complexity and uniqueness of human natural language. Analogies with everything else, games, instruments, and vehicles are based only on partial resemblances designed to bring out one or another aspect of language. For example, one obvious and significant weakness to the language-as-vehicle analogy is that natural language is not an artifact, in the sense that it is not intentionally made. Yet, the analogy works in many other respects. Competing motivations when applied to words and cars may, for example, work in the same way: a longer, polymorphemic word, just like a large car, may be more convenient, in that it is motivated and thus easier to remember (Fr. *parapluie, parasol*), but it is less economical.

On the issue of autonomy, presumably the structure of an engine can be studied in isolation, ... but up to a point, i.e., up to the moment when we start asking what the input is, whether the engine is powered by electricity, oil, steam, wind. etc.. Needless to say, the structure of the engine will depend on the input. Moreover, a description of the parts of an engine without reference to the forces by which they are moved and to the purpose they serve seems totally unilluminating and unscientific. There is no need to belabour the point here. What is surprising is that linguistics has to renew the same debate every twenty years or so. This is what G. Leech had to say in the early eighties before concluding that "the correct approach to language is both formalist and functionalist":

> On the face of it, the two approaches [formalism and functionalism – A.S.] are completely opposed to one another. In fact, however, each of them has a considerable amount of truth on its side. To take one point of difference: it would be foolish to deny that language is a psychological phenomenon, and equally foolish to deny that it is a social phenomenon. Any balanced account of language has to give attention to both these aspects: the 'internal' and 'external' aspects of language. (Leech 1983: 46).

We fully subscribe to everything in this quotation. The issue that needs to be discussed, from our point of view, is not whether there is an alternative to integrational linguistics, but rather the degree of explanatory adequacy.

6.   Degrees of explanatory adequacy with examples from aspectology

In some cases an internal explanation is quite sufficient: for example, when having to account for the fact that while the substitute of an NP is a 'pronoun', the substitute of a VP in English had to be called a 'propredicate', because the slot 'proverb' had already been occupied. This is, of course, a very simple example of a system-internal constraint. In other cases, what is adequate as an explanation is often determined by the theoretical model that has been adopted. This point can be illustrated by comparing a Jakobsonian explanation of the category of aspect with that suggested in Stoevsky 2001.

Roman Jakobson has definitely succeeded in making linguistics a much more disciplined place by consistently applying the theory of oppositions to grammatical categories and by distinguishing invariant from contextual meanings. As is well-known, the type of opposition that is central to his theory is the privative opposition, in which one member is marked and more restricted in meaning, while the other member is unmarked and less restricted in meaning. Distinctions in terms of markedness and invariant meanings have proven very useful not only in language-specific studies, but also in contrastive linguistics. In an important paper on aspect Dušková (1983) points out that while there may be a good deal of similarity between the progressive form in

English and imperfective aspect in Czech in that "both forms present verbal action as such, without indicating its beginning and/or termination, and hence usually as incomplete…, the principle feature being action in progress," there are also differences, in that the progressive indicates temporary duration, while the "imperfective aspect refers not only to temporary actions but to general actions as well". The aspectual asymmetry between the two languages is illustrated with the example *Jan kouři* which translates into English either as *John is smoking* or *John smokes*. Duškova goes on to point out that "the unmarked member of the English opposition is the simple form, which is more general, whereas the progressive form with its more specific meaning is the marked member of the opposition." By contrast, in the Slavic languages, as has been repeatedly stressed (not least by Jakobson 1984: 3; 1984: 47), though not without some dissenting voices (Kučera 1981: 187; Bache 1985: 68, 72), the imperfective is the unmarked member of the opposition, "since under certain conditions it can refer to a completed act (completion may be indicated by the situation or the context), e.g. *Proč jsi je zvala* (imperfective)? 'Why did you ask them to come?' (Duškova 1983). So, what the Jakobsonian type of analysis helps us to see and formulate explicitly is that despite some similarities between the progressive and the imperfective, there is a fundamental typological distinction between the aspectual oppositions in English and the Slavic languages. There is a risk, however, of construing the distinction simply as a case of reversed polarity: **progressive**/nonprogresssive, imperfective/**perfective**. This would correctly predict the existence of aspectual asymmetry between English and the Slavic languages, because the unmarked members, which cover more semantic ground, do not stand on the same side of the oppositions; at the same time it would obscure the fact that the principle on which the oppositions are based is not the same. Having reached this stage, we may want to go one step further and ask why is it that the principles on which a particular type of category (say, aspect) is based vary from language to language. Sometimes the motivation may be system-internal, and a Jakobsonian model can account for it, but often it is not. Then we need to look for an explanation somewhere else.

What Stoevsky 2001 sets out to do is establish a correlation between aspectual markedness and perceptual saliency. Some such correlation seems only logical, bearing in mind that aspect is concerned with the grammaticalization of perspectives on a particular situation. Studies on aspect in Slavic consistently claim that the marked form, the perfective, indicates "the absolute *limit* of the action" [emphasis added] (Jakobson 1984: 3), 'the situation *in its totality*', etc. On the other hand studies in perception have shown that "*shape* is the most informative visible property" [emphasis added](S. Palmer 1999: 363), and similarly, that "for humans a *line sketch* of an image often conveys most of the essential information" (Hidreth and Ulman 1993: 584). Numerous experiments, including one of our own, have shown that when presented with a figure-ground situation, humans normally focus their attention on the figure(s), though they can do otherwise if needed. Further evidence for the saliency and significance of complete shapes comes from Gestalt psychology and from the fact that all languages have the grammatical class of nouns. In this very synoptic presentation of Stoevsky 2001 many details which are part of the argumentation have been left out, yet the main conclusion regarding Slavic aspect should be obvious: the indication of "absolute limit", of totality, by the perfective in Slavic can be related to the saliency of contours/shapes in visual perception.

Turning our attention now to the marked member in the English aspectual opposition, we find that the progressive is characterized in terms of a number of features. Leech (1971: 15) and Quirk et al. (1985: 198) suggest a set of three – [DURATION], [LIMITED duration] [NOT NECESSARILY COMPLETE], adding that the first two "add up to the concept of TEMPORARINESS". Huddleston and Pullum (2002: 163) suggest a set of six – [IN PROGRESS, ONGOING], [IMPERFECTIVE], [MID-INTERVAL], [DURATIVE], [DYNAMIC], [LIMITED DURATION], the third and the last being implicatures. Quirk et al. also point out that the three features are actually context-sensitive, since "not all … need be present in a given instance". The invariant meaning in Quirk et al. (1985: 197) is given as "happening in PROGRESS at a given time", Huddleston and Pullum (2002: 162) determine "the basic use" as "the expression of progressive aspectuality", which subsequently is defined in terms of the six features already mentioned. What should be obvious is that if we have to deal with a whole set of features, rather than just one, the task of having to establish some sort of correlation between grammatical markedness and perceptual saliency becomes very difficult. So feature reduction based on implicational relations and the categorization of contexts becomes essential. In trying to identify the core meaning of the progressive many English grammars are in fact integrational, in the internalist sense, because they examine the interaction between aspectualities on the grammatical and the lexical levels. The most revealing part of this interaction is that the lexical meaning of some groups of verbs prohibits them from occurring in the progressive. Thus the progressive is shown to be hostile to stativity, respectively to be associated with *dynamic* situations (cf. Quirk et al. 1985: 201). Also revealing are the contexts in which the progressive and non-progressive are in contrast, in particular the so-called 'actual use' referring to an act of perception of an *ongoing dynamic situation*. The necessary and sufficient number of features for the characterization of such a situation is a combination of two features: [[+change], [+duration]], i.e., the reduction of the sets of features above cannot be carried any further. What is interesting about the English progressive is that the element [+ change] can be construed both as characterizing the internal dynamics of a situation (*She was brushing her teeth vigorously*), as well as contrasting this situation to some larger situation (*These days he is spending all his money on food*). The element of [change] is by far the most salient feature linguistically and extralinguistically. In perceptual terms the combination [[+change] [+duration]] characterizes the movement of objects. Various authors have noted that while stationary objects may remain unnoticed, a moving object calls for immediate attention (cf. S.Palmer 1999: 14). Gregory suggests an evolutionary explanation:

Detection of movement is essential for survival. From the animals lowest on the evolutionary scale to man, moving objects are either likely to be dangerous or potential food, so rapid appropriate action is demanded, while stationary objects can generally be ignored. (Gregory 1990: 93).

To sum up. Two of the most salient visual markers in the environment are *limits* (contours, edges, shapes) and *movement*. Languages vary in their aspectual choices, in that some have grammaticalized the indication of limits (e.g. the Slavic languages), while others have grammaticalized movement (e.g., English). As might be expected the aspectual meanings have become much more abstract as a result of grammaticalization. The distinction which we have noticed can explain why one and the same type of situation, e.g., a dynamic imperfective situation, as in *I am talking to my brother on the phone* is aspectually marked in English, but not in Bulgarian *Govorja s brat si po telefona*. In both languages the choices are psychologically motivated, but there is an element of randomness in which of the two will become conventionalized in a language; this is just another reminder of the social aspect of language. These last few paragraphs were intended to show that external explanations do have a role to play in integrational linguistics. The general philosophy of this paper, however, has been to stress the need for a balanced integrational approach.

References

Bache, Carl. 1985. *Verbal aspect. A general theory and its application to Present-Day English*. Odense: Odense University Press.

Benveniste, Emile. 1971. "The levels of linguistic analysis". *Problems of general linguistics*, ed. by Emile Benveniste, 101–111. Coral Gables: Miami University Press.

Bever, Thomas, Jerrold Katz and D. Terence Langendoen (eds.). 1976. "Introduction". *An integrated theory of linguistic ability*, 1–10. Hassocks, Sussex: Harvester Press.

Bybee, Joan. 2006. "Language change and universals". *Linguistic Universals,* ed. by Ricardo Mairal and Juana Gil, 179–194. Cambridge University Press.

Bybee, Joan. 2005. "The impact of use on representation: Grammar is usage and usage is grammar". *Presidential address at the Annual Meeting of the Linguistic Society of America,* January 8, 2005.

Carey, Kathleen. 1990. "The role of conversational implicature in the early grammaticalization of the English Perfect". *Proceedings of the Annual Meeting of the Berkeley Linguistic Society* 16: 371–380.

Chomsky, Noam. 2000. *New horizons in the study of language and mind*. Cambridge: Cambridge University Press.

Croft, William. 1995. "Autonomy and functional linguistics". *Language* 71(3): 490–532.

Duškova, Libuše. 1983. "Has the English verb system the category of aspect?" *Philologia Pragensia* 26(1): 14–23.

Gregory, Richard L. 1990. *Eye and brain. The psychology of seeing*. Oxford and New York: Oxford University Press.

Grice, H. Paul. 1975. "Logic and conversation". *Syntax and semantics* 3: *Speech acts*, ed. by Peter Cole and Jerry Morgan, 41–58. New York: Academic Press.

Harris, Roy. 1981. *The language myth*. London: Duckworth.

Harris, Roy. 1998a. *Introduction to Integrational Linguistics*. Oxford: Elsevier Science.

Harris, Roy. 1998b. "The integrationist critique of orthodox linguistics". *Integrational Linguistics: A first reader*, ed. by Roy Harris and George Wolf, 15–26. Oxford: Elsevier Science.

Harris, Roy. 1998c. "Three models of signification". *Integrational Linguistics: A first reader*, ed. by Roy Harris and George Wolf, 113–125. Oxford: Elsevier Science.

Hidreth, Ellen C. and Shimon Ullman. 1993. "The computational study of vision". *Foundations of Cognitive Science*, ed. by Michael Posner, 581–630. Cambridge, Mass.: MIT Press.

Huddleston, Rodney and Geoffrey Pullum. 2002. *The Cambridge grammar of the English language*. Cambridge: Cambridge University Press.

Jakobson, Roman. 1984. *Russian and Slavic grammar studies 1931–1981*. Edited by Linda Waugh and Morris Halle. Berlin: Mouton.

Johansson, Stig. 1992. "Comment to 'Using corpus data in the Swedish Academy Grammar'". *Directions in corpus linguistics. Proceeedings of the Nobel symposium 82, Stockholm, 4–8 August 1991*, ed. by Jan Svartvik, 332–334. Berlin: Mouton de Gruyter.

Katz, Jerrold. 1980. "Chomsky on meaning". *Language* 56: 1–41.

Katz, Jerrold and Postal, Paul. 1964. *An integrated theory of linguistic descriptions*. Cambridge, Mass.: The MIT Press.

Koerner, E. F. Konrad. 2004. *Essays in the history of linguistics*. Amsterdam: John Benjamins.

Kučera, Henry. 1981. "Aspect, markedness and t_0". *Syntax and Semantics, vol.14. Tense and aspect*, ed. by Philip Tedeschi and Annie Zaenen, 177–189. New York: Academic Press.

Lakoff, George. 1974. Interview with Herman Parret. *Berkeley Studies in Syntax and Semantics*, vol. I, ed. by Charles Fillmore, Robin Lakoff and George Lakoff, XI-1 – XI-43.

Langendoen, D. Terence and Thomas Bever. 1976. "Can a not unhappy person be called a not sad one?" *An integrated theory of linguistic ability*, ed. by Thomas Bever, Jerrold Katz and D. Terence Langendoen, 239–260. Hassocks, Sussex: Harvester Press.

Leech, Geoffrey. 1971. *Meaning and the English verb*. London: Longman.

Leech, Geoffrey. 1983. *Principles of pragmatics*. London: Longman.

Lieb, Hans-Heinrich. 1983. *Integrational Linguistics. Volume I: General outline*. CILT 17. Amsterdam: John Benjamins.

Lieb, Hans-Heinrich. 1992. "Integrational Linguistics: Outline of a theory of language". *Prospects for a New Structuralism*, ed. by Hans-Heinrich Lieb, 125–182. CILT 96. Amsterdam: John Benjamins.

Newmeyer, Frederick. 2000. *Language form and language function*. Cambridge, Mass.: MIT Press.

Newmeyer, Frederick. 2001. "The Prague School and North American functionalist approaches to syntax". *Journal of Linguistics* 37: 101–126.

Newmeyer, Frederick. 2003. "Grammar is grammar and usage is usage". *Language* 79(4): 682–707.

Newmeyer, Frederick. 2005. "A reply to the critiques of 'Grammar is grammar and usage is usage'". *Language* 81(1): 229–236.

Palmer, Stephen E. 1999. *Vision Science. Photons to phenomenology*. Cambridge, Mass.: MIT Press.

Quirk, Randolph, Sidney Greenbaum, Geoffrey Leech, Jan Svartvik. 1985. *A Comprehensive grammar of the English language*. London: Longman.

Saussure, Ferdinand de. 1974 [1916]. *Course in general linguistics*. Bungay, Suffolk: Fontana/Collins.

Smith, Neil. 1999. *Chomsky. Ideas and ideals*. Cambridge: Cambridge University Press.

Stoevsky, Andrei. 1983. "Use of lexical additives in the elicitation of grammatical meanings". *University of Sofia English Papers*, vol.2, 238–266.

Stoevsky, Andrei. 1992. "Tense meaning and pragmatics". *Current advances in semantic theory*, ed. by Maxim Stamenov, 399–416. CILT 73. Amsterdam: John Benjamins.

Stoevsky, Andrei. 2001. "Aspect, perception, and markedness". Paper presented at the conference "Perspectives on aspect", Utrecht, December 12–14, 2001.

Traugott, Elizabeth. 1989. "On the rise of epistemic meanings in English: An example of subjectification in semantic change." *Language* 65: 31–55.

Traugott, Elizabeth. 2001. "Legitimate counterexamples to unidirectionality". Paper presented at Freiburg University, October 17th 2001.

Expressing past habit in English and Swedish.

A corpus-based contrastive study

Bengt Altenberg
University of Lund

English has no single verb expressing habitual aspect. Instead, habitual behaviour is indicated in various ways, e.g. by *will* (predictable or timeless habit), by *used to* and *would* (habit in the past), or simply by means of the simple present or past tense, often combined with a temporal adverb (*usually, normally*, etc). The choice of construction is partly determined by tense and aktionsart (state vs activity), but otherwise the ways of expressing habit in English are not well investigated. By contrast, Swedish makes use of a single auxiliary, *bruka*, to express both past and present habit. This cross-linguistic difference is a fruitful starting point for a corpus-based contrastive investigation. In the present study the means of expressing past habit in the two languages are explored on the basis of the English-Swedish Parallel Corpus, a bidirectional corpus of English and Swedish texts and their translations into the other language. Starting from constructions with *brukade* in Swedish original texts and translations the corresponding expressions in English translations and source texts are examined. The perspective is then reversed: using the English habitual marker *used to* as a point of departure the Swedish equivalents are investigated to determine if other forms than *brukade* are used in Swedish. The study reveals a complex cross-linguistic picture where aktionsart, generic subject, temporal specification and other contextual features are shown to be important factors determining the choice of habitual expression in the two languages.

1. Introduction

The linguistic expression of habit is generally regarded as an aspectual category, but the definition of habituality varies. Brinton (1988: 53), for example, describes it as a category that "views a situation as repeated on different occasions, as distributed over a period of time." Comrie (1976: 27 f.), on the other hand, offers a much broader definition:[1]

> [Habituals] describe a situation which is characteristic of an extended period of time, so extended in fact that the situation referred to is viewed not as an incidental property of the moment but, precisely, as a characteristic feature of a whole period.

Like most aspectual categories, habituality tends to be expressed differently in different languages (see e.g. Dahl 1985: 95 ff., Bybee et al. 1994: 151 ff.). This is evident if we compare two such closely related languages as English and Swedish.[2] In both languages the simple present and past tense can be used to express habitual meaning, often specified by a suitable time adverbial:

(1)   *He (often) travels/travelled to London on business*
(2)   *Han reser/reste (ofta) till London i affärer*

Both languages also use auxiliary verbs as overt habitual markers. In Swedish, both present and past habit can be expressed by the auxiliary verb *bruka*:

(3)   *Han brukar/brukade resa till London i affärer*

English has no corresponding verb to indicate present habit, but past habit can be expressed by two verbs, *used to* and *would*. Both can be used to indicate repeated events, but (unlike *would*) *used to* can also express a past state that is contrasted with the present (cf. Leech and Svartvik 1994: 72):

(4)   *I used to know her well (when I was a student)*

Would tends to indicate personal habits or characteristic behaviour (cf. Quirk et al 1985: 228):

(5)   *He would wait for her outside the office (every day)*

This use of *would* is typical of written narrative style (see Leech and Svartvik 1994: 73), while *used to* is especially common in conversation (Biber et al. 1999: 489 f.).

---

1.   Comrie's much-quoted definition of habituality is wide enough to capture not only repeated events but also continuous states in the past (e.g. *the Temple of Diana used to stand at Ephesus*). As we shall see, this broad definition seems more appropriate for English than for Swedish. For other definitions, see e.g. Dahl (1985: 97), Brinton (1987) and Bybee et al. (1994: 151). Most writers emphasize the interaction between habitual aspect, tense and the 'aktionsart' of the verb (e.g. stative/dynamic). Teleman et al. (1999: 510 f.) describe the Swedish habitual verb *bruka* largely in terms of aktionsart.

2.   For English, this summary is based on the descriptions given in Quirk et al. (1985), Leech (1987), Leech and Svartvik (1994), Svartvik and Sager (1996) and Biber et al. (1999). The Swedish habitual verbs *bruka* and *pläga* (rare) are mentioned briefly in Teleman et al. (1999: 510 f.) but their use and distribution have not, to my knowledge, been investigated empirically.

The cross-linguistic situation is summarised in Table 1.[3] As we can see, the main difference between the languages lies in the use of overtly marked expressions: while Swedish has one verb *bruka* which can be used for both present and past habit, English has two verbs, *used to* and *would*, but these are only available for the expression of past habit.

Table 1. Main expressions of habit in English and Swedish

	English		Swedish	
	Marked	Unmarked	Marked	Unmarked
Present	–	simple present	*brukar*	simple present
Past	*used to, would*	simple past	*brukade*	simple past

However, even if the chief ways of expressing habit in English and Swedish are well known, comparatively little is known about the distribution of the different options and their cross-linguistic correspondence. The aim of this study is to explore the expressions of past habit in the two languages on the basis of a bidirectional translation corpus (see section 3 below) and to find out to what extent such a corpus can contribute to a better understanding of their use.

2. The choice of past habituals in English

Before we turn to the corpus data, however, it is necessary to examine what is known about the choice of habitual expressions in greater detail. As there are no empirical studies of Swedish habituals, the focus will be entirely on English.

The three main forms used to express habitual past situations in English – *used to*, *would* and the simple past – are often, but not always, interchangeable. Various factors affecting the choice of form have been suggested in the literature, but few empirical investigations have been devoted to all three forms. One exception is a recent study by Tagliamonte and Lawrence (2000) who examined various factors influencing the choice of habitual form in a corpus of recorded British English conversations. Starting from the observation that the choice of expression is mainly determined by the interaction of two factors, the 'aktionsart' of the verb (stative vs. dynamic) and some contextual indication of time (frequency or past time), they distinguish four basic habitual situations in which one, two, or all three variants seem to be permitted. These

---

3.   Some less common constructions available for expressing habit are ignored here. For example, in English temporary habit can be expressed by the present progressive (e.g. *I'm playing golf regularly these days*). In both English and Swedish, characteristic behaviour in the present and past is sometimes expressed by the auxiliary *can* : *kunna* (e.g. *She can/could sit for hours watching the birds in the park* : *Hon kan/kunde sitta i timmar och se på fåglarna i parken*).

situations are not clearly specified but can be interpreted roughly as indicated in Table 2 (cf. Tagliamonte and Lawrence 2000: 331 ff.).

Table 2. Contexts affecting the choice of habitual past expressions in English

Situation	Used to	Would	Simple past
Event + indication of frequency	+	+	+
Event without indication of frequency	+	+	–
Discontinued past state	+	–	+
State/event + indication of duration	–	–	+

Using Comrie's definition to identify habitual situations in their corpus, Tagliamonte and Lawrence found that 70% of the situations were realised by the simple past, 19% by *used to*, 6% by *would* and the remaining 5% by various other constructions, such as the progressive form and combinations with verbs like *tend to*, *keep* (*on*), etc. By means of a multivariate statistical technique they also examined the effect of various contextual factors on the choice of construction in the most common habitual situations.[4] The factors and their effect on the choice of construction are presented in broad outline in Table 3 (where '+' indicates a favourable factor, '(+)' a weakly favourable factor, and '-' an unfavourable factor).

Table 3. Factors affecting the choice of habitual past expression (simplified summary of Tagliamonte and Lawrence 2000)

Contextual factors	Used to	Would	Simple past
Negative clause	–	(+)	+
1st pers. subject	+		
2nd pers. (indef.) subject			+
3rd pers. subject		+	
Stative verb	–		+
Inanimate subject	–		+
Short duration		+	(+)
Co-occurring frequency adverbial			(+)
Sequence initial or alone (no sequence)	+		
Sequence internal		+	+

---

4.   The study was restricted to the two most common habitual situations described in Table 2, viz. those where all the forms could be used and those admitting the simple past or *used to* (see Tagliamonte and Lawrence 2000: 333 f.). Contexts admitting *used to* and *would* but not the simple past and contexts admitting only the past were found to be rare (7%).

The table shows that, in the situations examined, *used to* tended to be favoured with 1st person subjects, when it occurred initially in a sequence of habitual events in discourse and when it did not occur in a sequence, but was disfavoured in negative clauses, with stative verbs and with inanimate subjects. *Would* tended to be favoured with 3rd person subjects, in situations of short duration, non-initially in sequences and (weakly) in negative clauses. The simple past tended to be favoured in negative clauses, with stative verbs and inanimate subjects, sequence-internally, and (weakly) in situations of short duration and with frequency adverbials.

Some of the tendencies revealed in Tagliamonte and Lawrence's study confirm earlier observations. For example, the tendency to avoid *used to* in non-affirmative contexts is well known (see e.g. Quirk et al. 1985: 140, Biber et al. 1999: 165). Others are more surprising. For example, *used to* is generally described as having spread historically from 1st person subjects and dynamic situations to a much more extended – and grammaticalised – use (see Bybee et al. 1994: 155 f.), but turned out to be still very much restricted to its original use in these respects. Moreover, the importance of the position of a habitual expression in a sequence of repeated habitual events in discourse is revealing. Hence, although these tendencies do not reflect all possible habitual situations and are based on conversational data only, they are nevertheless interesting because they demonstrate the importance of the context for the selection of habitual expression and the range of factors involved. I shall return to some of them in the following sections.

3.   Material and method

The present study is based on the English-Swedish Parallel Corpus. This is a bidirectional translation corpus consisting of samples from a wide range of text types in each language and their translations into the other language. Care has been taken to create a balanced and comparable corpus where different types of fiction and non-fiction texts are represented in roughly equal proportions in both languages. Source texts and translations are aligned at sentence level. The present size of the corpus is 2.8 million words. For detailed information about the corpus, including the text codes used in this paper, see Altenberg and Aijmer (2000) and Altenberg et al. (2001).

The structure of the corpus is shown in Figure 1. As indicated, the corpus can be used for many different types of searches and comparisons. For example, by searching for a word or phrase in the original texts we get a list of its translation variants. Conversely, by searching for an expression in the translations we can study its sources in the original texts.

For practical reasons, the starting point of the study will be the marked forms *used to* in English and *brukade* in Swedish. Since the habitual use of the other past forms (*would* and the simple past) cannot be identified by form alone, they will be considered only to the extent that they occur as correspondences (translations and sources) of *used to* and *brukade* in the corpus.

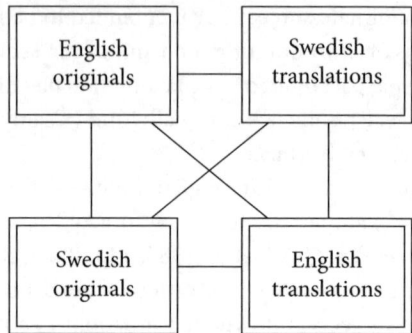

Figure 1. Structure of the English-Swedish Parallel Corpus

4.   *Used to* and *brukade* in original texts and translations

Let us first take a brief look at the relative frequency of the past forms *used to* and *bru-kade* in the original texts and translations. As shown in Table 4, Swedish *brukade* is more common than English *used to* in both the original texts and the translations.

Table 4. Frequency of *used* to and *brukade* in original texts and translations (occurrences per 100,000 words)

	Original texts	Translations
Used to	12.8	14.1
Brukade	15.1	21.4

This indicates that *brukade* is a more dominant marker of past habit in Swedish than *used to* is in English. This is what we might expect since *brukade* is the sole overt marker of past habit in Swedish, while *used to* competes with *would* as a means of expressing past habit in English.

Another notable feature in Table 4 is that both *used to* and *brukade* are more common in the translations than in the original texts. This 'overuse' in the translations may reflect a tendency among the translators to resort to the dominant expression in each language. Another possibility is that the translators have a tendency to be more explicit, i.e. to render a past habitual situation that is unmarked in the source language by means of an explicitly marked expression in the translations (on translation effects of this kind, see e.g. Baker 1996, Laviosa 1998a, b). However, the tendency to 'overuse' the marked habitual form is greater in the Swedish translations than in the English ones.

This may well be another reflection of the system difference mentioned above, viz. that *brukade*, the dominant Swedish form, is used as a translation of several competing English forms, in particular *used to* and *would*.

To explore these differences further we must examine the various means of expressing past habit that are available in the two languages, how often they are used, and what factors determine the choice between the different alternatives.

5. English correspondences of *brukade*

Let us first examine the English correspondences of Swedish *brukade* in the corpus. Table 5 displays the English translations of *brukade* in the Swedish original texts and the English sources of *brukade* in the Swedish translations.

Table 5. English correspondences of *brukade*

English correspondences	English translations		English sources	
	n	%	n	%
(a) Simple past	43	43	32	22
with time adverbial	34	34	20	14
without time adverbial	9	9	12	8
(b) *Used to*	34	34	37	25
(c) *Would*	5	5	66	45
(d) Adjective	5	5	3	2
(e) Noun	4	4	3	2
(f) Lexical verb	1	1	0	0
(g) Other	8	8	7	5
Total	100	100	148	100

Seven types of English correspondences can be distinguished. Three of these are relatively common, as translations and/or as sources: (a) the simple past form of the main verb, often specified by a time adverbial (denoting frequency or past time), (b) *used to*, and (c) *would*. These are illustrated in examples (6)–(8), respectively. The original text, marked by a text code, is placed first with the translation in the right-hand column:

(6) *Då och då satte han i gång någon ny bantningskur men **brukade** snart ge upp.* (SW1)   *Every now and then he would go on some new diet, but he **generally gave up** pretty quickly.*

(7) *Hans bästa vänner **brukade** säga att*   *His best friends **used to** say he was a*
     han var en latmask som sålde sin   *lazybones selling his Muse piecemeal,*
     Musa bit för bit, i munsbitar. (SCO1)   *in mouthfuls.*

(8) *Dit **brukade** denne sadist skicka en-*   *Thither **would** this sadist direct Eng-*
     gelsmän som diskret undrat var de   *lishmen who discreetly wondered*
     kunde tvätta händerna någonstans.   *where they could wash their hands.*
     (IU1)

Three less common types mark the habitual aspect by means of (d) an adjective, (e) a noun, and (f) a lexical verb. These are illustrated in examples (9) – (11), respectively:

(9) *De **brukade** ägna sig åt att trakassera*   *They were **given** to harassing their less*
     mindre framstående landsmän på ön.   *distinguished compatriots here on the*
     (LH1)   *island.*

(10) *Hon kom från fuset, hon hade värmt*   *She had come from the byre and had*
     *mjölken åt kalvarna, hon **brukade** stå*   *warmed the milk for the calves; she*
     därvid kalvarna timtals. (TL1)   *was in the **habit** of stopping with the*
                                                    calves for hours.

(11) *Hon **brukade** bli ful i mun när hon*   *Sara Sabina **tended** to spout off when*
     blev retad och kunde dra till med hela   *someone annoyed her, and knew*
     ramsor av grova matare. (KE2)   *whole litanies of crude words.*

Other variants of types (d) and (e) are the adjectival expressions *be wont to* and *be fond of* and the nominal phrase *be the custom to*.

A seventh type, called 'Other' in the table, contains examples in which no English form corresponding to *brukade* can be identified, either because the English version is reduced (e.g. to a non-finite expression) or because there is no translation. This type will be ignored here.

The habitual nature of the examples is often reinforced by a time adverbial in both languages. The role played by time adverbials with different types of habitual expression will be examined in section 9.

Returning to Table 5, we notice that some of the English correspondences have strikingly different frequencies as translations and as sources of *brukade*. *Used to* is relatively more common as English translations than as English sources (34% vs. 25%). The same is true of the simple past accompanied by a time adverbial, which is comparatively rare as the English source of *brukade* (14%) but often serves as a translation of *brukade* (34%). By contrast, the frequency of *would* exhibits an even more dramatic difference in the other direction: it is rarely used to translate *brukade* (5%) but is the most common English source of *brukade* (45%).

It is not entirely clear how these differences should be explained. If we assume that the English source texts give a better reflection of the normal distribution of the different habitual verbs in (written) English than the translations, we can conclude that the

English translators tend to avoid *would* in favour of *used to* or the simple past.[5] A possible reason for this can be seen if we compare the options confronting the English and Swedish translators. English translators rendering *brukade* have a choice between three main alternatives: *used to*, *would* and the simple past. Of these, *would* also has other functions (e.g. to express condition, intention and prediction) and cannot always be used to render habit unambiguously. By comparison, *used to* and the simple past specified by a time adverbial mark habitual meaning more unambiguously and may consequently appear to be safer and more convenient to use. The Swedish translators, by contrast, only have two options: *brukade* or the simple past supported by an appropriate time adverbial. Both are 'safe' options and consequently a common rendering of *would*. The reason why the English simple past is rarely the source of *brukade* may simply reflect the fact that it tends to be rendered by the simple past in Swedish too, in which case it would not turn up in the data. However, the role played by adverbials in marking habituality is slightly different in English and Swedish and I shall therefore return to this issue in section 9.

6.   Swedish correspondences of *used to*

Let us now reverse the perspective and look at the Swedish correspondences of English *used to*. As shown in Table 6, these are roughly of the same types as the English correspondences of *brukade*. The difference is that while the English habitual system includes three common types of expression (cf. Table 5), Swedish only makes use of two: (a) the simple past, often specified by a time adverbial, as illustrated in (12), and (b) *brukade*, as illustrated in (13). As a result, each of these types takes up a larger proportion of the total number of Swedish examples, in the translations as well as in the source texts.

(12)   *But Oliver **used to** correct me and ex-   Men Oliver **sa jämt** ['said always'] att*
       plain that you are whoever it is you're   jag hade fel: man är den man låtsas
       pretending to be. (JB1)   *vara.*

(13)   *Ethan **used to** say that Edward walked   Ethan **brukade** säga att Edward gick*
       as if he had sand in his bathing suit.   som om han hade fått sand i simbyxo-
       (AT1)   *rna.*

---

5.   However, the assumption that *would* is the most common habitual verb in English original texts is not supported in the material used by Tagliamonte and Lawrence (2000), where only 6% of the examples were realized by *would* (see section 2). A possible reason for this difference may be that their conversational material is less narrative in character than the present corpus (see section 10).

Table 6. Swedish correspondences of *used to*

Swedish correspondences	Swedish translations		Swedish sources	
	n	%	n	%
(a) Simple past	49	54	59	56
with time adverbial	37	41	41	39
without time adverbial	12	13	18	17
(b) *Brukade*	39	43	36	34
(c) Noun	1	1	0	0
(d) Adjective	0	0	2	2
(e) Lexical verb	0	0	2	2
(f) Other	1	1	6	6
Total	90	100	105	100

The remaining types – involving a noun, adjective or lexical verb – are comparatively rare. They are illustrated in the following examples:

(14)   *In the winter business was quieter, and Arthur **used to** like to spend Tuesdays and Thursdays from November through to March, when his wife Jane was helping out at the Junior School, with whoever it was it happened to be.* (FW1)

På sommaren flockades turisterna där, men på vintern var det lugnare, och Arthur hade tagit för **vana** att tisdagar och torsdagar från november till mars ägna sig åt små snedsprång med någon lämplig älskarinna.
(Lit. '… Arthur had adopted the habit …')

(15)   *He had just told her he had inherited a pair of shoes from Franz Antonsson, who **used to** be shop manager but had gone home to his mother's and died of consumption.* (KE2T)

*Nyligen hade han berättat för henne att han fått ett par skor efter **förre** bodbetjänten Franz Antonsson som dött hemma hos sin mor i lungsjuka.*
(Lit. '… former shop manager …')

(16)   *His mother **used to** sit by his bed, looking down at him as he lay there snuffling his way through his sound health-giving sleep.* (MR1T)

*Det **hände** att hans mamma satt vid hans säng då han snusande givit sig hän åt en stärkande sömn och såg på honom.*
(Lit. 'It happened that …')

Unlike the English correspondences of *brukade*, the Swedish correspondences of *used to* do not display any dramatic differences in frequency as translations and as sources. The main exception is *brukade*, which is comparatively more common in the Swedish translations than as a Swedish source of *used to*. As suggested in section 4, this translational 'overuse' of *brukade* may be seen as a tendency among the Swedish translators to favour an overtly marked habitual expression. The same tendency can be observed if we look at the Swedish sources of *used to*. A fairly common starting point of *used to* is an unmarked construction without either *brukade* or a time adverbial (17%). In other words, the English translators, too, seem to prefer a clearly marked habitual alternative. This is illustrated in the following examples:

(17) *Killarna **tråkade** ['teased'] mig i all*   *The lads **used to** tease me, in a good-*
      vänlighet, tyckte att jag lät som en   *natured way, reckoned I sounded like*
      uppslagsbok när jag kom i gasen. (PP1) *an encyclopaedia once I got going.*
(18) *Min fru **vävde** ['wove'] trasmattor.* (SC1) *My wife **used to** weave rag rugs.*

7. Mutual correspondence

If we compare Tables 5 and 6, we see that the mutual correspondence (or intertranslatability) of *used to* and *brukade* is comparatively low: they are used as translations of each other in little more than a third (38%) of the total number of examples (on the concept of 'mutual correspondence', see Altenberg 1999). The main reason for this is the frequent use of the simple past as an alternative translation: it is in fact the most common translation in both languages.

We can also see that the simple past (with or without a time adverbial) takes up a larger share of the Swedish examples (translations as well as sources) than of the English ones. This indicates that *brukade* is comparatively less common in Swedish than the combined use of *used to* and *would* in English. In other words, there seems to be an area of habitual usage that is expressed by an overt habitual marker in English but not in Swedish. This will be examined more closely in the following section.

8. Stative vs. dynamic situations

One important difference between *used to* and *brukade* is that the former can refer to both habitual events (19) and continuous states (20) in the past, whereas *brukade* (like *would*) chiefly refers to habitual events:

(19) *His hair, which Sarah **used to** cut for*   *Håret, som Sarah **brukade** klippa på*
      him, jutted over his forehead like a   *honom, sköt ut över pannan som en*
      shelf. (AT1)   *hylla.*

(20)   *You say nothing's changed, but you're*   *Du säger att ingenting har förändrats,*
       wrong, everything's changed. I used to   *men du har fel, allt har förändrats.*
       admire you. Now I despise you. I used to   *Förut beundrade jag dig. Nu föraktar*
       find you amusing. Now you bore me. I   *jag dig. Förut tyckte jag att du var*
       used to love you. Now I just feel sorry for *rolig. Nu tråkar du ut mig. Förut äl-*
       you." She smiled apologetically. "I also   *skade jag dig. Nu tycker jag bara synd*
       used to think you'd make it. (MW1)   *om dig." Hon log ursäktande. "Förut*
                                                    trodde jag också att du skulle bli något.
                                                    (Lit. 'Before admired I …'; 'Before
                                                    found I …', etc.)

As a result, *brukade* can only be used to translate *used to* in examples like (19), whereas in examples like (20) the simple past reinforced by a suitable time adverbial is preferred. This difference between the two verbs is clearly demonstrated by their tendency
to co-occur with stative and dynamic verbs in the corpus. While *used to* occurs with
stative verbs in 47% of the examples in the English original texts, the corresponding
figure for *brukade* in the Swedish original texts is only 27%.[6] The difference can be seen
even more clearly in the Swedish translations of *used to*, as shown in Table 7. In dynamic contexts *used to* is translated by *brukade* in 72% of the cases, but in stative contexts the proportion drops to 12%.

Table 7. Swedish translations of *used to* in stative and dynamic contexts

Swedish translations	Dynamic		Stative	
	n	%	n	%
Brukade	34	72	5	12
Simple past	13	28	36	88
Total	47	100	41	100

Yet, although *brukade* is mainly used in dynamic situations, it sometimes does occur
in stative contexts. However, in such cases the reference is not to a single continuous
state but to a stative situation that is repeated on different occasions:

(21)   *Tidningspojkarna brukade stå i en*   *The paperboys used to stand in a*
       frysande och huttrande flock ute på   *freezing, shivering group out on the*
       perrongen och vänta på att mor-   *platform waiting for the morning train*
       gontåget från Västerås skulle komma   *from Västerås to come in.*
       in. (LG1)

---

6.   The comparatively frequent occurrence of *used to* with stative verbs in the corpus (47%)
disagrees with Tagliamonte and Lawrence's (2000) finding that *used to* is disfavoured with stative verbs in English conversation (see section 2).

(22) *She and Porter's wife and Sarah **used** *Hon och Porters hustru och Sarah*
to sit around the kitchen – this was ***brukade** sitta kring köksbordet – det*
before Porter's wife got her divorce – *var innan Porters hustru också hade*
and they'd go on and on about the *tagit ut skilsmässa – och gå på i all*
Leary men. (AT1) *evighet om pojkarna Leary.*

We can now reformulate the restriction on the use of *brukade*: it cannot be used in situations referring to a single continuous state in the past. In such cases the simple past must be used. This can be demonstrated if we try to replace the simple past in Swedish translations of *used to* in stative contexts:

(23) *I remembered that Jess **used to** like his* *Jag minns att Jess **tyckte om** ['liked']*
mom's Swiss steak, so that's what I *sin mammas kalops, så det är vad jag*
brought. (JSM1) *tog med mig.*

(24) *He **used to** be a neo-realist, before* *Han **var** ['was'] neorealist innan neo-*
neo-realism came in, painting pedan- *realismen blev modern, och målade*
tic little interiors, hygienic still lifes, *pedantiska små interiörer, hygieniska*
toothpaste tubes and linoleum tiles, *stilleben, tandkrämstuber och linole-*
then moved on to collages of furry felt *umgolv, för att sedan övergå till col-*
and plastic flowers and bits of looking *lage av lurviga tygbitar och plastblom-*
glass. (MD1) *mor och bitar av spegelglas.*

In both these examples *brukade* would be odd. In (23) it would suggest that Jess didn't always like his mom's Swiss steak, an unlikely interpretation. Similarly, in (24) *brukade* would turn the past state into an irregular activity, again an unlikely reading.

However, there are exceptional cases where *brukade* does seem to refer to a continuous state:

(25) *Their wedding picture **used to** sit on* *Deras bröllopsfoto **brukade** stå på*
the piano in their living room, and *pianot i deras vardagsrum, och även*
though Pete put on less weight over *om Pete gick upp mindre i vikt under*
the years than any of us, he looked *årens lopp än någon av oss andra, så*
less like his youthful self than any of *var han mindre lik sitt ungdomliga jag*
us – his face was lined and wrinkled *än någon av oss andra – hans ansikte*
from the sun, his hair was bleached *var fårat och rynkigt av solen, hans*
pale, his body was knotted and stiff *hår var blekt och färglöst, hans kropp*
with tension. (JSM1) *var knotig och stel av spänningar.*

Here the meaning of *brukade* seems close to that of *used to*: the implication is not that the picture frequently stood on the piano or that it stood there on many different occasions, but that it had a temporally extended and characteristic position there. This is not the normal meaning of *brukade*, yet the translation sounds quite natural and, in fact, better than the simple past which might be misunderstood as referring to a single situation in the past. However, the notion of 'irregularity' that is normally associated with *brukade* is difficult to escape and it is impossible to interpret the situation as representing a continuous state. The impression is rather that the picture could be seen on the piano 'whenever "any of us" happened to visit the house and look into the living room'. Interpreted in this way, the use of *brukade* in (25) is not really an exceptional case. Rather, it supports the observation that 'recurrence' is an essential feature of *brukade* and that this cuts across the stative/dynamic dichotomy. In stative contexts we look for a way to interpret the situation that is compatible with this basic meaning.[7]

In dynamic contexts, on the other hand, Swedish translations with the simple past can usually be replaced by *brukade*:

> (26) *The big dyeing job was done twice a*   *Två gånger om året lät hon färga det*
> *year at the hairdresser's, but every*   *hos hårfrisörskan, men ungefär en*
> *month or so in between, Mrs Worm-*   *gång varannan månad* **sköljde**
> *wood* **used to** *freshen it up by giving it*   *['rinsed'] hon igenom det i handfatet*
> *a rinse in the washbasin with some-*   *för att det inte skulle förlora färgen, och*
> *thing called* PLATINUM BLOND HAIR-   *då använde hon sig av något som på*
> DYE EXTRA STRONG. (RD1)   *etiketten kallades* PLATINABLONT HÅR-
>   FÄRGNINGSMEDEL EXTRA KRAFTIGT.

Here *brukade* would clearly mark the habituality of the event, but since the time adverbial already indicates that the rinsing is a recurrent activity *brukade* is not needed.

However, there are also dynamic situations where *brukade* cannot be used:

> (27)   *"I studied with a man who* **used to**   *"Jag har varit elev hos en man som*
>   *train attack dogs," she said.* (AT1)   **dresserade** *['trained'] skyddshun-*
>   *dar", sade hon.*
>
> (28)   *In 1869 the Cutty Sark* **used to**   *1869* **gick** *Cutty Sark med te från*
>   *bring in tea from China and wool*   *Kina och ull från Australien och*
>   *from Australia and was the fastest*   *var sin tids snabbaste clipper.*
>   *sailing clipper afloat.* (SUG1)   (Lit. '1869 went Cutty Sark with
>   tea ...')

In (27) *brukade* would imply that the man did not train attack dogs as a regular occupation. Similarly, in (28) the Cutty Sark must be understood as involved in a regular activity, a situation which clashes with the notion of habitual 'irregularity' inherent in *brukade*. Hence, the use of *brukade* cuts across the stative/dynamic dichotomy. It cannot be used to refer to a single continuous state but it can refer to a state that is repeated on different occasions. It is normally used in dynamic situations except when

---

7.   However, it seems that *brukade* can be used in stative contexts that are more difficult to explain. The following (fabricated) example does not sound unnatural:

    Här **brukade** *järnvägsstationen ligga, men nu är den nerlagd.*

    (Lit. 'Here *brukade* the railway station lie, but now it is closed down.')

Exactly how this example should be explained is unclear.

the activity referred to is regular. In other words, *brukade* denotes a habit that is 'irregular' in some sense, either because it is recurrent but not continuous or regular.

9.   The role of time adverbials

Another difference between *used to* and *brukade* emerges if we examine the temporal expressions associated with the two verbs. As we have seen, the choice of habitual expression in the two languages is greatly dependent on contextual cues, especially temporal adverbials specifying the nature of the event or state indicated by the verb. In this section I will briefly examine the interaction between the choice of habitual expression (marked or unmarked) and temporal adverbials occurring in the immediate context.

It is natural to assume that there is less need for temporal specification if the habitual nature of the situation is already clearly indicated by a habitual verb like *used to* and *brukade*. Also, since *used to* and *brukade* are both unambiguous markers of habitual aspect we can expect them to be accompanied by a temporal specification less often than *would* (cf. Quirk et al. 1985: 229), which has a number of other functions in English, such as indicating hypothetical meaning, volition and future time. Moreover, in a sequence of habitual events the recurrent nature of each event may not have to be specified if the habitual nature of the situation is announced at the beginning of the sequence or otherwise indicated in the context. Hence, we can expect a close interaction between the verb and various time expressions in the context.

Let us first look briefly at the tendency of English *used to* and Swedish *brukade* to co-occur with a time adverbial in the same sentence in the original texts and translations. For comparison, *would* will be included when it is used as the English source of *brukade*, and the simple past when it is used as the source and translation of *used to* and *brukade*. Two types of adverbial will be considered, those indicating frequency (e.g. *usually, normally, often*) and those indicating an indefinite time in the past (e.g. *once, ten years ago, in the forties, as a child*).

The tendencies are shown in Table 8. As indicated by the percentages in the rightmost column, all the habitual verbs co-occur with a time adverbial in about a third of the examples, in the original texts as well as the translations. Somewhat surprisingly, the tendency is weakest with *would*, which we assumed above would have the greatest need for temporal specification. I will return to this question in section 11.

Table 8. Habitual expressions co-occurring with a time adverbial in original texts and translations

	Expression	Total	Co-occurring adverbial		No	%
			Frequency	Past time	adverbial	adverbial
English	Used to (orig.)	90	19	11	60	33
	Used to (transl.)	105	20	14	71	32
	Would (orig.)*	66	18	1	46	29
	Simple past (orig.)*	32	19	1	12	63
	Simple past (transl.)	43	31	3	9	79
Swedish	Brukade (orig.)	100	25	5	70	30
	Brukade (transl.)	148	47	7	94	36
	Simple past (orig.)**	59	9	32	18	69
	Simple past (transl.)	49	7	30	12	77

* English source of Swedish *brukade*; ** Swedish source of English *used to*.

However, in examples with the simple past the tendency to specify the habitual mean-ing by means of a time adverbial is much stronger in both languages. This tendency is evident in the original texts (63% of the English simple past examples that are the sources of *brukade* and 69% of the Swedish simple past examples that are the sources of *used to*) but it is especially strong in the translations (79% in the English simple past translations of *brukade* and 77% in the Swedish simple past translations of *used to*). This demonstrates two things. First, when the writers of the original texts do not use a habitual verb to mark the habitual meaning, they tend to rely on a suitable time adver-bial instead, as illustrated in (29) and (30):

(29)   *It was an Americanism he himself used often, but it produced no re-sponse. (DF1)*   *Det var ett uttryck som han själv ofta ['often'] brukade använda, men det gav inget gensvar.*

(30)   *Många gånger satt mor vid hans säng och baddade hans rygg där piskrap-pen fått skinnet att lossna och randat blodiga strimmor. (IB1)* (Lit. 'Many times sat mother …')   *Mother often used to sit by his bed, bathing his back where the carpet beater had loosened the skin and streaked his back with bloody weals.*

Second, the translators of such examples normally preserve the time adverbial in their translations, as in (29) and (30), but more importantly, they often use a time adverbial to render the meaning conveyed by a habitual verb in the source text, as in (31) and (32):

(31)   *But Oliver used to correct me and explain that you are whoever it is you're pretending to be. (JB1)*   *Men Oliver sa jämt ['said always'] att jag hade fel: man är den man låtsas vara.*

(32)   *En hypotes var en hypotes,* **brukade**   '*A hypothesis is a hypothesis,*' he <u>com-</u>
       han hävda, ingenting annat. (BL1)   <u>monly</u> *declared.*

In other words, the translators sometimes express the habitual meaning of the original twice, as in (29) and (30) where either the habitual verb or the frequency adverbial would have been sufficient, and sometimes they replace the habitual verb of the original by a frequency adverbial in the translation, as in (31) and (32) where a habitual verb would have been a possible alternative. There are also cases where an adverbial in the source text is replaced by a habitual verb in the translation, as in (33):

(33)   *There was a lot more underneath, stuff*   *Det stod en massa mer text, det som*
       Roger <u>always</u> *referred to as the blah-*   *Roger* **brukade** *kalla blähä-et, men*
       blah, but the copy set in boldface was   *överskriften i halvfet stil var det som*
       the real hooker. (SK1)   *hade gjort annonsen lyckad.*

Hence, in situations referring to habitual events and activities, habitual verbs and frequency adverbials have very similar functions and are often interchangeable.

The type of adverbials used in the two languages is also revealing. The adverbials occurring in the English translations and sources of *brukade* are nearly always adverbials of frequency (see Table 9 where some recurrent examples are listed).[8] This is the case whether they co-occur with *used to* or *would*, as in (34) and (35), or whether they occur in simple past constructions and thus 'replace' *brukade*, as in (36):

(34)   <u>*På nätterna*</u> *när jag låg vaken* **bru-**   <u>*At night*</u> *when I lay awake I* **used to**
       kade *jag lyssna på olika stationer.*   *listen to different stations.*
       (JMY1)

(35)   <u>*I normala fall*</u> **brukade** *syster hjälpa*   <u>*Normally*</u> *Sister* **would** *help me and*
       mig medan jag låtsades som om jag   *I'd pretend that I was in another*
       var i ett annat rum. (RJ1)   *room.*

(36)   *Just på fönsterbrädet där klockan stod,*   *On the windowsill, just where the*
       brukade *det bli så hett att det riktigt*   *clock was standing, it* <u>usually</u> *got boil-*
       gassade. (MG1)   *ing hot.*

The close association of *brukade* with frequency adverbials underlines the notion of 'recurrence' inherent in the verb.

Would, which has only been examined as a source and translation of *brukade* in the corpus, is also typically associated with frequency adverbials. Normally, an adverbial that is present in the source text is preserved in the translation, as in (37), but occasionally a frequency adverbial is added (38) or omitted (39) in the translation:

---

8.   Apart from the recurrent examples listed in Table 9, a wide range of non-recurrent adverbials are used to indicate frequency in the English texts, such as *commonly, occasionally, at tea-time, each term, every evening* (time, etc), *five days a week, in the autumn* (mornings, etc), *on Saturdays*, and subordinate clauses introduced by *as* and *when* (e.g. *when I grumbled about it*).

Table 9. Recurrent time adverbials in English translations and sources of *brukade*.

Adverbials	n
usually	16
always	12
often	7
at night	3
generally	3
normally	3
sometimes	3
each/every day	2
each/every year	2
never	2
regularly	2

(37) *"Quite often," she wrote, "when Mr. Flower needed an extra order of hay delivered, he and his wife **would** drive out on a Sunday to give the order and have a visit with old friends."* (RL1)

*"Ganska ofta när mr Flower behövde en leverans av ett extra lass hö", skrev hon, "**brukade** han och hans hustru fara ut på söndagen för att göra beställ-ningen och hälsa på gamla vänner."*

(38) *Detta var unikt i Europa, men som Sten Sture d.ä. själv **brukade** säga: – Det som rör alla bör av alla samty-ckas.* (HL1)

*This was a unique situation in Europe, but as Sten Sture the Elder **would** often say: That which concerns all should be assented by all.*

(39) *Mrs Fletcher felt that she belonged to Khartoum Road rather than Arblay Street; when asked for her address she **would** always quite unnecessarily point out that she lived on the corner.* (MD1)

*Mrs Fletcher kände att hon mer hörde hemma på Khartoum Road än på Ar-blay Street; när hon tillfrågades om sin adress **brukade** hon alldeles i onödan meddela att hon bodde i hörnet.*

The adverbials associated with *used to*, on the other hand, differ in character from those associated with *brukade* and *would*. As indicated in Table 10 which lists some recurrent examples occurring in the Swedish translations and sources of *used to*, a few adverbials denote frequency, but the majority refer to an indefinite time in the past, emphasizing that the situation continued for some time but then ceased to exist.[9]

Table 10. Recurrent time adverbials in Swedish translations and sources of *used to*.

Adverbials of frequency	n	Adverbials of past time	n
aldrig 'never'	5	*förr* 'formerly'	16
ibland 'sometimes'	5	*förut* 'formerly'	8
alltid 'always'	2	*tidigare* 'earlier'	8
		en gång 'once'	3
		på den tiden 'at that time'	3
		en gång i tiden 'once in the time'	2
		en gång i världen 'once in the world'	2
		förr i världen 'formerly in the world'	2

Adverbials of frequency predominate when *used to* corresponds to *brukade* in the Swedish sources and translations, i.e. when it refers to a recurrent situation, as in (40) and (41):

(40) *Själv hade hon något ledsamt färglöst   She herself had a few pitiful, mousy
      hängande där uppe, som hon **brukade**   strands on top that she **used to** try and
      försöka ändra på till lördagarna.*   spruce up <u>on Saturdays</u>.
      (PP1)

(41) *He said, "I **used to** work <u>five days a   Han sa: "Jag **brukade** arbeta <u>fem da-
      week</u>".* (JSM1)   gar i veckan</u>".*

When *used to* corresponds to a Swedish simple past construction, both adverbials of frequency (42) and adverbials of past time (43) occur:

(42) *I **used to** hear her laughing with him   Ibland hörde jag henne skratta tillsam-
      <u>sometimes</u> in the garden.* (MW1)   mans med honom i trädgården.*

---

9.   As in the English texts, a wide range of non-recurrent adverbials are also used to indicate frequency in the Swedish texts, such as *jämt* 'constantly', *många gånger* 'many times', *om kvällar-na* 'in the evenings', *varannan månad* 'every other month', *varje dag (år, termin, etc)* 'every day (year, term', etc), adverbial clauses of time (e.g. *när det var dimma* 'when there was a fog') and condition (e.g. *om jag sagt mot henne* 'if I had said anything against her'). Some adverbials indicate frequency without being strictly speaking time adverbials, such as *för aftonbruk* 'for evening use'. The past time adverbials exhibit the same variation. Some non-recurrent examples are *förr i tiden* 'formerly', *för tio år sedan* 'ten years ago', *i början* 'at the beginning', *som barn* 'as a child', and *tills helt nyligen* 'until quite recently'.

(43) *And these days you can't just take the*   *Och nu för tiden kan man inte bara*
      speedometer out and fiddle the num-   *plocka ut vägmätaren och fiffla tillbaka*
      bers back like you **used to** *ten years*   *siffrorna som man kunde för tio år*
      ago. (RD1)   *sedan.*

However, adverbials of past time are especially common where they have been added in a Swedish simple past translation, i.e. where they can be said to 'replace' *used to*:

(44) *his father and grandfather [...] had*   *hans far och farfar [...] hade arbetat*
      worked on the ships that **used to** *dis-* *på de båtar som från Crossness på*
      appear secretly up the Thames and out   *andra stranden av Themsen förr i*
      to sea to dump their, in those days,   *världen ['formerly'] diskret försvann*
      untreated load. (MD1)   *neråt floden och ut till havs för att*
                                                   dumpa sin på den tiden helt obehand-
                                                   lade last.

This correspondence between *used to* and a Swedish past time adverbial is particularly striking in the Swedish sources of *used to*, all of which denote a period of time in the past rather than frequency. Two examples are:

(45) *I början ['To begin with'] gjorde dom*   *They* **used to** *make boots and shoes,*
      ju skor och stövlar, men sen har ju   *but of course shoes and materials have*
      skorna och materialet förändrats.   *changed since then.*
      (SC1)

(46) *Han, Torsten, körde ut tidningar på*   *He, Torsten,* **used to** *take the papers*
      den tiden ['at that time'], på en stor   *out on a big old bike of his mother's.*
      gammal damcykel som var hans
      mammas. (LG1)

The reason for this is the notion of 'discontinuity' that is associated with *used to*. As pointed out by Leech (1987: 54), *used to* "typically points a contrast with a present state or habit". Another way of expressing this is to say that *used to* carries an implicature that the habitual situation it refers to no longer holds (cf. Comrie 1976: 28f.). This contrast is explicit in the English versions of (43) and (45), but implicit in (44) and (46). Swedish *brukade* does not carry the same implicature and the contrast therefore has to be expressed by the simple past and a clarifying past tense adverbial. As a result, a past time adverbial is typically added in the Swedish translations of *used to*, as in (44), but omitted in the English translations with *used to*, as in (45–46).

The sense of 'discontinuity' inherent in *used to* can also be conveyed by an aspectual shift from the past tense to the past perfect in Swedish:

(47)   *While he was away with his commit-*   *När han var borta på sina kommittéer*
       tees and meetings at weekends my   *och möten under helgerna försökte*
       mother tried to do with us the things   *min mor göra de saker med oss som vi*
       *we all **used to** do together.* (NG1)   *tidigare hade gjort ['formerly had*
                                                 done'] tillsammans.

(48)   *The material didn't have any colour*   *Tyget hade ingen färg men när ljuset*
       but when the light was on you could   *var tänt kunde man se att blommorna*
       *see that the flowers **used to** be col-* *hade varit ['had been'] i färg.*
       oured. (RDO1)

(49)   *She thought of the corridors lined with* *Hon tänkte på korridorerna som kan-*
       *closets where her clothes **used to** hang* *tades av garderober där hennes kläder*
       in colour co-ordinated rows. (ST1)   *hade hängt ['had hung'] i färgkoordin-*
                                                 erade rader.

In (47) the translator has made two changes to capture the discontinuity signalled by *used to*: insertion of the adverb *tidigare* 'earlier' and a shift to the past perfect. In (48) and (49) the aspectual shift has been judged sufficient to indicate that the state referred to no longer exists.

We can interpret these tendencies as follows. *Brukade* typically expresses recurrent events and states in the past. As a result, adverbials occurring in the English translations and sources of *brukade* are typically frequency adverbials. Conversely, when *brukade* is used to translate *used to* no adverbial needs to be added since the habitual meaning is inherent in *brukade* (although an adverbial in the English source is often retained in the Swedish version).

Used to, on the other hand, has two functions: it either indicates repeated events or states in the past (frequency) or a discontinued past state. In the former sense it is typically rendered by *brukade* and/or a frequency adverbial in Swedish; in the second sense it normally corresponds to a simple past construction specified by a past time adverbial or an aspectual shift in Swedish.

Despite the differences in habitual marking in the two languages, one common tendency should be emphasized: the habitual nature of a situation is generally marked in some way, either by means of a habitual verb (*used to*, *would* or *brukade*) or by a suitable time adverbial. If it is not, there is a risk that the situation is misunderstood as non-habitual. This can be seen in the following example. If we replace the habitual verb by the simple past (in either language), the verb might easily be misunderstood as referring to a single specific occasion in the past:

(50) *Harold Clark and my father **used to***   *Harold Clark och min far **brukade***
      argue at our kitchen table about who   *sitta vid vårt köksbord och diskutera*
      should get the Ericson land when they   *vem som skulle få Ericsons mark när*
      finally lost their mortgage. (JSM1)   *banken till sist sa upp deras lån.*
      *Harold Clark and my father argued   **Harold Clark och min far satt …*
      …

10. The quantifying use of *brukade*

As we have seen, habituality is clearly a temporal phenomenon, i.e. it displays a situation as distributed over a period of time. However, in stative situations *brukade* can also have a quantifying function:

(51) *I en tid då inte ens stormannadöttrar*   *At a time when not even the daughters*
      ***brukade** kunna läsa eller skriva, dik-*   *of great men in the realm could read*
      terar hon under många år en ström av   *or write she produced a multitude of*
      texter, totalt över 800, som översätts   *scripts, more than 800 over the years,*
      till dåtida Europas största språk och   *which were translated into the princi-*
      fortfarande räknas till medeltidens   *pal languages of mediaeval Europe*
      världslitteratur. (HL1)   *and are still regarded as major literary*
                                                        works from that time.

(52) *Röster i telefoner **brukade** förutsätta*   *Voices on the telephone seemed to take*
      alltför mycket som självklart. (LG1)   *too much for granted.*

Here *brukade* does not indicate that the subjects are involved in irregularly repeated states but rather that the state referred to does not have general (or generic) validity. Hence, in (51) the inability to read or write does not apply to all 'daughters of great men in the realm' but to most of them. Similarly, in (52) the point is that many – but not all – voices on the telephone took too much for granted. In other words, *brukade* does not express 'irregularity' in a temporal sense but rather in terms of applicability or validity.

We can explain this shift in meaning as an example of pragmatic reinterpretation. Since *brukade* cannot have its normal sense of (temporal) habituality, we are forced to search for an alternative interpretation that satisfies the strong notion of 'irregularity' inherent in the verb. The only possible reading that fits the context is 'irregular' validity. And since the examples only differ from generic ones in having less than generic validity, we can describe them as 'near-generic'.

That there is a close relationship between habituality (temporal irregularity) and near-genericness (quantitative irregularity) is demonstrated by the fact that *brukade* in examples like (51) and (52) can be paraphrased by either a multal quantifier or a frequency adverbial with little difference in meaning:[10]

(51') (a) *I en tid då inte ens de flesta stormannadöttrar kunde läsa eller skriva ...*
            (Lit. 'At a time when not even most daughters of great men ...')
       (b) *I en tid då inte ens stormannadöttrar vanligen kunde läsa eller skriva ...*
            (Lit. 'At a time when not even daughters of great men usually could ...')

The quantifying use of *brukade* can only be demonstrated clearly in contexts describing a continuous state. In dynamic situations of a generic character, where the notion of recurrence is natural, a habitual (i.e. temporal) interpretation of *brukade* always seems possible:

(53) *"Gud hjälpe den som ska genom Rö-*   "God help anyone whose way lies
      vargången", brukade folk säja, och då   along Robbers' Walk," people said,
      menade de det trånga bergspasset   talking of the narrow mountain pass
      mellan Borkaskogen och Mattisskogen.   between Borka's Wood and Matt's
      (AL1)   Wood.

Here a habitual reading ('usually') is at least as natural as a quantifying one ('most').

There is no clear evidence in the material that *used to* has the same quantifying potential as *brukade*. If this had been the case, we would expect a high degree of correspondence between *brukade* and *used to* in near-generic examples in the corpus, i.e. we would not expect any shifts to the generic simple past (without any other contextual indication) in either direction. Conversely, there should be no shifts from a generic simple past to a habitual verb. However, such shifts are common in the material. The English translations of *brukade* in (51)–(53) above are good illustrations of this: the use of the simple past renders the English versions fully generic, although the addition of *seemed* in (52) appears to be an attempt to capture the restricted validity of the Swedish original.

Conversely, when an example of a generic simple past in Swedish is translated by *used to* in English, we would expect the change to have a near-generic effect:

(54) *Där står en indian av trä, sådana hade*   There's a wooden Indian, like the ones
      man förr i tiden ['such had one for-   they used to have in front of cigar stores.
      merly'] utanför tobaksaffärer. (JMY1)

---

10. The parallelism is of course equally obvious in the present tense, the typical form of generic statements:
    (a) Svenskar brukar vara långa och blåögda. 'Swedes brukar (pres.) be tall and blue-eyed'
    (b) Svenskar är ofta långa och blåögda. 'Swedes are often tall and blue-eyed'
    (c) De flesta svenskar är långa och blåögda. 'Most Swedes are tall and blue-eyed'
On the relationship between frequency adverbials and quantifiers in generic expressions in English, see Quirk et al. (1985: 549 f.).

However, unlike *brukade, used to* is commonly associated with situations denoting a continuous state and so does not invite a quantifying reinterpretation. Instead, what *used to* conveys in such cases is rather the notion of temporal 'discontinuity' that we have seen is an essential feature of the verb. This is also clearly the case in (54) where *used to* captures the meaning of the adverbial *förr i tiden* ('formerly, once') in the Swedish original.

What further complicates the analysis is that habituality and near-genericness are sometimes difficult to distinguish. There are in fact few unambiguous examples of near-genericness in the corpus. The safest conclusion that can be drawn on the basis of the material is therefore that *brukade* tends to adopt a quantifying function in situations describing a continuous state. Whether *used to* has a similar effect is doubtful. To explore this question must be left for future research.

11. *Would*

Although *would* mainly turns up as a source of *brukade* in the present material, a few observations can be made. *Would* does not carry the sense of discontinuity inherent in *used to* and the two verbs are therefore not always interchangeable. Moreover, *would* tends to indicate characteristic or predictable behaviour (Quirk et al 1985: 228) and is especially common in written narrative style (Leech and Svartvik 1994: 73). The latter tendency is clearly evident in the present corpus. The great majority of the *would* examples occur in fiction texts (61% of the examples) and in (auto)biographical narratives (38%).

As we have seen, *would* is also predominantly used with dynamic verbs (91%), but this does not mean that it cannot indicate recurrent states:

(55)   *And the dog, most often, **would** be lying on top of his feet.* (AT1)   *Och hunden **brukade** oftast ligga ovanpå hans fötter.*

(56)   *This instrument **would** be on a table, and he played it with little mallets, and called off the dances as he played.* (RL1)   *Det där instrumentet **brukade** ligga på ett bord och han spelade på det med små klubbor och ropade ut danserna när han spelade.*

According to Tagliamonte and Lawrence (2000: 342 ff.) *would* is especially common non-initially in a sequence of habitual events. This tendency is also borne out in the present corpus. A few examples will suffice to illustrate this:

(57) *Lauretta rarely features in Miller's many accounts of his childhood. Here and there he mentions occasions when he had to fight other children who liked to taunt her by calling her "crazy Lauretta". Usually when he brings up her name it is to recall with anger and disappointment the way his mother* **used to** *treat her:*
I'll never forget my mother standing over Lauretta in the kitchen, trying to teach her the simplest things on a little blackboard. In one hand she held a piece of chalk, in the other a ruler. "What's two and two?" she'd ask. And Lauretta, who knew what was coming, **would** *begin to rattle off any answer she could think of. "Three, no five, no three..." and the harder she'd try the crazier my mother* **would** *get. It always ended up with a beating, then mother* **would** *turn to me with this exasperated look on her face, and she'd throw her hands up in despair. "What did I do to deserve this?" she'd ask me, as if I were God and had all the answers, me, a little boy! (RF1)*

Lauretta [...] förekommer sällan i Millers många olika beskrivningar av sin barndom. På några ställen nämner han tillfällen då han tvingades slåss med andra barn som retade henne och kallade henne "Toklauretta". Vid de tillfällen då han nämner hennes namn minns han oftast med vrede och besvikelse hur hans mor **brukade** *behandla henne:*
Jag ska aldrig glömma hur min mamma stod lutad över Lauretta i köket och försökte lära henne några enkla saker med hjälp av en liten svart tavla. I ena handen hade hon kritan, i den andra en linjal.
"Hur mycket är två och två?" **brukade** *hon fråga. Och Lauretta, som visste vad som väntade, började haspla ur sig det första som kom för henne. "Tre, nej fem, nej tre. . ." och ju mer hon ansträngde sig desto ilsknare blev mamma. Det slutade alltid med stryk och sedan vände sig mamma mot mig med uppgiven blick och slog ut med armarna i en desperat gest. "Vad har jag gjort för att förtjäna detta?"* **brukade** *hon fråga mig, ungefär som om jag vore Gud och kunde svara på allting, jag, en liten pojke!*

(58) *The waitress was the sort to stand and talk, mulishly deaf and blind to summonses from older, less flirtatious men at other tables.*

Servitrisen hörde till dem som gärna stannade och pratade utan att vare sig höra eller se vad de äldre och inte fullt så flörtiga herrarna vid andra bord önskade.

"*Those spoonwood leaves*", *she said,* | "*De där lagerbladen är giftiga*", *sa hon.*
using once again the country term, | "*Det kommer att rinna både upptill*
"*are poisonous. You'll run both ends.*" | *och nertill på er.*" *Uppmuntrad av män-*
Encouraged by their laughter, she em- | *nens skrattsalvor började hon berätta*
barked upon a tale of how the women | *en historia om hur kvinnorna i hennes*
in her village **used** *once* **to** *boil the* | *by en gång i tiden* **brukade** *koka giftet*
poison out of laurel leaves. They'd soak | *ur lagerblad. De lät giftet sugas upp i*
the poison into bread, she said, to bait | *bröd för att locka råttor och möss i*
the rats and mice: "A woman my | *fällan. "En kvinna som min farmor*
grandma knew made chicken soup | *kände gjorde kycklingsoppa med bär*
with laurel seeds and laurel sap. | *och sav från lagern. De* **brukade** *an-*
They'd use it as fox bait." (JC1) | *vända det för att locka räven med.*"

Examples (57) and (58) each contain a narrative sequence of habitual events in the past. The habitual nature of the events is clearly established at the beginning of each sequence, by "Usually when he brings up her name it is to recall the way his mother used to treat her" in (57) and "she embarked upon a tale of how the women used once to boil …" in (58). In both cases the first event is signalled by *used to* while subsequent events are expressed by *would*. In the Swedish versions *brukade* alternates with the simple past.

In the following scene, which describes the recurrent features of a man's sleepless nights, the habitual nature of the scene is first signalled by "his nights were terrible". Then *would* initiates the sequence of events (slightly abbreviated here) and dominates the rest of the narrative, only occasionally interspersed with the simple past. Again, *brukade* is the dominant Swedish translation:

(59) *But his nights were terrible.* | *Men nätterna var förfärliga.*
It wasn't that he had trouble getting to | *Inte så att han hade svårt att somna.*
sleep in the first place. That was easy. | *Det var en enkel sak. Han* **brukade**
He'd watch TV till his eyes burned; | *titta på TV tills det sved i ögonen, och*
then he'd climb the stairs. […] Gener- | *då gick han upp i övre våningen. […] I*
ally some black-and-white movie was | *allmänhet visades det någon film i*
running – men in suits and felt hats, | *svartvitt – män i kavajkostym och*
women with padded shoulders. He | *filthatt, damer med axelvaddar. Han*
didn't try to follow the plot. […] He | *gjorde inget försök att följa med i han-*
absently stroked the cat, who had | *dlingen. […] Omedvetet smekte han*
somehow crept into his lap. […] | *katten, som på något sätt hade ham-*
And the dog, most often, **would** *be* | *nat i knät på honom. […]*
lying on top of his feet. "It's just you | *Och hunden* **brukade** *oftast ligga*
and me, old buddies," Macon **would** | *ovanpå hans fötter. "Det är bara vi tre,*
tell them. | *gamla kompisar*", **brukade** *han säga.*

*At last he **would** slip out from under the animals and turn off the TV. He **would** put his glass in the chlorine solution in the kitchen sink. He **would** climb the stairs. He'd stand at the bedroom window looking over the neighborhood – black branches scrawled on a purple night sky, a glimmer of white clapboard here and there, occasionally a light. (AT1)*	*Till slut **brukade** han lirka sig ifrån djuren och stänga av TV:n. Ställde ner glaset i klorlösningen i diskhon. Gick uppför trappan. Sedan **brukade** han ställa sig vid fönstret i sovrummet och se ut över omgivningen – svarta trädgrenar mot en purpurfärgad natthimmel, en glimt av vitt trävirke här och där, någon gång ljus i ett fönster.*

These examples have one thing in common: once the habitual nature of the sequence has been established by means of *used to* and/or some other information in the context, the following events can be expressed by *would*. This may explain why *would* is less often accompanied by time adverbials than *used to* (and *brukade*). In a sequence of habitual events there is generally no need for additional temporal marking if the habitual nature of the sequence is clearly marked from the beginning.

12. Other factors

Some other conditioning factors explored by Tagliamonte and Lawrence (2000) in their spoken English corpus can also be examined cross-linguistically in the present (written) corpus. Three factors will be touched upon briefly here.

12.1   Correlation with the grammatical person of the subject

According to Tagliamonte and Lawrence (2000), 1st person subjects tend to favour *used to* while 3rd person subjects favour the use of *would*. As shown in Table 11, *used to* also has the strongest tendency to co-occur with 1st person subjects in the present corpus. However, as 3rd person subjects dominate with all three verbs, the grammatical person of the subject does not emerge as an important conditioning factor in the present corpus.

Table 11. Correlation with the grammatical person of the subject

	1st pers.	2nd pers.	3rd pers.	Total
Brukade (Sw. orig.)	9 (9%)	0	91 (91%)	100
Used to (Eng. orig.)	27 (30%)	1	62 (69%)	90
Would (source of *brukade*)	7 (11%)	0	59 (89%)	66

12.2 Correlation with animate subject

In Tagliamonte and Lawrence's study inanimate subjects were found to disfavour *used to* but to have no affect on the use of *would*. These results were taken to indicate that *used to* had not expanded its original use as much as expected and that therefore the grammaticalisation of *used to* had not advanced as far as that of *would*.

In the present corpus animate subjects dominate greatly with all the verbs, but all verbs also occur with inanimate subjects (see Table 12). *Would* has a greater tendency to cooccur with animate subjects than the other verbs. Hence, the present corpus does not seem to confirm Tagliamonte and Lawrence's results.

Table 12. Correlation with animate subject

	+ Animate	– Animate	Total
Brukade (Sw. orig.)	83 (83%)	17 (17%)	100
Used to (Eng. orig.)	70 (78%)	20 (22%)	90
Would (source of *brukade*)	63 (95%)	3 (5%)	66

12.3 Non-assertive contexts

Since *used to* is a past tense form taking the *to*-infinitive, it is felt to be awkward in negative and interrogative clauses where it either has to be used as an operator (e.g. *he use(d)n't to do it; used he to do it?*) or as a full verb with *do*-support (e.g. *he didn't use(d) to do it; did he use(d) to do it?*). As a result it tends to be avoided in non-assertive contexts (see Tagliamonte and Lawrence 2000: 337, Biber et al. 1999: 165). This is revealed in various ways in the corpus. Although neither *used to* nor *brukade* is very common in non-assertive contexts, it is significant that *used to* only occurs once with *not*-negation:

(60) *She **used** not **to** worry about this uncertainty, but worry has been forced upon her by what Hugo has not entirely seriously labelled her mid-life crisis.* (MD1)   *Tidigare har hon inte funderat särskilt mycket över denna kluvenhet, men Hugo har genom att påstå att hon befinner sig i vad han halvt på skämt etiketterar som en typisk medelålderskris tvingat henne in i självprövning.*

In the remaining negative examples *never* is used instead of *not* (61), or else the simple past supported by a frequency adverbial is preferred to *used to* (62):

(61) *"He never **used to** do this."* (AT1)   *"Så här brukar han aldrig ['never'] göra."*

(62)   *He didn't <u>usually</u> come to those, and*   *Han **brukade** inte <u>ofta</u> ['often'] vara*
       didn't seem at ease with the family.   *med och verkade inte känna sig hem-*
       (RDA1)   *ma i familjen.*

The strategy of using the simple past and a time adverbial is also evident in interrogative contexts:

(63)   *"When Greville came to see his hors-*   *"När Greville kom för att titta på sina*
       es," I asked, "did he <u>ever</u> bring anyone *hästar", sa jag, "**brukade** han då*
       with him?" (DF1)   *<u>ibland</u> ['sometimes'] ha med sig*
                                                         någon?"

The same strategy is seen very clearly in the English translations of *brukade* in non-assertive contexts: *used to* is avoided and the habitual meaning of the Swedish original is conveyed by the simple past (64), usually reinforced by an adverbial indicating frequency (65) or some similar notion (66):

(64)   ***Brukade** gemene man förvara slad-*   *Did ordinary people have such things*
       dlampor hemma hos sig? (LG1)   *at home?*
(65)   *De var söderut och västerut och **bru-***   *They were down South and out West*
       ***kade** inte lämna sin adress ens utan*   *and <u>usually</u> didn't even leave their*
       Gunnar sade att Karna var duktig och   *address. Gunnar said Karna was ca-*
       nog kunde klara det hela med huset   *pable and could take care of the house*
       och mig och ungarna och allt tillsam-   *and me and the little girls and every-*
       mans med Ingrid. (JMY1)   *thing with Ingrid.*
(66)   *Nöjd **brukade** kanske inte bli*   *Perhaps Allwright was not a man to*
       förvånad. (SW1)   *be <u>easily</u> surprised.*

13. Conclusion

As this study has demonstrated, English *used to* and Swedish *brukade* only display partial correspondence. Although they can each be regarded as the prototypical habitual form in the two languages, their mutual correspondence is low (38%). The existence of *would* as an alternative marked form in English does not change this picture: though common as a source of *brukade* in the Swedish translations, it is surprisingly rare as a translation of *brukade*.

One reason for the low correspondence of *used to* and *brukade* is that the simple past is frequently used to express habituality in both languages. It is in fact the most common translation equivalent in both languages. However, being unmarked for habituality, the simple past is a possible option only in cases where the habitual nature of the situation is indicated in the context, typically by a time adverbial.

But the choice of expression is also determined by other factors. An essential difference between the languages is that *used to* is common in both stative and dynamic situations, whereas *brukade* (like *would*) is usually restricted to dynamic situations. Yet, the stative/dynamic distinction alone is never quite decisive: both verbs can be used in either context. Instead, the choice between the marked and the unmarked expression in the two languages can be explained in terms of three other factors that cut across the stative/dynamic dichotomy. These are indicated in Table 13.

Table 13. Factors affecting the choice of habitual expression

Habitual form	Temporal extension	Recurrence	Discontinuity
used to	+	±	+
brukade	+	+	±

Both *used to* and *brukade* refer to a situation that has 'temporal extension', i.e. a situation that is viewed as "characteristic of an extended period of time" in the past (cf. Comrie 1976: 27 f.). This is why neither verb can be replaced by the simple past without some contextual indication of habituality. If there is no such indication the clause may easily be misinterpreted as referring to a single occasion, i.e. as non-habitual.

However, unlike *used to*, *brukade* can only be used about a situation that is viewed as 'recurrent', i.e. to a state or event that is not continuous or regular but recurs on different occasions. *Used to* is not constrained by this feature and can refer to both recurrent and continuous situations. In addition, *used to* strongly suggests that the past situation is 'discontinued', i.e. that it no longer applies and therefore contrasts with the situation at the moment of speaking. This meaning is not equally obvious in *brukade* and to express the same contrast in Swedish the simple past and a past time adverbial are generally preferred.

Other factors have little or no effect on the choice of expression. *Used to* is not readily accepted in non-assertive clauses with *do*-support, but this is a rare feature in the material. The animacy and grammatical person of the subject do not seem to affect the choice of expression in either language.

Would has only been examined as a source of *brukade* in the Swedish translations in the corpus. Although it is rarely used as a translation of *brukade*, the two verbs have at least one feature in common: both are mainly used to describe recurrent events in dynamic situations. *Would* is however more restricted in its distribution: it is typically used to describe characteristic behaviour and it is especially common in sequences of habitual events in narrative contexts.

However, this study also raises an important question. How can 'habituality' be defined in a language-neutral way? The *tertium comparationis* that emerges from the material is determined by the two habitual forms – *used to* and *brukade* – that were used as the point of departure of the comparison, and these two forms clearly identify different notions of 'habituality'. If we return to the two definitions cited at the beginning of the paper, we find that these, too, describe the notion of habituality differently. Comrie's definition is wide enough to include continuous past states in the notion of habit. In a Swedish perspective this seems odd and anglocentric and it is tempting to suspect that Comrie allowed the function of English *used to* to influence his definition. Brinton, by contrast, regards habits and states as mutually exclusive (1987: 199) and restricts habituality to situations that are viewed as "repeated on different occasions", which excludes continuous states. This definition agrees much better with the use of Swedish *brukade* and seems less dictated by formal considerations, but it excludes an essential function of English *used to*.

The question is how these definitions could be reconciled. From a Swedish point of view *used to* must be regarded as polysemous, but it is obvious that a comparison of two languages alone will not give us a satisfactory answer. To arrive at a general language-independent definition of habituality we need to compare a wide range of languages. Then we might be able to define some prototypical notion of habituality that is shared by a large number of languages and regard deviations from this notion as extensions or restrictions of this prototypical idea. What is clear, however, is that such comparisons must be based on authentic texts revealing the use and correspondence of habitual forms in the compared languages. Parallel corpora involving other language pairs or multilingual translation corpora allowing cross-linguistic comparisons of several languages will be useful resources for such research in the future.

References

Altenberg, Bengt. 1999. "Adverbial connectors in English and Swedish: Semantic and lexical correspondences". *Out of corpora. Studies in honour of Stig Johansson*, ed. by Hilde Hasselgård and Signe Oksefjell, 249–268. Amsterdam: Rodopi.

Altenberg, Bengt and Karin Aijmer. 2000. "The English-Swedish Parallel Corpus: A resource for contrastive research and translation studies". In *Corpus linguistics and linguistic theory*, ed. by Christian Mair and Marianne Hundt, 15–33. Amsterdam: Rodopi.

Altenberg, Bengt, Karin Aijmer and Mikael Svensson. 2001. *The English-Swedish Parallel Corpus: Manual*. Department of English, University of Lund. Available at www.englund.lu.se/research/corpus/corpus/espc.html.

Baker, Mona. 1996. "Corpus-based translation studies: The challenges that lie ahead". *Terminology, LSP and translation. Studies in language engineering in honour of Juan C. Sager*, ed. by Harold Somers, 175–186. Amsterdam: John Benjamins.

Biber, Douglas, Stig Johansson, Geoffrey Leech, Susan Conrad and Edward Finegan. 1999. *Longman grammar of spoken and written English*. Harlow: Longman.

Brinton, Laurel J. 1987. "The aspectual nature of states and habits". *Folia Linguistica* 21: 195–214.

Brinton, Laurel J. 1988. *The development of English aspectual systems*. Cambridge: Cambridge University Press.

Bybee, Joan L., Revere D. Perkins and William Pagliuca. 1994. *The evolution of grammar: Tense, aspect, and modality in the languages of the world.* Chicago: University of Chicago Press.

Comrie, Bernard. 1976. *Aspect: An introduction to the study of verbal aspect and related problems.* Cambridge: Cambridge University Press.

Dahl, Östen. 1985. *Tense and aspect systems.* Oxford: Blackwell.

Laviosa, Sara. 1998a. "Core patterns of lexical use in a comparable corpus of English narrative prose". *Meta* XLIII (4), 557–570.

Laviosa, Sara. 1998b. "The English Comparable Corpus: A resource and a methodology". *Unity in diversity? Current trends in translation studies,* ed. by Lynne Bowker, Michael Cronin, Dorothy Kenny and Jennifer Pearson, 101–112. Manchester: St Jerome Publishing.

Leech, Geoffrey N. 1987. *Meaning and the English verb.* London: Longman.

Leech, Geoffrey and Jan Svartvik. 1994. *A communicative grammar of English.* 2nd edn. London: Longman.

Quirk, Randolph, Sidney Greenbaum, Geoffrey Leech and Jan Svartvik. 1985. *A comprehensive grammar of the English language.* London: Longman.

Svartvik, Jan and Olof Sager. 1996. *Engelsk universitetsgrammatik.* 2nd edn. Stockholm: Almqvist and Wiksell.

Tagliamonte, Sali and Helen Lawrence. 2000. "I used to dance, but I don't dance now". The habitual past in English. *Journal of English Linguistics* 28: 324–353.

Teleman, Ulf, Staffan Hellberg and Erik Andersson. 1999. *Svenska Akademiens grammatik. 4. Satser och meningar.* Stockholm: Norstedt.

Do cognate and circumstantial complements of intransitive verbs form one 'Range'?

A corpus-based discussion

Kathleen Rymen and Kristin Davidse
University of Leuven

In this article we examine the question whether cognate complements (as in *dance the tango*) and circumstantial complements (as in *climb stairs*) can be regarded as expressing the same semantic role. Halliday has proposed that they do: in his view they both delimit the 'extent', or 'Range', of the process. Traditionally, however, they have been regarded as distinct grammatical categories. Assuming, like Halliday, that grammatical categories are form-meaning couplings, we investigate in corpus data the two types of formal evidence proposed by him for the unified Range category: alternations and selection restrictions on determiners and modifiers. By quantifying the relative frequencies of the alternate constructions, we have found that clauses with cognate complements form the marked option in comparison with intransitives. Clauses with circumstantial complements, by contrast, alternate with intransitive clauses as well as with clauses with prepositional phrase in varying proportions. This shows that the notion of 'location involved in process' can be more strongly or weakly present in the semantics of verbs taking circumstantial complements. The determiners and modifiers of cognate and circumstantial complements also reflect different semantic relations of the complement to the process expressed by the verb. Cognate complements are predominantly indefinite and circumstantial complements more often definite, because the former typically construe a 'new' instance of the process, whereas the latter often express pre-existing locations. Attributive modifiers of the two complement types differ both quantitatively and qualitatively. Cognate complements take more qualitative adjectives, which tend to express the manner in which the process takes place. Circumstantial complements have much less qualitative modification and often express the resistance or facilitation offered by the location to the action being carried out on it. We conclude that the two types of complements express different sorts of entities with different relations to the process.

1.   Introduction[1]

In this article, we will be concerned with the semantic role of the 'Range' of intransitive verbs, proposed by Halliday (1967: 58–62, 1985: 134–137, 151–152) as a category of the 'experiential' grammar of the clause. In Halliday's functional grammar, the 'experiential' meaning of the clause is constituted by the relations between the process (expressed by the lexical verb) and its participants (designated by nominals), as modified by circumstantial elements (typically expressed by PrepPs and adverbials).

Halliday (1967: 58ff) introduced the Range as grammatically and semantically distinct from the other non-agentive roles Goal and Beneficiary. Whereas the latter two represent entities participating in the process, the Range is only a "pseudo-participant" in the process and specifies "the extent of its scope" (1967: 58). Within the Range, Halliday distinguishes two subtypes, one re-labelling the process as in (1), and one indicating the domain over which the process takes place as in (2).

(1)   *Koya women in the congregation linked arms at Yuniah's instigation, made a circle and danced* **a Koya dance.** (CB)

(2)   *The first American to climb* **Mt. Everest** *was James W. Whittaker.* (CB)

The most important difference between Halliday's and other approaches in the literature to these clause types is that the Range is put forward as one unified category. Yet, traditionally, the postverbal NPs in (1) and (2) are viewed as instances of two distinct categories: *a Koya dance* is generally known as a 'cognate object', while *Mt. Everest* has been described as a 'transitivizing object' (Massam 1990), a NP turning an intransitive verb into a transitive one. In this article, we will consider the question whether Halliday is justified in regarding the Range as one unified category in English. So as not to forestall the discussion terminologically, we will refer to the postverbal NP in (1) as a cognate complement and to that in (2) as a circumstantial complement[2].

The structure of the article will be as follows. In section 2 we will look at the formal recognition criteria and the semantic characterization proposed by Halliday for the Range category. The formal claims made by Halliday basically fall into two groups: on the one hand, they relate to alternations of Range-constructions, such as its highly

---

1.   In spite of (or perhaps because of) her modesty, Angela Downing has always been a formidable model of professionalism. She has never failed to take the challenges of linguistic investigation very seriously and has brought many others to high-quality research. Talking about her ongoing work on the functional description of English, she once exclaimed: "There is still so much work to be done!" Thanks to enthusiastic and hard working students like Kathleen Rymen, some of the research needs identified by Angela Downing are being met. In recognition of Angela Downing's great inspirational role, Kathleen Rymen and I dedicate this article to her.

2.   In the expressions "cognate complement" and "circumstantial complement", "complement" is used in the sense of a nominal elaborating and completing the meaning of the verb, as in Langacker (1987).

marked passive; on the other, they are to do with determiners and modifiers occurring in the NPs realizing Ranges. In sections 3 and 4, we will check these claims empirically in extended data sets collected by Rymen (1999) from the COBUILD corpus. In section 5 we will discuss to what extent these quantified data analyses can help us with regard to the question whether or not cognate and circumstantial complements of intransitive verbs form one category.

2.   Halliday on Range

Halliday (1967, 1985) sets up the Range as a specific semantic role which may be either Complement of the active (*everyone plays football*) or Subject of the passive (*football is played by everyone*). Even though these look like transitive clauses, he stresses that they are semantically intransitive. In "Notes on Transitivity and Theme" (1967: 58) he advanced the Range's inability to be reflexive as the main indication that it is not targeted by the action. Whereas Goal and Beneficiary display the paradigmatic contrast between non-reflexive and reflexive – Actors can take themselves as Goal or Beneficiary of the action -, the Range cannot be co-referential with the Actor:

(1)   b.   *They danced themselves.*

(2)   b.   *The first American to climb himself* […]

In *Introduction to Functional Grammar* (1985), Halliday reiterated the claim that clauses with Range are semantically non-transitive, but now he adduced the fact that these clauses have very uncommon and marked passives as formal evidence. This argument has to be seen against the more general tenet that possibility of an unmarked passive is a crucial symptom of a clause's semantic transitivity (Halliday 1985: 151ff), i.e. of action being carried over from an Agent onto a Patient. Within a cognitive framework, exactly the same correlation between passivizability and transitivity has been pointed out by Langacker (1987) and has been elaborated in more detail by Rice (1987).

   In support of the Range's non-transitive semantics Halliday also points out that, unlike a real Patient, it cannot be probed by *do to* or *do with*, as shown by 3b,

(3)   a.   *Have they dug up the road yet? – No, but they are doing the pavement.* (Halliday 1967: 61)
       b.   *Have they crossed the road yet? – *No, but they are doing the pavement.* (Halliday 1967: 61)

and it cannot be followed by a depictive (4b) or resultative (5b) attribute:

(4)   a.   *He made the box big.* (Halliday 1967: 61)
       b.   *He made the mistake big.* (Halliday 1967: 61)

(5) a. *They trampled the field flat.* (Halliday 1985: 148)
     b. **They crossed the field flat.* (Halliday 1985: 148)

He characterizes the general meaning of the Range as a non-patientive "extension" (1967: 59, 61) of intransitive processes, and then goes on to distinguish two semantic subtypes. In the first type, the Range is "co-extensive with, is indeed merely a nominalization of the process" (1967: 59). It is, therefore, either lexically cognate in the strict sense with the verb (e.g. *smile a smile*) or it is a lexical collocate of the verb (as in *play a game*). This subtype also subsumes the specific case in which "the process... is entirely expressed in the nominal element, the verb merely specifying that there is a process involved: *he had a bath, he took a dislike, he made a mistake*" (1967: 60). The latter construction does not alternate with the intransitive of the general verb (such as *have, take* and *make*), but, if anything, with the intransitive of the verb corresponding to the Range NP. The second type of Range is an entity which exists independently of the process but which indicates "the domain over which the process takes place" (1985: 134), as in *he walked the streets* (1967: 59). This type tends to alternate with intransitives plus PrepP, often allowing for a number of different prepositions in that alternate.

This binary distinction is cross-classified by Halliday with a "further distinction (...) between quality range and quantity range" (1967: 59). The former specifies type, as in *he played tennis, he climbs mountains*, or quality, as in *he played a good game*. The latter specifies measure, as in *he jumped the wall, he played five games* (1985: 135). Even though the quality-quantity distinction is linked to formal realizations such as numeratives and qualitative adjectives, it is clearly not meant as a mutually exclusive classification. In our reading of Halliday, these two functions can instead be seen as uniting the two types of Range.

We thus see how Halliday grounds the delineation and semantic elucidation of the Range-category in 'formal' features in the broad sense, viz. alternations of the Range-construction and tendencies with regard to the modification of Range-NPs. This is in keeping with his adherence to the tenet that grammatical meaning is naturally construed by grammatical form (Halliday 1985: xxxii). However, his points about alternations and modifiers imply claims about quantitative occurrence for which he does not adduce empirical evidence. This is what, on the basis of Rymen's (1999) quantified corpus study, we will do in the next two sections. In section 3, we will look at the alternations manifested in usage by the two types of Range-constructions, referring also to Levin (1993). In section 4, we will confront claims by Halliday and other authors regarding the modification of Range-NPs with quantified corpus data. The results will be brought to bear on the question whether or not cognate and circumstantial complements of intransitive verbs can be viewed as forming one category.

3. Alternations of constructions with cognate and circumstantial complements: a quantified approach

In section 2, we saw how Halliday bases both the identification and the semantic interpretation of the Range on claims such as impossibility of corresponding reflexives and resultatives, systematic alternation with intransitives or intransitives plus PrepPs, and marked status of the passive. In sections 3.2 and 3.3, we will report on Rymen's (1999) quantified corpus study of the alternations of cognate and circumstantial complement respectively. In section 3.1, we will first briefly outline our theoretical position with regard to the semantic relevance of transitivity alternations and of their quantitative instantiation in actual usage (for a more detailed discussion, see Davidse 1998).

3.1 Transitivity alternations

Transitivity alternations constitute the **verb-specific** alternations of clause structures, i.e. alternations determined by the lexical verb used in the clause (Levin 1993; Van den Eynde 1995). Depending on general transitivity distinctions, e.g. whether the verb is intransitive, transitive or compound transitive, a clause can be related to very different networks of possible and impossible transitivity alternations. For instance, intransitives in English cannot be passivized or causativized: *I went, *I am being gone, *They went me* (Whorf 1956: 80).

Clauses also have general alternations which do not depend on verb meaning and apply very regularly, such as the possibility of construing a polar interrogative or a clause with fronted object. In Halliday's layered functional framework, these general alternations are the clause variants described within the 'mood' and 'textual' component of clause grammar.

Because they are verb-specific, transitivity alternations are fairly generally recognized to be semantically revealing about the process-participant configurations being depicted. However, views differ as to what semantic aspects of process-participant relations they are most revealing of.

Lexicalist approaches within Government and Binding have stressed their heuristic value with regard to verb meaning and verb classes. For instance, Levin (1993: 9–10) argues that verbs manifesting the ergative alternation, such as *break*, depict change of state (*The window broke*) and the causation of change of state (*The little boy broke the window*).

Within the more constructional Hallidayan approach – which emerged in "Notes on Transitivity and Theme" (1967, 1968) – transitivity alternations have been used as a heuristic for the semantic relations between verbs and their participant roles. In our view, the most important thing transitivity alternations may reveal is the "inherent voice" (Halliday 1968: 196) between process and participants, for instance, whether nominals relate as 'entities verb-ing' or 'entities being verb-ed' to the verb. Thus, the alternations of *John marched the prisoners*

(6) *What John did to the prisoners was march them. – The prisoners marched.*
(Halliday 1968: 196)

reveal that *the prisoners* have both an undergoing and a doing relation to the process. By contrast, with *John hit the ball*, the impossibility of an intransitive with *the ball* as Actor

(7) *What John did to the ball was hit it. – *The ball hit.* (Halliday 1968: 196)

shows that it has a purely undergoing relation to the process.

Finally, the relative frequency of occurrence of alternates in extended data bases has also been used as a clue to certain semantic aspects of verb-participant configurations. As noted in section 2, Halliday (1985: 151–153) correlates the semantic transitivity of a process-participant relation with the availability of an unmarked passive. In the Systemic Functional tradition, 'markedness' has always been linked to frequency. In this tradition, a dimension of variation is interpreted as the 'terms' of a 'system'. The relative markedness of these terms can then be assessed by frequency of attestation in random samples displaying the variation in question. According to Halliday and James (1993), the quantitative patterns thus obtained tend towards either an **equal** distribution, in which case there is no difference in markedness, or a **skewed** one, with 90% versus 10% considered the ideal skew for the unmarked versus the marked option. The passive is a special case as it is itself the marked way of construing a transitive relation. Svartvik (1966: 46) found a proportion of 93%, 95%, 68% actives versus 7%, 5%, 32% passives in his data sets, the first two of which were novels and the last a scientific text. The average, which can be presumed to neutralize register differences, comes close to an 'ideal' skewed system: 88% actives versus 12% passives.

Assuming these views about the heuristic value of transitivity alternations, we can now turn to Rymen's (1999) quantified study of cognate and circumstantial complement alternations.

3.2   Cognate complement alternations

Helped by Levin's (1993: 95) list, Rymen selected nine intransitive verbs which have typically been associated with 'cognate objects' in the literature, viz. *breathe, cough, dance, die, dream, smile, sneeze, sniff, waltz.* All these verbs also have a cognate noun allowing quantification of the alternation with delexicalized verb. Rymen made exhaustive extractions from the COBUILD corpus for *sneeze, sniff, waltz* and *cough,* and extended random samples for *breathe* (and noun *breath*), *dance, die* (and noun *death*) and *smile.* She then quantified the relative occurrence of intransitive clauses, clauses with lexical verb and cognate complement, and clauses with general verb and cognate complement. This led to the results set out in Table 1. It has to be noted that, by limiting the third set of data to examples with a strictly cognate noun (as in *to dance – to do a dance*), the results are representative only of the lexical set described above. In the general semantic domain of, for instance, 'dancing', the construction with general verb and deverbal complement is likely to be more frequent than in this data set, as it also includes expressions such as *to do a waltz, to do a jig*, etc.

Table 1. Relative frequency of cognate complement constructions vis-à-vis intransitives

	intransitive	lexical verb + cognate complement	general verb + cognate complement
breathe	94.8% (1754)	4.1% (75)	1.1% (20)
cough	97.1% (402)	0.7% (3)	2.2% (9)
dance	94.6% (558)	5.1% (30)	0.3% (2)
die	98.8% (247)	0.8% (2)	0.4% (1)
dream	97.4% (634)	1.7% (11)	0.9% (6)
smile	98.5% (532)	1.3% (7)	0.2% (1)
sneeze	98.9% (98)	0% (0)	1% (1)
sniff	95.9% (446)	0% (0)	4.1% (19)
waltz	96.3% (78)	1.2% (1)	2.5% (2)
total	**96.1% (4749)**	**2.6% (130)**	**1.2% (61)**

We are immediately struck by the great quantitative homogeneity of these results. For all verbs concerned, there is a very clear and strong skew, with the intransitives by far the most frequent option and a relatively small percentage of cognate complement constructions. The average proportion of intransitive versus cognate complement clause is 96.1% versus 3.9%. This shows that the option of 'restating' the intransitive process in a cognate complement is very infrequently taken and constitutes the marked option for the representation of such processes.

As we saw in section 2, Halliday (1985) strongly emphasizes the semantic intransitivity of the cognate complement construction and adduces its marked passive as a piece of evidence for it. Rymen therefore dredged her data sets for passives of cognate complement constructions of the nine verbs investigated and found exactly two occurrences in the *dance*-corpus.

(8) *[...] after the Second World War with a performance on February 20 of The Sleeping Beauty, the same ballet **that** was danced on the night of February 20, 1946.* (CB)

(9) *After five short abstracts, the entire company moves into the second part, where **the work** is danced, often contrapuntally to the passionate Fearful Symmetries by John Adams.* (CB)

That, i.e. *the same ballet* in (8) and *the work* in (9) are interesting in that, on the one hand, they do designate an instance of 'dancing', but on the other, they also refer to the pre-existing abstract choreography. According to Rymen (1999: 119), it is due to this latter feature that these cognate complements behave more like 'normal' Patients, and hence allow the passive.

Still, in Rymen's cognate complement data, passives form only 1% versus 99% of actives. According to Halliday and James (1993), this is the sort of relative frequency characteristic of marked options **within** marked options. And this confirms Halliday's claim that clauses with cognate complement have a marked passive. Consequently, Halliday's point about the semantic intransitivity of this construction type is also given support: clauses with cognate complement do not depict actions which target and/or affect entities.

3.3   Circumstantial complement alternations

With reference to Levin (1993), Rymen also selected seven intransitive verbs which can take bare nominals to express the domain over which the action takes place: *bicycle, climb, descend, jump, prowl, row* and *skate*. She made complete extractions from the COBUILD corpus for *bicycle, descend, prowl* and *skate*, but worked with a random sample for the very frequent *climb* and *jump*. Levin (1993: 43) indicates that these verbs participate in the "locative preposition drop alternation" and she therefore relates them to intransitives with PrepP. However, in Halliday's approach, as they are part of the Range category, they are also said to fundamentally alternate with intransitives. Hence, Rymen quantified the relative occurrence of intransitive clauses, clauses with PrepP, and clauses with circumstantial complement, as manifested in her data set. She obtained the following results:

Table 2. Relative frequency of circumstantial complement constructions vis-à-vis intransitives and intransitives with PrepP

	intransitive	intransitive + PrepP	circumstantial complement construction
bicycle	86.4% (70)	13.6% (11)	0% (0)
climb	22.8% (160)	33.1% (232)	44.1% (309)
descend	50.4% (333)	39.2% (259)	10.4% (69)
jump	66.7% (352)	27.5% (145)	5.9% (31)
prowl	41.1% (7)	11.8% (2)	47.1% (8)
row	80.9% (195)	16.6% (40)	0.4% (1)
skate	87.7% (414)	11.9% (56)	0.4% (2)
total	57 % (1531)	27.5% (745)	15.5% (420)

Clearly, we get a much more diffuse picture here than with the cognate complement clauses, both with regard to the proportion of intransitives versus intransitives plus PrepP and circumstantial complement clauses, and with regard to the distribution of these structure types over the individual verbs. Whereas *bicycle* has no circumstantial complement clause at all in the COBUILD corpus, *row*, *skate* and *jump* have a minority of circumstantial complement clauses, somewhat comparable to the small proportion of cognate complement uses found with the intransitive verbs in section 3.2. *Bicycle*, *row* and *skate* also skew rather strongly towards intransitive use. By contrast, with *jump* and *descend*, the intransitive uses take up only 66.7% and 50.4% respectively. The circumstantial complement construction with *climb* is very frequent (44.1%), and can barely be regarded as a marked option. It scores higher than both the PrepP (33.1%) and the intransitive (22.8%) options. *Prowl*, with a much more limited data set, mirrors this sort of distribution. We have to conclude that the option of a bare intransitive clause, an intransitive clause with PrepP, and a clause with circumstantial complement does not manifest predictable frequencies with these verbs, and that the circumstantial complement constructions cannot be regarded as an intrinsically marked option, as witnessed by their frequency with *climb* and *prowl*.

The next question is then whether their passive construal in English gives any indication of them approximating a form of transitivity comparable to transitive clauses in the full sense. Rymen (1999: 72) found only three passives in her whole database, two examples like (10) with *climb* and a metaphorical one with *jump* (11).

(10)   *Fortunately, **most mountains** can be climbed the pretty way: up a footpath, and when you get to the top the views are just the same.* (CB)

(11)   *[...] **the fences** that need to be jumped.* (CB)

Passives thus constitute an equally small fraction in the circumstantial complement data (0.7%) as in the cognate complement data (1%). Hence, circumstantial complement constructions seem to be as semantically intransitive as cognate complement constructions. Clauses with circumstantial complements do not depict the affecting of an entity, or the targeting of action onto an entity.

4.   Identifiers, quantifiers and other modifiers in cognate complement and circumstantial complement-NPs

4.1   Introduction

Halliday (1985: 135) characterizes the Range as a device allowing for detailed specifications of quality and quantity impossible in clauses with intransitive verb only. He does not make any principled distinction between the two types of Ranges in this respect and does not suggest that for instance cognate Ranges attract more expressions of quality and circumstantial Ranges, more expressions of quantity. By contrast, with regard to the literature in general it could be said that the notions of quality and quantity have been more typically associated with cognate complements and circumstantial complements respectively. For instance, Poutsma (1904: 76–77), Stein (1979), Rice (1988) and Massam (1990) have all stated that cognate complements typically take modifiers such as prenominal adjectives. On the other hand, Jackendoff (1985), Dixon (1991) and Langacker (1991) have attributed a general 'holistic' effect to the circumstantial complement-construction, which the related construction with PrepP lacks: if the location is expressed by a NP, the clause tends to entail complete coverage of that entity. While the concept of holicity implies quantity, no claims concerning numeratives in the circumstantial complement-NP have been associated with this.

With regard to the definiteness of cognate complements rather contradictory claims have been formulated in the literature. Whereas Halliday (1967), Moltmann (1989) and Massam (1990) state that cognate complements are typically indefinite, Rice (1987) suggests that definite or demonstrative determiners, like qualitative modifiers, may 'improve' the acceptability of cognate complements. According to Halliday (1985) cognate complements cannot be personal pronouns and are normally not modified by a possessive. The issue of definiteness has been less explicitly looked at for circumstantial complements, but the examples typically discussed have definite NPs, including proper names.

To check such claims empirically, and to obtain a more systematic picture of identification, quantification, quality- and class-specifications in 'Range' NPs, Rymen carried out a systematic quantified analysis of these modifiers in her data sets of cognate and circumstantial complements.

4.2   Identifiers, quantifiers and other modifiers in cognate complement NPs

Rymen's data contained 130 examples of cognate complement constructions with lexical verbs and 61 with general verbs. Tables 3 and 4 list the main types of modifiers whose occurrence in these data she investigated and they indicate in what percentage of the data each type of modification was manifested.

Firstly, she analysed and quantified identifiers and quantifiers. Within the identifier types, definite article (12), demonstrative determiner (13), possessive determiner (14), indefinite article (15) and zero-article (16) were distinguished.

(12)   *[...] you travelled round the world on a cruise ship playing tenniquoits in the sun, eating three five-course meals a day, dancing **the tango and charleston** with strangers and going ashore to see the pyramids.* (CB)

(13)   *Orphan said soothingly, I've had **those same dreams**.* (CB)

(14)   *And I dream **my dream** even though I have divined that their secret can only be one of five possible secrets.* (CB)

(15)   *But just when Shane Warne and Tim May thought they were safe to breathe **a sigh of relief**, they were called back from the dressing room gates [...]* (CB)

(16)   *Formula One boss Bernie Eccelstone and Max Mosely [...] breathed **collective** **sighs of relief** as the premier championship bounced back.* (CB)

Cognate complements with proper names (17) and pronouns (18) were analysed separately.

(17)   *Which trio were dancing **The Resurrection Shuffle** in 1971.* (CB)

(18)   *[...] I had to choreograph a ballet and then dance **it** [...]* (CB)

Quantifiers in cognate complement examples included cardinal numbers, non-specific absolute quantifiers and relative quantifiers, as exemplified in (19), (20) and (21) respectively.

(19)   *Kip took **one disgusted sniff**, left the bin in the front garden and walked calmly into the house.* (CB)

(20)   *When you have a difficult feeling, take **several slow, deep breaths**.* (CB)

(21)   *You're fearful all the time as you take **every breath**, [...]* (CB)

Cardinal numbers and their non-specific counterparts such as *several* assess the intrinsic size of the quantity. Relative quantifiers such as *every* invoke a reference mass and measure off a proportion of that reference mass (Langacker 1991).

It has to be noted that Rymen analysed the *primary* determiners of the cognate complements. The identifier and quantifier types listed in Table 3 were thus applied as mutually exclusive categories.

It turned out that only 4.5% of the cognate complements contained explicit quantifiers. As for identification, 77.8% had indefinite identification and only 17.7 % definite identification. The cognate complements of lexical verbs had a noticeably larger proportion of definite NPs than those of general verbs. The former had 12.3% cases with definite article, 6.9% with possessive determiner, as well as some pronouns and proper names. By contrast, Rymen's database contained only two examples of definite cognate complements with general verbs.

These results show that quantity specification is not very common with cognate complements. The oft-made claim that cognate complements are typically indefinite is confirmed, but definite identification does not constitute an extremely exceptional option.

In the second place, Rymen also investigated the occurrence of classifiers (22), prenominal attributes (23) and postmodifiers (24), whose use in cognate complement data is illustrated in the following examples:

(22)   *She does erm **worship dance** which is dancing in churches.* (CB)

(23)   *So if I [...] only have eight beds [...] that's not going to be able to cope with ongoing deaths so the only other way to ensure that they have **a really good death** is to [...]* (CB)

(24)   *Harriet smiled **a smile that never quite touched her eyes**.* (CB)

Table 3. Relative frequency of identification and quantification types in cognate complements

	cogn. co. + lexical verb	cogn. co. + general verb	total
proper name	3.1% (4)	0% (0)	2% (4)
pronoun	1.5% (2)	0% (0)	1% (2)
definite article + cognate complement	12.3% (16)	1.6% (1)	9% (17)
demonstrative determiner + cognate complement	0.8%(1)	1.6% (1)	1% (2)
possessive determiner + cognate complement	6.9% (9)	0% (0)	4.7% (9)
indefinite article + cognate complement	65.4% (85)	78.7% (48)	70% (133)
zero-article + cognate complement	7.7% (10)	9.8 (5)	7.8% (15)
subtotal identifiers	97.7% (127)	90.1% (55)	95.5% (182)
cardinal number + cognate complement	0.8% (1)	3.3% (2)	1.5% (3)
indefinite absolute quantifier + cognate complement	1.5% (2)	3.3% (2)	2% (4)
relative quantifier + cognate complement	0% (0)	3.3% (2)	1 % (2)
subtotal quantifiers	2.3% (3)	9.9 % (6)	4.5 % (9)
total	100% 130	100% (61)	(100%) 191

Attributes ascribe a gradable quantity to the instances depicted by the NP, while classifiers add subtypes to the types designated by the head noun (Halliday 1985). Some cognate complements contain both classifying and quality-specifying elements, as in (25), and the categories listed in Table 4 are therefore not mutually exclusive.

(25)   [...] the Brisbane Blazers will breathe *a huge sigh of relief.* (CB)

Table 4. Relative frequency of other modifiers in cognate complements

	cogn. co. + lexical verb	cogn. co. + general verb	total
classifier	4.6% (6)	4.9% (3)	4.7% (9)
attribute	33.8% (44)	63.9% (39)	44.9% (83)
postmodifier	56.9% (74)	16.4% (10)	44.4% (84)

As shown in Table 4, modifiers expressing type and quality specifications of the process are frequent in cognate complements. Cognate complements without modifiers are relatively rare. This confirms that one of the main reasons why cognate complement constructions exist is to enable quality and type specifications of intransitive processes.

4.3 Identifiers, quantifiers and other modifiers in circumstantial complement NPs

Rymen's extractions on the keywords *bicycle, climb, descend, jump, prowl, row* and *skate* threw up 410 examples of circumstantial complement constructions. She analyzed and quantified the occurrence of identifiers, quantifiers, and class- and quality-specifiers in these data in the same way as she did in cognate complement constructions.

Table 5 represents the relative occurrence of the main identifying and quantifying types in the circumstantial complement corpus. Identification types include the types distinguished for the cognate complement data, proper name (26), personal pronoun (27), definite article (28), demonstrative determiner (29), possessive determiner (30), indefinite article (31) and zero-article (32), as well as interrogative determiner (33) and genitive (34). All these uses are illustrated in the examples below.

(26) *[...], so when I walked across Ireland I had to climb **Carrauntoohil**.* (CB)

(27) *Climb **them** [the Malvern Hills] from Great Malvern or Colwall Stations.* (CB)

(28) *[...] she became unable to look out of the windows, and even found descending **the stairs** a nightmare.* (CB)

(29) *Not only can you take to climbing **this unbelievable landmark** [...] but you can study its history [...]* (CB)

(30) *We'd climb **our tree** and act out fantasies.* (CB)

(31) *[...] the zoo population of Siberian tigers – each large, expensive to keep, needing **an area** to prowl, and a diet of high quality meat – could soar in two decades to 6500.* (CB)

(32) *[...] people ascended and descended **stairs** from level to level [...]* (CB)

(33) *After a scant breakfast of squirrel caught and roasted the day before, they discussed **which of the two lower peaks** to climb.* (CB)

(34) *Few people achieve the mix of mis-spent youth, talent and motivation necessary to climb **rock's greasy pole,** but most yearn for it.* (CB)

Quantification types likewise parallel those for cognate complements: cardinal numbers (35), non-specific absolute quantifiers (36) and relative quantifiers (37).

(35) *They have jumped **1,128 fences** the equivalent to lapping Newcastle racecourse more than 100 times.* (CB)

(36) *And, besides, there were **a few more local hills** I wanted to climb.* (CB)

(37) *Fortunately, **most mountains** can be climbed the pretty way: up a footpath, and when you get to the top the views are just the same.* (CB)

Table 5. Relative frequency of identification and quantification types in circumstantial complements

proper name	8.1% (34)
personal pronoun	8.1% (34)
definite article + circumstantial complement	36.7% (154)
interrogative determiner + circumstantial complement	0.2% (1)
demonstrative determiner + circumstantial complement	2.9% (12)
possessive determiner + circumstantial complement	1.4% (6)
genitive + circumstantial complement	1.7% (7)
indefinite article + circumstantial complement	15.2% (64)
zero-article + circumstantial complement	16.7% (70)
subtotal identifiers	91% (382)
cardinal number + circumstantial complement	4.7% (20)
non-specific absolute quantifier + circumstantial complement	2.4% (10)
relative quantifier + circumstantial complement	1.9% (8)
subtotal quantifiers	9% (38)
total	**100% (420)**

Quantifiers appear to be only marginally more frequent in circumstantial complements (9%) than in cognate complements (4.5%). The 'extent' meaning of circumstantial complements thus turns out not to be strongly reflected in the presence of quantifiers in the strict sense. With regard to identifiers, circumstantial complements differ more strongly from cognate complements, which were predominantly indefinite (77.8%). Circumstantial complements have twice as many definite identifiers (59.1%) as indefinite ones (31.9). Circumstantial complements have a definite article in 36.7% of the cases, and are more commonly realized by proper names and pronouns than cognate complements.

Table 6 lists the occurrence of classifiers, prenominal attributes and postmodifiers with circumstantial complements, which are illustrated by the following examples:

(38)   *[...] and Tour de France riders still descend **mountain roads** flattened over handlebars.* (CB)

(39)   *But it [the river] could spread across the beaches, climb **the mighty dunes** and flood the whole valley.* (CB)

(40)   *Er at the moment this team is attempting to climb **the world's fifth highest mountain which is Mackaloo.*** (CB)

Table 6. Relative frequency of other modifiers in circumstantial complements

classifier	9.9% (42)
attribute	14.6% (62)
postmodifier	12% (51)

Table 6 shows that circumstantial complements differ from cognate complements mainly in two respects. Firstly, the majority of circumstantial complements have no type or quality modification at all, as in (41)

(41) *You'll be healthier and breathe more easily – for example when you climb* **stairs** *or run for a bus.* (CB)

Secondly, prenominal attributes are noticeably less common – only 14.6% in comparison with 44.9 % with cognate complements. Hence, circumstantial complements in general attract many fewer specifications of class and quality than cognate complements.

4.4 Conclusion

What conclusions can we draw from the quantitative results discussed in sections 4.2 and 4.3? The quality-quantity distinction, when linked to realization by qualitative versus numerative modifiers in the complement NP, does not seem to provide strong arguments for either similarity or distinctness of the two subtypes: the proportion of explicit numeratives is comparable for both types, but cognate complements have more quality-modification. However, in Section 5, we will argue that the function of specifying 'quality' is a relatively superficial generalization and that the 'qualitative' adjectives in cognate complements express a different basic meaning than those in circumstantial complements, thus arguing for the distinctness of the two subtypes. The most important numerical difference revealed in section 4 concerns definiteness: cognate complements have predominantly indefinite identification, whereas circumstantial complements are more often definite. This distinct definiteness status also argues for the distinctness of the two types, which will be interpreted further in the next section.

5. The distinct relation of cognate and circumstantial complements to the intransitive process

In this section we will put together the most important results from sections 3 and 4. As will become obvious throughout the discussion, the alternations of cognate and circumstantial complement clauses and the modification patterns of the complements point to a different semantic relation of the two complements to the process.

The most striking result of the quantification of alternations in section 3 was the extremely infrequent passive for both cognate and circumstantial complements. This confirms, in our view, Halliday's point that both cognate and circumstantial complements are **semantically non-transitive**. Hence, any discussion of cognate complement and circumstantial complement constructions has to take as starting point the basic intransitivity of the semantic configurations depicted. Beyond this, the different networks of alternations in which the two constructions partake suggest different semantics.

The two types of cognate complement constructions (with lexical and with general verb) alternate with intransitive clauses: the cognate complement constructions form a – very homogeneous – minority, averaging 3.5 % in Rymen's data. Halliday's characterization that cognate complements are 're-labellings' of an intransitive process is spot-on. Cognate complements used with general verbs such as *take, do, have* are intrinsically **de-verbal**. This probably explains their virtual ban on definiteness: they introduce instances of the process being carried out rather than referring to things that exist in the world. All semantic specifications about the intransitive process are given by the cognate complement, not by the general verb.

Cognate complements used with lexical verbs also depict an instance of a process, as clearly illustrated by examples such as

(42)   *Shakyamuni lay down between two sala trees near Kusinagara and prepared to breathe **his last**.* (CB)

(43)   *The exhaust coughed **an extra beat** and quickened its note [...]* (CB)

In this construction the verb itself already specifies the type of intransitive process involved. The cognate complement can be realized by a greater variety of nouns than are found in the constructions with general verbs and it is also more often definite. Strictly cognate nouns not infrequently have definite determiners and then depict an instance of an act which can be related to other instances of that act by the same or another actor.

(44)   *I smiled **the same smile**.* (CB)

(45)   *Then Lyman danced **his own rough struggle** from the freezing muscle of water where he had jumped in to grab Henry back, and failed.* (CB)

Another recurring use of definite cognate complements designates both the pre-existent 'script' or 'plan' and one of the concrete processes realizing it.

(46)   *During the Stuttgart's Kennedy Center engagement, Hayden's partner, Richard Cragon, won't be dancing **the prince** in 'Sleeping Beauty'.* (CB)

Finally, against Halliday's statement to the contrary (1985: 136), possessive determiners do occur in this type of cognate complement. They refer to the actor of the intransitive act.

(47)   *I smiled **my assent**, then left in a hurry, by the back door.* (CB)

The fact that cognate complements always depict an instance of a process has important consequences for the semantic interpretation of descriptive modifiers in them. As pointed out by Stein (1979: 109), qualitative adjectives often express the manner in which the actor carries out this process. For instance,

(48)   *Brian sweetly smiles **his modest smile**.* (CB)

(49)   *He was dancing **a rather clumsy waltz** with Violet.* (CB)

Rymen calculated that 67% of all qualitative adjectives in her cognate complement data express manner.

Likewise, descriptions which are to do with 'quantity' in a broad sense tend to specify aspects of the act depicted by the cognate complement such as iterativity or (relative) temporal location in time. For instance,

(50)   *Close your eyes, take **one or two deep breaths** through your noise.* (CB)

(51)   *There were pictures as we said our vows, as we climbed into the limo, cut the cake, waltzed **the first dance**.* (CB)

In other words, these 'quantitative' descriptions also have to be interpreted as applying to the intransitive acts described.

Circumstantial complement constructions alternate with intransitives plus PrepP and intransitives as such in varying proportions. The alternation with intransitives plus PrepP is the one most semantically revealing for circumstantial complement constructions.

In intransitive clauses with PrepP, the PrepP expresses a locative domain (Langacker 1991: 66). The preposition expresses a locative relation such as 'upward directionality', 'contact with surface', of which the prepositional complement expresses the specific coordinates, e.g. *up the mountain, on the lake*. Thus a locative domain is evoked within which acts and events are depicted as taking place, as in *climb up the mountain, row on the lake*.

In the circumstantial complement construction, by contrast, there is no preposition indicating a locative domain independent of the intransitive act. The verbs patterning with circumstantial complements incorporate locative notions such as 'upward directionality' (*climb*), 'downward directionality' (*descend*), 'contact with a surface' (*row, skate*, etc.) in their lexical semantics. This explains why prepositions are not strictly necessary with them. By the same token, verb and circumstantial complement (have to) share more semantic features and tend to constitute more fixed collocations than in an intransitive clause with PrepP. For instance, it is possible for people to *row on a lake, off the Point, at the Games, to Russia, under the bridge*, etc – in other words a great variety of locative relations and entities specifying the locative domain may be involved. However, circumstantial complement constructions are restricted to expressing the water expanse rowed on or the distance covered, as in *row the lake, row the whole course*, etc.

As a result of there being no preposition, the location in circumstantial complement constructions is not evoked as an independent locative domain. Only that part of
the location co-extensive with the process is part of the meaning profiled by a circumstantial complement clause. It is this that may lead to the much discussed 'holicity' effect of circumstantial complement constructions. If the part evoked coincides with the
full extent that can or has to be covered, as in

(52)   *They will row **the course** and follow the tasks as outlined in the diagram to the
right.* (Google)

then the circumstantial complement construction will entail a 'holistic' reading. However, the parts of the location involved in the intransitive act do not necessarily form the
whole distance that can or has to be covered, as in (53), where there is no holicity effect.

(53)   *Marlin and sailfish tend to prowl **the edges of these streams**.* (CB)

The semantic relation of 'location involved in process' also influences the choice of
quantitative and qualitative descriptive modifiers in circumstantial complement constructions. These modifiers often indicate the extent or the height of the location (54),
or its resistance to or facilitation of the act (55).

(54)   *You can climb **its 6,900 ft**, but it is steep, so you may want to take the cable car.*
(CB)

(55)   *Anti-lock brakes overcome the problem of front wheel locking, when descending
slippery hills [...]* (CB)

The identifying types found in circumstantial complements can also be explained with
reference to the semantic relation of the latter to the verb. Definite circumstantial complements, including proper names, typically refer to concrete, identifiable locations or
landmarks.

(56)   *[...], so when I walked across Ireland, I had to climb **Carrauntoohil**.* (CB)

On the other hand, there is also a sizeable minority of indefinite and otherwise un-
modified circumstantial complements, as in (57). These merely indicate the type of
location involved in the process.

(57)   *These shrubs [...] are able to climb **walls and trees**.* (CB)

6.   Conclusion

In this article we have subjected the Hallidayan category of Range to closer scrutiny.
Halliday's approach is unique in the literature in that it collapses two grammatical
categories, cognate object and transitivizing object, which have traditionally been kept
separate. In section 2, we have looked at Halliday's formal and semantic characteriza-

tion of the Range and noted the necessity of verifying the quantitative hypotheses implied by these descriptive claims. In sections 3 and 4, we have reported on Rymen's quantified corpus study of the alternations of cognate and circumstantial complements, and of the types of modification found in those two types of complement.

These quantifications and observations of corpus data progressively adduced arguments for the position that cognate and circumstantial complements, despite both being part of a semantically intransitive configuration, have a different semantic relation to the verb. Cognate complements re-label the intransitive process (as stressed by Halliday) and this fundamentally affects the interpretation of their identifiers, quantifiers and other modifiers. For instance, so-called 'qualitative' adjectives in cognate complements often express the manner in which the intransitive process is carried out. Circumstantial complements profile the part of the location involved in the intransitive process. This also influences the choice of identifiers, quantifiers and other modifiers. For instance, attributes may indicate how extended or difficult to negotiate that location is.

Hence, while recognizing that Halliday contributed some very good observations, we conclude that it seems best to work with two distinct categories, as is customary in the literature. Analyses of the cognate complement have to take into account that the unit [verb + [adjective + cognate complement]] is basically semantically equivalent to [adverb + intransitive verb]. Circumstantial complements, by contrast, are not restatements of the process and their locative relation to the verb is an important semantic component. We also hope that our discussion has made clear that further data-driven work needs to be done to characterize the different semantic relations of cognate and circumstantial complements to the verb in greater detail and with more precision.

References

Davidse, Kristin. 1998. "Agnates, verb classes and the meaning of construals: the case of ditransitivity in English". *Leuvense Bijdragen (Leuven Contributions in Linguistics and Philology)* 87(3–4): 281–313.

Dixon, Robert. 1991. *A new approach to English grammar, on semantic principles.* Oxford: Oxford University Press.

Halliday, Michael. 1967. "Notes on transitivity and theme in English 1". *Journal of Linguistics* 3: 199–244.

Halliday, Michael. 1968. "Notes on transitivity and theme in English 3 ". *Journal of Linguistics* 4: 179–215.

Halliday, Michael. 1985. *An introduction to functional grammar.* London: Arnold.

Halliday, Michael and Zoë James. 1993. "A quantitative study of polarity and primary tense in the English finite clause". *Techniques of description: Spoken and written discourse: A festschrift for Malcolm Coulthard*, ed. by John McH. Sinclair, Michael Hoey and Gwyneth Fox, 32–66, London: Routledge.

Jackendoff, Ray. 1985. "Multiple subcategorization and the theta-criterion: the case of *climb*". *Natural Language and Linguistic Theory* 3: 271–295.

Langacker, Ronald. 1987. *Foundations of cognitive grammar. Vol. 1. Theoretical prerequisites.* Stanford: Stanford University Press.

Langacker, Ronald. 1991. *Foundations of cognitive grammar. Vol. 2. Descriptive application.* Stanford: Stanford University Press.

Levin, Beth. 1993. *English verb classes and alternations: A preliminary investigation.* Chicago: University of Chicago Press.

Massam, Diane. 1990. "Cognate objects as thematic objects". *Canadian Journal of Linguistics* 35: 161–190.

Moltmann, Friederike. 1989. "Nominal and clausal event predicates". *Papers from the regional meeting of the Chicago Linguistics Society* Part 1: 300–314.

Poutsma, Hendrik. 1904. *A grammar of Late Modern English.* Groningen: Noordhoff.

Rice, Sally. 1987. "Towards a transitive prototype: evidence from some atypical English passives". *Proceedings of the annual meeting of the Berkeley Linguistics Society* 13: 422–434.

Rice, Sally. 1988. "Unlikely lexical entries". *Proceedings of the annual meeting of the Berkeley Linguistics Society* 14: 202–212.

Rymen, Kathleen. 1999. A constructional approach to Ranges: The Promoted Circumstance Range and the Cognate Object Range. M.A. Thesis. University of Leuven.

Stein, Gabriele. 1979. *Studies in the function of the passive.* Tübingen: Gunther Narr.

Svartvik, Jan. 1966. *On voice in the English verb.* The Hague/Paris: Mouton.

Van den Eynde, Karel. 1995. "Methodological reflections on descriptive linguistics. Knud Togeby's principles and the pronominal approach". *Studies in valency,* ed. by Lene Schøsler and Mary Talbot, 111–131, Odense: Odense University Press.

Whorf, Benjamin L. 1956. *Language, Thought and Reality: Selected Writings of Benjamin Lee Whorf,* ed. by John B. Carroll. New York: Wiley.

The UNCONSCIOUS, IRRESPONSIBLE CONSTRUCTION in Modern Icelandic

Enrique Bernárdez
Universidad Complutense, Madrid

The Icelandic language possesses a number of constructions whose function it is to express the degree of agentivity or lack of agentivity of a process. This paper analyses a specific construction built with the auxiliary verb *verða* 'to become' plus an experiencer or affected entity in the dative and a lexical verb in the neuter form of the past participle; the construction is used to mean that the human experiencer is unconscious of the onset of the process leading to a new state as a result. For instance, *mér verður litið*, meaning 'I happened to look'. The assumed agent of the resulting state is conceptualized as an involuntary experiencer, not responsible for the resulting action or process. This construction has not been the object of systematic analysis before and this paper intends to offer a preliminary analysis from a semantic perspective. The construction is set in relation with the other Icelandic constructions of 'reduced agentivity'.

1. Introduction

The construction analysed in this paper is exemplified in (1):

(1) … nú **verður mér** af tilviljun **litið** framaní þennan mann.
     now **becomes me**-DAT by chance **looked** in-face this man-ACC
     'I happened to look at this man in the face, by sheer chance.' (Laxness, p.162).

It is used to express an action that has taken place without the person involved – marked in the case normally used for the experiencer, i.e. the Dative – being in control or even conscious of the process leading to the result marked by the Past Participle of the verb. In (1), the fortuitous nature of the process is further signalled by the adverbial construction, *af tilviljun*, 'by chance', but in most cases no special element is used to reinforce this meaning.

This is one of many 'impersonal' expressions in Icelandic, which enable the speaker to avoid mentioning the agent: a process is portrayed as taking place without any intervention on the part of the person affected.

In Section 2 some of the very few comments on this construction in the linguistic literature will be reviewed. Section 3 then offers a detailed analysis of the construction. Section 4 tries to put it in relation with other Icelandic constructions used to demote or eliminate the agent, and Section 5 will present the conclusions of this paper and the prospects for future research.

2.   Previous scholarship on the construction

This construction has not been the object of much research. We can find brief references in the standard dictionaries. Sigfús Blöndal's Dictionary includes this reference under the auxiliary, *verða*:

> *e-m verður litið til e-s*, en kommer til at se hen til en; *honum varð reikað* (el. *gengið*) *þangað*, han gik af en Hændelse derhen, det hændte sig, at han gik derhen. (Vol. 2, p. 927)[1]

Another reference is found under *líta* 'to look at' which, as we shall see, is one of the most frequently used verbs in this construction:

> *e-m verður litið*, en kommer til at se (n-t el. i en vis Retning): *mjer varð litið á hann*, mit Blik traf ham tilfældigvis. (Vol 1, p. 502)[2]

Among the grammars, only Kress (1982: 150) makes brief reference to this construction, which is not mentioned in e.g. Árnason (1980) or Einarsson (1945):

> Die Verbindung von *verða* + NSN des Part. Prät. mit einem Dativ der beteiligten Person ist eine eigenartige Passivbildung; sie deutet an, daß die betreffende Aktion von einer magischen Kraft ausgeht: *Mér varð hugsað til hans*, 'Ich mußte plötzlich an ihn denken, er fiel mir plötzlich ein.' *Henni varð litið á hann*. 'Sie mußte zu ihm hinblicken. Ihr Blick fiel auf ihn.' *Honum varð gengið þangað sem gullið lá*. 'Es zog ihn dorthin, wo das Gold lag.'[3]

---

1.   "*E-m verður litið til e-s*, one happens to look at something; *honum varð reikað* (or *gengið*) *þangað*, he went there without having planned it, it happened that he went there." [All translations by E. Bernárdez]

2.   "*E-m verður litið*, one happens to see/look (something or in a certain direction): *mjer varð litið á hann*, my eyes met him accidentally."

3.   "The union of *verða* + of the Past Participle with a Dative for the affected person is a peculiar passive construction; it signifies that the action goes out from a magic force: *Mér varð hugsað til hans*, 'suddenly I had to think of him.' *Henni varð litið á hann*. 'She had to look at him.' *Honum varð gengið þangað sem gullið lá*. 'He was drawn towards the place where the gold was.'"

The other Icelandic grammars do not mention the construction (Árnason 1980, Einarsson 1945, Halldórsson 1950, Pétursson 1981). The abundant literature on the impersonal constructions of Icelandic, which will be briefly mentioned later in more detail, also fails to consider it, probably because of the exclusively syntactic interest that motivates it.

3.   The unconscious, irresponsible construction (UI)

3.1   Initial characterisation

The form of UI can be initially characterised as follows:

(2)   N:EXPERIENCER:DATIVE   *verða*:3rdSG   V:PASTPART-NEUTER

The noun must have a human referent; *verða* is only used in the third person singular, present or past, and the lexical verb has to be chosen from a small group of verbs licensed for this construction.

3.2   Verbs licensed in the construction

In order to identify the verbs allowed in UI, and to increase the number of examples found in the literary texts considered in the first steps of this research, a Google-search was carried out. Our limited corpus does not allow any statistically valid – or useful – results, which, in any case, are not very important in the present context, as the construction itself is of low frequency. The only verbs found were the following:

> *líta*: to look at, watch
> *hugsa*: to think, ponder, consider
> *bregða*: to startle
> *ganga*: to go

Let us first see a few examples of usage with these verbs; they are from our Google-search, unless noted otherwise.

3.2.1   Líta
Líta is probably the most frequently used verb, so much indeed that it found its way to the dictionary as a kind of idiomatic expression.

(3)   ***Mér varð litið*** *upp fyrir okkur og sá þar beint fyrir ofan hausana á okkur...*
'I happened to look up before us and saw directly in front of our heads...'

(4) *Rétt áðan varð mér litið í spegil (...) og, VOILA! sá mig. ... Mér allavega varð litið í spegilinn og sá brjálaðar krullur prýða mitt fagra höfuð.*
'Just a minute ago, I happened to look at the mirror and VOILÀ! (I) saw me... I really **happened** to look at the mirror and saw some crazy curls decorating my beautiful head.'

(5) *Mér varð litið í kringum mig.... Með Bessastaði í hægra eyranu varð mér litið út yfir bílastæðið.*
'I happened to look around me... With Bessastaðir[4] on the right I happened to look out over the car park.'

(6) *Mér varð litið út um gluggann. Fyrstu sólargeislarnir voru að paufast upp yfir sjóndeildarhringinn.*
'I happened to look out of the window. The first sunrays were sneaking about over the horizon.'

(7) *Mér varð litið á sjónvarpið rétt í þessu.*
'I happened to look at the TV-set at that precise moment.'

(8) *Honum varð litið upp í fjallið og sá...*
'He happened to look up at the mountain and saw...'

(9) *En í því varð honum litið við.*
'But at that precise moment he happened to look at it.'

(10) *Honum varð litið í kringum sig.*
'He happened to look around him.'

(11) *Honum varð litið til baka.*
'He happened to look back.'

(12) *Þegar okkur varð litið út um gluggan árla morguns þann 1. júní...*
'When we happened to look out of the window in the early morning of that 1st of June...'

(13) *Er henni varð litið yfir ána...* (Jón Thorodssen: *Piltur og stúlka*[5])
'When she happened to look over the river...'

As seen in this selection, the affected person has to be in the first or third persons, singular or plural. No second person affected was found in the Google search or in the literary works.

The verb *líta* is always followed by an expression of direction, i.e., the accidental looking signified by the construction always takes place in a certain direction: one's attention is drawn toward some specific place, person, or object. Quite frequently, that leads to seeing something special, unexpected, strange, etc. The auxiliary *verða* can be

---

4.   Bessastaðir is the official residence of the President of Iceland.

5.   *Piltur og stúlka* (A boy and a girl) is a classical 19th century novel, written by Jón Thorodssen. However, this excerpt was accessed via Google, hence no bibliographical reference is offered.

understood as fulfilling a double, even a triple, function: on the one hand, as marking the obligatoriness of the action of looking – which probably led Kress to his 'magical' interpretation; secondly, as marking the change of state typical of the basic meaning of *verða*: in the initial stage the affected person is not seeing X, after the ('magical'?) process this situation has changed. The third value of the auxiliary is that of forming a peculiarly impersonal passive.

Therefore, the original formulation of the form of the UI Construction as proposed in (2) can now be developed as (14); a general definition of the meaning of this sub-construction with *líta* is included.

(14)   N:EXPERIENCER:DATIVE:1st/3rd   *verða*:3rdsG   *líta*:PASTPART-NEUTER-DIRECTIONAL

Someone is compelled to look in a certain direction; as a result, that person sees something anomalous, or unexpected. The action of looking begins suddenly and unwillingly at a very precise moment.

3.2.2   *Hugsa*

The second most frequently used verb in UI is *hugsa* 'to think, ponder'. As is also the case with *líta*, an active, personal construction is possible and quite common, too; *hugsa* refers to the conscious, reflexive process of active thinking, in the same way that *líta* points to the conscious activity of looking at something. In both cases, the person can be conceptualised as being in full control of the activity and therefore has most of the features of an active, conscious agent. Now, both *líta* and *hugsa* are seen in this construction as lacking any agent and simple affecting the person who, in the 'normal' use of the verb, would be active and conscious. See the following examples with *hugsa*:

(15)   *Á ítalíuárunum **varð mér** oft **hugsað**:* ... (Bergsson, p. 115)
       'In my Italian years, I often happened to think: ...'

(16)   *Kanski ætti ég að stelast þángað einhverja nótt þegar aftur fer að dimma, **varð mér** stundum **hugsað**. En þá duttu mér í hug næturverðirnir.*
       'Maybe I should have to sneak there some night when nights begin to be dark again, I thought sometimes, unwillingly. But then the night-guards came to my mind.' (Laxness, p. 159).

(17)   ***Mér varð** strax **hugsað** til vina minna, Baskanna, sem ég kynntist í Edinborg.*
       'My mind was immediately drawn toward my friends, the Baskirs, who I met in Edinburgh – I happened to think of...'

(18)   *Ég veit ég er fyrstur með fréttirnar, en **mér varð hugsað** um þetta í dag.... Ég ætlaði að þrífa bílinn í dag, en **mér varð hugsað** til þess að það er...*
       'I know I am the first with the news, but I happened to think of this today... I was going to go and get the car today but I suddenly came to think that...'

(19) *Mér varð hugsað til hins daglega nútímalífs og fólks sem verður að þjást veg-na... Mér varð hugsað til fólks í mannkynssögunni sem leið þjáningar vegna...*
'I came to think of the everyday life of today of those people who have to suffer because... I came to think of the people in human history we under-went suffering because...'

(20) *Mér varð hugsað til þessara orða þegar ég vafraði um netið í dag.*
'I came to think of these words when I was surfing in the Net today'.

(21) *Okkur varð hugsað til Stebba Páls.*
'We came/happened to think of S.P.'

3.2.3   *Other verbs: bregða and ganga*

Much less frequent are the verbs *bregða* and *ganga*:

(22) *Mér varð svolítið brugðið sjálfum er ég leit þetta skeyti augum.*
'I was a little startled although I was looking at this very attentively.'

(23) *Nú líður frammundir miðjan aftan, og verður ömmu minni geingið útúr ko-tinu að líta á kálið í góða veðrinu...*
'Now the day passes on until mid evening and my grandma goes out of the kitchen, by sheer chance, to (have a) look at the vegetables in the good weather.' (Laxness, p. 44).

3.3   Discussion: Common features of the UI Construction

As can be seen, the main features of UI that have been identified reappear in these two verbs: a process with no initiator, effector, or agent, that affects a person – first or third person only – usually but not always (cf. 23) represented by a pronoun, that leads to some new situation. In (22) and (23), however, the resulting, conscious action is not exactly of the same kind as the unconscious one. That is, in e.g. (8) above, repeated here,

(8) *Honum varð litið upp í fjallið og sá...*
'He happened to look up at the mountain and saw...'

there is a first unconscious, non-volitional process which compels the individual to look at something; then, the resulting state or process (*sá*: he saw) is consciously felt by the individual, as just said. With *hugsa* things are slightly different, as the construction identifies the origin of a thought, idea, etc., as alien to the individual, who then can entertain the idea in a conscious way. With *bregða*, the process of being startled is due to something in the 'resulting' state, in such a way that a certain situation, etc., pro-vokes a kind of 'coming into conscience' on the part of the affected person, who then continues in the same situation but in a qualitatively new way: the new state is only internal, not externally perceivable.

The use of *ganga*, on the other hand, implies that the movement is involuntarily initiated: this sub-construction is also telic, in the sense that there is a certain movement towards a destination; in this case the destination is a physical location, whereas in the other cases (*líta*, *huga* and *bregða*) the destination is some mental or perceptive state. All this allows us to (still provisionally) rephrase our definition of UI in a more precise way, as (24):

(24) N:EXPERIENCER:DATIVE:1st/3rd   *verða*:3rdSG   V:PASTPART-NEUTER-
DIRECTIONAL
N: human
V = *líta, huga, bregða, ganga*

Someone is compelled to initiate a process in an undesired, unplanned, unconscious manner, which is however closely related to the initial state; as a result, that person ends up in a new, initially unexpected state which s/he can now be conscious of.

The reason why only first and third person referents are used in UI is rather straightforward: one can assert this type of situation about oneself, as the process referred to is an internal one, not accessible to observation. Except, that is, in narratives, where narrators can 'look inside' their persons and identify their motivations. We can see the rationale for Kress' interpretation: it is, in fact, 'as if' some magical force were at play here. In a future article the traditional collections of Icelandic tales and stories will be analysed in order to see whether the construction is associated with magic or other somehow supernatural situations and processes. But of course, neither in the novels by Laxness or Bergsson, nor in the internet web-pages accessed, was any magical element to be found.

The explanation, in my opinion, may lie in something quite different from magic but deeply entrenched in Icelandic culture[6]: the feeling that things 'just happen' with no explanation. In fact, in the two novels this 'principle' is pervasive, although with a slight difference: in Laxness' *Brekkukotsannáll* (translated in English as *The Birds Can Sing*) things happen, although in this sense *Sjálfstætt fólk* (*Independent People*) could be the best example of the impossibility of understanding things. In Bergsson's *Lömuðu kennslukonurnar* (*The Paralytic Teachers*; no translation has been published yet), as in so much of his literary production, it is mainly thinking that is produced in an unconscious, unexplainable way: our mental life has a life of its own, as shown by the author in so many of his novels (see also Bjarnadóttir 2003).

---

6.   And elsewhere, of course; see Bernárdez (2001).

4. Other constructions with demotion of the agent

The UI Construction is not at all isolated, but shows a number of features that are also independently present in other Icelandic constructions. In fact, UI serves, as one of its main purposes, the function of demoting the agent to its complete deagentivisation, i.e., the complete absence of an agent or responsible effector, a process also quite apparent in other languages, like Spanish (Bernárdez 1997). I shall very briefly sketch the main types of construction related to the one analysed in this paper, in order to try and ascertain its place within the system of agent-demotion constructions or, in more syntactic terms, the 'impersonal construction(s)', so abundant in this language. As Barðdal points out in the introduction to her research project on "The Impersonal Construction in Icelandic/Scandinavian/Germanic and its Development"[7]:

> The impersonal construction is an Indo-European inheritance, which in Germanic has survived only in three languages, i.e. Icelandic, Faroese and German. New research has revealed that impersonal predicates are much more frequent in Modern Icelandic than, for instance, in Old Swedish, Old English and Modern High German.

4.1   The passive(s)

A first type of agent-demoting construction is, of course, the passive, together with the typically Nordic medio-passive. The passive is usually formed with the auxiliary *vera* 'to be', as in (25):

(25)   *Ég var barinn.*
       'I was hit.'

The second passive form is built with the verb of change of state, *verða*, as in (26)

(26)   *Ég varð barinn.*
       I became hit
       'I was hit.'

This second form is historically more recent (see Nygaard 1906) and the two passives show a difference in meaning; Einarsson considers the *verða* passive to include a reference to the future[8]; Kress (1982: 150, § 396) explains that future meaning as a consequence of the basic meaning of this passive, which he defines as follows:

> Neben dem Passiv mit *vera* 'sein' wird auch ein Passiv mit *verða* in der Bedeutung 'getan werden können, zu tun sein' gebildet, z.B.: *Hann lét kaupa allt sem í varð náð.* 'Er ließ alles aufkaufen, was erlangt werden konnte, was man bekommen

---

7.   In her web-page: http://www.hf.uib.no/i/Nordisk/ansatte/Barddal/Impersonal%20Construction.

8.   Remember that German uses the cognate verb, *werden*, to mark both the passive and the future tense.

konnte, was zu bekommen war.' Diese Passivbildung ist nur im Präsens und Prä-
teritum üblich und häufig negiert: *Það verður ekki tekið alvarlega.* 'Das kann nicht
ernst genommen werden, das kann man nicht ernst nehmen.' *Í fylgsni sínu urðu
þjófarnir ekki séðir.* 'In ihrem Versteck konnten die Diebe nicht gesehen werden.'[9]

Both passives share a general meaning which is defined by Kress (ibid.) in the following way:

> Das Passiv des Isl. dient als Mittel, den Urheber eines Tuns anonym bleiben zu
> lassen, d.h. ihn zu verschweigen…. Man kann das isl. Passiv treffend als Anony-
> mum bezeichnen.[10]

In addition to these two constructions, an additional 'impersonal passive' is used as in
other Germanic languages (Kress 1982: 151; see also Grebe et al., eds., 1966; Van Valin
and LaPolla 1997):

(27) *Meðfram veggjunum var raðað kistum og koffortum.*
      alongside the-walls was-3rdSG placed-NEUT.SG boxes-DAT and trunks-DAT
      'Trunks and boxes were placed alongside the walls.'

(28) *Nú heyrir Jón, að setzt er í körfustólinn*
      now hear-3rdSG Jón that sit-PAST.PART.NEUT is in the-wicker.chair
      'Now J. hears that somebody seats himself in the wicker chair.' (Einarsson
      1945: 148)

UI can be seen as a special case of (a) the passive with *verða*, and (b) the impersonal
passive (although impersonal passives are usually constructed with the usual auxiliary,
vera, as in the examples above).

4.2   Other uses of the auxiliary *verða*

For an adequate understanding of the functions of *verða*[11], it is convenient to summarise its use. As a lexical verb it is defined in Árnason (ed., 2002: 1726) as "eiga sér stað,
koma fyrir", i.e. 'take place, happen'; it is based on Blöndal's definition: "finde Sted,

---

9.   Together with the passive with *vera*, 'to be' another passive is built with the verb *verða* and
the meaning 'to have something done, to be done', e.g. *Hann lét kaupa allt sem í varð náð* 'he had
bought everything that could be bought, that could be got.' This passive construction is used
only in the present and the past tenses and is frequently negated: *Það verður ekki tekið used* 'that
cannot be taken seriously, that is not to be taken seriously.' *Í fylgsni sínu urðu þjófarnir ekki séðir*
'in their hideout, the thieves could not be seen.'

10.   The Icelandic passive is used in order to leave the effector of an action nameless, i.e. not
mentioned. … It is therefore right to define the Icelandic passive as an 'anonymous' form.

11.   A cognate of German and Dutch *werden*, and of Old English *weorðan*, going back to an Ide.
root *wer- meaning 'turn, bend' as in Latin *verto*, which also appears in the directional *–ward* in
e.g. *towards.* (Watkins 2000: 99)

foregaa, hænde, ske" (same as above). Both dictionaries point to its use as a marker of future states, as was pointed out above in relation to the *verða*-passive.

As an auxiliary, and in addition to its use in the passive forms just sketched, it is also employed in one of the obligative constructions, pointing to the need that a later, different state will be achieved by the subject. Thus:

(29)   *Hann verður að fara.*
       'He must go.' (Einarsson 1945: 166).

Other obligative constructions, such as the one using *eiga* 'have, own', as in (30):

(30)   *Ég á að fara.*
       'I have to go.'(Einarsson 1945: 164),

show differences in meaning that need not occupy us here. Suffice it to emphasise the idea of 'change of state', thus implicit futurity, of *verða*.

In UI, as already pointed out, the different senses of this verb are used: change of state, and therefore futurity, as well as obligation: the person cannot help doing what s/he is somehow 'compelled' to do.

4.3   The medio-passive

Icelandic, like the other Nordic languages, has a medio-passive historically built with the reflexive pronoun, later grammaticalised in a non-transparent ending and with a variety of non-reflexive meanings (Nygaard 1906: 155ff); this led to the development of new reflexive verbs, which use the common reflexive forms of the personal pronouns, as *spegla sig* 'watch oneself in the mirror', literally 'mirror oneself' or *hefna sig* 'take revenge', literally 'revenge oneself'. Again in Kress' words (1982: 143):

> An die Stelle reflexiver Verben treten mediale Verben, wenn bezeichnet werden soll, daß das Subjekt einer Aktion diese ohne seinen Willen an sich erfährt (unfreiwillige, passive reflexive Bedeutung). Im Deutschen entspricht in der Regel ein reflexives Verb; weniger glücklich ist die Wiedergabe durch das Passiv. Die Bedeutung der isl. medialen Verben trifft man am ehesten mit intransitiven Verben des Deutschen.[12]

This typically Nordic construction, which in part parallels the Spanish *se*-constructions, has been the object of fairly intensive study and it needs not detain us here.

---

12.   "Instead of the reflexive verbs medial verbs are used whenever it is to be signified that the subject of an action experiences this against his will (involuntary, passive reflexive construction). In German the usual correspondence is a reflexive verb; less adequate is the correspondence with the passive. The meaning of the Icelandic medial verbs is usually to be found in German intransitive verbs."

4.4   'Proper' impersonals

The passive and medial forms have as their main function the demotion of the agent of transitive verbs, but for the same purpose other constructions, properly called 'impersonal', are also used. Here are some (edited) examples of the various impersonal constructions, taken from Minger (2002), who groups them according to the case in which the *subject* is marked.

4.4.1   *DATIVE*

(31)   *Mér er illt í höfði.*
       me-DAT is painful in head
       'I have a headache.'

(32)   *Þykkir mér.*
       thinks me-DAT
       'I think.'

(33)   *Mér er kalt.*
       me-DAT is cold
       'I am (getting) cold.'

(34)   *Mér sjárnaði það.*
       me-DAT grieved it
       'It grieved me/It gave me pain/It hurt me.'

(35)   *Barninu batnaði veikin.*
       child.the-DAT recovered-from disease.the-NOM
       'The child recovered from the disease.'

4.4.2   *ACCUSATIVE*

(36)   *Mig þyrstir.*
       me-ACC is thirsty/thirsts
       'I am thirsty.'

(37)   *Mig langar í sígarettur.*
       me-ACC wants for cigarettes
       'I want cigarettes.'

(38)   *Mig vantar peninga.*
       me-ACC lacks money-ACC
       'I lack money.'

4.4.3   *GENITIVE*

(39)   *Verkjanna gætir ekki.*
       pains.the-GEN is-noticeable not
       'The pains are not noticeable.'

Einarsson (1945: 167ff) provides a general classification according to the semantic domains where impersonal constructions are mostly used. He establishes the following groups[13]:

a. **Nature.** "Verbs expressing processes of nature (…), variations of day and night, the seasons, the weather take either the indefinite subjects *það, hann*, or none at all":

(40)   *Nú snjóar.*
now snows
'It is snowing now.'

(41)   *Daginn lengir.*
day.the-acc lengthens
'The day(s) grow(s) longer.'

b. **Happenings**, etc.: "Verbs expressing not too well defined happenings, turning, beginning and end, events, passing of time, difference and lack…":

(42)   *Hér lýkur sögunni.*
here ends story.the-DAT
'Here the story ends.'

(43)   *Nú var komið að kveldi.*
now was come-PAST.PART-NEUT at evening
'Now it was near evening.'

c. **Mind**, etc.: "Verbs expressing processes of the mind, sensations, thoughts, feelings, etc. are often impersonal. With these verbs the logical subject (the man who senses, thinks, feels) is put in the accusative or the dative, while the sensation, thought, feeling often is treated as a subject…. That the accusative or dative is the logical subject is indicated by its fairly consistent position before the verb":

(44)   *Mig syfjar.*
me-ACC get.drowsy-3rd-PRES.
'I get drowsy.'

(45)   *Mér þykir vænt um hann.*
me-DAT seem nice-NEUT about him-ACC
'I like him.'

(46)   *Mér sýnist, að…*
me-DAT seem-3rdSG-MEDIAL, that…
'I think that …'

UI shares with this last group of medial verbs an inner-psychological element: the process is seen as being restricted to the affected person (in the accusative or, much more frequently, the dative). Similarly, in UI the process is totally limited to the inner

---

13.   I include only those immediately related to the purpose of this paper.

of the subject; the difference is mainly that in some cases an externally perceivable final state can be produced: the individual is looking at and seeing something, or is visibly startled, or in a different location than he was before. Only the sub-construction with *huga* 'think' remains merely internal, of course. UI is also part of a wider system Icelandic has as its disposal to express nuances regarding both perception and, most importantly, mental activities. These issues will be dealt with in future papers.

There exists a significant number of 'proper' impersonal constructions whose *experiencer* or *affected* person is in the dative or accusative case and no explicit subject in the nominative case is used. The already rich literature on this type of construction in Icelandic is basically restricted to its syntactic analysis, as summarised in Minger (2002; see also Andrews 1982, Barðdal 2000, 2001, Van Valin 1991, Zaenen et al. 1985; Barðdal 1997, Eythórsson 2000, Rögnvaldsson 1996, Mørck 1992, and Barðdal and Eythórsson 2003, among others, analyse the issue from a historical perspective: it certainly goes back to the oldest written forms of the Nordic languages). The main point of interest was the interpretation of the experiencers in these constructions as subjects, in spite of their not being in the nominative, the usual case for subjects in Icelandic. As we have just seen in the quotes from Einarsson above, this interpretation has rather old roots although in different terms: 'logical subject'. Sentence (3) above, for instance, shows that the Dative Noun in the first clause (*mér*), which is followed by the impersonal *verða*, is further followed by the verb *sjá* 'to see' in the 1st person singular of the past tense: *sá*. There seems to be no option except to consider the dative *mér* as the subject of *sá*.

Anyway, in this paper we are not interested in these syntactic issues. I shall refer to this supposed subject as the *experiencer*, although on occasion the semantic function may not coincide exactly with that one (both *theme* and *patient* have been proposed, for instance; see Barðdal 2004).

5. Conclusions and prospects

The construction I have termed UNCONSCIOUS, IRRESPONSIBLE is a special case among the many Icelandic constructions expressing the demotion of the agent or full deagentivisation. The following elements have been identified:

1. **Use of the dative to mark the individual as en experiencer,** even with verbs that would otherwise appear with a subject in the nominative: controlled, conscious actions as 'looking', 'thinking' or 'going' are reconceptualised as internal processes that affect the individual that would normally be the agent.
2. **Use of the verb *verða* to mark the compulsory character of the individual's involuntary action,** as well as the implicit change of state.
3. **Use of the neuter Past Participle of the lexical verb,** which thus contributes to building a construction which stands formally – and semantically – quite close to an impersonal *verða*-passive.

4.   **Absence of a 'regular' (i.e., nominative) subject**, thus contributing to the idea that the experiencer's action 'comes out of nowhere'.

IU shares these elements with other Icelandic constructions. Also some which have not been mentioned in this paper but which show striking similarities although they do not fully conform to the formal characterisation given above. I mean expressions like (47):

(47)   *Mér varð hverft við, þegar ég vaknaði.*
       'I was suddenly startled when I woke up.'

In spite of the external similarity, *hverft* is NOT the Neuter Past Participle of the verb *hverfa*, 'to oscillate, doubt' but the neuter of an adjectiv *hverfur* – derived from *hverfa*. The whole construction is listed in Blöndal's, Árnason's, and Sigurðsson's dictionaries as an idiom. The semantic similarity with *bregða* and the formal connection of *hverft* with neuter participles may lead to the speakers' conceptualising both in a similar way – but this has to be empirically proved.

Something similar happens with the neuter adjective *ágengt*, as in (48):

(48)   *Honum varð ágengt.*
       'He became aggressive'.

What is intriguing in (47) and (48) and brings both together with IU, is the fact that the adjective is in the neuter singular and the person affected by fright (47) or aggressivity (48) is set in the dative case. It is perfectly possible, and usual, to say *hann varð ágengur* 'he became aggressive', but the, in Kress' words, 'magical' agency typical of the UI Construction would then be left unexpressed.

A number of general cognitive principles are at action here, then. Seeing mental and perceptual processes as due to nothing at all, i.e. to be uncaused, is basic in any psychological 'folk theory': in English or Spanish we can say something like

(49)   *No lo pensé, la idea se me vino, simplemente.*
       'I did not think it, the idea just came to me.'

And in certain situations (50) can be heard among Spanish speakers:

(50)   *Yo no lo pensé, se me pensó*
       I did not think it, it thought-itself to me
       'I did not intend to think about that; I just got that idea.'

And in German the following can be mentioned in this context:

(51)   *Er dachte besser als andere, denn er dachte außen und innen. Es wurde gegen seinen Willen in ihm gedacht. Er sagte, Gedanken würden ihn gemacht.* (Musil 240 [the page reference is to the 2003 edition])
       'He thought better than the others, because he thought outside and inside. It was thought in him against his will. He said, thoughts were made for him.'

References

Andrews, Avery D. 1982. "The Representation of Case in Modern Icelandic". *The mental representation of grammatical relations*, ed. by Joan Bresnan, 427–503. Cambridge, Massachusetts: The MIT Press.

Árnason, Kristján. 1980. *Íslensk málfræði* (2 vols). Reykjavík: Iðunn.

Árnason, Mörður (ed.). 2002. *Íslensk orðabók*. Reykjavík: Edda.

Barðdal, Jóhanna. 1997. "Oblique subjects in Old Scandinavian". *Working Papers in Scandinavian Syntax* 60: 25–50.

Barðdal, Jóhanna. 2000. "Oblique subjects in Old Scandinavian". NOWELE 37: 25–51.

Barðdal, Jóhanna. 2001. "The perplexity of Dat-Nom verbs in Icelandic". *Nordic Journal of Linguistics* 24: 47–70.

Barðdal, Jóhanna. 2004. "The semantics of the impersonal construction in Icelandic, German and Faroese: Beyond thematic roles". *Focus on Germanic Typology*, ed. by Werner Abraham, 105–137. Berlin: Akademie Verlag.

Barðdal, Jóhanna and Thórhallur Eythórsson. 2003. "The change that never happened: the story of oblique subjects". *Journal of Linguistics* 39: 439–472.

Bergsson, Guðbergur. 2004. *Lömuðu kennslukonurnar*. Reykjavík: JPV Útgáfa.

Bernárdez, Enrique. 1997. "A partial synergetic model of deagentivisation". *Journal of Quantitative Linguistics* 4: 53–66.

Bernárdez, Enrique. 2001. "Cultural determination of cause-effect. On a possible folk model of causation". *C.L.A.C.* Vol. 6. (http://www.ucm.es/info/circulo/index.htm)

Bjarnadóttir, Birna. 2003. *Holdið hemur andann. Um fagurfræði í skáldskap Guðbergs Bergssonar*. Reykjavík: Háskólaútgáfan.

Blöndal, Sigfús. 1920–1924. *Islands-dansk Ordbog*, 2 vols. Reykjavík: Verslun Þórarins B. Þorlákssonar & København: Gutenberg.

Einarsson, Stefán. 1945. *Icelandic*. Baltimore: The John Hopkins Press.

Eythórsson, Thórhallur. 2000. "Dative vs. nominative: Changes in quirky subjects in Icelandic". *Leeds Working Papers in Linguistics* 8. 27–44.

Grebe, Paul et al. (eds.). 1966. *Grammatik der deutschen Gegenwartssprache*. Mannheim: Bibliographisches Institut.

Halldórsson, Halldór. 1950. *Íslenzk málfræði*. Reykjavík: Ísafoldarprentsmiðja.

Kress, Bruno. 1982. *Isländische Grammatik*. Leipzig, Verlag Enzyklopädie.

Laxness, Halldór. 1957. *Brekkukotsannáll*. Reykjavík: Vaka-Helgafell, 2000.

Minger, David L. 2002. *An analysis of grammatical relations and case marking in Icelandic*. PhD Thesis, University of California, Davis.

Mørck, Endre. 1992. "Subjektets kasus i norrønt og mellomnorsk". *Arkiv för nordisk filologi* 107: 53–99.

Musil, Robert. 1930–1932. *Der Mann ohne Eigenschaften*. Hamburg: Rowohlt.

Nygaard, M. 1906–1966. *Norrøn syntax*. Oslo, Aschehoug.

Pétursson, Magnús. 1981. *Lehrbuch der isländischen Sprache*. Hamburg: Buske.

Rögnvaldsson, Eiríkur. 1996. "Frumlag og fall að fornu". *Íslenskt mál* 18: 37–69.

Sigurðsson, Arngrímur. 1983. *Íslenzk-ensk orðabók*. Reykjavík: Ísafoldarprentsmiðja.

Van Valin, Robert D., Jr. 1991. "Another Look at Icelandic Case Marking and Grammatical Relations". *Natural Language and Linguistic Theory* 9: 145–194.

Van Valin, Robert D., Jr. and Randy J. LaPolla. (1997). *Syntax: Structure, meaning and function*. Cambridge: Cambridge University Press.

Watkins, Calvert. 2000. *The American Heritage dictionary of Indo-European roots*. Boston: Houghton Mifflin.

Zaenen, Annie, Joan Maling and Hölskuldur Thráinsson. 1985. "Case and grammatical functions: The Icelandic passive". *Natural Language and Linguistic Theory* 3: 441–483. (Reprinted in *Modern Icelandic Syntax* (Syntax & Semantics 24), ed. by Joan Maling and Annie Zaenen, 1990, 95–136.)

Modelling 'selection' between referents in the English nominal group

An essay in scientific inquiry in linguistics

Robin P. Fawcett

Centre for Language and Communication Research, Cardiff University

This paper addresses two issues, one descriptive and one methodological. It offers a description of part of the English nominal group (aka noun phrase) that greatly extends the traditional concept of 'determiner'. More specifically, it describes an integrated semantics and functional syntax for the quantifying and deictic determiners, based on the concept of 'selection'. This approach has the advantage over standard representations that, when analyzing (1) *five books*, (2) *those books* and (3) *five of those books*, the words *five, those* and *books* expound the same element in each case. The paper then shows how this approach can be extended to eight other determiners and their associated uses of *of* (and, incidentally, the structure for its remaining uses). But there is equal emphasis on the methodology used to establish which of three possible types of structure should be used to model such examples, and the paper concludes by suggesting that the ultimate criteria are those of elegance in the operation of the grammar.

1. Aims and scope

It is a very great pleasure to contribute to this volume in honour of Angela Downing.[1] In this 'essay in scientific inquiry', I start from the assumption that a linguist is some-

---

1. The research that is drawn on here was in large measure carried out as part of the COMMU-NAL Project. COMMUNAL was supported by grants from the Speech Research Unit at DRA Malvern for over ten years, as part of Assignment No. ASO4BP44 on Spoken Language Understanding and Dialogue (SLUD), by ICL and Longman in Phase 1, and throughout by Cardiff University. I would also like to express my personal thanks to the two friends and colleagues to whom I am most indebted. The first is Michael Halliday, the 'father' of Systemic Functional Linguistics and the linguist to whom I, like many others, owe the basis of my current model of language. The second major debt is to Gordon Tucker, who has worked with me in (i) developing the version of Systemic Functional Grammar (SFG) that has come to be known as the Cardiff Grammar, and (ii)

one who adopts a scientific approach to the goal of understanding the nature of language – and Angela Downing is a particularly fine linguist. She is committed to the tasks of making viable, theory-based descriptions of languages, of making those descriptions available for use by others (notably in Downing and Locke 1992, 2006), and of encouraging other scholars. Furthermore, she is committed to that great undoer of theories and descriptions: the data of real-life texts, whether selected by the individual linguist (e.g. Downing 1991) or taken from one of the great computer corpora (e.g. Downing 1996).

The primary aim of this paper is to consider the alternative possible structures for the syntax of a central area of English grammar that is still surprisingly under-represented in the great descriptive grammars of English, and to present the syntax through which I consider that these structures can most insightfully be modelled. This will in turn require me to discuss the criteria that we use to decide between alternative structures. In this research, I have drawn extensively on corpus studies, the results of which have significantly extended the model – but ultimately, as we shall see, we also need to bring very different sources of evidence to such decisions: principally, in this case, the evidence inferable from how the language works. Here, then, a language is seen not as an abstract object but as a tool with which to do things – and so, in the metaphor of the computer, as a program.

The second aim of this paper is therefore to show that having a clear, working model of how language works can make a crucial contribution to the process of deciding between alternative syntactic representations of sequences of items. In this paper I shall illustrate this principle from a grammar of some central aspects of the **English nominal group**. The theory of language within which this grammar is set is **systemic functional linguistics** (SFL) – but the general principle – and probably some of the detailed description of the structure – is equally relevant to any theory of language that is both functional and one that aims at providing an overall model of language and its use (e.g. the theories described in Butler 2003a, 2003b).

The best way to indicate the parts of the nominal group on which we shall focus is to invite you to inspect the examples in the next section. But a full description and justification of even this limited set of data would require too much space, and for this see Chapter 7 of Fawcett (forthcoming). Here we shall focus on the relationship between what we shall term the **quantifying determiner** and the **deictic determiner** – and so on the **semantic** and **syntactic** relationships that hold between them. Then I shall show how the grammar adopted for this relationship can be extended to the many other similar relationships found in the meanings and forms of the English nominal group – but without spelling out the argument for the model in these later cases. It will by then be evident, I

implementing it in the COMMUNAL computer model of language. But I am also very grateful to Chris Butler for his acute comments, questions and suggestions during the particularly troublesome birth of this paper, which have led to very many improvements.

think, that the reasoning that underlies the description of the relationship between the quantifying and deictic determiners also applies to those other cases.

2.   Some data in need of explanation

2.1   The data and some questions that they raise

The questions to which this paper seeks to provide answers are:

1.   'How should we model the **syntax** of examples (1) to (11) below?'
2.   What **semantic** features do these items and their associated structures realize?
3.   What is the nature of the rules that relate the **semantics** to the **syntax**?

In preparation for the discussion of these matters, Section 2.2 will give a brief selective overview of the relevant literature, and Section 3 will introduce the necessary background concepts. The substantive issue will be addressed in Section 4, and Section 5 will then show how the principle established there can be extended to cover no less than ten structurally distinct determiners. Finally, Section 6 will present my conclusions.

Sections 4 and 5 summarize a description of the English nominal group that provides for the cases exemplified in (1) to (11) – among many others that appear to have similar structures.

(1)	*all*	*(of)*	*those children / them*
(2)	*five*	*of*	*those children / them*
(3)	*hundreds*	*of*	*those children / them*
(4)	*a crowd*	*of*	*those children / them*
(5)	*five*	*of*	*the youngest of those children / them*
(6) *the front of*	*a group*	*of*	*the youngest of those children / them*

The layout of (1) to (6) is significant, as Sections 4 and 5 will demonstrate – and so is the optionality of *of* in (1). But many other items are optional in these examples, in the sense that they can be removed and still leave a valid nominal group, e.g. *those* in (3) and *the youngest of* in (6).

However, any adequate description of the English nominal group must also model the expression of what we shall term 'representation', as in the underlined nominal groups in (7) and (8), and 'typicity', as in (9) and in (10) – both of which appear to use broadly the same structure – several times, in the case of (10). In contrast, consider the structure of (11), which clearly has essentially the same meaning as (9), but which does not use this structure – whatever that structure is.

(7)   *This is <u>a photo of my daughter</u>.*
(8)   *What's <u>your idea of an ideal partner</u>?*

   (9)   *Toyota have brought out <u>a new type of car that is more eco-friendly</u>.*
   (10) *This is <u>an example of one of the first of the new varieties of GM wheat</u>.*
   (11) *Toyota have brought out <u>a new car that is more eco-friendly</u>.*

Exploring and assessing the evidence related to the question of what the structure of
(1) to (11) should be is the main focus of Sections 4 and 5, and so of this paper.

2.2   The paucity of the literature

There is nothing unusual about (1) to (11), and yet – surprisingly – there is still, so far
as I am aware, no published grammar that explains their syntax in a principled way –
let alone their semantics.

   This strong statement takes account of the three most recent comprehensive grammars of English, i.e. Quirk et al (1985: 248–252), Biber et al (1999: 256–270) and Huddleston and Pullum (2002: 352–353 and 411–413) – and many other works. These include four recent functionally-oriented grammars: Halliday's *Introduction to
Functional Grammar* (Halliday 1985), and so the virtually unchanged descriptions in
Halliday (1994) and Halliday and Matthiessen (2004), henceforth *IFG*; Downing and
Locke 1992 and 2006, Sinclair (1990); and Matthiessen (1995). Two papers by Sinclair
(1991: 81–98) and Prakasam (1996: 567–583) provide interesting discussions of the
problem of how to analyze *of* in nominal groups but, while Prakasam suggests quite a
range of possible structures, neither paper provides a full grammar for (1) to (11) and
the many related phenomena. In Fawcett (forthcoming, in preparation), however – to
which this paper provides an introduction – I offer a comprehensive systemic functional grammar that does this.

   The approach to the English nominal group to be presented in Sections 3 to 5 is set,
broadly, within the theory of syntax first presented in Halliday (1961/1976) – while differing significantly from the later version found in *IFG*. Most of the proposals in Sections
3 and 4 have been published earlier in outline form – first in Fawcett (1974–1976/1981)
and then, in a slightly revised version, in Fawcett (1980). The current version is far more
comprehensive, and includes full system networks and realization rules. It was developed
as part of the COMMUNAL Project (see Footnote 1), with many important inputs from
Gordon Tucker (e.g. for modifier sequence see Tucker 1998: 204f.). It is also described
briefly in Fawcett (2000: 203–204, 297–302 and 304–307) and in Butler (2003a: 309–313)
– but most fully in Fawcett (forthcoming, in preparation).[2]

---

2.   In addition, I have presented the concept of 'selection in the nominal group' in (i) papers
and workshops at several International Systemic Congresses; (ii) guest lectures at the Universities of Macquarie (Sydney), Doshisha (Kyoto) and Gent (Belgium); and, with colleagues, (iii)
undergraduate and postgraduate courses at Cardiff.

Interestingly, other scholars have adopted aspects of the model of 'selection' in the English nominal group presented here.[3] Downing and Locke (1992: xix) acknowledge Fawcett (1974–1976/1981) as a source, and in their Module 47, in both the 1992 and 2006 editions, the terms 'selecting' and 'particularizing' are used in essentially the senses used here.[4]

Matthiessen has adopted even more of my concept of 'selection' (1995: 655–657) – though only, it appears, when the relevant determiner is filled by a nominal group. So for him *a pack of cards* involves 'selection' but *fifty-two cards* does not – presumably because of the presence of *of* in the former. I show in Section 4 that the syntax of the two should be broadly similar – though not identical.[5]

However, the concept of 'selection' is absent from all three editions of *IFG*.[6] It nonetheless includes two related concepts proposed in Fawcett (1974–1976/1981) and included here (though under different names from mine). The first is the concept of 'Measure', as in *a pack of* cards and *another three cups of* that good strong tea (Halliday 1994: 195). The first is said to function as a 'Numerative' while the second, for unexplained reasons, is described differently, i.e. as a 'Pre-numerative'. The second concept is that exemplified in *the front of* the house. In the 1994 edition of *IFG* this is described as a 'Pre-Deictic', but in the 2004 edition it becomes a 'Facet'. A further problem is that Halliday's analysis of *of* as PART OF the 'Numerative', 'Pre-Numerative', 'Pre-Deictic' or 'Facet' leaves the reader asking 'What is the unit of which the word *of* is an element?' This area of the *IFG* grammar appears to need substantial revision if it is to account consistently for the data to be discussed here.

The published literature, then, is largely unhelpful, so we must develop our own analysis for such examples. The first step is to establish the grammatical framework to be used.

---

3. Note that this is a syntagmatic sense of the term *selection*, and that it is to be distinguished from the use of *select* in the context of 'selecting between options in a system network'. However, the option to choose to 'select' from within a referent - e.g. by 'quantity' - is itself an option in a system, as we shall see.

4. Further work in the COMMUNAL Project on the nature of the referents of nominal groups has persuaded me to change my position on my earlier assumption (in Fawcett 1980) that 'particularization' is itself a type of 'selection'. Logically that approach makes sense, but the way that the grammar of English (and every other language I know of whose grammar foregrounds this concept) actually operates is, I have come to realize, to treat 'particularization' as PART OF THE MEANING OF WHAT WE SHALL REFER TO AS THE 'WIDEST REFERENT'. Essentially, this is because there is no possibility of operating the concept of 'selection' when we use inherently 'particularized' items such as the 'third person' pronouns. (See Section 4.1.)

5. Perhaps this apparently illogical difference in structure is adopted out of deference to Halliday's early analysis of one-item quantifying expressions as 'numeratives'. But that analysis fails to capture the important generalizations that the present analysis captures.

6. This is even true of the 2004 edition, in which Matthiessen was a 'co-reviser' with Halliday. But it was in fact Halliday who was responsible for the chapter on groups (Matthiessen, personal communication).

3.   The necessary background concepts

3.1   Alternative models of Systemic Functional Grammar (SFG)

The version of SFG with which I work is, as Halliday has said (1994: xii), "based on the same systemic functional theory" as his. However, as a result of the extensive work by the team at Cardiff since the late 1980s, there are now two fairly comprehensive versions of SFG, with some significant differences from each other. The two models are generally referred to by their academic bases, i.e. as 'the Sydney Grammar' and 'the Cardiff Grammar'. Butler (2003a, 2003b) provides fairly full descriptions of both versions (as well as two other 'structural-functional' models), and he reaches the encouraging conclusion that "in my view the Cardiff model represents a substantial improvement on the Sydney account" (2003b: 471).

3.2   How a systemic functional grammar works

I shall now provide a brief overview of how a SFG works. Here we assume a model in which the **system network** that models the 'meaning potential' of a language constitutes its **semantics**.[7]

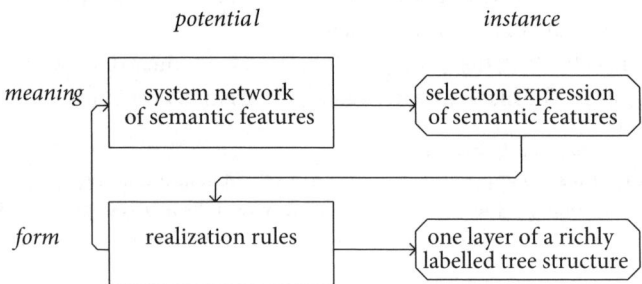

Figure 1. The main components of a Systemic Functional Grammar and their outputs

Figure 1 shows the two main components of the grammar of a language (on the left), and their outputs (on the right). The grammar contains two 'potentials': one at each of the two levels of

---

7.   See Chapter 5 of Fawcett (2000) for a discussion of the broad similarities and the relatively minor differences between the generative versions of the Sydney Grammar and the Cardiff Grammar. In the Cardiff Grammar we interpret the system networks of choices in TRANSITIVITY, MOOD, THEME and so on as the semantics, while the current version of the Sydney Grammar (e.g. as proposed in Halliday and Matthiessen 1999) treats them as the lower of TWO networks that specify 'meaning potential' - a controversial proposal that is as yet unsupported by a description of either a reasonably full set of networks at the higher level or how their output determines the choices in transitivity, etc.

meaning and **form**. The process of generation is controlled by the **semantic system network**, which models the language's 'meaning potential' (see Figures 4 and 8 for examples).

Figure 1 also shows the two types of 'instance' – i.e. the outputs from each of the two components. Each traversal of the network results in a **selection expression** of the features chosen on that traversal. The **realization rules** refer to these as they specify the output. An output consists of a **syntactic unit**, its **elements**, and the **items** that expound them – unless one of its elements is to be filled by a further **unit**, in which case the rule specifies **re-entry** to the network (note the arrow on the left).

Each traversal of the network chooses features relevant to one semantic unit, and each generates one syntactic unit. The first traversal typically generates a **clause**, and later traversals generate the **nominal groups** (and other units) that will fill some of its elements.

Thus a 'grammar' is essentially a model of the sentence-generating component of a full model of language and its use. So the term 'grammar' is used here as a short form for **lexico-grammar** – a term that usefully reminds us that the system network covers meanings realized in lexis, as well as in syntax and in grammatical items (as in a narrower sense of 'grammar').

We shall see examples of this model at work in Sections 3.4, 4.2.2 and 4.4.7.[8]

3.3   An introductory outline of the English nominal group

While the **semantics** of the English **nominal group** (henceforth usually **ngp**) involves several different strands of meaning (as does the clause), these are integrated, at the level of **form**, into a single structure.

This consists of four broad types of element: **determiners** (e.g. the **deictic determiner** so **dd**), **modifiers** (**m**), the **head** (**h**) and **qualifiers** (**q**). Consider (12) in Figure 2.

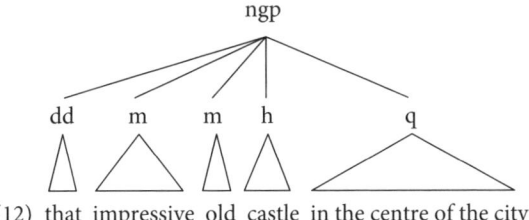

(12) that impressive old castle in the centre of the city

Figure 2. The primary structure of a simple nominal group

Note the following points:

1. Each ngp has at least one **referent**, which is typically 'singular', 'plural' or 'mass'. (I say 'at least one', because we frequently find that a ngp contains one or more em-

---

8.   For a fuller discussion of the implications of Figure 1, see Chapter 3 of Fawcett (2000), and for a full account of how a SFG works see Fawcett, Tucker and Lin (1993).

bedded ngps (e.g. the ngp *the centre of the city* in Figure 2) and so another referent. And in Section 4.4 we shall meet the idea that a ngp that contains 'selection' has more than one referent – WITHOUT NECESSARILY INVOLVING EMBEDDING. (See Section 4.1 for a fuller account of what a 'referent' is.)

2. When discussing the English ngp, we shall use the following technical terms and abbreviations (as specified in, for example, Fawcett 2000). Using (12) as our example, we can say: 'This **unit** is a **ngp** that has as its **elements** a **deictic determiner** (**dd**), two **modifiers** (**m**), a **head** (**h**) and a **qualifier** (**q**). The deictic determiner is **expounded** by the item *the* and the head by the item *castle*. The qualifier (whose internal structure is not shown) is **filled** by a **prepositional group** (**pgp**) (*in the centre of the city*). Each of the two modifiers is filled by a **quality group** (**qlgp**) (also not shown), their apexes being expounded by the items *impressive* and *old*.'[9]

3. A ngp may contain many types of determiner and modifier and several qualifiers, but it can have only one head.

4. Each determiner, modifier and qualifier is a separate element of the ngp, and each realizes a different type of meaning.

5. With only very minor variations, the sequence of the elements is fixed.

6. The presence of the head element is almost OBLIGATORY (though we shall shortly meet an exception to this generalization). There are three main types (and some less frequent ones that we shall omit here):

    (i) heads that state the **cultural classification** that is being assigned to the referent by a choice in the vast system network of noun senses that a language makes available to its users ('common nouns');[10]

    (ii) heads that refer to their referent by a **token cultural classification** ('third person pronouns'); and

    (iii) heads whose referent is **named** ('proper nouns').

    Here we shall be concerned with Types (i) and (ii) – as in Examples (1) to (6).

7. All elements other than the head are structurally OPTIONAL, with Type 1 allowing far the widest range of elements.

8. The general function of both modifiers and qualifiers (which precede and follow the head) is to **describe** the referent. Both answer the general question 'What sort of object?', and there are specialized questions for each subcategory of modifier and qualifier ('What colour?' etc). But modifiers also serve one (typically) of three broad functions: in principle, all modifiers can be used to **classify** the referent, but some simply **depict** (cp. 'defining' and 'non-defining') – and some are **affective** (*nice, nasty*).

---

9.   We recognize the presence of a qlgp here because almost all such cases can be preceded by a **temperer**, e.g. *very*. For the fullest grammar yet published of the grammar of the **quality group** (the unit whose pivotal element is an adjective or adverb), see Tucker (1998).

10.   For an excellent introduction to this important SFL concept, including a survey of the literature up to the time, see Tucker (1996).

3.4   The semantics and realization rules for the ngp and its head

In this section (and two later ones) I shall demonstrate how a systemic functional grammar works. I shall illustrate this by showing how simple realization rules generate the central parts of the example in Figure 2. This section will therefore illustrate the model of language in Figure 1 at work.

Why do we need to go into such detail? The reason is that our goal in this paper is to decide between several possible alternative structures that might be used to model the concept of 'selection' – and to do this we need to know how the grammar works. If we didn't, we wouldn't be able to understand why one structure is preferable to another. So the four key concepts, as in Figure 1, are (i) the **system network** that defines the language's meaning potential, (ii) the **selection expression** of features chosen from it on any one traversal of it, (iii) the **realization rules** that these trigger, and (iv) the **structure** that is their output in any one instance, consisting of **syntax** and **items**.

The process of generation within the lexicogrammar begins with the **system network**. (In a full model of how we produce texts, e.g. as described in Fawcett, Tucker and Lin (1993), there are several stages before this, but I omit these here.) The **entry condition** to this vast network of semantic features is the feature [**entity**], and the first system is a choice between the principal semantic units – so between [**situation**], which is typically realized in a **clause**, and [**thing**], which is typically realized in a **nominal group** – and a few others, which I shall omit here to keep things simple.[11] And for the same reason I won't attempt to display this part of the very large system network to which [thing] leads. But we can nonetheless get a good picture of its size, if we look at the **selection expression** of features that results from a traversal of it. Here, with some omissions, is the 23-feature pathway through the network that generates (i) the unit **ngp** in Figure 2, and (ii) the noun that functions as its **head (h)** i.e. *castle*:

> [entity, thing (56),.... (6 features).... cultural classification,.... (8 features).... building,.... (4 features).... castle-c (74.6917)].

There are two points to note. First, the suffix '-c' on the final feature indicates that this is a 'count' thing, so ensuring that [castle-c] – together with all the other 'cultural classifications' that are 'count' – is given the feature [count-cc], and so enters the system where the choice is between 'singular' and 'plural'. ('Mass' things similarly receive the feature [mass-cc].) Second, the numbers following the features [thing] and [castle-c] are those of their realization rules. The rules themselves are shown below.[12]

---

11.   Semantic features that occur in running text are normally shown in square brackets, as here; sometimes, however, a meaning is represented informally by using single quotation marks.

12.   The other features have no realizations - but in many cases another feature in the system in which they occur does - so motivating the inclusion of the feature. (Having a realization rule is only one among several reasons for including a feature in a system network.)

Each **realization rule** is composed of one or more **statements**. Their purpose is to specify one or more **operations** that are to be executed when that feature is selected. They are therefore 'statements' about what is to be done – so that they function as commands.

> 60:   thing: insert ngp, h @ 66.
> 74.6917: castle-c: h < "castle".

Here is the 'translation' of Rule 60, which contains two 'statements':

1. If the feature [thing] is selected, insert a nominal group (ngp) into the structure – i.e. to fill the element (e.g. a Complement) for which the grammar is currently generating a unit.
2. Then insert a head (h) at Place 66 of the ngp.

This shows that there are 65 Places at which different preceding elements may be located. However, very few of them are ever generated together on one traversal of the network. The role of the numbered Places is to get the elements in the right order, and after this has been done the unused ones are stripped away – so producing representations like that in Figure 2 (though with more detail).

Rule 74.6917 simply says:

If the **feature** [castle-c] is selected, the **head (h)** is to be **expounded** by the item "castle".

So these two rules generate, for the example in Figure 2, (i) the unit, (ii) its pivotal element and (iii) the item that expounds it. Here we shall ignore the generation of the modifiers and the qualifier, but in Section 4.2.2 we shall see (i) how the plural form of *castle* would be generated (if required), and (ii) how the **deictic determiner** is generated. Then in Section 4.4.7 we shall see how the grammar models the semantics and the syntax of 'selection between referents'.

Before we go further, however, it will be useful to address an issue in the description of English concerning the item *of*.

3.5   The use of *of* in structures other than 'selection'

As the examples in Section 2.1 showed, this paper is about a set of uses of *of* in English. The item *of* is in fact the second most frequent item in English after *the*, and it comprises about two per cent of all words in all types of text (Sinclair 1991: 84, 143).

While it expresses several different semantic relationships, in the grammar presented here these are realized in EITHER ONE OF JUST TWO TYPES OF STRUCTURE. One is the 'selection' structure to be introduced in Section 4.4.6. In the other one, *of* functions, at the level of form, as a **preposition** in a **prepositional group**.[13] There it is used to express sev-

---

13. Our term 'prepositional group' is essentially the same as 'prepositional phrase', as used by Halliday in *IFG*.

eral different semantic relationships – two of the most frequent being 'personal relation-ship', as in (13), and the relationship of a Participant Role to its Process, such as we find in the **nominalization** of the experiential meaning of an **event** (which is typically realized in a clause), as in (14).[14] We shall call this the 'prepositional group as qualifier' structure.

(13)   *(He was) the confidant of three prime ministers.*
(14)   *(It was) the clash of two cultures.*

Currently, most linguists – other than those who use the approach described in Fawcett (1974–1976/1981, 1980, 2000) and here – appear to make the unquestioned assump-tion that the 'prepositional group as qualifier' structure should be used for modelling ALL instances of *of*.[15] Since we ourselves will shortly be considering the possible use of this structure to model the 'selection' meaning of *of*, you may find it helpful to familiar-ize yourself with the analysis in Figure 3 and its Key.

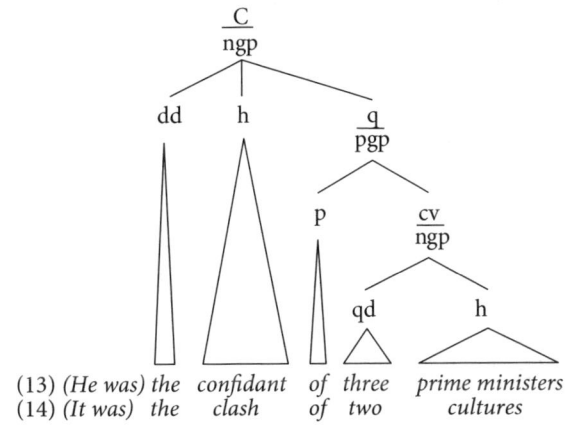

Key (new elements): pgp = prepositional group
p = preposition   cv = completive   qd = quantifying determiner

Figure 3. The 'prepositional group as qualifier' construction

---

14.   Thus the function of *of* in a nominalization is to mark what follows as a Participant Role (PR) in the Process that is expressed (or partly expressed) in the head. So in *the clash of two cultures (with each other)*, 'two cultures' functions as a PR in the Process of 'clashing' that is realized in *clash*. Another use of *of* as a preposition occurs when it realizes part of the meaning of a Process in examples such as *I'm thinking of you* and *I'm aware of the problem* (where 'thinking of' and 'being aware of' are the Processes).

15.   One group whose members don't is Sinclair and his team. Interestingly, Sinclair (1990) lists the cases where the Birmingham group use a prepositional group (or 'phrase') to represent the structural relationships around *of* (which however include some that are handled here as types of 'selection'). Disappointingly, they don't say what they think the structural relationship between *of* and its neighbouring elements is in cases such as *five of them* or *a pile of books*. Nor does Sin-clair (1991). Perhaps this implies an openness to the structure proposed here?

I should make it clear that I consider the analysis shown here to be fully appropriate to each of the two cases illustrated. Section 4 will consider how far it is also appropriate to use it for examples with *of* in its 'selection' sense – as well as considering two other possible structures.

4.   The semantic relationship of 'selection': Its realization in the relationship between the quantifying and deictic determiners

This section summarizes an approach to the structure of an important aspect of the ngp which will be new to many readers, and which therefore needs justifying. Here we only have space to illustrate and justify the most frequent type, but essentially the same principles apply to the other types to be introduced in Section 5 – and there is a fuller account of these in Chapter 7 of Fawcett (forthcoming). However, while this approach to analyzing ngps has not been widely publicized in text books, it has been employed by those using the Cardiff Grammar for over thirty years – both for extensive text analysis and for generating text-sentences in the computer.

4.1   A note on the concept of 'referent'

The concept of a **referent** will play a central role in what follows, so I shall begin by explaining the sense in which the term is used here. Consider the meanings of the underlined portions of the following examples (spoken by two friends in an art gallery):

(15)   A: *I just love <u>this portrait</u>!*
(16)   B: *Actually, I prefer <u>these landscapes</u>.*
(17)   A: *Well, yes, <u>they</u>'re pretty good too.*
(18)   B: *But really I prefer <u>still lifes</u>.*
(19)   A: *What I like best is <u>icecream</u>!*

We shall say that the underlined portion of each example has a **referent**. There are three points to note. The first is that in each case the expression refers to a **single referent** – in a sense of 'single' which is clearly NOT the same as 'singular'. In other words, it is not only *this portrait* (which clearly refers to a 'singular' object) that has a single referent; so too do *these landscapes* and *they*, even though they refer to 'plural' objects. And sometimes a Performer refers to a 'whole class' of 'count things', as in *still lifes* or a 'whole class' of a 'mass' object, as in *icecream* (aka 'generic reference').

Secondly, we must be clear about where the referent of a ngp is located. We need a model of 'reference' which recognizes that it is in the mind of the Performer (i.e. the person who produces the ngp). There may or may not be a corresponding **object** in the real world (objects being 'concrete' or 'abstract'), but there is always one in the Performer's mind – even when no such object exists, as when I say *That's a griffin.*

Thirdly, (15) to (19) illustrate the difference between a referent that is **particularized** (aka 'definite') and one that is **unparticularized**. It is those of (15) to (17) that are particularized, and those of (18) and (19) that are not. In cases such as *they* in (17), we shall say that the word *they* identifies a **single particularized referent**, and in cases such as (15) and (16) we shall say that the two words *this portrait* or *these landscapes* combine to refer to a single particularized referent. The difference between (15) and (16) on the one hand and (17) on the other is that in (17) the **Performer (P)** is referring to a referent that P is presenting to the **Addressee (A)** as something that P expects A to be able to identify, given only the two meanings that the referent is (i) presented by P as being 'identifiable' by A – and so 'recoverable' – and (ii) 'plural'. A little redundancy in a text is a good thing, but when saying or writing (17), P is implying that P considers (or purports to consider) that it would be excessively redundant to specify the 'class of thing' by supplying a lexical item (e.g. as P does in *those landscapes*).

In contrast, the referent of a ngp such as *still lifes in* (18) is simply 'members of the class of "still life" pictures'. (Interestingly, a subsequent reference to such a referent may take the form of *they* which is typically used for particularized referents.)

In the next few sections we shall consider two important types of determiner and the types of meaning that they realize – first individually and then in combination as the most frequent type of **selection** in the nominal group.

4.2   Particularization: meanings realized in the deictic determiner

4.2.1   *The data to be modelled*
The **deictic determiner (dd)** is by far the most frequent type of determiner – especially when it is expounded by *the*, as it is over 90% of the time. Indeed, *the* is more than twice as frequent as any other word in English, and instances of *the* comprise roughly four per cent of all types of text (figures derived from Sinclair 1991: 18 and 143).

When there are other determiners in the same ngp, the **dd** is always the last one before the **modifiers** (if there are any) and the **head**. It is this that enables us to treat the **dd** and what follows it (e.g. *those landscapes*) as having a single referent, in the same way that we treat *they* (which may replace *those landscapes*), as a single referent.

The **dd** answers the question: 'Which (or whose) thing?' Typical examples of a **dd** in a ngp are (with the semantic features that specify the type of 'particularization' shown in brackets):

(20)   *(Don't look at)* <u>*the*</u> *sun.*   [recoverable]
(21)   <u>*That*</u> *book (belongs to me).*   [by location relative to performer]
(22)   *(Is that)* <u>*your*</u> *new dishwasher?*   [by association with possessor]

In over 99% of cases the **dd** is **expounded** by an **item** i.e. (i) the word *the*, or (ii) a 'demonstrative' (*this, that, these, those, which* or *what*), or (iii) a 'possessive' (*my, your, his, her, its our, their, whose*). But occasionally it is **filled** by a **unit**, which is here termed a

genitive cluster. This unit typically expresses a 'possessive' meaning, e.g. *Fred's*, *the new doctor's* (see Fawcett 2000: 212, 307).

4.2.2   *The semantics and realization rules for the deictic determiner*

We saw in Section 3.4 the rules by which the **ngp**, its **head** and the **item** that expounds it are generated. We also saw that the semantic features in the network for the 'cultural classification' of things lead to one or other of the feature [count-cc] or [mass-cc], and Figure 4 takes up the traversal of the network from that point.

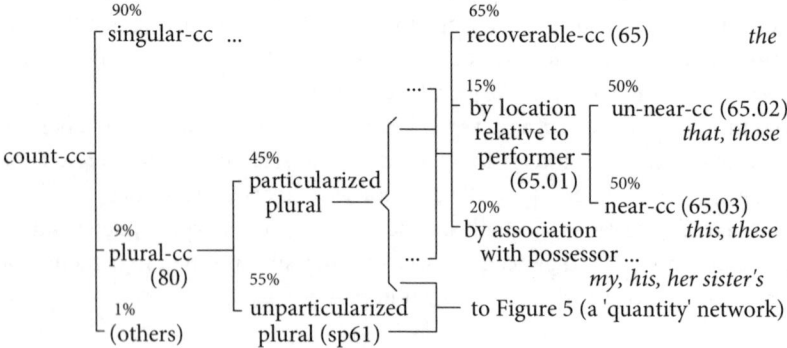

mass-cc ... (to a network partly like that for [plural-cc], but smaller)

Figure 4. Part of the system network for 'particularization'

Here I can illustrate only part of the network entered from [plural-cc]. Notice first that it is this feature from which the 'plural' form of the head is generated, e.g. *castles* or *books* (as shown in Rule 80, which is given below).

The two main systems offer choices between (i) providing 'particularization' and not doing so, and (ii), if 'particularized' is selected, between the three main types of particularization. The sub-network for types of 'possessor' is omitted, but examples of the two main types of structure that it generates are given – *her sister's* being a **genitive cluster**.[16] (The rule 'sp61' will be explained in Section 4.4.7.)

The key concepts are: (i) the system network is traversed from left to right; (ii) a right-opening square bracket is a **system** and it means 'or'; (iii) a right-opening curly bracket means 'and', so that it means that both paths must be followed; and finally (iv)

---

16. The probabilities on the features in the system network are derived from various sources. In this case, those for [singular-cc] v [plural-cc] are derived from Biber et al (1999: 334), and the others are from the Fawcett-Perkins-Day corpus (Day forthcoming). The present figures are those for casual spoken discourse, and where they are different in a different register, the grammar changes the probabilities. The grammar is therefore sensitive to register differences. This important refinement is however omitted here to simplify matters.

a left-opening square bracket means 'or', i.e. it is **a disjunctive entry condition** to the system to the right.

As the simple realization rules below show, 'particularization' is expressed by first locating a **deictic determiner (dd)** at Place 27, and then expounding it by any of the forms specified in Section 4.2.1.

65:       recoverable-cc: dd @ 27, dd < "the".

65.01:   by location relative to performer-cc: dd @ 27.

65.02:   un near-cc:
          if (singular-cc or mass-cc) then dd < "that",
          if plural-cc then dd < "those".

65.03:   near-cc:
          if (singular-cc or mass-cc) then dd < "this",
          if plural-cc then dd < "these".

80:       plural-cc: if not ['irregular noun senses'] then h <+ "+s".[17]

Please look first at Rule 80. It is this rule that would have generated the *s* on *castles* in Figure 2, if it had been required. Notice that BOTH of the features in Figure 4 that are dependent on [plural-cc] go on to Figure 5, which presents choices in 'quantification'. Thus a thing may be 'quantified' both when it is 'particularized' and when it is not. As we shall see, this is a central concept in the way in which 'selection' is modelled in this grammar.

Notice the conditions in Rules 65.02 and 65.03, through which the grammar neatly generates the four items *this, these, that* and *those* from just two rules. It does this by referring to two features that occur elsewhere in the sub-network and that are needed in any case.[18]

Here we have looked at the sub-network for 'plural' things. But what about 'singular' and 'mass' things? Both enter the same sub-network for 'particularization' as 'plural' things – as the conditions in 65.02 and 65.03 show (and as the 'compound' entry to the sub-network also suggests). However, each leads on to very different options in 'quantity' from [plural-cc] – those open to [singular-cc] being very few indeed. Using 'dependence' between systems to organize this part of the grammar keeps the overall structure of the grammar clearer and makes it easier to maintain and extend.[19]

---

17.   The plural forms of 'irregular nouns' such as *man, woman, child* and *species* are generated by a different rule, which consults a table of 'irregular' forms.

18.   I have omitted the details of the network dependent on [by association with possessor] - but, to complete the picture, we should note that it generates EITHER an **item** such as *my, your* etc, OR, after re-entering the network, a **genitive cluster** such as *my brother's* that fills the **dd**.

19.   It also enables the linguist to add to the grammar the useful refinement that the probabilities on more 'delicate' features in the network can be changed by special rules on the less delicate features (as we shall see in Section 4.4.7).

In the next section we shall look at the meanings and forms found in the quantifying determiner.

4.3   Quantification: Meanings realized in the quantifying determiner

The second most frequent type of determiner is the **quantifying determiner**. It is half as frequent as the **dd** but over twenty times more frequent than any other determiner.

The question it answers is 'How many (or much)?' – but this raises the question 'Of what?' At this point I shall provide a temporary answer, which is: 'Of whatever is specified in the part of the ngp that follows it'. (Section 4.4 will give a better answer.) Usually what follows is simply a **head** (possibly preceded by one or more **modifiers**). But it can also be a **dd**, this being followed in turn by a head, as in *five of those books*. Section 4.4 will address the central question of this paper, i.e. how to model examples of this sort.

But first let us look at the forms that a **qd** may take. There is a probability of around 90% that it will be directly **expounded** by an **item**. Here are some typical examples, followed by the semantic features that specify the type of 'quantification':

one, two, three... ninety-nine[20]	[cardinal plural]
some (weak form, so pronounced *s'm*)	[recoverable quantity]
much, many	[approximate quantity]
more, less, fewer	[comparison]
all, most, some (strong form), *few, no*	[proportion]

We come now to the items *a* and *an* – which we shall treat as a single item, represented as *a(n)*. It is the fourth most frequent word in English (figures derived from Sinclair 1991: 143).[21] Almost all other grammars label *a(n)* as the 'indefinite article' and *the* as the 'definite article'. But it is simply not the case that what differentiates *the* and *a(n)* is the presence or absence of the feature 'definiteness' – which is what their traditional labels suggest. Here, drawing on the evidence of (i) the classes of item that *one* and *a(n)* occurs with, (ii) their meanings, (iii) their history, and (iv) their phonology, we treat *the* as a **dd** (as we saw in Section 4.2) and *a(n)* as a **qd**. More precisely:

(i)   the item *the* can precede a 'singular', 'plural' or 'mass' head, but *a(n)*, like the cardinal numeral *one*, can only precede a 'singular' head;

(ii) the meaning of *a(n)* is that it is the 'unmarked' version of 'one', in the sense that it is this meaning that is chosen unless there is good reason to bring out the 'cardinality' of the meaning by using *one*;

---

20. In *IFG*, Halliday and Matthiessen analyze *one* both as a 'Deictic' (2004: 315) and as a 'Numerative' (2004: 318) - without giving any explanation for this. Again, this suggests the need for a revision of the account of this area of the grammar in the Sydney Grammar.

21. Sinclair, working purely at the level of form, counts them separately, so that for him *an* is fifth and *an* is forty-first (with two punctuation marks ahead of it - a comma and a dash).

(iii) this is what we should expect, because *a(n)* is derived historically from *one* (so that the spelling rule for *a* v. *an* should not be that we add 'n' before a vowel, as school-children are usually taught, but that we remove 'n' before a consonant);

(iv) the 'unmarked' status of *a(n)* is reflected in the phonology, in that it is an inherently weak (aka 'unstressed') syllable, while *one* is inherently strong (aka 'stressed').

Compare the meanings and forms of (23), (24) and (25), where [cardinal one] and [unmarked one] are features in the same system – a system that is only open to things that are 'singular'.

(23)   *(I can see)* <u>*one*</u> *ant.*   [cardinal one]
(24)   *(I can see)* <u>*an*</u> *ant.*   [unmarked one]
(25)   *(I can see)* <u>*a*</u> *soldier ant.*   [unmarked one]

In this grammar, therefore (though not in most others), the close semantic, historical and phonological relationships between *a(n)* and *one* are matched by the similarity of their syntax.

In around 10% of cases, however, a **qd** is not directly expounded by an **item**, but is **filled** by a **group**. This may be a **ngp**, as in (26) and (27), or a **quantity group (qtgp)**, as in (28) – or indeed both (a **ngp** within a **qtgp**), as in (29).[22]

(26)   <u>*five hundred*</u> *children*   [cardinal plural]
(27)   <u>*two cups*</u> *of tea*   [measured by unit]
(28)   <u>*very many*</u> *people*   [approximate quantity]
(29)   <u>*roughly two dozen*</u> *youths*   [rough numeral unit, adjusted].[23]

When we were considering 'particularization' in Section 4.3, we moved directly from a summary of the data to the grammar that would generate it. We have now considered the data of 'quantification', so you might now expect an equivalent specification of its generative grammar.

However, you will have to wait for this until Section 4.4.7. The reason is that the way in which the system network for 'quantification' and its realization rules operate presuppose a decision on precisely the question to be addressed in the next section – that of which of three alternative structures for representing examples such as *five of those books* is to be preferred. However, this decision is itself influenced, as we shall shortly see, by the way the grammar works.

---

22. This requires a re-entry to the network to generate the nominal or quantity group that fills the **qd** - and a second re-entry in the case of (29) to generate the embedded **ngp**. For a brief account of the **quantity group** (a vital but overlooked unit in English syntax), see Fawcett (2000: 207–209, 307). For a much fuller description, see Fawcett (forthcoming).

23. For a fuller picture of (i) the rich variety of units that may fill the **qd** and (ii) the semantics and syntax of the quantity group, see Fawcett (forthcoming).

4.4   Selection by quantity from a particularized referent

4.4.1   *The data to be modelled*

We come now to a type of nominal group that has TWO REFERENTS. For reasons that will become clear shortly, we shall call the first (or leftmost) referent in such a ngp the **substantive referent**, and the last (or rightmost) one the **widest referent**.[24]

We shall begin with the **widest referent**. Its two most frequent types are:

1. an unparticularized referent – which, if it is not preceded by a determiner, carries the meaning that the whole class of such objects is the referent (aka 'generic reference'), as (30) below, and
2. a particularized (aka 'definite') referent, as in (31).

> (30)   *books*   [whole class][25]
> (31)   *these books* [particularized]

Now we are ready to look at 'quantity' as a type of 'selection'. For most of Section 4 we shall be concerned with examples that express **selection by quantity** from a **particularized** referent. Our two key examples are (32) and (33) below. Then in Section 4.5 we shall consider examples of 'selection by quantity' from an **unparticularized referent.**

> (32)   *five of those books*   [particularized, quantified]
> (33)   *a large number of those books* [particularized, quantified]

To keep things simple, we shall focus initially on (32). However, since *five* and *a large number* are realizations of two meanings with a fairly close systemic relationship (i.e. both state the 'number' of a plural 'referent'), we shall assume that the overall structure that we establish for (32) must also be appropriate for (33) – even though in (33) the quantifying expression introduces a new **unit** (i.e. the ngp *a large number*), rather than being a single **item** (*five*).

If we were to look only at (33), we might be tempted to formulate the problem – as many linguists have in the past – like this:

'What is the most appropriate way to relate the two ngps of *a large number* and *those books* syntactically – while also finding some existing syntactic category in which to place *of*?'

But to ask this question is to foreground the patterns at the level of **form**. A more insightful question to ask is:

---

24. The reason not to refer to the 'last referent' as the 'second referent' is that in Section 5 we shall go on to consider cases that have three or even more referents.

25. The feature 'whole class' is one of the 'others' in Figure 4.

'How should we relate a quantifying expression such as *a large number, very many, five* and so on to what follows it (e.g. *those books*) – while also identifying the semantic and syntactic functions of *of*?'

4.4.2   *The semantics of 'selection by quantity' from a 'particularized' referent*

Here is my answer to the second question – which also, incidentally, answers the first. I suggest that the key concept in understanding the meaning of examples such as *five of those books* is that of 'selection' – in the sense that one referent is being 'selected' from 'within' (in a broad sense of that term) another referent. In the present example we have a case of 'selection by quantity', but there are other types, as Section 5 will show.

The concept of 'selection' appears at every level of representation. It is present in the **systemic functional logical form** that represents the **input** to the lexicogrammar (which we will omit here to keep things simple); it is then reflected in the system networks at the level of **semantics** (as we shall see in Section 4.4.7); and finally it is realized in the **syntax** through which such meanings are realized. Here, then, we are describing the **semantics** of **selection**.

In a wording that keeps close to the items at the level of form, we might say that, in *five of those books, five* is selected from *those books*. But it would in fact be more accurate to say that the **referent** of *five of those books* is selected from the **referent** of *those books*. In what follows, however, I shall for brevity sometimes write as if an expression such as *five* – and so *a large number* – had a referent.

4.4.3   *Three alternative structures for representing 'selection'*

How is the **meaning** of 'selection' itself realized at the level of **form**? Clearly, this is the role of the item *of*. That is the easy part of the answer; the harder task is to identify the **structure** that most appropriately represents the relationships between *of* and its neighbouring elements.

Let's consider the alternative structures for (32) above – and so for (33) above. In broad terms, there are three: in Option A *of* and *those books* form a unit; in Option B *five* and *of* do; and in Option C *of* is a sister element to both *five* and *those books*.

We shall find that the reasoning in the three next sub-sections relates – as statements about syntax naturally do in a functional grammar – to the meaning, and so to whatever rules relate meaning to form. And our experience of seeing the grammar at work in Sections 3.4 and 4.2.2 has prepared us for this. Thus, we have already seen (i) how the grammar inserts a **unit** (here a **ngp**) into the structure (e.g. to fill an element of a clause such as a **Complement**), then (ii) how it gives the unit the **elements** that are required by the meanings that are to be communicated, and finally (iii) how it expounds an element by an **item**. And we have also noted one case in which (iv) a realization rule instructs the grammar to **re-enter** the network and to choose certain options, in order to generate a new **unit** that will **fill** an **element** of the one currently being generated. This was in Section 4.2.1, where we noted that a **dd** is sometimes filled by a unit (here termed the **genitive cluster**) with its own internal structure, as in *her sister's partner.*[26]

4.4.4   *Problems with Option A: the 'prepositional group as qualifier' construction*

The structure favoured by the general consensus in published grammars is that of **Option A**. This is the 'prepositional group as qualifier' construction that we first met in Figure 3. There, however, it was being used as the realization of two very different semantic relationships, neither of which resembles 'selection'. To see what Option A would look like if it was used to represent the relationship of 'selection' between a 'quantity' and the 'particularized' referent in the ngp, please inspect the two examples in Figure 5.

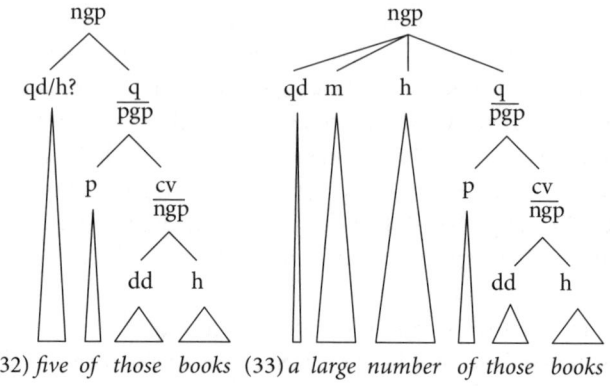

(32) *five of those books* (33) *a large number of those books*

Figure 5. Option A: The use of the 'prepositional group as qualifier' construction to represent 'selection'

There are at least the following four problems with this approach. While I shall describe them in SFL terms, there would be equivalent problems in any functionally-oriented model of language – though they would naturally be expressed in a different vocabulary.

1.   The first problem is that, while (33) appears to match the pattern found in Figure 3 quite well, (32) does not. The question is 'Is *five* in (32) functioning as a **head** – perhaps on the generally assumed (but unexplained) grounds that a ngp has to have a head – or does *five* directly expound a quantifying determiner – as most linguists would agree that it does in *five books*?' With Option A, then, we have to choose between (i) maintaining the general rule that a ngp always has a head and (ii) having a rule which states that *five* expounds the **qd**. The grammar cannot have both. This is a small but significant problem, then, for the many linguists who be-

---

26.   See Appendix A of Fawcett (2000) for a slightly fuller explanation of how a SFG works, and Fawcett, Tucker and Lin (1993) for a much fuller one.

lieve that every ngp must have a head. (In the grammar for 'quantity' to be presented in Section 4.4.7, the simple rule for generating *five* covers (32).)[27]

2. The most serious disadvantage of Option A is that *books*, i.e. the **noun** which states the 'cultural classification' of the referent of the **matrix ngp** (or 'mother' ngp), would in this analysis be buried TWO LAYERS BELOW the matrix ngp. Yet it normally functions as its **head** – and, as we shall see, for good reasons. But if its location in the structure were to be as in Figure 5, the grammar would need to have one rule for placing *books* in the structure when it was generating *those books* (when it would be the head of the matrix ngp) and another rule when generating *five of those books* or *a large number of those books* (when it would be the head of a ngp two layers below). And, as if that were not bad enough, there would need to be yet another rule for each of the eight further cases (all types of 'selection', I suggest) that we shall meet in Section 5, since each would similarly be modelled by a ngp in a pgp that functioned as qualifier to the head on its left. Option A therefore misses a very important generalization. The ideal, of course, is to have one rule that covers all cases, whether there is 'selection' or not – so long as this doesn't cause other problems. The present grammar has such a rule.

3. The second very serious problem is also caused by the location of the noun in a ngp two layers below the matrix ngp. In this case what matters is that it expresses the widest referent's 'number' – i.e. whether it is 'mass', 'singular' or 'plural'. The reason for the problem is that the grammar contains three very different 'quantity' networks: one for each of 'singular', 'plural' and 'mass' things (with the 'plural' network being by far the largest). So the question is: 'How is the grammar to know that it must enter the 'plural' sub-network for 'quantity', to generate *five* and other 'plural' expressions to expound the **qd** of the matrix ngp?' The difficulty is that, at the point when it should be entering the network, it wouldn't know what the semantic features that specify the embedded head will be – and so whether or not 'plural' should be chosen (since 'number' depends on the 'cultural classification'). This situation arises because units in the LOWER layers of a structure are generated later than those ABOVE them. In other words, the features associated with the embedded ngp *those books* in (32) wouldn't be known at the point in the generation process at which they would be needed to guide choices in 'quantity' – because that part of the grammar wouldn't yet have done its work.[28] What we need, therefore, is a grammar

---

27. Notice that the supposed similarity between (33) and the examples in Figure 3 depends crucially on agreeing that the little word *of* always functions as a preposition. Indeed, Sinclair suggests (1991: 83) that "it may ultimately be considered distracting to regard *of* as a preposition at all". As will be clear, my position on this matter is (as it has been since Fawcett 1974–1976/1981) that I accept that the 'prepositional group as qualifier' construction is appropriate for SOME uses of *of*, including the two uses in the examples in Figure 3 – but NOT for modelling the syntax of 'selection'.

28. It is a basic principle of this grammar (and almost all that I know of) that the planning - and so the generation - of a text-sentence begins with larger units and works its way down to the more detailed decisions. This is generally thought to correspond roughly to how we plan text-

which FIRST selects the features associated with the head (e.g. its 'cultural classification' as 'book' and its 'number' as 'plural'), and that ONLY THEN chooses in the appropriate type of 'quantity' sub-network.[29] To summarize: if the particular sub-network for 'quantity' from which *five* and *a large number* are generated is to be entered, the grammar must have first selected the feature 'plural' – either earlier in the traversal of the network or while generating a higher unit. The need to provide for this gives us a third reason to reject Option A in favour of B or C.

4.   A fourth reason to reject Option A is the following. The grammar operates most economically IF IT INTRODUCES THE ITEM *of* BY THE SAME RULE AS THE QUANTIFYING EXPRESSION. In other words, one rule should generate both the **qd** and, when *of* is required (as it typically is), the element that *of* expounds. (This is achieved here in Rule 61.02, as we shall see in Section 4.4.7.) But this requires the two elements to be sister elements of the same unit, as in Option C.

In summary, we can say that, while Option A will feel familiar to most readers because of its wide use in most theories, it has two major disadvantages and two lesser ones. And it also suffers from a fifth problem, as we shall see when we consider Option B.

4.4.5   *Problems with Option B: the structural inverse of Option A*

We have now seen four good reasons for rejecting Option A. So should we use **Option B** instead? Structurally, it is the mirror image of Option A, so we might at first expect it to have similar shortcomings.

As Figure 6 shows, it involves attaching *of* to the preceding ngp as a 'postposition' – like *ago* in *many years ago*. One minor problem is that there is no obvious name for the element labelled '?' in both examples.

While Option B may strike us as a bit of an oddity, we should nonetheless give it a fair assessment. For a start, it has the considerable advantage over Option A that the noun expressing the 'cultural classification' would in this case be the head of the matrix

---

sentences. Alternatives have been proposed, of course - principally 'dynamic', 'left-right' generation (to borrow the terminology of computational linguistics) - but I know of no evidence which shows that an overall 'top-down, left-right' model is misguided. Indeed, it too can function 'dynamically', in the sense that, in mid-generation, it can be sensitive to earlier decisions. After three decades of work on modelling the generation of text-sentences and considering alternative models, this still feels the most insightful overall model - which is itself a kind of evidence!

29.   There are two main ways in which the grammar can control entry to a sub-network. The first is to ensure that the sub-network is entered from the key feature, which in this case is [plural-cc] - or alternatively from a feature that is itself dependent on it. (As you will see in Section 4.4.7, this is the solution in the present case, the reason being that it enables the grammar to capture far more generalizations than would otherwise be possible - as described in the first objection to Option A). The second way to control entry to a sub-network is to locate the **unit** in which the choices in the sub-network will be realized AT A LOWER LAYER IN THE STRUCTURE, and a realization rule on the key feature ensures that the right sub-network is entered on re-entry to the network to generate the lower unit.

ngp – so that the two most serious problems with Option A would not apply to it. In this model, it is the ngps containing *five* and *a large number* that are buried two layers down. And this rearrangement of the layers of structure at which the units occur suits the direction of the dependencies between features that were serious problems for Option A – because the features realized in *books* would be generated well in advance of the rules that generate *five* and *a large number* – rather too well in advance, in fact. This is because dependencies between the semantic features of units AT DIFFERENT LAYERS OF THE STRUCTURE always make the grammar more complex – and in this case they would be TWO layers apart. But option B is at least implementable.

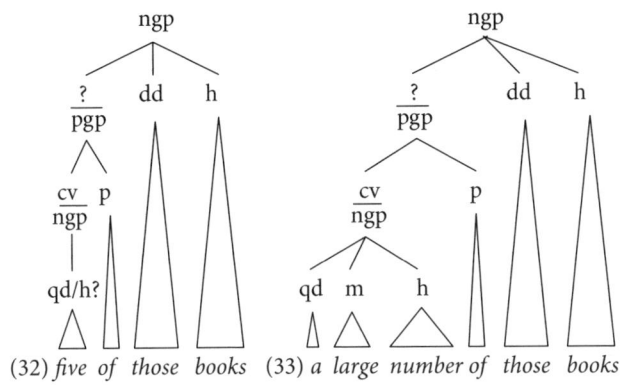

Key (new elements): ? = new name for element required
pgp = pre-/post-positional group p = pre-/post-position

Figure 6. Option B: The use of a pre-head 'postpositional group' construction to represent 'selection'

However, there are still two problems with Option B. The first is rather like the fourth problem with Option A. It is that, in examples such as the short version of B's reply in (34), the grammar needs to be able to generate the item *five* – but WITHOUT ALSO GENERATING *of*. And this suggests that *of* should not be in a postpositional group with *five*, but should instead function as an element of the matrix ngp – as does *them* in (34).

(34)   A: *How many of these apples* would you like?
       B: *I'd like five (of them).*

Option B's second disadvantage is the general reason that it requires TWO MORE LAYERS OF STRUCTURE than Option C – a disadvantage that also applies to Option A. The relevant principle is that additional structure that is not justified by the requirements of the grammar should be avoided. And there are no such requirements in the present case. So, while it would be POSSIBLE to implement Option B in the generative version of the grammar, there would be a cost in additional complexity over Option C – and for no clear purpose.

4.4.6   *Option C: a more elegant solution*

Option C brings the enormous advantage that NEITHER *those books* NOR *five* is buried.

In this option the meaning of 'cultural classification' is always expressed in the head of the matrix ngp, and the 'relating' element *of* is treated as AN ELEMENT OF THE SAME UNIT AS THE TWO ELEMENTS THAT IT RELATES – the **qd** and the **dd** – so neatly meeting all the requirements that have emerged in the discussions of Options A and B.[30]

The structure used in the Cardiff Grammar is therefore that shown in Figure 7. Moreover, this structure functions equally neatly for ALL examples of selection between a **qd** and a **dd** – so, for example, for (33) as well as (32). For obvious reasons, we call the element expounded by *of* the **selector (v)**.[31]

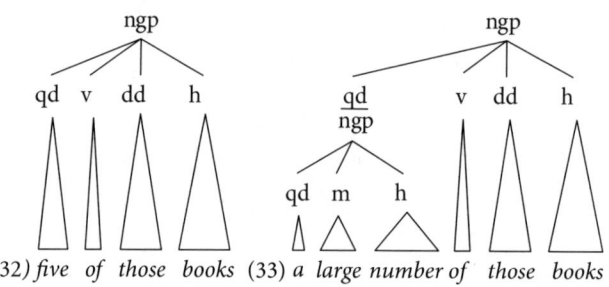

(32) *five of those books*   (33) *a large number of   those books*

Figure 7. Optionc C: The structure of two nominal groups with 'selection'

Generating *a large number* does of course add an extra layer to the structure – as it would in any model, since it is a full nominal group.[32]

In this grammar, then, the structure shown in Figure 7 is not just a structure that is used when the **qd** is filled by a ngp (which appears to be Matthiessen's position (1995: 655)), but a structure that is capable of handling ALL cases of quantification. It is this structure that enables the grammar to handle the many examples where *of* occurs

---

30. In this respect it plays a role with similarities to that of a 'relational' Process such as 'being' and 'having' in the clause. Compare the interesting analysis in Prakasam (1996: 57–58) of a subset of ngps in which *of* is analyzed, as a lexical verb would be, as the element 'Process'.

31. However, the reason for using 'v' to represent the selector in a diagram may be less obvious. Why not use 's'? The answer is that (i) a capital 'S' is already in use for the Subject and (ii) there is another group element whose name begins with 's' (the **scope** in a **quality group**). So here we use 'v' - because it represents the minimal phonetic representation of *of*.

32. The potential semantic - and so syntactic - complexity within it is enormous; consider for example *a small number, a pretty big number, a greater number (of books) than I have ever seen in one room*, etc.

between the **qd** and the **head**, even when it is NOT filled by a ngp – as in the cases of *plenty of books* and in all of the relatively frequent cases like *five of them, two of us*, and so on. And, as we shall see in Section 5, it handles various other types of selection equally neatly.

Now that we have a structure in which the **qd** and the **dd** occur in the same ngp, we can introduce the terms 'substantive referent' and 'widest referent' in their natural context. The referent of the first (or leftmost) determiner is the **substantive referent**. Often it is literally 'substantive' – e.g. if you say to a greengrocer *I'd like a kilo of those potatoes*, what you will get is not 'those potatoes' (i.e. all of them), but just 'one kilo' of them. And the referent of the last (or rightmost) referent (excluding referents embedded in qualifiers) is termed the **widest referent**, because it is the most comprehensive one. In a simple example such as *these books*, then, the widest referent is also the substantive referent. (See Section 4.5 for the reason why this is not the case with *five books*.)

Finally, note that there are THREE major ways in which a **particularized** widest referent is manifested in a ngp with 'selection'. Consider (35) to (37):

(35)   *I'll take five of those bananas.*   [cultural classification]
(36)   *I'll take five of them.*   [token cultural classification]
(37)   *I'll take five.*   [token cultural classification unrealized]

In each the **qd** is expounded by *five*, and so in each it is the same rule that generates *five*. Thus (37) has no head and no selector.

To enable you to check that these claims actually work, I must now provide the essentials of the grammar for 'quantification'.

4.4.7   *The semantics and realization rules for 'selection by quantity'*

Please now inspect the system network and its associated realization rules for yourself. If you wish, you can combine them with those in Sections 3.4 and 4.2.2 to generate various ngps with a full **qd v dd h** structure.

The network in Figure 8 has a similar overall organization to that in Figure 4, and the realization rules apply in a similar way. The unlabelled network entered from [particularized plural] is simply a reminder of the sub-network for types of 'particularization' that we met in Figure 4 – and most of the rest of Figure 8 is an indication of the very large sub-network for meanings of 'quantity' to which Figure 4 leads.

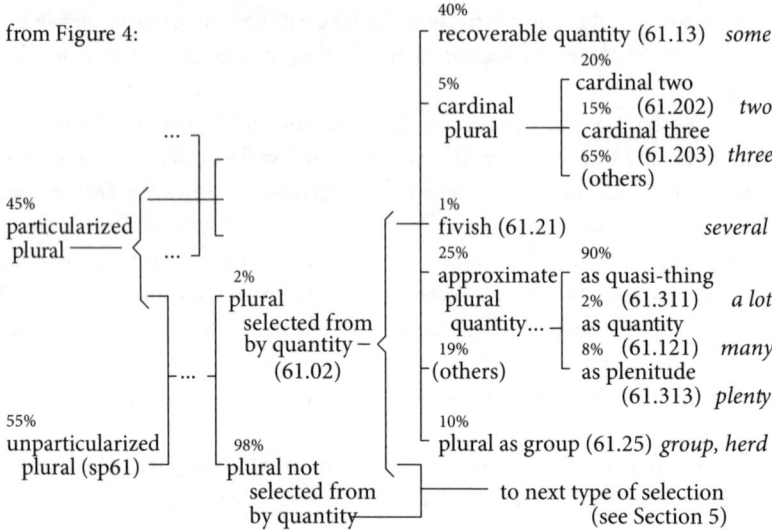

sp61 : unparticularized plural :
   for same pass prefer [plural selected from by quantity].

Figure 8. Part of the system network for 'quantification'

The realization rules are:

61.02: plural selected from by quantity:
   qd @ 15,
   if particularized plural then (qv @ 16, qv < "of"),
   if (unparticularized plural and
      (as quasi thing or plenitude or plural as group etc))
   then (qv @ 16, qv < "of").

61.13: recoverable quantity: qd < "some".

61.202: cardinal two: qd < "two".

61.203: cardinal three: qd < "three".

61.21: fivish: qd < "several".

61.311: as quasi thing: qd < "a lot".

61.312: as quantity: qd < "many".

61.313: as plenitude: qd < "plenty".

61.45: plural as group:
   for qd prefer [features leading to 'group' / 'crowd' / 'herd' etc],
   for qd re-enter @ entity.

The key system is the choice between [plural selected from by quantity] and [plural not selected from by quantity]. If [plural selected from by quantity] is chosen, Rule 61 inserts a **quantifying determiner (qd)** into the nominal group at Place 16 – and, if certain other features are chosen, it will also insert the associated **quantifying selector (qv)** at Place 16. More specifically, it states that if [particularized plural] has also been selected, ALL types of quantification require the selector *of*, but if [unparticularized plural] has been chosen, it is only required when one of quite a large sub-set of quantifying expressions is used. These include certain frequent expressions of 'approximate plural quantity', including from Figure 8: (i) [as quasi thing], which is realized as *a lot (of)*; and (ii) [as plenitude] which generates *plenty (of)*.[33] Figure 8 also includes (iii) [plural as group], which, after re-entry to the network via Rule 61.45, generates embedded nominal groups such as *a group (of), a very large crowd (of), a small herd (of)* – and all other 'collective' nouns.[34] Other features omitted here include those from which lots (of), *tons (of), dozens (of), two kilos (of)* etc are generated. All of these require the selector *of*, EVEN WHEN THERE IS NO **dd**. Many other features, however, do not – including those in Figure 8 that generate *some, two, three, several* and *many*. The situation is complicated, and Rule 61 provides neatly for both cases, i.e. those where 'selection' is realized by *of* and those where it is not.

The next point illustrates one of the ways in which probabilities are modelled in this grammar. Notice that the two entry conditions to Figure 8 are the two central features from Figure 4. So, irrespective of whether the 'thing' was 'particularized' in that prior system, it enters the system for 'selection by quantity' (or 'quantification'). Some systemic linguists may be inclined to protest at this layout, suggesting that the two systems for 'particularization' and 'quantification' should be entered simultaneously, both from the feature [plural-cc]. But such a grammar would be unable to express the probabilities that this grammar seeks to model.

The reason for showing the relationship as we do (i.e. as **dependence** rather than **simultaneity**) is as follows. The probabilities in the system for 'particularization' (in Figure 4) are fairly evenly weighted. So, if [particularized plural] is selected (so generating a **dd** such as *the*), there should be only a relatively low probability of generating another determiner – SINCE MOST NGPS HAVE ONLY ONE DETERMINER. This is why the probability on [plural selected from by quantity] is set at 2%. Thus, while the network is able to generate examples on the pattern of *five of those books* – it does so with only 2% of **dds**.

But what happens if [unparticularized plural] is chosen instead? Then a 'same pass' rule (sp61) is immediately activated. Note that this is quite different from a realization rule. Its effect, as you can see from the **sp rule** immediately below the network, is to

---

33.   These features are entered from [approximate large quantity], which is a feature in the system dependent on [approximate plural quantity] and is omitted here to save space.

34.   Our earlier example of *a large number (of)* is another realization of [approximate plural quantity] - one that is realized through re-entry to the network to generate a ngp.

change the probabilities in the system for 'quantification' – and rather drastically. It changes the probability on [plural selected from by quantity] from 2% to 100%, so ensuring that a **qd** will be generated. In this way the rule neatly ensures that the nominal group will have either a **qd** or a **dd** – or, occasionally, both.[35]

'Selection by quantity' is a complex part of the language, as we have now seen, so it is unsurprising that it has an equivalently complex grammar.

4.5   Corollary: selection by quantity from an unparticularized referent

We have now established the pattern for 'selection by quantity' from a 'particularized' referent. But what is the semantics of examples such as those in (38) and (39), in which the referent is NOT 'particularized'?

(38) *five books / five thousand books*
(39) *many books / several books*
(40) *five of those books* (originally introduced as (32))

The answer, as you may have realized, is that the relationship between *five* and *books* in (38) is essentially the same as that between *five* and *those books* in (40). The only difference between them is that the referent of *those books* in (40) is a **particularized** set of 'books' (which could instead have been referred to by *they*) while *books* in (38), in 'unparticularized'. Thus the last section has already provided the grammar that generates examples such as *five books*. And it follows from this that *one book* – and so also *a book* – has the same syntax as (38), i.e. **qd h**.

In all these cases 'selection' occurs without being made overt in the word *of*. But there are many types of 'selection' with which *of* is obligatory. Interestingly, several have a semantically similar form that does not use *of*, so that the two semantic features occur in the same system or sub-network. As (41) shows, *of* is required with *plenty* but not with *many*, and (42) to (44) illustrate similar pairs with meanings that are closely related semantically – and so systemically – but which differ with respect to the presence or absence of *of*.

(41) *many books / plenty of books*
(42) *much grass / lots of grass*
(43) *several thousand books / several thousands of books*
(44) *all those children / all of those children*

The difference that is common to all of (41) to (44) is that in the first of each pair of examples the relationship of 'selection' is **covert**, while in the second it is **overt**.

---

35.   If what was wanted had been *books*, this would be have generated from the feature [whole class]. This is an option among the 'others' in Figure 4, and the series of systems we are considering here would not have been entered.

These close semantic similarities suggest that in all of the above examples – so irrespective of whether 'selection' is realized by *of* – the grammar should (i) treat the word expressing the cultural classification as the **head** of the matrix ngp, and (ii) treat the quantifying expression and the optional selector as sister elements to it – so as **qd** and **v**, as in Figure 7.

As will now be clear, any other decision would add a great deal of unnecessary complexity to the realization rules that convert the features in the system network into structures at the level of form. So such examples are powerful evidence that Option C is the most appropriate of the three syntax models considered in Section 4.4.

4.6   Summary so far

The reasoning presented here has been in terms of SFL, but the same principles are likely to apply to any grammar that takes seriously its responsibility to provide an account of language at the two levels of **meaning** and **form**.

The advantages if using Option C rather than either Options A or B to represent the syntax of examples such as *five of those books* will now be clear.

In this approach to the structure of the English ngp, then:

1. the noun that expresses both the 'cultural classification' and the 'number' of the widest referent always expounds the head of the matrix nominal group (and so is never buried inside a 'prepositional group as qualifier' structure);
2. the deictic determiner that realizes the various meanings of 'particularization' is similarly always an element of the matrix ngp (and so never buried in a qualifier);
3. the quantifying determiner that realizes a wide range of meanings of 'selection by quantity' is also always a direct element of the matrix ngp (and so is not forced to function as a head); and – coming now to the part of the structure that is furthest from the approach found in traditional grammars -
4. the selector *of* is a direct element of the matrix ngp.

As Sections 4.4 and 4.5 have shown, this structure – and so the concept of 'selection' that it realizes – expresses clearly both the similarities and the differences between *those books*, *five books* and *five of those books,* and the similarities and differences between *five books* and *a large number of books* – and so on. And capturing generalizations such as these should gladden the heart of any functional linguist!

5.   The other determiners

5.1   Selection by 'superlative'

We shall now make a quick tour of the other relationships of 'selection' that are recognized in the Cardiff Grammar. There is no space, sadly, to do more than hint occasionally at the reasons for adopting this description.

As a way in, consider the relationship between the familiar example in (45) and the more complex structure in (46):

(45)   *five of those books*
(46)   *five of the most interesting of those books*

Our now well-established analysis of (45) was given in Figure 7 – and I introduce here an equivalent LINEAR REPRESENTATION that is more economical with space:

(47)   ngp: *five* [qd] *of* [v] *those* [dd] *books* [h]

But how should we analyze (46) above? The two instances of *of* suggest that the referent of *five* is selected from the referent of *the most interesting (ones)*, and that this is in turn selected from the referent of *those books*. So we have here a second type of selection – and the analysis is as in Figure 9.

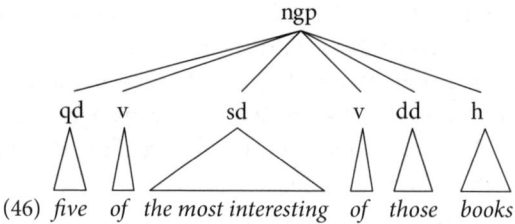

Figure 9. The structure of a nominal group with two types of 'selection'

Thus the **superlative determiner (sd)** occurs BETWEEN the **qd** (if there is one) and the **dd** (if there is one) – with the **sd** being filled by a **quality group** (Tucker 1998, Fawcett 2000: 206–7, 307).[36] And, to be consistent – and so to keep the realization rules simple

---

36.   This is a special type of qlgp that has, in addition to an **apex, degree temperer, finisher** etc, a **quality group deictic (qld)**. This use of *the* must therefore be distinguished from *the* as a **dd** in text analysis (which usually isn't difficult). When *the* functions as a **qld**, it can sometimes be replaced by a possessive expression, but *this, that, these* and *those* sound very odd indeed.

– the structure that realizes *the most interesting books* must be as in (48) – again, with a quality group filling the **sd**.[37]

(48)   ngp: *the most interesting* [sd] *books* [h]

The SEQUENCE of the three determiners in relation to each other is fixed as **qd (v) sd (v) dd (m) h**. The model therefore predicts that these elements will always occur in this sequence.

5.2   Two apparent counter-examples that are not: Selection by 'totality'

I shall now briefly explain how two apparent counter-examples are to be analyzed. Each uses words that typically occur as a **qd** – but here they serve a different function.

We have seen that the sequence among the determiners introduced so far is **qd v sd v dd h**. The first apparent counter-example is the occurrence AFTER the **dd** of words such as *few, many* and cardinal numerals, as in *her <u>five</u> grandchildren*. You might be tempted to analyze this as **dd qd h**. But now consider (49):

(49)   *One of her <u>five</u> grandchildren (is here).*

In (49), the **qd** *one* is the **substantive referent** (as the verb *is* shows). So what is *five*? It is a **quantifying modifier (qtm)**. This relatively infrequent modifier, like *elderly* in *her elderly father*, almost always serves the **depicting** function (for which see Section 3.3).[38]

Example (50) illustrates a second apparent counter-example. Here *all*, which is typically a **qd** and so typically precedes the **sd** (as we saw in Section 5.1), occurs AFTER it.

(50)   *one of the most generous of <u>all</u> (of) his benefactors*

As in (49), *one* is the **qd**. The function of *all* is not to 'select by quantity', but to emphasize that what follows refers to the 'full total' of the referent. This is the **totalizing determiner (tod)**, and it can only be expounded by *all*. Now compare (50) with the apparently related (51):

(51)   *all (of) his benefactors*

The test to discover whether *all* is a **tod** or a **qd** is to try replacing it by *some* or *most*. In (50) it cannot be replaced, but in (51) it can – so proving that in (51) *all* is a **qd**.

5.3   Selection by 'fraction'

We come next to the **fractionative determiner (fd)**. This answers the question 'What fraction of it (or them)?' about whatever is specified to the right of it. It is often ex-

---

37.   Thus (48) is not, as you might at first think, similar in structure to *these very interesting books* - the latter being simply ngp: *these* [dd] *very interesting* [m] *books* [h].

38.   It is this relatively infrequent element (rather than the **qd**) that appears to correspond, positionally, to the 'Numerative' in *IFG*.

pounded directly by *half*, but it may also be filled by a **ngp**, such as *three fifths, three in / out of (every) five* and *sixty per cent*. It is rare for it to co-occur with 'quantification'. Its place in the sequence of determiners is shown in (52):

(52)   *a third* [fd] *of* [v] *his set* [qd] *of* [v] *the best* [sd] *of* [v] *the* [dd] *prints* [h]

5.4   Selection by 'order'

The **ordinative determiner (od)** answers the question 'Which thing is being uniquely identified in terms of its position in a sequence?' Like the superlative determiner (with which it rarely occurs, since both identify 'uniquely') it is filled by a **quality group**. Its typical position among the determiners is shown in (53):

(53)   *one* [qd] *of* [v] *the first* [od] *of* [v] *the fastest* [sd] *of* [v] *the* [dd] *runners* [h]

5.5   Selection by 'part'

The **partitive determiner (pd)** answers the question 'What part or parts of it (or them)?' A **pd** is invariably filled by a **ngp** whose **head** denotes a part of something, e.g. *the back* of a the house, *the head* of the valley, *the head* / *president* of the company, *the peaks* of the mountains, the *centre* of the city (as in Figure 3). The place in sequence of the **pd** is shown in (54):

(54)   *the porches* [pd] *of* [v] *ninety per cent* [fd] *of* [v] *those* [dd] *houses* [h]

5.6   Selection by 'qualification'

The eighth determiner is the **qualifier-introducing determiner (qid)**. It is the least frequent of all, and seems always to be expounded by *those*, as in (55). Its sole function is to signal that the **cultural classification** in the head is about to be **sub-classified** by additional information in a **qualifier**. As (55) shows, it can co-occur with a **dd**, so showing that it is a different element. The test to discover whether *those* is a **tod** or a **dd** is to try replacing it by *these* – and if it cannot be replaced it is a **tod**.

(55)   *those* [qid] *of* [v] *her* [dd] *family* [h] *who are mentioned in her will* [q]

5.7   Selection by 'representation'

Semantically, the **representational determiner (rd)** is unlike any determiner that we have met so far, in that 'selection by representation' does NOT identify a referent that is A SUB-SET OR A PART of what follows it. It is not 'selection' as an 'extraction' of the referent from a wider referent, but an 'abstraction' of it – in this case by 'representation'. And yet it functions in the grammar of English as if it was a type of 'selection'.

The test for it is that it answers 'Yes' to the question 'Is this a representation of the referent of the following part of the ngp?' It is filled by a **ngp** whose head may express a **physical** representation, as in *a map* of the world, *a recording* of her voice and (56) below, or a **mental** representation, as in *the concept* of liberty or *an example* of this construction.

(56)   *(This is) a photo* [rd] *of* [v] *the back* [pd] *of* [v] *our* [dd] *house* [h]

One indication that *house* is the head of the full ngp in (56) is the fact that the 'representation' may be merely **covert**. Thus you can show someone a photo and say *This is the back of our house.*[39]

The **rd** precedes all the determiners considered already. This means that if one of them APPEARS to occur before the **rd**, it is in fact **embedded** in it (as described in Section 5.9).

5.8   Selection by 'typicity'

The **typic determiner (td)** has much in common with the **rd**. It answers the question: 'What type or types of thing?'. Typical examples of 'typic ngps' are shown in the underlined portions of (57) and (58):

(57)   *Scientists have discovered two new types of ant(s).*
(58)   *This is a different brand of oil.*

Interestingly, different dialects of English represent the head differently, with some of them copying the plurality of the head of the ngp that fills the **td** onto the head of the matrix ngp, as in (57). With 'typicity', the choice between its being 'overt' or 'covert' is built into the grammar, as (59) and (60) suggest:

(59)   *Scientists have discovered two new ants.*
(60)   *This is a different oil.*

In (60) the concept of 'typicity' is explicitly marked by the treatment of *oil* (a 'mass' thing) as 'singular' – as shown by the item *a*. But in (59) the 'typicity' isn't expressed, so (59) is, in principle, ambiguous.[40]

The **td** is like the **rd** in never being preceded by a selector. So what is the structure of examples such as (61)? See Section 5.9 for the answer.

(61)   *This is one of the first of the new varieties of GM wheat.*

---

39. This option is one of the earliest that we teach our children, i.e. when looking at a picture book with a year-old child we say *What's this? It's a cow*, and so on - not *It's a picture of a cow.*

40. Two other common typic nouns are *sort* and *kind* - but about half of the occurrences of *kind of* and *sort of* are what Biber et al term 'vagueness markers' (1999: 257).

5.9   Sequence, embedding and discontinuity within the determiners

It is rare for more than three determiners to occur as elements of the same ngp, but when they do they occur in the following sequence (with only occasional minor variations):

td/rd v pd v fd v qd v od v sd v tod v qid v dd.... h [41]

However, there are two complications to this relatively simple picture.

The first arises because many of the determiners are filled – either always or sometimes – by a ngp. So this question arises: 'Can an embedded ngp, such as those found in the **td**, the **rd**, the **pd**, and the **qd**, contain a further embedded ngp?' The answer is that they can – and they quite frequently do.

Consider the underlined portions of the following two examples, each of which contains a **rd** and a **qd** that is filled by a ngp:

(62)   A: *What I liked best was <u>that simple picture</u> of <u>a bowl</u> of fruit.*
(63)   B: *Which one? – There are <u>several roomfuls</u> of <u>pictures</u> of fruit!*

Since the **rd** and **qd** in (62) are already in the predicted sequence, there is no problem. But in (63) they are not. The present model can nonetheless handle this, however, because it allows embedding where this is justified by the nature of the relationships – as in Figure 10.

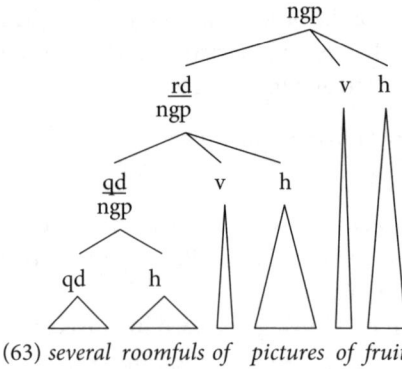

(63) *several roomfuls of   pictures of fruit*

Figure 10. Embedding within the representational determiner

Here, the matrix ngp tells us that the two primary referents are 'fruit' (the 'cultural classification') and 'pictures (of the fruit)'. But because 'pictures' is 'quantifiable', we can say 'how many' pictures are involved. And one way of measuring the 'quantity' of the pictures is in terms of the number of 'roomfuls' of them. Hence the structure in Figure 10.

---

41. There is a need for more work, perhaps using very large corpora, to check on the sequence suggested here.

Finally, the linear representations of (61) (from Section 5.8) are:

(64)   matrix ngp: *one of the first of the new varieties* [td] *of* [v] GM *wheat* [h]

(65)   ngp at **td**: *one* [qd] *of* [v] *the first* [od] *of* [v] *the* dd] *new* [m] *varieties* [h]

Now for the second complication. Consider the underlined portion of (66):

(66)   *The picture of the fruit <u>that I like best</u> is this one.*

The words *that I like best* are clearly functioning as a qualifier – but does it describe 'the picture' or 'the fruit'? It could be either – so the syntax must allow for the qualifier to be a sister element to either *picture* or *fruit*. And in the former case the ngp *the picture.... that I like best* is **discontinuous**. In a full representation of such examples, therefore, the line joining the qualifier to the rest of its ngp crosses the triangles symbolizing 'exponence' above *of, the* and *fruit*.

That concludes our whirlwind tour of the 'other determiners' – 'other' that is, than the **dd** and **qd** – and our introduction to the use of the concept of 'selection' in modelling the relationships between their referents.

6.   Conclusions

6.1   Criteria for determining structure

The description of the English ngp on which this paper draws were originally prepared as part of the 'guidelines' for use by members of my research team on a large text analysis project (Fawcett and Perkins 1980a-d, 1981), and parts of it have appeared in Fawcett (1974–1976/1981, 1980, 2000). But here, for the first time, I have given the reasons why we who work in the framework of the Cardiff Grammar use this model of the English nominal group.

In Section 4.4 we considered carefully the three main possible structures for *five of those books*, and we saw how a fully explicit – so generative – SFG that uses the structure that we labelled Option C works. Crucially, this demonstrated the interdependence of the structure itself with the way that the realization rules operate – and I suggested that the recognition of this principle is relevant to the evaluation of alternative structures in any functional model of language. It might be going too far to say that the ONLY criterion for deciding between alternative structures should be how elegantly the structures, the semantic features and the realization rules operate with each other – but it is only a little too far! Another criterion that we might invoke, at least in general 'hunch' terms, is how transparently the structure at the level of **form** reflects our perception of the logical structure of the **input**, when generating text-sentences. But this 'transparency' criterion should be seen as part of the general criterion of elegance (so economy and clarity) in the operation of the overall model. This consists essentially of (i) the input in terms of a logical representation, (ii) the mechanisms by which this determines which semantic features get selected (both bring omitted here for reasons of space), (iii) the semantics, (iv) the realization rules, and (v) the structures and items of the output. Indeed, we should expect the operation of every part of the model of language to depend on – and to affect – every other part. *Tout se tient*, as Meillet (1937) has nicely expressed it.[42]

The next section summarizes the set of concepts that are required to realize the concept of 'selection'.

6.2   A summary of the 'selection principle'

The set of concepts that underlie the description of the ten determiners summarized here constitutes the **selection principle**. This states that:

1.   Each **determiner, pronoun** and **proper name** has an associated **referent** that is expressed in that element (and in what follows it, if anything does).
2.   The last (or rightmost) part of the nominal group refers to the **widest referent**, e.g. *books* in *five books, them* in *five of them* and *the book*s in *five of the books*. It is the referent of EITHER (i) the **deictic determiner** (if there is one) plus any following modifiers, head and relevant qualifiers, OR (ii) the **pronoun** or **proper name** that is the head, plus any relevant modifiers or qualifiers.
3.   The referent of the **last determiner** (if any) that occurs before the widest referent is treated as being **selected** from the widest referent.
4.   This relationship of **selection** is repeated for the referent of the **second last determiner** (if any) before the widest referent, then for the referent of the **third last determiner** before it, and so on, each being selected from the referent of what follows to the right of it.
5.   The first (or leftmost) referent is the **substantive referent**, the others being simply other referents from which it is selected. The substantive referent may be realized in a nominal group that is **embedded** within another determiner (see 9 below).
6.   The type of 'selecting relationship' between the referent of the determiner and the referent of what follows varies according to the type of meaning that the determiner realizes.
7.   The meaning of 'selection' is frequently not expressed overtly – especially when a **qd, od** or **sd** is the last determiner before an unparticularized widest referent. But when the relationship of 'selection' is realized the **selector** is always expounded by *of*.
8.   It is rare for more than three determiners to co-occur, but when they do they typically occur in the following sequence:

    td/rd v pd v fd v qd v od v sd v tod v qid v dd.... h

---

42.   The model presented here has passed the additional test of being implemented in the computer, as part of the COMMUNAL Project. This doesn't 'prove' that it is 'right', of course, but it does at least demonstrate that the principles on which it operates have been thought through sufficiently - and made sufficiently clear - for them to be implemented in a computer program.

9. When a **nominal group** fills a determiner, **embedding** occurs, thus occasionally permitting what may at first appear to be a non-canonical sequence of determiners.

6.3   A 'text-descriptive' summary

From the viewpoint of the requirements of a text-descriptive grammar – i.e. one that is adapted for use in describing texts – we can summarize the proposals for modelling the overt forms of the determiners as follows (the elements being listed in the sequence in which they occur in the matrix ngp):

element	item	unit (s)
typic determiner		ngp (h < *type,* etc)
representational determiner		ngp (h < *photo.* etc)
partitive determiner		ngp (h < *back,* etc)
fractionative determiner	*half* or	ngp (h < *fifth* etc)
quantifying determiner	item or	ngp or quantity group
ordinative determiner		quality group (apex < *fifth* etc)
superlative determiner		quality group (apex < *finest* etc)
totalizing determiner	*all*	
qualifier-introducing determiner	*those*	
deictic determiner	item or	genitive cluster
head	noun	ngp (occasionally)

With the knowledge of (i) the probabilities of what may fill each type of determiner (an item, a set of items or a unit) and (ii) the tests for each given in Section 5, the analysis of nominal groups that contain these structures is a manageable task.

6.4   A 'theoretical-generative' summary

A grammar that provides only structures (such as the first two editions of *IFG*) can provide a viable framework for describing text – so long as its criteria for identifying categories are sufficiently clear. This is a **text-descriptive grammar**. But until its creators publish both its system networks and its realization rules – i.e. until it is presented as a **theoretical-generative** grammar – we do not have a clear idea of how it actually works. (See Fawcett 2000: 78–81 for the distinction between 'theoretical-generative' and 'text-descriptive' aspects of linguistics, and so types of grammar.)[43]

The best way to summarize the way in which the small portion of a generative SFG presented here works is to invite you to look again at the following:

---

43. The 2004 edition of *IFG* adds some networks, but there is no attempt to provide systematic coverage of ALL the networks, nor to provide realization rules. This is regrettable but understandable, since that work's goal is to be a text-descriptive grammar, not a theoretical-generative one.

1. Section 3.2 and Figure 1 for the overall model of the language itself,
2. The selection expression and realization rules in Section 3.4,
3. The system networks and realization rules in Sections 4.2.2 and 4.4.7, and
4. The diagrams of the structures generated, e.g. Figures 2, 7 and 8.

This model, then, has served those working in the framework of the Cardiff Grammar well for over three decades of work in text analysis and computer generation. And, when minor additions such as the **tod** (*all*) and the **qid** (*those*) were required, it was able to accommodate them without difficulty.

6.5   Methods of inquiry

Finally, we turn to the methods used in this investigation – and their lessons for future work. In the 1970s, when I began developing the model described here, much of my evidence was drawn from (i) the everyday language in use around me, and (ii) the real life texts that my students and I were trying to analyze. I also consulted (iii) the literature on English grammar available at the time, notably Quirk et al (1972) (the first of the big modern grammars) – though the literature, as we saw in Section 2.2, was then and still is very little help in this case. And, like other linguists, I also used (iv) 'thought experiments' to produce test examples – this being the only way to work out the sequences of the determiners.

What other evidence might we use to decide between various possible structures? Traditional 'formal tests' still have a role to play in deciding between alternative structures in a 'text-descriptive' grammar that doesn't have a 'theoretical-generative' counterpart, and they still play a minor role in my research as 'pointers' and 'checks' when considering what the structures required as outputs from the realization rules should be.

Since the late 1980s, however, I have increasingly given weight to two other research methods. The first is the data extracted from the large corpora (COBUILD and, increasingly, the vast corpus available on the internet through Google). These are a wonderfully challenging source of data – but they don't necessarily suggest what the syntax should be.[44]

The second research method that I have adopted since the 1980s is that of building explicit grammars. I now recognize that the most influential criteria in deciding between alternative structures must be those of elegance (i.e. economy and clarity) in the operation of the grammar – and not merely in its representations. To this I would wish to add the principle of maximizing the transparency of the structure at the level of form as a reflection of the relationships within the representation (in an appropriate logic) of the input – via the semantic features of the system networks. This is, in fact, which is

44. We should note that evidence from corpus linguistics is increasingly available through what Neale (2005) has called 'the "second level" use of corpora', e.g. as found in the *COBUILD Dictionary* (Sinclair 1987/1995), Francis, Hunston and Manning (1996, 1998), and Biber et al (1999). (However, these have not been much help in the present study, as we saw in Section 2.2.)

really just a particularly rewarding type of elegance. And these criteria should, it seems to me, be paramount in a functional model of language for the twenty-first century.

References

Biber, Douglas, Stig Johansson, Geoffrey Leech, Susan Conrad and Edward Finegan. 1999. *Longman grammar of spoken and written English*. Harlow: Pearson.

Butler, Christopher S. 2003a. *Structure and function: An introduction to three major structural-functional theories. Part 1: Approaches to the simplex clause*. Amsterdam: John Benjamins.

Butler, Christopher S. 2003b. *Structure and function: An introduction to three major structural-functional theories. Part 2: From clause to discourse and beyond*. Amsterdam: John Benjamins.

Day, Michael D. Forthcoming. *A corpus-consulting probabilistic approach to parsing: the CCPX parser and its complementary components*. PhD Thesis. Cardiff: Dept. of Computer Science, Cardiff University, Cardiff.

Downing, Angela. 1991. "An alternative approach to theme: A systemic-functional perspective". *Word* 42(2): 119–143.

Downing, Angela. 1996. "The semantics of *get*-passives". *Functional descriptions: Theory in practice*, ed. by Ruqaiya Hasan, Carmel Cloran and David Butt, 179–206. Amsterdam: John Benjamins.

Downing, Angela and Philip Locke. 1992. *A university course in English grammar*. New York: Prentice Hall.

Downing, Angela and Philip Locke. 2006. *English grammar: A university course*. 2nd edn. Abingdon: Routledge.

Fawcett, Robin P. 1974–1976/1981. *Some proposals for systemic syntax*. Cardiff: Polytechnic of Wales (now University of Glamorgan).

Fawcett, Robin P. 1980. *Cognitive linguistics and social interaction: Towards an integrated model of a systemic functional grammar and the other components of an interacting mind*. Heidelberg: Julius Groos and Exeter University.

Fawcett, Robin P. 2000. *A theory of syntax for Systemic Functional Linguistics*. Amsterdam: John Benjamins. [Current Issues in Linguistic Theory 206].

Fawcett, Robin P. Forthcoming. *Functional syntax handbook: Analyzing English at the level of form*. London: Equinox.

Fawcett, Robin P. In preparation. *Functional semantics handbook: Analyzing English at the level of meaning*. London: Equinox.

Fawcett, Robin P. and Michael R. Perkins. 1980a-d. *Child language transcripts 6–12, Volume 1: Six year olds, Volume 2: Eight year olds, Volume 3: Ten year olds, Volume 4: Twelve year olds*. Pontypridd, Wales: Polytechnic of Wales (now University of Glamorgan).

Fawcett, Robin P. and Michael R. Perkins. 1981. "Project report: Language development in 6- to 12-year-old children". *First Language* 2: 75–79.

Fawcett, Robin P., Gordon H. Tucker and Yuen Q. Lin. 1993. "How a systemic functional grammar works: The role of realization in realization". *New concepts in natural language generation*, ed. by Helmut Horacek and Michael Zock, 114–186. London: Pinter.

Francis, Gill, Susan Hunston and Elizabeth Manning. 1996. *Collins COBUILD grammar patterns 1: Verbs*. London: HarperCollins.

Francis, Gill, Susan Hunston and Elizabeth Manning. 1998. *Collins COBUILD grammar patterns 2: Nouns and adjectives*. London: HarperCollins.

Halliday, Michael A. K. 1961/1976. "Categories of the theory of grammar". *Word* 17: 241–292. Reprinted as Bobbs-Merrill Reprint Series No. Language 36, and in part in Michael A. K. Halliday, 1976, *System and function in language: Selected papers by M. A. K. Halliday*, ed. by Gunther R. Kress, 84–87. London: Oxford University Press.

Halliday, Michael A. K. 1985. *An introduction to functional grammar*. London: Arnold.

Halliday, Michael A. K. 1994. *An Introduction to functional grammar* 2nd edn. London: Arnold.

Halliday, Michael A. K. and Christian M. I. M. Matthiessen. 1999. *Construing experience through meaning: A language-based approach to cognition*. London: Cassell Academic.

Halliday, Michael A. K., and Christian M. I. M. Matthiessen. 2004. *An introduction to functional grammar* 3rd edn. London: Arnold.

Huddleston, Rodney D. and Geoffrey K. Pullum (principal authors). 2002. *The Cambridge grammar of English*. Cambridge: Cambridge University Press.

Matthiessen, Christian M. I. M. 1995. *Lexicogrammatical cartography: English systems*. Tokyo: International Language Sciences Publishers.

Meillet, Antoine. 1937. *Introduction a l'étude comparative des langues Indo-Européennes*. 8th ed. Paris: Librairie Hachette.

Neale, Amy. 2005. "Matching corpus data and system networks". *System and corpus: Exploring connections*, ed. by Geoffrey Thompson and Susan Hunston, 143–163. London: Equinox.

Prakasam, V. 1996. "'NGp of NGp' constructions: A functional-structural study". *Meaning and form: Systemic functional interpretations*, ed. by Margaret Berry, Christopher S. Butler, Robin P. Fawcett and Guowen Huang, 567–583. Meaning and Choice in Language: Studies for Michael Halliday. Norwood, NJ: Ablex.

Quirk, Randolph, Sidney Greenbaum, Geoffrey Leech and Jan Svartvik. 1972. *A grammar of contemporary English*. London: Longman.

Quirk, Randolph, Sidney Greenbaum, Geoffrey Leech and Jan Svartvik. 1985. *A comprehensive grammar of the English language*. London: Longman.

Sinclair, John (editor-in-chief). 1987/1995. *Collins COBUILD English language dictionary*. London: Collins.

Sinclair, John (editor-in-chief). 1990. *Collins COBUILD English grammar*. London: HarperCollins.

Sinclair, John. 1991. *Corpus, concordance, collocation*. Oxford: Oxford University Press.

Tucker, Gordon H. 1996. "Cultural classification and system networks: A systemic functional approach to lexis". *Meaning and form: Systemic functional interpretations*, ed. by Margaret Berry, Christopher S. Butler, Robin P. Fawcett and Guowen Huang, 533–536. Meaning and Choice in Language: Studies for Michael Halliday. Norwood, NJ: Ablex.

Tucker, Gordon H. 1998. *The lexicogrammar of adjectives: A systemic functional approach to lexis*. London: Cassell Academic.

Problems in NP structure

An example from British tabloid journalism

Eirian Davies
Department of English, Royal Holloway, University of London

This paper considers a textual example of the nominal group found in a British tabloid daily newspaper (*The Sun*), with a view to examining how far two standard treatments of nominal group/noun phrase structure, directed at a student readership, account for the pattern of pre-modification found in it. The two works referred to are, Greenbaum, S. and R. Quirk (1992) *A Student's Grammar of the English Language*, and, Halliday, M.A.K. and C.M.I.M. Matthiessen (2004) *An Introduction to Functional Grammar* (3rd edn). Halliday's functional category of 'classifier' and Greenbaum and Quirk's category of 'noun pre-modifier' largely overlap, and rules for the relative sequence of different elements in NP/nominal group structure in these two accounts have a good deal in common. Problems with the analysis of the chosen example exist for both. The main distinction between these accounts with respect to pre-modification lies in Halliday's proposal of a division between a logical and an experiential basis for nominal group analysis. Using the example given, the suggestion is made that these two dimensions are not mutually independent, and that a case can be made that it is set inclusion attributes of the experiential structure that determine the features dealt with under the heading 'logical structure' in Halliday's account.

1. Introduction

This paper is devoted to the discussion of a single example of a noun phrase, namely *a canal barge dwelling white Rasta rich bitch*. This was taken from *The Sun* newspaper[1], and brought to my attention by a student[2] who used it, among several others found in the tabloid press, to make the claim that the noun phrase in English shows complica-

---

1. 20th February 1999, p.25.

2. Dong Chang Moon, who was awarded an MA in Modern English Language at Royal Holloway, University of London, UK.

tions beyond anything explained in the handbooks. In that respect it raises some interesting issues, but it also shows *The Sun* at its most unpleasant. Probably, the main drift of the cultural attitudes implied is an aggressive antipathy towards 'radical chic'. My aim, though, has been to look at the ideational and structural aspects, rather than at markers of evaluation, although they all interact. I have tried to remain detached from the insult conveyed, and the identity of its unfortunate victim is lost in time. In the discussion that follows I refer mainly to the treatment of the noun phrase / nominal group in two works with somewhat different approaches: one, the standard account within systemic linguistics (Halliday and Matthiessen, 2004), and the other the more eclectic approach of Quirk *et al* (1985) as somewhat revised and updated, with students specifically in mind, in Greenbaum and Quirk (1990).

2.   Constituents

I want to begin by identifying what seem to be the constituents of this noun phrase (internally uninterruptible elements), and to make some informal observations on each:
1.   *a*
2.   *canal barge dwelling*
3.   *white Rasta* (?)
4.   *rich*
5.   *bitch.*

2.1   Constituent 1: *a*

The indefinite article here is capable of contrasting with the definite article on the 'uniqueness'/ 'inclusiveness' criterion as distinguished by Lyons (1999: 2–15). Compare: *The canal barge dwelling white Rasta rich bitch!* used as a free-standing exclamation. This conveys that the person referred to is not only already familiar to, and identifiable by, the addressee, but also that she is unique in Lyons' terms. This use of the definite article is mainly associated with insults (whether real, *The young hooligan!* or (partly) simulated, *The old devil!*), and so might relate to evaluation, and the interpersonal component. On the other hand, *a young hooligan/ an old devil/ a man of parts,* seem to convey non-uniqueness, and by virtue of this, a plurality of *young hooligans/ old devils/ men of parts,* of which the individual concerned is just one. But such expressions can also be used of an already identified individual, as in a caption to a photograph, where it might be argued too that reference is to an unique individual in that context. So, the contrast between *a* and *the* here seems to have something to do with the 'size' of the set of individuals to which reference is made (one (*the*), vs. many (*a*), members).

2.2   Constituent 2: *canal barge dwelling*

Canal barge dwelling comes under the heading of what Halliday and Matthiessen (2004: 322) describe as 'some part of the experiential structure of a clause (here Complement + Verb)[being] downgraded to function as Epithet or Classifier'. On the *very/more* test they propose (320), it would be a Classifier here. For Greenbaum and Quirk (1990: 146–7) it would be a premodifier participle, typically occurring in zone III ('postcentral') position. They distinguish between –*ing* participles which have the potential to indicate a permanent or characteristic feature and those which do not, and associate the indefinite article with the habitual or permanent and the definite article with the specific or temporary. How 'permanent' is perhaps open to question in our example, but 'habitual' seems a fair description of *canal barge dwelling*, which is nongradable (and not capable of intensification by *very*).

2.3   Constituent 3: *white Rasta*

White Rasta presents various problems of analysis, one of which is the question of interruptibility. It does in fact seem possible to insert an adjective between the two items, as in *white young Rasta*. If so, *white Rasta* is not a compound word, and the further question arises of whether or not it realizes a single element of structure. For Greenbaum and Quirk (1990: 146–7), *white*, as a colour adjective, typically occurs in zone III, postcentral position; for Halliday and Matthiessen (2004: 319) it is an experiential epithet, because potentially defining. The status of *Rasta* as a noun, as opposed to an adjective, is perhaps open to debate. As a contraction of *Rastafarian* (which is formally similar to, and behaves in the same way as, *Christian* or *Australian*) it could be either: *Rastafarian culture/ I am a Rastafarian*. As an adjective, it would be classed as one of provenance by Greenbaum and Quirk (1990: 391), like *Russian/ Gothic*, and as non-gradable. *Rasta* cannot take submodification by *very* here; but that feature is not much help in distinguishing between noun and adjective since either may take *very* in (similar) limited conditions (*cf. That's a very <u>London</u> attitude to the countryside / That's a very <u>Gothic</u> building style);* and neither does so easily elsewhere. I would want to say that *Rasta* is probably behaving as a noun here, rather than as an adjective of provenance. If so, it follows the general rules for relative sequence in the premodifier set out in Greenbaum and Quirk (1990: 392) in relation to what precedes it (*white*), but not in relation to what follows it (*rich*). By contrast, *white* follows these rules with respect to what follows it (*Rasta*), but not in terms of what precedes it (*canal barge dwelling*). Both *white* and *Rasta* could occur without the other in this construction: *a canal barge dwelling white rich bitch/ a canal barge dwelling Rasta rich bitch*, which again argues for their separability, and for the view that there are two elements here rather than one. However, it seems to me that both these variants sail closer to the wind in terms of the race relations act than the original. If so, this is perhaps some **semantic** evidence for a single element.

2.4   Constituent 4: *rich*

It seems to me that the position of *rich* in relation to the other elements in the (pre-) modifier is probably the most interesting feature of this example. Stylistic motivations for placing it last seem almost certainly to include the fact that it rhymes with the head word *bitch*; but whatever the reasons, its placement here has the effect of dislocating what both Greenbaum and Quirk, and Halliday and Matthiessen see as the typical sequence of elements in the (pre-)modifier. For Greenbaum and Quirk (1990: 146–7) *rich* is a central, gradable adjective which typically occurs in zone II (and should therefore come before the colour adjective *white* (zone III), as well as before a participle, *canal barge dwelling* (also zone III), as also before a denominal adjective denoting nationality or ethnic background (zone IV), and certainly before a noun: *Rasta*, however analysed). In this example, *rich* immediately precedes the head, and is in 'classifier' position for Halliday and Matthiessen (2004: 319–20) and in 'zone IV', 'prehead' position for Greenbaum and Quirk (1990: 146–7). As such, it should not be able to take a sub-modifier indicating degree or intensification; but in this example the acceptability of inserting *very* before *rich* seems uncontroversial (although it would make an already long modifier that much more so). *Rich* seems to be behaving here in its ordinary use as a gradable central adjective. However, there is also the possibility that *rich bitch* should be treated as a compound noun. I am indebted to Angela Downing for pointing out its similarity to *fat cat* as evidence for this view, and to Christopher Butler for providing the results of a search of the British National Corpus that shows that both these expressions sometimes appear as hyphenated forms[3], again suggesting compound status in each case. It is also true that *rich bitch* can occur as a compound adjective, as in, *She's a (very) rich(-)bitch dresser*; and so can *fat cat*, as in, *He's a (very) fat(-)cat CEO*. To treat *rich bitch* as a compound noun here would substantially simplify the structure of the nominal group, especially if *white Rasta* were also treated as a compound, and would remove the dislocation in the typical sequence of elements in the (pre-)modifier found if *rich* is treated as a separable central adjective. However, in our example, indications to the contrary include the possibility of pre-modification by *very*, and the interruptibility test, which allows not only, *rich white Rasta bitch*, but also, *a rich canal*

---

3.   In the 7 concordance examples found by a search of the British National Corpus for *rich* and *bitch* within 5 words of each other, these two items were contiguous in all cases and hyphenated in three, of which two were compound nouns and the other a compound adjective. None of the examples referred to a female dog. In a search defined in the same way for *fat* and *cat*, of the 39 examples found 8 referred to the four-legged animal, and of those which did not, 9 were hyphenated, of which 5 were compound nouns and 4 were compound adjectives. In a similar concordance for *Rasta(farianism)*, which found 98 instances, there was just one example of *white rastas*, which nicely illustrates the meaning it has in our example: *It was a weird time, with white rastas, art-school escapees, old rockers*. I take these results to indicate that *rich bitch* can occur as a compound, either noun or adjective; but would still want to argue that it does not yet always do so, as in our current example.

barge dwelling white Rasta bitch. Fat cat is a semantically exocentric compound noun, but the case for claiming this status is less clear for *rich bitch*. *Fat cat* as a compound seems to be currently used mostly with reference to men, whereas *cat* in isolation may be used to refer either to women (with derogatory connotations) or to men (with approbatory associations), and is gender neutral when used to refer to the four-legged animal. *Rich bitch* is generally used to refer to women, and so is *bitch*, which is also female-gender specific when used to refer to dogs. That is, *rich bitch* is more semantically endocentric. If we substitute *fat cat* for *rich bitch* in our example, it fails the interruptibility test: * *A canal barge dwelling fat white Rasta cat*, is probably a kind of four-legged animal, or at least an overweight female person; but not an overpaid/ greedy business man. Similarly, *fat cat* cannot be pre-modified by *very* in this context and retain its human reference: *A canal barge dwelling white Rasta very fat cat* would have four legs. That is, *fat cat* emerges as a compound noun on both these tests, while *rich bitch* does not do so on either of them. On these grounds, then, I will treat *rich* in this example as a separate adjective.

2.5   Constituent 5: *bitch*

The head word, *bitch*, is the only unambiguously derogatory term in this phrase: compare, *a canal barge dwelling white Rasta rich stockbroker.* Other terms seem to acquire derogatory connotations in proportion to their nearness to the head, so that *rich* acquires the most.

It might be useful at this point to reorder the example in terms of what Greenbaum and Quirk regard as the typical relative sequence of elements in the premodifier. If *white* and *Rasta* are analysed as separate elements, this would give: *a rich white canal barge dwelling Rasta bitch.* If *white Rasta* is analysed as a compound (either adjective or noun), we would have: *a rich canal barge dwelling white Rasta bitch.* In both cases, *Rasta* immediately precedes the head, and would be a classifier in Halliday and Matthiessen's terms. If it is actually the case that premodifiers acquire connotations associated with the head in proportion to their nearness to it, then both these re-orderings are more evaluatively negative with respect to *Rasta* than the original.

3.   Ordering of elements and the 'logical structure' of the nominal group

I want now to pursue the question of relative ordering of elements in this nominal group. The considerations involved are essentially to do with what Halliday and Matthiessen deal with under 'logical structure' (2004: 329–31).

Permutations, treating *white Rasta* as a single element:

(i)   *a canal barge dwelling white Rasta rich bitch* (1,2,3,4,5)
(ii)   *a white Rasta canal barge dwelling rich bitch* (1,3,2,4,5)

(iii)	*a rich white Rasta canal barge dwelling bitch* (1,4,3,2,5)
(iv)	*a white Rasta rich canal barge dwelling bitch* (1,3,4,2,5)
(v)	*a rich canal barge dwelling white Rasta bitch* (1,4,2,3,5)
(vi)	*a canal barge dwelling rich white Rasta bitch* (1,2,4,3,5)

We might add a further 18 permutations here, based on treating *white* and *Rasta* as interruptible separate constituents:

(vii)	*a canal barge dwelling white rich Rasta bitch* (1,2,3a,4,3b,5)
(viii)	*a canal barge dwelling Rasta rich white bitch* (1,2,3b,4,3a,5)
(ix)	*a canal barge dwelling rich Rasta white bitch* (1,2,4,3b,3a,5)
(x)	*a canal barge dwelling Rasta white rich bitch* (1,2,3b,3a,4,5)
(xi)	*a white rich canal barge dwelling Rasta bitch* (1,3a,4,2,3b,5)
(xii)	*a white rich Rasta canal barge dwelling bitch* (1,3a,4,3b,2,5)
(xiii)	*a white canal barge dwelling Rasta rich bitch* (1,3a,2,3b,4,5)
(xiv)	*a white canal barge dwelling rich Rasta bitch* (1,3a,2,4,3b,5)
(xv)	*a Rasta rich canal barge dwelling white bitch* (1,3b,4,,2,3a,5)
(xvi)	*a Rasta rich white canal barge dwelling bitch* (1,3b,4,3a,2,5)
(xvii)	*a Rasta canal barge dwelling white rich bitch* (1,3b,2,3a,4,5)
(xviii)	*a Rasta canal barge dwelling rich white bitch* (1,3b,2,4,3a,5)
(xix)	*a Rasta white canal barge dwelling rich bitch* (1,3b,3a,2,4,5)
(xx)	*a Rasta white rich canal barge dwelling bitch* (1,3b, 3a,4,2,5)
(xxi)	*a rich canal barge dwelling Rasta white bitch* (1,4,2,3b,3a,5)
(xxii)	*a rich Rasta white canal barge dwelling bitch* (1,4,3b,3a,2,5)
(xxiii)	*a rich Rasta canal barge dwelling white bitch* (1,4,3b,2,3a,5),

together with the already mentioned:

(xxiv)	*a rich white canal barge dwelling Rasta bitch* (1,4,3a,2,3b,5)

None of these examples, (vii) – (xxiv), seems grammatically unacceptable as an English phrase, which tends to substantiate my student's complaint; but I shall only attempt to touch on one or two of them. My main focus will be on examples (i)–(vi).

I want to dig a little deeper into Halliday and Matthiessen's account of what they call the 'logical structure of the nominal group'. The gist of my argument will be that this structure relates directly to the content of what is conveyed, and cannot be separated from experiential meaning.

Halliday and Matthiessen (2004: 329–35) treat the recursive modification which they postulate for the structure of the nominal group modifier as being a matter of sub-categorization: '*a* is a subset of *x*'. Any subset of a given set is included in that set; and any given set includes itself. This means that, if a given set, A, is included in a set, B, then A is either smaller than B or the same set as B. What I am driving at relates, I suspect, to the difference between a modifier + head structure and a compound word at head: to the difference between 'a black bird' (as opposed to a green or yellow bird) and 'a blackbird' (as opposed to a wren). In the first case, the set of birds referred to (those which are black) is included in the set of birds, but is not the same. In the second, the set of birds referred to is the same as the set of blackbirds. The first, in the process of referring, specifically allows for a subset of birds which are not black; but the second refers only to a single species, which does not, in itself, specifically call attention to the idea that other related species may exist. Recursive modification in the nominal group is of the first kind. (I ignore complexities of sub-modification for the present.) I shall use the idea that (pre-) modification in the nominal group involves the inclusion of a subset within a set other than (and so, larger than) itself to explore differences in the experiential implications conveyed by different relative orderings of the elements within it. I shall of course adopt the interpretation which shows recursive set inclusion moving leftwards from the head of the nominal group (equivalent to a right branching tree).

There are two aspects of the case where set A is included in, but is not the same as, set B which concern us. Firstly, there will be some individual member(s) of set B which are not also (a) member(s) of set A. So, one or more members of set B who are not members of set A are 'allowed for'. (If $A \subseteq B$ and $A \neq B$, then '$x \in B$ & $x \notin A$' is allowed for.) Secondly, if a given individual is a member of set A, then that individual must also be a member of set B. If we take the nominal group *a blue dress* as a simple example, this approach will lead us to say that this conveys that the set of *blue dresses* is included within the set of *dresses*, that, if a given item is a member of the set of *blue dresses* it is also a member of the set of *dresses*, and that a set of *dresses* which are not *blue* is allowed for. If we took, *a small blue dress*, this would be taken to convey that there is a set of *blue dresses* which is included in the set of *dresses*, and a set of *small blue dresses* which is included in the set of *blue dresses*, thereby allowing for some *dresses* which are neither *blue* nor *small,* and also for some *dresses* which are *blue,* but are not *small*. What isn't allowed for in the reference made here is a *dress* which is *small* but is not *blue*. And if x is a member of the set of *small blue dresses,* x is a member of the set of *blue dresses*.

We can use this approach in a further attempt to decide whether or not *white Rasta* in our original example, (i), should be regarded as **semantically** unified (and therefore 'compound' on that criterion), or not. To do this, I shall compare it with (vii), where *white* and *Rasta* are separated by the insertion of *rich*. The problem can be posed as the question of whether or not (i) implies that there may be a set of *Rasta rich bitches* who are not *white*. (Both (i) and (vii) allow for a set of *bitches* who are all three things: *rich* and *white* and *Rasta*.)

In, (vii) *a canal barge dwelling <u>white rich Rasta</u> bitch*, I want to claim that there is an implication that the set of *rich Rasta bitches* includes the set of *white rich Rasta bitches*.

So, there may be (a) some *Rasta bitches* who are *rich* but not *white*. And, there may also be (b) some *Rasta bitches* who are not *rich* and are not *white*.

This differs from the original, (i) *<u>white Rasta rich</u> bitch*, where the implication is that the set of *rich bitches* includes the set of *white Rasta rich bitches*. So, there may be (c) some *rich bitches* who are not *white* and are not *Rasta*. (But, here, it is more difficult to suggest that a set of *Rasta bitches* who are not *rich,* whether *white* or not, is allowed for.) The form in (i) allows for (c) some *rich bitches* who are neither *white* nor *Rasta*. Whether or not it is taken to allow also for (d) *rich bitches* who are *Rasta*, but not *white*, depends on whether or not *white Rasta* is taken to be a compound word. If it is, then (i) does not allow for (d); if it isn't then (i) does allow for (d).

On that basis, then, if *white Rasta* is treated as two elements, both (i) and (vii) allow for a *bitch* who is both *rich* and *Rasta*, but not *white*; and (i), but not (vii), allows for a *rich bitch* who is neither *Rasta* nor *white*. But, if it is treated as a compound in (i), only (vii) allows for the former. In either case, only (vii) allows for a *Rasta bitch* who is neither *rich* nor *white*. If *white Rasta* is treated as a compound, then (i) allows for a *rich bitch* who is not a *white-Rasta*, but not for any of the other possibilities mentioned. By contrast, (vii) does not provide for a *rich bitch* who is not *Rasta*.

This exploration does not decide the question of +/- compound status; but it does perhaps provide a basis on which to argue for one interpretation rather than another, taking what we know of the cultural context of (i) into account. Young women with a lot of money of their own, as a class, could perhaps be expected to arouse hostility in many typical readers of *The Sun;* so that a general derogatory label for them as a set of dislikeable individuals might be predicted. On that basis, the analysis above would lead to interpreting *white Rasta* as **semantically** a compound.

However, if (vii) is acceptable, then *white Rasta* is interruptible, and, so not grammatically a compound word on that criterion. If, as just suggested, it is semantically unified, then we are left with the sort of conflict between these two different kinds of criteria which is also found in the case of many potential phrasal verbs. I shall adopt the analysis of it as a compound in the remainder of this discussion and treat it as such in considering permutations (i) – (vi).

These permutations form 3 pairs, according to the constituent which comes last in the premodifier, immediately before the head. This is: *rich*, in (i) and (ii); *canal barge dwelling*, in (iii) and (iv); and *white Rasta, in (v) and (vi)*. In this way, only (i) and (ii) allow for a set of *rich bitches* who are neither *white Rasta* nor *canal barge dwelling*. Only (iii) and (iv) allow for a set of *canal barge dwelling bitches* who are neither *white Rasta* nor *rich*; and only (v) and (vi) allow for a set of *white Rasta bitches* who are neither *canal barge dwelling* nor *rich*.

In the first pair, (i) allows for a *white Rasta rich bitch* who is not *canal barge dwelling*; and (ii) allows for a *canal barge dwelling rich bitch* who is not *white Rasta*. In the second pair, (iii) allows for a *white Rasta canal barge dwelling bitch* who isn't *rich*; and (iv) allows for a *rich canal barge dwelling bitch* who isn't *white Rasta*. In the third pair, (v) allows for a *canal barge dwelling white Rasta bitch* who isn't *rich*; and (vi) allows for a *rich white Rasta bitch* who isn't *canal barge dwelling*.

Both (i) and (vi) allow for a *bitch* who is both *white Rasta* and *rich*, but not *canal barge dwelling*. Both (iii) and (v) allow for a *bitch* who is both *white Rasta* and *canal barge dwelling*, but not *rich*. Both (ii) and (iv) allow for a *bitch* who is both *canal barge dwelling* and *rich* but is not *white Rasta*. These pairings derive from what comes **first** in the nominal group, immediately following the definite article.

In the first pair, (i) allows for a *bitch* who is *rich*, but not *white Rasta*; and (vi) allows for a *bitch* who is *white Rasta*, but not *rich*. In the second pair, (iii) allows for a *bitch* who is *canal barge dwelling*, but not *white Rasta*; and (v) allows for a bitch who is *white Rasta*, but not *canal barge dwelling*. In the third pair, (ii) allows for a *bitch* who is *rich* but not *canal barge dwelling*; and (iv) allows for a *bitch* who is *canal barge dwelling*, but not *rich*.

We could summarize these comparisons, together with those of the nine other pairings we could consider, by saying that the relative sequencing of elements in the premodifier of the nominal group affects the experiential content of what is conveyed by its utterance. That is, such linguistic structuring conveys an implicit structuring of extralinguistic reality, for the purposes of a given act of referring. In this way, it provides a mechanism by which the cultural attitudes of the speaker can be conveyed in a given instance without explicit mention; and by which, in some contexts, appeal can be made to any such cultural attitudes assumed to be shared by the addressee.

We have already compared our original example, (i) *a canal barge dwelling white Rasta rich bitch*, with two of the other permutations where *white Rasta* is treated as a compound: (ii) and (vi). I want to conclude by examining the remainder.

Of these, it is (v), *a rich canal barge dwelling white Rasta bitch*, which represents what both Greenbaum and Quirk, and Halliday and Matthiessen would regard as the unmarked sequence. (v) differs from (i) only with respect to the position of *rich*: the other two elements in the premodifier remain in the same sequence relative to each other. (i) allows for a set of *rich bitches* who are neither *canal barge dwelling* nor *white Rasta*; but, in (v), the only kind of *rich bitches* provided for in the reference made are those who are both *canal barge dwelling* and *white Rasta* (a rather specialized group!). We could attempt to re-phrase this by saying that, in (i), what we are talking about is *a rich bitch*, whereas, in (v), what we are talking about is *a white Rasta bitch*. This would be to follow Halliday and Matthiessen in giving a different semantic status to the classifier, as opposed to epithets. We could describe this by saying that the classifier gives a **defining** property of the set at head, as opposed to an epithet, which gives only a non-defining characteristic. But, to do this would not fit altogether easily with a view of all premodifying elements working in exactly the same way as each other to subcategorise progressively, working leftwards from the head of the nominal group. The descriptive problems involved in such an approach, if adopted, would involve the difficulties which Halliday and Matthiessen allude to in distinguishing between an epithet and a classifier.

Variant (iii), *a rich white Rasta canal barge dwelling bitch,* has exactly the reverse order of elements in the premodifier as compared with (i) (and pairs with (v) with respect to the position of *rich*). If we retain our progressive sub-categorization approach for the moment, (iii) allows for a *canal barge dwelling bitch* who is neither *white Rasta* nor *rich*; and, as in (v), the only kind of *rich bitch* referred to is also both *canal barge dwelling* and *white Rasta*. In contrast with both (i) and (v), (iii) does not allow for *a white Rasta bitch* who is not *canal barge dwelling*, though like (v), but unlike (i), it does allow for one who isn't *rich*.

Variant (iv), a *white Rasta rich canal barge dwelling bitch,* contrasts with (i) only with respect to the position of *canal barge dwelling.* Unlike (i), (iv) doesn't allow for a *white Rasta bitch* who isn't *canal barge dwelling.* Like (iii) and (v), but unlike (i), (ii) and (vi), (iv) allows for a *canal barge dwelling bitch* who isn't *rich.*

It seems to me that the main point of interest in this series of comparisons relates to the different positions of *rich.* I have argued that *rich bitch* in this example is not grammatically a compound word, as shown by both the *very* and interruptibility tests; and it is not a classifier for Halliday and Mathiessen on the intensifier criterion. Nevertheless, their gloss for a classifier, which would give, 'bitch classified as rich', does not seem inappropriate for (i) and (ii), where it immediately precedes the head, and which we have already compared in terms of progressive sub-categorization. It is perhaps worth considering whether, in an adjective + noun sequence, a strong lexical prediction between them might be one factor 'pushing' the adjective towards functioning as a classifier. Given our earlier speculations about the prejudices of some readers of *The Sun*, this might be a factor at issue here.

We could approach the relative sequencing of *rich* in the remaining permutations (iii) – (vi) in two different ways: either in terms of the identity of the constituent which immediately follows it, or in terms of its place in relation to the initial article. The first gives us the two pairs: (iii) and (vi), where it is followed by *white Rasta;* and (iv) and (v), where it is followed by *canal barge dwelling.* The second gives us the two pairs: (iii) and (v), where *rich* immediately follows the indefinite article; and (iv) and (vi), where *rich* is separated from *a* by an intervening constituent.

Let us take first the two pairs identified in terms of the succeeding constituent: (iii) and (vi), (iv) and (v). In (iii), *rich white Rasta canal barge dwelling bitch* allows for a set of *white Rasta canal barge dwelling bitches* who are not *rich,* and for a set of *canal barge dwelling bitches* who are neither *white Rasta* nor rich. In (vi), *canal boat dwelling rich white Rasta bitch* allows for a set of *rich white Rasta bitches* who are not *canal boat dwelling,* and for a set of *white Rasta bitches* who are neither *canal boat dwelling* nor *rich.* Both (iii) and (vi) allow for a set of *rich white Rasta bitches*; but in (iii) these constitute a subset of *canal boat dwelling bitches,* and in (vi) these form a set which itself **includes** a subset of *canal barge dwelling bitches.* So, (iii) allows for a set of *canal barge dwelling bitches* who are not *rich* or *white Rasta*; but not for a set of *rich white Rasta bitches* who are not *canal barge dwelling.* In contrast with this, (vi) **does** allow for a set of *rich white Rasta bitches* who are not *canal barge dwelling*; but does **not** allow for a set of *canal barge dwelling bitches* who are not *rich* or *white Rasta.* In this way, the implications of (iii) and (vi) are in some sense opposed: (iii) implies that if x is *a rich white Rasta bitch* then x is *canal barge dwelling*; but, (vi) implies that if x is *a canal barge dwelling bitch* then x is *a rich white Rasta.* 'Any *rich white Rasta bitch* referred to is *canal barge dwelling*':: 'Any *canal barge dwelling bitch* referred to is a *rich white Rasta*'.

In (iv), *white Rasta rich canal barge dwelling bitch* allows for a set of *rich canal barge dwelling bitches* who are not *white Rasta* and for a set of *canal barge dwelling bitches* who are neither *white Rasta* nor *rich*. In (v), *rich canal barge dwelling white Rasta bitch* allows for a set of *canal barge dwelling white Rasta bitches* who are not *rich*; and for a set of *white Rasta bitches* who are neither *canal barge dwelling* nor *rich*. Both (iv) and (v) allow for a set of *rich canal barge dwelling bitches*, but this set is potentially smaller in (v) than in (iv), because they are all *white Rasta* in (v), whereas (iv) allows for some who are not *white Rasta*.

If we compare these four permutations with (i) and (ii), where *rich* is potentially a classifier, it can be seen that it is only there, with *rich* in the immediately pre-head position, that allowance is made for *rich bitches* who are not *white Rasta* and not *canal barge dwelling*.

Let us now take the pairs of permutations distinguished by the distance of *rich* from the initial indefinite article: (iii) and (v), adjacent; as opposed to (iv) and (vi), separated. Given the nature of the other components in this nominal group, the position immediately following the article is the one predicted for *rich* here by both Greenbaum and Quirk, and Halliday and Matthiessen. (iii) and (v) differ, as discussed above, in terms of what follows *rich*. But, in both, if the referred to *bitch* is *rich* she is also *white Rasta* and *canal barge dwelling*. In this respect, (iv) and (vi) offer a contrast with the first pair. In (iv), if the referred to *bitch* is *rich*, she is also *canal barge dwelling*, but not necessarily *white Rasta*. In (vi), if she is *rich*, she is also *white Rasta*, but not necessarily *canal barge dwelling*. In (i) and (ii), if the referred to *bitch* is *rich*, this implies nothing else at all about her being +/- *white, Rasta,* or *canal boat dwelling.*

4.   Conclusions

The set inclusion relations in our original example, (i) *A canal barge dwelling white Rasta rich bitch* are such that, in extralinguistic reality, the set of 'canal barge dwellers' is potentially much larger than the set of 'white Rasta' and than the set of 'rich' people, with which it perhaps only minimally intersects, while the set of 'white Rasta' is probably smaller than the set of 'rich' people, which in turn may be either larger, or smaller, than the set of 'bitches'. My point here is that any of the orderings of these elements in the pre-modifier that we have discussed represents the imposition of some structuring in terms of experiential meaning. It is not the case that the Head, *bitch,* which is here also the 'Thing' in Halliday and Matthiessen's terms (2004: 331–3), denotes a member of an objectively larger set, which is then progressively sub-categorized. There is no 'passive' mirroring of reality. What we are presented with in (i) as the referent that we are talking about is a member of the sub-set of 'bitches' who are rich. What we are not talking about is any 'canal barge dwelling bitches' who are not 'white Rasta' and 'rich', or any 'white Rasta bitches' who are not 'rich'. Logical structure expresses, and arises out of, experiential structure.

In summary, there are two conclusions, of different kinds, that I would like to draw from this exploration of a single example.

The first is theoretical in nature: namely, that if we apply the notion of sub-categorization as an explanation of recursive premodification in the nominal group, we emerge with distinctions attributable to it which are surely experiential in nature. For Halliday and Matthiessen, *canal barge dwelling, white Rasta* and *rich* could all be classifiers. The different permutations of their relative sequence that we have explored, by expressing different orders of progressive sub-categorization, yield different analyses of extralinguistic reality in terms of hierarchies of the sets of referents that we are talking about. That is, one of the most important aspects of the experiential analysis is realized by the ordering of elements in recursive premodification.

The grounds for distinguishing between an experiential and a logical component here are obscure to me. The main attraction of distinguishing a Head, associated with the logical structure, from a Thing, associated with the experiential component, seems to lie rather narrowly in cases where these can be said not to coincide, as in *cup of tea*, where *cup* is said to be the Head, and *tea* the Thing (Halliday and Matthiessen, 2004: 333). In terms of 'logical structure', this is post-, as opposed to pre-modification, and it does not seem necessary to extrapolate from this and extend the distinction to cases of premodification where the Head and Thing coincide. Rather, it seems that what is needed is a more developed model of experiential meaning in this area.

The second conclusion is stylistic. I am told that several journalists write for both the British national daily papers that are owned by Rupert Murdoch: *The Sun* and *The Times;* and that of these, writing for *The Sun* is considered more difficult. At the end of our exhaustive examination of the other permutations available to the author of our original example, it seems reasonable to be left with a feeling of admiration for the skilful economy with which s/he conveys cultural attitudes, if not for the attitudes themselves.

Finally, I would claim that the answer to my student's complaint about the variety of acceptable possibilities for ordering elements in the NP/nominal group (pre-)modifier is that this variety provides for the realization of some subtle semantic distinctions. It all depends on what the speaker means and wishes, implicity, to convey. As such, ordering of this kind in texts should be of major interest to those studying markers of evaluation.

References

Greenbaum, Sidney and Randolph Quirk. 1990. *A student's grammar of the English language.* London: Longman.

Halliday, Michael A. K. Revised by Christian M. I. M. Matthiessen. 2004. *An introduction to functional grammar.* 3rd edn. London: Arnold.

Lyons, Christopher 1999. *Definiteness.* Cambridge: Cambridge University Press.

Quirk, Randolph, Sidney Greenbaum, Geoffrey Leech and Jan Svartvik. 1985. *A comprehensive grammar of the English language.* London: Longman.

Double-possessive nominalizations in English

J. Lachlan Mackenzie
Honorary Professor, Vrije Universiteit Amsterdam

Double-possessive nominalizations such as *Iraq's invasion of Kuwait* have played
a prominent role in the history of linguistics. However, this construction is not
only cross-linguistically rare but also the least used form of nominalization
in English texts. The question is addressed of the circumstances under which
double-possessive nominalization is used. What emerges from corpus analysis
is that the construction is employed above all to designate mental processes
and that its occurrence differs from that of its clausal analogue in occurring
in certain syntactic positions in which clauses are excluded. The article also
contains discussion of such matters as the semantic categories of entity proposed
by Functional Grammar, the interaction of nominalization and psych verbs and
the effect of syntactic 'priming'.

1. Introduction

Nominalizations have played a prominent part in the development of linguistic theory.[1]
They were among the first phenomena to be analysed in early syntactic studies, with
Chomsky (1964) proposing a generalized transformation of 'nominalization', which was
to be developed and refined by Lees (1966). The grammar of nominalizations was also
fundamental to the rise of X–bar Syntax (Chomsky 1970, elaborated in Jackendoff 1977),
after Chomsky had noted that the transformational rule was too powerful. The range of
nominalizing constructions in English was identified by Ross (1973) as a prime case of a
'squish', leading to the prototype view of syntactic categories characteristic of cognitive
grammar. Typological work on nominalizations (Koptjevskaja-Tamm 1993) has revealed
a structured range of variation across languages, one that is remarkably similar to the
range identified for the nominalization-rich language English. In semantics, work since
Vendler (1968) has shown that the meanings of nominalizations can be categorized ac-

---

1.   The research for this article was conducted in the framework of the project *Discourse Analysis in English: Aspects of cognition, typology and second language acquisition*, funded by the
Spanish Ministry of Science and Technology (MCYT, grant reference BFF2002-02441), with
further support from the Xunta de Galicia (XUGA, grant reference PGIDIT03PXIC20403PN).

cording to a layered hierarchy (cf. Mackenzie 1996, 2004), and more generally Halliday has pointed out that "[n]ominalizing is the single most powerful resource for creating grammatical metaphor" in rewording processes and properties, congruently worded as verbs and adjectives respectively, as nouns (Halliday and Matthiessen 2004: 656). Heyvaert (2001) breaks new ground in asserting that nominalizations, in the Systemic Functional Grammar (SFG) approach she adopts, involve interpersonal functions of Subject/person deixis and finite/non-finite grounding. Moving out into textuality, Downing (2000) explores the specific functions of nominalizations in headlines and the leads of newspaper articles, while Albentosa Hernández and Moya Guijarro (2000) and Banks (2001) examine the role of nominalizations in English scientific prose. Pérez de Ayala Becerril (2002), finally, shows how nominalizations in English and Spanish, which 'encapsulate' and thereby background potential important participants (Downing 1997), may mystify the reader of journalistic texts (see also Halliday and Matthiessen 2004: 657 on nominalizing writers' use of power and prestige to "mark off the expert from those who are uninitiated").

All of the themes mentioned will return in the following, which presents an initial investigation of double-possessive nominalizations, i.e. such constructions as in (1) and (2):

(1)   *Caesar's destruction of the city*

(2)   *My understanding of the assignment*

I shall call them double-possessive because the head (*destruction* in (1) and *understanding* in (2)) is both preceded and followed by a possessive phrase. The preceding possessive phrase may, as in (1), take the form of a phrase with the enclitic postposition *'s* (or its phonologically zero allomorph), or of a possessive determiner, as in (2); the following possessive phrase always takes the form of a prepositional phrase introduced by *of*. The equivalence of postpositional phrases with *'s* and prepositional phrases with *of* has been argued on many occasions (cf. Mackenzie 1985); consider, for example, the semantic equivalence of (3) and (4):

(3)   *The destruction of the city*

(4)   *The city's destruction*

Nominalization will be analysed as involving the assimilation of a non-nominal to a nominal lexeme (cf. Mackenzie 1996: 325). Thus the noun *destruction* is linked through nominalization to the verb *destroy*, and the noun *understanding* to the verb *understand*. What I take to be characteristic of nominalization is thus the syntactic categories of the lexemes at issue. My position therefore differs from that taken by Halliday, who sees nominalization as covering cases in which "a group, phrase or clause comes to function as part of, or in place of (i.e. as the whole of), a nominal group" (Halliday and Matthiessen 2004: 358). This leads him to see embedding in English as "a form of nominalization". In contrast, I shall be concerned with nominalization as an alternative to embedding (or indeed subordination in general), i.e. with the language user's 'choice' between a nominalized and a non-nominalized formulation of a syntactically subordinated predication. To take an example from the corpus (see below for details), the issue is the co-availability of nominalized (as in (5)) and non-nominalized (as in (6)) formulations:

(5) *before his invasion of Kuwait* (corpus)

(6) *before he invaded Kuwait* (invented)

It is the transparent similarity of such examples as (5) and (6) that has encouraged linguists to regard the nominal and verbal forms as being very closely related, either by transformation (as in Chomsky 1964) or through the assignment of the same abstract syntactic schema, as in X-Bar Theory (Chomsky 1970). After all, both *invasion* in (5) and *invade* in (6) appear to have the same valency, i.e. a requirement to take two arguments expressing the Agent and Patient respectively. This is also the position taken in standard works in Functional Grammar (FG). Dik (1997: 165) postulates parallel 'predicate frames' (i.e. valency structures) for nominal and verbal lexemes linked through nominalization. In Role and Reference Grammar (RRG), too, "deverbal nominals have the same logical structure in their lexical entry as the corresponding verb" (Van Valin and LaPolla 1997: 186), although the authors recognize (1997: 60) that not every noun phrase that is structurally akin to (1) has a clausal equivalent, their example being *yesterday's shelling of Paris*; this point will be expanded in Section 3 below.

However, the analysis of nominalizations as semantically and syntactically parallel to verbal clauses runs into various difficulties (cf. Mackenzie 1996, and also Butler 2003: 270–278 for a lively account of the nominalization debate within FG). Firstly and morphosyntactically, an explanation is needed for the occurrence of (double) possessive marking in the English noun phrase. Whereas Dik (1997: 158) appeals to a principle of formal adjustment in the expression rules whereby the predication is squeezed (as well as possible) into the mould of the unmarked NP, Mackenzie (1996) argues that the phrases are true – if metaphorical – Possessors, a position that chimes with Halliday's above-mentioned view of nominalizations as metaphorical, and that the two constructions should receive distinct representations.

Secondly and semantically, equating nominalization with subordination fails to explain the meaning difference between the abstract noun and its verbal congener, a difference in the nominalization that Lehmann (1982) has characterized as 'typification', the creation of a concept that is not specific to the situation at hand. Typification links both to the function of nominalizations in headlines, calling up a concept that will be given specific detail in the newspaper article to follow (Downing 2000), and to the use of nominalizations to withdraw from reality and thereby mystify the reader (Pérez de Ayala Becerril 2002).

Thirdly and textually, no explanation is offered by the proponents of full valency for the fact that in actual usage nominalizations occur overwhelmingly with less than the full complement of adnominal elements. Whereas finite, active uses of a verb such as *destroy* will come accompanied by both arguments (Agent and Patient), examination of the British National Corpus (BNC) with the VIEW Concordancer (see below) reveals that of the corpus's 2315 occurrences of *destruction*, 1258 (50.0%) occur with no adnominal elements, while 1144 (49.4%) occur with only one adnominal element (of these 65 are preposed, e.g. *our destruction*, and 1079 postposed, e.g. *destruction of that relationship*). Crucially, there are only 13 (0.6%) instances in which *destruction* occurs with equivalents of both Agent and Patient, e.g. *their destruction of the Burgundian kingdom in the mid-430s*.

The major conclusion from these figures (which can be replicated for any nominalization in English) must be that the construction on which the edifices of many theoretical approaches to nominalization have been built, that exemplified in (1) above, is by far the most infrequent among nominalizations. Whereas this may be unproblematic from a formalist viewpoint (which is concerned with accounting for the **possible** constructions in language), from a functionalist viewpoint (which seeks to account for which constructions are **normal** in a given communicative context) we must prefer an analysis in which the most frequent construction (that without any adnominal material) is basic, and in which constructions with gradually more adnominal elements are seen as elaborations of that basis (for just such an account, see Mackenzie 1996).

The frequency observations for English are mirrored by the rarity of the double-possessive construction in the languages of the world (Comrie and Thompson 1985). It is perhaps the fact that English unusually has two positions within the NP available for possessives (*the horse's mane, the mane of the horse*) that makes the construction possible at all. It appears, then, that the Anglocentricity of linguistic theorizing may have played tricks on those who regard double-possessive nominalizations as unmarked.

In the remainder of this article, I shall pursue the analysis of the double-possessive construction on the basis of data derived from application of the Variation in English Words and Phrases (VIEW) Concordancer available on the Internet at http://view.byu.edu/ to the 100-million-word British National Corpus (http://www.natcorp.ox.ac.uk/). Since the Concordancer sometimes yields double responses and does not respond in the given time to more complex search instructions, I shall not be presenting quantificational data, but rather shall use the results to indicate trends in the data and also for qualitative analysis. Another reason why raw statistics cannot be used is that a search instruction like [*'s *ion of] retrieves strings which satisfy the formal criteria but are irrelevant to the research question, e.g. *today's generation of cars*. Forms in *–ion* and *–ing* will accordingly be considered only if they are closely related in meaning to the verbal stem to which the suffixes attach.

Verb-to-noun non-agentive nominalization of the kind to be investigated here can be signalled by a range of suffixes including *–ment* (*government*), *–al* (*proposal*) and *– ance/ence* (*allowance, preference*) as well as zero (*approach*). However, the investigation will be limited to instances with either the most frequent nominalizing suffix *–ion* (as well as its various allomorphs *–tion, –sion* etc.) or the suffix *–ing*, which is the morphologically most productive in being theoretically affixable to any verbal stem. The premodifying possessive phrase will take the form either of an NP with the enclitic postposition 's (or its zero allomorph) or a possessive determiner (*my, your, his, her, its, our, your* or *their*); the post-modifying possessive phrase will always be a PP introduced by *of*.

The fundamental research question is the following: under what circumstances is this textually infrequent and typologically unusual construction used? In order to provide an answer to this question, we shall first consider, in Section 2, the semantic properties of double-possessive nominalizations as evinced in the corpus data. Then we can progress in Section 3 to the analysis of the syntactic environments in which double-possessive nominalizations occur and in Section 4 to the conclusions that can be drawn from that analysis.

2. The semantic properties of double-possessive nominalizations

An important insight of FG, first set out in Hengeveld (1989), is that subordinate constructions, i.e. those that depend for their occurrence upon other constructions, may be associated with different kinds of entity. Thus Hengeveld analyses an instance of direct speech introduced by the verb *say* as being in correspondence with a 'speech act', a clause subordinated to the verb *know* with a 'potential fact', and a clause subordinated to the verb *see* (in its visual sense) with a 'state-of-affairs'. With regard to (7) and (8), examples taken from Katz and Postal (1964: 123 ff.), Hengeveld observes that nominalizations, which are also subordinate constructions, may be associated with potential facts (as in (7)) or states-of-affairs (as in (8)):

(7)   *I dislike John's carelessly driving the car.*

(8)   *I dislike John's careless driving of the car.*

Further development of Hengeveld's ideas by various scholars in FG has led to the elaboration of a more complex typology of semantic categories in Hengeveld and Mackenzie (2006: 673), as set out in Table 1:

Table 1. Semantic categories

Semantic category	Variable	Examples
Individual	x	chair, brother_of
State-of-Affairs	e	meeting, cause_of
Propositional Content	p	idea, belief_in
Property/relation	f	colour, fond_of
Location	l	garden, top_of
Time	t	week, end_of

The various categories proposed here appear to correspond *grosso modo* with various suffixation and word formation strategies in English, as shown in Table 2, also from Hengeveld and Mackenzie (2006: 673):

Table 2. Suffixation and word formation strategies

Semantic category	Examples
x	mean-ness, kind-ness, false-ness
e	writ-er, employ-er, sing-er
p	explora-tion, deci-sion, deple-tion
f	hope-Ø, wish-Ø, belief-Ø
l	brew-ery, bak-ery
t	summer-time, day-time

Table 2 suggests that nominalizations in *–ion* designate states-of-affairs (e). This is true of (9), which like all following numbered examples is drawn from the corpus:

(9)   *Iraq's invasion of Kuwait was simple theft.*

However, by various processes of metonymy, such nominalizations can also come to designate entities of other kinds. Thus in (10), *conception* designates a propositional content (variable: p), one that results from the action of conceiving:

(10)   *In acquiring one's conception of the world, …*

And in (11), *collection* designates not the activity of collecting but the totality of objects collected, i.e. the individual (variable: x) that results from the activity:

(11)   *the British Museum's collection of seventy Zapotec ceramics*

The same kind of metonymic extension is observable in nominalizations formed with the suffix *–ing*. This suffix is familiar from the formation of gerundive constructions such as (12):

(12)   *the myth of Athena growing a beard*

In addition, the suffix is employed to form nominalizations whenever there is a lexical gap, i.e. no well-formed word with a derivational suffix such as *–ion*. This becomes particularly clear from the corpus analysis, in which there is a relation of complementary distribution between the verbs nominalized with *–ion* and those nominalized with *–ing*. (13) gives a sample of the verbs underlying the most frequently encountered double-possessive nominalizations in *–ion*, and (14) a sample of the verbs underlying the most frequently encountered double-possessive nominalizations in *–ing*. The reader will be able to determine not only that the two sets do not overlap but also that the verbs in (14) lack a corresponding nominalization in –*ion* (or indeed one with any other relevant suffix):

(13)   *acquire, allege, allocate, annex, apply, appreciate, assume, collect, comprehend, condemn, consider, consume, conceive, construct, create, define, denounce, describe, discuss, estimate, evaluate, examine, expect, explain, explore, express, impress, intend, interpret, introduce, invade, invent, investigate, observe, occupy, perceive, possess, predict, present, produce, provide, recognize, recollect, reject, represent, select, suspect*

(14)   *cross, find, handle, hold, learn, link, loathe, market, name, pattern, plan, play, rate, read, record, report, restructure, sell, set, teach, tell, training, understand, use, view, write*

Although it is true that all the verbs in (13) have a Latinate origin, the choice of suffix does appear to be a matter of morphological blocking rather than historical roots since there are also several Latinate items in (14): note in particular how the ill-formedness of *restructuration (quite acceptable in French) entails the use of *restructuring* in (15):

(15)   *Our restructuring of the support arrangements also means that …*

Two instances of –*ing* were found, it should be said, where –*tion* would have been possible:

(16)   *… some liberals had pushed their rationalizing of the Christian faith to the extreme.*

(17)   *we will give you help in your resolving of any claim you may have.*

and there appeared to be some hesitancy about the form *rendition* (with truncation of the final syllable of *render*), with as many as 121 instances of *rendering of* in the BNC as against 82 of *rendition of.*

Returning to the matter of metonymic extension, we observe the same pattern among the double-possessive nominalizations in –*ing*. Alongside examples like (8), in which the nominalization designates a state-of-affairs, in (18) we see *understanding* designating a propositional content (p):

(18)   *a new idealism and optimism transformed man's understanding of himself.*

and in (19) *drawing* designating an individual (x):

(19)   *what looked like a child's drawing of a ladder lay across it.*

In Mackenzie (1998), I proposed adding a further semantic category to the six listed in Table 1, that of manners (m), pointing out that we regularly refer to the way in which states-of-affairs are carried out. Among the linguistic techniques available to us to do this are (a) manner adverbs (typically ending in –*ly*), (b) prepositional phrases introduced by *like, in the manner of,* or *a la* and (c) finite clauses introduced by *the way* or *how.* Consider in this light examples (20) and (21), with *–ion* and *–ing* nominalizations respectively:

(20)   ... *has more to do with people's perception of George Michael than anything else.*

(21)   *Americans liked Reagan's personality and his handling of the economy and foreign policy.*

Note that *people's perception of George Michael* is equivalent to *the way people perceive George Michael* and *his handling of the economy and foreign policy* is equivalent to *how he handled the economy and foreign policy.*

The provisional conclusion is that double-possessive nominalizations, and probably nominalizations in general, designate the semantic category state-of-affairs (e) but that the designation can also be metonymically extended to three other semantic categories, p, x and m, to use the FG variables. The data suggest, however, that we need to consider a fourth metonymic category, one that has not been mentioned in the existing literature. Consider such examples as the following:

(22)   ... *then continued to augment his holdings of land and office.*

(23)   ... *are worried about the size of their allocation of FA Cup final tickets.*

What is augmented in (22)? What has size in (23)? The answer surely is not a state-of-affairs or any of the semantic categories mentioned above. What is designated here is an amount (in the case of uncountables, like *land and office* in (22)) or a number (in the case of countables, like *tickets* in (23)), since (22) must be interpreted as 'continued to augment the amount of land and office he held' and (23) as 'worried about the size of the number of the FA Cup Final tickets allocated to them'. Let us for such cases add the semantic category 'quantity' (with the variable q; cf. Hengeveld and Wanders 2007:221 for this variable). This category may also be relevant for instances like (24):

(24)   ... *gruesome details of their combination of sexual and dietary depravity*

Here the meaning is merely that the people were both sexually and nutritionally depraved, not that there was any state-of-affairs of (wilful) amalgamation of the two.

A construction found very frequently in the data is that found in (25), an apparent double-possessive nominalization with the head *feeling*:

(25)   ... *her feeling of remorse at the kind of marriage she could offer Stanley.*

Although it is certainly the case that 'she felt remorse', and *her feeling of remorse* would represent a regular nominalization of that clause, I am loath to analyse it as a double-possessive nominalization. Note that *feeling* can here be paraphrased as 'sense' and in *her sense of remorse*, *remorse* would be in apposition to *sense*. This would then be the correct analysis of (25): 'her feeling (namely remorse at ...)'. This is also connected to the constraint whereby non-controlled, non-dynamic states-of-affairs (such as 'feeling remorse') are found to be ungrammatical in double-possessive nominalization: *his knowing of the answer, *her resembling of her mother, etc (Naumann 1998).

Let us now consider the types of 'process' that predominate among the double-possessive nominalizations in the data. In terms of Halliday's typology of process types (Halliday and Matthiessen 2004: 171), there is a goodly number of material processes involved, but mental processes clearly predominate, with a smattering of verbal processes too, as a glance back at (13) and (14) will reveal. The fact that the nominalization *Iraq's invasion/annexation/occupation of Kuwait* occurs 50 times in total should perhaps be ascribed to the political circumstances at the time of data-gathering. Otherwise, it is mental processes, 'concerned with our experience of the world of our own consciousness' (Halliday and Matthiessen 2004: 197), that are in the majority, with such heads as *perception, conception, expectation, interpretation, understanding* and *appreciation* being among the most common.[2] By far the most frequent combination, with 352 tokens (as against 51 of *my understanding of …*, for example), is *our understanding of …*, where *our* is in almost all cases to be understand as 'human beings", for example in (26):

(26) … *so that we can improve our understanding of naturally occurring phenomena.*

The predomination of mental processes in the data is surprising, since it has long been supposed that nominalization applies most freely to highly effective verbs, i.e. to those that induce a change of state in the **second** argument, the Patient. Hence, presumably, the preponderance of examples such as (1) in the nominalization literature. Mental processes, however, typically involve a change in the **first** argument (in Halliday's parlance, the Senser; Halliday and Matthiessen 2004: 201). With verbs such as *perceive, conceive, interpret*, etc., it is a matter of how the Senser is altered (mentally) as a result of interacting with the phenomenon. This may also explain why such verbs predominate in double-possessive nominalizations. In single-possessive nominalizations of material verbs, as in (3) and (4) above, it is the verb's second argument that is expressed as the possessor, since it undergoes the change and its mention is therefore more crucial. The title of the film *The Killing of Sister George* is in principle ambiguous between a reading of *Sister George* as Agent or Patient; but the preferred interpretation will be as Patient (being the more affected role) – and this is indeed what is intended by the title! However, with mental verbs such as *interpret*, it is the first argument that has the more affected role: when a student interprets a text, s/he is affected by that experience, not the text. Nevertheless, with single-possessive nominalizations of material processes of the type shown above, it is again the second argument that occurs in possessive form: *the perception of reality, the interpretation of the text*. The rationale for the double-possessive nominalization is therefore particularly strong in such cases, since it allows mention of the more affected role, the Senser.

---

2. Although low in control, these are dynamic processes, and thus do not fall foul of the above-mentioned constraint on the nominalization of [−con, −dyn] verbs.

Those mental processes which do have the Senser in single-possessive nominalizations, characterized by the so-called 'psych verbs' (cf. Grimshaw 1990), understandably fail to show up in the data because the Phenomenon appears after a preposition other than *of*, e.g. *Laurie's frustration at Sue's indifference, Noel's satisfaction with his exam results*. One interesting exception is *impression*, as in (27):

(27) *That is my impression of the situation.*

Here *my* is the Senser and *the situation* is the Phenomenon, but the nominalization is not in correspondence with **I impressed the situation*, but rather with *(how) the situation impressed me*. This inverted relationship qualifies *impress* as a psych-verb. However, a frequent collocation in the corpus is with *artist's*, as in (28):

(28) *Our artist's impression of Lucan as he might look today ...*

Here, I would argue, there has been a shift of sense, so that *impression* here means 'portrayal', with *our artist* as Agent and *Lucan* as Patient. This then allows the expression to occur as an argument of a verb of visual perception, i.e. an individual (x-entity), as in (29):

(29) *... poring over a damp dog-eared artist's impression*

in which, it should be said, *artist's* is to be analysed as a classifying rather than specifying genitive.

To summarize this section's semantic analysis, then, we have found that double-possessive nominalizations in English designate states-of-affairs but also can be extended metonymically to designate individuals, propositions, manners, and quantities. The other major finding is that such nominalizations predominantly designate dynamic mental processes, involving a change of state in the individual designated by the preposed possessive.

3. The syntactic properties of double-possessive nominalizations

The formal parallelism between double-possessive nominalizations and two-argument clauses has led many grammarians to assume that such nominalizations are alternatives to a subordinate clause. This seems to me as true of formalist appeals to structural analogues as of functionalist claims of a 'congruent' congener to metaphorical nominalizations. There are indeed cases in which the nominalized and non-nominalized versions do appear to be little more than stylistic variants, for example after temporal conjunctions, as in (30):

(30) *His parents had sent him to Oslo immediately after Hitler's annexation of Austria.*

This could have been formulated as … *immediately after Hitler annexed Austria.*[3] This kind of homology also applies to the analysis of such nominalizations as in (31), where there is equivalence with an embedded presupposed object clause of the form *that British Steel has "abruptly" announced the closure of the Ravenscraig plant:*[4]

(31)   *It also calls on the general assembly to deplore British Steel's "abrupt" closure announcement of the Ravenscraig plant.*

Nominalizations in English are typically associated with presupposed information, and equivalence with the complement of a 'factive' verb such as *deplore* is therefore to be expected.

There is also frequent equivalence with manner clauses introduced by *how*. This appears to link up with the presupposed status of nominalizations, since such clauses presuppose the event, and focus attention on its execution. Consider (32), in which the nominalization is equivalent to *how he investigated various aspects of the negative attraction rule*:

(32)   *Labov's (1973) account of his investigation of various aspects of the negative attraction rule …*

At the same time, the nominalized form seems to emphasize more strongly the results of Labov's work than does the clausal version.

The data also display several instances in which there is equivalence with a non-finite clause, either a gerundive or an infinitive. Consider the following examples:

(33)   *… films that were quite forthright in their condemnation of social vices*

(34)   *Annadale continued their domination of the men's 1500m*

where there is equivalence with *… in condemning social vices* and *… to dominate the men's 1500m* respectively.

Nevertheless, there are a number of syntactic circumstances under which nominalizations do not have well-formed clausal equivalents. Thus although there is equivalence when a subject clause is found in clause-initial position, only the nominalization is available when clause-initial position is assumed by another element:

(35)   *Their exploitation of this recently opened path aroused jealousy among the knights.*

The double-possessive nominalization is equivalent to the clause *that they were exploiting this recently opened path* but this is not possible in the interrogative analogue *Did their exploitation …*: cf. **Did that they were exploiting this recently opened path arouse*

---

3.   This also suggests a close link between prepositions (such as *after* in (30)) and conjunctions (*after* in the alternative formulation), as explored by Hengeveld and Wanders (2007).

4.   The nominalization in (31) in unusual in that the postposed possessive is to be understood as an argument of *closure*, the modifier within the nominal compound *closure announcement*.

jealousy? A corpus example of the effect of the cleft construction, in which the Focused subject is moved away from clause-initial position by *It* + BE, is (36), where again paraphrase with **It was that Germany declared war on Russia* ... is ill-formed:

(36)   *It was Germany's declaration of war upon Russia which led to France and Britain declaring war.*

Similarly, the occurrence of a grammatical preposition (as opposed to the lexical preposition in (30) above) such as *to* in the prepositional verb *lead to* enforces the choice of a gerundive or a nominalization, as in the following case, where a finite clause is impossible:

(37)   *This protest ... led to his foundation of the Lake District Defence Society.*

Where a concept that could be expressed with a clause is related by coordination or contrast to another that is inherently an NP, then there appears to be pressure for nominalization. Consider the following example, in which the NP *the programmes* 'primes'[5] the choice of a nominal expression of the second conjunct, which could have been expressed clausally as *how we understand the facilities available to you*:

(38)   *... summarising the programmes and our understanding of the facilities available to you.*

Similar remarks apply to example (39), which could, perhaps more straightforwardly, have ended with *the fact that he does not possess a Ph.D.*:

(39)   *Swallow's predicament is a familiar one in British universities, as is his non-possession of a Ph.D.*

The presence of a nominal head in a nominalization opens up the possibility of adjectival modification. In many cases, the adjective in a double-possessive nominalization is equivalent to an adverb in the corresponding clause. These may be a manner adverb (*forcibly* in (40)), a temporal adverb (*subsequently* in (41)), an evidential adverb (*allegedly* in (42)), or even possibly an illocutionary adverb (*bacteriologically* in (43)) – i.e. the adverb may occur at any of the four layers distinguished in FG:

(40)   *the Communist Party's forcible suppression of opposition in 1948*

(41)   *Foucault's subsequent repudiation of the central thesis of Madness and Civilization*

(42)   *Japan's alleged obstruction of foreign investment plans ...*

(43)   *Robert Koch's bacteriological explanation of cholera*

---

5.   There is increasing evidence for 'priming', i.e. the notion that the production of a certain formal structure encourages the production of a subsequent element with similar structure (Pickering & Branigan 1999).

In addition, the corpus shows instances in which the adjectives correspond with a verb and its clausal complement. Here the relationship between nominalization and clause is already looser. For example, the combination of adjective and head in (44) corresponds to the finite catenation *continues to dominate*, in (45) to *planned to invade*, and in (46) to *amended how they define*:

(44) *the USSR's continued domination of her neighbour*

(45) *Edward's planned invasion of France*

(46) *Schrager and Short's amended definition of corporate crime*

However, there are also instances in which the adjective is inherent to the nominalization and there is no adverbial equivalent, e.g.:

(47) *the ordinary courts' particular interpretation of all of these terms*

(48) *other relations enter into our various conceptions of these things*

(49) *his well-known discussion of the function of the category of time*

(50) *their entire production of a line of woollen garments*

These adjectives fall into the class recognized by Halliday and Matthiessen (2004) as post-Deictics: they occur immediately after the determiner and serve to indicate a property of the 'thing' designated by the noun: small wonder, then, that they have no equivalent in the clausal expression.

This section has argued that the relation between the double-possessive nominalization and its clausal equivalent is, at best, a loose one. There are several syntactic environments in which nominalization is required or at least preferred to clausal expression. In addition, nominalizations can display properties, such as the presence of post-Deictics, for which there is no clausal equivalent.

4. Conclusion

Nominalization is a prominent device in contemporary English. Halliday and Matthiessen (2004: 657) remark that it "probably evolved first in scientific and technical registers" but "has gradually worked its way through into most varieties of adult discourse", where "it tends to become merely a mark of prestige and power". Nominalization typically involves a degree of implicit communication, since in almost all cases at least one of the arguments of the nominalized predication is lost. Where this exceptionally does not happen, we have double-possessive nominalization, the object of this article. The argument, set in a functional framework inspired by Dik (1997) and Halliday and Matthiessen (2004), has used a corpus methodology to derive some observations about the properties of this construction, which has all too easily been assumed to have characteristics analogous to those of the full clause. The indications are that double-possessive nominalizations have a range of metonymically linked designations and refer above all to mental processes. Syntactically, they are not in free variation with full clauses (as a reduction of their function to merely that of marking prestige would presuppose): rather, the use of the nominalized form is obligatory in certain definable circumstances and also permits the expression of certain meanings that are inexpressible in clausal form.

References

Albentosa Hernández, José Ignacio and Arsenio Jesús Moya Guijarro. 2000. "La reducción del grado de transitividad de la oración en el discurso científico en lengua inglesa". *Revista Española de Lingüística* 30: 445–468.

Banks, David. 2001. "Vers une taxonomie de la nominalisation en anglais scientifique". *Le groupe nominal dans le texte spécialisé*, ed. by David Banks, 53–64. Paris : L'Harmattan.

Butler, Christopher S. 2003. *Structure and function: A guide to three major structural-functional theories. Part 2: From clause to discourse and beyond.* Amsterdam: John Benjamins [Studies in Language Companion Series 64].

Chomsky, Noam. 1964. "A transformational approach to syntax". *The structure of language*, ed. by Jerry A. Fodor and Jerrold J. Katz, 119–136. Englewood Cliffs NJ: Prentice-Hall.

Chomsky, Noam. 1970. "Remarks on nominalization". *Readings in English Transformational Grammar*, ed. by Roderick A. Jacobs and Peter S. Rosenbaum, 184–221. Waltham MA: Ginn.

Comrie, Bernard and Sandra A. Thompson. 1985. "Lexical nominalization". In *Language typology and syntactic description. Volume 3: Grammatical categories and the lexicon*, ed. by Timothy Shopen, 349–398. Cambridge: Cambridge University Press.

Dik, Simon C. 1997. *The theory of Functional Grammar. Part 2: Complex and derived constructions*, ed. by Kees Hengeveld. Berlin: Mouton de Gruyter [Functional Grammar Series 21].

Downing, Angela. 1997. "Encapsulating discourse topics". *Estudios Ingleses de la Universidad Complutense* 5: 147–168.

Downing, Angela. 2000. "Nominalization and topic management in leads and headlines". *Discourse and community: Doing functional linguistics*, ed. by Eija Ventola, 355–378. Tübingen: Gunter Narr.

Grimshaw, Jane B. 1990. *Argument structure.* Cambridge MA: MIT Press.

Halliday, Michael A. K. and Christian M. I. M. Matthiessen. 2004. *An introduction to functional grammar.* 3rd edn. London: Arnold.

Hengeveld, Kees. 1989. "Layers and operators". *Journal of Linguistics* 25(1): 127–157.

Hengeveld, Kees and J. Lachlan Mackenzie. 2006. "Functional Discourse Grammar". *Encyclopedia of language and linguistics*, 2nd edn, vol. 4, ed. by Keith Brown, 668–676. Oxford: Elsevier.

Hengeveld, Kees and Gerry Wanders. 2007. "Adverbial conjunctions in Functional Discourse Grammar". *Structural-functional studies in English grammar: In honour of Lachlan Mackenzie*, ed. by Mike Hannay and Gerard J. Steen, 211–227. Amsterdam: John Benjamins.

Heyvaert, Lisbeth. 2001. "Nominalization as an 'interpersonally-driven' system". *Functions of Language* 8(2): 287–324.

Jackendoff, Ray. 1977. *X-bar syntax: A study of phrase structure.* Cambridge MA: MIT Press.

Katz, Jerrold J. and Paul M. Postal. 1964. *An integrated theory of linguistic descriptions*. Cambridge MA: MIT Press.

Koptjevskaja-Tamm, Maria. 1993. *Nominalizations*. London: Croom Helm.

Lees, Robert B. 1966. *The grammar of English nominalizations*. The Hague: Mouton.

Lehmann, Christian. 1982. "Nominalisierung: Typisierung von Propositionen". *Apprehension: Das sprachliche Erfassen von Gegenständen. Teil I: Bereich und Ordnung der Phänomene*, ed. by Hansjakob Seiler and Christian Lehmann, 64–82. Tübingen: Gunter Narr.

Mackenzie, J. Lachlan. 1985. "Nominalization and valency reduction". *Predicates and terms in Functional Grammar*, ed. by A. Machtelt Bolkestein, Casper de Groot and J. Lachlan Mackenzie, 29–47. Dordrecht: Foris. [Functional Grammar Series 2].

Mackenzie, J. Lachlan. 1996. "English nominalizations in the layered model of the sentence". *Complex structures: A functionalist perspective*, ed. by Betty Devriendt, Louis Goossens and Johan van der Auwera, 325–355. Berlin: Mouton de Gruyter. [Functional Grammar Series 17].

Mackenzie, J. Lachlan. 1998. "On referring to manners". *English as a Human Language: In Honour of Louis Goossens*, ed. by Johan van der Auwera, Frank Durieux and Ludo Lejeune, 241–251. Munich: Lincom Europa.

Mackenzie, J. Lachlan. 2004. "Entity concepts". *Morphology: a handbook on inflection and word formation*, ed. by Geert Booij, Christian Lehmann, Joachim Mugdan and Stavros Skopeteas, 973–982. Berlin: Mouton de Gruyter.

Naumann, Ralf. 1998. "A dynamic temporal logic of events, intervals and states for nominalization in natural language". *The computational treatment of nominals*, ed. by Federica Busa, Inderjeet Mani and Patrick Saint-Dizier, 10–19. Montréal: Université de Montréal [COLING-ACL'98].

Pérez de Ayala Becerril, Soledad 2002. "Nominalization as impersonalization strategy: Some corpus notes for the study of agency mystification". *Conceptualization of events in newspaper discourse: Mystification of agency and implication in news reports*, ed. by Juana I. Marín Arrese, 55–70. Universidad Complutense de Madrid.

Pickering, Martin J. and Holly P. Branigan. 1999. "Syntactic priming in language production". *Trends in Cognitive Sciences* 3(4). 136–142.

Ross, John Robert. 1973. "Nouniness". *Three dimensions of linguistic theory*, ed. by Osamu Fujimura (ed.), 137–257. Tokyo: TEC.

Van Valin, Robert D., Jr. and Randy J. LaPolla. 1997. *Syntax: Structure, meaning and function*. Cambridge: Cambridge University Press.

Vendler, Zeno. 1968. *Adjectives and nominalizations*. The Hague: Mouton.

Pragmatics, word order and cross-reference

Some issues with pronominal clitics in Bulgarian

Svilen B. Stanchev
University of Veliko Turnovo, Bulgaria

There is an apparent ambivalence in the lexico-grammatical status of pronominal clitics in Bulgarian. They have the features of pronominal forms on the one hand and grammaticalized markers on the other. The present analysis builds on my previous publications in the field of Bulgarian clitics, sentence pragmatics and word order, but it also takes into account other recent publications on the subject. I adopt the view that Bulgarian pronominal clitics have grammaticalized to a degree where they function as cross-reference markers of the object, identical with verbal inflexions which cross-reference the subject. This approach makes it possible to account for the use of clitics both in their object-reduplicating function and as separate short pronominal forms. In correlation with prosody and special sentence positions, clitics play an important role in the pragmatic organization of the expression as markers of object topicalization. Basing my pragmatic analysis on the general schema of pragmatic positions in the Bulgarian sentence (cf. Stanchev 1997), in this article I present an outline of the major patterns of Topic and Focus assignment involving constructions with reduplicating clitics (CRCs).

1. Introduction

Pronominal clitics in Bulgarian have specific functions in the organization of the linguistic expression, as has been noted in the 'traditional' literature from the 1960s and 70s. Discussions of clitic constructions have led to conclusions that [paradoxically] "...the short pronominal forms seem to be more closely associated both phonetically and semantically with the verb rather than with the noun..." (Ivanchev 1978: 196–7). The moot point here is the fact that although clitics are originally pronominal, i.e. they relate to (and may substitute for) nominal terms, they nevertheless pertain syntagmatically to structures centred on the verbal predicate, as can be seen in (1)–(3):

(1) *Davam   ti   ya*   *knigata.*
give-1SG you-DAT.CL it-FEM.ACC.CL book-DEF.FEM
I give it to you, the book.

(2) *Knigata   ti   ya   davam*   *na teb.*
book-DEF.FEM you-DAT.CL it-FEM.ACC.CL give-1SG to you
The book, I give it to you.

(3) *Davam   ti   ya.*
give-1SG you-DAT.CL it-FEM.ACC.CL
I give it to you.

Cases like these have led Pashov (1978) to the conclusion that short pronominal forms "...have developed into grammaticalized markers of some kind and are similar to particles which 'signal' the direct and the indirect object in much the same way as the verbal inflexion 'signals' the subject" (Pashov 1978: 347). Adopting that point of view would mean assuming a certain dualism of pronominal clitics – pronominal arguments with full pronominal correspondences (e.g. *mene*$_{Full}$ – *me*$_{CL}$ 'me'; *tebe*$_{Full}$ – *te*$_{Cl}$ 'you'; *nego*$_{Full}$ – *go*$_{CL}$ 'him' etc.) on the one hand, and something like 'object markers' in the ad-verbal clitic cluster on the other. In the latter function they resemble, to a certain extent, verbal inflexions. Consider also the following examples:

(4) a. *Udarixa   me.*
hurt-PST.3PL me-ACC.CL
They hurt me / I got hurt.

   b. *Udarix   se.*
hurt-PST.1SG se-REFL.CL
I got hurt.

In (4a.) the subject is not overtly expressed but is 'indexed' on the verbal predicate by the PST.3PL inflexion '-xa' and, in a similar manner, *me* cliticized to the verb 'indexes' the object. Cases with the reflexive clitic *se*, as in (4b), have been discussed within the framework of Functional Grammar (cf. Stanchev 1990) and *se* has been shown to have acquired the characteristics of a grammaticalized marker with ad-verbal cliticization. Similarly, personal pronominal clitics in Bulgarian seem to have evolved into (semi-) grammaticalized ad-verbal markers. As such they seem to have acquired a certain pragmatic significance –that of object topicalization markers.

I shall address the issue about the status and pragmatic functionality of clitics in Bulgarian, primarily in view of their use as object-reduplicating items. I will argue that pronominal clitics in Bulgarian have departed from their original (pro)nominal status as argument position fillers and have developed into some kind of 'agreement markers' with pragmatic and cross-referencing significance. When needed, but not exclusively, the discussion will resort to the framework of Functional Grammar (FG) with special regard to its treatment of pragmatic functions (cf. Dik 1989, Dik 1997a) and of the cross-referencing relation between predicates and terms as outlined in Dik (1989: 132–135), for which Bulgarian offers a favourable testing ground.

2.   Some general characteristics of Bulgarian clitics as ad-verbal markers

Like, for instance, English, Bulgarian is an analytical language with no case marking on nominal constituents. Unlike English (and some other analytical languages) however, Bulgarian word order allows for a considerable degree of variation which is widely employed for pragmatic purposes. This high degree of flexibility and word order variation is supported by structural and prosodic means for the syntagmatic and pragmatic organization of the expression. Along with the paradigm of verbal inflexions, Bulgarian pronominal clitics are a major structural means of indicating the syntagmatic relations in the expression.

2.1   Verbal inflexions

Verbal inflexions code subject-predicate concord and the subject need not be fully specified as a term structure if it is deducible from the inflexion, cf. (5a) and (5b):

(5)   a. *Az vidyax   deteto.*
        I   saw-PST.1SG child-DEF
        I saw the child.

     b. *Vidyax   deteto.*
        saw-PST.1SG child-DEF
        I saw the child.

The PST.1SG inflexion codes the subject term on the verb *vidyax* in (5b), and an overt (pro)nominal realization of the subject term (as in (5a)) may be considered redundant. According to Dik (1989: 133) languages where this can be the case are termed 'Pro-Drop' type (e.g. Italian, cf. Matthews 1997: 251), as opposed to 'Non-Pro-Drop' languages (e.g. English, ibid.). In the latter type the subject constituent cannot be 'dropped'. The optional character of the subject term in Pro-Drop languages makes it possible to use the 'full' expression with an overt subject for pragmatic purposes, notably for emphasis on that overt Subj. constituent, as is the case in (6):

(6)   a. *AZ vidyax deteto.*
        I saw the child.

     b. *Imenno az vidyax deteto.*
        It was *I* who saw the child.

In cases with an overtly expressed subject like (6a,b), prosodic and structural means – emphatic stress as in (6a), or special focus constructions as in (6b) may be employed to 'highlight' the subject constituent in the expression.

2.2   Clitic pronominal forms

Pronominal clitics may occur independently, as short pronominal arguments of the predicate – an alternative to full pronoun forms, as e.g. *Az vidyax deteto*$_{NP}$ 'I saw the child' – *Az vidyax nego*$_{Full\ Pron}$ 'I saw it' – *Az go*$_{CL}$ *vidyax* 'I saw it'. In the latter case *go* takes the pre-verbal (but never clause-initial) position typical of the clitic cluster (see footnote 16). In addition, there is also the object reduplicating use of pronominal clitics in Bulgarian[1], as is the case in (7)–(9) below:

(7)   *Az deteto   go   vidyax.*
      I   child-DEF it$_{CL}$ saw-1SG
      I saw the child.

(8)   *Az go   vidyax   deteto.*
      I   it$_{CL}$ saw-1SG child-DEF
      I saw the child.

(9)   *Deteto   az go   vidyax.*
      child-DEF I   it$_{CL}$ saw-1SG
      I saw the child.

As can be seen from (7)–(9), Bulgarian word order is flexible and dynamic: these examples are word order variations which, without further prosodic specification / emphatic stress, largely correspond to the English 'I saw the child' where the short pronominal accusative[2] form *go* 'it' reduplicates the direct object. It is cliticised to the verb as some kind of ad-verbal marker of an 'accusative' relation between the verbal predicate and an object term. Pragmatically, these are instances with topical subject and object constituents and a focal predicate. A more extensive analysis of the pragmatics of expressions like (7)–(9) will be given in 3.3 below.

Bulgarian pronominal clitics code information about person, number and gender and are also case-sensitive (see footnote 2). Clitic object reduplication is a characteristic feature of Bulgarian which can also be found in other languages of the *Balkansprachbund*, such as Romanian or Greek, but also in Romance languages like Spanish and French. There is a connection between object reduplication and the development of a

---

1.   The clitic can reduplicate both direct and indirect objects. The direct vs. indirect object distinction is of no relevance for the discussion here and I shall adhere mostly to cases with direct object reduplication as representative of the general pragmatic and structural characteristics of Bulgarian clitics.

2.   There are vestigial accusative and dative case forms for the pronominal clitics in Bulgarian.

language to analyticism, as is noted in diachronic descriptions of Balkan and Romance languages (cf. Pashov 1978, Ivanchev 1978).

As already mentioned, not only the direct (Goal/Patient) but also the indirect (Recipient) object can be reduplicated, consider (10) and (11):

(10) *Na Petar mu   izpratixa pokana.*
      to Peter him$_{DAT.CL}$ sent-3PL invitation
      They sent Peter an invitation. / Peter was sent an invitation.

(11) *Na momcheto mu   e studeno.*
      to boy-DEF him$_{DAT.CL}$ is cold
      The boy is cold.

Examples (10) and (11) illustrate different instances of 'dative' clitic reduplication. In (10) an indirect object is located in an atypical pre-verbal position with accompanying clitic reduplication. Just like cases with direct object reduplication, the expression in (10) pragmatically corresponds to an English passive, as suggested in the translation of the example. Example (11) is an instance of a set impersonal collocation with obligatory clitic reduplication; such cases are outside the scope of the present study. In general, indirect object reduplication will be mentioned only briefly and will not be analysed in detail here (see footnote 1 above).

Before proceeding further, it should be noted that clitic reduplication is part of an intricate marking system in Bulgarian and "[a]lthough subject to stylistic and dialectal variation and deplored as illogical by prescriptive grammarians, [it] is a robust feature of Bulgarian grammar. In certain situations, it is even obligatory" (Franks and Rudin 2005: 2).

In the next section I shall outline the functionality of clitic reduplication with regard to word order and pragmatics in Bulgarian.

3. Word order and pragmatics with clitic reduplication

3.1 Some preliminaries

It has been generally accepted that Bulgarian is a language with a predominant S–V–O order of constituents (cf. Avgustinova 1997: 114; Dyer 1992: 63; Stanchev 1987: 34). Despite its lack of case marking Bulgarian is characterized by a very dynamic word order; subject to structural and prosodic marking along with contextual factors, a great number of word order variations are possible in Bulgarian (cf. Siewierska and Uhlirova 1998: 107–110). Clitic reduplication is just one of the structural/marking means for making it possible to depart from the basic 'neutral' S–V–O order and have a preverbal (O–V) object as is the case in (7), (9) and (10). In fact, some word order patterns are not possible, not 'licensed' (Jaeger and Gerassimova 2002: 4), without clitic reduplication.

Even at first sight, it becomes apparent that the analysis of structures with reduplicating clitics will have to deal with the following major issues: a) the pragmatic organization of the expression, i.e. what the reduplicating clitic 'signals' in terms of pragmatics and to which pragmatic dimension the reduplicated constituent should be relegated – topical, focal, extra- or intra-clausal; b) what the structural status of reduplicating clitics is and how these correlate with other pronominal constituents. The 'pragmatics issue' with reduplicating clitics will be addressed further in 3.3. I shall resort to the theory of Functional Grammar because its pragmatics component subsumes in a relatively structured manner not only the clause-internal pragmatic functions but also the correlation to extra-clausal constituents which is relevant to the description of constructions with reduplicating clitics (henceforth CRC). A brief outline of FG tenets regarding the pragmatic organization of the linguistic expression is given in 3.2 below.

3.2   Pragmatics and Functional Grammar

For the pragmatic analysis of linguistic expressions in Functional Grammar (cf. Dik 1989, 1997a,b) a distinction is made between clauses and extra-clausal constituents and, respectively, between intra-clausal and extra-clausal pragmatic functions.

Within the clause, constituents may be divided into those presenting already *given* information on the one hand, and those presenting *new* information on the other, and partially corresponding to that distinction are the dimensions of *topicality* and *focality* respectively. In addition, "[t]opicality concerns the status of those entities "about" which information is to be provided or requested ... [it] concerns the participants..., the "players" in the play staged in the communicative interaction. Focality attaches to those pieces of information which are the most important or salient ... with respect to the further development of the discourse.... [It] concerns the "action" of the play" (Dik 1997a: 312). This approach to Topic and Focus is pretty much mainstream and established in current linguistics. In addition, a brief mention should be made of the fact that FG adopts various subtypes of Topic (e.g. *New Topic, Given Topic, Discourse Topic*) and Focus (e.g. *Completive, Contrastive* etc.) and that there is a certain area of overlap between *topicality* and *focality*, i.e. certain topical elements can be at the same time focal (cf. Dik 1997a: 312–335).

Along with the intra-clausal Topic and Focus, FG posits special functions for the *extra-clausal constituents* which are typically dislocated, or 'bracketed off,' from the clause by prosodic means. The extra-clausal functions Theme and Tail are important for the 'management' and the organization of the content of the expression with regard to the context where it occurs (see Dik 1997a: 310–311). A Theme is a 'left-dislocated' constituent which pertains to the general domain of 'orientation' preceding the clause-proper. It introduces entities "... with respect to which the following clause is going to present some relevant information [as e.g.] [t]he initial constituent in ... the following [expression]: [...] *That guy, is he a friend of yours?*" (Dik 1997b: 389).

The pragmatic function Tail is assigned to extra-clausal 'right-dislocated' constituents, loosely adjoined and adding some further information or 'afterthought.' Tail constituents are typical of unplanned spoken language and they represent some kind of 'repair mechanism', used most often when further specification and clarity is deemed necessary, as e.g. *He is a nice chap, your brother* (see Dik 1997b: 401–403).

This brief outline of pragmatics in FG should serve as a general framework for the analysis of sentence pragmatics in expressions with CRCs further on in the discussion.

3.3   Pragmatic organization of sentences with CRCs

Most current accounts of CRCs have focused on the importance of reduplicating clitics for word order dynamism and the pragmatic organization of the expression in Bulgarian. Authors have focused on different aspects of the role of reduplicating clitics in the expression3. The first obvious observation is that clitic reduplication is indispensable in cases of deviation from the basic S–V–O order when an object is given prominence in pre-verbal position as in (7) and (9). Consider also the following examples:

> (12)   a. *Te   pokanixa   Petâr na večerya*   – basic S–V–O pattern
> they invited-3PL Peter to dinner
> They invited Peter to dinner.
>
> b. *(Te) Petârgo   pokanixa   na večerya*   – 'deviant'(S)–O–V pattern
> (they) Peter him$_{Cl.}$ invited-3PL to   dinner
> They invited Peter to dinner. / Peter was invited to dinner (by them).

The passive English interpretation in (12b) renders the pragmatic contents of the Bulgarian expression in a more adequate manner than the active one (see also (10) above). The clause-initial A^2 (Patient) constituent in (12b) is a topical object signalled by a reduplicating clitic; in the English correspondence the A^2 (Patient) is also topical, only here it is coded in the 'inherently topical' syntactic function Subject. Apparently, along with the structural object marking function in the 'deviant' O–V word order pattern, a major pragmatic function of reduplicating clitics (as illustrated in (12)) is that of object (whether direct or indirect) topicalization marker; I shall pursue this line of reasoning further on in the analysis.

For greater detail in the analysis of word order and pragmatic issues related to clitic reduplication, the discussion below will be organised with regard to the pre-verbal vs. post-verbal position of the reduplicated constituent and its pragmatic functionality.

3.3.1   *Pre-verbal reduplicated constituents and topicality*
Examples (7), (8) and (9) illustrate constituent order variations in Bulgarian where the object *deteto* can be placed in different clausal positions. Stanchev (1997: 128–129) accounts for the differences between cases like (7), (8) and (9) in the following manner: (7) is a case of intra-clausal multiple topical constituents – (Subj.–Obj)$_{Top}$–CL–V,

---

3.   For a summary and analysis of the basic ideas underlying various accounts related to Bulgarian reduplicating clitics see Jaeger and Gerassimova (2002: 6–9).

whereas (8) and (9) are seen as instances of extra-clausal clitic-reduplicated Tail (Subj.–CL–V–Tail) and Theme (Theme–Subj.–CL–V) respectively. There are inherent problems with such an approach which I shall try to resolve through a unified analysis of all clitic occurrences further on in the discussion. In this section only cases like (7) and (9) will be discussed since they are instances of CRC with a pre-verbal reduplicated object, and (8) will be accounted for in 3.3.3.

Previous research on the interplay between sentence pragmatics and special sentence positions in Bulgarian (cf. Stanchev 1997) has shown that in Bulgarian it is possible to have multiple topical constituents in one predication and that there is no 'general' structural marker for Topic assignment, apart from special Topic positions, in the sentence.[4] Both the extra-clausal Theme and topical intra-clausal constituents are defined in the FG literature on the basis of criteria such as "aboutness," "with respect to…" (see 3.2 above). For these reasons it is difficult to make a hard-and-fast distinction between topical and Theme constituents in the pre-verb field. Expressions (7)–(9) would be typical responses to questions regarding *deteto* 'the child' as a topical constituent about which information is to be provided. On the other hand, the speaker (in this case *az* 'I') is always accessible in the communicative situation and is thus also topical. Hence, both *az* 'I' and *deteto* 'the child' are 'given' topical constituents. Since a prosodic boundary between Theme and the rest of the sentence is not always distinctly marked, in cases with clitic reduplication and with multiple 'given' constituents in sentence-initial position the dividing line between 'topical' and 'thematic' becomes 'fuzzy'. In view of this, the question arises whether to analyse (7) as an expression with multiple Topic $(Subj–Obj)_{Top}–V_{Foc}$, and (9) in a similar fashion, however with a reverse order of constituents, i.e. $(Obj–Subj)_{Top}–V_{Foc}$.

The answer to the question posed above will depend on the view adopted about the status of reduplicating clitics – are they short pronominal arguments, or are they merely agreement/cross-referencing markers? There is a certain duality of Bulgarian clitics with respect to that problem. To treat the reduplicated object in (9) as a left-dislocated Theme means to recognize the reduplicating clitic *go* as a pronominal argument in the clause to which that extra-clausal Theme refers. And this would be logical having in mind that reduplicating clitics are after all pronominal constituents. They have full pronominal correspondences with which they can be substituted (in keeping with the structural laws of cliticization) in their non-reduplicating occurrences, e.g. *Az vidyax deteto*$_{NP}$ 'I saw the child' vs. *Az vidyax nego*$_{Full}$ / *Az go*$_{CL}$ *vidyax* 'I saw it'.

4.　In connection with the extreme ease of constituent order variation in Bulgarian, several Topic–Focus configurations are possible. Along with the canonical clause-initial Topic and postverbal Focus, various other patterns occur, especially in spoken language. To capture these patterns one needs to postulate multiple configurations with special positions P_0 through P_4 in the Bulgarian sentence (cf. Stanchev 1997: 132).

However, a counterpoint to the above consideration is that there are instances where reduplicating clitics and their full pronominal correspondences co-occur in one and the same expression, as in (13) below:

(13) a. *Deteto,   az nego go vidyax.*
        child-DEF I   it$_{FULL}$ it$_{CL}$ saw-1SG
        The child, I saw it.

     b. *Deteto,   nego az go vidyax.*
        child-DEF it$_{FULL}$ I   it$_{CL}$ saw-1SG
        The child, I saw it.

Bulgarian allows expressions like (13a, 13b), although they are mostly restricted to informal oral discourse. In such cases the reduplicated constituent *deteto* 'the child' is clearly extra-clausal and intonationally 'bracketed off' as a Theme. It correlates with the intra-clausal full pronominal object *nego* and there is also the reduplicating clitic *go* which is coreferential with the full pronominal *nego*. The existence of cases like (13a,b) where the 'Theme vs. multiple-Topic' ambiguity is clearly resolved, points to a conclusion that reduplicating clitics are not arguments proper since they have their full pronominal correspondences for that function, and this leaves the clitics with the function of ad-verbal cross-referencing/agreement markers. In terms of intra-clausal organization, the difference between (13a) and (13b) is identical to that between (7) and (9), i.e. it is just a matter of reversed order of the intra-clausal multiple topical constituents; however there is in addition an extra-clausal Theme *deteto* 'the child' in (13a) and (13b).

The comparison between (13a)–(13b) and (7)–(9) leads to the conclusion that the latter are instances of multiple topical constituents in clause-initial position, and the former are identical expressions but 'extended' with a Theme. In that intricate correlation (7) and (13a) represent the more canonical $A^1 > A^2$ word order pattern in the clause whereas (9) and (13b) are the 'deviant' $A^2 > A^1$ variations.

From the analysis presented above it is apparent that both (7) and (9) are to be treated as cases with multiple topical constituents (Subject and Object) in clause-initial position albeit with different constituent orders.[5]

The observations so far lead to the generalization that the main function of clitics in CRCs (as illustrated in (7), (9), (10), (13) etc.) is to signal the topicality of pre-verbal objects. This is supported by other accounts of Bulgarian CRCs: clause-initial object topicalization accompanied by clitic reduplication has been noted in one way or the other in the 'traditional' literature (cf. Georgieva 1974, Ivanchev 1978, Popov 1963: 167). This prime function of clitics is also taken as a key point for a formalized account of clitic reduplication and word order in Jaeger and Gerassimova (2002: 6–9) as based on a hypothesis suggested in Leafgren (1997a, 1997b). Object topicalization goes along with a 'deviant' word order where the object is shifted to pre-verbal/clause-initial position. It has

---

5.   In Stanchev (1997) the matter was left open; the current analysis is seen as an 'upgrade' on the discussion presented there (ibid. 128–129).

been suggested (cf. Popov 1963: 229–230, Georgieva 1974: 75) that reduplicating clitics signal deviations from the basic S–V–O word order pattern and help avoid ambiguity. This is however not the whole truth because object reduplication operates along with an intricate system of other markers for the disambiguation of clausal functions. When other oppositions, such as the person-number marking, are neutralised, the CRC alone is insufficient to disambiguate the expression, as in (14a) and (14b):

(14) a. *Gostite   gi   vidyaxa decata.*
         guests-DEF them$_{CL}$ saw-3PL children-DEF
         The guests saw the children. / The children saw the guests.

      b. *Decata   gi   vidyaxa gostite.*
         children-DEF them$_{CL}$ saw-3PL guests-DEF
         The children saw the guests. / The guests saw the children.

The ambiguity in such cases stems from the fact that both NPs in the expression are 3PL and the reduplicating clitic may refer to each one of the two; the reduplicated object may be either in the pre-verb or in the post-verb field (cf. (9) vs. (8)), i.e. word order is not indicative either. Disambiguation in such cases is possible only with the help of prosodic marking and the context of the expression.

In an overview of major hypotheses underlying various accounts of Bulgarian CRCs, Jaeger and Gerassimova (2002: 6–9) note that, among others, object reduplicating clitics have been classified by different authors also as case markers of the doubled constituent, markers of definite and of specific objects – claims which, I think, focus more on the 'side effects' rather than the essence.

It is true that pronominal clitics are case-sensitive, but that's only a vestige from Old-Bulgarian and case marking is not their main function in current Bulgarian. I would rather say that reduplicating clitics 'agree with' the object, rather than 'mark its case'.

That reduplicating clitics are markers of definiteness/specificity of the reduplicated object is, in my opinion, again a 'side-effect' rather than a main function of clitic reduplication; that it is mostly definite objects that are eligible for clitic reduplication is noted in standard Bulgarian grammars. Definiteness marking is however not the *raison d'être* of CRCs; reduplicating clitics typically refer to topical constituents which are inherently 'given' and thus definite. What is more, non-definite objects can also be clitically reduplicated. Determination by at least the indefinite article *edin*$_{Masc}$ / *edna*$_{Fem}$ / *edno*$_{Neut}$ 'one'[6] is a minimal prerequisite for clitic reduplication, as is the case in (15a).

---

6.   Bulgarian count nouns have the property of **optional** indefinite article determination. Thus the difference between
      V stayata   ima   Ø kotka and *V stayata   ima   edna   kotka*
      in room-DEF there is cat   in room-DEF there is a/one-FEM cat
woke would translate as 'There is a cat in the room' vs. 'There is some / a certain cat in the room', both expressions being perfectly grammatical and quite common; Ø signals the absence of any article and *edna* is the feminine form of the indefinite article, which in Bulgarian is identical with the numeral for 'one'.

The indefinite article *edin / edna / edno* determines the NP as 'specific' which allows for clitic reduplication[7] (cf. (15a)). The absence of that minimal determiner renders the expression unacceptable (cf. (15b)):

(15) a. *Edna kotka ya   goni   kuče.*
       A/one cat   her_{CL} chase-3SG dog
       A cat is being chased by a dog.

      b. **Kotka ya   goni   kuče.*
       Ø cat   her_{CL} chase-3SG dog

A typical discourse context for (15a) is when the non-definite (i.e. not 'given') object *edna kotka* 'a cat' refers to a specific / identifiable entity, as presented in (16) and in (17) below:

(16) *Na dvora   ima   množestvo kotki. <u>Edna kotka ya   goni   kuče</u>,*
       in the-yard there is multitude cats a/one cat   her_{CL} chases dog
       druga   kotka e   na dârvoto, a   ostanalite sa do ogradata
       another cat   is on tree-DEF and the-rest are by the-fence
       There is a great number of cats in the yard. One cat is being chased by a dog,
       another cat is on the tree, and the rest are by the fence.

Albeit non-definite, the reduplicated object in the underlined CRC in (16) is still topical since it qualifies as Sub-Topic (cf. Dik 1997a: 314, 323–325) – part of a set of entities already introduced in the discourse. The intended English translation is best rendered with a passive.

There are cases with CRCs where the reduplicated object is on the borderline between topicality and focality, i.e. where the 'givenness' parameter is not met, as is the case in a discourse situation presented in (17):

(17) *Na dvora   stavat   razni nešta: <u>edna kotka ya goni   kuče</u>,*
       in the-yard happen-3PL various things a/one cat   her chases dog
       dete rita topka…
       child kicks ball
       Various things are happening in the yard: a cat is being chased by a dog, a
       child is kicking a ball…

The communicatively adequate English correspondence in (17) is again a passive clause where the A^2 is coded as topical Subject. The reduplicated object in the underlined CRC in (17) is not 'given' in the preceding context, yet it is what the ensuing expression is about. It is thus a New-Topic – inferred from the contextual setting, about which information is to be provided in the predication (cf. Dik 1997a: 312–313). *Edin*

---

7. That indefinite specific (as determined by the indefinite article *edin / edna / edno*) objects can be reduplicated is suggested in Leafgren (1997b: 122) and is also supported by data in the present study.

'a/one' is not the only non-definite determiner which may 'allow' clitic reduplication of the fronted object. Consider (18) below:

(18)   *Nyakakva /edna   žena   ya   otkrila policiyata v gorata   snošti.*
        some   one-FEM woman her$_{CL}$ found police-DEF in forest-DEF last night
        A / Some woman was found by the police in the forest last night.

Arguably, *nyakakva žena* 'some woman' in (18) is not 'given' but nevertheless topical, since it is 'what the predication is about'. It is indefinite but specified[8] as indicated by the determiner *nyakakva* 'some / a certain' or *edna* 'a / one'.

As is seen from the English translations of cases like (15) through (18), the 'pragmatic scope' of CRCs correlates to that of passives – topicalization of a non-A^1 constituent.[9] Thus CRCs are in rivalry with passives as a means of Patient and Recipient topicalization. Despite the pragmatic parallels between CRCs and passive structures however, there is a major difference between the two in terms of the Subject–Object configuration.[10] Communicatively, CRCs are preferred in spontaneous oral discourse whereas passives occur mostly in formal written texts (cf. Jaeger and Gerassimova 2002: 4).

From the discussion so far it has become apparent that reduplicating clitics are associated with topicalization of the object in pre-verbal position. Since 'fronting' of the object is a deviation from the basic S–V–O constituent order pattern, the CRC functions as a marker to resolve the A^1 – A^2 relation in the expression. *Definiteness* is not a strict prerequisite for the reduplication of pre-verbal objects; non-definite specific objects with Sub-Topic or New Topic pragmatic function can also be reduplicated.

Clearly, there is a correlation between pre-verbal object topicality and clitic reduplication in the sense that reduplicated fronted objects in a Bulgarian expression will invariably have topical status, and vice versa – reduplicating clitics may be considered 'diagnostic markers' of topical objects.

3.3.2   *Topicality versus focality of pre-verbal reduplicated constituents*

An object in the pre-verb field of a Bulgarian expression is dislocated from its unmarked clause-final position in the basic S–V–O pattern. This dislocation signals that

---

8.   Research focused on formal linguistic accounts of Bulgarian word order and clitics (cf. Avgustinova 1997 i.a.) has sought a greater detailing of the classificatory parameters allowing object reduplication. In the present pragmatically oriented functional account this is not deemed essential. As already observed, it is primarily topical definite / specified objects that are clitically reduplicated. This is in line with the generalization suggested in Jaeger and Gerassimova (2002: 8) that non-specific (and non-generic) NPs cannot be reduplicated.

9.   Since reduplication of the 'dative' A^3 object, along with the 'accusative' A^2 one, is also possible (cf. footnote 1), it is more precise to say that CRCs signal the topicalization of non-A^1 constituents.

10.   In FG passives are tackled within the concept of alternative assignment of the perspectivizing / syntactic function Subject.

the object (an A² or A³ constituent) is given some communicative salience in terms of the pragmatic organization of the expression.

It was shown in 3.3.1 that when the fronted dislocated object is marked by clitic reduplication (along with a definite or 'specific' determiner) it is topicalized and there may be alternative topical configurations in the pre-verb field – (S–O)$_{Top}$ or (O–S)$_{Top}$, as in (7) and (9) respectively.

Topicality with fronted objects is not limited to the prototypical cases of definite 'given' topical elements; there are instances of fronted object with clitic reduplication which are in the area of overlap with focality. Such is the case with non-definite, non-'given' New Topics which are only contextually inferable as in (17) above.

Another possibility for a focal constituent to be reduplicated in pre-verbal position is in cases like (19):

(19) A: *Kakvo stana   sâs zakuskata?*
          what happened with breakfast-DEF
          What happened with the breakfast?

      B: *Soka   go izpix,   a   šokolada   go pribrax.*
          juice-DEF it$_{CL}$ drank-1SG and chocolate-DEF it$_{CL}$ put away-1SG
          The juice I drank and the chocolate I put away.

The example in (19) demonstrates that Contrastive Focus constituents – *soka* 'the juice' and *šokolada* 'the chocolate' – may also get clitic reduplication. Since these are also partly topical (on this 'dualism' cf. Dik 1997a: 312 – 313) this claim does not contradict the observations made so far.

Expressions with a clause-initial Focus object are a regular pattern in Bulgarian. In such cases the pre-verbal object is not marked by clitic reduplication but it has to be given prosodic accentuation. As a departure from the 'neutral' basic word order pattern this signals special Focus salience of the non-reduplicated fronted object, see (20):

(20) A: *Ti kakvo pročete – vestnika ili knigata?*
          What did you read – the newspaper or the book?

      B: *KNIGATA*$_{Foc}$ *pročetox.*
          book-DEF   read-PST-1SG
          I read the BOOK. / It was the book that I read.

The fronted object in (20B) without clitic reduplication has to be given prosodic salience signalling its Focus assignment in a marked word order pattern. Now see (21) and consider the difference between (20B) and (21B):

(21) A: *Ti pročete li knigata?*
          Did you read the book?

      B: *Knigata*$_{Top}$ *ya pročetox   minalata sedmica.*
          book-DEF it$_{CL}$ read-PST.1SG last   week
          I read the book last week./ The book, I read it last week.

The reduplicated clause-initial object (underlined in (21B)) is a Topic in a prosodically neutral word order.

The discussion of these cases leads to a conclusion that the pre-verbal object functions in an environment characterized by the privative opposition [+/– clitic reduplication] i.e. it may or may not be reduplicated. The pre-verbal object is reduplicated in the communicatively (and prosodically) 'neutral' case when it is Topic, which seems to be the 'default value' of the opposition. A 'fronted' object with no clitic reduplication on the other hand is signalled by prosodic salience and functions as Focus. Hence, *pre-verbal object position + clitic reduplication* seems to be a productive means of assigning the Topic function to object constituents in Bulgarian.

In connection with these observations I refer to the following general schema which is postulated for Bulgarian in Stanchev (1997: 132):

(22) $_{P2}\{\text{Theme}\}_{P2}, {}_{P1}\{\text{Top/Foc}\}_{P1} - {}_{P4}\{\text{Foc}\}_{P4} - \text{V} - {}_{P0}\{\text{Foc/Top}\}_{P0}, {}_{P3}\{\text{Tail}\}_{P3}$

where P0, P1, P2, P3 and P4 are special sentence positions with relevance to pragmatic function assignment.

In an attempt to capture the possible variations in the largely free order of constituents, the schema in (22) shows that, apart from the extra-clausal Theme, in the pre-verb field of the Bulgarian expression there is a special position P1[11] which may be filled either by a Topic or a Focus. In addition, there is also a pre-verbal Focus position P4.[12] The P1–P4 configuration is essential for the pragmatics of the pre-verbal field in Bulgarian.

As a result of the analysis in this paper the general schema (22) can be further refined as follows:

–   when a non-A[1] object is fronted in the P1 position, it is singled out for special treatment subject to further specification by structural and/or prosodic marking;
–   clitic reduplication marks Topic assignment to the fronted object (cf. (21B))
–   prosodic prominence without clitic reduplication marks Focus assignment to the fronted object (cf. (20B))

Prosodic prominence seems to be a general marker of Focus since it is applicable to subjects (cf.(23b)) and pre-verbal peripheral constituents (satellites) (cf.(23c)) in P1, but also to post-verbal constituents (cf. (23d)):

(23)   a. *Ivan pristigna   včera.*
          Ivan arrive-PST-3SG yesterday
          Ivan arrived yesterday.

       b. *IVAN pristigna včera.*
          It was IVAN who arrived yesterday.

---

11.   The first special position in the sentence postulated in the 'classical' FG literature; in the case of P1 numbering also reflects the pragmatic importance of that clause-initial position.

12.   The 'late' numbering in this case reflects not so much the pragmatic status of P4 as the fact that it was postulated later than the 'original' P1, P2, and P3 (cf. Stanchev 1997).

c. *VČERA pristigna Ivan.*
   YESTERDAY did Ivan arrive. / It was yesterday that Ivan arrived.

d. *Ivan pristigna VČERA.*
   Ivan arrived YESTERDAY.

Focus salience of the subject *Ivan* (23b) and the Temp satellite *včera* 'yesterday' (23c) and (23d) is marked by an intonation accent noted in capitals and rendered by the focus construction or accentuation in the English correspondence.

In addition, a Topic–Focus (in that order!) group configuration is also possible in the pre-verb field of the Bulgarian expression. Without clitic reduplication the pre-verbal object must be marked as Focus by accentuation, consider (24):

(24) *Petâr*$_{Top}$ *KÂŠTATA*$_{Foc}$ *prodade*   (*a   ne   kolata*).→ P1$_{Subj-Top}$ – P4$_{Obj-Foc}$ – V
      Peter   house-DEF   sold-3SG   (but not car-DEF)
      Peter sold the HOUSE (not the car)./It was the house that Peter sold (and not the car).

Example (24) illustrates the concurrent filling of P1 and P4 in the general schema (22) with a Subj-Top – Obj-Foc respectively.

With clitic reduplication it is possible to assign the preverbal object in P1 as Topic and the subject is then assigned accentuated Focus in the pre-verbal P4, consider (25):

(25) *Kufara*   *ŽENATA*   *go donese*   → P1$_{Obj-Top}$–P4$_{Subj-Foc}$–CL–V
      suitcase-DEF woman-DEF it$_{CL}$ brought-3SG
      It was the woman who brought the suitcase.

Preverbal Topic assignment of the object in P1 may also allow for Focus assignment of the subject in the post-verbal P0 position, see (26):

(26) *Kufara*   *go donese*   *ŽENATA*.   → P1$_{Obj-Top}$–CL–V–P0$_{Subj-Foc}$
      suitcase-DEF it$_{CL}$ brought-3SG woman-DEF
      It was the woman who brought the suitcase.

Invariably, clitic reduplication of a P1 object in cases like (25) and (26) indicates Topic assignment on that object; when P1 is taken by an Obj-Top, the subject may be assigned the Focus function either pre- or post-verbally –in P4 or in P0 respectively.

3.3.3 *Post-verbal reduplicated constituents*

When the reduplicated object is in the post-verb field of the expression, e.g. in cases like (8), it may be analysed as a Tail constituent (cf. Stanchev 1997), provided the reduplicating clitic is treated as a short pronominal form with argument status just like its full pronominal counterpart. However, adopting a view that Bulgarian reduplicating clitics are not arguments proper but object cross-reference markers, makes it more viable to look for a substantiation of the claim that with post-verbal reduplicated objects too (cf. (8)) clitics are again markers of topicalization, as is the case with pre-verbal reduplicated objects.

In the post-verbal field the object is in its 'default' unmarked position in accordance with the basic word order sequence S–V–O. If there is no special prosodic marking, this ordering correlates with the 'natural' *Topic > Comment / Focus* pragmatic sequence, as is the case in (27a); prosodic prominence of the object (cf. (27b)) would single it out as Focus in much the same manner as in English:

(27) a. *Az vidyax deteto.*   b. *Az vidyax DETETO.*
         I saw the child.   I saw the CHILD.

In (27b) the post-verbal object *deteto* 'the child' is assigned the Focus function through prosodic accentuation. In such cases it cannot be reduplicated since, as already noted, clitic reduplication is not possible with Focus constituents.

Intonational accentuation on the subject *az* 'I' will mark the latter as Focus and the post-verbal object will then pertain to the topical constituents of the expression, see (28):

(28) AZ_{Foc} *(go) vidyax deteto*$_{Top}$.
        I   it$_{CL}$ saw-1SG child-DEF
        It was I who saw the child.

In (28) clitic reduplication is optional and it apparently augments the topicality of the post-verbal object[13]. Reduplication in such cases is however the preferred option when the verbal predicate itself is focused by prosodic accentuation, consider (29):

(29) *Az (go) VIDYAX*$_{Foc}$ *deteto*$_{Top}$.
        I it$_{CL}$ saw-1SG   child-DEF
        I SAW the child.

It is possible to have the expression in (29) without clitic reduplication but the 'reduplicated variant' is the option where the object is explicitly marked as Topic.

The multiple topical constituents[14] may be positioned on both sides of the verbal centre, as in (29) (or, for that matter, (8)), in which case the predicate itself is focal. This pattern yields a "topical– focal– topical" configuration. Or else, the topical constituents can be grouped in the pre-verb field in an S–O or O–S order, as in (7) and (9) respec-

---

13. A clitically reduplicated object in clause-initial position (cf. (9)) will be 'more topical' than the same constituent in non-clause-initial preverbal position (cf. (7)) or in post-verbal position, as in (8). It seems that clitic reduplication may contribute jointly with special sentence position towards Topic assignment. This assumption needs to be substantiated by further research.

14. I have been discussing cases with a topical 'group' involving only the subject and object but the group may also include topical satellites of time, location etc. (cf. Stanchev 1997). This extension however does not appear to reflect in any significant manner on the general constituent order pattern and will not be discussed here.

tively. Grouping of multiple topical constituents is also possible in the post-verb field; consider (30) and (31):

(30)   *Vidyax*$_{Foc}$ *(go) az*$_{Top}$ *deteto*$_{Top}$.
        saw-1SG it$_{CL}$ I   child-DEF
        I saw the child.

(31)   *Vidyax*$_{Foc}$ *(go) deteto*$_{Top}$ *az*$_{Top}$.
        saw-1SG it$_{CL}$ child-DEF I
        I saw the child.

The word order variations in (30) and (31) are a matter of style and 'ornamentation of the narrative'; clitic reduplication is optional and is only felt as an additional enhancement of the object's topicality. Arguably, this again may be considered Topic assignment marking on the object (see footnote 13 above); the latter claim is yet to be further substantiated by an analysis of representative corpus data.

There is no clitic reduplication of 'partly-focal' (e.g. Contrastive Focus) constituents in post-verbal position. As with other focused constituents, post-verbal Focus too is marked by intonational accentuation whereby clitic reduplication is not possible.

In general, clitic reduplication of the post-verbal object is mostly optional, its main function again being to indicate the topical status of the object constituent. Since post-verbal position of the object does not run against the grain of the basic word order pattern in Bulgarian, clitic reduplication here is not a major means of disambiguation (as is the case with pre-verbal objects) but simply an additional (sometimes redundant) object topicality indicator. In compliance with the general *Topic > Focus* tendency, the basic S–V–O sequence will naturally present the post-verbal object as focal in prosodically neutral cases such as (27a). Prosodic salience will assign Focus on the post-verbal object as in (27b); intonational accentuation on some other constituent – the A¹ subject (cf.(28)), the verbal predicate (cf.(29)), or some satellite, will in turn assign Focus on them and the post-verbal object is then topical – with or without clitic reduplication.

As can be seen from (22), various pragmatic configurations are possible with the highly dynamic Bulgarian word order. Typically, focal and topical elements will be 'balanced' on the two opposing poles of the expression whose pivot is the verbal predicate. In the canonical instances of prosodically neutral expressions there seems to be a tendency for topical constituents to be placed in clause initial position thus preceding focal ones no matter whether the latter are pre- or post-verbal. The great number of possible combinations has led to the conclusion that the basic word order pattern in Bulgarian seems to be largely subject to the influence of pragmatic factors rather than to syntactic or semantic ones.[15] There seems to be only one major pattern excluded by

---

15.   As pointed out in Jaeger and Gerassimova (2002: 14), Leafgren (1997c: 5ff.) shows that to-pic-before-comment seems to be the more important ordering mechanism in Bulgarian than subject-before-object or agent-before-patient. This claim is substantiated in the quoted source by extensive statistical data.

the general schema in (22): although Topic and Focus may co-occur in the pre-verb field, they can not be 'grouped together' in the post-verb field of the expression. The various examples adduced so far show that a general marker of focality for various clausal constituents is prosodic accentuation, whereas clitic reduplication seems to function as a general marker of object topicality – either obligatory for disambiguation in the pre-verb field, or optional (augmentative) with post-verbal objects.

4.   Bulgarian reduplicating pronominal clitics and cross-reference

4.1   Verbal inflexions and clitic cross-reference

With regard to the outlines of cross-reference between predicate and terms in FG, as suggested in Dik (1989: 133–134), it appears that Bulgarian reduplicating clitics are items with cross-referencing characteristics. Cross-reference is an appositional relation "…found in many languages, and … its occurrence is not restricted to the relation between Subject and predicate" (Dik 1989: 134). As already mentioned, reduplicating clitics in Bulgarian are 'paradoxical' because despite their pronominal origin they attach to the verbal predicate while relating to arguments of that predicate. Just like case marking and adpositions, clitics signal relations between predicate and terms, but while the former are term/argument markers (i.e. 'dependent-marking' items, cf. Dik (1989: 134–footnote 13)), reduplicating clitics in Bulgarian are markers on the predicate (i.e. 'head-marking items', cf. Dik (ibid.)) and in this they resemble verbal inflexions.

Since Bulgarian is a Subject Pro-Drop language, an expression is complete without an overtly specified subject; verbal inflexions cross-reference the subject constituent on the verbal predicate (cf. (32a, 32b)):

(32)   a. *Az piša   dobre.* – *Ti   pišeš   dobre.*
   I   write-1SG well   you write-2SG   well
   I write well.   You write well.

  b. *Piša   dobre.* – *Pišeš   dobre.*
   write-1SG   well   write-2SG   well
   I write well.   You write well.

In addition to the cross-referencing of the subject by means of verbal inflexions, in Bulgarian it is possible to cross-reference also the A^2 and the A^3 object by means of reduplicating clitics, see (33):

(33)   a. *Petâr mu   ya   dade   knigata   na učitelya.*
   Peter him-DAT.CL   it-ACC.CL   gave-3SG book-DEF   to   teacher-DEF
   Peter gave the book to the teacher.

b. *Petâr mu*   *ya*   *dade.*
   Peter him-DAT.CL   it-ACC.CL gave-3SG
   Peter gave it to him.

In (33b) the nominal object forms are dropped and only the cross-referencing clitics suffice to make the expression complete. In an analogy with (32b) we can say that cross-referencing reduplicating clitics enable Object Pro-Drop phenomena in Bulgarian. Now turning to example (3) at the beginning, it is obvious that this is a case of a 'minimally complete' predication featuring both Subject and Object Pro-Drop where the arguments are not overtly realized but only marked on the predicate by cross-referencing items. These parallels show that the system of cross-reference in Bulgarian involves verbal inflexions for subject cross-reference (cf. (32)) and reduplicating clitics for object (direct or indirect) cross-reference (cf. (33)).

Within the clitic cluster the A^3-marking 'dative' clitic will invariably precede the A^2-marking 'accusative' one, no matter whether they are in pre- or post-verbal position, consider (34) which presents curtailed variants of (33):

(34)   a. *Toi mu   ya*   *dade.* → pre-verbal clitic cluster
          he him-MASC.DAT.CL it-FEM.ACC.CL gave-3SG
          He gave it to him.

       b. *Dadox   mu   ya.*   → post-verbal clitic cluster
          gave-1SG him-MASC.DAT.CL it-FEM.ACC.CL
          I gave it to him.

In (34b) I have used the 1SG form of the verb since it is referentially unequivocal, unlike the 3SG which may also mark 2SG. The clitic cluster is post-verbal only when the subject is not overtly expressed, in which case the verb takes the clause-initial position as in (34b). Whether pre- or post-verbal, the ordering of clitics within the cluster remains constant: 'dative'/A^3 clitic before 'accusative'/A^2 clitic. This clitic IO–DO sequence runs counter to the general S–V–DO–IO pattern.[16]

An interesting phenomenon in canonical CRCs with a pre-verbal clitic cluster and post-verbal reduplicated objects is the concentric tendency[17] of constituent ordering around the verbal predicate – clitics before the verb and (pro)nominal terms after the verb in a $A^3 > A^2 - V_{A1} - A^2 < A^3$ pattern, see (35):

---

16. A simplified generalization from extensive research on word order and the clitic cluster suggests that Bulgarian shows preference for a Subj-V-DO-IO order and the clitic cluster is mostly pre-verbal but it cannot be clause-initial–in such cases the verb is preposed to the clitic cluster (cf. Jaeger and Gerassimova 2002: 4–5).

17. A pre-verbal clitic cluster with post-verbal reduplicated object(s) tends to be felt by native speakers as the "default" ordering of constituents; in view of the great variety of possible word order patterns this is just a tendency with no claims of absolute validity. See also footnote 16 above.

(35)

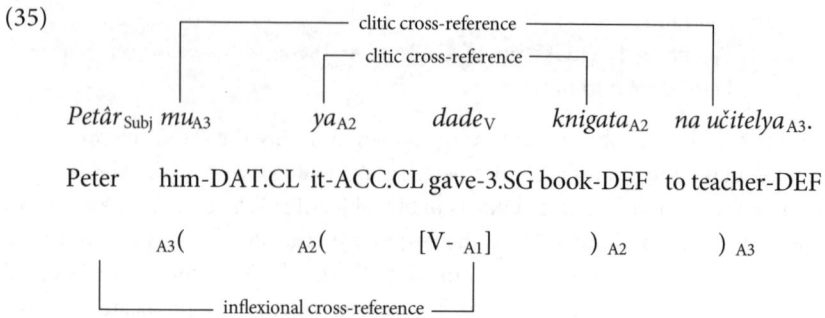

As suggested in Dik (1989: 134), the Semantic Function Hierarchy (ibid. Section 10.4.2) may have some bearing on the way semantic functions are cross-referenced on the verb. The concentric ordering tendency demonstrated in (35) may also be sensitive to the Semantic Function Hierarchy as a manifestation of the A^1 (Agent) > A^2 (Goal / Patient) > A^3 (Recipient) precedence with relation to the verbal predicate. The general validity of this claim however needs to be substantiated by corpus-based research.

4.2   On the status of pronominal clitics in Bulgarian

There may be different ways to account for the inherent 'dualism' in the status of pro-nominal clitics (here I subsume Bulgarian pronominal clitics in all their occurrences, not just in CRCs). One way is to adopt a scalar approach, where they are regarded as argument position fillers of some 'special' kind: on the one hand, as minimal argu-ments, they can make a Bulgarian expression complete just like nominal and full pro-nominal constituents do, but on the other, they are (semi-) grammaticalized markers of person, number, gender and case, structurally dependent on other constituents. In a scalar approach the 'full' (pro)nominal constituents may be thought of as *maximal* argument position fillers whereas clitics are to be regarded as *minimal* argument posi-tion fillers. In this system of minimality and maximality of arguments the much dis-puted reflexive clitic *se* would occupy the lowest end of a 'maximality hierarchy': it doesn't mark person, number or gender but just signals 'reflexivity'. In FG accounts the use of the Bulgarian *se* has been shown to display the properties of a general intransi-tivisation/argument reduction marker along with its vestigial reflexive pronominal characteristics (cf. Stanchev 1990). Thus *se* is lowest on a scale of argument position fillers in Bulgarian: *argument reduction marker se* → *pronominal clitics* → *full (pro)nominal constituents*. This sequence is just a rough sketch because impersonal pronominal and other 'dummy' arguments should also be located in the continuum; nevertheless it gives a general idea of the scalar approach. However, this approach to clitics poses some problems because it presupposes a dualistic account of the functions of the same structural constituent – the pronominal clitic.

To avoid the inherent ambivalence in the traditional treatment of Bulgarian clitics as essentially pronominal constituents, it is necessary to account both for their use as reduplicating clitics and as independent short pronominal forms in a sustained unified manner. For this purpose one needs to assume that even in their independent use pronominal clitics have drifted away from the pronominal system of language and are currently used as object agreement markers in the overall system of cross-reference. Numerous examples throughout the discussion so far (cf. e.g. 4.1 above) indicate that in all uses of Bulgarian pronominal clitics there are parallels with verbal inflexions in their function as cross-referencing items on the verbal predicate; in addition, 'full' pronominal forms have assumed the function of lexical arguments in the predication, thus leaving their clitic correspondences with a primarily 'marking' function (cf. e.g. (13)). All this vindicates the claim about the grammaticalized status of clitics in Modern Bulgarian.

Assuming the predominantly grammaticalized status of Bulgarian clitics makes it also possible to sustain the argument about their specific pragmatic function as object topicalization markers in CRCs. Such an approach is also in accordance with other recent accounts of Bulgarian clitic reduplication.

The analysis of CRCs in Stanchev (1997) is based on a more traditional approach to clitics as elements pertaining to the pronominal system of language and having the characteristics of arguments in the predication. As already pointed out, this approach is less felicitous because of its inherent dualism: it hampers a straightforward analysis of sentence pragmatics because it presupposes the need to analyse some instances of the reduplicated objects as intra-clausal topical constituents while relegating others to the domain of extra-clausal Theme and Tail.

The 'topicalization marker cross-reference' approach adopted for the present analysis allows for a unified and comprehensive, yet precise, account of Bulgarian clitics both as reduplicating elements and in their independent use.

5.   Summary and conclusions

The approach to clitics as grammaticalized markers is applicable both to their use as separate pronominal forms and as reduplicating clitics. Bulgarian is a Pro-Drop language and it is possible to produce complete predications when argument positions are 'minimally' filled by verbal inflexions for A^1 and ad-verbal clitics for A^2 and A^3. Such expressions are the minimal realization of fully specified predications.

In the field of pragmatics, clitics are again best analysed as grammaticalized ad-verbal markers rather than 'full' arguments. In Stanchev (1997) the latter approach was adopted, which led to some inconsistencies and open questions in the analysis. Pragmatically, reduplicating clitics clearly display features of 'object-topicalization markers.'

The main implications and conclusions from the analysis of reduplicating clitics as factors for word order and pragmatics in Bulgarian are:

- The 'default' constituent in preverbal position is the subject; when an object is dislocated to preverbal position it is in a 'deviant' word order pattern; in this a-typical position the object must be marked either by prosodic accentuation or by clitic reduplication.

- A fronted object without clitic reduplication is accentuated and assigned the Focus function in P1 (see (22)); incidentally, accentuation will also assign Focus to a P1 or post-verbal subject, or a post-verbal object, or a satellite; thus prosodic promi-nence seems to be the general focalization marker in the clause, whereas clitic re-duplication is the topicalization marker for objects.

- With clitic reduplication the preverbal object is assigned the Topic function in P1 (see (22)) when the subject is an accentuated Focus either in the next preverbal special position P4 or in the post-verbal P0 position.

- When the verb itself is accentuated as Focus, the reduplicated preverbal object is part of a 'multiple topical group' together with the subject in a random *Subj.–Obj.* or *Obj.–Subj.* ordering before or after the verb; or else the topical constituents are split on both sides of the verbal predicate.

- As predicted by the general schema (22), Topic and Focus may appear together pre-verbally (only in a *Topic>Focus* order), or they can be 'balanced' on both sides of the verbal predicate (either as *Top–V–Foc*, or as *Foc–V–Top*) but they do not appear jointly in the post-verbal field; in all occurrences of the object as pre-verbal Topic, clitic reduplication is obligatory because it serves to resolve the subject / object ambiguity inherent to the pre-verb field in Bulgarian.

- With post-verbal objects clitic reduplication is mostly optional and has 'augmen-tative' function as a marker of object topicality.

- Communicatively, CRCs are in rivalry with passive structures as a means of Topic assignment to non-A^1 constituents: the former occur mainly in spontaneous oral discourse whereas passives are typical of written texts.

Abbreviations and symbols:

A^1, A^2, A^3 – first, second, third argument of the verbal predicate in FG (see below) in terms of their 'centrality', correlating largely to the Agent, Goal, Recipient semantic func-tions respectively

ACC – 'accusative' (of clitic forms in Bulgarian)

CL – clitic pronominal form (short form personal pronouns)

CRC – construction with reduplicating clitic(s)

DAT – 'dative' (of clitic forms in Bulgarian)

DEF – definite article (suffixed in Bulgarian)

DO – direct object

Fem – feminine

FG – Functional Grammar in the tradition of Simon Dik (1989, 1997)

Full – full pronominal form (long form personal pronouns)

IO   – indirect object
Masc   – masculine
Neut   – neuter
PL   – plural
PST   – past tense form of verbs
SG   – singular

References

Avgustinova, Tania. 1997. "Word Order and Clitics in Bulgarian". *Saarbrücken dissertations in computational linguistics and language technology, Volume 5.* DFKI, Saarbrücken.

Dik, Simon C. 1989. *The theory of Functional Grammar. Part 1: The structure of the clause.* Dordrecht: Foris. [Functional Grammar Series 9].

Dik, Simon C. 1997a. *The theory of Functional Grammar, Part 1: The structure of the clause.* 2nd revised edition. Berlin: Mouton de Gruyter.

Dik, Simon C. 1997b. *The theory of Functional Grammar, Part 2: Complex and derived constructions.* Berlin: Mouton de Gruyter.

Dyer, Donald L. 1992. *Word order in the simple Bulgarian sentence: A study in grammar, semantics and pragmatics.* Amsterdam: Rodopi.

Franks, Steven and Catherine Rudin. 2005. "Bulgarian clitics as K⁰ heads". *http://www.cogs.indiana.edu/people/homepages/franks/fasl13.f-r.final.pdf.*

Georgieva, Elena. 1974. *Slovored na prostoto izrečenie v bălgarskija knižoven ezik* (Word order of the clause in Standard Bulgarian). Sofia: BAN.

Ivanchev, Svetomir. 1978. "Nablyudeniya vârxu upotrebata na člena v bâlgarski ezik" (On the use of the article in Bulgarian). *Pomagalo po bâlgarska morfologiya* (A textbook of Bulgarian morphology), ed. by Petar Pashov, 186 – 212. Sofia: Naouka i Izkoustvo.

Jaeger, Florian T. and Veronica A. Gerassimova. 2002. "Bulgarian word order and the role of the direct object clitic in LFG". *http://cslipublications.stanford.edu/LFG/7/lfg02jaegergerassimova.doc.*

Leafgren, John R. 1997a. "Definiteness, givenness, topicality and Bulgarian object reduplication". *Balkanistica* 10: 296–311.

Leafgren, John R. 1997b. "Bulgarian clitic doubling: Overt topicality". *Journal of Slavic Linguistics* 1(5): 117–143.

Leafgren, John R. 1997c. "Topical objects, word order, and discourse structure in Bulgarian". (Presented at the AAASS 1997) Quoted from Jaeger, Florian T. and Veronica A. Gerassimova. 2002. "Bulgarian word order and the role of the direct object clitic in LFG". *http://cslipublications.stanford.edu/LFG/7/lfg02jaegergerassimova.doc.*

Matthews, Peter. 1997. *The concise Oxford dictionary of linguistics.* Oxford: Oxford University Press.

Pashov, Petar. 1978. "Za 'padežite' na mestoimeniyata v sâvremenniya bâlgarski ezik" (On the 'cases' of pronouns in current Bulgarian). *Pomagalo po bâlgarska morfologiya* (A textbook of Bulgarian morphology), ed. by Petar Pashov, 340–356. Sofia: Naouka i Izkoustvo.

Popov, Konstantin. 1963. *Sâvremenen bâlgarski ezik: Sintaksis* (Syntax of Modern Bulgarian). Sofia: Naouka i izkoustvo.

Siewierska, Anna and Uhlirova, Ludmilla. 1998. "Word order in Slavic languages". *Constituent Order in the Languages of Europe*, ed. by Anna Siewierska, 105–150. Berlin: Mouton de Gruyter.

Stanchev, Svilen. 1987. "Some observations on the order of constituents in Bulgarian". *Getting one's words into line. On word order and Functional Grammar*, ed. by Jan Nuyts and Georges de Schutter, 33–43. Dordrecht: Foris Publications. [Functional Grammar Series 5].

Stanchev, Svilen. 1990. "Bulgarian se-constructions in Functional Grammar." *Working with Functional Grammar: Descriptive and computational applications*, ed. by Mike Hannay and Elseline Vester, 17–30. Dordrecht: Foris. [Functional Grammar Series 13].

Stanchev, Svilen. 1997. "Pragmatic functions and special sentence positions in Bulgarian". *Discourse and pragmatics in Functional Grammar*, ed. by John H. Connolly, Roel M. Vismans, Christopher S. Butler and Richard A. Gatward, 121–135. Berlin: Mouton de Gruyter. [Functional Grammar Series 18].

Patterns of multiple theme and their role in developing English writing skills

Mike Hannay
Vrije Universiteit, Amsterdam

This paper looks at patterning in multiple themes in written English. Adopting a view of theme in declarative SVO clauses which extends up to the grammatical subject and its non-restrictive postmodifications, and building on an earlier study by Smits (2002), it uses corpus data to identify three major patterns, labeled "stepwise", "focalizing" and "grounding". All three patterns are used by advanced learners of English in their writing, but the stepwise pattern is significantly overused while the others are underused. In light of the relevance of these patterns for writing text conforming to the C levels of the Common European Framework of Reference, the paper argues for the development of study and exercise material making use of data from learner corpora.

1. Introduction[1]

It is a particular merit of Downing and Locke's *English grammar: A university course.* (2006, the second edition of Downing and Locke 2002) that grammar comes to life as a result of aptly chosen examples of linguistic phenomena being presented in their actual context of use. This shows how strongly Angela Downing subscribes to the idea that one can come to understand the nature of language by investigating how people use it, and by studying the communicative effects that the use of particular linguistic structures may have. The present contribution draws its inspiration from this functional approach to language and takes as its subject the topic of Theme, in the systemic-functional sense, which has held Angela's particular interest: she has applied it in the study of literary text (Downing 1995), she has contributed to the theoretical debate (Downing 1991), and she has paid specific attention to it in the context of advanced language learning (Downing and Locke 2002, 2006). My aim in this contribution is to argue for paying more focused attention to specific thematic patterns in university courses on "syntax for writing", an area of interest which is emerging from corpus and genre-based studies into the linguis-

---

1.   I would like to thank Lachlan Mackenzie for comments on an earlier version of this text.

tic features of native speaker and learner writing (cf. for example Hinkel 2002, 2004); more in particular, I argue that learner corpora can be used to great benefit as the source of exercise material.

One specific type of theme that has started to attract interest over the last few years is that of multiple theme. Assuming an approach whereby theme extends up to the first ideational element (Halliday 1994: 53), the elements in bold in (1) and (2), taken from (Downing and Locke 2002: 233), represent multiple themes:

(1)   *Much to our surprise, though, the show* was a flop.

(2)   *Technologically, then*, it is admirable.

There are three basic categories of theme: textual, interpersonal, and ideational (or experiential). In (1) and (2), *much to our surprise* and *technologically* are interpersonal, *though* and *then* are textual, and *the show* and *it* are ideational themes. A multiple theme can be seen as presenting a complex framework for the interpretation of what follows in the rest of the sentence (cf. Fries 1995: 4). Gómez-González (1998, 2001, 2004) studied the occurrence of multiple themes in spoken data, and looked in detail at the ordering of thematic elements which preceded and followed the experiential theme. By contrast, Smits (2002) looked at multiple themes in the written English of native speakers and advanced learners. The scope of her study is more limited than that of Gómez-González, in that it only covers combinations of two or more adverbial expressions preceding the subject in declarative S-V-O clauses. However, what is interesting is that she identifies five separate patterns, each of which reflects a different kind of complex orientation and typically involves specific grammatical forms.

The idea that thematic elements combine in specific patterns to provide a framework for sentence interpretation may be of considerable interest in the context of developing writing skills materials. First of all, just three of the patterns account for approximately 90% of the multiple themes in Smits's data. Moreover, two of these three patterns are much underused by advanced Dutch learners of English, while the other is much overused (cf. Smits 2002: 161).

However, in order to be able to determine the focus of any study materials, it would be necessary to consider the three major patterns in a wider context, given the limited nature of Smits's study. On the one hand this would allow us to assess the centrality of the three major patterns she distinguishes, and possibly introduce refinements, and on the other hand it would grant a fuller overview of the kind of grammatical structures which make specific contributions to multiple themes.

Accordingly, the text is organized as follows. Section 2 describes the basic patterns of multiple theme distinguished by Smits (2002) on the basis of her corpus study. Section 3 then defines a broader approach to the scope of theme in English, based on Downing (1991), and goes on to discuss additional thematic material to that studied by Smits, taken from a small sample of English texts. Finally, section 4 considers the role which thematic patterns can play in the context of advanced writing courses, against the backdrop of the Common European Framework (CEF), in particular with regard to the development of discourse competences required to perform at levels C1 and C2.

2. Complex beginnings in written English

In her corpus study of what she calls complex beginnings in English native speaker and learner texts, Smits (2002) looks at combinations of two and more adverbial elements before the grammatical subject in sentences with a S-V declarative main clause. She distinguishes five basic types of complex beginnings employed by writers of English, based on a corpus of 500,000 words with texts drawn more or less evenly from (a) newspapers and magazines, (b) academic journals, and (c) fiction. These patterns are illustrated below.[2]

The first type is itself labeled 'complex', and is illustrated in (3) and (4):

(3) *In the matter of trout fishing, of course, things are much more predictable.*
[NEC 53–185]

(4) *By the early 1970s, however, this attitude was changing and Sir Robert Mark, who took over as Metropolitan Police Commissioner, promised to do away with corruption within the force.* [NEC 119–329]

In the case of (3), the second element, *of course*, modifies the first, and the two elements together provide a complex orientation for the message to follow. The function of the modification is to focalize the initial thematic element. With regard to (3), for instance, the core message of this sentence is that in the matter of trout fishing things are much more predictable; moreover, this is obviously the case, and this obviousness is to be understood precisely in terms of it being trout fishing we are talking about. Of the 496 multiple themes in the corpus, 168 (=33.8%) belong to this complex category, and 98% of them have an adverbial such as *however, of course, though, for example,* as second element.

The next type is called 'grounded'; examples are (5) and (6):

(5) *Later, with England converted to Christianity, the daughters of the great Anglo-Saxon noblemen were sent abroad to France to be educated in the Christian and classical mode.* [NEC 3–21]

(6) *On Christmas Eve, when it had become clear that the paper was not going to be scared away, Yeo authorized a statement, published two days later, accepting responsibility for the child.* [NEC 179–513]

---

2. Examples with a NEC coding label are from the corpus compiled by Smits (2002). NEC stands for native speaker corpus. The example is number 185 and comes from text 53. I would like to express my thanks to Aletta Smits for making her database available.

With the grounded type, the second expression further specifies the first, usually by mentioning an event which allows the reader to gain a greater understanding of the relevance of the particular setting for understanding the message to come. The two orientational expressions can usually be paraphrased as a kind of orientational proposition, so that (5) might be interpreted as "Later England was converted to Christianity, and in that situation the following happened". There are 95 grounded beginnings in the corpus, making up just over 19% of the whole. A common syntactic device for the grounding element are full clauses, as in (6), which because of their array of functional slots have excellent grounding potential (Smits 2002: 60), and account for 48% of all cases of grounding. A further 44% of grounding elements are prepositional phrases.

In the third type, 'composite', the second element also modifies the first, but this time in such a way that a fusing of the two frames emerges. Usually this composite theme is made up of time and place expressions, as in (7) and (8):

(7)   *At a conference in London today, Mr Whiskin will stand up and ask his audience to change their minds too.* [NEC 164–390]

(8)   *Two years ago in Dublin I said if you don't have something that is perceived to be inclusive you've had it.* [NEC 219–479]

This type is quite rare in the corpus, occurring 24 times (=4.8%).

The complex beginnings in (3–8) have in common that the second adverbial modifies the first. The final two types do not have this feature. First of all there is the "compound" type, exemplified in (9) and (10):

(9)   *Stripped of his army rank, hair falling over his collar, Anthony Dryland presents an unlikely figure of retribution.* [NEC 112–319]

(10)   *Elevated to a university syllabus, condemned for blighting marriage, Mills and Boon is a publishing success story that leaves Booker winners in the shade.* [NEC 222–70]

Compound beginnings involve two pre-subject elements which could be coordinated. The complex framework they provide is thus created simply by an add-on process. They occur only 17 times (=3.4%) in the corpus.

Finally, stepwise orientations, as in (11–13), provide two separate orientations to the content of the main clause:

(11)   *On the St Petersburg waterfront, if you don't pay off the right people, you may find that the crane operator will drop your cargo in the water.* [NEC 138–127]

(12)   *All being well, at the beginning of next month Suzanne will start a series of injections to stimulate her ovaries to produce the eggs needed to make embryos.* [NEC 124–423]

(13) *In fact, according to Tim Newburn, a criminologist at the Policy Studies Institute and co-author of a government-commissioned report, Persistent Young Offenders, such a group is very hard indeed to identify.* [NEC 162–398]

The stepwise category is the largest of the five types, with 192 examples (=38.7%) in the data. There are two main categories. First of all, 69% have a textual or interpersonal adverbial expression as first thematic element; example (13) falls under this type. Of the remaining cases a lot of examples present an all-encompassing domain within which the rest of the sentence can be interpreted. This domain can then be further restricted, for instance by a circumstantial theme such as in (11) or (12).

In all, the vast majority of these multiple themes – 455 of 496 themes with two adverbials – belong to the complex, grounded and stepwise categories, and academic texts contain more complex beginnings overall than news texts and fiction. A particularly interesting feature is the pair formed by complex and stepwise orientations. On the one hand, the two kinds can operate in tandem, as the following example with three initial elements shows:

(14) *By early 1980, however, with all the worldwide editorial coverage The Trinity was getting, the designers suddenly felt they couldn't afford not to have The Trinity on the catwalk.* [NEC 89–17]

The initial experiential theme *by early 1980* provides a temporal setting for the whole sentence. The second thematic element, *however*, relates the message to come to the preceding discourse, and precisely in terms of the contrast presented by the initial temporal setting. Together, these two elements form a complex orientation, and this orientation is then itself grounded by means of the prepositional phrase, which describes a situation that provides the relevance of early 1980 for understanding the import of the main message.

On the other hand, if the two orientational elements in a complex multiple theme are reversed, the outcome is almost always a theme which one would associate with a stepwise interpretation. By analysing the contexts in which these two types occur, Smits (2002: 118f.) shows that the choice of each type is determined by organizational principles at a higher level of discourse. For instance, complex themes like (4), repeated here for convenience, will tend to appear in a context where the discourse is progressing by chronological development, whereas stepwise themes like (4') would be more likely to occur where the discourse is progressing by rhetorical development.

(4) *By the early 1970s, however, this attitude was changing and Sir Robert Mark, who took over as Metropolitan Police Commissioner, promised to do away with corruption within the force.* [NEC 119–329]

(4') *However, by the early 1970s this attitude was changing and Sir Robert Mark, who took over as Metropolitan Police Commissioner, promised to do away with corruption within the force.*

What is interesting from a language learning perspective here is that a comparison of native speaker data and essays written by advanced Dutch students of English reveals a significant difference in use with regard to the grounded, complex and stepwise patterns. To start with, students use very few grounded themes compared to native speakers (Smits 2002: 157). Moreover, they use many more stepwise themes while native speakers use relatively more complex themes (Smits 2002: 151). One possible explanation for this latter fact, Smits argues, is that students find stepwise themes in some way easier to produce: in cognitive terms, dealing with one thing at a time may be cognitively less demanding. Another possible reason is that university writing instruction tends to emphasize the value of signposting to aid text processing, and signposting may be seen as something that is preferably done sentence-initially.

The findings on overuse and underuse are in themselves enough to suggest that language curricula, and writing programmes in particular, should pay attention to thematic patterns, all the more because Smits's data also reveal that a high percentage of first year learners – some 39% – produce no complex beginnings at all. However, it will be recalled that Smits's study was confined to an analysis of pre-subject adverbial expressions, and before looking at the role of thematic patterns in university writing programmes we therefore have to consider such patterns in a wider syntactic perspective.

3.   An expansion of complex beginnings

Smits' data collection is limited in two main respects. First of all, the constituents she considers are restricted to those with an adverbial function, which means that for instance standard relative clauses, appositions and independent parenthetical clauses are not taken into account. These are illustrated by the italicized elements in the following examples:

(15)   *Because it was a major international intellectual centre, **which has quickly come to rival Paris itself**, Cologne was able to absorb its Scottish contingent.* [ORC A-1–22] [3]

(16)   *In Australia, **traditionally the best market for fiction from Britain**, the hardback sales were proportionally lower.* [ORC A-4–34]

(17)   *Afterwards, at the other end of his life (**it seems that the future cannot be restrained, and insists on seeping back into the past**), when he got his name into all the papers over the scandal of the headless murders, the custom official's daughter Farah Rodrigues unlocked her lips and released from her custody the story of the day on which the adolescent Omar Khayyam, even then a fat fellow*

---

3.   Examples with an ORC coding come from the additional text sample used for this study. A-1–122 means that the example is number 22 in text 1 from the academic articles. In other examples, M stands for in-flight magazines, P stands for political commentary, F stands for fiction, and C for charity mail.

with a missing shirt-button at navel height, had accompanied her to her father's
post at the land border forty miles to the west of Q. [ORC F-4–21]

Second, Smits does not consider the grammatical subject itself. Now, the extent of the
theme is a much debated subject within systemic functional linguistics (cf. Downing
1991; Fries 1995; Berry 1996; Gómez-González 2001; and for an overview of the issues
involved Butler 2003: 129ff), but one of the more widespread views is that the theme
should in standard S-V declarative clauses be taken to include the subject. Downing
(1991: 125) takes *Freud* in (18) to belong to the theme in spite of the initial prepositional phrase being an experiential element as well:

(18) *Towards the end of his life, Freud concluded that he was not a great man, but*
      he had discovered great things.

For her it is important to distinguish between the circumstantial frameworks set up by
spatiotemporal and situational thematic elements and the individual frameworks set
up by participants. This means that for any sentence where the subject is the first obligatory constituent of the main clause, the subject is part of the theme. However, on
this approach a full understanding of thematic patterning also requires that we look at
the way in which subject themes are postmodified, just as Smits does with pre-subject
thematic elements. I will take this idea on board, and call the resulting sentence segment the theme zone, following Hannay (1994) and Gómez-González (2004). Note
that although Gómez-González includes the postmodifications of circumstantial
themes in the theme zone, she does not extend the theme zone up to the grammatical
subject in all cases. Also, note that this approach to theme does not include all elements
that Hartnett (1995) assigns to the "pit" following the theme, since she also considers
elements which relate to the following main predicate as well as postmodifications of
the subject. To clarify, the theme zone in (19–21) is italicized:

(19) *Indeed, even middle-class, Guardian-reading liberals, especially in the inner*
      cities, deny their own actions in worshipping at the shrine of their comprehen-
      sive ideals whilst sending young Charlotte or Thomas to a private or out-of-
      borough grant-maintained school; they explain that, much as it pains them,
      their local school is not good enough. [ORC P-5–18]

(20) *But if our lords and masters have their way, the proposed amendment to the*
      defamation bill, which has just completed its passage in the Lords, will enable
      MPs to waive parliamentary privilege, individually not collectively, and as when
      they choose, to sue newspapers if the individual MP sees fit. [ORC P-7–29]

(21) *Some pages later, Maud (unaware, of course, unlike Possession's readers, of*
      Val's remark) rereads the suicide note of Blanche Glover, LaMotte's companion
      in the house they have shared in Putney. [ORC F-4–51]

To start to get a picture of the situation in written English I compiled a small sample of
texts from five different genres, namely newspaper political commentaries, chari-

ty mail, academic articles, in-flight magazine articles, and fiction. The sample comprises a total of 39 texts comprising 2627 sentences. The elements in the theme zone of each text sentence were classified according to their syntactic status and analysed further in terms of Smits' thematic patterns.

The text sample contains just 10 cases where pre-subject thematic elements are modified by non-adverbial forms. Because of the small number – four independent clauses, three relative clauses and three appositions – I will not consider them further here. However, there are 122 cases where the grammatical subject in declarative SV clauses has some form of non-restrictive postmodification, amounting to 4.6 cases per 100 sentences. This group needs to be looked at in greater detail. The syntactic make-up of the group is presented in (22):

(22)   **Syntactic characteristics of non-restrictive subject postmodifiers**

Relative clause	16
Identificational apposition	31
Property-assigning apposition	13
Adverb or adverb phrase	16
Adverbial clause	04
Prepositional phrase	11
Participial clause	10
Non-verbal clauses	07
Independent clause	07
Other	07
Total	122

Let us consider some of the most important of these modification types in more detail and look at the functions which they perform in context, starting with relative clauses. Duurkoop (2001) analysed about 150 non-restrictive relatives following initial adverbials and grammatical subjects, and found that 85% of these clauses have a grounding function in that they help the reader to gain a fuller understanding of the message, or an element of the message, contained in the matrix clause. We can understand this in two ways. First of all consider (23):

(23)   *The US-based International Women's Media Foundation (IWMF), which recently honoured Kim Bolan and several other women with 'Courage in Journalism' awards during an international conference in Washington, also think it matters.* [ORC M 5–13]

This sentence comes from an in-flight magazine article about female journalists. The IWMF is introduced for the first time, so the reader may not know what it is, and more importantly, will not know why it is being introduced at this point, as a result of which it is potentially highly uninteresting to state that the IWMF thinks that something matters. For the message to be seen as relevant, the IWMF itself has to be seen as relevant, and that is the function of the relative clause here. This is very close to the function fulfilled by relative clauses and other structures in Smits's grounded themes, for instance (5–6) above.

In other cases it is not so much the relevance of the subject referent on the scene that is established by the relative clause but rather a fuller understanding of the message as a whole, the relationship that in Rhetorical Structure Theory is known as background (cf. Mann and Thompson 1987). In (24) the relative clause gives the reader information about Balloch which helps him understand why it was almost certain that he died of natural causes.

(24)   *Yakoob Balloch, who had been suffering for some time from sporadic pains in the region of the appendix, almost certainly died of natural causes.* [ORC F-4–15]

The main syntactic category in subject post-modifications is apposition. Appositions can have different functions in discourse, and following the basic categories proposed in Hannay and Keizer (2005) I distinguished two specific kinds of apposition use in the data here, identificational and property-assigning appositions. Let us consider identificational appositions first, exemplified by (25) and (26).

(25)   *About the time that Athilmer returned to Scotland, one of his protegés, **Thomas Baron**, was elected dean (9 October 1448)…* [ORC A-1–12]

(26)   *One backbencher, **Kenneth Lewis**, declared acidly at a meeting of the 1922 committee that the leadership was on a leasehold, not a freehold, basis.* [ORC P-9–34]

With this kind of apposition the function is to help the reader identify the subject referent. The apposition does not really ground the referent, but rather specifies it so that the reader has a better chance of identifying it. As such, it is rather like the specifying elements identified by Smits to which she ascribes a minimal grounding function, but which she includes under her grounding type. An example is (27):

(27)   *Then, a month later, Charles Wilson appeared at an art exhibition being held by a friend of mine at her studio.* [NEC 111–325]

Here the adverbial expression *a month later* serves to make the reference more precise, but it does not make it clear what is relevant about the time of the event described in the main clause. By contrast, consider now (28) and (29), which are examples of property-assigning apposition:

(28)   *However, around this time, the Rijksdienst van Monumentenzorg (RDMZ), **a government agency responsible for preserving Holland's cultural heritage**, embarked upon a scheme to take an inventory of buildings from the period 1850–1940, a period which had hitherto been neglected.* [ORC M-1–1]

(29)   *Samuel Johnson, perhaps the most eloquent of all defenders of artists' rights, accepted the logic of 50-year copyright.* [ORC P-1–3]

In (28), the apposition might at first appear also to just provide a further specification of the subject term, describing the function of the agency concerned for readers who are unable to derive this from the Dutch title. However, the RDMZ has not been mentioned in the text before, and the description given allows the reader to assess the importance and relevance of the agency in the context. This relevance-creating function is more clearly present in (29), which comes from an article about Brussels pressure to extend artists' copyright from 50 to 70 years. The writer wishes to quote Samuel Johnson, but the reader needs to know why it should be relevant to mention Samuel Johnson at all, and that is what the apposition does here. As such, it has a grounding function that is equivalent to the relative clause in (23).

Finally, let us look at the use of adverbial expressions and participial clauses, of which there are 26 examples in the sample. Here are some examples:

(30)   *The danger, though, is clear: Singapore-type provident funds could be progressively used to replace existing welfare structures, with their accompanying need for a redistributive tax system.* [ORC P-4–14]

(31)   *'Selection', however, is bad, ignores the needs of the less academic, and leads to a divided society.* [ORC P-5–16]

(32)   *That, briefly, is the structure of Europe.* [ORC P-6–22]

(33)   *The first ballot, then, is a vote of confidence in the leadership, a vote to determine whether the leader has sufficient authority to continue.* [ORC P-9–36]

(34)   *The new generation of Tory parliamentary candidates, receiving no signal to reprogramme their reflexes, have continued as unreconstructed Thatcherites – or after her laying on of hands, Portilloites.* [ORC P-2–8]

(35)   *Now Barnby, feeling that he could do with a holiday, was in this bloody villa.* [ORC F-2–6]

In addition to those cited in the examples, the adverbials include *obviously, too, of course, for example, by contrast, certainly* and *at any rate*. All these adverbials serve to focalize the subject element, just as they do with pre-subject thematic expressions. By contrast, the work done by participial clauses appears closely related to that carried out by the relative clause in (24) – providing background information about the subject referent so that the message in the main clause can be better understood.

What these two adverbial structures have in common is that the vast majority of them (the adverbs *though, too* and *then* are restricted to a postmodifying function) could just as easily have appeared sentence-initially, before the subject. Consider (36) in this regard:

(36)   *Scrimgeour, certainly, was a former student at Paris, but Atholl's first university, from which he held the degree of B.Dec, as early as 1409, is unknown.* [ORC A-1–1]

(36')   *Certainly, Scrimgeour was a former student at Paris …*

The ordering in (36) strongly resembles Smits' complex orientation, while that in (36')
resembles her stepwise orientations. The difference in discourse context which often
gives rise to the choice of pattern with the stepwise and focalizing patterns is relevant
here too. Here is (36) in its wider context, (36"):

(36") *The earliest Scots to arrive in Cologne were apparently drawn by its faculties of
        law: Nicholas Atholl and James Scringeour were already graduates when they
        matriculated at Cologne in 1419. Scrimgeour,* **certainly,** *was a former student
        at Paris but Atholl's first university, from which he held the degree of B.Dec. as
        early as 1409, is unknown.*

The function of *certainly* in this position is to relate the message to come to the preceding discourse, and precisely in terms of the entity referred to by the subject. By focusing on Scrimgeour in this way, the writer sets up a contrast with Atholl, having introduced the two together in the previous sentence. However, if the writer had used (36')
in the same context, then the focus on Scrimgeour would have been less clear. The ordering in (36) is thus in accordance with a pattern of thematic progression which high-
lights the various Scots who were among the first to arrive in Cologne.

 In sum, we have seen in this section that by expanding the area of analysis to include non-adverbial thematic elements as well as all forms of non-restrictive post-
modification of the subject, we find general confirmation of the thematic patterns
identified by Smits. In addition to the non-modifying stepwise pattern, there are two
basic patterns, involving grounding and focalizing. The grounding pattern can be analysed as involving two subtypes, one where the modifier has a specifying function,
serving to identify and characterize the theme element more precisely, and one where
the modifier has a relevance-creating function.

 It might indeed be interesting to investigate the extent to which post-modification
of later elements in the clause, outside the theme zone, has a markedly different function, as Duurkoop (2001) found for non-restrictive relative clauses and as has been
noted for various other clause types (cf. Thompson (1985) for purpose clauses and
Chafe (1984) for adverbial clauses in general). This would be an interesting way of testing the validity of non-restrictive subject postmodification as a boundary between the
theme zone and rheme zone of the sentence, but unfortunately that is beyond the scope
of the present paper.

 If we look at the syntactic configurations, we can detect a number of dominant
patterns associated with each thematic pattern. These are summamrized below using
constructed examples.

Stepwise

(37) *However, after the riots had died down the Lib Dems never looked back.*

(38) *At election time, if you start a riot, you should be very aware of the dangers
       involved.*

Grounding and specifying

(39)   *In Britain, where the Constitution riots started, the Liberal movement had begun to stagnate.*

(40)   *Later, after the riots, people started taking the LibDems more seriously.*

(41)   *The riots, the first in London for years, really shook the capital.*

(42)   *The riots, which started in London but soon spread to Paris, made Brussels sit up and listen.*

Focalizing

(43)   *The riots, however, made people take the LibDems more seriously.*

(44)   *After the riots, of course, people started taking the LibDems more seriously.*

(45)   *If the riots had not come when they did, however, the LibDems might not have won the election.*

To round off this section I now turn briefly to students' use of non-restrictive post-modification of the subject. In order to compare the situation with native speaker text I took a sample of 41 texts from the Dutch section of the International Corpus of Learner English (cf. Granger et al. 2003). All texts were between 400 and 1500 words long and were written by students with a maximum of two years of university English study behind them. There was no time pressure, no exam conditions, and reference works could be consulted. Each of the 1925 sentences was annotated for the syntactic status of constituents in the theme zone, as defined above. The result in terms of subject postmodification is that there are just 66 cases, which is 3.5 per 100 sentences. Their syntactic status is presented in (46):

(46)   apposition   26
       adverbial phrase / clause   28
       relative clause   10
       participial clause   2
                    total   66

Two remarks can be made about this. First, there is a difference in frequency compared to the native speaker texts in the sample (3.5 vs. 4.6 per 100 sentences). Second, the main devices which students use are the same as can be found in the native speaker texts, but the native speaker texts include a greater variation of devices. This latter difference may of course be due to differences in genre, but in general the data would suggest that students do not make as much use as native speakers of the opportunity to mark backgrounded information and to focalize individual notions by lexical and syntactic means.

4. Thematic patterns and writing skills

Traditional writing guides acknowledge the value of both varying one's sentence openings and using subordination devices to background less important ideas, but advice is typically general in nature. With regard to sentence openings, Watkins and Dillingham (1996: 120) and Kane (1988: 174), for instance, advise students to change the order of elements occasionally in order to avoid monotony, and provide examples of different syntactic elements before the subject, but go no further. Where writing guides include exercise material, practice is given on the mechanics of clause combining and the embedding of information into single clauses. However, although the value of mechanical clause combining exercises cannot be underestimated, since it is essential that beginning writers learn to use the phrasal and clausal options available in any language for packaging information into compact moulds, such exercises do not take as their input sequences which students actually produce or sequences which one might realistically expect to appear in students' first drafts. Hannay and Mackenzie (1990: 233–234) argue for clause combining which concentrates on linking devices that are problematic, a phasing of exercises to promote retention of form, and most important, backgrounding in sentence production in the context of the textual unit, so that learners need to make a decision on how and what to combine.

In the last few years, corpus linguistics has begun to show new possibilities for developing language teaching material which can fulfil these requirements. The basis, and the stimulus, has been provided on the one hand by detailed descriptions of the dominant linguistic characteristics of specific genres, and on the other hand by studies of learner corpora which reveal overuse and underuse of specific lexical and syntactic phenomena. For instance, Biber et al. (2002) provide general characterizations of the different genres produced by students in their study environment, on the basis of clusters of linguistic features. More specifically, Hinkel (2002) carried out a detailed study of the individual linguistic and rhetorical features of L2 writing, and concluded that more emphasis needs to be put on syntactic structures which play a specific role in writing, a position partly motivated by the wide range of studies that make it clear that mere exposure to L2 grammar and discourse is not the most effective means of achieving academic L2 proficiency (Hinkel 2004: 5).

From the point of view of learner corpora, quite a few studies have concentrated on specific linguistic features typically associated with written language (cf. for instance various contributions in Part II of Granger 1998), and more recently attention has also focused on the use of corpora in foreign language teaching (cf. for instance the contributions in Part III of Granger et al. 2002). Significantly, there has also been considerable interest in determining the linguistic traits of the written English produced by students in all kinds of tests such as TOEFL and IELTS tests. The particular value here is that texts which have been assessed as belonging to a certain level of proficiency can be characterized according to specific arrays of linguistic features (for an overview of the value of corpus linguistics for testing, see for example Hawkey and Barker 2004).

The potential of corpus linguistics in the area of language teaching and language testing is clearly demonstrated by the recently started British Academic Written English Corpus (BAWE) project at the Universities of Warwick, Oxford Brookes and Reading in England. The aim of the project is to compile a corpus of written assessed English http://www2.warwick.ac.uk/fac/soc/celte/research/projects/bawe/ (accessed 13 April 2005) so as to provide a database "for use by researchers who are investigating the nature of academic writing, and also by tutors who are designing teaching and assessment materials for their students".

The relevance of thematic patterns in this context can be assessed by considering the can-do statements for the two highest, "proficient user" levels within the Common European Framework of Reference (CEF) (Council of Europe 2001: 62) with regard to report and essay writing:

> C2 (mastery): Can produce clear, smoothly flowing, complex reports, articles or essays which present a case, or give critical appreciation of proposals or literary works. Can provide an appropriate and effective logical structure which helps the reader to find significant points.

> C1 (operational proficiency): Can write clear, well-structured expositions of complex subjects, underlining the relevant salient issues. Can expand and support points of view at some length with subsidiary points, reasons and relevant examples.

In general terms C1 is geared towards the ability to produce expository text while C2 involves the ability to produce argumentative texts. Both levels involve the production of complex texts, and in terms of the management of information flow both involve the ability to draw the reader's attention to the important information in the text. One consequence of this will be that in syntactic terms students at this level can effectively deploy a wide range of structures including different kinds of subordination. It is also important that students have a sufficient command of the techniques associated with exemplification and with causal relationships.

On the basis of the data presented in previous sections, it will be clear that thematic patterns have a role to play here. Their effective use can thus be seen as a particular feature of discourse competence, which the CEF sees as part of the pragmatic component of communicative competence and defines as "the ability of a user/learner to arrange sentences in sequence so as to produce coherent stretches of language" (Council of Europe 2001: 123). This is stated as involving such matters as topic/focus, given/new, and rhetorical effectiveness. In terms of coherence and cohesion, students at C2 level can "create coherent and cohesive text making full and appropriate use of a variety of organisational patterns and a wide range of cohesive devices" (Council of Europe 2001: 125).

So how might corpora help with developing material for thematic patterns? To try and answer this question, let us have a closer look at the grounding pattern. This is a pattern which in contrast to native speaker texts occurred quite rarely in Smits's corpus and which was also found in limited numbers in the additional text sample which looked at postmodification of the subject. First, here are two further examples from Smits' native speaker corpus:

(47) *Some six weeks ago, when Diana agreed to be interviewed by the programme about every aspect of her life, the 'scandal' of her friendship with Will Carling was blazing across the front pages.* [NEC 81–303]

(48) *On July 11, while Ashby's death warrant was being routinely prepared for the signature of Trinidad's figurehead president in Port of Spain, Candace Carrington-Scott took her three-year-old daughter to a swimming lesson.* [NEC 96–355]

These examples have a similar structure which is quite common in the data: an initial temporal adverbial, modified by a prepositional phrase or adverbial clause expressing an event which anchors the initial adverbial, and then the subject. For each of these it is possible to deconstruct the clause combination and see how the information in the second element provides grounding for the initial element and at the same time helps the reader to understand the import of the message. The result is given in (47') and (48'):

(47') *Some six weeks ago, Diana agreed to be interviewed by the programme about every aspect of her life. At that time the 'scandal' of her friendship with Will Carling was blazing across the front pages.*

(48') *On July 11, Ashby's death warrant was routinely prepared for the signature of Trinidad's figurehead president in Port of Spain. At that time Candace Carrington-Scott took her three-year-old daughter to a swimming lesson.*

One way of determining whether learners produce structures that might be 'ripe for clause combining', as it were, might be to search for structures which bear features of these deconstructed sequences. Accordingly, as a first step I searched the 41 essays from the ICLE corpus referred to in section 3 above for sentences beginning with *in* and *at*, as one albeit limited way of identifying time and place expressions functioning as theme. I then analysed the status of the sentence in its context to see if the sentence itself presented background information and to see if the following sentence presented information which had a more nuclear role in the rhetorical development of the paragraph. Here are two cases in point, in their context; interestingly, both in fact involve not two sentences but just one, with two main independent clauses conjoined by *and*.

(49) *But before one can speak of any conservatism, one must at least have some notion of the past, of how sexuality was the last decades. **In the 1960s the sexual revolution took place and phenomena such as partner swapping, group sex and communes became a common feature.** The seventies allowed every-*

thing and sex was a must; it did not matter in fact with whom. <ICLE-DN-NIJ-0003.7>[4]

(50)   *A good example of this can be found at the English Departments of Dutch Universities. At these departments all students are lectured to in English and it appears that they have a better knowledge of the language than students of, for instance, Business Communication English (a study for which English is also very important) who are lectured to in Dutch.* So apparently English lectures do help. <ICLE-DN-NIJ-0002.7>

In both cases the situational thematic elements in absolute initial position have scope over both the independent clauses which follow, and in both cases the first clause provides the background for the information in the coordinated clause. A grounding pattern would reflect the status of the information more clearly and would also serve to add pace to the text, as in (49') and (50'):

(49')   *In the 1960s, when the sexual revolution took place, phenomena such as partner swapping, group sex and communes became a common feature.*

(50')   *At these departments, where all students are lectured to in English, it appears that they have a better knowledge of the language than students of, for instance, Business Communication English (a study for which English is also very important) who are lectured to in Dutch.*

Another case did not involve coordinated clauses but two separate sentences:

(51)   *By way of contrast you could say that people should not be held responsible because they might have voted for someone from a smaller political party and that party might not have any great political influence. In the Netherlands, for instance, one party never has an absolute majority. A large number of people vote for smaller parties and they cannot be held responsible because the party they chose for has only so much influence. Or Great Britain where voting goes by district. This means that the biggest party in a district gets to send a representative to parlement.* <ICLE-DN-NIJ-0011.6>

Here the sentence *In the Netherlands, for instance, one party never has an absolute majority* does not constitute a major point in the light of the previous sentence. Rather, it provides a framework for understanding the information in the following sentence, which can be seen as an attempt to support the argument in the opening sentence. Again, a grounding pattern, this time combined with a focalizer, can clarify the relationships involved:

---

4.   Examples with an ICLE coding come from the International Corpus of Learner English (Granger et al. 2003).

(51') *In the Netherlands, for instance, where one party never has an absolute major-*
ity, a large number of people vote for smaller parties and they cannot be held
responsible because the party they chose for has only so much influence.

Another kind of grounding comes from appositions relating both to subject themes as
well as circumstantial themes. Here is an example of property-assigning apposition
from the data:

(52) *In this day and age it's hard to believe that these diseases are still killers. But*
between them, they cause the deaths of over 1.5 million chilldren and paralyse
another 100,000 every year. Maria Sapateiro, a young mother from Mozam-
bique, suffered her own agonies as she watched five of her children die. One by
one, as each tiny infant she cradled grew weaker from diseases like measles and
tuberculosis, she prayed desperately for the power to stop them from dying.
[ORC C-5–2]

Again we can deconstruct, giving us something like (52'):

(52') *Maria Sapateiro is a young mother from Mozambique. She suffered her own*
agonies as she watched her children die.

What is striking here is that in the deconstructed version, the sole function of the first
sentence is to characterize Maria Sapatiero. If this sequence had appeared in its context
like this, the reader might be justified in asking whether the initial sentence was informative enough to warrant sentencehood. The original version is clearly more compact, gives more speed to the text, and backgrounds the unimportant information
while promoting the important information. In this case I searched the subcorpus for
a particular kind of copula construction: all sentences beginning with the indefinite
article or with *another* and which continued with a copula and a noun phrase. This is a
construction for introducing a new referent into the discourse. Here is an example:

(53) *But within Labour there are also supporters of the ruling. Tony Blair himself is*
reviewing the all-women policy. He has never been a real protagonist of it, and
now he has a good reason to abandon it. He will not enter the election with an
illegal selection procedure of his candidates. **Another supporter of the ruling is**
Mr. Geach, a former member of Labour. *He said that the ruling will certainly*
send a message to the Labour Party, which has a sexist policy in place [an-
nouncement of quote from Geach at this point, not included in corpus, MH].
Roy Hattersley, a former deputy leader, called the all-women policy a silly poli-
cy. He called on Tony Blair to abandon it. All these different reactions to the
tribunal's ruling show that Labour hasn't decided how to react. <ICLE-DN-
GRO-0002.1>

In this case there is no great need to make a special point of the introduction of Geach
into the discourse: he is mentioned very briefly as an example and does not return in

the next couple of paragraphs. If the writer had used an apposition, he could have appropriately downgraded Geach's status. Here are two alternative reformulations:

(53')   *Another supporter of the ruling, Mr Jim Geach, a former member Labour MP, said that the ruling will certainly send a message to the Labour Party, which has a sexist policy in place.*

(53")   *Another supporter of the ruling, the former Labour politician Jim Geach, said that the ruling will certainly send a message to the Labour Party, which has a sexist policy in place.*

It is conceivable that the writer shied away from the first alternative so as not to have to use a double apposition, but a double apposition does not really disturb the flow of the sentence here, and the restrictive apposition within the non-restrictive apposition is also not too heavy.

Now consider (54), which is slightly different but again includes a copula construction which introduces a new discourse referent in a rather prominent fashion:

(54)   *I think that the Food and Drug Administration, an institution that creates regulation concerning their field of expertise, will have a tough job on campaigning against the cigarette companies. The FDA is now trying to make smoking look like it is sort of the same thing as drugs <R>.* **A new regulation is an ID rule.** *This rule says that without a driver's license or any other legal identification card that states that one is 21 or older the youth cannot buy cigarettes. More new regulations are on the way and are all based on trying to reduce the smoking habits among young teenage kids.* <ICLE-DN-GRO-0004.1>

There are a number of possible alternatives here which allow the writer to say what he wants in one sentence and move the discourse along. First, (54') involves a focalization with *for example*, which foregrounds the ID rule, while (54") uses an identificational apposition to put the ID rule into the background.

(54')   *The ID rule, for example, is a new regulation that says that without a driver's license or any other legal identification card that states that one is 21 or older the youth cannot buy cigarettes.*

(54")   *One new regulation, the ID rule, says that without a driver's license or any other legal identification card that states that one is 21 or older the youth cannot buy cigarettes.*

Finally, here is a case of a copula construction where the newly introduced referent appears as subject:

(55)   *When a criminal had killed someone he was killed too. As the saying goes; an eye for an eye, a tooth for a tooth. Nowadays this doesn't happen anymore. Most countries abolished capital punishment and if they didn't they practically don't issue it anymore. There are also countries though where this is different.*

> *The United States is an example of that. In the US there are several states that still have capital punishment, and criminals were killed recently.* [ICLE-DB-KVH-0052.2]

Here again the text slows down as a result of relatively unimportant information being given sentence status, but expressing exemplification by means of a focalizer allows everything to be formulated in one sentence and to fit into the preceding context, which invites the mention of examples:

(55') *There are also countries though where this is different. **In The United States, for example, there are several states that still have capital punishment, and criminals were killed recently.***

In the first instance these data from student essays suggest that students are indeed missing opportunities in their writing to use the thematic patterns available to good effect. But they also show us that students produce specific sequences of information formulated using syntactic devices which are not the most effective for distinguishing between foregrounded and backgrounded information. Indeed, further research might also be expected to reveal more sequences of this kind.

Examples of these sequences might provide excellent teaching and exercise material for advanced courses in "syntax for writing". First, of course, the student has to be shown the individual syntactic structures which are involved. Then the major thematic patterns must be presented, along with the functions which these patterns perform and the contexts in which these patterns are relevant. In terms of practice, students may be given recognition tasks, clause-combining tasks and more open-ended writing tasks, but at advanced levels a special role can be played by editing tasks based on data from learner corpora. This may help to focus the writer's attention on the importance of using the theme zone of the sentence to provide an appropriate and effective framework for the interpretation of the relatively more important information to come.

In this context it is interesting to note that Smits (2002: 159) found that while first and second year university students significantly underused her complex beginning category (see (2) above), this underuse had become much less apparent in the writing of third and fourth year students, who used them roughly to the same extent as native speaker writers. This development makes it on the one hand important to pay attention to thematic patterns in the first place, but it is also suggestive that certain kinds of patterning might be a trait of writing at a higher level of attainment. This may be relevant in the light of the remark that users of the CEF should consider "how qualitative progress in the pragmatic component can be characterized" (Council of Europe 2001: 130).

5.   Conclusion

The thematic patterns discussed in this paper provide different means of creating a complex framework for the interpretation of sentences. For each pattern it is necessary for the learner writer to have a command of the most common syntactic background-ing devices, of which there is a considerable range. Another important point is that where modifiers can change position – something we saw with stepwise and focalizing patterns, as well as with post-subject modification – the preferred position appears to be governed by the role of the modified element in the discourse. This suggests that a considerable degree of discourse competence is required to use these patterns effec-tively, but by the same token that the effects that can be achieved are indicative of re-fined argumentation.

The underuse of these thematic patterns by advanced learners of English can best be addressed by means of explicit instruction. This is necessary because of the strength of evidence which suggests that exposure to syntactic structures relevant for specific genres is not enough, even for advanced students. But in addition to explicit instruc-tion, exercises must concentrate on contextualized work, which means that we need to make use of data from learner corpora. In doing so it will be necessary to pay sufficient attention to the qualitative analysis of structures used in learner writing, since a certain sequence of sentences may be quite appropriate in one context but may be a candidate for clause combining in another. I have suggested a small number of sentence sequenc-es in learner text which might benefit from investigation in order to provide contextu-alized exercise material for clause combining geared towards the production of com-plex thematic patterns; further research is needed to establish the relevance of these sequences and to identify more.

All in all, I hope to have shown that thematic patterns, with their different rhe-torical features and syntactic realizations, have an important place in a writing-ori-ented university course in English grammar.

References

Berry, Margaret. 1996. "What is Theme? A(nother) personal view". *Meaning and form: systemic functional interpretations. Meaning and choice in language: Studies for Michael Halliday*, ed. by Margaret Berry, Christopher S. Butler, Robin Fawcett and G. Huang, 1–64. Norwood, NJ: Ablex.

Biber, Douglas, Susan Conrad, Randi Reppen, Patricia Byrd and Marie Helt. 2002. "Speaking and writing in the university: A multi-dimensional comparison". *TESOL Quarterly*: 36(1), 9–48.

Butler, Christopher S. 2003. *Structure and function. A guide to three major structural functional theories. Part 2: From clause to discourse and beyond*. Amsterdam: John Benjamins.

Chafe, Wallace, L. 1984. "How people use adverbial clauses". *Proceedings of the Xth annual Meet-ing of the Berkeley Linguistics Society*: 437–449.

Council of Europe 2001. *Common European framework of reference for languages.* Cambridge: Cambridge University Press.

Downing, Angela. 1991. "An alternative approach to theme: A systemic-functional perspective". *WORD* 42(2): 119–143.

Downing, Angela. 1995. "Thematic layering and focus assignment in Chaucer's *General Prologue* to *The Canterbury Tales*". *Thematic development in English texts*, ed. by Mohsen Ghadessy, 147–163. London: Pinter.

Downing, Angela and Philip Locke. 2002. *A university course in English grammar.* London: Routledge.

Downing, Angela and Philip Locke. 2006. *English grammar: A university course.* 2nd edn. London: Routledge.

Duurkoop, Kirsten. 2001. *The discourse functions of non-restrictive relative clauses in written texts.* MA thesis. Vrije Universiteit, Amsterdam.

Fries, Peter H. 1995. "A personal view of theme". *Thematic development in English texts*, ed. by M.Ghadessy, 1–19. London: Pinter.

Ghadessy, Mohsen (ed.) 1995. *Thematic development in English texts.* London: Pinter.

Gómez-González, Maria de los Ángeles. 1998. "A corpus-based analysis of extended multiple themes in PresE". *International Journal of Corpus Linguistics.* 3(1): 81–113.

Gómez-González, Maria de los Ángeles. 2001. *The theme-topic interface: Evidence from English.* Amsterdam: John Benjamins.

Gómez-González, Maria de los Ángeles. 2004. "Functional Grammar and the dynamics of discourse". *A new architecture for Functional Grammar*, ed. by J. Lachlan Mackenzie and María A.Gómez-González, 211–242. Berlin: Mouton de Gruyter.

Granger, Sylviane (ed) 1998. *Learner English on computer.* London: Longman.

Granger, Sylviane, Estelle Dagneaux and Fanny Meunier (eds.). 2003. *The International Corpus of Learner English. Handbook and CD-ROM. Version 1.1.* Louvain-la-Neuve: Presses Universitaires de Louvain.

Granger, Sylviane, Joseph Hung and Stephanie Petch-Tyson (eds). 2002. *Computer learner corpora, second language acquisition and foreign language teaching.* Amsterdam: John Benjamins.

Halliday, Michael A. K. 1994². *An introduction to functional grammar.* 2nd edn. London: Edward Arnold.

Hannay, Mike. 1994. "The theme zone". *Nauwe betrekkingen. Voor Theo Janssen bij zijn vijftigste verjaardag*, ed. by Ronny Boogaart and Jan Noordegraaf, 107–117. Amsterdam: Stichting Neerlandistiek Vrije Universiteit and Munster: Nodus Publikationen.

Hannay, Mike and M. Evelien Keizer (2005). "A discourse treatment of English non-restrictive nominal appositions in Functional Discourse Grammar". *Studies in Functional Discourse Grammar*, ed. by J. Lachlan Mackenzie and María A.Gómez-González, 159–194. Bern: Peter Lang.

Hannay, Mike and J. Lachlan Mackenzie. 1990. "The writing student: From the architect of sentences to the builder of texts". *The writing scholar. Studies in academic discourse*, ed. by Walter Nash, 205–235. Newbury Park CA: Sage.

Hartnett, Carolyn.G. 1995. "The pit after the theme". *Thematic development in English texts*, ed. by Mohsen Ghadessy, 198–212. London: Pinter.

Hawkey, Roger and Fiona Barker. 2004. "Developing a common scale for the assessment of writing". *Assessing Writing* 9/2: 122–159.

Hinkel, Eli. 2002. *Second language writer's text: Linguistic and rhetorical features.* NJ: Lawrence Erlbaum.

Hinkel, Eli. 2004. *Teaching academic ESL writing: Practical techniques in vocabulary and grammar*. NJ: Lawrence Erlbaum.

Kane, Thomas S. 1988. *The new Oxford guide to writing*. Oxford: Oxford University Press.

Mann, William C. and Sandra A. Thompson. 1987. "Rhetorical Structure Theory: A theory of text organization". *Information Sciences Institute Research Report:* 87–190. 4676 Admiralty Way, Marina del Rey, CA 90292-6695.

Smits, Aletta M. 2002. *How writers begin their sentences: The discourse functions of complex beginnings in written English*. Utrecht: LOT. [LOT dissertation series 69].

Thompson, Sandra A. 1985. "Grammar and written discourse: Initial vs. final purpose clauses in English". *Text* 5(1/2): 55-84.

Watkins, Floyd C. and William B. Dillingham. 1996. *Practical English handbook*. Boston, Mass: Houghton Mifflin.

Interactive solution-problems

A set of structures in general and scientific writing

Michael P. Jordan
Queen's University at Kingston

The theory of problem-solution patterning is already well established for a wide range of genres and at macrostructure and microstructure levels of communication. That theory has, however, largely failed to account for interactive solution-problems: where a solution is or causes a problem to another person, group or thing. This chapter establishes the major parameters of this sub-theory of problem-solution structures and the related grammar and signalling. For informal writing in the natural sciences, solution-problems are shown to apply to environmental concerns, predator-prey relations and cause-effect relations. More generally the principles are extended to cover third-party involvement, friends and enemies and iatrogenic solution-problems. The sub-theory of structures and linguistic signalling outlined here applies to many genres – not just those in the natural sciences, but also in news and business reports, and general journalism. Studies of the structures and signalling of politics and fictional works (cartoons, sitcoms, soap operas, movies, novels, etc.) would be natural extensions for the principles explained.

1. Background

1.1 Macrostructure Framework

Van Dijk (1977, 1981, 1985) and Kintsch and van Dijk (1978) show that any text has an overall "macrostructure" or "superstructure" representing the types of information in the document and the sequence of these information types. Van Dijk's macrostructure is "a global level of semantic description" (1977: 6) that "defines its global coherence" (1985: 115). Several such rhetorical structures have been noted. An early multi-item sequence is Burke's (1945, 1969) "dramatistic pentad" of 'Act-Agent-Scene-Agency-Purpose' based on analysis of stage events. Beardsley (1950) and then Young and Becker (1966) note the sequence 'Topic-Restriction-Illustration,' and Labov and Waletsky (1967), elaborated later by Labov (1972), identify the pattern 'Abstract-Orientation-

Complication-Action-Evaluation-Result/Resolution-Coda' in oral narratives. Longa-cre (1972) identified a similar pattern for some narratives: 'Aperture-Setting-Inciting moment-Developing conflict-Climax-Dénouement-Final suspense-Closure'. van Dijk (1977) discusses the typical narrative structure 'Setting-Complication-Resolution-Evaluation-Moral', and Corbett (1977) uses the framework of 'Problem-Analyze the Problem-Hypothesis-Test Hypothesis' as a framework for structured analytical writing. Although all these structures can be applied to texts outside the dramatic and narrative genres, they are not ideal for that purpose.

The more specific 'Problem-Solution' pattern, however, has been applied to other genres. Grimes (1975: 211) claims broad genre universality for this two-part structure by noting that "Both the plots of fairy tales and the writings of scientists are built on a response pattern. The first part gives a problem and the second its solution." Likewise, Werlich (1976: 106) notes that "In either of the two text forms [*comment* and *scientific argument*] the encoder starts from the implicit or explicit statement of a *problem*." The claim of broad applicability for such structures is also supported by van Dijk (1977), who notes that the structure of an argument should be assigned independently of whether it is about engineering, linguistics or child-care. Mann and Thompson (1987, 1989) include the Problem-Solution pair (which they call "Solutionhood") as one of their semantic relations. More recently, Trott (2000: 52) claims that the argument in Banting and Best's paper (1922) on the discovery of insulin can best be described as Problem-Solution. Wagner (1995: 225–228) shows that the macrostructures of some engineering telephone conversations follow the problem-solution pattern, while Gray (1977: 291–311) notes that the subdivisions of a "composition" are the problem (exposition) and a solution (argument).

Hutchins (1977) also uses the problem-solution structure to explain the overall organizational structure for scientific discourse, and especially as the basis for abstracting (1987) although Cremmins (1982) and Jordan (1991a) show prevalence of the broader structure 'Scope-Purpose-Method-Results-Conclusions in abstracts. Winter (1976) had earlier used the 'Problem-Solution' pair as the core of the broader pattern of discourse 'Situation-Problem-Solution-Evaluation' for technical reports, while van Dijk (1977) suggests the 'Introduction-Problem-Solution-Conclusion' pattern for scientific discourse. These are essentially the same, but the difference is important. The "problem" in science is an intellectual need to understand or explain something, and the "solution" is an explanation, model or formula; in engineering, however, the "problem" is a practical need to design something and the "solution" is the completed product (Jordan, 2000: 94–95). Hoey (1979, 1983) and Jordan (1980, 1984a) both use Winter's four-part pattern as the basis for analyzing texts from many genres, while Halliday (2002 [1985]: 276) uses the four-part structure 'the situation, the problem, its solution, and the process of problem-solving'. Rino and Scott (1994, 1996) show the usefulness of the 'Problem-Solution' structure for the creation of summaries – especially those generated by computers. Porush (1995: 67) includes "statement of problem" as an essential element in the parts of a research paper, with "interpretation of data" as the implicit solution to this intellectual problem.

1.2   Problem-Solution and Purpose-Means

Burke (1945, 1969) had recognized that parts of his dramatistic pentad formed couplets of information (which he called "ratios"), but his emphasis was more on the 'Purpose-Means' pair rather than 'Problem-Solution,' as seen by his explanation of the pentadic model. In an explanation of the rhetorical structures for biblical translation purposes, Beekman and Callow (1974: 317) emphasized the means and purpose elements of the discourse in the following example:

(1)   a. *(Christ) has now reconciled you (to God)*
       b. *by* means *of dying physically*   MEANS of 1.
       c. in order *that you will be holy*   PURPOSE of 1.

The close connection between the 'purpose-means' and 'problem-solutions' pairs can be seen in the following example:

(2)   To *counteract the* problem *of accidental ignition of fluid in spray when using hydraulic fluids, the British Standards Institute has produced a new draft for development, DD 61 'Flammability for hydraulic fluids.'* (*Safety*, April 1979: 8 – from Jordan, 1984a: 78–79)

While the whole of the introductory subordinate clause is the purpose, the problem is contained within it as the object of the to-infinitive; the main clause provides both the solution to the problem and the means of achieving the purpose. Thus the purpose is broader than the problem, as it is a stated determination to overcome the problem. Thompson (1985), Jordan (1996) and Hwang (1997) provide analyses of the 'purpose-means' microstructure, and the wider 'Purpose-Means-Evaluation' structure is discussed in Jordan (2000: 103–105).

1.3   Basic Problem-Solution Structures

Working with Winter, Hoey (1979) identified how writers produce signalling in discourse for 'Situation-Problem-Solution-Evaluation' texts and elaborated on the principles by explaining many of the complications that occur "on the surface of discourse" (1983), expanding the fourth category to include the "Result" of remedial action. Jordan (1980) demonstrates the 'Problem-Solution' principles within a broader 12-part structure and even very short texts including summaries and titles are shown to follow problem-solving principles, as in (3)

(3)   *Peening Process Prevents Intergranular Corrosion of Stainless Steels* (Jordan 1981)

Here the subject is the solution, the verb is the evaluation, the object is the problem, and the adverbial is the situation. As engineering is essentially a problem-solving activity, the system is ideal for explaining almost any text beyond those that deal solely with description or evaluation. A simple three-part problem-solution example in engineering is:

> (4)   *Today's bearings are intrinsically reliable machinery components.* **Nevertheless,** *some bearings fail before their design service life. Of these failures, 16% have been attributed to incorrect installation and a further 36% to inadequate lubrication. In other words, the* **problem** *is human* **error.** *Bearing mounting and dismounting using equipment* **unfit** *for the purpose often results in* **premature failure. To overcome this** *and ensure trouble-free operation, SKF has developed a range of products designed to ease the tasks of mounting and maintenance, minimize the risk of failure, and so reduce downtime....* (Machinery and Equipment, April 1995: 6 – from Jordan 2000: 97).

The transition word *Nevertheless* mediates between the situation in the first sentence and the coming problem, which is strongly signalled by *fail, failures,* the prefixes *in* and *un, problem, error* and *premature failure.* With *this* re-entering the whole of the complex problem to provide macrostructure cohesion, *To overcome this* indicates that details of the solution are about to be given – and also the intended purpose of the design work. The positive evaluation of the solution is inherent in the details provided.

Principles of problem-solution patterns are important because they represent the assessments, decisions and actions of those involved in the account – even for engineering documents, where human involvement may not be overtly indicated. To follow the approach of using such structures in general discourse and writing in the natural and human sciences however, we need to recognize other patterns and signalling that extend the basic problem-solution structures into areas of interactional assessments and related actions. When natural, medical, social and human sciences are involved, solutions affect animate objects, which often assess what is being done to them – and sometimes take remedial action. Thus, we are here seeking to develop an extended sub-set of language structures and related signalling that enables us to describe and explain such systems of interactive thought and action. As Selzer (1993) notes "[i]n the study of the rhetoric of science, we need analytical techniques as sophisticated and as powerful as the texts they are designed to describe". We need a powerful method of explaining texts involving "interactive solution-problems".

2.   Interactive Problem-Solutions

2.1   Unintentional Interactive Solution-Problems

For examples (3) and (4), the theory of problem-solution texts is essential for an understanding and explanation of the overall semantics, structure, cohesion and signalling of the communication; an explanation of the grammar alone is insufficient. The concepts in engineering are relatively simple because we are dealing with inanimate objects, which do not have their own assessments and actions included as part of the document. That is, as the topics discussed are things, they cannot agree with, or object to, actions being taken that affect them. When actions that are taken as solutions or attempted solutions **do** affect others, those actions may be perceived as, or may cause, an unpleasant, undesirable or unwanted situation (i.e., a problem). This relationship, initially labelled "people problems" (Jordan 1981: 445; 1984b: 65–66), can be seen in:

(5) *Vickers is laying off 350 workers at its Elswick defence system plant.* **Not enough** *orders.* (*The Economist*, 29 March 1980: 85 – from Jordan 1984a: 46)

This is a solution-problem text, in which the action taken by Vickers is an attempted solution to the problem they face; the problem is signalled by *Not enough*. However, Vickers' action would be assessed negatively by (i.e., be a problem to) the workers who are being laid off. Solutions that are, or that cause, a problem to others are here called "solution-problems." They are "interactive" because they involve two or more participants, as shown by:

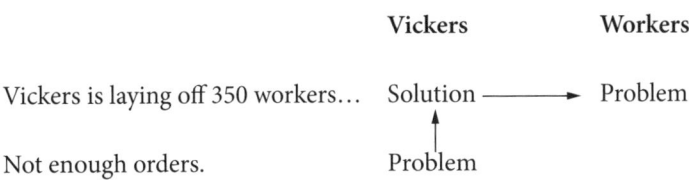

Although in example (5) Vickers is not deliberately trying to present a problem for its workers, its action nevertheless does this. In this text no further action by the workers is noted and the text ends there.

Those who undertake necessary solutions that cause problems to others may feel they need to apologise for their actions:

(6) *Attention Customers*
 Due *to severe losses, we will no longer be able to accept cheques as payment for purchases (prescriptions excluded). We are sorry for any inconvenience that this may* **cause.** (Herbie's Drug and Food Warehouse, Kingston, Canada, 18 March, 2005)

The first sentence has a problem-solution structure, which is also basis-assessment (Jordan 2001) signalled by *Due to*; the inherent purpose is to reduce the losses (the problem), making the solution also a means of achieving the purpose. The solution is re-entered by *this* as subject of the restrictive relative clause within the complex nominal complement of the second sentence. The prefix of *inconvenience* indicates the problem caused to shoppers, *sorry* expresses the apology, and *cause* notes the cause-effect relation between the solution as cause and the inconvenience as the effect. This brief example shows how the clause relations occur: between sentences, between clauses of a sentence, between subject and complement, and even within a complex nominal group. See Jordan 1998 for details of the cause-effect relation at all such levels.

2.2　Deliberate Interactive Solution-Problems

Often, however, action is taken as a deliberate act to present a problem to those creating a problem – often in an effort to remedy problematic behaviour or an undesirable situation:

(7) **Complaints** *have been received by the Health Education Council and television networks* **after** *the screening of an* **anti-smoking** *film which showed a young child sucking crayons imitating smoking....Many of the parents who complained were reported to be smokers who felt that they were in no position to admonish their children.* (*Here's Health*, June 1980: 77 – from Jordan 1984b: 65–66)

The Health Education Council felt that smoking at home was a problem, although perhaps not all the parents assessed their behaviour in that way. The *anti-smoking* film was an attempt to make parents feel guilty about their behaviour – and perhaps to change it. The parents presumably felt guilty (a problem to them), and their *Complaints* were an attempt by some parents to alleviate this problem by having it withdrawn:

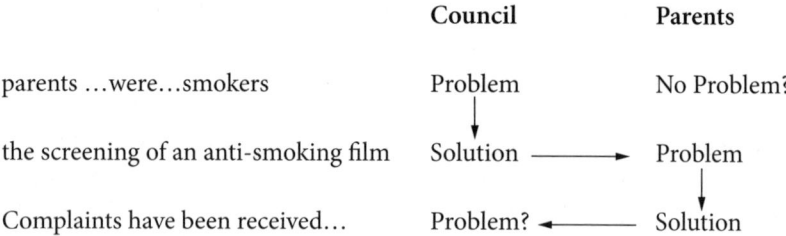

	Council	Parents
parents ...were...smokers	Problem	No Problem?
the screening of an anti-smoking film	Solution ⟶	Problem
Complaints have been received...	Problem? ⟵	Solution

In example (7), the group who were the target of the solution-problem responded by trying to have it removed; the signal for this basis-assessment relational pair is the time adverbial *after*, a typical signal of logical connection in news reporting (Jordan 1997). When the two sides are seeking to create problems for the other side in an effort to achieve their overall purpose, strings of sequential solution-problems can occur. Texts describing union/management conflicts, wars, and chronic disagreements are just a few examples that lend themselves to this sort of analysis, which is arguably the central recurring relational structure in all novels, movies and soap operas. However, solution-problems can eventually give rise to a resolution of the initial difference in perception:

(8) *The letter in your June/July issue about how to keep your man in shape reminded me: Mine refused to admit he was gaining a spare tyre* **until***, every time I got romantic and gazed lovingly into his eyes, I also knowingly grabbed a handful of spare flesh. This brought him down to earth with a bump and shamed him into*

eating more sensibly. Now not only is he slimmer and fitter, but there also seem to be more of those romantic moments. (Slimming Naturally, October/ November 1979: 13 – Jordan 1984a: 25)

Although the spare tyre was not a problem for the man, it was for the writer, who sought to solve it by deliberately creating a problem for the man. The man's action leads to a positive result that solves his problem (the flesh grabbing) as well as the writer's (the spare tyre):

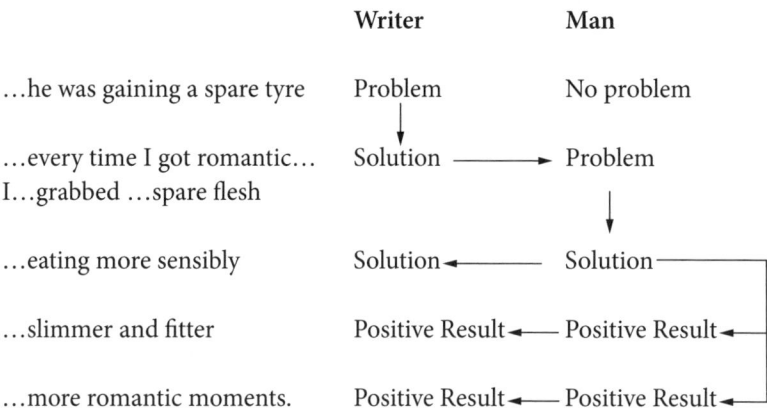

	Writer	**Man**
…he was gaining a spare tyre	Problem	No problem
…every time I got romantic… I…grabbed …spare flesh	Solution ⟶	Problem
…eating more sensibly	Solution ◄—	Solution
…slimmer and fitter	Positive Result ◄—	Positive Result ◄—
…more romantic moments.	Positive Result ◄—	Positive Result ◄—

Rather than escalate the disagreement (by, for example, seeking a partner who would not grab spare flesh during such moments), the man chose to co-operate in solving the problem caused by the writer – and this also solves the writer's initial problem. The comparative results of *slimmer and fitter* and *more romantic moments* also solve other unstated problems. The relation between eating more sensibly and becoming slimmer and fitter is a cause-effect relation as it is an "unwitting (generally inanimate) cause of an event" Quirk *et al.* (1985:351), whereas the one between the flesh grabbing and eating more sensibly involves basis-assessment as reason and thought are involved (Anscombe, 1957).

Some words always indicate interactive problem-solutions because at least two people or groups are always involved in a distasteful action, e.g., *abuse, accuse, arrest, assault, complain, harass, kill, molest, persecute, reject, sue.* Others only indicate interactive problem-solutions if an animate recipient is given a problem, but not if the solution is to *ignore* a rain shower, *hit* a nail, *scream at* the waves, etc. In example (8), the whole main clause *I…spare flesh* has to be interpreted within its context as being undesirable or embarrassing (i.e., a problem) to the man.

2.3   Threats, Warnings and Retaliations

It may be enough merely to *threaten* to take action to solve a problem, as warnings present a problem to the person being threatened. Even veiled threats can be quite effective:

(9)   *Polite Notice*
Customers are requested, in their own interests, not to park on the pavement as this is causing an inconvenience to residents. (Trawlerman Fish Bar, Hatfield, England, August 1980 – from Jordan 1981: 415)

Parking on the sidewalks is a solution for the drivers, who need to leave their cars before going into the shop to buy fish and chips. However, this action is a problem for the residents as it makes it *in*convenient for them to walk to and from their houses. The *Polite Notice* (perhaps deliberately like *Police Notice*) is the attempted solution: for drivers not to park there, thus solving the residents' problem. The phrase *in their own interests* is a veiled threat that residents might do something unpleasant (for the car owners) to the cars representing the inconvenience. If the threat fails, action might be taken to create a more substantial problem to the car owners.

The presence of cars on the sidewalk *is* perceived as a problem (a cognitive mental process) rather than *causing* something to happen (a material process) that is perceived as a problem; see Thompson's (1996: 76–116) explanation of the importance of these and other distinctions in systemic-functional grammar.

It is the Fish Bar owners, not the residents, who are requesting/warning/threatening customers not to create a problem for residents. The Fish Bar owners presumably do not wish their customers to be presented with solution-problems (scratches, smashed lights, etc.) by irate locals, as that might lead to the customers' solution of going elsewhere for their fish and chips – a problem for the Fish Bar owners!

3.   Solution-Problems in Science Writing

3.1   More than People Problems

Although many interactive solution-problem structures involve people, others do not, and the wider term *interactive solution-problems* is more appropriate. Problem-solutions figure significantly in a trilogy of papers dealing with openings (titles, abstracts, introductions) in science writing (Jordan, 1991b, 1991c, 1993), especially the section of informal science texts dealing with "Openings with Interactive Problems." Although the emphasis there is on problem-solution interactions between people, one example identifies solution-problems affecting insects:

(10)   *Cooked Cockroaches*
   A pest control company had found a way to exploit insects' vulnerability to heat ***in order*** *to* ***kill*** *common house pests.* (*New Scientist*, 17 February 1990: 35)

The pests – what they do or perhaps simply their presence – are a problem to house owners, who seek to solve their problem by killing the pests; this "ultimate solution" is, of course, the ultimate problem for the pests. Widening the scope of the framework described here to include other than human involvement enables us to understand structures with interactive texts about nature and the environment.

3.2   The Interactive Component in Problem-Solution Texts

As noted earlier, simple problem-solution structures occur frequently in many types of texts. Here is an example that clearly follows Grimes's 'Problem-Solution' definition:

(11)   *The streams and rivers in and around Atlanta have become a* ***dumping ground*** *for thousands of tons of waste, including tires, household appliances, cars, batteries, and mattresses. For one year, city-contracted crews for the Stream Clean-up project will remove trash and debris from 37 miles of Atlanta waterways. Crews completed work on the first creek (7.8 miles long) in December and hauled away 205.37 tons of trash.* (*Environment*, May 1999: 23)

The first sentence is the problem, and the remainder of the text provides details of the solution and the result of the work so far. For such non-interactive texts, the recognition of the problem is expressed as sufficient motivation to solve it. In interactive texts, however, the motivation comes from another person or group who recognizes the original problem and intervenes by creating another problem to pressure someone into solving the problem. The actual text here started with:

(11a)   ***In response*** *to a number of water violation* ***suits*** *against the city of Atlanta, Georgia, Atlanta mayor Bill Campbell is leading an aggressive environmental cleanup campaign.*

It is now clear that the cleanup was not simply a solution to the dumping problem, but was primarily an attempt to solve the interactive problem of the lawsuits. The Stream Cleanup Project is intended as a solution to the environmental problem and also the interactive legal problem presented by the lawsuits. In this text, an element of nature is unable to speak for itself or present an interactive problem in an effort to protect itself. The dumping of refuse may appear unsightly, but it might not present a tangible (or serious enough) problem to city authorities, who may thus be inclined not to spend the necessary funds to correct the situation. Improvement was brought about not by the existence of the problem itself, but on the basis of the interactive legal problem presented by the environmentalists on behalf of nature.

In other texts, however, the element of nature that is adversely affected presents an interactive problem by itself. That is, the environmental problem "demands" resolution because it is seriously affecting quality of life:

> (12) *Forest fires and urban pollution are wreaking havoc in Southeast Asia*
> *The region has been hit by atmospheric pollution at levels seriously affecting mil-*
> *lions of people, with hundreds of **deaths**...The calamity highlights two severe*
> *problems. One is potentially **lethal smog** that has arisen due to a combination of*
> *factors...Added to that the plumes of **forest fires** now raging in upwind Indone-*
> *sia and it is small wonder that world **pollution** records are being broken. The*
> *only silver lining...is that it could put additional pressure on rapidly developing*
> *nations to clean up their act. (Nature, 25 September 1997: 315)*

The environmental degradation is being caused by solutions to modern-day needs (forest fires and the need for personal transportation and industrial development). This time, though, the environmental problem demands resolution because it is a problem not just for the environment, but also for everyone living in the area:

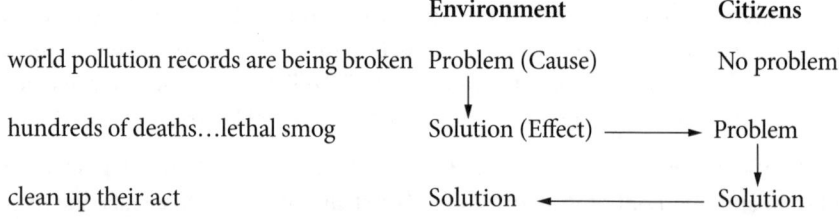

The final embedded clause (*it...act.*) signals the problem the deteriorating environment is presenting to developing nations. As the environment is inanimate, it cannot deliberately kill hundreds of people or create lethal smog as a purposeful interactive solution-problem to encourage action to solve its own problem. Instead there is a cause-effect relation between the initial problem and the interactive solution-problem. In human (and animal) thinking situations, the solution-problem is basis-assessment, where the initiating problem is the basis and the solution-problem is the considered decision or assessment. For other situations, the initiating problem is the cause and the problem-solution is the effect.

3.3   Problem Identification, Study and Resolution

The sequence of events in any assessment-basis type of problem-solution activities involves at least: (a) problem recognition; (b) studying the problem to determine its extent, cause, seriousness, etc.; (c) the decision to solve the problem, (d) determination of possible solutions and their refinement; (e) the decision on the final solution and its final development; and finally (f) the implementation of the solution and perhaps its evaluation. Assessments and testing are important aspects of most of these stages. This overall "design process" in engineering, described for example by Earle (1977), is reflected in all texts that describe the thought/action patterns of those involved in any multi-stage problem-solution sequence (Jordan 1980).

Some texts describe the whole (completed) sequence of thoughts and actions, whereas others describe the thoughts and actions up to a given point in the procedure. Here is a text at the early stage of problem identification:

(13) *What's twice the size of the United States and under water? According to Elliott A. Norse of the Marine Conservation Biology Institute in Redmond, Washington, the answer is the area of the seabed destroyed by fishing trawlers. Fishing boats in search of deep-sea delicacies such as shrimp and flounder disturb ocean floor colonies, which are more vulnerable than their counterparts closer to shore. The species diversity in these areas dips markedly after trawlers pass through. Norse suspects that in addition to being extensive, the damage may prove to be long lasting. (Environment, March 1999: 22)*

Deep sea fishing with trawlers is a solution to the need or desire to catch shrimp and flounder, but it is also proving to be a problem to many of the species that live there. This text identifies this interactive solution-problem and provides a clear indication of its extent and seriousness. The next step is for environmentalists to find a solution to this problem on behalf of the fisheries – and that will very likely present an interactive problem to the deep-sea fishers.

Once a problem has been identified, it needs to be studied with a view to determining whether it really needs to be solved. The next text illustrates this stage of the problem-solution procedure:

(14) *Cell phone towers, housing the antennae that make the cell phones work, have been cropping up all across the country...Angry citizens and even whole municipalities have revolted against tower placements. The city of Medina, Washington, instituted two consecutive 6-month moratoriums on the building of new towers to study the problem, and other cities across the country are following its lead. (Environment, June 1999: 23)*

The new towers are a solution to the commercial needs of the cell phone companies, but are perceived as a problem by citizens and municipalities. The revolt and moratoria against the towers are attempted solutions by the citizens – and also a problem to the companies. The problem is being studied with a view to determining a solution to the citizens' problem that will also satisfy the cell phone companies:

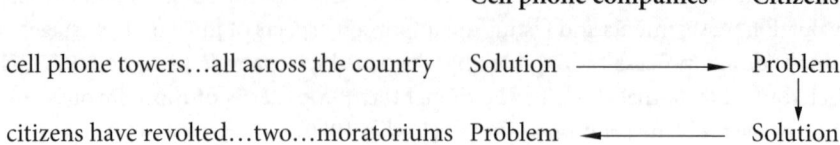

	Cell phone companies	Citizens
cell phone towers…all across the country	Solution ⟶	Problem
citizens have revolted…two…moratoriums	Problem ⟵	Solution

A successfully completed interactive solution-problem is shown by:

(15)   *Home Depot, currently the largest retailer of old-growth wood products in the world, has announced that it will **stop** carrying such products by the end of 2002. This decision comes **after** an intensive, two-year protest spearheaded by Rainforest Action Network.* (*Environment*, November 2000: 8)

The sale of old-growth wood products is part of the company's solution to their need to earn money for shareholders, but it is a problem to those seeking to protect the old-growth trees – and to the trees themselves of course. The Network's *protest* (their solution and an interactive problem for Home Depot) has led the company to agree to *stop* selling those products; this is a solution to the Network's problem and also to their own interactive problem (the protest):

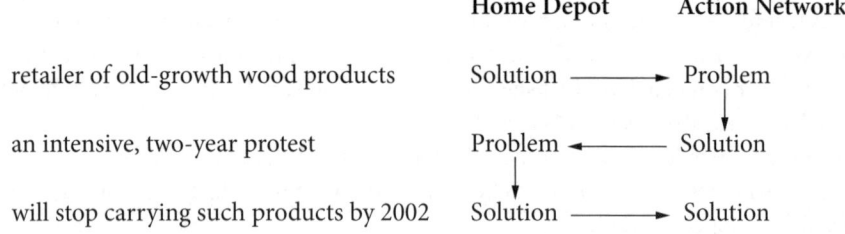

	Home Depot	Action Network
retailer of old-growth wood products	Solution ⟶	Problem
an intensive, two-year protest	Problem ⟵	Solution
will stop carrying such products by 2002	Solution ⟶	Solution

3.4   Predator-Prey Patterns

The natural sciences abound with situations where one species preys on others, and this is reflected in the contents and structure of the documents that describe these activities. Humans, of course, are the most significant predators of all, preying on many animals and fish and thus presenting their prey with the ultimate problem: their very lives. As we saw in example (10), about the cooked cockroaches, humans often kill other species when they are or they cause a problem to us. In example (13), we saw how trawling fishers preying on certain species cause an unintended "collateral" problem to other species in that area. And of course any killing of animals or fish presents a problem to the creatures affected, whether the motivation is to obtain food, or for the joy some people find in hunting and killing. Some species (e.g., frogs, turtles, salmon) find a solution to their predation problem by producing very large numbers of offspring so that the small proportion that survive are enough to continue the species; such action is a solution-solution as it adds to the availability of prey. Other animals, birds and fish seek to avoid predation through speed, camouflage, immobility, poison, spines, colour warnings, etc. Such "escape behaviour" presents a problem to the predator:

(16) *At least one species of clupeid fish can detect sound up to 180 Hz. We speculate that clupeids are able to detect the ultrasonic clicks of one of their major predators, echolocating cetaceans….Shad readily detect echolocating pulses of dolphins, and like moths, the response to the detection of such sounds is **escape behaviour**.* (*Nature*, 25 September 1997: 341)

The interactive solution-problems here are shown by:

	Cetaceans	**Shad**
one of their major predators	Solution ⟶	Problem
able to detect the ultrasonic clicks	Problem ⟵	Solution

3.5 Friends and Enemies

Left on their own, predators and prey usually develop a balanced ecosystem, in which enough prey are eaten to sustain the predator, but not enough to endanger the prey as a species – and thus present a problem to the predator. Humans often intervene, however, to protect domesticated animals and birds, or preferred or endangered species. The structures that mirror the natural predator-prey forces and the related human aims and desires can become very complicated, especially when two or more human groups with conflicting interests become "friends" with the sides and therefore become "enemies":

(17) *In Britain, the hen harrier, Circus cyaneus, is a beautiful but scarce bird of **prey**, today found mainly on moorland in Scotland. The hen harrier's big **problem** is that it **eats** chicks and adults of the red grouse, Lagopus lagopus scoticus. The grouse-shooting industry is of some economic significance, directly generating a gross revenue of more than $16 million a year [and]…management of moorland estates for grouse has helped **protect** large areas of Britain's uplands, and their native vegetation from **overgrazing** or **disappearing** under gloomy plantations of sitka pine or other exotic tree species. But successful management of the grouse-shooting industry…depends on high population densities of grouse. So the hen harrier's depredations are understandably viewed with **disfavour** by moorland managers. Although hen harriers and their nests have received full legal **protection** since 1954, there are abundant anecdotal reports of their **persecution**….We have a real **problem** here, with conservation interests on both sides: the grouse-shooting industry helps to conserve traditional British uplands and their vegetation, which would otherwise be likely to **disappear** under pine plantations; but the economic viability of this industry is seen by some of its practitioners to require the illegal **killing** and **harassment** of birds of prey. Underlying*

*this dilemma, Etheridge et al. observe that "the sport shooting of red grouse and other game birds may not continue to be acceptable to the general public if its proponents argue that it can be sustained only by the **persecution** of rare birds of prey." (Nature, 25 September 1997: 331)*

Although the central issue is concerned with the predator-prey relationship between the hen harrier and the red grouse, different groups of humans have intervened on behalf of the two sides – for two quite separate and (to them) justifiable reasons. The hen harrier's initial problem is its need for food, and it solves this by eating red grouse. This is obviously a problem for the red grouse and also to those who need large numbers of grouse to shoot, a clear instance of an interactive solution-problem. The solution for supporters of red grouse is to persecute and kill hen harriers to help protect the red grouse so that enough red grouse will be raised to allow them to be shot without seriously depleting their numbers. (Whether this is really a solution for the grouse is problematic!) The persecution is also stated as a solution to two other problems: the need to continue the revenue derived from hunting grouse, and the need to retain the present varied vegetation. The legal protection is intended as the environmentalists' solution to the persecution, but that is apparently only partially successful: it is a problem for the grouse managers, but they continue the persecution anyway. The final observation involves the possible problem created to the general public by the grouse managers' actions and views.

4.   Cause-Effect Relations in Interactive Solutions

4.1   Basic Cause-Effect Elements

The cause-effect relation figures prominently in science and therefore also in texts that describe it. The causes of an interactive solution-problem are identified in:

(18)   *Burning trash in backyard barrels, though legal in many rural areas, emits more dioxins and furons than a municipal waste incinerator serving tens of thousands of households. Lower incineration temperatures and poor combustion conditions seem to be the **culprits**. (Environment, April 2000: 6)*

Burning trash in backyard barrels is a solution to the problem of trash disposal, but it is also a problem for the environment (and people generally) as it emits more noxious products than does municipal waste incineration. The second sentence identifies the two causes (the *culprits*) for the difference in toxic emissions.

Solution-problems were defined earlier as solutions which **are** or which **cause** a problem for someone or something else. In example (18), the burning of trash might well have been a problem by itself because of the smoke or smell of the burning, but it is the problem to the environment **caused** by the two factors of the backyard burning that is emphasised. In example (14), about the placement of cell phone transmission towers, we are told that citizens are *angry* (an assessment), but we are not told the precise basis (reason) for their anger. Is it the unsightly appearance of the towers (i.e., that the towers themselves **are** a problem), or is it that the towers are **causing** a problem through television reception interference – or perhaps both? For all possibilities, the placement of the towers creates a solution-problem for the local citizens.

Cause-effect and a solution-problem lead to a further solution-problem in:

(19) *Half of all U.S. residents have switched brands **after** learning that a particular product, its packaging or the company that makes it is **harming** the environment. The products affected range from common household items such as food and cleaning products to pesticides, computers, and even automobiles. More than 40 percent of those surveyed said they would **switch** to products made by companies working to improve the environment. (Environment, January/February 1999: 22)*

In the first sentence, three factors harm the environment. As the first two (the product and packaging) are inanimate, they are **causes** of the harm; but the third factor (the company) is assumed animate and therefore this is presumably making a conscious choice (as a solution) to harm the environment. The brand switching is an interactive solution-problem intended to present a problem to the companies to try to convince them to stop harming the environment. The opposite structure occurs in the final sentence: a positive incentive is offered to companies who are working to improve the environment. Thus many U.S. residents are collectively using their purchasing power to punish those who harm the environment and to reward those who improve the environment, the aim being to improve the environment.

4.2   Appearance of Environmental Reaction

When environmental harm becomes serious, it becomes a problem to those who have harmed it – and to others of course. As we saw with the discussion for example (12) (about the forest fires), such relations are cause-effect as the environment is inanimate. However, they may **appear** as interactive solution-problems – as if the environment were consciously fighting back against those causing it harm. We could thus regard the environment as a "person" in structural diagrams of interactive solution-problems. A complex cluster of such cause-effect relations occurs in the following example:

(20) *Salt in the subsoils of Western Australia is rising to the surface **as** farmers upset the water balance **by** chopping down trees to grow more crops. The water table rises and capillary action brings salt to the surface, where it forms a hard, white crust. Rising salt **kills** vegetation, encouraging **erosion** and the formation of **deserts**. Hundreds of thousands of hectares of Western Australia have already been **poisoned** by salt....Salt has turned a third of the state's streams*

*brackish, making them unfit for drinking or for irrigating crops. The trees
shown here near Perth have been planted in **an effort** to bring salt lands back
into productive use.* (Photograph caption, *New Scientist*, 9 February 1991: 23)

Although the purpose of the means clause is to grow more crops, it results in the upsetting of the water balance. This adverse change enables capillary action to bring salty water to the surface, where it evaporates and leaves the soil salty. The salt has two effects: it kills vegetation, which leads to soil erosion, which causes desert formation; and it turns streams brackish, which leads to unfit water for drinking or irrigation. The purpose of the tree planting is to reverse the problems caused by the original felling of trees.

4.3   Iatrogenic Solution-Problems

Solutions do not always work, and failure leaves the problem unresolved. Even worse, the attempted solution can actually make the situation worse by causing an additional problem, even if it solves or partly solves the original problem. Although only a single person or group may be involved, such "iatrogenic" solutions are solution-problems as they rebound on those seeking the initial solution. Example (20) shows the highly undesirable iatrogenic effects of the attempted solutions of chopping down trees to grow more crops. Iatrogenic solution-problems are common in medicine, e.g., the taking of ASA to thin blood but perhaps resulting in stomach ulcers, operations that lead to complications or even death, cold remedies that cause sleepiness.

Many actions taken to avoid or solve a problem could lead to additional problems, perhaps also while leaving the original problem unresolved:

(21)   *For years, employees at Mitsubishi Motors Corp. **tucked complaints about
auto defects away** by the dozen in a special place....The complaints stayed
filed, awaiting clarification, explanation or documentation that usually never
came. The **defects** were fixed on **a case-by-case basis to avoid humiliating
recalls**. As it announced another recall yesterday affecting 88,000 cars and
trucks, half of them in the United States, Mitsubishi acknowledged the long-
time cover-up.* (The Kingston Whig Standard, 23 August, 2000: 14)

Car and truck owners had a problem with *auto defects* in their vehicles and sought to solve them by the *complaints*. These presented a problem to Mitsubishi, who sought to solve it *on a case-by-case basis* and *tucked...away* the complaints *to avoid* the bigger solution-problem of *humiliating recalls*. However, this *long-time cover-up* led to the 88,000 recall. Details later in the text explain that, after the news became public, the company's value fell by 30%, the president was forced to resign, and criminal prosecution is pending. Clearly, the company's attempted solution created a far greater problem for itself than the original problem.

5.   Interactive Problem-Solutions as Macrostructures

5.1   Titles with Summaries

Most of the examples in this chapter are short extracts of larger texts, showing the need for any meaningful explanatory model to include the principles of interactive problem-solutions described here. As with all clause-relations, however, interactive problem-solutions can also dominate the overall structure of a text. This can often be seen from the titles, summaries and initial paragraphs of texts (see Jordan 1991b, 1991c, 1993) as in:

(22)   *OSC moves against Black*
Seeks heavy fines, trading bans
Former executives face hearing
Ontario's stock watchdog is seeking **huge fines, permanent trading bans and the**
return of $11 million *in controversial "non complete" payments from media mogul Conrad Black and three close associates.*
The Ontario Securities Commission announced late yesterday it will start **pro-ceedings against** *Black and three other former Hollinger Inc. executives in con-nection with a series of newspaper asset sales between 1998 and 2001.*
OSC staff allege the foursome...put themselves in conflicts of interest, didn't dis-close information on numerous occasions, breached their fiduciary duties and acted contrary to the public interest. (Toronto Star, 19 March, 2005: A1)

The alleged actions of Black and his associates were presumably solutions to needs they had at the time, but they were problems to the public the OSC represents. In response, the OSC will start *moves against* them in an effort to recover by *heavy fines* $11 million inappropriately or illegally gained and to further punish them by *trading bans*. The OSC actions present significant problems to the respondents. The macrostructure of the total text available on this subject is shown in the three titles and is given some substance in the short summary that follows.

5.2   Macrostructure in Titles

Even when there is no summary that details the interactive problem-solutions, the ti-tles themselves may be sufficient to indicate that the macrostructure is dominated by them, as in the following example. Whenever one person or side perceives a problem and takes action to solve it, that action might create a problem for those who do **not** perceive the *status quo* as a problem and who thus regard the action as a threat:

(23)   Female-led Muslim Service **sparks anger**
Amina Wadud trying to foster equality
Violates tradition, Islamic leaders say (*Toronto Star,* 19 March, 2005: A12)

Perceiving gender inequality in Islamic prayer, Amina Wadud and her followers seek to *foster equality* by leading a mixed-sex prayer service. This attempted solution to their perceived problem of inequality is a problem to those who believe it *violates tradition* of male prayer leadership and single-sex prayer meetings; their *anger* sparked (caused) by the attempted solution is noted in the main headline.

The macrostructures of texts such as those indicated by examples (22) and (23) are dominated not just by the semantics of problem and solution, but also by the interactive nature of the solution being or creating a problem to another person, group or thing.

6.   Review and Conclusions

This chapter has extended the established theory of 'problem-solution' analysis by adding an important sub-set of structures that occurs when a solution to one problem simultaneously is or causes another problem. Usually the solution-problem is to another person, thing, or group (interactive solution-problems), as opposed to iatrogenic solution-problems, for which the solution-problem adversely affects the initiator of the original solution. The earlier theoretical framework and the extension discussed here both explain the types of information present in many texts, the way these information types are connected to create typical patterns of text, and the related signals of text connection.

Solution-problems occur at both macrostructure and microstructure levels of documents. For some texts, the principles of solution-problem connectivity are the main mechanism of binding the various types of information into a coherent overall message, and they are essential components of any adequate textual explanation. For other texts, solution-problems form a smaller part of the overall document, and other mechanisms of analysis play more important roles in their understanding. Some descriptive and evaluative texts, of course, contain no solution-problems.

The examples and discussion in this chapter show how solution-problems occur in informal writing in the natural sciences, often together with the prevalent cause-effect relation. Third-party (and higher level) involvement, and iatrogenic effects add to the power of this model of textual explanation, while solution-solutions show connectivity with the related area of symbiotic, co-operative behaviour. Friend/enemy principles allow the sub-theory to account for the adverse or beneficial effects of solutions on others who are not directly involved, but who are empathetically or antagonistically engaged by the benefit to or pain of others.

Although there is some emphasis here on the genre of informal scientific prose, other examples have been taken from general journalism and business to show that the principles described here are relevant to a number of genres. Interactive problem-solutions appear ideal (perhaps essential) for a deeper understanding of the contents, structure and signalling of non-fictional works, such as soap opera, sitcoms and movies. It also seems likely that the principles of solution-problems could considerably enrich the understanding and interpretation of literary works.

References

Anscombe, Gertrude E. M. 1957. "Intention". *Proceedings of the Aristotelian Society* 57: 321–323.

Banting, Federick G. and Charles H. Best. 1922. "The internal secretion of the pancreas". *Selected papers of Charles S. Best*, ed. by Charles H. Best, 43–60. Toronto: University of Toronto Press.

Beardsley, Monroe C. 1950. *Practical logic*. New York: Prentice Hall.

Beekman, John and John Callow. 1974. *Translating the word of God*. Grand Rapids, MI: Zondervan.

Burke, Kenneth. 1945, 1969. *A grammar of motives*. Berkeley: University of California Press.

Corbett, Edward P. J. 1977. *The little rhetoric and handbook*. New York: John Wiley.

Cremmins, Edward T. 1982. *The art of abstracting*. Philadelphia: ISI Press.

Earle, James H. 1977. *Engineering design graphics*. New York: Addison Wesley.

Gray, Bennison 1977. *The grammatical foundations of rhetoric*. The Hague: Mouton.

Grimes, Joseph 1975. *The thread of discourse*. The Hague: Mouton.

Halliday, Michael A. K. 2002 [1985]. *Dimensions of discourse analysis: Grammar*, 29–56. *On grammar*, ed. by Jonathan J. Webster, 261–290. London: Continuum. (Originally published in *Handbook of discourse analysis, Vol. 2: Dimensions of discourse*, ed. by Teun A. van Dijk, 29–56. London: Academic Press, 1985).

Hoey, Michael P. 1979. *Signalling in discourse*. Birmingham, England: English Language Research Centre, University of Birmingham. [Discourse Analysis Monographs No. 6].

Hoey, Michael P. 1983. *On the surface of discourse*. London: George Allen and Unwin.

Hutchins, William J. 1977. "On the structure of scientific texts". *University of East Anglia Papers in Linguistics* 5 (3): 18–39. Norwich, Norfolk: University of East Anglia.

Hutchins, William J. 1987. "Summarisation: Some problems and methods". *Meaning: The frontier of informatics*, ed. by Kevin P. Jones, 151–173. London: Aslib.

Hwang, Shin J. J. 1997. "Purpose clauses in English and Korean". *The 23rd LACUS Forum*, ed. by Alan K. Melby, 495–508. Chapel Hill, NC: The Linguistic Association of Canada and the United States.

Jordan, Michael P. 1980. "Short texts to explain problem-solution structures – and vice versa". *Instructional Science* 9: 221–252.

Jordan, Michael P. 1981. "Structure, meaning and information structures of some very short texts". *The 11th LACUS Forum*, ed. by Waldemar Gutwinski and Grace Joly, 410–417. Columbia, SC: Hornbeam Press.

Jordan, Michael P. 1984a. *Rhetoric of Everyday English Texts*. London: George Allen and Unwin.

Jordan, Michael P. 1984b. "Structure, style and word choice in everyday English texts". *TESL Talk* 15 (1&2): 60–67.

Jordan, Michael P. 1991a. "The linguistic genre of abstracts". *The 17th LACUS Forum*, ed. by Angela M. Della Volpe, 507–527. Lake Bluff, IL: LACUS.

Jordan, Michael P. 1991b. "Openings in informal scientific texts". *Technostyle* 9(2): 1–19.

Jordan, Michael P. 1991c. "Openings in quite formal scientific texts". *Technostyle* 9(3): 18–37.

Jordan, Michael P. 1993. "Openings in formal scientific and engineering texts". *Technostyle* 11(1): 1–28.

Jordan, Michael P. 1996. "To-infinitive groups as clauses and post-modifiers". *The 21st LACUS Forum*, ed. by Mava-Jo Powell, 258–268. Lake Bluff, IL: LACUS.

Jordan, Michael P. 1997. "Subtle signalling of logical relations in news reporting". *The 23rd LACUS Forum*, ed. by Alan K. Melby, 325–340. Chapel Hill, NC: LACUS.

Jordan, Michael P. 1998. "Pragmatic, stylistic and grammatical limitations on choice: A study of cause-effect signalling in English". *Linguistic choice across genres: Variation in spoken and written English,* ed. by Antonia Sánchez-Macarro and Ronald Carter, 66–86. Amsterdam: John Benjamins.

Jordan, Michael P. 2000. *The language of technical communication.* 2nd edn. Kingston, ON: Quarry Press.

Jordan, Michael P. 2001. "Some discourse patterns and signalling of the assessment-basis relation". *Patterns of text,* ed. by Mike Scott and Geoff Thompson, 159–192. Amsterdam: John Benjamins.

Kintsch, Walter and Teun A. van Dijk. 1978. "Toward a model of discourse comprehension and production". *Psychological Review* 85: 363–394.

Labov, William 1972. *Language of the inner city: Studies on the Black English Vernacular.* Philadelphia, PA: University of Pennsylvania Press.

Labov, Wiliam and Joshua Waletsky. 1967. "Narrative analysis: Oral versions of personal experience". *Essays on the verbal and visual arts,* 12–44. Seattle, WH: University of Washington Press.

Longacre, Robert E. 1972. *Hierarchy and universality of discourse constituents in New Guinea languages.* Georgetown: Georgetown University Press.

Mann, William C. and Sandra A. Thompson. 1987. "Rhetorical Structure Theory: A framework for the analysis of texts". *Technical Report ISI/RS:* 87–185. Marina del Rey, CA: University of Southern California. Also in *Discourse Processes* 9(1): 57–90.

Mann, William C. and Sandra A. Thompson. 1989. "Rhetorical Structure Theory: A theory of text organization". *Technical Report ISI/RS:* 87–190. Marina del Rey, CA: University of Southern California.

Porush, David. 1995. *A short guide to writing about science.* New York: Harper Collins.

Quirk Randolph, Sidney Greenbaum, Geoffrey Leech and Jan Svartvik. 1985. *A comprehensive grammar of the English language,* London: Longman.

Rino, Lucia H. M. and Donia Scott. 1994. "Content selection in summary generation". *Report ITRI-94-9, Technical Report Series.* Brighton, Sussex, England: Information Technology Research Institute.

Rino, Lucia H. M. and Donia Scott. 1996. "A discourse model for gist preservation". *XIII Simpósia Brasileiro de Inteligência Artificial.*

Selzer, Jack (ed.). 1993. *Understanding scientific prose.* Wisconsin: University of Wisconsin Press.

Thompson, Sandra A. 1985. "Grammar and written discourse: Initial vs. final purpose clauses in English". *Text* 5: 55–84.

Thompson, Geoff. 1996. *Introducing functional grammar.* London: Arnold.

Trott, Christine. 2000. "Rhetorical invention in the discovery of insulin". *Technostyle* 16(1): 50–64.

van Dijk, Teun A. 1977. *Text and context: Explorations in the semantics and pragmatics of discourse.* London: Longman.

van Dijk, Teun A. 1981. *Studies in the pragmatics of discourse.* The Hague: Mouton.

van Dijk, Teun A. 1985. *Semantic discourse analysis.* London: Academic Press, Harcourt Brace Jovanovich.

van Dijk, Teun A. and Walter Kintsch. 1983. *Strategies of discourse comprehension.* New York: Academic Press.

Wagner, Johannes. 1995. "'Negotiating activity' in technical problem solving". *Discourse of negotiations: Studies of language in the workplace,* ed. by Alan Firth 223–246. Oxford: Pergamon.

Werlich, Egon 1976. *A text grammar of English.* Uni-Taschenbücher 597, Heidelberg: Quelle and Meyer.

Winter, Eugene O. O. 1976. *Fundamentals of information structure*. Hatfield, Herts: School of Humanities, The Hatfield Polytechnic (now Hertfordshire University).

Young, Richard E, and Alton L. Becker. 1966. "The role of lexical and grammatical cues in paragraph recognition". *Studies in language and language behavior. Progress report No. 2*. Ann Arbor, MI: University of Michigan, Center for Research on Language.

The English Contrastive Discourse Marker *instead*

Bruce Fraser
Boston University

This paper examines the English Contrastive Discourse Marker *instead* as it occurs both in written and spoken discourse. I conclude that there are two primary uses for *instead*: a "pseudo-action" use, where *instead* signals a contrast between a non-occurring action and an occurring action; and an "actual-action" use, where it signals a contrast between two occurring actions. I then discuss the semantic restrictions on the discourse segments contrasted with each of these two uses and find them mutually exclusive. Finally, I look at *instead* in combination with *and*, *but*, and *so*.

1. Introduction

The class of English Contrastive Discourse Markers (CDMs) consists of lexical expressions such as *but, conversely, instead*, and *on the contrary* that typically signal a contrast between adjacent discourse segments, S1 and S2. Within this class, two types of contrasts are signaled: **DIRECT CONTRAST** and **INDIRECT CONTRAST**[1].

DIRECT CONTRAST, illustrated in (1),

(1) a. *I could take my vacation is Florida.* **On the other hand,** *I could take it in Jamaica.*
b. *Most basketball players are tall.* **In contrast,** *most divers are relatively short.*
c. *All athletes are not intellectuals.* **Conversely,** *all intellectuals are not athletes.*
d. *Susan is thin* **but** *John is fat.*

occurs when the hearer is able to compare an aspect (or aspects) of the explicit interpretation of the second discourse segment, S2, with (a) corresponding aspect(s) of the explicit interpretation of the first segment, S1, and thereby derive a meaningful seman-

---

1. See Fraser (2006a) for a theory of discourse markers within which this analysis is carried out. For details on the notion of Contrastive Contexts, see Fraser (2006b). I assume that when a CDM occurs the sequence is well-formed and interpretable into one of the two types of contrast. I use "interpretation" in contrast to "semantic meaning" to signify the semantic meaning of a segment modified by pragmatic factors.

tic contrast between the two segments. For the purposes of this paper, by "meaningful" I mean that the contrast must "make sense" in that specific discourse context. Thus, if in (1d) Susan was *thin* but John was *joyful*, a direct contrast, signaled by the Discourse Marker (DM) *but*, would not be present unless the hearer could construe a meaningful contrast between *thin* and *joyful*. This is a possibility, but not very likely.

A direct contrast may arise when S2 contains a single concept with a specific value (e.g., in (1a), LOCATION: "Florida") which is compared with the same concept in S1, but with a different value (LOCATION: "Jamaica"). Alternatively, a direct contrast may arise when S2 contains two or more concepts with specific values which are compared with the corresponding concepts and their values in S1, as in (1b): TYPE OF ATHLETE; HEIGHT. Both the specific details of the interpretation of the direct contrast as well as whether one or more concepts must be in contrast is a function of each particular CDM.

INDIRECT CONTRAST occurs when a CDM is present but the hearer is unable to construe a meaningful direct contrast between S2 and S1. In this case, the hearer must find an indirect message which can be derived from the explicit interpretation of S1 (a contextual implication, an entailment, a presupposition, or a felicity condition), which the explicit interpretation of S2 denies. The resulting interpretation is that the indirect message of S1 is rejected. This case is illustrated in (2).

(2)   a.   [IMPLICATION]
          A: *I'm a certified nurse. B: **However**, my husband won't permit me to work.*
      b.   [ENTAILMENT]
          A: *Why did he kill the President? B: **But** the President's not dead, only sleeping.*
      c.   [PRESUPPOSITION]
          A: *When did he die? B: **Except** he didn't die. He just left town.*
      d.   [FELICITY CONDITION]
          A: *I'm giving you a car for your graduation. B: **But** you know you can't afford to do that.*

In (2a), for example, the explicit interpretation of S2 ("My husband won't permit me to work") is compared with a contextual implication of "I'm a certified nurse," namely, "I can work." The result is that S2 denies the implication of S1, resulting in a direct contradiction, and the interpretation of the sequence is that the implication is rejected.

One group of CDMs signals direct contrast only (*conversely, in comparison, in contrast*, and *on the other hand*); one group signals indirect contrast only ((*al)though, despite, except, in spite of that, only, nevertheless, still*, and *yet*), and one group signals both direct and indirect contrast (*but, however, instead, on the contrary*, and *rather*)[2].

This brief paper is about the CDM *instead*. In contrast to the CDM *but*, which has received considerable research over the years, this is to my knowledge the first treat-

---

2.   A number of these CDMs have variations in form (e.g. *despite/in spite of*) which may be accompanied by different restrictions on both their function as well as the syntactic privileges of occurrence. These are not considered here.

ment of the marker *instead*. I begin by characterizing the two different uses of *instead* and the semantic requirements *instead* places on each use, then look at the related variation form *instead of*, and finally examine the sequences of *instead* with the primary DM is English: *and, but,* and *so*. My intention is to sketch out the different uses of *instead* when it signals direct contrast and the contexts in which they occur, so that future work might reveal how this marker both differs and is similar to other CDM in English and in other languages.

In gathering the data for this paper I examined more than 500 sequences involving *instead* taken at random from the British National Corpus, from MICASE (the Michigan Corpus of Academic Spoken English), newspapers such as the Boston Globe, overheard conversations, and self-constructed examples. Once my tentative analysis was completed, I examined primarily the BNC for several sequences which would illustrate the point. In most cases, I abbreviated the examples for the sake of exposition but attempted to maintain their integrity. Where no indication of source is given, the example is constructed.

2. The two uses of *instead*

The following examples illustrate the first use of *instead*.

(3) a. *We don't do drugs, drink, or use profanity.* **Instead***, we instill morals and values in our boys by raising them right.* (BNC)
  b. *In the 16th century, Elizabethans rarely cleaned their teeth.* **Instead** *they gargled with sugar water to sweeten the breath.* (BNC)
  c. *I should have sent back the drinks.* **Instead** *I looked upon them as a windfall in our rather strained circumstances.* (BNC)
  d. *Mehan expected to win easily last year, given his previous showing.* **Instead***, he lost by a large margin.* (Boston Globe)

From these examples we see that this use of *instead* requires that the prior discourse segment S1 specify – sometimes explicitly, sometimes implicitly – an action that is not done (We *don't do drugs*), an action that is seldom done (Elizabethans *rarely* cleaned their teeth), should be done (I *should have sent back* the drinks) or was not done (Mehan *didn't win*). The use of *instead* requires, in addition, that the second segment of the sequence, S2, specify a different action that was done, will be done, should be done, or was done. I shall refer to this use of *instead* as the PSEUDO-ACTION USE, and for the sake of exposition, henceforth only speak of an action that "was done" or "was not done."

The second use of *instead* is exemplified in the following example sequences.

(4) a. *The church should get out of the business of acting as an agent for the state in legalizing marriage.* **Instead** *it should create a variety of ways in which people can covenant together.* (BNC)

b. *He should stop digging up the garden. He should/could now start planting* **instead.** (BNC)

c. *Mark talked at length with the police.* **Instead,** *he should have kept quiet.* (C)

d. *They criticized his artwork mercilessly.* **Instead,** *they might/could have been a little more sensitive.* (BNC)

In this use of *instead* there an action explicitly specified in S1 which has occurred. In addition, *instead* requires that S2 specify a different, viable action that serves as an alternate for the action specified in S1. By 'viable' I mean that the S2 action must 'make sense' as an alternative in the particular discourse context. I will refer to this as the ACTUAL-ACTION USE of *instead*.

While the declarative–declarative sequence occurs most frequently, I have found all combinations of declarative, interrogative, and imperative syntactic sequences. Moreover, not just any sequence of actions can be related by *instead*; they must deal with the same general topic, a general property of direct contrast sequences. We can see from (5)[3],

(5) a. *He expected to win easily.* **Instead,** *he lost by a large margin.* (C)

b. *He expected to win easily.* **#Instead,** *he climbed Mt. Rushmore last week.*

that it is difficult if not impossible to get a reasonable interpretation of (5b). In addition, the time of S1 must not be subsequent to that of S2,

(6) *John didn't participate in the festivities.* **#Instead,** *he's just going to watch.* (C)

and furthermore, *instead* is inherently anaphoric and we find many sequences like that in (7).

(7) a. *I didn't go.* **Instead** *(of going/of doing that), I just stayed at home.*

b. **Instead of going,** *I just stayed at home.*

This topic is touched on below. Finally, *instead* can occur initially, medially, and finally, as the examples in (8) show[4].

(8) a. *He expected to win easily.* **Instead,** *he lost by a large margin.* (C)

b. *Ok, we are going to use the new method. Really. What we should use* **instead** *is the old tried and true way.* (BNC)

c. *You think it's incomprehensible that maybe two plus two doesn't equal four but equals seven* **instead.** (MICASE)

---

3.   I use the # to indicate discourse unacceptability and * to indicate grammatical unacceptability.

4.   The majority of sequences with S2 being an interrogative have the *instead* in segment-final position as in (8c).

3. Semantic conditions for the use of instead

3.1 The PSEUDO-ACTION USE of instead

There are three main ways in which the speaker may convey to the hearer that the action specified in S1 is a pseudo-action. One way is by using an explicit negative marker. This may be accomplished in two ways. First, the verb or some other constituent in S1 can be negated, as in (9).

(9) a. *Courbet's canvases are **not** about imitation of nature. **Instead** the artist is inserting himself and inserting the fact that art is a made thing.* (BNC)
   b. *You **can't** give me an answer to this question in the paper. It is an interesting question. Put it in a footnote **instead**.* (MICASE)
   c. ***Nobody** listens. **Instead** they stare out of the window at the countryside.* (BNC)
   d. ***Don't** dwell on what went wrong. **Instead**, focus on what to do next. Spend your energies on moving forward toward finding the answer.* (BNC)

There are several restrictions on this negation. First, negative morphological incorporation is not permitted, as the examples in (10) illustrate.

(10) a. *I disagree. #I have to side with Harry **instead**.*
   b. *They discouraged him from going. #**Instead**, the counseled him out of the program.*

Presumably these negative-incorporated forms are not acceptable because to *disagree*, for example, is considered an action performed while to *not agree* is considered not performing the act of *agreeing*.
   A second restriction occurs when S2 contains an emphatic stress,

(11) a. *He didn't **TAKE** the letters. #**Instead**, he **DID** photograph them.*
   b. *John didn't eat the cookies. #**Instead**, **HE** ate the cake.*

though the sequences seem fine with the CDM *but*. Finally, if the verb is negated, S1 must specify an action. Whereas with *rather*, S1 may specify a state, *instead* does not permit a state to be represented in S1.

(12) a. *This job is not possible. #**Instead/Rather**, it's tedious.*
   b. *He wasn't actually crazy. #**Instead/Rather**, he was just a little drunk.*
   c. *It is not the government which is to blame. #**Instead/Rather** it's the politician.*

The second way of using a negative marker to convey the pseudo-action *instead* is accomplished by with a negative adverb such as *few, gone, hardly ever, rarely, seldom, without,…*, as shown in (13).

(13) a. *Company cultures are like country cultures. **Never** try to change one. Try, **instead**, to work with what you've got.* (BNC)

    b. *Toothpaste today contains cement and seaweed. In the 16th century, Eliza-*
      *bethans **rarely** cleaned their teeth. **Instead** they gargled with sugar water to*
      sweeten the breath. (BNC)

    c. *After all, political correctness is/was in many ways an attempt by the puri-*
      *tan left to rein vent Victorian morality **without** any reference to God or*
      *religion or tradition, rooting it **instead** in victimology and neo-Romanti-*
      cism. (BNC)

A second means of conveying a pseudo-action in S1 is by using a verb which such as *anticipate, ask, be tempted, expect, implore, hope* which, when it is used as the main verb in the sequence, implies a negative complement, thereby establishing a negative implication that the action which follows did not occur.

(14) a. *I **asked** him to stop singing, since I was trying to sleep. [=>He didn't stop]*
      ***Instead** he continued singing even louder.* (MICASE)

    b. *Marx and Engels **dreamed** of the emergence of a very utopian kind of soci-*
      *ety. [=>It didn't happen.] **Instead** what emerged in the Soviet Union by the*
      nineteen thirties was totalitarianism. (BNC)

    c. *Television was **supposed** to be a national park. [=>It hasn't become that.]*
      ***Instead** it has become a money machine. It's a commodity now, just like*
      pork bellies. (BNC)

    d. *Many thoughtful pacifists **hoped** that the appeasement of Germany's Ver-*
      sailles grievances would serve to moderate, or even undermine, the Nazi
      *regime. **Instead**, it only aggravated the situation.* (BNC)

S2 must specify an action which in treated as an alternate to the pseudo-action of S1. Thus, in (14a) we have *stop* vs. *continue*, in (14b) *emergence of Utopia* vs. *emergence of totalitarianism*, and so forth.

    A third means of conveying pseudo-action is to have the speaker use the conditional forms *could, should, might* (optionally in conjunction with *have*) to provide a negative implication[5].

(15) a. *I **should have** sent the drinks back.* [=> I didn't send them back] *Instead I*
      looked upon them as a windfall in our rather strained circumstances. (MICASE)

    b. *Okay, we **could** use the old tried and true method.* [=>We aren't going to
      use it] *Instead, what we're gonna do is use an experimental method and see*
      what happened. (BNC)

    c. *There was a point at which, you know, they **might have** just been abolished*
      entirely. [=>It wasn't abolished] *Instead, they were reconfigured.* (BNC)

---

5.   The conditional modal *would* is unacceptable here, as (a) shows,
(a) I **would** have done it. #**Instead**, I just sat there and watched.
(b) I **would** have done it. **But** I didn't. **Instead**, I just sat there and watched.
but if the denial expression is made explicit, as it is in (b), then the *would* is acceptable.

Here, again, S2 s required to specify an action has taken place.

Notice that in these last two cases, the contrast is indirect, not direct. In (14a), for example, there is no direct contrast available, and S2 ('I asked him to stop singing...') is compared with the implication 'He didn't stop singing'. Similarly, in (15a), S2 ('I looked upon them as a windfall...') is being compared with an implication of S1 ('I didn't send the drinks back.')

3.2   The actual-action use of *instead*

Recall that this use of *instead* is created by S1 specifying an action which has occurred while S2 specifies a viable alternative action, which also has occurred. There are three means for conveying this.

First, a negative interpretation of S1 may be conveyed by using an inherently negative verb such as *deny, fail, forget, refuse, reject* (e.g., *deny = not accept*).

(16) a. *Many African-American women had **rejected** the kind of hair straightening and processing products promoted in this ad. **Instead**, in this time period, they chose a more natural look as a symbol of pride in race and African origins.* (BNC)
      b. *I was **denied** permission to take the exam. **Instead**, I was sent to the principal's office for the day.* (C)
      c. ***Forget** the lottery. Bet on yourself **instead**.* (BNC)

Second, the actual-action use may be signaled by having S1 consist of a positive, non-conditional segment, while S2 contains a conditional form *might, should,* or *could* (with an optional *have*) and offers an alternative action[6].

(17) a. *Mark talked at length with the police. **Instead**, he **should have** kept quiet.* (C)
      b. *The trouble with music appreciation, in general, is that people are taught to have too much respect for music. They **should** be taught to love it **instead**.* (MICASE)
      c. *They criticized/condemned his artwork mercilessly. **Instead**, they **might have** been a little more sensitive.* (BNC)
      d. *Today, people are obsessed with movie stars. **Instead**, they **should** pity them.* (Boston Globe)

Finally, the third way for signaling an actual-action in S1 is to indicate (either directly or by implication) that the action specified should be stopped, with S2 again offering an alternative action. The examples in (18) illustrate this.

---

6.   I realize that this is an oversimplification of the details which are not important for the purposes of this paper.

(18) a. *You would be amazed how many important outs you can get by working the count down to where the hitter is sure you're going to throw to his weakness.* **Instead**, *you throw to his power.* (Boston Globe)
      b. *The church should get out of the business of acting as an agent for the state in legalizing marriage.* **Instead** *it should create a variety of ways in which people can covenant together.* (BNC)
      c. *I just had to wonder if/whether we could get our guys to give up those football games. Would they listen to Strauss* **instead**? (MICASE)
      d. *He stopped digging up the garden and started planting* **instead**. (BNC)

To sum up, *instead* has two functions: the first, the PSEUDO-ACTION USE, is to signal that S1 specifies an action which did not occur, while S2 specifies an action which did occur; and the second, the ACTUAL-ACTION USE, is to signal that S1 specifies an action while S2 specifies alternative action.

4.   The variant *instead of*

A variation of *instead* is *instead of (V-ing/doing that)*. Anaphoric, it selects that action of S1 – the text in bold in (19) – which is either a pseudo-action (19a-b) or an actual-action (19c-d), converts it into a positive gerund form, as shown. The negative adverbs, the conditional form and the like are just ignored and only the main action of S1 is selected.

(19) a. *We don't do drugs, drink, or use profanity.* **Instead of doing drugs,..,** *we instill morals and values in our boys by raising them right.*
      b. *In the 16th century, Elizabethans rarely cleaned their teeth.* **Instead of cleaning their teeth,** *they gargled with sugar water to sweeten the breath.*
      c. *The church should get out of the business of acting as an agent for the state in legalizing marriage.* **Instead of acting as an agent,** *the church should create a variety of ways in which people can covenant together.*
      d. *Every waking moment should have been concentrating on the race which I was convinced I could win.* **Instead of concentrating on the race** *I was getting myself into an increasingly confrontational situation, a battle of wills, with the Director of Coaching.* (BNC)

There are various orders of the *instead of*, as shown in (20).

(20) a. *I didn't go.* **Instead of going,** *I just lounged around at home.* (C)
      b. **Instead of going,** *I just lounged around at home.*
      c. *I just lounged around at home,* **instead of** *going.*

5. *But* as a surrogate for *instead*

The CDM *but* signals "simple contrast" (see Fraser 2005). As such, it is more general than the other direct contrast CDMs, which specify more precisely the nature of their contrast. It is usually assumed that *but* can be a surrogate for each of the direct contrast CDMs. Thus, in (21),

(21) a. *Among South American hunters and gatherers, women are actively excluded from hunting large animals.* **On the other hand/But** *they are expected to supply the basis of daily sustenance through the gathering of vegetable products, an activity which men affect to despise.* (BNC)
   b. *Most basketball players are tall.* **In contrast/But**, *most divers are relatively short.*
   c. *All athletes are not intellectuals.* **Conversely/But**, *all intellectuals are not athletes.*

the interpretation of the relationship of S2 to S1 in the three examples is the same, irrespective of whether, for example, *on the other hand* or *but* is present.

However, the meaning of *but* does not change when it appears in these sequences; rather (note: not *instead*), the linguistic and discourse context created the contrastive context in which the meaning of the more specific marker (e.g., *conversely*) was simply redundant. For example, in (21c), the linguistic context provides what is required by *conversely* (but not *in comparison* or *in contrast*) and thus when the *but* is present, the interpretation is as if *conversely* were there.

This is what occurs with pseudo-action use of *instead*. As the examples in (22a-c) illustrate, the presence of *but* rather than *instead* does not appear to change the interpretation of the sequence[7].

(22) a. *Most great men and women are not perfectly rounded in their personalities.* **Instead/But** *they are people whose one driving enthusiasm is so great it makes their faults seem insignificant.*
   b. *Marx and Engels dreamed of a very utopian kind of society.* **Instead/But** *what emerged in the Soviet Union by the nineteen thirties was totalitarianism.*
   c. *Okay, we* **could** *use the old tried and true method.* **Instead/But** *what we're gonna do is use an experimental method and see what happened.*

For the actual-action use, *but* is not acceptable as a surrogate for *instead*, and the interpretation is different, if it is good at all.

(23) a.) *Many African-American women had rejected the kind of hair straightening and processing products promoted in this ad.* **#But/Instead** *in this time period, they chose a more natural look as a symbol of pride in race and African origins.*
   b. *The trouble with music appreciation, in general, is that people are taught to have too much respect for music.* **#But/Instead** *they should be taught to love it.*

---

7. I say "appear" since there is controversy on the acceptability of these examples.

c. *The church should get out of the business of acting as an agent for the state in legalizing marriage. #But/Instead the church should create a variety of ways in which people can covenant together.*

6. *Instead* in combination with *and*, *but*, and *so*

I turn now to the use of *instead* in combination with the three primary discourse markers in English: ELABORATION: *and*; CONTRASTIVE: *but*, and INFERENTIAL: *so*[88]. The acceptability of the combination of *but...instead* in (24a-b) and the unacceptability in (24c-d) reflect the facts just discussed: a combination of *but...instead* may occur just in case the *but* can occur as a surrogate for *instead*.

(24) a. *Most great men and women are not perfectly rounded in their personalities. **But, instead** they are people whose one driving enthusiasm is so great it makes their faults seem insignificant.*
b. *Company cultures are like country cultures. Never try to change one. **But** try to work with what you've got **instead.***
c. *Many African-American women had rejected the kind of hair straightening and processing products promoted in this ad. #**But, instead,** in this time period, they chose a more natural look as a symbol of pride in race and African origins.*
d. *The church should get out of the business of acting as an agent for the state in legalizing marriage. #**But** the church should create a variety of ways in which people can covenant together **instead**.*

Turning to the *and...instead* sequence, we see that replacing the *but* in the above sequences with *and* will not result in acceptable sequence. However, there are examples that are quite acceptable with *and* but not *but*, as in (25).

(25) a. *You would be amazed how many important outs you can get by working the count down to where the hitter is sure you're going to throw to his weakness **and/*but** then throw to his power **instead**.*
b. *This figure reflects the difference between the earnings I will get if I keep working, **and/*but** the retirement benefits that I will get if I retire now **instead**.*
c. *I just had to wonder if/whether we could get our guys to **give up** those football games **and/*but** listen to Strauss **instead**.*
d. *Illusions commend themselves to us because they save us pain **and/*but** allow us to enjoy pleasure **instead**. We must therefore accept it without com-*

---

8.   There are other DM – *instead* sequences, such as "I don't want to go to the this movies this evening. However, I will agree to watch TV instead" which will require further examination.

plaint when they sometimes collide with a bit of reality against which they are dashed to pieces. (BNC)

Notice also that all of the above example are cases of the actual-action use of *instead* and, in general, the *and...instead* combination is acceptable with the actual-action use of *instead* whereas with the pseudo-action use it is not, revealing what concepts underlies the actual-action use of *instead*: "Stop this *and* do that *instead*."

The third primary DM in a sequence with *instead* is *so*, the primary inferential marker, which signals that the message in S2 is justified by the message in S1. Consider the examples in (26).

(26) a. *I'd go in if Marie was with me, but I'm on my own and I might have a bit of difficulty with the menu. So **instead**, what I do is just stand outside and look through the window.* (BNC)
b. *As a child she had not had time for many fairy stories and did not now know them to tell to her daughter. So **instead**, she showed her the pictures.* (BNC)
c. *At the request of the Catholic Church, a three-day sex orgy to be held near Rio de Janeiro was cancelled last Friday. So **instead**, I spent the weekend cleaning my apartment.* (Boston Globe)

In each case the action specified in S1 justifies the reactive action in S2, thereby justifying the *so*. In addition, in each case the action specified in S2 is a viable alternative action to that of S1, thereby justifying the *instead*.

If the action in S2 in examples (26) were as in (27), for example,

(27) a. *I'd go in if Marie was with me, but I'm on my own and I might have a bit of difficulty with the menu. So #**instead**, I'm not going to go inside.*
b. *As a child she had not had time for many fairy stories and did not now know them to tell to her daughter. So #**instead**, her daughter was never exposed to this childhood luxury.*
c. *At the request of the Catholic Church, a three-day sex orgy to be held near Rio de Janeiro was cancelled last Friday. So #**instead**, I spent the weekend cleaning my apartment.*

the *so* would be justified as the DM relating the two actions, but the *instead* would not be acceptable since the S2 action specified was not a viable alternative in place of the S1 action.

It is interesting that although *so* and *because*, both Inferential Discourse Markers, have a complementary distribution when used in what Sweetser (1990) calls the semantic/propositional sense.

(28) a. *John came back **because** he loved her.* (C)
b. *John loved her **so** he came back.*

However, this distribution does not carry over if an **instead** is present.

(29) a. *Her owner felt she had neither the skill nor the courage to ride her. So in-stead, a confident horseperson was engaged to do battle with Honey.* (BNC)

　　　b. *#Instead, a confident horseperson was engaged to do battle with Honey because her owner felt she had neither the skill nor the courage to ride her.*

　　　c. *It's a good idea to carefully check the identity of the artifact for authenticity because you might find you've got a fake **instead**.* (BNC)

　　　d. *#You might find you've got a fake **instead** so it's a good idea to carefully check the identity of the artifact for authenticity.*

7. Conclusion

I have no illusions that the foregoing constitutes a complete and accurate presentation of the Contrastive Discourse Marker *instead*. I do think, however, that it is a good start on the analysis of this CDM. I also think that each and every DM will have to be subjected to a high degree of scrutiny if we're going to understand the breadth and complexity of these functional expressions. In addition, since some of the more robust DMs (e.g., *and*, *but*, *so*) appear to be universal (or nearly so) across language, a cross-language examination must be undertaken to see just how similar they are. These chores await.

References

Fraser, Bruce. 2005. "The English contrastive discourse marker *but*". Unpublished manuscript.
Fraser, Bruce. 2006a. "Towards a theory of discourse markers". *Approaches to discourse particles, 1*, ed. by Kerstin Fischer, 189–205. Amsterdam: Elsevier.
Fraser, Bruce. 2006b. "On the universality of Discourse Markers". *Pragmatic markers in contrast, 2*, ed. by Karin Aimer and Anne-Marie Simon-Vandenbergen, 73–93. Amsterdam: Elsevier.
Sweetser, Eve. 1990. *From etymology to pragmatics.* Cambridge: Cambridge University Press.

Global and local attention in task-oriented conversation

An empirical investigation

Julia Lavid
Universidad Complutense de Madrid

The genre of task-oriented conversation has not received much attention within the linguistic literature, but its study is highly relevant for spoken dialogue systems, where dialogue is focused on accomplishing a concrete task. Using a sample of 30 dialogues, randomly selected from a larger corpus of appointment-scheduling dialogues, this paper investigates how speakers focus their global and local attention as the dialogue progresses. It is expected that the results of this empirical investigation will shed light on the global and local attentional features of this type of task-oriented conversations and will contribute to a better understanding of this important cognitive component of discourse processing.

1. Introduction[1]

The attentional state is a fundamental component of discourse structure which affects both the production and the understanding of various grammatical and discourse phenomena, being also crucial for the development of natural language processing systems as well as of theoretical import across the cognitive and linguistic sciences.

This important cognitive component has been studied by different disciplines and from different perspectives, but, to date, there is a lack of a unified framework which takes advantage of the advances within each field.

---

1.   As a former student and disciple, I would like to dedicate this paper to Professor Angela Downing, whose work on functional grammar and discourse has exerted a great inspirational role on several generations of functional linguists in Spain, and which I greatly admire.

A preliminary version of the research reported in this paper was presented at the 3rd Workshop of *the Systemic Functional Research Community on Ideational and Interpersonal Grammar,* an international research network jointly coordinated by the Universities of Leuven, Antwerpen and Ghent, and with the Universidad Complutense de Madrid as one of its international partners.

Within computational accounts (Grosz and Sidner 1986), the attentional state is one of the three interrelated components of discourse structure, the other two being the structure of the sequence of utterances (called the linguistic structure), and a structure of purposes (called the intentional structure). The linguistic structure consists of segments of the discourse into which the utterances naturally aggregate. The intentional structure captures the discourse relevant purposes, expressed in each of the linguistic segments as well as relationships among them. The attentional state is an abstraction of the focus of attention of the participants as the discourse unfolds, and is concerned with the dynamic recording of the objects, properties and relations that are salient at each point in the discourse. In its global conceptualization, the attentional state is responsible for the global coherence of discourse, while in its local dimension researchers have concentrated on its relationship with the perceived local coherence of a given stretch of discourse.

Within linguistics the perspective has been basically static, concentrating on the information structure of utterances in discourse from different angles (Firbas 1964; Sgall et al. 1986; Halliday 1994; Jackendoff 1972; Vallduví 1994; Steedman 2000, to mention a few), and using a variety of different terms to refer to interrelated notions such as theme-rheme, topic-focus, given-new, among others (see Lavid 2000). Interestingly, recent research within linguistics on conversational topics (Downing 2000; Downing et al. 1998; Givón 1997) seems to be moving towards a more dynamic viewpoint in studying how topics are introduced, developed and closed over a stretch of discourse. This tendency points towards relevant points of contact which can be useful for both research communities.

A fundamental distinction which seems to be operational for the study of the attentional state is its global or local perspective. This distinction has been explicitly established in the CL field, but has also been present in sentential (local) or discoursal (global) linguistic analyses.

In this paper, some preliminary steps are taken to integrate the global and the local aspects of the attentional state by concentrating on a subtype of task-oriented conversation, namely, appointment-scheduling dialogues. This conversational genre has not received much attention within the linguistics literature (cf. Taboada and Lavid 2003), but is the natural research context for most of the work on conversational human-computer interaction. More precisely, research efforts on building spoken dialogue systems which emulate human performance in conversational interaction concentrate on what are called practical dialogues, i.e. dialogues focused on accomplishing a concrete task (Allen et al. 2001). It is expected, therefore, that the research reported in this paper will be of relevance both for the wider linguistic community on conversational analysis as well as for computational efforts on human-computer interaction.

The research questions investigated in this paper are the following: how is attention organised globally and locally as dialogue progresses in this conversational genre? More specifically, how can the cognitive notions of global and local attention be operationalised in terms of linguistic categories? How are such linguistic categories distributed throughout the conversations and what is their function? Are there any typical realization mechanisms for expressing them? What is the relationship between attentional state and the generic task-structure which characterises this type of conversations? I believe that answers to these questions will reveal aspects of the attentional state of discourse, and, more specifically, of this of type of task-oriented conversation, not fully addressed in previous work.

The investigation of these issues will be presented as follows. First, the materials and the methods used in this empirical investigation are described in section 2: the sample corpus is presented in 2.1 and the procedure used to analyse the data in 2.2. Section 3 presents the results of the empirical analysis, and finally, section 4 discusses the research findings and provides some concluding remarks.

2.   Materials and methods

2.1   Materials

A sample consisting of thirty dialogues, randomly selected from the English part (881 dialogues) of a large corpus of appointment-scheduling dialogues, was used for this study. This sample is part of a large scheduling corpus from the Interactive Systems Laboratories, recorded mainly in Pittsburgh from the conversations of native speakers of either English or Spanish. The large corpus from which the sample was drawn was collected under laboratory conditions for the purpose of training a speech recognition system. An example of a dialogue from the sample corpus is presented below:

Example dialogue (1):

OPENING
A: Rob {comma}
TASK PERFORMANCE
PROPOSAL
how about the /uh/ {comma} afternoon of the sixteenth {period} /h#/ hum# {seos}

ACCEPTANCE OF PROPOSAL
B: okay Alan {comma} {seos}
that'll @that will@ be great {comma} actually {comma} {seos}
remarkably {comma} <it's @it is@> i'm @i am@ free {comma} that afternoon {comma} {seos}

PROPOSAL
how about /uh/ /ls/ say {comma} from two to four {period} {seos}

ACCEPTANCE OF PROPOSAL
A: two to four is fine {period} {seos}
/ls/ let's @let us@ do it {period} hum# {seos}

CONFIRMATION OF ACCEPTANCE
B: /h#/ okay {comma}
+QUESTION ABOUT PLACE
where would you like to meet {period} /h#/{seos}

PLACE PROPOSAL
A: /h#/ my office is fine {period} /h#/{seos}

ACCEPTANCE OF PROPOSAL
B: /h#/ okay {comma} excellent {period} {seos}

CLOSING
I will see you then {period} /h#/{seos}

This dialogue exemplifies the main characteristics of the sample corpus used in this study: dyads of two speakers with conflicting schedules that cover a two-to-four-week period. The speakers' task consisted in scheduling an appointment lasting for at least two hours during that period. The interaction took place in a recording laboratory, where the speakers, equipped with headsets and a microphone, did not face each other, thus resulting in dialogues similar to telephone conversations.

Also, as illustrated by example dialogue (1), the sample dialogues used in this study include an annotation of their generic stages, which specified their function (in capital letters in example dialogue 1) with respect to the whole.[2] The generic structure of the sample conversations can be graphically represented as in Figure 1 below.

As shown in the figure, dialogues consist of three main generic stages: an Opening stage, a Task-Performance stage, and a Closing stage. The Opening stage varies in length and content. It goes from a simple *hello*, or just a throat-clearing noise, to a lengthy exchange involving questions about the other person's health, work, family, etc. The Task-Performance stage itself is composed of different substages: first, one of the interlocutors makes a proposal for a meeting. His/her interlocutor will then reject or accept the date proposed. If the proposal is accepted, details about the meeting place or other particulars may follow. Speakers would then move to the Closing stage, where the speakers usually confirm the date agreed upon, say good-bye and close the conversation.

---

2.   I would like to thank the Interactive Systems Laboratory of Carnegie Mellon University and its director, Alex Waibel, for permission to access the corpus used in this study. The sample used in this study was previously annotated in terms of rhetoric and thematic patterns to derive a generic characterisation of the conversations (see Taboada and Lavid 2003). This proved to be an advantage for the analysis of the attentional structure investigated in this paper.

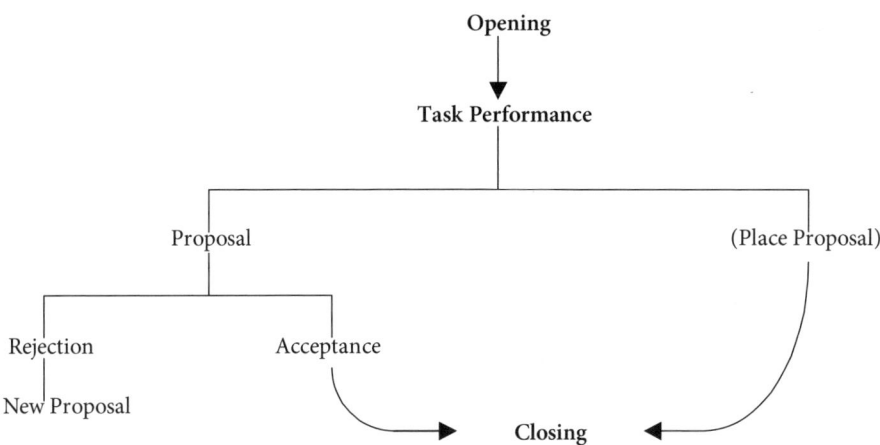

Figure 1. Graphic representation of generic structure of sample conversations

2.2   Procedure

In order to investigate the research questions formulated in the introduction, the notions of global and local attention were operationalised in terms of linguistic categories which allowed qualitative and quantitative analyses of the sample corpus. Thus, global attention was operationalised in terms of the (discourse) topics which are mutually constructed by participants as the discourse progresses (Linell and Korolija 1997; Chafe 1997, among others). Local attention was operationalised in terms of Focal Points, i.e. those entities, properties or relations upon which the speaker focuses within a discourse segment concerned with a specific Topic, and which are considered to be more salient / relevant for that Topic.[3]

On the basis of these operationalisations, the corpus analysis phase proceeded as follows:

1.   With respect to the global attentional state, a systematic search for Topic Types (TTs) and Topic Shift Candidates (TSCs) was carried out throughout the different stages of the generic structure of the conversations, using the classification illustrated in Table 1 below.

---

3.   The category of Focal Point used in this study is similar to the definition of psychological focus provided by J. Gundel (1999: 294): "an entity is in psychological focus if the attention of both speech participants can be assumed to be focused on it because of its salience at a given point in the discourse."

Table 1. Proposed classification of TTs and TSCs

TOPIC TYPES	TOPIC SHIFT CANDIDATES (TSCs)
OBJECT	Function of the object
	Attributes of the object: function, price, owner, user, availability
	Actions the object plays a prominent role in: enable, results, problem(s)
ATTRIBUTE	Objects which have the attribute; more specific attribute
ACTION	Actor, object, etc... of the action; any participant role
EVENT	Next event, preceding and enabling events
	Circumstances associated with the event: place, date, time, manner, reason(s), etc...
	History of the event
	Results and effects associated with the event

TTs were defined in this study as those input topics which speakers select at the beginning of these conversations, and TSCs were defined as those topic categories which are appropriate sequences to a given input topic. The latter are an extension and a reformulation of the conversational association categories (CACs) proposed by Schank (1982). They are concerned with the semantics of conversation and are based on contextual selection rules which specify the appropriate responses to a given input TT. Thus, for example, if the TT of a given discourse segment is of the Event type, the TSCs will be either Next event, or Preceding and Enabling Events, or Circumstances associated with the Event (e.g. place, date, time, etc.), history of the Event, or Results and Effects associated with the Event.

2.   With respect to the local attentional state, the analysis searched for Focal Points (FPs), concentrating both on their distribution and progression patterns throughout the conversations, and on the realisation mechanisms used to express them.

3.   Results

The presentation of the findings will begin with the global attentional component and will then focus on the local attentional one.

With respect to the global attentional state, the analysis revealed the following findings:

1.   The initial input Topic which characterises this type of conversations is an Event TT, more specifically, the meeting that the interlocutors have to arrange in a two-to-four-week period. This type of topic is often implicit, and can be considered as the conversational macrotopic which characterises this type of conversations.

2. The typical TSCs in the sample conversations are circumstances associated with the initial input topic, such as the date, the time and the place where the meeting will take place.
3. TTs and TSCs are not distributed randomly throughout the conversations but follow a hierarchical plan or topic trajectory which progresses from the date and the time to the place of the meeting.
4. TSCs structure the sample dialogues into characteristic Topic Spaces, an organisational category of the global attentional state.
5. Topic Spaces tend to correlate with the different stages of the generic structure of the task, but their scope may cover wider segments of the conversation.

Example dialogue (2) below will be used to exemplify the results of the analysis carried out on the corpus sample. As in example (1) above, the elements of the generic structure are identified at the beginning of each discourse segment in capital letters. The elements in bold identify the Focal Points which will be studied later in this section.

Example dialogue (2)

OPENING (empty)
TASK PERFORMANCE

A: /ls/ /h#/ #microphone# maybe we should get <[s(ome)] {comma}>
together some time {comma} and talk about this a little longer {period} {seos}

PLACE PROPOSAL
/h#/ /ls/ do you have anything free in your schedule {comma}
/uh/ from {comma} #microphone# /ls/ *THE DAY AFTER TOMORROW ON*   {quest}
#key_click# #noise# {seos}

REJECTION OF GENERAL PROPOSAL
B: /h#/ well I'll @I will@ be on vacation the {comma}
/uh/ *SECOND* {comma} *THIRD* {comma} and *FOURTH* {period} {seos}
I'm @I am@ taking the family to Cancun {period} {seos}

    + 2 NEW PROPOSALS
    /ls/ /h#/ /um/ /ls/ how 'bout *THE SEVENTH* {period} or *THE NINTH* {period}

    or maybe even *THE FOURTEENTH OR SEVENTEENTH*   {period}
    /h#/ #key_click# /h#/ {seos}

REJECTION OF NEW PROPOSAL 1
A: #begin_microphone# /h#/ /ls/ well it looks like I'm @I am@
out of town {comma} on *THE SEVENTH AND THE NINTH*   {comma}

+ACCEPTANCE OF NEW PROPOSAL 2 + QUESTION
but *THE FOURTEENTH* is open {comma} {seos}

/uh/ *WHAT TIME* suits you then {period} #end_microphone# #key_click# {seos}

TIME PROPOSAL
B: /ls/ /h#/ how 'bout *TWO O'CLOCK IN THE AFTERNOON*   {period}
/h#/ #key_click# {seos}

ACCEPTANCE OF TIME PROPOSAL + QUESTION
A: /h#/ *TWO O'CLOCK IN THE AFTERNOON*   sounds fine {period}

TOPIC SPACE 1

TOPIC SPACE 2

{seos}   *WHERE* would you like to meet {period} #key_click# # {seos}

PLACE PROPOSAL
B: /h#/ we'll @we will@ meet at   *YOUR OFFICE*   <[i(f)] {comma}>
if you don't @do not@ mind {period} #key_click# {seos}

A: #microphone# do you still know where *IT* is from last time {quest}
or is this something new {period} #key_click# /sniff/ #microphone# {seos }

B: /h#/ nope {comma} I still remember where *IT* is {period} {seos}

CLOSING
I'll @I will@ see you*THERE* {period} #key_click# #paper_rustle# {seos}
A: /ls/ see you*THERE* {comma} /h#/ #key_click# {seos}

TOPIC
SPACE 3

With respect to the results presented above, example dialogue (2) illustrates that the initial input Topic is an Event TT, since both participants are engaged in arranging a meeting in a two-to-four-week period. The TSCs are circumstances associated with this Topic, more specifically, the date, the time and the place where the meeting will take place. The distribution of these TTs and TSCs is not random but follows a hierarchical plan or topic trajectory which progresses from the date and the time to the place of the meeting. Also, as illustrated by the markup, the dialogue is structured into three Topic Spaces, which partially correlate with the different stages of the generic structure of the task: Topic Space 1 is concerned with the negotiation of a date to meet; Topic Space 2 is concerned with negotiation of time; and Topic Space 3 deals with the place to meet.

Each of these Topic Spaces partially correlates with the main different Proposal stages of the more general Task Performance stage. Topic Space 1 correlates with the Date proposal stage consisting of a series of proposals followed by rejections and a final acceptance of date to meet. Topic Space 2 correlates with the Time Proposal stage which consists of a first proposal by speaker B followed by an acceptance by speaker A. Topic Space 3 correlates with the Place Proposal stage.

However, as illustrated by example dialogue (2) the correlation between generic stages and Topic Spaces is partial, since the semantic scope covered by a Topic Space may extend to discourse segments belonging to more than one generic stage of the conversations. Thus, for example, Topic Space 3 partially correlates with the Place Proposal stage but extends to discourse segments belonging to the Closing stage. Also, Topic Space 2 covers the question about time uttered by speaker B after the Acceptance of the Date proposal.

Figure 2 below graphically represents the generic and the topic structures of example dialogue (2):

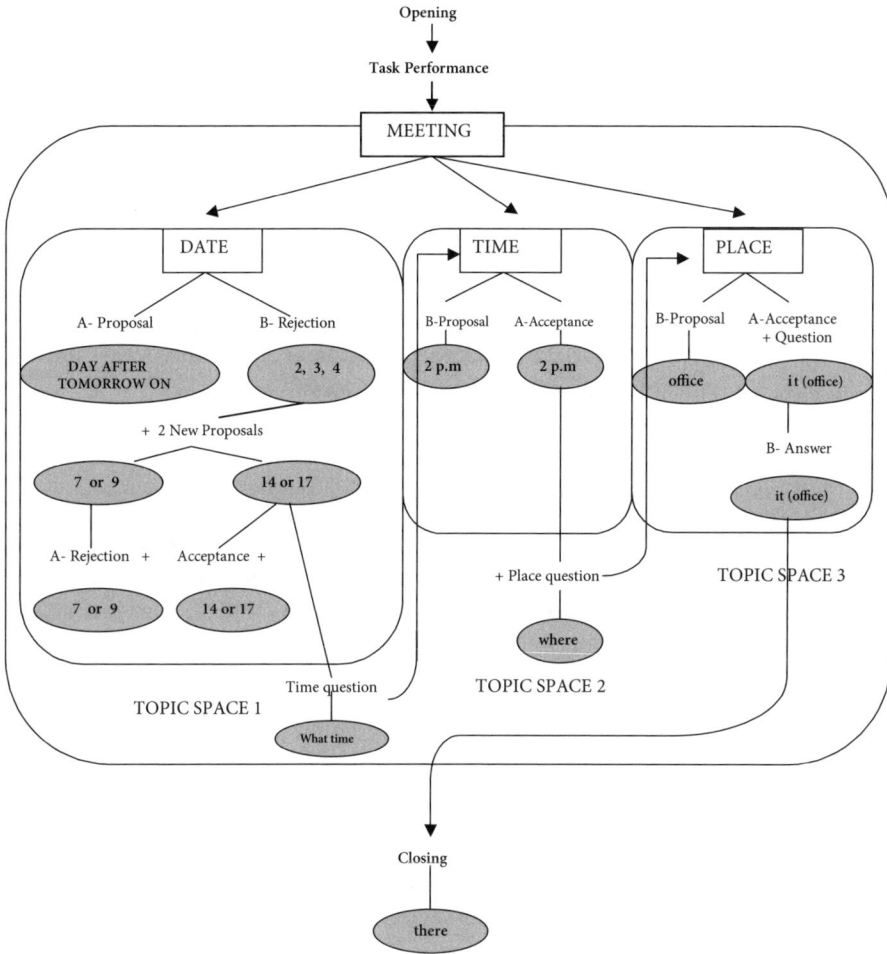

Figure 2. Graphic representation of generic and topic structures of example dialogue

As shown in the figure, there are three Topic Spaces emerging out of each of the three TSCs (date, time and place). Topic Space 1 is the wider one, and involves a recursive cycle of Proposals followed by Rejections followed by New Proposals until the Acceptance of a New Proposal is obtained by one of the interlocutors. More specifically, the negotiation which takes place in this Topic Space is as follows: first, an initial *Date Proposal* is made by A, which is followed by a *Rejection* by B. This same interlocutor makes then two *New alternative Proposals*, one of which is rejected by A and the other one is accepted. This *Acceptance* closes up Topic Space 1, and gives way to Topic Space 2. The transition from 1 to 2 is explicitly marked by the question posed by A which introduces a new TSC, the time of the meeting. Topic Space 2 opens up with a *Time Proposal* by B, followed by an *Acceptance* by A. This, again, closes up Topic Space 2 and gives way to Topic Space 3. The Place Question posed by A immediately after his Acceptance functions as a transition from the current Topic Space 2 to the next. Finally, Topic Space 3 opens up with a *Place Proposal* by B, followed by an *Acceptance* by A, which later asks additional details about the location of the Place.

With respect to the local attentional state, the analysis revealed the following findings:

1.   Topic Spaces center on specific Focal Points (FPs).
2.   Focal Point distribution and progression in the sample dialogues was not random but was found to correlate with certain stages of the conversation, and to function as linguistic signals of the Topic Space segmentation.
3.   Two main types of FP progression patterns were observed in the sample corpus:
     a.   FP continuation, correlating with the Rejection or Acceptance stages following a specific Proposal within a given Topic Space.
     b.   FP Shift, used to indicate when a New Proposal was made (within the same Topic Space) or when a New Topic Space was opened. It was also used to indicate a transition between two different Topic Spaces.

The analysis of the corpus also revealed several lexicogrammatical mechanisms selected by interlocutors to realise Focal Points. These mechanisms are: thematization, lexical cohesion (especially repetition), use of determiners, and pronominalisation. These mechanisms work simultaneously to achieve local attentional effects in the sample of conversations.

Example dialogue (2) above also serves as an illustration of these results. Thus, each Topic Space in the dialogue centers on specific Focal Points, i.e. entities, properties or relations which are considered to be more salient and relevant for that Topic Space. In example dialogue (2) above the elements in bold and italics are the Focal Points within each Topic Space. In Topic Space 1, concerned with the date of the meeting, the Focal Points are "the day after tomorrow on", the "second, third and fourth", the "seventh", "ninth" and the "fourteenth or seventeenth". In Topic Space 2, concerned with the time of the meeting, elements such as "what time" and "two o'clock in the afternoon" are Focal Points. In Topic Space 3, elements such as "your office", "it", or "there" (where the pronouns "it" and "there" refer to the office) are Focal since they are more salient to the place TT.

With respect to the distribution and progression of these Focal Points in example dialogue (2), one can observe that the two main types of FP progression patterns correlate with specific substages of the generic structure of the conversations. Thus, FP continuation correlates with Rejection or Acceptance stages following a specific Proposal within a given Topic Space. This is illustrated in Topic Space 2 where the FP continuation - realized by the repetition of the FPs "two o'clock in the afternoon"- correlates with the Acceptance substage following the Time Proposal stage.

FP shift is used to indicate when a New Proposal was made (within the same Topic Space) or when a New Topic Space was opened. The former is illustrated by the shift from FPs such as "the second" "the third" and "the fourth" in the Rejection stage to the

FPs "the seventh" or "the ninth" which indicate a New Proposal within Topic Space 1. The latter is illustrated by FPs such as "what time" which opens Topic Space 2, or "where" which opens Topic Space 3. These correlations are specified in Table 2 below:

Table 2. Correlations between dialogue stages and FP Progression Patterns

DIALOGUE STAGES	FP PROGRESSION PATTERNS
Rejection	FP Continuation
Acceptance	
New Proposal	Focal Point Shift
New Topic Space	

As to the realisation of FPs, example dialogue (2) also illustrates the use of some of the mechanisms mentioned before. For example, a good number of the FPs in the example dialogue are thematised. This is a frequent realisation mechanism used in the sample corpus (40 percent of the FPs are thematised), probably used as a textual device to bring to focus those elements which are more salient within a Topic Space.

Other realisational mechanisms are lexical cohesion, especially the repetition of lexical items in Acceptance stages to confirm a time or a date, as illustrated by the repetition of "two o'clock in the afternoon" in the Acceptance stage of Topic Space 2 in the example dialogue. Other cohesive mechanisms such as the use of referential expressions (determiners, adverbs, pronouns), as illustrated by the pronoun "it" referring to "your office", work in conjunction with thematisation and repetition to achieve local attentional effects in the sample of conversations.

4.   Discussion and concluding remarks

As the results of the empirical analysis of the sample dialogues have shown, the global and local attentional components of task-oriented conversation are not isolated functional components of dialogue but can be integrated into a unified model which accounts for the relationships which exist between the categories involved. Thus, it was found that TSCs (such as the date, the time, or the place of the meeting) structure the sample dialogues into characteristic Topic Spaces, an organisational category of the global attentional state which emerged from the analysis. Topic Spaces can be considered as context segments where FPs operate, and can be provisionally defined as mental/cognitive territories whose landmarks or centers are specific Focal points. In fact, one of the observed functions of Focal Points was to signal transitions between Topic Spaces. It was also observed that the distribution of Topic Spaces was not random but followed a plan or trajectory which progressed from the date and the time to the place of the meeting, and that there were characteristic correlations with the different stages of the generic structure of the task, although the scope of Topic Spaces could cover wider segments of the conversation. Similarly, it was observed that FP distribution and progression patterns correlated with specific substages of the generic structure of the sample conversations; thus FP continuation correlated with Rejection or Acceptances stages within a given Topic Space, while FP shifts were used to indicate when a New Proposal was made (within the same Topic Space) or when a new Topic Space was opened. The analysis also revealed characteristic realisation mechanisms for FPs in the sample corpus.

These findings are not only relevant for the linguistic characterization of task-oriented conversation but may guide computational implementations for many natural language applications, where the recognition and analysis of the document topics is an important task. For example, in interactive dialogue systems whose main task is to answer requests made by customers, the response strategy employed may depend on the topic types of the request (Lagus and Kuusisto 2002). In order to recognize these topic types dialogues are first split into topically coherent segments and then organized on a document map. The document map thus forms a kind of topically ordered semantic space. In large vocabulary speech recognition knowledge of the topic can, in general, be utilized for adjusting the language model used (see Iyer and Ostendorf 1999). Identification of topics is, therefore, important for sentence comprehension and dialogue strategy selection. Moreover, topic information has been used as one type of contextual information to maintain robustness in spoken dialogue systems and to improve recognition accuracy of spoken utterances (Jokinen et al. 1998).

In all these tasks, models of global and local attention based on empirical analysis, such as the one outlined in this paper, may prove to be useful for the construction of modules which can be adapted to different system needs. For example, if the application context is natural language generation, it would be possible to represent the categories studied as declarative attentional resources which could then be used by a planning algorithm distributed along different components of the generation process (cf. Lavid 2003), following the text planning methodology investigated by the author and colleagues (Hovy et al. 1992).

A detailed account of implementation possibilities, however, is beyond the scope of this study. It is expected, however, that the results of this empirical investigation will shed light on the global and local attentional features of this type of task-oriented conversations and will contribute to a better understanding of this important cognitive component of discourse processing.

References

Allen, James F., Donna K. Byron, Myroslava Dzikovska, George Ferguson, Lucian Galescu and Amanda Stent. 2001. "Towards Conversational Human-Computer Interaction". *AI Magazine* 22 (4): 27–35.

Chafe, Wallace. 1997. "Polyphonic topic development". *Conversation. Cognitive, Communicative and Social Perspectives*, ed. by Talmy Givón, 41–54. Amsterdam: John Benjamins.

Downing, Angela. 2000. "Talking Topically". *Text and Talk*, ed. by Angela Downing, Jesús Moya, and José I. Albentosa, 31–50. Cuenca: Universidad de Castilla-La Mancha.

Downing, Angela, Joanne Neff, Marta Carretero, Elena Martínez-Caro, Soledad Pérez de Ayala, Juana Marín and José Simón. 1998. "Structuring and signaling topic management". *Lacus Forum XXIV*, ed. by Samuel Embleton, 267–278. Chapel Hill, North Carolina: The Linguistic Society of Canada and the United States.

Firbas, Jan. 1964. "On defining the Theme in Functional Sentence Analysis". *Travaux Linguistiques de Prague* 1: 267–280.

Givón, Talmy (ed.). 1997. *Conversation: Cognitive, Communicative and Social Perspectives*. Amsterdam: John Benjamins.

Grosz, Barbara and Candice Sidner. 1986. "Attention, Intentions, and the Structure of Discourse". *Computational Linguistics* 12: 175–204.

Gundel, Jeanette K. 1999. "On different kinds of focus". *Focus in natural language processing*, ed. by Peter Bosch and Rob van der Sandt. 293–305, Cambridge: Cambridge University Press.

Halliday, Michael A. K. 1994. *Introduction to functional grammar*. London: Arnold.

Hovy, Eduard, Julia Lavid, Elisabeth Maier, Viphu Mittal and Cécile Paris. 1992. "Employing knowledge resources in a new text planner architecture". *Aspects of Automated Natural Language Generation (Lectures Notes in Artificial Intelligence)*, ed. by Robert Dale, Eduard Hovy, Dietmar Rösner y Oliviero Stock, 57–72. Springer-Verlag.

Iyer, Rukmini M. and Mari Ostendorf. 1999. "Modelling long distance dependencies in language: Topic mixtures versus dynamic cache model". *IEEE Transactions on Speech and Audio Processing*, 7(1): 30–39.

Jackendoff, Ray. 1972. *Semantic interpretation in generative grammar*. Cambridge, MA: MIT Press.

Jokinen, Kristiina, Hideki Tanaka and Akio Yokoo. 1998. "Context management with topics for spoken dialogue systems". *Proceedings of COLING-ACL 1998*, 631–637. Montreal (Quebec, Canada), August 10–14, 1998.

Lagus, Krista and Jukka Kuusisto. 2002. "Topic identification in natural language dialogues using neural networks". *Proceedings of the 3rd SIGdial Workshop on Discourse and Dialogue*, Philadelphia.

Lavid, Julia. 2000. "Linguistic and computational approaches to information in discourse: Theme, Focus, Given and other dangerous things". *Revista Canaria de Estudios Ingleses* 40: 355–369.

Lavid, Julia. 2003. "Modelling the attentional state of discourse: towards an integration". Paper presented at the *8th International Cognitive Linguistics Conference*. Logroño (Spain). July 2003.

Linell, Per and Natascha Korolija. 1997. "Coherence in multi-party conversation". *Conversation: Cognitive, communicative and social perspectives*, ed. by Talmy Givón, 167–205. Amsterdam: John Benjamins.

Schank, Roger C. 1977. "Rules and Topics in Conversation". *Cognitive Science* 1: 421–441.

Sgall, Petr, Eva Hajičová and Jarmila Panevová. 1986. *The Meaning of the sentence in its semantic and pragmatic aspects*. Prague: Academia.

Steedman, Mark. 2000. "Information structure and the syntax-phonology interface". *Linguistic Inquiry* 34: 649–689.

Taboada, Maite and Julia Lavid. 2003. "Rhetorical and thematic patterns in scheduling dialogues: A generic characterization". *Functions of Language* 10(2):147–178.

Vallduví, Enric. 1994. "The dynamics of information packaging. Integrating information structure into constraint-based and categorial approaches". *DYANA-2 Report R1.3B*, ed. by Elisabeth Engdahl. Amsterdam: ILLC.

Metadiscursive and interpersonal values of pronominal topics in spoken Spanish

Raquel Hidalgo Downing and Laura Hidalgo Downing
Universidad Complutense de Madrid and Universidad Autónoma de Madrid

This paper presents a discussion on the interactive and textual functions of pronominal marked topics in spoken Spanish. The study is a continuation of an empirical analysis based on Marcos Marín's *Corpus oral de referencia de español contemporáneo* (Marcos Marín 1992), in which we have examined the formal types and pragmatic functions of marked topics in peninsular spoken Spanish, applying a conversational approach to topic (Hidalgo Downing 2003). According to the results of that study, Spanish speakers use marked topics to signal different types of movements in topic sequencing, such as topic introduction, framing, shading and closing. A large group of marked topics in spoken Spanish is composed of pronouns, which are informationally given elements by definition. In Spanish then, marked topics are not restricted to the introduction of referents which are not completely recoverable to the hearers, as other studies have suggested (Geluykens 1992), but rather, serve interactive and textual functions. In this paper, we aim to examine the discourse functions of personal and demonstrative pronouns, and to discuss the organizational and interpersonal nature of such functions. The idea we would like to explore is that topic signalling can be studied as a metadiscursive device, where the different functions of pronouns serve as orientation to hearers in the organization, regulation and interpretation of discourse.

1. Introduction

The purpose of this paper is to examine the discourse functions of pronominal marked topics in contemporary spoken Spanish, and to relate them to the interpersonal and metadiscursive component of discourse. In section 3 we will briefly present the basic features of marked topics in spoken Spanish. In section 4 we introduce the idea of topics as metadiscursive orientation, first (4.1) discussing the metadiscursive value of some topic moves such as framing of topic reintroduction. Then in section 4.2. we examine in detail the discourse functions of personal and demonstrative pronouns. We conclude the paper with a discussion in which we establish the connection between informational status and organizational values in discourse.

2. Grammar and conversation

Topic-marking constructions have received wide attention within different linguistic theories, and in particular, in functional approaches to language study. Despite the natural differences in foci of interest, there are several commonalities, such as the description of formal and functional properties of marked syntax, and the connection between marked syntax and informative status of discourse referents. On the other hand, a very promising type of study has explored the interactive aspects or word order, an approach initiated by Duranti and Ochs (1979) and more recently continued by Geluykens (1992) and Barnes (1985). These studies examine word order changes through some regulatory, interactive devices such as turn-taking. In this paper we also apply a conversational treatment to topic-marking constructions, but it is our purpose to take the connection between grammar and conversation further than such previous studies.

As a matter of fact, linguistic studies present grammar and discourse organization as two separate things. For instance, functional studies on word order have often centred their attention on the examination of the conditions which explain the appearance of marked syntax, such as whether the referents are recoverable or accessible to the hearer or not, or whether the referent has been mentioned, when and how many times, in the text before. In other words, the predominant interest in functional studies has been to relate marked syntax to the speaker's assessment of information in discourse.

Conversational analysis, on the other hand, has studied those aspects of interaction which regulate the speakers' interventions in terms of adequate points of transition, type, possible extension, by such means as turn-taking, discourse markers, preferred and dispreferred reactive moves, and so forth. Thus, an important contribution to the study of spoken interaction has been, precisely, the recognition and analysis of the organizational and regulatory roles played by much of the linguistic material used by speakers in face-to-face interaction.

Within conversational analysis, the idea of such an intersection is implicit in the approach to the study of spoken language. Conversional analysts do not study the content of discourse as something discrete, which can be easily identified, isolated and separated from the mechanisms which make content manifest. In other words, conversational analysis examines how, rather than what, we speak.

Recently, there have been interesting attempts to examine aspects of grammar from an interactive approach; in particular, there is a growing interest in including the interpersonal component in the study of grammar. For instance Dahl (2000) studies the egophoricity of discourse, i.e. the statistically relevant occurrence of discourse participants in spoken discourse, in comparison with written discourse. Haiman (1995) proposes the suggestive idea of a divided self in the grammar of reflexives, where the point of view of the speaker consists in a process of self-awareness, where she presents herself doubled and divided, in comparison with the perfect fusion between reality observation and speaker which can be found in omniscence. Schmid (1999) examines some aspects of word order in German written texts in the light of subjectivity, subjectivization (Langacker 1990) and Kuno's (1987) idea of empathy. In particular, she analyses the German constructions of subject inversion in certain types of texts. Sheibman (2002), on the other hand, examines the dimension of subjectivity in the grammar of spoken English; her study is a statistical account of the frequency and use of personal pronouns and types of verbs in spoken discourse. Her findings show that most of our interventions in conversation are clearly subjective; that is to say, that we present utterances with verbs of cognition, propositional attitude and speech, such as *know, think,* or *believe* to present subsequent predicates. In other words, spoken discourse is built through the speaker's point of view rather than otherwise.

The approach of some of these studies is connected, although not always in a direct and homogeneous fashion, to studies on subjectivity and subjectivization (Langacker 1990), which have proved to be particularly productive in their application to linguistic change. For instance, in the process of grammaticalization described by Traugott (1982), there is a gradual change from lexical meanings to pragmatic strengthening. The historical development consists in a process whereby the meaning of a lexical item progressively bleaches into textual or interpersonal meanings, as in the evolution of full verbs to modal auxiliaries.

We would like to show that a similar process may be also found synchronically: in the double nature, informative and interpersonal, of the discourse contexts and functions of marked topics in spoken Spanish.

3. Marked topics in spoken Spanish

The construction examined in this study presents a constituent which appears to the left of the clause, detached from the predication by prosodic pause or the presence of syntactic material, and often copied in the predication by a pronoun:

(1) *La reflexión sobre la política parlamentaria de nuevo, la pongo, o sobre la legitimidad democrática, la pongo en relación con lo que ya he dicho.*
The reflection on parliamentary policy, again, I relate it, or on democratic legitimacy, I relate it to what I have been saying.

(2) *Oye y la revista esta, ¿cada cuánto la sacáis?*
Look, this journal of yours, how often do you publish it?

In examples (1) and (2) the detached constituent marks the topic of the utterance, that is to say, what the utterance is about; since in this construction the topic is marked unambiguously, it is said to be marked or syntactic (Gundel 1998; Reinhart 1982)[1].

This construction presents interesting formal and functional properties, which co-incide with the properties described in other languages for the pragmatic function topic (Li and Thompson 1976, Lambrecht 1981, Barnes 1985). For instance, in spoken Spanish, the constituent can be left out of the illocutionary form of the predication – as in (2) – and can play the different major syntactic functions, such as subject and complements, – as in (2), (3) and (4). There is often grammatical distance between the detached constituent and the predication via insertion of linguistic material, such as embedded clauses, as in (3) and (4). The constituent often appears in the nominative form, that is to say, without any case marking, as in (5). Also, there can be more than one topic to the left of the clause, as in (6)[2]:

(3)   *Pablo imagino que estará por aquí.*
      Pablo I imagine he is around.

(4)   *Pero los libros que yo quería hacer en esta vida, pues los he hecho y ahí están.*
      But the books I wanted to write in my life, well I have written them, so there they are.

(5)   *Porque hoy los hombres, nos ponen el delantal, nos ponen a fregar los platos, nos ponen con el carrillo de la compra.*
      Because men nowadays, they make us cook, they make us wash the dishes, they make us do the shopping.

(6)   *Entonces yo, este abrigo que traigo hoy, lo he hecho porque reconozco que es superbarato.*
      Then I/ this coat that I have brought today, I have brought it because it is really cheap.

In addition to the interesting formal properties of the construction, marked topics are relevant to the sequential organization of discourse. In particular, since the constituent presents what the utterance is about, detachment is used by speakers as a conversational, negotiated device of managing discourse topic development[3], and of offering orientation on how the discourse topics should be interpreted and continued. In the following sections, we will examine framing and topic reintroduction of detached NPs, where the speaker's intention of offering orientation is particularly clear. Then we will

---

1.   The construction is also named "left-dislocation" (Ochs and Duranti 1979), or topic (Lambrecht 1994, Cadiot 1992).

2.   For a full description of formal and functional properties of detached constituents in spoken Spanish, see Hidalgo Downing (2003: 117–209).

3.   For more details on the idea of marked topics as a conversational strategy, see Geluykens (1993:188) and Hidalgo Downing (2003: 233–243).

look at pronominal detachment, where the interpersonal and textual values are especially evident and interesting.

4. Topics as metadiscursive orientation

4.1 Framing and topic reintroduction

The metadiscursive value of detached NPs can be seen in some strategies of topic
change, such as framing and reintroducion.

Conversational analysis describe frames as prefaces or introductory movements,
which represent a closed repertoire of discourse markers such as *well* or *ok* which mark
boundaries in accordance with topic segmentation (Francis and Hunston 1992). However, frames may also include, as Goutsos (1997: 48–49) suggests, an open class of
metadiscursive expressions which, in common with discourse markers, "orient the
hearer on the sequential organization of the text". In our data, frames accompany topic
introduction, and serve the purpose precisely of preparing the hearer for the introduction of a new topic:

(7)   *Bueno, voy a hacer alguna consideración.* **La primera,** *el aspecto exterior de los*
      ejércitos engaña. Y **la muestra más palpable la** *estamos teniendo ahora todos*
      los días, cuando vemos el aspecto exterior del ejército israelí. **El ejército israelí**
      no se puede decir que dé un aspecto exterior de disciplina, uniformidad, y sin
      embargo es un ejército eficaz.

      Well, I would like to make a few comments. The first, the appearance of armies
      is misleading. And the most evident proof/we have it in front of our eyes,
      when we see the Israelian army. The Israeli Army/ it cannot be said that its
      apperance is of discipline, uniformity, and nevertheless it is an efficient army.

The speaker in (7) starts his intervention with the discourse marker *bueno* and the metadiscursive expresion *voy a hacer alguna consideración*, both elements which frame the two
detached NPs, *la muestra más palpable* and *el ejército israelí*, which introduce the new topic
in the discourse. A similar framing function can be found in the metadiscursive expressions *en cuanto a* (*with regard to*), often associated to detachment constructions:

(8)   **En cuanto a lo que estás planteando de las minorías,** *en estos casos cuando*
      sustenta una mayoría a nivel local o provincial o regional, **los partidos minori-**
      tarios, *pues tienen pocas opciones de sacar sus proyectos adelante.*

      With regad to what you are asking about minority parties, in these cases when
      there is a local, provincial or regional parliamentary majority, minority par-
      ties, well they do not have many chances to put their projects forward.

Expressions of the type *en cuanto a* are in fact specialized in preparing a move of topic
introduction by providing a frame, which responds to the speaker's intention of opening

a new domain and signalling a new discourse topic. In examples like (8), also, such an expression goes along with a metadiscursive device whereby the speaker links his intervention to that of previous speakers, signalling that his intervention is relevant to what has been said before. Since topic introduction is a quite radical strategy of topic shift, modifying the course of conversation and introducing a new matter which may not be completely accessible to the other interlocutors, the speaker feels the need to provide indications on the coming shift, in order to prepare the other speakers for the change.

A similar process of metadiscursive elaboration is found in topic reintroduction, where the speaker brings forward a discourse topic which has been temporarily abandoned or left in the background by other discourse topics. Reintroduction of an old subject has in common with framing the high degree of elaboration, which the speaker produces in order to orient the hearer into the new direction of the conversation, making sure that the content of his intervention will be accepted as relevant:

> (9)   *Soy un romántico, y entonces cuando yo leo, pues estoy dentro; cuando yo veo una película, pues estoy dentro.* **Lo que pasa** *es que,* **ahora que estamos hablando** *de los suramericanos y de lo que yo decía antes, de* **la moda... o el esnobismo,** *pueden dañar la literatura.*
> I am quite romantic, and when I read a book, I get really involved; when I see a film, I get really involved too. The thing is that, now that we are talking about Latin American [writers] and as I was saying before, fashion or snobbish attitudes, they can harm literature.

The speaker uses a detached constituent *la moda o el esnobismo/pueden dañar la literatura* to introduce a new topic in the conversation, but he does so preparing the introduction through a metadiscursive elaboration which links the content of this topic to what has been said before. Again, the speaker uses this device to indicate the connection to the previous discourse.

Similarly to framing, topic reintroduction in our data is always accompanied by metadiscursive expressions which make the function explicit, such as *como hablábamos* o *decíamos*, as in (10) and (11):

> (10)   **El lince europeo, el que decíamos** *que es otra especie, desapareció básicamente porque se le cazaba.*
> The European lynx, that one we were saying that it belongs to a different species, disappeared basically because it was hunted.

> (11)   **Como estábamos hablando de la paletilla,** *se puede hacer rellena, tranquilamente. Ahora, también existe la costumbre del cordero lechal asarlo entero o por cuartos.*
> As we were talking about [lamb] shoulder, you can fill it, that's fine. However, baby lamb/ we roast it, either the whole lamb or in pieces.

In fact, these can be considered metadiscursive expressions, in Goutsos' terminology, specialized in marking the topic reintroduction, symmetrical to framing.

4.2   Pronominal Topics

In spoken Spanish, pronouns can also appear to the left of the clause, detached from the predication and copied anaphorically through a co-indexed clitic. Detached pronouns found in the corpus data are of the two kinds, personal and demonstrative, and can also appear as multiple topics, that is, with more than one pronoun in that position, or combined with a detached NP or a cleft-clause:

(12)   *Yo eso no me lo habían hecho nunca.*
      I/that/they had never done it to me.

(13)   *Yo lo que acaba de decir Armando estoy completamente de acuerdo.*
      I/what Armando has just said/I completely agree.

(14)   *Yo la moto no me la llevo.*
      I/the motorbike/ I am not taking it.

Personal and demonstrative pronouns represent a significant number of detachments in Spanish[4]; such high frequency coincides with similar studies done in French (Barnes 1985), which distance this type of construction from English, where pronouns cannot be detached this way (Geluykens 1992). Other studies of spoken Spanish have noted the importance of such a construction, although a thorough analysis of the discourse functions has not been pursued. For instance, Vigara Tauste acknowledges that in colloquial Spanish the first person subject pronoun[5] often appears slightly separated from the verb, without syntactic agreement inside the predication; therefore she considers that such pronoun is an "emphatic pronoun" (Vigara Tauste 1992:84) starting the utterance but with no syntactic link with the clause.

   Pragmatic and discourse properties of pronouns differ slightly from those of the topicalized NPs seen in the previous section. Pronouns represent given information by definition; in particular, personal pronouns represent the discourse participants, therefore we can consider they are maximally given (Barnes 1985).

   In contrast with this property, studies on word order have centred their attention on the assessment of information in discourse, suggesting that marked syntax somehow correlates with informative tension or less accessible referents (Prince 1984, Geluykens 1992). However, if detached pronouns amount to an important group of marked topics, then these cannot be restricted to the introduction of information in discourse. On the contrary, as we shall see, discourse functions of pronouns are regulatory, textual and interpersonal, rather than informative.

---

4.   In Marcos Marín's *Corpus oral de referencia de español contemporáneo* (1992), pronouns amount to the 40% of detachments. Of these pronominal detachments, 68% corresponds to personal pronouns, whereas the remaining 31.8% is composed of demonstrative pronouns (Hidalgo Downing 2003:200).

5.   Although, in principle, all subject pronouns can be detached, the overwhelming majority are represented by the first person pronoun *yo*.

4.2.1   *Discourse functions of personal pronouns*

In the data, personal pronouns have been found in the following discourse contexts: (i) turn-boundary, (ii) topic shift to the speaker as topic, (iii) hedging. These functions are regulatory in that they have to do with the management of turns in speech, topics being a grammatical device of self-selection used by speakers, and interpersonal, since they present the speaker's topic. We will discuss both aspects in this section and the following.

About half of the pronominal topics coincide with turn-taking positions. In this context, the pronominal topic appears at the beginning of the speaker's intervention, and introduces the speaker's utterance, typically in a conversation with different participants:

(15)   *S1: Yo no... no vamos. Por supuesto que no puedo defender a Dionisio por co-*
       meter un delito. Me parece que, bueno, es un delito.
       S2: Yo...sobre el comentario que le hacían a Dionisio sobre defender a sus com-
       pañeros o no defenderlos, la mayor parte de las empresas de seguridad, sólo
       17 estaban cumpliendo el convenio.
       S3: Yo lo que acaba de decir Armando estoy completamente de acuerdo.
       S1: I no..not really. Of course I cannot defend Dionisio for having commited
       a crime. Because I think, well, what he has done is a crime.
       S2: I ...with regard to the comment that they made to Dionisio on whether he
       should defend his workmates or not, the majority of security companies,
       only 17 were observing the agreement.
       S3: I/ what Armando has just said/ I completely agree.

In the three interventions, speakers use the detached pronoun to signal that they are taking the conversational floor. The initial position of the pronoun, opening the speaker's contribution, supports the idea of an interactive function for these topics, associated to the turn-boundary and to a competitive strategy, in this context of a multi-party conversation, of assertively taking the floor. This interactive role is particularly evident in those cases where the pronoun is not generated in the predication, and has no grammatical continuation in any of the arguments of the predication, as happens in the second intervention. These pronouns are "utterance topics" (Morris 1998) or "individual frames" as described by Chafe (1976) rather than subject marking pronouns. In contexts of the type of (15), the speaker seems to have followed the strategy: first mark my turn, then introduce the utterance. This conversational strategy may explain the fact that the pronoun often does not mark agreement inside the predication, giving the impression that the predication itself has been formulated independently from that first pronominal topic.

Although there are many pronouns in turn-taking positions, it is not the only position found for these topics. Speakers also use other means to mark their turns, such as the discourse markers *bueno* or *pues*, as in examples (16) and (17):

(16) *Pues yo quería contestarle...hay dos tipos de robos.*
Well I would like to answer to you...that there are two types of thefts.

(17) *Bueno, yo creo que es un espectáculo, como dice Armando de Miguel, que pro-duce alarma.*
Well, I think that, as Armando de Miguel says, it is a quite alarming show.

On the other hand, pronominal topics are also found in oral genres where the speaker does not need to compete for the conversational floor, like interviews or lectures. In (18), for instance, the speaker is being interviewed by a journalist and uses the detached pronoun *yo* several times, even if he doesn't need to mark his turn:

(18) a. *Yo de momento ya he roto esa frustración, que era escribir un libro.*
I/ for the time being/ have overcome that frustration, which was to write a book.

   b. *Yo concretamente he hablado con ellos de este tema, y estamos encantados.*
I/ specifically/I have talked to them about this, and we are delighted.

   c. *Yo me gustaría que la gente viera lo que he escrito por una necesidad, como decía antes.*
I/ I would like people to see my book because I need them to, as I have said before.

From this we can note that the pronoun signals the speaker's contribution and often intervenes in the process of speakers' self-selection in conversation. However, the use of the pronoun is best seen as a general strategy of marking the speaker's intervention rather than a specific turn-taking or competitive strategy, since it also appears in medial positions and in spoken genres, such as interviews, where the speaker does not need to compete for the floor.

In many contexts of appearance, the detached pronoun responds to a strategy of topic shift. The pronoun modifies the topic of the previous discourse, marking not so much a change in a general topic, but a more local shift to the speaker-as-topic. A typical example can be seen in (19), where the two speakers, in the context of a radio programme, are talking about a fur coat manufacturer.

(19) S1: *No es un visón de bueno...eh....de muchas ofertas que puede haber por ahí y que yo he visto y tal y que, bueno, no voy a mencionar a nadie, ni nos interesa...*
S2: *No, no..tampoco pasa nada.*
S1: *Bueno, me gusta recordar que es un buen abrigo de visón. Entonces yo, este abrigo que traigo hoy, lo he hecho un poco porque reconozco que es superbarato.*
S2: *Éste que te has traído, que yo, además, me lo probé también porque es largo, amplísimo, precioso.*
S1: It is not one of those coats...well...you know...that you find in one of those sales and that I have seen and, well, I am not going to mention any names, we are not interested...

S2: Oh no, that's fine.

S1: Well, I would like to remind everyone that it is a good mink coat. Then I/ this coat that I am wearing today/ I have brought it because I admit that it is really cheap.

S2: This one, which you have brought today, I/ also/ I tried it on too because it is long, loose-fitting, really beautiful.

The two speakers use detached pronouns in their interventions, and in both cases, the pronoun introduces a topic shift to the speaker as topic. By this device, the speakers can keep talking about the general topic of the conversation, while at the same time shifting the local utterance topics. In other words, we can consider that the detached *yo* here responds to a local operation of topic shift, in which the speaker signals the transition to the speaker himself as topic, but at the same time maintains a global or general topic, which is continued by the other speakers. Barnes (1985:39) finds that this context is very frequent in French, in which detached pronouns, rather than changing the global topic, mark "the speaker's contribution to the discourse topic".

The function described by Barnes is reinforced by the fact that many of the contexts where topic shift occurs initiate illocutionary speech acts such as opines, comments, evaluations, justification or explanations; in other words, interventions in which the speaker typically expresses his/her opinion or contributes with his judgement, experiencie or point of view. Verbs of saying (*say, make clear*), influence (*insist*) and propositional attitude (*believe, think, seem*) are particularly frequent, as Bentivoglio (1987) has also found in her quantitative study on the first person pronoun in Venezuelan spoken Spanish:

(20)   *Bueno, yo a mí me parece que la primera concienciación nos corresponde a nosotras, las mujeres.*
Well/ I to me/ it seems that awareness should start among us women.

(21)   *Yo personalmente no me creo lo del [periódico] semanario.*
I/ personally/ I do not believe the conversion into a weekly paper.

(22)   *Yo lo primero que quisiera dejar claro a todos los oyentes, es que huyan de cualquier tipo de ganga.*
I/ the first thing/ I would like to make clear to the audience is that they should avoid all kinds of bargains.

(23)   *A mí eso, insisto que no me parece mal.*
To me that/ I insist that it doesn't seem at all bad.

In such contexts of appearance, the pronoun is separated from the predication through the insertion of linguistic material of various kinds, such as utterance adverbs, cleft-clauses, or copulative clauses introduced by *es que*, the latter amounting to a meaningful group:

(24)   *Yo es que he venido a la biblioteca, pero así, a lo del departamento no he venido yo.*
I/ the truth is/ that I came to the library, but not to the department.

(25) *No, **yo** es que tengo una niña y le doy de comer a las cuatro.*
No/ I/ my problem is/ that I have a baby and I feed her at four.

(26) ***Yo** es que a las cuatro me es imposible venir.*
I/ my problem is/that I can't come at four.

The purpose of such linguistic material is "hedging", expressed here by formulas such as *yo es que, yo me parece que* or *yo personalmente*, which are particularly frequent with opines; that is, when the speaker expresses his opinion or attitude towards something or someone.

4.2.2 *The speaker's voice*

From the functions seen so far, detached personal pronouns do not fit the definition of topic in terms of aboutness, since they do not really introduce "what the utterance is about". Rather, they are best seen as "utterance topics" (Morris 1998) or even as "individual frames" in the sense of Chafe (1976). As we have noted above, one property of utterance topics is that they allow speakers to speak topically in a global sense, that is, to produce utterances which are relevant to what is being talked about, while at the same time they introduce the speaker's personal view, experience or attitude with regard to that subject. The frequent, although not exclusive, use of pronouns at the beginning of interventions, coinciding with turn-boundaries, reinforces the idea that these pronouns serve to construct the speaker's perspective in interaction.

The general use of pronouns to construct the speaker's subjectivity has been noted by Benveniste (1966), and more recently has been studied quantitatively by Scheibman (2002). In her study on the patterns of subjectivity in spontaneous conversation, Scheibman shows that the highest frequency of utterances in spoken discourse are represented by personal pronouns and certain semantic types of verbs, such as cognitive, verbal and interactional.

The function of expressing the speaker's subjectivity is particularly evident and interesting in the case of detached, marked personal pronouns. As we have argued, detached pronouns are associated to opines, evaluations, and hedging: speakers use the pronoun to introduce a subjective frame for their contribution, thus marking the speaker's involvement in the event.

One of the ideas which best suit the functions seen for pronominal topics in spoken Spanish is Kuno's notion of "empathy" (Kuno 1987, Kuno and Kaburaki, 1977). Empathy is defined as the speaker's degree of identification with the event expressed in the utterance, and can be illustrated by the analogy with cinematographic perspective: empathy is the camera angle adopted by the speaker to produce his utterance: "Empathy is the speaker's identification, with varying degrees (from 0 to 1) with a person who participates in the event that he describes in the sentence" (Kuno and Kaburaki 1977: 628). For instance, in (27a) the speaker looks at the event objectively, without establishing empathy relations with any of the participants, while in (27b) the speaker approaches John more than Mary, establishing the empathy relation John > Mary:

(27)   a. *John loves Mary.*
       b. *John loves his wife.*

On the other hand, in utterances such as (28), the speaker does not establish empathy relations with the participants, but describes his own action:

(28)   *I spoke to John about his wife.*

The empathy relation here is the following: *Speaker > John > John's wife.* This relation corresponds to the principle described by Kuno as the "Speech Act Empathy Relation", which reads as follows: "The speaker cannot empathize with someone else more than with himself. E (speaker) > E (others)" (Kuno 1987: 212).

This identification with the speech act of the speaker describes precisely the use of the detached pronouns discussed in the previous section. The detached pronoun, as "utterance topic", signals that the speaker commits himself to the illocutionary act of the utterance, and expresses his perspective, voice or identity. In other words, the utterance is thus part of the "speaker's sphere" and what comes after that is the "speaker's topic" in the sense of Brown and Yule (1983).

(29)   *Yo personalmente no me creo lo de la conversión [del periódico] al semanario.*
       I personally/ I do not believe the conversion into a weekly paper.

(30)   *Yo lo primero que quisiera dejar claro a todos los oyentes, es que huyan de cualquier tipo de ganga.*
       I/ the first thing I would like to make clear to the audience is that they should avoid all bargains.

(31)   *A mí eso, insisto que no me parece mal.*
       To me that/ I insist that it doesn't seem at all bad.

The pronominal topic allows the speaker to present the utterance divided in two distinct parts: first, the "speaker's speech act" expressed by the detached pronoun, and the second part, which introduces the predication containing the event coded and the participants, who do not necessarily coincide with the speaker. As we have noted in the previous section, the data reveal interesting examples of pronominal topics with no grammatical agreement inside the predication, such as (32) and (33):

(32a) *Yo mucha gente me ha comentado.*
       I/ many people have told me...

(33b) *Yo eso nunca me lo habían hecho.*
       I/ that/they had never done it to me.

In (32) the empathy relation is as follows: *E (speaker) > gente (people)*, and in (33) the relation is: *E (speaker) > E eso (that) E > ellos (they)*.

If we compare these utterances with their canonical counterparts, it shows that the grammatical subjects are not good candidates for prominence in discourse, since they are generic, anonymous, undifferentiated:

(32b)   *Mucha gente me ha comentado...*
    Many people have told me...

(33b)   *Nunca me habían hecho eso.*
    They had never done that to me.

Therefore, the speaker does not change the syntactic coding of the predication but chooses a pragmatic device, which is to precede the utterance by the pronominal topic, thus indicating that the speaker is a more prominent entity than is suggested by the syntactic coding of the utterance (a direct object).

In his study on reflexives, Haiman (1995) proposes that the reflexive sentences with the nominal reflexive, such as *I expect myself to win* somehow express the speaker's "divided self"; that is to say, a perspective operation of self-representation whereby "the speaker sees himself/herself as an actor (sees himself, indeed, as others see him) on a stage shared by others. S/He is an actor on the world stage: but s/he is also a critic" (Haiman 1995: 223). The non-reflexive counterpart, on the other hand, consists in a "non-representation of the self, which corresponds to Langacker's (1985: 122) objective scene" (Haiman 1995: 217).

Fronted, detached pronouns also represent a perspective operation by which the speaker presents her "social I" separately from the predication which follows. The utterance is divided in two parts, precisely the same as the most commonly found definition for the topic-comment structure, in which the first part describes the topic, "what the utterance is about", and the second contains the comment, which is "what is predicated of the topic". The difference here is that the first part introduces the speaker, and the second, the speaker's speech act; therefore if we asked "what the utterance is about", we would have to say that the utterance is about the speaker. As a matter of fact in (31) and (32), the utterance does not talk about "the people" or "they" but, as Haiman would put it, about the speaker who sees himself as an actor on the (discourse) stage.

To sum up, the detached first person pronoun in spoken Spanish shows some very interesting discourse functions, which are not really informative in the sense of introducing information into speech. On the contrary, the pronoun is an important interactive and interpersonal device, which serves to mark local topic sequencing, turn-boundaries, and the construction of the speakers' intersubjectivity in discourse.

4.2.3   *Discourse functions of demonstrative pronouns*

Demonstrative pronouns also represent an important group of marked topics in spoken Spanish. Although the different forms of demonstrative pronouns would be, in principle, adequate candidates to appear in the spoken language, the corpus data reveal an overwhelming presence of the two neuter variants *esto* and *eso*:

(34) *Esto lo hemos oído.*
      This/ we have heard it.

(35) *No, eso no lo sabía.*
      No, that/ I didn't know it.

(36) S1: *Esto, ¿lo ponemos en bolsa o lo dejamos fuera?*
      S2: *No, eso guárdelo usted.*
      S1: This, shall we put it in the bag or leave it aside?
      S2: No, that, put it away, please.

This preference can be explained if we take into account that the demonstrative pronoun often does not stand for an entity mentioned before, but rather for a discourse fragment, understood as a whole. This is so even in those cases in which the demonstrative is used deictically, as in (36): S1 asks where he should put some objects, but he uses the neuter pronoun rather than the plural with gender agreement *estos* or *estas*, therefore generically including the set of referents he has in his hands. By this property, described by Halliday and Hasan (1976: 52–53) as "extended reference", the demonstrative can refer not only to the concrete entity mentioned before, but also to the generic class the referent stands for.

Demonstrative pronouns can be separated from the predication by different means, such as illocutionary force (36), prosody (37) or grammatical distance (38). However, the distance between the pronominal topic and the predication is smaller compared to other marked topics. Frequently, demonstrative topics are rather cohesive, somehow integrated in the predication, as in (39). This is probably due to the givenness of such pronouns, but also, as we will see, to the functions they display, metatextual in nature.

(37) *A mí eso, insisto que no me parece mal.*
      To me that, I insist that I think it is fine.

(38) *Y eso sí que creo que es algo que hay que tener en cuenta.*
      And that, yes I think that it is something that should be taken into account.

(39) *Eso lo dice mucha gente.*
      That, many people say it.

Similarly to personal pronouns, demonstratives do not introduce new referents in discourse, their discourse functions being textual, metadiscursive, rather than strictly informative. In particular, in the data, demonstrative pronouns appear as the following: (i) first reference to previous discourse content as a whole, thus recognizing it as a discourse topic; (ii) closing, (iii) evaluation of a discourse topic, and (iv) encapsulation.

In the first function, the demonstrative topic presents some propositional content, which has been mentioned before, as a whole, thus recognizing and conceptualizing this content as unitary. From that segment on, it can be treated as a discourse topic:

(40)   *Si hay confabulación, si hay algún tipo de delito, si hay alguna actuación legal,*
       ***eso** tendrá que determinarlo la justicia.*
       If there has been a conspiracy, if any crime has been committed, if there will
       be legal proceedings, /that/ the justice will have to determine it.

On the other hand, in closing contexts, the demonstrative topic includes the discourse
content which has been built up through the speaker's intervention. The speaker takes
the topic to its closing by offering a summary of the content which has built up throughout the speaker's contribution (41):

(41)   *Pero la sociedad hasta ahora ha estado hecha para los hombres, porque antes ha*
       dicho que si las mujeres no hacen la mili. Las mujeres hacemos: de pediatra, de
       geriatra, porque ¡ay cuando los padres se nos ponen viejos! Nos tenemos que
       hacer cargo de ellos, el hombre se va a trabajar fuera de casa, y la mujer se
       queda con el mogollón. Tenemos que gestionar todas las cosas burocráticas de los
       *colegios, de papeleos de cuarenta mil cosas. **Eso** todo lo hace la mujer.*
       But society is organized to suit men, at least up until now; he said that women
       do not do military service. But women do many other things: they are paedia-
       tricians, geriatricians; as a matter of fact, who takes care of our parents when
       they get old? We take care of them, while men go and do their jobs, and wom-
       en stay at home, with all those tasks. We manage all bureaucracy related to the
       childrens' schools, and paperwork of all sorts. All that/ women do it.

In the closing context, the demonstrative appears at the end of the speaker's intervention, marking retrospectively the end of it, therefore giving indications of a possible
"point of transition" (Schegloff and Sacks 1973), which can be used by other speakers
to take the turn. The metadiscursive function is particularly evident in contexts such as
(42), where S2 actually interprets the demonstrative as a signal of topic closing, therefore rapidly taking the turn and introducing a new topic, which is here marked with
the discourse marker *oye*:

(42)   S1: *Yo de momento ya he roto esa frustración que era escribir un libro, y os*
           *aseguro que no sabéis lo que es tener el volumen en las manos, y decir, **esto***
           ***lo he hecho yo**, qué barbaridad.*
       S2: *Oye, Millán. ¿Cómo es posible que una tierra que hasta ahora ha dado*
           gañanes y pastores, como es La Mancha, de pronto aparecen una serie de
           personajes como Almodóvar?
       S1: I/ for the time being/ have overcome that frustration I had, which was to
           write a book, and I can tell you it is really exciting to have the volume in
           your hands and say, this/ I have done it myself/it's amazing.
       S2: Listen, Millán. How can you explain that a land such as La Mancha, which
           up until now hasn't given us anything but boors and shepherds, suddenly
           gives celebrities like Almodóvar?

A similar function we have identified as evaluation. The speaker makes an evaluative comment on the previous speaker's intervention. The context of appearance is at the beginning of the speaker's intervention, often marking disagreement:

(43)   S1:   *Yo el otro día estuve leyendo un libro sobre psicología infantil, y decía que aún teniendo mellizos, nunca deben ir vestidos igual, y nunca deben dormir en la misma habitación..*
       S2:   *Pero es que...*
       S1:   *ni ir al mismo colegio porque la personalidad de uno puede influir sobre la personalidad del otro. (...)*
       S2:   *Pero es que **eso...eso** a mí me parece un...un poco de majadería, ¿eh?, porque realmente...*
       S1:   *Yo estoy de acuerdo.*
       S2:   *O sea, **yo eso** lo discutiría con cualquiera.*
       S1:   I was reading a book on child psychology, and it said that, if you have twins, they should never dress the same or sleep in the same bedroom..
       S2:   But the thing is...
       S1:   they shouldn't even attend the same school, because one's personality could influence the other.
       S2:   But that...that/ I think that's nonsense, really, because
       S1:   I agree.
       S2:   Well, I/ that/ I would question it to anybody.

The demonstrative here introduces the speaker's reaction to the immediately previous intervention, performed by a different speaker: the demonstrative creates a cohesive link between two adjacent interventions. As opposed to the closing function, the demonstrative appears at the beginning of an intervention, which is a reactive move. Since associated to reaction, it often appears with opines, advice, judgements, such as examples (44) and (45):

(44)   ***Eso** yo creo que deberías hacerlo ya.*
       That I think you should do it now.

(45)   ***Y esto** que estoy diciendo a lo mejor es un poco grave, pero creo que hay que decirlo.*
       And this which I am saying may sound a bit serious, but I think it must said.

The last function found for the demonstratives is encapsulation. In the interpretation of certain pronouns, such as demonstratives, Halliday and Hasan (1976: 52–54) make a distinction between "extended reference" and "textual reference". While in the first reading the pronoun refers to an entity, or the class of entities evoked by the referent, in the second the pronoun refers back to what has been said, understood as metaphenomenon. In Halliday and Hasan's examples, *that* in (46.a) refers to *the vase*, while in (46b) refers to "the fact of having broken the vase".

(46) *They broke a Chinese vase.*
  (a) *That was very valuable.*
  (b) *That was very careless.*

The demonstrative pronouns found in the Spanish corpus present the two possibilities described by Halliday and Hasan, as examples (47) and (48) respectively show. However, in the topicalized construction the second use, the "textual reference"reading, is by far more frequent.

(47) S1: *Lo único que he tomado es Nolotil, el típico calmante de dolores.*
   S2: *Yo **eso** no lo probé.*
   S1: The only thing I have taken is Nolotil, a typical painkiller.
   S2: I/ that/ I haven't tried it.

(48) *En cambio, el conjunto de países árabes, incluso los más ricos, serán países endeudados y además dependientes. Y **eso** sí que creo que es algo que hay que tener en cuenta.*
   On the contrary, the group of Arabic countries, even the wealthiest ones, will be indebted, dependent countries. And that/ I do think it is something that should be taken into account.

In terms of topic sequencing and organization, this second use of the demonstrative is the most interesting, implying that the demonstrative serves as a device used to reformulate discourse contents and to retrospectively link discourse fragments. The higher frequency of the neuter forms of the demonstrative *esto/eso* reinforces its metatextual rather than deictic functions. This function has been described as encapsulation (Downing 1997b, Goutsos 1997). Through encapsulation, the speaker includes propositional, discourse content and expresses it in reduced, condensed form through different types of nominalization. The demonstrative pronoun can include discourse contents, "creating a cohesive link with a fragment of previous discourse, and not only with the immediately previous clause. In this use, the demonstrative includes the previous discourse and closes a transition area, giving way to a new topic introduction" (Goutsos 1997: 53):

(49) *El hecho de que la esposa, o una de las esposas, lo ignoro pero bueno, la conocida...Sul, me parece que se llamaba, ¿no? La esposa de Mao tuviera...o por lo menos en Occidente nos ha llegado que tuvo una cierta relevancia en vida e incluso después de la muerte de Mao; **eso**, ¿tuvo alguna influencia para que las reivindicaciones de las mujeres tuvieran mayor presencia en la revolución?*
   The fact that his wife, or one of his wives, I don't know but anyway, the one who was well known, ... Sul, I think was her name, wasn't it? Mao's wife had... or at least in the West the idea has reached us that she was a very important public figure during Mao's life and even after his death; **that**, did it have any

influence on the fact that women demands had more presence in the revolution?

As shown in the use of the demonstrative in (49), encapsulation has a double nature, retrospective and prospective: "once it appears as encapsulation, the information so expressed is given or presupposed, and will appear as background; at the same time, it is expected that it will be the point of departure for the introduction of new information" (Downing 1997b:151). By including the previous discourse, the demonstrative creates a retrospective link, looking back in the text. But, at the same time, the demonstrative closes a fragment, some discourse content, pushing the information to the second part of the speaker's intervention, opening a new topic.

The speaker uses the encapsulated demonstrative here in order to build the presupposed knowledge and move forward, mostly with the function of pushing prospectively the subsequent discourse.

To conclude, the demonstrative pronouns are also given by definition. However, as opposed to personal pronouns, they do not represent discourse participants, but entities of the extralinguistic context and, more frequently, discourse contents which have been expressed before. It is actually this property of the demonstrative which accounts for the important metatextual role it plays, linking discourse fragments which appear in adjacent utterances but also at long distance.

5.   Conclusions

Detachment of NPs and pronouns to the left of the predication, marking the topic of the utterance, displays a complex set of discourse functions in contemporary spoken Spanish, functions which are not always related to the assessment of the novelty of information in discourse, but to the organization of such discourse. In particular, we have explored the idea that a syntactic topic does not mark "what the utterance is about" but is a metadiscursive device, by which the speaker offers the hearer orientation on the sequencing and interpretation of on-going discourse, indicating how the utterance should be interpreted and what may be coming next.

The metadiscursive component of detached NPs can be noted in general in topic introduction, but particularly in frames and topic reintroduction. In these occasions, the detached constituents introduce some information in the discourse, the referents being unknown to the hearer, but, at the same time, offering indications on the topic sequencing of interventions.

Pronouns, on the other hand, which have taken up most of the discussion, offer interesting insights into the interpersonal and organizational value of word order. Demonstrative pronouns, rather than introducing referents, play textual roles, such as closing and encapsulation, and interpersonal, such as evaluation and recognition of discourse contents. The first person pronoun, on the other hand, does not introduce what the utterance is about but the speaker's voice in discourse.

The distribution of discourse functions goes parallel to the decrease in informative tension, as shown in Table 1 and Table 2.

Detached NPs introduce new referents in discourse – a lexical and informative type of meaning – while also organizational and metadiscursive – frames, for instance – as shown in Table 1. Pronouns, on the other hand, shift to textual meanings – demonstratives – and attitudinal – personal pronouns.

In table 2, on the other hand, we can note the functions associated to the informative and organizational component of discourse, respectively.

Table 1. Discourse functions of detached constituents

Discourse functions	NPs	Demonstrative pronouns	First person pronoun
Lexical and informative	– Introduction of new referents; – Reintroduction of abandoned referents	– First reference to a discourse topic; – Recognition of a discourse content as topic	
Organizational	Frames	Closing	Topic and turn-boundaries; Speaker's self-selection
Textual and Interpersonal		Evaluation of a discourse topic; Encapsulation	Empathy, speaker's perspective or voice

Table 2. From the informative to the organizational component of discurse

Informative	Organizational component of discourse
Introduction of totally and partially new referents	a. Negotiated introduction of referents in discourse b. Frames c. Encapsulation d. Perspective, speaker's voice

The distribution suggests that when the referents are given, as in demonstrative and personal pronouns, syntactic topics do not introduce information in discourse anymore but their functions become purely organizational: interactive, textual and interpersonal. It is, in synchronic terms, a similar process to the "pragmatic strengthening" described by Traugott (1982: 248) when historical grammaticalization takes place: "*In the process of grammaticalization, lexical items tend to move from ideational/ propositional to textual/cohesive and interpersonal/expressive meanings. Each of these steps represents a change from less personal meaning to meaning that is more anchored in the speaker's relation to the utterance*".

References

Barnes, Betsy K. 1985. *The pragmatics of left detachment in spoken standard French*. Amsterdam: John Benjamins.

Benveniste, Émile. 1966. "La naturaleza de los pronombres". *Problemas de lingüística general I*, 172–178. México, Siglo XXI, 1971.

Bentivoglio, Paola. 1987. *Los sujetos pronominales de primera persona en el habla de Caracas*. Caracas: Universidad Central de Venezuela.

Brown, Gillian and George Yule. 1983. *Discourse analysis*. Cambridge: Cambridge University Press.

Cadiot, Pierre. 1992. "Matching syntax and pragmatics: A typology of topic and non-topic related constructions in spoken French". *Linguistics* 30: 57–88.

Chafe, Wallace, 1976. "Givenness, contrastiveness, definiteness, subjects, topics and point of view". *Subject and Topic*, ed. by Charles N. Li, 25–55. New York: Academic Press.

Dahl, Östen. 2000. "Egophoricity in discourse and syntax". *Functions of Language* 7: 37–77.

Downing, Angela. 1997a. "Discourse pragmatic functions of the Theme constituent in Spoken European Spanish". *Discourse and pragmatics in Functional Grammar*, ed. by John H. Connolly et al, 137–161. Berlin: Mouton de Gruyter.

Downing, A. 1997b. "Encapsulating discourse topics". *Estudios Ingleses de la Universidad Complutense* 5: 147–168.

Duranti, Alessandro and Elinor Ochs. 1979. "Left-dislocation in Italian conversation". *Syntax and semantics. Discourse and syntax, vol.12*, ed. by T. Givón, 377–416. New York: Academic Press.

Francis, Gill and Susan Hunston. 1992. "Analysing Everyday Conversation". *Advances in spoken discourse analysis*, ed. by M.Coulthard, 123–182. London: Routledge.

Geluykens, Ronald. 1992. *From discourse process to grammatical construction. On left-dislocation in English*. Amsterdam: John Benjamins.

Geluykens, Ronald 1993. "Topic introduction in English conversation". *Transactions of the Philological Society* 91–92: 181–214.

Goutsos, Dyonisos. 1997. *Modelling discourse topic: Sequential relations and strategy in expository text*. Norwood, NJ: Ablex.

Gundel, Jeanette. 1988. "Universals of topic-comment structure". *Studies in syntactic typology*, ed. by M. Hammond et. al., 209–239. Amsterdam: John Benjamins.

Haiman, John. 1995. "Grammatical signs of the divided self: A study of language and culture". *Discourse grammar and typology: Papers in honor of John W. M. Verhaaer*, ed. by Werner Abraham, T. Givón and Sandra Thompson, 213–234. Amsterdam: John Benjamins.

Halliday, Michael A. K. and Ruqaiya Hasan. 1976. *Cohesion in English*. London: Longman.

Hidalgo Downing, Raquel. 2003. *La tematización en el español hablado*. Madrid: Gredos.

Kuno, Susumo and Etsuko Kaburaki. 1977. "Empathy and syntax". *Linguistic Inquiry* 8(4): 627–72.

Kuno, Susumo. 1987. *Functional syntax: Anaphora, discourse and empathy.* Chicago/London: Chicago University Press.

Lambrecht, Knud. 1981. *Topic, antitopic and verb agreement in non-standard French.* Amsterdam: John Benjamins.

Lambrecht, Knud. 1994. *Information structure and sentence form.* Cambridge: Cambridge University Press.

Langacker, Ronald. 1985. "Speculations on subjectivity", *Iconicity in syntax*, ed. by J. Haiman, 101–150. Amsterdam: John Benjamins.

Langacker, Ronald. 1990. "Subjectification". *Cognitive Linguistics* 1(1): 5–38.

Marcos Marín, Francisco. 1992. *Corpus oral de referencia de español contemporáneo.* Madrid: Universidad Autónoma de Madrid.

Li, Charles, and Sandra Thompson, 1976. "Subject and topic: A new typology of language", *Subject and Topic*, ed. by Charles N. Li, 457–490. New York: Academic Press.

Morris, Terry. 1998. "Topicity vs. thematicity: Topic-prominence in impromptu Spanish discourse". *Journal of Pragmatics* 29: 193–203.

Prince, Ellen. 1984. "Topicalization and left-dislocation: A functional analysis". *Discourses in Reading and Linguistics. Annals of the New York Academy of Sciences*, vol. 433: 213–225.

Reinhart, Tania. 1982. "Pragmatics and linguistics: An analysis of sentence topics". *Philosophica* 27: 53–94.

Schegloff, Emmanuel, and Harvey Sacks. (1973). "Opening up Closings". *Semiotica* 7: 289–327.

Scheibman, Joanne. 2002. *Point of view and grammar. Structural patterns of subjectivity in American English Conversation.* Amsterdam: John Benjamins.

Schmid, Monika. 1999. *Translating the elusive. Marked word order and subjectivity in English-German translation.* Amsterdam: John Benjamins.

Traugott, Elizabeth. 1982. "From propositional to textual and expressive meanings: Some semantic-pragmatic aspects of grammaticalization". *Perspectives on Historical Linguistics*, ed. by Winfred Lehmann and Yakov Malkiel, 245–271. Amsterdam: John Benjamins.

Vigara Tauste, Ana María. 1992. *Morfosintaxis del español coloquial.* Madrid: Gredos.

Phatic communion and small talk in fictional dialogues

Ludmila Urbanová
Masaryk University Brno

Phatic communion and small talk in fictional dialogues are governed by two opposing tendencies which coexist in dialogic structure known as verisimilitude and defamiliarization (see Fowler 1996). On the one hand, fictional dialogues make use of features present in authentic, spontaneous face-to-face conversation, e.g. loose syntactic structure, ellipsis, interjections, informal phraseology etc., to sound close to real-life situations. On the other hand, however, the author utilizes casual exchanges to create new, unconventional meanings frequently carrying differing points of view which are expressions of heteroglossia defined as "polyphony of social and discursive forces" (Holquist 1994: 69). My findings present the results of an analysis of fictional dialogues in the novel *Heat Wave* by Penelope Lively. Phatic communion and small talk are understood as two different, though mutually related notions. Small talk seems to reflect a broader concept of socialization, while phatic communion is considered to be part of small talk.

1. Phatic communion as social ritual

The functioning of the language means used in conversation is determined by "the general principle of maintaining a social equilibrium" (Leech 1980: 94). At the same time, conversational behaviour tends to be ritualistic. Established patterns of phatic behaviour are recurrent, and are in harmony with the existing social norms and social and cultural expectations. Phatic communion and small talk can be characterized as phenomena which are universal, although certain aspects can be identified as culture-specific.

The ritualistic substance of speech behaviour has attracted the attention of many linguists dealing with language as social action, for example Malinowski (1972), Firth (1964), Sapir (1949[1921]), Leech (1980), Halliday (1990) etc. In my contribution I will attempt to juxtapose several theories which tackle the role of phatic communion in fictional dialogues. My aim is to show that on the one hand phatic devices used in conversation are represented by a rather restricted repertoire of recurrent patterns, and that, on the other, however, a great variety of meanings and ways of expression can be achieved through the use of phatic devices in different contexts. Instances of phatic communion will be interpreted with due regard to sociolinguistic criteria of **solidarity, status and formality**.

A significant layer of discourse in which phatic devices are exploited, both in authentic conversation and in fiction, is connected with **re-accentuation** and **defamiliarization** strategies producing distinctions in key, namely irony. In such occurrences the interpretation of the message is context-sensitive.

1.1   Phatic communion re-defined

In the Routledge Dictionary of Language and Linguistics (1996), phatic communion is defined as

> Malinowski's term used for communicative acts that fulfill an exclusively social function, that is, acts that serve to confirm "ties of union" such as the more or less formal inquiry about one's health, remarks about the weather, or comments on trivial matters.

Malinowski defines phatic communion as "free, aimless, social intercourse" (1999: 302), the function of which is primarily based on the process of establishing and maintaining social contact. Firth (1964) stresses the existence of typical situational contexts within the context of culture which give rise to the language ritual. In the same vein, Sapir develops his idea of speech as an acquired "cultural" function claiming that "Speech is a human activity that varies without assignable limit as we pass from social group to social group, because it is a purely historical heritage of the group, the product of long-continued social usage" (1949[1921]: 4).

1.2   The substance of phatic communion

Let me explain the nature of phatic communion in some detail. In Malinowski's words "The breaking of silence, the communion of words is the first act to establish links of fellowship, which is consummated only by the breaking of bread and the communion of food" (1999: 303). The notion of communion is connected with the fact that in the particular instance of small talk or chat "...bonds of personal union" are created by a mere exchange of words (Malinowski 1999: 304). Thus language used in such speech situations means sharing rather than exchanging ideas, feelings and emotions with the interlocutor(s). Lyons (1981: 143) stresses the function of the social ritual: "This felicitous expression...emphasizes the notion of fellowship and participation in common social rituals..."

By contrast, Bakhtin (1999:127) sees striking differences and individual variation even in **genres of everyday life**, i.e. in the domain of language ritual, which is in harmony with the understanding of language use as an act of individual choice:

A large number of genres that are widespread in everyday life are so standard that the speaker's individual speech is manifested only in its choice of a particular genre, and, perhaps, in its expressive intonation. Such, for example, are the various everyday genres of greetings, farewells, congratulations, all kinds of wishes, information about health, business, and so forth. These genres are **so diverse** because they differ depending on the situation, social position and personal interrelations of the participants in the communication.

1.3   Factors constituting phatic devices

In my understanding of the notion of phatic communion I do not support Malinowski's claim that "language here is not dependent upon what happens at that moment, it seems even to be deprived of any context of situation. The meaning of any utterance cannot be connected with the speaker's or hearer's behaviour, with the purpose of what they are doing" (1999: 302). In this article I will try to justify the claim that phatic communion cannot be dissociated from the context of situation. My hypothesis is that phatic communion is the product of the contextual specifications in the process of communication.

Malinowski's term phatic communion is related to the notion of **mutual knowledge**. The term has been widely used in the pragmatic literature, together with the alternative terms **background knowledge** or **common ground**. Blakemore (1992: 8) understands mutual knowledge as tied to assumptions from memory which

> ...include memories of particular occasions and about particular individuals, general cultural assumptions, religious beliefs, knowledge of scientific laws, assumptions about the speaker's emotional state and assumptions about other speaker's perception of your emotional state.

The layer of context which is labelled **the context of general experience** (Firbas 1992) is particularly dominant in the phatic sphere. Our background knowledge, i.e. the experience of the world around us, enables us to use recurrent patterns of linguistic and non-linguistic behaviour. In agreement with Lyons (1977: 574) the notion of context is a complex phenomenon comprising features, which, in my view, have a direct bearing on the choice of the means of expression used in the phatic communion. The aspects which are considered to be crucial in the employment of phatic devices in the speaker-hearer interaction are the following:

1. social role and status
2. knowledge of spatial and temporal location
3. knowledge of formality level
4. knowledge of the medium (i.e. the appropriate code or style)
5. knowledge of the subject matter
6. knowledge of the appropriate province determining the register.

1.4   Phatic maxim or phatic principle?

At this point I would like to question the interpretation of the phatic function as an inherent component of the Politeness Principle introduced in Leech (1983). In Leech's chart featuring Interpersonal Rhetoric (1983:149) the Phatic Maxim is ranked among the maxims of tact, generosity, approbation, modesty, agreement and sympathy.

In my view, Leech's question mark accompanying the phatic maxim in the chart entails the possibility of a different, more radical evaluation. I would advocate the interpretation in which the phatic maxim is re-evaluated as an independent pragmatic principle.

The Phatic Principle can thus be defined as a principle which enhances social contact, which helps to facilitate the smooth flow of communication and the successful mediation of the message.

2.   Role of phatic devices in fictional dialogues

In my investigation the contradictory standpoints of Malinowski and Bakhtin are confronted and examined with respect to phatic communion and small talk in different social contexts. I am inclined to take the view that the context of situation necessarily influences the choice of the phatic communion devices, since "...the use of words in live speech communication is always individual and contextual in nature" (Bakhtin 1999:129).

Moreover, shifts of meaning occur when defamiliarization takes place: "...the generic form of greeting can move from the official sphere into the sphere of familiar communication, that is, it can be used with parodic-ironic re-accentuation" (Bakhtin 1999:127).

2.1   Avoiding sensitive topics

In Example 1 the speakers can be characterized as equal with regard to status, showing solidarity and sharing a high degree of mutual knowledge. The style of speech is colloquial. The phatic discourse is used to establish an atmosphere of mutuality creating common ground. At the same time, phatic strategies are used to avoid sensitive topics, which is in harmony with the Pollyanna Principle.

(1)   *Pauline offers her plate. Hugh helps himself to a forkful of terrine. "Mmn. Very nice. I should have had that – the seafood is a touch boring. So... how's Teresa?"*
"Teresa's fine," says Pauline. Hugh looks closely at her, as though the reply was not quite satisfactory. "Nothing wrong, is there?"
"Nothing at all. The weather's gorgeous. At weekends we go and look at tourist attractions in the interests of scholarship. Maurice's scholarship."

2.2   Phatic device as topic mediator

Conversation about the weather is considered to be culture-specific, because it is considered to be typical of English speakers. As such it is often mocked and ridiculed by foreign learners of English. A passage from George Mikes' book *How to Be a Brit* (1986: 139–140) is a proof of the mocking attitude:

> The main and the most glorious achievement of television is that it is killing the art of conversation. If we think of the type of conversation television is helping to kill, our gratitude must be undying.

In Example 2 the weather is not the focus of conversation, since it mediates another topic, the harvest.

(2)   *"No sign of rain," says Pauline, who knows the correct language.*
"Too late for rain, anyway," Chaundy replies, surly. It is of course the wheat that is under discussion, standing stiff and motionless around them.
What would rain do now?" inquires Pauline.
"Knock it down, won't it?" says Chaundy. "One good thunderstorm and that lot'll be flattened."

3.   Level of formality in phatic communion

My assumptions follow Bakhtin's above-mentioned view of the dependence of the means of expression on the choice of speech genre (1999: 127). I assume that basic distinctions in the nature of phatic devices occur at the level of formality. Varied degrees of formality can be reflected in them, as well as changing degrees of facticity on the one hand and emotiveness on the other. Predictability with regard to the choices made bears witness to the existence of a ritual in instances of verisimilitude. On the other hand, defamilarization devices are used by the author to "force us to look, to be critical" and make us "question the naturalness of a coded concept" (Fowler 1996: 57–58). Let me tackle the controversial interpretation of phatic devices in the verification of my hypothesis that phatic communion is context-dependent.

3.1   Reflection of status in greetings

Phatic devices are utilized in fiction to indicate differences in the relationship between the participants. In the introduction ritual, in the same context of situation, use is made of greetings which differ as to their level of formality. *Hi* is informal and rather familiar, whereas ***hello*** is "the usual word used when greeting someone" (the definition is taken from *Longman Dictionary of English Language and Culture*).

The difference in the choice reflects the difference in the status of the participants in communication: *hi* being used among friends whereas **hello** is used by Carol to greet an elderly person, Teresa's mother. This example shows that the same context of situation can produce different choices in the phatic strategy. Bakhtin's view that it is not only the situation as such but also the social positions and personal interrelations of the participants in the communication which trigger different solutions with regard to phatic devices is thus verified.

(3) *"Hi, James. Hi, Carol,"* says Maurice. *"This is Pauline, Teresa's mother".*
"Hello," says Carol. *The beam loses its intensity. She is not interested in someone's mother, it would seem.*

3.2 Reflection of status in address

The contexts presented in examples (4) and (5) are different as to the level of formality. In the first example the interlocutor is addressed directly in a familiar way as Mum, in the second the form of address *mother* is indirect and formal. Although the relationship between mother and daughter remains the same, the different contexts of situation, however, produce different forms of address.

(4) (daughter speaking to mother)
"Come in. Mum- could you hold Luke for a minute?"

(5) (daughter speaking to friends)
"See you tonight, then. My mother's coming over for supper".

3.3 Shifts in key

In small talk **irony** can be produced through sequencing speech acts which have a contrastive meaning. Lack of compatibility in the interpretation of the meaning of the message in speaker-hearer interaction creates a **paradox.**

(6) *"Why?" she said to Teresa, clenched in disbelief and dismay.*
"Why get married?"
"I'm in love with him," said Teresa, incandescent with happiness.
"Think about it for a bit," wailed Pauline.
"You can't think when you're in love," said Teresa, reasonably enough.

In example (7), irony is signalled by **exaggeration** expressed by the emotive expressions *rotten cynic* and *fraud*. The intonation described by the comment *says James amiably* shows a positive attitude of the speaker which modifies the illocutionary force of the remark. The meaning of the utterance thus becomes **re-accentuated.**

(7)   *"You're a rotten cynic, Maurice," says James amiably. He seems to have recovered his good humour, if it was ever really lost.*
"Ooh... you fraud, Maurice," says Carol.

In informal dialogues instances of small talk are frequently utilized by the author to create an atmosphere of intimacy and closeness. The discourse tactic of **teasing** produces irony as "an apparently friendly way of being offensive" (Leech 1983: 144). The use of the speech act of directing *Go right ahead and interrupt* differs from social expectations in such a communicative situation.

(8)   *"It's me", says Hugh. "Am I interrupting?"*
"Go right ahead and interrupt. I'm procrastinating as it is."

Stereotypical exchanges are replaced by more lively and more sophisticated contributions reflecting either the feeling of solidarity or an atmosphere of tension between the participants in conversation. Defamiliarization is based on the **contrast** and **non-observance** of the maxims of the Politeness Principle.

(9)   *"James has this aunt coming from Bournemouth," Carol explains. "We've got to give her tea. What a bore. Couldn't we have got flu?"*
"No," says James. "This is an aunt I like."
Carol pulls a face across the table, a mock spoiled-child face.

In **sequencing the speech acts** in the dialogic structure the author tends to use strings of ironical remarks to depict intricate relationships between the protagonists, creating gradation of meaning.

(10)   *"Gorgeous apple tart," says Carol. "Apples out of the garden?"*
"Of course," says Maurice. "Dew-picked at dawn."
"You don't pick apples in July," says Teresa. "Sainsbury's."
"Whoops!" says Carol. She points a finger at Maurice. "You did that on purpose – leading me on."
"On the contrary," says Maurice. "I have no idea when you pick apples.".
"And here you are writing an enormous book on country life," she continues, beaming. "Shame on you!"
"My task is the deconstruction of a myth," says Maurice. "Not horticultural information." He grins back at her.

3.4   Asymmetrical relationships

Asymmetry in sharing a communicative situation reflects **the status gap** and/or **lack of mutual knowledge** between the participants, leading to misunderstanding which has a humorous effect.

(11)   "*It's me,*" *says Chris Rogers.* "*I just wanted to say I think I may have made a breakthrough.*"
"*Ah,*" *says Pauline.* "*That chapter?*"
"*No, no. With my wife.*"
"*Of course,*" *says Pauline.* "*Forgive me. She's coming back?*"
"*Well, let's say she is beginning to make some very promising noises. And one of the children has got a temperature, which helps. She's a bit fazed about that.*"

4.   Conclusions

In my analysis of fictional dialogues in the novel *Heat Wave* by Penelope Lively, my hypothesis that phatic devices are context-dependent has been proved. A great variety of phatic devices has been utilized by the author to make the dialogues sound authentic in using elements of spoken language. The most significant feature of the spoken mode used in the fictional discourse under analysis is represented by **ellipsis**. The frequent occurrence of elliptical sentence structures represents a major contribution to the high degree of inherent authenticity and intimacy in fictional dialogues. The sequencing of speech acts is another important tool used by the author to create contradiction, tension and implicature in fictional dialogues. The analysis verifies the assumptions expressed in Fowler (1996: 131):

> The types of greetings used, the forms of questions asked, even the speed and intonations of contributions, intricately manage the sharing of a conversation between participants. Even a tiny interchange uses structure very precisely to govern what happens, how much is said, and who says it.

In the choice of phatic devices the relationships between participants in terms of status and solidarity versus distance play a crucial role. The degree of formality in these devices varies considerably in the discourse under investigation. Speech behaviour showing a combination of informal and formal ways of expression is utilized by the author to illustrate the way of thinking and personal characteristics of the protagonists.

Politeness strategies used in fictional dialogues vary considerably; preference is given to **mock-politeness strategies** rendering irony and detachment. Shifts in key within the dialogic structure are closely connected with defamilarization strategies.

References

Bakhtin, Mikhail M. 1999. "The Problem of Speech Genres". *The discourse reader*, ed. by Adam Jaworski and Nikolas Coupland, 121–132. London: Routledge.
Blakemore, Diane. 1992. *Understanding utterances*. Blackwell.

Firbas, Jan.1992. *Functional Sentence Perspective in written and spoken communication.* Cambridge: Cambridge University Press.

Firth, John R. 1964. *Papers in linguistics.* Oxford: Oxford University Press.

Fowler, Roger. 1996. *Linguistic criticism.* 2nd edn. Oxford: Oxford University Press.

Halliday, Michael A. K. 1990. *Spoken and written language.* Oxford: Oxford University Press.

Holquist, Michael. 1994. *Dialogism. Bakhtin and his world.* London: Routledge.

Leech, Geoffrey N. 1980. *Explorations in semantics and pragmatics,* Amsterdam: John Benjamins. [Pragmatics and Beyond 5].

Leech, Geoffrey N. 1983. *Principles of Pragmatics.* London and New York: Longman.

Lyons, John. 1977. *Semantics.* Cambridge: Cambridge University Press.

Lyons, John. 1981. *Language and linguistics.* Cambridge: Cambridge University Press.

Malinowski, Bronislaw. 1972. "Phatic communion". *Communication in face-to-face interaction,* ed. by John Laver and Sandy Hutcheson, 146–152. Harmondsworth: Penguin.

Malinowski, Bronislaw. 1999. "On Phatic Communion". *The discourse reader,* ed. by Adam Jaworski and Nikolas Coupland, 302–305. London: Routledge.

Mikes, George. 1986. *How to be a Brit.* London: Penguin Books.

Sapir, Edward. 1949[1921]. *Language.* London: Harvest Books. [Originally published by Harcourt, Brace and World, New York, 1921].

Literature Analysed

Penelope Lively. 1997. *Heat Wave.* Penguin Books

Literature Consulted

Longman Dictionary of English Language and Culture
Routledge Dictionary of Language and Linguistics

Mister so-called X

Discourse functions and subjectification of *so-called*

Lieven Vandelanotte
University of Namur

In this paper, I explore the usage range of the pattern *Mister so-called X* on the basis of internet data. In a first step I argue that framing adjectives such as *so-called, alleged,* and *purported* involve interpersonal rather than representational meaning and structure. Secondly, of the different framing adjectives, *so-called* is shown to be the one which has come to be used most often with dissociative affect, a development which is co-enabled by its high frequency and its lack of very strong register preferences and collocates. Finally, in a set of 88 observations of the pattern *Mister so-called X* collected through WebCorp [www.webcorp. org.uk], I distinguish different usage patterns and relate these in terms of subjectification.

1.   Introduction[1]

It is widely recognized that our everyday discourses have embedded within them many prior or potential other discourses (Bakthin 1984, Mey 1999). Perhaps the most obvious linguistic manifestations of this polyphony are constructions like direct and indirect speech or thought and intermediate forms of these, in which the content of a speech or thought act is depicted in the reported clause. However, in many constructions which lack reported clauses, reportative 'signals' can nonetheless be discerned (Authier-Revuz 1995, Thompson 1996), as with the use of verbs indicating that a speech act has taken place (1) (cf. Leech and Short's [1981] 'narrative report of a speech

---

1.   I thank Kristin Davidse for her comments on an earlier version of this paper.

act'), of adverbs like *apparently* or *reportedly* (2), of adjuncts like *according to X* (3), of clauses like *rumour has it* (4), or of adjectives like *alleged* and *so-called* (5):[2]

(1) *But as Kiesler drove him back to the hotel after* **he'd thanked** *Maria profusely for her fine meal, Brand couldn't rid himself of the feeling that the actor's motive was somewhat stronger than the mere fact that he'd liked the cut of his jib.* (CB, ukbooks)

(2) *However, the prize for most eccentric Cornish behaviour must be awarded to a nutty vicar of times past. The distinguished Rev Robert Hawker* **apparently** *dressed up as a mermaid and swam out to a rock off the Bude coast, singing melodiously to the astonished local fishermen!* (CB, ukmags)

(3) **According to Mr Lubbers**, *co-operation in this field could greatly help in other areas, particularly environmental and transport policy.* (CB, bbc)

(4) *Rod's still a God. How old is Rod Stewart these days?* **Rumour has it** *he swam away from the Titanic.* (CB, sunnow)

(5) *Today, metal cans are subjected to the most thorough and objective environmental studies which take account of the energy required at all stages of can production and use. These* **so-called** *"cradle-to-grave" studies take into account the energy used to mine and transport raw materials, produce the metal, manufacture the can, fill it (in the case of steel this could be with food, drinks, toiletries or even paint), transport it to a shop and, ultimately, recycle it.* (CB, ukephem)

In this paper, I would like to focus on adjectives which, like *so-called* in (5), serve to conjure up a distinct discourse or 'mental space' (Fauconnier 1985) and which I have previously called 'framing adjectives' (Vandelanotte 2002) because they serve not to describe a 'referential' property, but rather to set something apart as belonging to a 'second-order' reality, viz. the reality of another's discourse (McGregor 1997: Ch. 6). They include among others *putative, purported, alleged* and *so-called*, and it is to this last item that the bulk of this paper will be devoted.

In the second section, I will argue that framing adjectives in general are 'different' semantically as well as structurally from ordinary qualifying adjectives: they seem not so much to ascribe permanent or temporary qualities to a head noun, but rather put the designated entity in a certain perspective. As a structural corollary, they will be argued to involve interpersonal rather than representational combinatorics. In a third section, I will briefly discuss some framing adjectives in terms of frequency, genre, collocation, and potentially 'dissociative' or ironic uses. *So-called* will turn out to have the greatest potential for dissociative 'prosody' (cf. Louw 1993), and this factor may help to explain the independent developments that the constructional template *mister so-called X* seems to undergo in present-day English. These developments will form the

---

2.   Examples marked 'CB' were extracted from the Cobuild Bank of English corpus by remote log-in and are reproduced here with the kind permission of HarperCollins Publishers. For glosses of the subcorpora tags, see the "Data sources" section.

topic of the fourth section of this paper, and they will be explicated in terms of 'subjectification' in Traugott's sense (e.g. 1982, 1989, 1995, 2003). The main conclusions will be summarized in a fifth section.

2.   Framing adjectives: meaning and structure

2.1   A functional interpretation of the noun phrase

Functionally, the structure of the English noun phrase can be understood in terms of the general schema of **the instantiation of a type of thing** (Langacker 1991: Ch. 2). In proper names and pronouns, these functions are incorporated in a single form: both proper names and pronouns by their very nature designate a single thing, but they do carry with them higher order type specifications such as "person", "river", or "animate thinking female" (compare *Mr Blair* to *The Thames* to *she*). It is these implied type specifications that allow us to wonder who will be *the next Tony Blair* or to say that since his operation, our neighbour is now *a she*.

With full NPs, on the other hand, the functions of instantiation and type specification can be explicitly distinguished. At the 'categorizing' or 'type specifying' end of the noun phrase, one finds the head noun with nominal or adjectival classifiers, and at the 'instantiating' end one finds qualifying adjectives, quantifiers, determiners, and postdeterminers like *usual* and *famous* (Halliday 1994 [1985]), which all work together to narrow down the general type of thing to the designated instance in the 'here and now' of the speech participants. It is the ultimate step of 'grounding' an instantiated type in a speech event which enables meaningful reference: *fluffy cat* for instance means little in isolation, but *the fluffy cat* singles out one instance which is signalled to be identifiable to the hearer, whereas *a fluffy cat* invites the hearer to think of any one 'fluffy cat' as an arbitrary instance of the set of fluffy cats (Langacker 1991: 103-107, 2002: 166-171). The canonical ordering of elements within the noun phrase can be argued to reflect iconically, from right to left, the move from a general type of thing to the instance being talked about in the ongoing discourse.

Within this functional interpretation of the noun phrase, adjectives can have different functions (and some adjectives are specialized for a given function, while others may perform different functions in different contexts). **Adjectival classifiers**, like nominal ones, serve a type-specifying function, since they delimit a subtype of the general type given in the head noun. For instance, the examples in (6) identify subtypes of the general type *train*, whereas those in (7) do not designate types of trains, but trains with certain properties:

(6)   *electric trains, steam trains, diesel trains*

(7)   *long trains, new trains, powerful trains, charming trains*

Compare, in this regard, the well-known tests of gradability and predicative construal (see Halliday 1994: 184f):[3]

(6a)   *a very electric train*

(6b)   *the train is electric*

(7a)   a very powerful train

(7b)   the train is powerful

According to Langacker (1991: 58-59), **qualifying adjectives** such as *long, new, powerful,* and *charming* in (7) also contribute to the type specification by virtue of further narrowing down the type of thing referred to. However, the fact that the adjectives in (7) allow a predicative construal as in (7b) seems to argue in favour of relating the function of the qualifying adjective *powerful* to an instance, and not a type, since this construal can only combine with a specific instance (***the train** is powerful*) and not with a non-instantiated type (**TRAIN** is powerful*). In more general terms, this means that qualities such as *long* or *charming* can only be ascribed to instances, not to types, because qualities are too incidental to square with the general validity of a type conception. This does not mean that a type conception does not imply certain qualities: a *dog*, for instance, is naturally four-legged. Precisely because this quality belongs to the type conception of *dog*, however, one will not normally ascribe the quality *four-legged* to an instance of a dog. It is only when as the result of some unfortunate accident or freak of nature a dog has only three legs that *three-legged* may appear as an adjective explicitly qualifying *dog*. From this brief discussion I conclude that unlike classifying adjectives, which specify a subtype, qualifying adjectives designate qualities of an instance of a (sub)type.

Postdeterminer uses of adjectives pertain to the instantiating function of the noun phrase: as suggested by Halliday's term 'secondary deictic', they aid the identification of the instance, typically by invoking relations such as fame or familiarity (*usual, famous*), sameness or difference (*same, other, different*), and 'intertextual' relations (*aforementioned*) (cf. Halliday 1994 [1985]: 183, Sinclair et al. 1990: 70). In (8) for instance, the use of the postdeterminer *usual* appeals to the hearer's knowledge of typical instances of excuses, and thereby identifies the excuses Homer might have made as being of the same kind. Similarly in (9), a constructed example, the correct instance of *pair of shoes* is identified by pointing out that it is of the same general type as some other instance with which the hearer is already acquainted, viz. that worn by the speaker (cf. Breban and Davidse 2003):

(8)   *The first time Homer skipped class, he didn't forge a note from his mother or provide any of the usual excuses.* (CB, npr)

---

3.   Note that there does exist a set of adverbs including *strictly, almost, fully,* and *utterly* which can be used to 'grade' or 'temper' classifying adjectives (see Sinclair et al. 1990: 95).

(9)   *When I saw him last week, it turned out my brother had bought the same pair of shoes as mine.*

It should be noted that adjectives used as postdeterminers often have qualitative uses as well. Historically in fact, it would seem that postdeterminer uses have often derived from more attributive or qualifying uses, as shown by Breban (2006) for adjectives of general comparison such as *other*.

Up to this point, it seems that different kinds of adjectives or adjectival uses can be related to the general functional schema of the instantiation of a type: classifying uses narrow down the type specification, qualifying uses predicate properties of the instantial set, and postdeterminer uses aid the identification of the intended instance. With this knowledge in mind, we can confront the question what function is fulfilled by 'framing' adjectives such as *so-called* or *alleged*.

2.2   Where do framing adjectives fit in?

From the preceding discussion, we can conclude that the main functions of a noun phrase are the following: to categorize the referent as being of a certain type, to attribute qualities to the referent, and to identify the instance of the type which the speaker wants to focus on (cf. Bache and Davidsen-Nielsen 1997: Ch. 10). If we assume that framing adjectives have a canonical function within the noun phrase, they would have to relate to one of these basic functions. Consider, in this regard, *alleged* in (10):

(10)   *In New Jersey today, a jury will hear closing arguments in the trial of four young men accused of raping a mentally retarded woman. The* **alleged** *rape took place in the suburban town of Glen Ridge, New Jersey, four years ago this week.* (CB, npr)

Applying the distinctions proposed in the preceding section, the question is whether *alleged* in (10) is a classifying or a qualifying adjective, or whether perhaps it functions as a postdeterminer. It seems intuitively clear that *alleged rapes* form no culturally entrenched subtype of *rapes*. Logically speaking, in fact, some alleged rapes turn out not to be rapes at all, so it would make little sense to distinguish, for instance, 'alleged rapes' and 'real rapes' as subtypes of rapes in the same way that 'the sciences' can be subdivided into, say, 'the social sciences' and 'the biological sciences'.

In similar vein, it seems difficult to maintain that *alleged* in (10) is a qualifying adjective: *alleged* does not describe some aspect of a rape, but bears on what one might call the reality status of the designated instance. Thus, while *a powerful train* allows the predicative alternate *the train (talked about) is powerful*, it makes little sense to say that *the rape (talked about) is alleged*. Full clausal alternates are possible if they provide some additional information (*the rape is alleged to have taken place in the suburban town of Glen Ridge*), but then *alleged* is a participial verb form rather than an adjective, and it is no longer clear whether *alleged* pertains only to the location of a rape which has really occurred, or whether it pertains to both the occurrence and the location of the rape.

Finally, an interpretation of *alleged* in (10) as a postdeterminer cannot be maintained, since *alleged* does not help to single out the precise instance of *rape* talked about.

The logical conclusion at this point is that framing adjectives escape the traditional categories and functions of adjectives. At one stage in his exposition of the functions of noun phrases, Langacker has in fact hinted at this: speaking of the examples *this damn spoon, those fuckin' chickens,* and *a so-called expert,* he notes that the adjectives in them do not fit his description of nominal functions, "representing instead an editorial comment by the speaker" (Langacker 1991: 59). In Vandelanotte (2002), I have proposed to deal with both expletive adjectives like *damn* and *fucking* and framing adjectives like *so-called* in terms of **interpersonal** rather than **representational** grammar (on interpersonal vs. representational grammar, see Halliday 1994 [1985], Hengeveld 1989, McGregor 1997). Representational grammar is concerned with how language users construe their experiences (things, situations, events), whereas interpersonal grammar is concerned with the ways in which these representations of experience get to be negotiated socially. For instance, the ordering and intonation of representational material may determine whether a statement is being made or a question asked (*He's mad at me* vs. *Is he mad at me?*). Interpersonal resources include those involved in the expression of negation, of modality and evidentiality, of speech function and of politeness marking.

Like modal auxiliaries, which influence the degree of likelihood or obligatoriness, or like speech functional adverbs like *frankly* or *honestly,* framing adjectives do not add to the complexity of the experience being represented. Rather, they give a different interpersonal orientation to the representation. In functional grammars like Halliday's (1994 [1985]) and especially McGregor's (1997), it is argued that interpersonal resources do not only involve different types of meaning, but also a different type of structure. In general terms, these different form-meaning pairings could be called **non-compositional**, as opposed to the compositional nature of representational form-meaning pairs. Let us consider briefly what is meant by this.

2.3   Interpersonal meaning and structure as 'non-compositional' meaning and structure

In order to illustrate the difference between compositional vs. non-compositional structure, consider the example in (11) and its expansions in (11a-c).

(11)   *We were playing*

(11a)   *We were playing* **football**

(11b)   *We were playing football* **in the hallway**

(11c)   **Honestly,** *we were* **only** *playing football in the hallway*
         (not setting fire to the dustbin)

To the initial representation of an activity, *We were playing*, is added in (11a) the comple-ment *football*, which explicitates the kind of playing involved, and in (11b) the modifier *in the hallway*, which gives the location for the event of football playing. Complementa-tion and modification are forms of representational or 'compositional' structure-build-ing: some structure is added which adds to the complexity of the situation. By contrast, in (11c), adding *honestly* and *only* does not in any way render the situation represented more complex. What *honestly* does is express the speaker's attitude towards the hearer (and possibly it also counters an implicit accusation of not being honest). *Only*, on the other hand, counters the hearer's expectation or assumption that more was going on than playing football (for instance in a context in which the person guilty of setting fire to a dustbin is being sought, as suggested by the parenthesis in 11c).

Honestly and *only* in (11c) are 'non-compositional' in that they do not combine with the representation in (11b) to form a more complex representation. Rather than specifying a participant or a circumstance of place, time, reason, and so on in a partly expounded representation, non-compositional expressions bear directly on a fully composed representation as a whole, and they discharge their meaning across this en-tire representational unit (cf. McGregor 1997: Ch. 6). This meaning which they dis-charge can be broadly characterized as 'interpersonal' because it relates to the interac-tion between the speaker and hearer in a speech event, by expressing a speaker's position or his or her attitude towards the hearer, or by appealing to the assumptions and expectations shared among speaker and hearer.

The idea that interpersonal resources 'overlay' their meaning across an entire rep-resentational unit is captured terminologically by McGregor (1997: Ch. 6) in his no-tion of **scopal structure**. Scopal structure in his sense of the term does not refer mere-ly to well-known applications of the term scope to such areas as quantification and negation, but to all cases of interpersonal, non-compositional structure. In my view, adjectives like *so-called* and *alleged* involve this kind of scopal structure, and thus are not representational 'modifiers' in the way that *powerful* in *a powerful train* is.

In fact, McGregor (1997: Ch. 6) distinguishes two types of interpersonal structure, scope and framing. Framing is the kind of structure involved, according to McGregor, in reported speech constructions such as direct and indirect speech or thought. One problem with the notion of framing as a kind of interpersonal structure is that, apart from the arbitrary criterion of involving reported speech or not, it is unclearly distin-guished from scope, with no operational criteria to distinguish one from the other. More importantly, I have argued against McGregor's treatment of reported speech con-structions in terms of interpersonal structure only (Vandelanotte 2005: Ch. 2, forth-coming): in my view, non-subjectified reporting clauses such as *he said* or *she thought* cannot be reduced to mere interpersonal operators, but rather have representational meaning and combine compositionally with the reported clause. For these reasons I do not adopt the two-way division in the domain of interpersonal structure between scope and framing. Even so, I have adopted the term 'framing adjective' as a convenient shorthand term, without however claiming a different type of interpersonal structure for these expressions compared to other interpersonal phenomena.

Turning to structural characteristics of interpersonal resources, what is striking is that they can often interact with a variety of structures of different size. This is not the case with representational structures, which interact syntagmatically with specific types of units. A predicate like *sing*, for instance, takes nominal (or nominalized) complements to code the singer and the song sung, and a modifier like *in the hallway* modifies an event or a situation (such as *we were playing football*). By contrast, consider the interpersonal adverb *possibly* in (12) and the subjectified reporting clause *I think* (functioning as a kind of hedge) in (13):

(12a)   *Mr Graham* **possibly** *has that in mind.* (CB qtd. Tucker 2001: 190)

(12b)   *It will end in imprisonment, torture,* **possibly** *death.* (CB qtd. Tucker 2001: 208)

(13a)   *And it's about three quid* **I think** *isn't it. About three quid each.* (CB, ukspok)

(13b)   *I wrote the first draft of this… I wrote the first draft of it in er* **I think** *seven pages and er they said that won't do at all* […]. (CB, ukspok)

In (12a) *possibly* has scope over the full finite clause, whereas in (12b) it only holds *death* in its scope. Similarly in (13a), *I think* expresses a lower degree of commitment or certainly vis-à-vis *it's about three quid*, whereas in (13b) it does so only with regard to *in seven pages* (with as focus of the scopal relationship *seven*).

The same kind of versatility as to the extent of the scope involved can be observed with scopal adjectives. Consider, in this regard, the examples involving *so-called* in (14):

(14a)   *They can get between $ 400 and $ 1000 for selling a stolen vehicle to* **a so-called expert** *who completely changes the vehicle's identity and resells it for a large profit.* (CB, oznews)

(14b)   *I think that one of the problems that has arisen with the very emotional and understandable response to seeing pictures of* **Romanian so-called 'orphans'** *is that people want to rush out and help there.* (CB, bbc)

(14c)   *This is* **a classic so-called Derridean question;** *whoever wrote it – and one cannot help suspecting Professor Taylor himself – is obviously well steeped in deconstructivist argot.* (CB, usbooks)

(14d)   *The west has no intention of saving the Muslims from genocide and this is reflected by the feeble response of* **the so-called United Nations** *which is dominated by the western powers.* (CB, ukmags)

In (14a), the unit that is scoped by *so-called* is not merely *expert* but *an expert*: *a so-called expert* is someone who calls themself *an expert* even though they may well be unreliable wheeler-dealers rather than real experts. In other words, in (14a) a full noun phrase is scoped by *so-called*. Note that a 'representational' dependency analysis would view *so-called* as a modifier of the head *expert*, and would thus miss the point that in fact what it holds in its scope is a fully grounded instance (i.e. an instantiated type with its determiner, tying the instance to a specific speech event).

In the other examples (14b-d), it is not the whole NP which is scoped, since in each case the focus is on a specific term which is suggested to be inadequate in some respect: *orphans* in (14b), *Derridean* in (14c), and *United* in (14d). Thus, the suggestion in (14b) that people are being misled by pictures of children does not question the nationality of the children, but only the claim that they are orphans. Similarly, in (14c) there is no question that the referent of *this* is indeed a classic question, but what is highlighted (somewhat ironically) is that it is a classic question 'of the Derridean type', i.e. phrased entirely in *deconstructivist argot*. Finally, in (14d), there is no doubt as to the name of the institution (*the United Nations*), but part of the proper name *United Nations* is being treated as a qualifying adjective, and *so-called* is used to criticize the institution for lacking in this property (unity) which forms part of its name. The type of 'selective domain of application' evidenced by *so-called* in (14c-d) is a phenomenon that is not found in representational (qualifying and classifying) adjectives,[4] which always combine either directly with the head noun or with the head noun and any intervening adjectives, and never only with an adjective. (These two options were referred to as 'independent' vs. 'recursive' modification in Vandelanotte 2002.)

What I have argued up to this point can be summed up as follows. Framing adjectives such as *alleged* and *so-called* transcend traditional adjective categories such as qualifying and classifying adjectives. In a functional interpretation of the noun phrase, they do not indicate a subtype of the general type of thing indicated in the head noun, nor do they help to identify the precise instance by designating some property of the intended referent. Rather, they function interpersonally, overlaying units of different sizes with their perspectivizing meaning, and can therefore be analyzed in terms of scopal rather than dependency structure. In the next section, I will briefly compare one particular framing adjective, *so-called*, to some of its near-equivalents in terms of their meaning and use. One feature, the possibility of using the framing adjective with dissociative or ironic overtones, will turn out to be particularly prominent in the use of *so-called*, and this will help to explain the different uses of *mister so-called* distinguished in section 4.

3.   *So-called* and its near-equivalents: distribution and function

Apart from *alleged* and *so-called*, of which examples have been given above, several other adjectives can be analyzed as framing adjectives because of a shared reportative

---

4.   I do not include postdeterminers under the heading of 'representational' adjectives because they work together with determiners to ground an instantiated type in a concrete speech event, and in this sense are interpersonal rather than representational. Therefore, the 'determining complex' (determiners + postdeterminers) can be analyzed in terms of scope rather than dependency (see Davidse 2004).

and evidential meaning, for instance *purported, pretended, (self-)professed, putative, self-styled,* and *supposed.* Their shared reportative-evidential meaning can tentatively be glossed as (15):

(15)   [FRAMING ADJECTIVE] X =
       stated by some, but not the speaker, to be X

In other words, framing adjectives make crucial reference to an external source (i.e. a source other than the speaker) which is held responsible for a given designation. With some, like *self-styled* or *(self-)professed,* this external source is the referent of the framed designation (as in *a self-styled messiah*) or the referent of the possessive determiner or genitive accompanying the framed designation (as in *her professed love of family*). With others, such as *alleged* and *supposed,* the external source is neither the speaker nor the immediately involved person (e.g. the rapist in *an alleged rapist*) but rather a kind of anonymous collective like the police or public opinion.

The formulation in (15) leaves the question as to whether the 'framed' designatum is veridically 'X' entirely open. With *so-called,* for instance, fully neutral uses occur quite frequently, i.e. uses in which, while the speaker is not strictly held to the applicability of the designation, there is no suggestion that this designation is unjustifiedly used. This is directly related to the lexical meaning of *so-called,* which in its most literal interpretation refers merely to the name given to a referent, as in (16):

(16)   *The Supreme Court has let stand a lower court ruling allowing states to have* **tough so-called 'lemon laws'** *to protect new car buyers.* (CB, npr)

The use of *so-called* in (16) merely perspectivizes *lemon laws* as a term devised especially to refer to laws protecting people who have the ill luck of having bought a lemon, i.e. a bad car. There is no question here of the proper or improper use of a term: it is only the explicit recognition that a special term is being used that prompts the use of *so-called.*

A different kind of neutrality seems to be involved with *alleged*: since an alleged murderer, for instance, may in the end be acquitted, it is the case that the veridical application of the designation *murderer* is at stake, whereas in (16) the applicability of the term *lemon laws* is not. However, in using *alleged,* the aim is to leave the matter of guilt or innocence to the judicial system, and thus to suggest neither of the two.

What can, then, be qualified as non-neutral uses are those in which a kind of affective distancing on the current speaker's part is involved, in the sense that he or she signals through the use of the framing adjective that the framed designation is not justifiedly or correctly used. In a case-study on *so-called* reported on in Mackintosh

(2003),[5] the proportion of such dissociative uses of *so-called* (as in 14a-b and 14d above) was 39% (in an extraction of 300 tokens from the Cobuild corpus), as against 61% of 'neutral' uses of the kind exemplified in (16). Some further examples of dissociative vs. neutral meaning are given in (17) and (18) respectively, so as to clarify the difference between the use of *so-called* to indicate that someone claims a certain term unjustifiedly, and the use to give a technical or precise name to some phenomenon, without any suggestion of dispute as to the use of this name.

(17) *Cobuild corpus examples of* DISSOCIATIVE *uses of* so-called

(17a) *The recent hijacking of the passenger jet in Algeria may reinforce our belief that violence is peculiar to the Muslim faith. However, the pre-Christmas mock shooting of Santa Claus in Lismore, the very real shooting in the US of an abortionist by* **so-called men of God***, the mindless brutality of the civil wars in Bosnia and Northern Ireland, and the obscene major conflicts down the centuries from the Crusades to the Vietnam War should show us that Christians of all denominations have been among the most prolific and the most inhumane willing killers in history.* (CB, oznews)

(17b) *My book was an angry response to the papers being published in* **so-called scientific journals** *saying Aids had started in Africa. When they say Africans they mean Black people wherever they are.* (CB, ukmags)

(17c) *Justice? Ah yes, that's when drug pushers like Lemmer get ten years in jail for destroying countless innocent lives with their filthy trade but are back on the streets five years later to carry on where they left off. And justice is jailing a terrorist for life for murdering innocent people in the name of some cause the anarchistic bastard doesn't even understand, then letting him go when more anarchistic bastards hold more innocent people to ransom. Why don't you ask the victims' families what they think of* **this so-called justice***?* (CB, ukbooks)

(18) *Cobuild corpus examples of* NEUTRAL *uses of* so-called

(18a) *If his Vive La France rhetoric is any guide, Chirac also would avoid transferring further powers to the European bureaucrats in Brussels. This gives hope to the anti-European Union people in Britain –* **the so-called sceptics** *– but Chirac is not thinking of Britain.* (CB, oznews)

(18b) *At one end of the scale, there are the stores of information in university computers (who first established the Internet to aid academic work). At the other, there*

---

5. Both Mackintosh (2003) and Vanaelten and van Osch (2003) are case studies supervised by me for the course *English Linguistics: Applied Linguistics* coordinated by Kristin Davidse at the University of Leuven. For *so-called* and *alleged*, the data set looked at by Mackintosh and Vanaelten and van Osch respectively consisted of 300 extractions on the relevant lexeme followed by either an adjective or a noun randomly drawn from the various Cobuild subcorpora. For *purported*, the Cobuild corpus returned only 36 tokens, but Vanaelten and van Osch additionally looked at the 50 tokens that could be obtained from the BNC sampler [http://sara.natcorp.ox.ac.uk/lookup.html].

are **the so-called "bulletin boards"**, *on which small groups of enthusiasts can exchange electronic messages.* (CB, ukephem)

(18c) *The British government, and Mrs Thatcher in particular, have always been hostile to the creation of a single currency throughout Europe, and the setting-up of one central bank to direct monetary policy in all the countries of the European Community – as foreseen by* **the so-called Delors Plan.** (CB, bbc)

Extending the meaning of the notion of semantic prosody (Louw 1993, Stubbs 1995) somewhat, cases like those in (17) could be grouped under dissociative prosody. In its strictest application, the notion of semantic prosody refers to the typical collocational association of a given word (for instance *utter*) with either positive or negative collocates (e.g. negative collocates in the case of *utter: confusion, contempt, despair, devastation*, etc.). In the sense intended here, dissociative prosody refers to the affective overtones which *so-called* acquires in cases like (17), in which its meaning could be paraphrased as *claimed to be X, but in the current speaker's opinion not really X, but something worse than X.* Thus, by killing a fellow man the *so-called men of God* in (17a) behave in rather ungodly ways; the *so-called scientific journals* in (17b) are suggested not to come up to the standards of scientific journals because of the unfounded assumptions on which articles in them are based, and in (17c) the *so-called justice* is suggested to be unjust, for letting convicted criminals free after a few years in jail.

Interestingly, in another case study dealing with *alleged* and *purported* (Vanaelten and van Osch 2003), it was found that these framing adjectives barely have dissociative uses like those in (17). In only a handful of cases (5 out of 300, or less than 2%) can it be argued that *alleged* means not only 'stated by others to be X', but also 'found by the current speaker not to actually be X, but worse than X'. Two of these are given in (19): in (19a) the speaker expresses self-irony in referring to himself as *the alleged celebrity*, and in (19b) *Joanna Trollope's alleged insights* are suggested not to exist or at least not to be very insightful at all.

(19a) *I know exactly when I had my best round. It was in 1988 in a charity golf game at the Alliss-Manitou Pro-Am, which used to be held every year at Ferndown, just outside Bournemouth. Ronan Rafferty was the pro, I was* **the alleged celebrity**, *and two guys called Phil and Ronnie, who were friends of Ronan's, made up the rest of our team in a field of about 20 or 30. It was one of those magical games of golf where everything went our way.* (CB, today)

(19b) *ITV's A Village Affair was lesbian love in a chocolate-box English village packed with braying snobs, cousins of those in The Choir. Delicately done and womanfully acted, though it was by Sophie Ward and Kerry Fox, I failed to grasp* **Joanna Trollope's alleged insights**. *Why, if the affair was so liberating, did the two women part at the end?* (CB, today)

The higher incidence of dissociative uses of *so-called* compared to *alleged* can be related to a number of interrelated factors. The combination of register and collocational patterning of the two adjectives suggests that *alleged* is more strongly associated with journalistic language, and collocates strongly with words denoting 'investigation' and 'the thing investigated' (viz. various kinds of criminal offences). *So-called*, on the other hand, shows a more varied distribution in terms of register as well as more diversified collocates.

As an indication of the register distribution, consider the data summarized in Table 1, which give the numer of tokens per million words across the different subcorpora of the 56 million word part of the Cobuild corpus. The total number of occurrences in the corpus of *so-called* followed by an adjective or a noun is 1517, that of *alleged* 1366. Bold type indicates higher frequency of one adjective compared to the other in the relevant subcorpus. With one important exception, *so-called* is less frequent in journalistic subcorpora, especially in Australian newspapers, *Today* and *The Sun*, and transcripts of BBC World Service broadcasts. Of the more or less 'journalistic' subcorpora, it is only in the American National Public Radio subcorpus that *so-called* is more frequent than *alleged*. One possible explanation for this might lie in the difference between American and British English, in that *alleged* may simply be less frequent in American English as such. Some confirmation of this can be gained from a comparison of the two adjectives in the US ephemera subcorpus, with 12 occurrences (9.80 per million) for *so-called* and none for *alleged*.

For books, transcribed informal speech, magazines, and ephemera, the higher incidence of *so-called* compared to *alleged* can be interpreted as follows: *alleged* is not only more frequent in journalistic language, but it is also more strongly restricted to such language, and much less common than *so-called* in other registers. In other words, *so-called* has a more varied profile in terms of register distribution.

Table 1. The distribution of *so-called* and *alleged* across different registers

Subcorpus	Number of occurrences per million words for *so-called* (N=1517)	Number of occurrences per million words for *alleged* (N=1366)
oznews	33.91	**51.90**
times	29.49	**30.54**
today	21.53	**40.97**
sunnow	18.54	**25.75**
bbc	74.72	**96.94**
npr	**60.72**	30.36
ukbooks	**28.95**	10.09
usbooks	**28.44**	8.89
ukspok	**8.84**	0.54
ukmags	**25.09**	16.73
ukephem	**8.96**	2.88
usephem	**9.80**	0.00

The registerial 'specialization' of *alleged* is reflected in its collocates ordered by t-score, a measure of "the confidence with which we can claim that there is some association" which identifies, according to Clear (1993: 281-282), "frequent and very reliable collocations". The collocates of *alleged* turn out to refer to different offences and the police's investigation of them. Lexically full words with a t-score of 4 or more include, in decreasing order from 6.10 down to 4.15, *victim, involvement, rape, offences, police, plot, corruption, investigation, victims, assault, attack, fraud, abuse, connection, drug, protest,* and *affair*. *So-called* only has a single lexically full collocate with a t-score of 4.60, viz. *experts*, and only *affair* and *friends* have a t-score higher than 3. Thus, of the fifty strongest collocates ordered by t-score (and including lexically 'empty' function words like *the* or *of*), *so-called* has 42 'collocates' with a score between 2 and 3, whereas all fifty strongest collocates of *alleged* have a score higher than 3.

This suggests that *so-called* has fewer and weaker collocates, and is thus less specialized both in terms of register and in terms of the words with which it combines. *Alleged*, on the other hand, is characterized by a more restricted meaning and use, and may therefore less easily be up for (affective) meaning developments than its more versatile near-equivalent *so-called*. Added to this is the different source orientation referred to above: *alleged* normally refers to an external, judicial source of the allegation, whereas with *so-called*, especially in its dissociative uses, it is often the person designated in the NP containing the adjective who is responsible for the designation (as in *a so-called expert*). It stands to reason that just anyone calling themselves an 'expert' or a 'friend' can more readily be criticized for using these terms if judged by others to be inappropriate, than the police or the court will be criticized for making accusations. The combination of their high frequency and their different meaning and use thus help to explain the different propensity of *so-called* versus *alleged* for developing dissociative meanings.

As for the remaining framing adjectives, adjectives like *purported* and *putative* are restricted in terms of genre, occurring mainly in books and also in newspapers, but hardly anywhere else. In addition, these adjectives are generally far less frequent, with *purported* and *putative* for instance occurring only a few dozen times in the Cobuild corpus, and therefore less likely to develop new, affective meanings. As is well known, less frequent words have a more strictly delineated and independent meaning (Sinclair 1991), and therefore partake less easily in meaning developments. More generally, more frequent items in a language are more easily accessed to form new utterances as well as new constructions, and thus higher frequency tends to correlate with higher degrees of grammaticalization (cf. Bybee and Hopper 2001). As Hoffmann (2004) has argued, this general mechanism cannot be applied in all contexts: when certain forms have a low absolute frequency but have a very high 'relative' frequency, i.e. are used overwhelmingly for the expression of a particular concept, they will be more prone to processes of grammaticalization and subjectification (examples include complex prepositions like *by dint of* or *in readiness for*, for which alternatives are few and far between). In the case of framing adjectives, however, clearly there are various alternatives to choose from to express the reportative-evidential concept involved, so the notion of relative, 'conceptual' frequency described by Hoffmann (2004) does not apply to low-frequency framing adjectives.

In sum, the frequency of *so-called*, along with the wide variety of registers in which it is used and the absence of strong collocational patterning, combine with its reportative-evidential meaning to enable the development of dissociative meanings often directed towards the person using a certain designation for him- or herself. This process can be seen as one involving **subjectification** to the extent that it constitutes a first remove from a more propositional meaning ('stated by some, but not the speaker, to be X') towards a more expressive, subjective meaning, based in the current speaker's beliefs ('in the current speaker's opinion in fact worse than X or not X at all') (cf. Traugott 1982, 1989, 2003). In the next section, I will focus on the constructional template *mister so-called X*, and argue that in some of its uses it represents a further remove from the more propositional meaning.

4. An emerging pattern: *Mister so-called X*

In Mackintosh's (2003) case study, there was one occurrence of *so-called* which, if taken literally, seemed almost absurd because the designation framed by it was, quite plainly, someone's proper name:

(20)   *TRUE STORIES. The column that wishes Carol Clerk and Nigel all the best! BUM GRAVY, FOREHEADS IN A FISHTANK, LOVECRAFT, ADORABLE, TERMINAL CHEESECAKE, THE SIDDELEYS, THE BRILLIANT CORNERS and MARTIN STEPHENSON. Just some of the people that weren't at last week's star-stuffed, celeb-rammed, decadence-drenched BRIT AWARDS. Well, that's a good enough reason for us to go, we though[t], as we walked out of the suite hire shop and into a passing black cab (it would have been so much easier if the cab had stopped, but anyway). Within an hour, TRUE STORIES was schmoozing and boozing with loads of DEAD IMPORTANT people giving us LITTLE CARDS with their names of them saying Actually, I think it'd be very valuable to your line of work if you kept in touch with me. Hmmm, I think not,* **MR SO-CALLED JAGGER!** (CB, ukmags)

Assuming that we are dealing in (20) with Mick Jagger (and not some impostor), the meaning of (20) cannot be understood as 'you may well call yourself Mr Jagger, but according to me you're not a real Mr Jagger'. While one can quite easily question someone's right to call themselves an expert or a friend, on the basis of properties defining expertise and friendship, it makes no sense to question someone's right to call themselves by their own names. Proper names by their very nature uniquely designate a person, and while they have grammatical and presuppositional meaning, they lack lexical meaning (Van Langendonck 1999): there are no properties defining 'Mr Jagger-ness' against which the degree of Mr Jaggerness can be measured.

A search on other occurrences of *mr so-called* (or *mister so-called*) yields only one additional case in the entire Cobuild corpus (*Sort out what's wrong in your own country first, Mr So-called Graham*, CB, ukbooks). While this shows that (20) is not a one-off, one is left to wonder whether the phenomenon is as unusual as suggested by its low incidence in the Cobuild corpus. One way of finding out is to use the internet as a source of data.

4.1   The internet as corpus?

In one familiar definition, a 'corpus' is described as a "collection of naturally occurring language text, chosen to characterize a state or variety of a language" (Sinclair 1991: 171). On various counts, the internet does not qualify as a corpus: while one could view it as a collection of naturally occurring texts, these texts have not been deliberately collected or chosen on the basis of certain criteria and with certain goals in mind. In addition, they have not, like many corpora, been enriched with several kinds of information, such as details on the source of the text or part of speech tagging. As the internet has increas-ingly been found a potentially interesting resource for data, an awareness has gradually grown of the many drawbacks involved in trying to use the internet as corpus (e.g. van Oostendorp and van der Wouden 1998, Janda et al. 2003, Renouf et al. 2004). In a cau-tionary note, Resnik and Elkiss (2004) have pointed out that

> current Web search methods are oriented more toward shallow information retrieval techniques than toward the more sophisticated needs of linguists. Using the Web in linguistic research is not easy.

Among the problems are limitations in query syntax (the popular search engine Goog-le does not even allow the use of wildcards), the lack of part of speech tagging (making research into more abstract constructional schemata well nigh impossible), the ab-sence of reliable information as to the authenticity and sociological embedding of the data (are native speakers involved or not, for instance), the difficulty in comparing us-age across different genres (since one can only limit searches to certain subdomains, which do not neatly correspond to a variety of genres), and the impossibility of obtain-ing accurate absolute frequencies (because, basically, one cannot know how many words are on the internet).

A number of these drawbacks are beginning to be addressed in projects such as WebCorp (Kehoe and Renouf 2002, Renouf et al. 2004, Renouf 2005) and The Linguist's Search Engine (LSE) (Resnik and Elkiss 2004). WebCorp in its currently available shape is built 'on top of' existing search engines such as Google,[6] but allows more complicated search queries using wildcards and complex pattern matching options, as in the example *the (boat|ship) s(u|a|i)nk**, in which the pipe | means 'OR' and * is a wildcard. This is achieved by expanding all possible combinations in a given query into an explicit statement of all the options (*the boat sank, the boat sunk, the boat sinks,* etc.) (Kehoe and Renouf 2002). In addition, WebCorp enables one to output concordances in a user-friendly format such as Keyword In Context (KWIC) tables. The LSE works rather differently (Resnik and Elkiss 2004): given an input sentence instantiating the pattern one wants to retrieve, its built-in parser builds up a syntactic tree which the user can edit down to the essentials (eliminating, for instance, dominating S nodes above VP nodes or any lexical material that is too specific). The resulting tree structure is what the software subsequently looks for in a collection of annotated data. The LSE comes with a data set of 3 million annotated sentences from the Internet Archive [www.archive.org], but it also allows the user to construct their own 'collections' of internet data by defining queries in Altavista, which are subsequently loaded into LSE and annotated.

The reason why, in spite of the many difficulties involved, projects such as WebCorp and LSE press on lies in the one important forte of the internet as an "accidental corpus" (Renouf et al. 2004), viz. the fact that material is constantly being added to it, which means that it holds good chances of reflecting very quickly new language developments which have not yet reached the corpora, and also of yielding more results for more or less recent developments for which corpora throw up only few results. It is also for this reason that in order to find relevant tokens of the pattern *Mr so-called X*, I have turned to the internet. The two Cobuild corpus examples are both from sources dated 1993, and if the intuition that the pattern is relatively recent and colloquial is correct, one might expect to find more data via a search of the web.

Before looking at the internet data, one more preliminary remark is in order. The internet contains texts of many different types, of which some closely resemble, or are even taken from, traditional printed or spoken media, while others are quite specific to it. Particularly these more specific resources, such as internet fora and online 'guestbooks', in which language users often identify themselves by means of nicknames, may influence the type of results you get. As we will see in the next section, this last point will prove relevant to the results for *Mr so-called X*.

---

6.   A new version of WebCorp is currently being prepared which is based on a tailored linguistic search engine, which will improve both the speed and the range of processing options of WebCorp (Renouf 2005).

4.2   *Mister so-called X* as an instance of subjectification

Using WebCorp, four concordances were made yielding a total of 88 relevant observations:[7] 49 for *Mr so-called*, 26 for *Mr so called* (without the hyphen), 8 for *Mister so-called*, and 5 for *Mister so called*. While this is already a considerable improvement compared to the two cases in the Cobuild corpus, it should be noted that a simple Google search on *"mr so called"* (yielding both examples with and without hyphen) in fact yields many more cases (for instance 979 hits on 4 May 2005). Since my aim is exploratory and qualitative only, and since the concordance output in KWIC tables is more easy to work with than unedited lists of Google search results, the WebCorp results are sufficient for my present purposes. However, it does remain difficult to understand why the discrepancy in the number of results for a straightforward Google search and a WebCorp search using Google should be so large.

Because some of the Google data in an earlier, random collection (built and saved on 23 October 2003) provide good examples of some of the categories I will discuss below, I will occasionally use such an example, indicating 'G' for 'Google' as its source. Examples from the WebCorp concordance of 88 tokens will be indicated by 'W'. Apart from a few cases in which the template *Mr so-called X* seems to be used neutrally, I will argue that at least three different meanings need to be distinguished for the pattern. In addition, I will show that some extensions and combinations of the three meanings occur.

4.2.1   *The ordinary dissociative use of* Mister so-called X

The predominant pattern seems to be that in which *Mr so-called* has the same kind of dissociative prosody as *so-called* in cases like *a so-called expert* or *a so-called scientific journal*: by saying *Mr so-called X*, the current speaker is in fact saying of someone that he or she is "not really X", "not a good X", "not much of an X". Unlike the case with proper names alluded to above, and to which I will return in a moment, there are in this '**ordinary dissociative**' use certain properties which define what it takes to be a real or a good X. Typical head nouns occurring in the template include *expert, war hero, president, police officer, Professor, lawyer man, academic, justice, doctor, Editor, solicitor,* and *adult webmaster*. Examples are given in (21) below. Clearly the suggestion in (21a), for instance, is that George Bush is, in the writer's opinion, "not much of a President" or "not a good President", just as the academic in (21b) is judged by a colleague not to be a good academic. (21c) is remarkable for its deliberate over-use of framing devices: *mr so-called "palestinian" so-called "refugee" quote unquote* combines the template *mr so-called X* with quotation marks, the *quote unquote* pattern, and a repetition of *so-called*. Arguably, the effect of such insistent use of multiple framing

---

7.   These Webcorp extractions were made on 25 and 27 April 2005. Examples left out of consideration included two cases involving someone by the name of *Mr So* (calling out to someone else), duplicate tokens, a few uninterpretable cases, and some examples discussed by myself on a course website [http://wwwling.arts.kuleuven.be/engling/appling/] under the heading "Google it!" [http://wwwling3.arts.kuleuven.be/engling_e/appling_e/google.htm].

devices is to create a heightened level of dissociation vis-à-vis the designation "pales-tianian refugee", and vis-à-vis the people who (unjustifiedly according to the writer of [21c]) apply this designation to themselves.

(21a)   *Then there is W. Bush's call for a Prime Minister of Palestine. A what??? Just where,* **Mr. So-Called President**, *is this country that needs a Prime Minister? Show me its boundaries. Did someone re-draw the world map while I was napping?*
[W – http://www.thehappyheretic.com/rabbit.htm – accessed 25 April 2005]

(21b)   *You lecture in "Social Psychology"? Me, too. The only difference is that I know what I am talking about. You don't think so? Well, my text is online. Try tearing apart the arguments I put forward in Chapters VI to IX. Just try,* **Mr. so-called "academic"**.
[W – http://www.shef.ac.uk/~psysc/psa-public-sphere/msg00295.html – accessed 25 April 2005]

(21c)   *I mainly bring up the issue of the refugee expulsions as a partial explanation of the persistence of Palestinian rejectionism. Damn right they would prefer to go back to their grandfathers [sic] house in Haifa, rather than resettle in some corrupt PLO state! Obviously the answer in most cases has to be "I'm sorry, but not any more." That's a different response than "tough shit, fuck you, join the hundred million other refugees in the world,* **mr. so-called "palestinian" [sic] so-called "refugee" quote unquote**."
[W – http://www.usefulwork.com/shark/archives/001255.html – accessed 25 April 2005]

In all, I have coded 41 tokens of the 88 contained in the WebCorp concordances as cases of this 'ordinary dissociative' meaning. Within this group, however, there are two special cases which can be viewed as extensions of cases such as (21). The first of these extensions involves **a different source of the designation** judged inappropriate by the current speaker. In the majority of cases, as in the examples in (21), the person responsible for the designation framed by *Mr so-called* is the referent of this designation: in (21a) President Bush, in (21b) an academic, and in (21c) potential Palestinian refugees. In two cases out of the 41 in this group, however, the designation framed by *Mr so-called* is not one used by its referent, but by other people. One fairly straightforward case is (22a), in which the source of the designation *King of R&B* is explicitly signalled not to be Bobby Brown, but Whitney (presumably Whitney Houston). The second case (22b) is more complicated:

(22a)   *Why is it that* **Mr. So-called King of R&B** *[according to Whitney] Bobby Brown gets to have his own dang reality show but I can't have one?*
[W – http://www.meacfans.com/ubb/ultimatebb.php/ubb/get_topic/f/27/t/00 5792/p/2.html – accessed 25 April 2005]

(22b)   *A friend of mine came out recently and I had no problem with it. My justification – I'd known him 13 years and done everything with the guy, played soccer,
hung out, went drinkin' etc. so the way I see it is that he's the same guy I've always
know [sic], just a little pinker around the gills now. But he does do things that
pi$$ me off too, at the same time. He somehow now thinks that he has a license
to act 'extremely' camp in public and constantly talk about having sex (a trait
that 100% of gay men I've met also have!!!). So, in a way, it might not be* **Mr.
So-called Homophobes** *[sic] fault that he's taking it badly, it might be down to
the way his newly come-out friend is acting. When you've known someone a
long time, and to see them acting like this is really a let-down. Its like when your
parents say to you "I'm not angry, I'm just disappointed". So spare a thought for
mr. homophobe, it may not be entirely his fault that he's acting like this.*
[W – http://www.boards.ie/vbulletin/archive/index.php/t-92192.html – ac-
cessed 25 April 2005]

(22b) is taken from an online discussion board in which the original poster (as the first
participant in a 'thread' or string of messages and replies is called) expressed his disap-
pointment about the negative reactions to one of his friends' coming out. What the
poster of the message in (22b) is arguing is basically that the *newly come-out friend* may
have given cause to these negative reactions himself by displaying irritating campy and
sex obsessed behaviour. In making this argument, the writer of (22b) suggests that
other participants in the thread on this topic may have been too quick in their judge-
ment as to the homophobia of the gay man's friends. When he refers to one of these
friends as *Mr so-called homophobe*, it is not the referent of the expression who refers to
himself as *homophobe*. Rather, it is other participants in the online discussion who
have, in preceding messages in the thread, done so, and this is what makes cases like
(22) different from (21).

A rather different kind of extension is found in 5 cases out of the 41 grouped under
the 'ordinary dissociative' meaning of *mr so-called X*. Each of these five cases involves
a combination of *Mr so-called* with a proper name, but each time in a situation in
which the person designated in the NP containing *Mr so-called* is accused of **assuming
someone else's (or simply a false) name**. Example (23a), for instance, is taken from a
lenghty correspondence between a London underground customer and its customer
service centre. The letter writer of (23a) has had an unsatisfactory correspondence
with a Mr Green, who has in his opinion never seriously replied to any of the points he
raised in his original letter of complaint, and who, as became clear through a wrongly
addressed e-mail, had even been forwarding and discussing the customer's e-mails
with a number of his friends. After several unanswered e-mails, the customer finally
received a reply not from Mr Green but from Mr Summers, and he questions the iden-
tity of this Mr Summers by using the pattern with *Mr so-called*:

(23a)   *Dear Mr Summers*
I would indeed be more than happy to remind you of the situation regarding my
correspondence with Mr Green. [...]
I also have to say, and damn the consequences, I also have to say that I have my
suspicions that you, Mr Summers, even exist. I have my suspicions, I say, that
you, **Mr so-called 'Summers'**, *are in fact Mr Green, merely posing as 'Mr Sum-*
mers', in order to weasel out of the moral obligation into which you have so fool-
ishly stumbled.
[W – http://www.thefridayproject.co.uk/pondlife/without_prejudice.php –
accessed 25 April 2005]

A similar though fictional case is presented by example (23b), taken from a mock website in which parts of the diaries of US Senator McCarthy, renowned for his anti-com-
munist witch hunts in the 1950s, are supposedly "revealed". Within the frame set by the
parody of McCarthy's diaries, McCarthy in (23b) calls into doubt the real identity of
Mr So-called Parks because *Mr Parks* is almost an anagram of *Karl Marx*:

(23b)   *Mr Parks at the store has agreed to let me work there after school and on week-*
ends. However, I am concerned. If you take the letters of the name Mr Parks
and rearrange them, you get Kr Marks (if you use the 'K' twice and ignore the
'P') which is almost 'Karl Marx'!!! Can this be a coincidence? I have my doubts.
I'll be keeping a close eye on **Mr So-called Parks**.
[W – http://www.gdm93.dial.pipex.com/mccarthy.htm – accessed 25 April 2005]

Other examples in the WebCorp concordance include *Mr so-called Fischer*, who is accused of using a Jewish sounding nickname on the internet while he is neither an Is-
raeli nor a Jew, and *Mr so-called Lincoln* used in a mock website in which a distinction
is made between the former and the real Lincoln. Perhaps the most curious example is
that of *Mr so-called Dan Hays*, in a context in which two people are called *Dan Hays*
and one is posing as the other:

(23c)   *And we found that in fact a London-based painter called Dan Hays is cynically*
passing himself off as Dan Hays by nicking Dan Hay's [sic] photographs off the
net and painting them under the nom-de-plume of Dan Hays. We say: WHO
DO YOU THINK YOU ARE **MR SO-CALLED DAN HAYS?**
[W – http://www.artrumour.com/Newsletter/newsletter10.htm – accessed
25 April 2005]

It will be clear that these five cases involve dispute as to whether someone justifiedly
uses a name or not, and therefore groups with the 'ordinary' dissociative uses, rather
than with cases like *Mr so-called Jagger* in (20) above, in which there is no question as
to the identify of the person referred to. It is to these cases that I now turn.

4.2.2   *The invective use of* Mister so-called *in combination with*
             proper names and nicknames

In cases like (20) above and (24) below, *Mr so-called* is used in conjunction with a proper name not in order to put up for debate the right of the designated referent to use this name, as in (23), but purely to express a dissociative attitude towards the referent. In effect, the kind of dissociative meaning is different from the 'ordinary' dissociative meaning, because the link with the general meaning of framing adjectives as stated in (15), 'stated by some, but not the speaker, to be X' is very weak and even lost. This is why cases like (24) do not allow paraphrases like *you're not much of a Mick Jagger, you're not a good Ronaldo*, or *you're not really Tony Blair (though some may call you so)*. I would propose to characterize the dissociative meaning in cases like (24) as **invective** (to different degrees) **vis-à-vis a person with name X**. A case like (24a) is very similar to (20), not only because both involve Mick Jagger, but also because they both occur in British music magazines, *Melody Maker* (20) and *NME* (24a), and most of all since they both seem very much in jest. In (24b) as well, no genuine contempt vis-à-vis the football player Ronaldo seems to be involved, and the use of *Mr so-called* is more provocative than contemptuous. In (24c), however, it is clear that Zimbabwe's president Mugabe is being contemptuous in referring to the British PM and his cabinet as *Mr so-called Tony Blair and his gay cabinet*.

(24a)   *Mick Jagger has spoken out.*
        The Daily Star (November 7) reveals today that Jagger, frontman with top selling boyband The Rolling Stones, thinks "it's stupid to behave like you're 17". Jagger's quotes come in the light of a recent survey that said "It's really intelligent to behave like you're 17." [...] Let me remind **Mr so called Jagger** *of one salient point. Of all the people that were surveyed, 87% said they believed it was really intelligent being 17.*
        [W – http://www.nme.com/news/49186.htm – accessed 27 April 2005]

(24b)   *In the second half, Wilmots scored on a bicycle kick (try that,* **Mister so-called Ronaldo!***), and once again Belgium were in full-dress entertainment mode.*
        [W – http://www.planetworldcup.com/GUESTS/peter20040419.html – accessed 27 April 2005]

(24c)   *Now Mugabe is unwilling to accept responsibility for ruining a once prosperous country, preferring to blame Zimbabwe's misfortunes on the machinations of '***Mr so-called Tony Blair** *and his gay cabinet'.*
        That he is an idiot is doubted by no one. But opinions about how best to deal with Mugabe, before too many of his countrymen die, vary.
        [G – http://www.westminsterwatch.co.uk/sketcharchive/emag_sketch020815. htm – accessed 23 October 2003]

In the WebCorp concordance, there are 33 (out of 88) observations involving an invective use (be it in jest or for real) of *Mr so-called* in combination with a name. It should be noted that the name need not be that of a famous person, as it is in examples (24a-c), but may just as well be the name of anyone who has their name mentioned on the internet. In one example, someone posted a comment on the website of someone called Uffe Høgh Olesen angrily addressing him as *Mr so called Olesen* [W – http://elfwood. lysator.liu.se/art/u/f/uffe2/uffe2.html – accessed 27 April 2005]. More importantly still, the category of invective uses with proper names includes cases in which the proper name is in fact a **nickname**, i.e. a name chosen by someone publishing their views on the internet but wishing to remain anonymous. Even though such nicknames might allow the 'ordinary' dissociative use in which the appropriateness of calling oneself X is questioned, I would argue that in many cases this is not an issue and nicknames form a perfect 'virtual' parallel to real proper names (see below, however, for 'mixed' cases involving both invective and a play on the lexical meaning of a given nickname). Thus, in examples (25a-b), no meanings of the kind 'you are not a real or not a good Felt Pelt/Nader '04' are involved, and what is expressed is merely exasperation with or contempt for online speech participants (more mildly or mockingly in [25a], more seriously in [25b]) having *Felt Pelt* and *Nader '04* as nicknames:

(25a) *While googling for information on the film, I found this brief mention on Ain't It Cool News [linked to the website http://www.aintitcool.com/display. cgi?id=17737&next=1, LV], and I am **not** amused to see that someone has coopted my patented "Memphis, crown jewel of Mississippi" line. You shall be hearing from my attorney, sir,* **Mr. so-called "Felt Pelt"**!
[W – http://www.portapulpit.com/2005_02_01_sisternovena_archive.html – accessed 25 April 2005]

(25b) So **Mr so called "Nader '04"** *does that mean in your twisted logic that your candidate, for recounting in New Hampshire is guilty of the crime of "wanting to know the truth about voting in the U.S." as well?*
Some people are seriously spinning a snazzy campaign of "hate the Greens, hate the Libs for wanting to count your actual votes" aren't they?
[W – http://portland.indymedia.org/en/2004/12/305654.shtml – accessed 27 April 2005]

In addition to the invective meaning, a metalinguistic comment as in (26) may be added. In commenting on a comical series in the tradition of *The Simpsons* and *Futurama*, but clearly judged to be an inferior rip-off by the commentator, the name of the main character is introduced as *Mr so-called 'Peter Griffin' (what an exciting name)*:

(26) *With that in mind let's start off by admitting to ourselves that this 'family guy' character,* **Mr so-called 'Peter Griffin'** *(what an exciting name), is nothing more than an ungodly hybrid of Homer Simpson and Hank Hill from King of the Hill and that that's all there is to it. That's all he is, in character and appearance. No more no less.*
[W – http://www.atlantismantis.com/familyguy.html – accessed 25 April 2005]

Clearly in (26) as in (25), a paraphrase such as *he's not really/not a good Peter Griffin* makes no sense, and a real 'proper name' case is involved. What precisely is reacted to with contempt is not only the character carrying this name (specifically the fact that it is *an ungodly hybrid* of existing characters), but also the unexciting nature of the name. Such a metalinguistic judgement is fundamentally different from the 'contentful' judgements involved in the ordinary dissociative uses such as *Mr so-called expert.*

If we now pause to compare the ordinary dissociative to the invective use of *mr so-called*, in which the latter combines with proper names and nicknames without question-ing the appropriateness of someone using these names, I think we have to conclude that the invective cases can be analyzed as **more subjectified** than the ordinary dissociative ones. While the latter of course already reflect the current speaker's attitudes, the purely invective cases focus **exclusively** on this subjective attitude. In other words, what they have lost in comparison with ordinary dissociative uses is the reliance on the proposi-tional meaning of the scoped headword (*expert, justice, academic,* etc.) on the basis of which criticism then gets to be voiced. It is, in the invective cases, not certain properties of experts, justices, academics, and so on of which the lack or paucity is criticized in the NP's referent. Rather, it is the whole person as such vis-à-vis whom negative attitudes such as contempt, disagreement, and dislike are expressed.

As suggested earlier, the two main categories distinguished so far – ordinary dis-sociative and invective vis-à-vis 'a whole person' with a certain name or nickname – are not mutually exclusive. There are in my data 5 cases for which I would argue that they involve a **combination** of the two categories: on the one hand, it is a proper name or nickname that is in the scope of *Mr so-called*, but on the other hand, this name or nickname has a lexical meaning of which the applicability to the NP's referent is ques-tioned. Thus, in using *Mr so-called reality* or *Mr so-called amazing* in reacting to some-thing posted on the web by people using *Reality* and *Mr amazing* respectively as their nicknames, both a 'pure' negative reaction towards these people and a play on the lit-eral meaning of *reality* and *amazing* are being voiced. The examples in (27) provide further illustration of this point. In (27a) in fact a real name of a hiphop or rap artist, Sage Francis, is involved. The ultimate conclusion of the example and of the review (*Sage Francis: Like Eminem, but clever*) from which it is taken is in fact positive, but in the extract in (27a) a possible reaction to some of Sage's lyrics is described in which someone who purports to see fully through these lyrics defiantly and confidently ad-dresses the singer as *Mr so-called Sage*, thus combining the 'pure' invective, person-directed meaning and a more contentful reflection on the appropriateness of the lexi-cal meaning of the name *Sage*. In example (27b), a more fully and straightforwardly negative attitude is expressed towards someone who first posted under the nickname *GeorgeW_Is_A_Nazi*, and subsequently under that of *Mr Cool* (as shown by the identi-cal Internet Protocol address of the two posters). Clearly this person is responded to negatively by the person with *geokstr* as a nickname, who calls him a liar and a fraud, and by the some token he is not considered to be 'cool' at all.

(27a)   *Sage, by contrast, confounds the listener at every turn.*
         Here's one, overly simple example. The track 'Kill Ya Momz' appears to be a
         parody of the Limp Bizkit, "Feel my paaaaiiiin!" skool of hip hop metal. But then
         it goes into a child's rap about how their mother is "The best mother/ There re-
         ally is no other". 'How sweet', you think. But then, an adult's voice – Sage's, you
         assume – comes in. "That's bull", it grunts. 'A-ha,' you think – gotcha! He's an-
         other Eminem, obsessed with his nasty mom – the only difference is that he
         swathes his oedipal complex in layers of irony – it's all become clear. What do you
         say to that, **Mr so-called Sage?**
         "Er, the line is 'That's all', not 'That's bull'."
         Bugger.
         [W – http://www.posteverything.com/sackbutblues/article.php?id=5577 – ac-
         cessed 25 April 2005]

(27b)   *– cool_person: Geokstr, I am a member of Mensa. There goes your theory. Get a*
         life virgin boy.
         – geokstr: **Mr. so-called Cool***: So you're "GeorgeW_Is_A_Nazi", eh? I guess be-*
         ing in Mensa doesn't necessarily mean one can't still be an absolute liar and a
         fraud, now does it?
         [W – http://www.factnet.org/discus/messages/5/2841.html?1103176134 – ac-
         cessed 25 April 2005]

4.2.3   *The neutral use of Mister so-called X with nicknames*

The invective uses of *Mr so-called* (either pure or combined with dissociative attitudes
vis-à-vis the lexical meaning of the name or nickname) should not be taken to mean that
any occurrence of *Mr so-called* with a name always expresses a negative attitude. Out of
the 88 WebCorp tokens, there are four cases for which a more **neutral** interpretation
seems justified; one of these is given in (28) below. In each of these cases, a nickname
rather than a real name is involved, and there are no indications in the context that anything like criticism or contempt is being expressed vis-à-vis the referent of the NP containing *Mr so-called*. In (28), for instance, it is the sister of the person being addressed
(sLiMdAvE) who posts a comment to his online guestbook, and she is amicably informal
but certainly not negative towards her brother in this message, adding even that she is
always there for him. Perhaps one could paraphrase 'friendly' uses of *Mr so-called* in
combination with nicknames as 'X, as apparently you call yourself on the internet'.

(28)   *Sup [what's up, LV]* **Mister so called sLiMdAvE**
        yo dude, do something about ur [your, LV] page it looks so plain. learn some html
        on htmlhelper to make ur page look nicer =P [smiley 'sticking one's tongue out', LV]
        can`t believe u [you, LV] and jj went out for two years already..i guess time flies.
        congratulations to u two =) [smiley, LV] Anyway, if u need anything, just come and
        ask me i`m always here for u. ur lil sis [your little sister, LV] Winnie

[W – http://guestbook.asianavenue.com/Members/MyPage/guestbook.
html?MEMBER=SlimDave – accessed 27 April 2005]

4.2.4   Mister so-called X *used with a current speaker's own contemptuous designation*

In the data, one final pattern manifested itself which has little in common with either the ordinary dissociative or the invective uses of *Mr so-called*. As a first example, consider (29), taken from the earlier, informal Google extraction:

(29)   *Now maybe you're thinking, "Wait a minute **Mr So-Called Know-it-All!** Even if all this stuff or material works and you can show me how to put it all together, I don't want to do this marketing work. I'm a solicitor. I'm paid to make clients [sic] legal problems either never surface or go away. Marketing is for somebody else or a slow peaceful rainy Thursday afternoon."*
[G – http://solicitorsinstitute.com/client.html – accessed 23 October 2003]

What is different about a case like (29) is that, unlike in the other uses, the designation that is in the scope of *Mr so-called* is not one used by the referent person nor by others to refer to him or her. Rather, it is the current speaker's own designation for this person: 'X, this is what I call you' rather than 'X is what you call yourself (as in *Mr so-called expert*), what others call you (*Mr so-called homophobe*), or simply what you *are* called (*Mr so-called Tony Blair*)'. Arguably, *Know-it-All* is not something one calls oneself nor something one wants to be known as. Instead, it reflects the judgement of the current speaker, i.e. the one using the phrase *Mr So-Called Know-it-All*. The attitude expressed in such a case is thus not one of implicit disagreement with the designation following *Mr So-Called*, as in the ordinary dissociative use, but the attitude is more explicitly given in a kind of name-giving act: 'I call you X, and in so doing I have expressed my judgement and criticism of you'.

In the WebCorp data, five of the 88 tokens were included in this '**name-calling**' use, in which the current speaker calls the referent person names. Three of these cases are given in (30) below. (30a) is taken from a column in which the author reports on an American survey in which 53 % of respondents said they thought the press had too much freedom, and only 65 % think that newspapers should be able to publish freely without prior government approval. In referring to an arbitrary instance of such a respondent as *Mr So-Called Conservative Who Wants to Censor the News Media*, it is clear that the designation is entirely the columnist's: it is the columnist who "assume[s] that many people who answered this poll consider themselves to be conservatives", and it is his choice of words to translate the alleged surplus of freedom into a desire to actively censor the news media. Put differently, it is unlikely that any of the respondents targeted by the columnist would choose to describe themselves as 'conservatives who want to censor the news media', and when prompted it seems unlikely that they would agree to being called this (even though following the columnist's reasoning, the conclusion seems logical enough).

(30a)   *Since conservatism seems to be the "default setting" of American politics [...],*
I'm gonna assume that many of the people who answered this poll consider
themselves to be conservatives. Isn't one of the Big Principles of conservatism
that the government should be as small and unobtrusive as possible? In that case,
I have a question. "Hey, **Mr. So-Called Conservative Who Wants to Censor the**
News Media," *I'd ask (in that charming way that I have). "Exactly how big a*
bureaucracy do you think it would take to pre-read and approve or censor every
news story in advance and who's gonna pay for this?"
[W – http://www.crankymediaguy.com/backissues/1999/070799.html – accessed 25 April 2005]

(30b) is taken from an online discussion forum dealing in this particular discussion
with the merits of Windows MediaPlayer 9, a piece of software made by Microsoft,
against the background of long standing discussions about the pros and cons of using
Windows or Linux as an operating system for one's pc. In (30b), someone with as nickname Neo Neko responds to a message by someone with Daybreak as a nickname.
Daybreak's main point was that people actually using any Microsoft products had no
right to criticize Microsoft products, since doing so is hypocritical. At no point has
Daybreak referred to himself as an idiot savant (let alone an idiot), so the designation
used in Neo Neko's reply is entirely his:

(30b)   *On the subject of ditching Windows toally [sic]. By your account* **Mr so called**
idiot savant, or perhaps idiot fits better. *If we were good Linux fanatic Win-*
dows bashers we should ditch Windows entirely. Forgive me for making you
look a bit ignorant,(believe me it was not hard) if I never ran windows at all
ever then how could I make any viable opinions/judgement on which is better.
[W – http://www.hydrogenaudio.org/forums/lofiversion/index.php/t3747.
html – accessed 27 April 2005]

Since an idiot savant is somebody with autism or mental retardation, but with exceptional mental abilities in one particular domain (for instance numerical calculation),
the designation is not unequivocally negative, and is replaced by an unmistakably negative and simpler alternative, *idiot*.

A final example of this perhaps least expected usage of *Mr so-called*, consider (30c).
The authors of (30c) are a group of kids who have participated in a TV show called
Singapore's Brainiest Kids, and they react against critical comments on this programme
made by the author of the blog (a kind of online diary) called *Confucius at Oxford*. In
hyphenating *confucius-who-did-not-speak-wisely-in-this-blog*, the authors of (30c) create a unit which as a whole can only be attributed to themselves: the blogger is not of
the opinion that he has spoken unwisely, and in fact in a later comment defends his
original criticisms.

(30c)   *Next time,* **Mr so-called confucius-who-did-not-speak-wisely-in-this-blog**,
watch what you say with your mouth, or rather, type with your fingers.

[W – http://www.thum.org/oxon/archives/000095.html – accessed 25 April 2005]

Inasmuch as *Confucius at Oxford* is the name of the blog, one might argue that (30c) involves not only the current speaker's name-giving act, but also the invective nick-name use discussed previously. However, *Confucius* is not actively used as a nickname; different messages posted onto the blog are signed with *PJ* rather than with *Confucius*. The fact that 'Confucius' is said not to have spoken wisely can be taken as a kind of play on the historical figure of Confucius, a wise ancient Chinese philosopher, and in this sense (30c) is also reminiscent of cases like *Mr so-called Dan Hays* (23c) or *Mr so-called Sage* (27a). However, in the final analysis the whole designation, including the choice to use Confucius even though it is only part of the blog's name, not the blogger's nick-name, reflects the choice of words of the authors of (30c) and can therefore best be included in the 'name-giving' category.

What is ultimately so strange about this use of *Mr so-called* is that from one per-spective, it radically opposes the meaning of *Mr so-called* in the ordinary dissociative use, as well as the general core meaning of framing adjectives (as formulated in 15 above), viz. 'stated by some (but not the speaker) to be X'. One way of making sense of this is to view the invective meaning in combination with proper names and nick-names as an intermediate step, in which the tie with any lexical properties (of experts, academics, and so on) that can be questioned by the current speaker, who does not associate with the designation framed by *Mr so-called*, is severed.

This line of analysis is represented in Figure 1. In going from the ordinary disso-ciative to the purely invective use, any accusation of 'pretense' is lost ('you're pretend-ing to be X, but you lack the right credentials/qualities/etc.'), and the dissociative or critical meaning of *Mr so-called* becomes purely invective, and is therefore more sub-jective. This absence of any specific allegation of pretense or undeservedly carrying a given name or title unites the invective and the name-giving uses, which are therefore both more subjective (less propositional) than the ordinary dissociative use. In going from the invective use with proper names and nicknames to the name-giving use, however, the invective meaning is **explicitated** in the name that is given (e.g. *Know-It-All* in 29). Particularly in Langacker's (1985) understanding of subjectivity and objec-tivity in terms of implicit, 'offstage' versus explicit, 'on stage' construal, this kind of explicitation could be taken to objectify to some degree the subjective meaning. Fol-lowing this line of reasoning, the name-giving pattern, while arguably the most devi-ant compared to the normal meaning of *so-called*, would be less strongly subjectified than the invective use with proper names and nicknames.

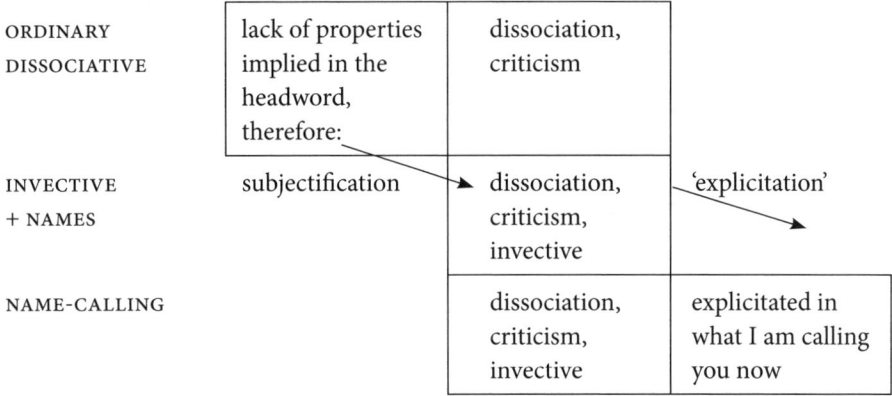

Figure 1. Meaning components of the three main usage patterns of *Mr so-called X*.

Arguably, one factor which co-enables severing the link with the lexical meaning of *so-called* in going from the ordinary dissociative to the invective and name-calling uses is the existence of the pattern *Mr X* with dissociative overtones (p.c. K. Davidse). Expressions such as *Mr Cool* or *Mr Know-it-all* may indeed be used dissociatively as such, and forms such as *Mr so-called Know-it-all* could then be viewed as a kind of blend of the dissociative *Mr X* pattern with the *Mr so-called X* pattern in its more 'lexical' meaning and use. The 'purely' dissociative meaning of *Mr X*, which does not have the lexical overtones of *Mr so-called X* in its ordinay uses, is then carried over into the resulting blend, which functions as an intensified variant of the dissociative *Mr X* pattern.

4.2.5 *Summary*

In Table 2 an attempt is made at summarizing the findings on *Mr so-called X* in the WebCorp dataset of 88 observations. It is immediately clear that two categories are very prominent: that in which the NP's referent is criticized for his or her lack of sufficient qualities or properties inherent in the head noun (or, in the few cases involving proper names, for a lack of the property of actually or rightfully having that name), and, on the other hand, that in which *Mr so-called* combines with a proper name or nickname of which the applicability is not at all disputed, but an invective attitude is expressed vis-à-vis the person carrying a certain name. If one adds up the invective category with the combined category involving dissociative reflections on the lexical meaning of names or nicknames, and with the neutral use of the pattern with nicknames, almost half of all data (42/88) turn out to use *Mr so-called* in combination with a name or nickname without the use of this name as such being questioned. This is remarkable since the core meaning of *so-called* and other framing adjectives, 'stated by some, but not the speaker, to be (called) X' becomes inert in such contexts. Equally remarkable, but for different reasons, is the remaining, infrequent pattern in which it *is* precisely the speaker, and no one else, who states that someone should be called X (as in *Mr so-called Know-It-All*).

Table 2. *Mr so-called X* in 88 WebCorp observations: summary of findings

Category	Meaning	Example	# (N=88)
Ordinary dissociative (lexical properties)	'you're not a real/not a good/not much of an X'	Mr. so-called "academic" (21b)	41
	Includes 2 cases in which others call the NP's referent X (e.g. Mr. so-called Homophobes fault, 22b), and 5 cases in which the NP's referent is accused of assuming a false name (e.g. Mr So-called Parks, 23b)		
Invective (with proper names and nicknames)	'X is your name or nickname, and I express contempt for/exasperation with you'	Mr so called Jagger (24a)	33
Dissociative + invective (names with lexical meaning)	'X is your name or nickname, I express contempt for/ exasperation with you, and I question the appropriateness of your name or nickname'	Mr so-called Sage (27a)	5
Neutral	'X is apparently your nickname on the internet'	Mister so called sLiM-dAvE (28)	4
Current speaker's dissociative name-giving act	'X is what I call you (contemptuously)'	Mr. So-Called Conservative Who Wants to Censor the News Media (30a)	5

4.3   Methodological afterthoughts

Before summing up the main conclusions of this paper, it is useful to reflect briefly on a few methodological issues pertaining to the use that has been made of internet data. The influence of the medium on the kinds of data retrieved has been evident throughout the above discussion: nicknames have formed an important part of my story, and among the prime loci for *Mr so-called X* on the internet are various forms of 'interactive' websites – discussion fora and guestbooks – as well as mock websites. All of this means that for every observation, it was necessary to see a lot of context in order to be able to interpret an example. In practical terms, this means that all website addresses returned in the Web-

Corp concordances have had to be visited and at least partially read, so as to determine, for instance, whether the designation within the scope of *Mr so-called* was a nickname, a proper name, a current speaker's designation, or what not.

In order to demonstrate the complexities that may be involved, consider examples (31-32). At face value, (31) might be taken as an example of the 'ordinary dissociative' use: some news reporter is called *Mr so called reporter* by someone who finds he lacks the right skills or credibility to be a reporter. On closer inspection, however, *reporter* turns out to be the nickname of someone (who presumably is not a reporter at all) simply posting onto a discussion forum. This is why (31) was coded as an 'invective' case, combining with a nickname, and not as an ordinary dissociative case.

(31)   *U [you, LV] only post anti-Jewish stuff* **Mr so called reporter**. *What is your agenda? I think therefor by definition u r [you are, LV] a racist and anti-semite. Hard to swallow?*
       [W – http://sydney.indymedia.org/front.php3?article_id=35833 – accessed 27 April 2005]

In (32), two different tokens of the same NP, *Mr so-called Lincoln*, are involved, but because of the different contexts in which they function they have received a different analysis. In (32a), the person referred to posted a message on a forum using the nickname *Abraham Lincoln*, and therefore this example was classed as an invective use with a nickname. The context for (32b), on the other hand, is rather complex. It is taken from a mock website in which both a 'real' Lincoln® and an impostor are assumed to exist. In referring to the impostor as *Mr. so-called Lincoln®*, the latter's right to use the name Lincoln® is being questioned, and therefore (32b) falls under one of the special cases subsumed under the ordinary dissociative pattern, viz. that in which someone is accused of falsely using a name.

(32a) *Now that is Friday, go sit on your couch over the weekend on your thumbs.* **Mr so called Lincoln**.
       [W – http://www.geek.com/news/geeknews/2005Jan/gee20050127028869. htm – accessed 27 April 2005]

(32b) *Then it occurs to one of us (I'm not certain which one – I always get us mixed up) that this fellow may not have been the real Lincoln®, but rather some kind of charlatan. And so, as I'm lying in bed listening to the alarm bell in the distance, I'm wondering if* **Mr. so-called Lincoln®** *has found himself another pile of money somewhere.*
       [W – http://www.biggreenhits.com/BackPages/march05.htm – accessed 25 April 2005]

One may also wonder to what extent the use of internet data distorts the results one obtains. On the one hand, of course, the reason for taking recourse to internet data lies in the scarcity of relevant data in classical corpora for certain kinds of problems, usually involving very recent developments in the language not yet reflected in corpora. For many topics, that internet data are used need not influence the type of results obtained so much as for this specific one: since *Mr so-called X* NP's are concerned with identifying and usually directly addressing persons, and since identity is such a central notion on the internet, in which people take on virtual identities, it should come as no surprise that the results reflect this. Arguably, this is not so much a distortion of reality, as a reflection of the fact that an expression like *Mr so-called X*, especially in its invective uses, may have a bigger role to play on the internet than in everyday 'offline' interaction.

This does not, of course, invalidate concerns as to how usable internet data ultimately are. Particularly the question as to the sources of the language samples remains a difficult and important one, considering the large amount of non-native speakers of English (with widely varying levels of proficiency) avidly using the means of communication offered by the internet. Either one has to accept that internet data yield samples of 'World English' or even 'Internet English', or one has to find ways to elicit native speaker data only, for instance through a combination of domain restrictions and manual sampling. For my present purposes, however, I believe that even the relatively few internet data that I have looked at in detail have proved to be interesting and helpful in linking up the neutral and dissociative meanings of the framing adjective *so-called* with the further developments it has undergone in the template *Mr so-called X*.

5. Conclusion

In this paper I have tried to relate the general meaning and specific discourse functions of the framing adjective *so-called* to a number of usage types which can be distinguished for the pattern *Mister so-called X* on the basis of internet data.

In section two, the point was made that framing adjectives like *so-called* are different from established adjective types such as classifying and qualifying adjectives and postdeterminers in contributing neither to the type specification nor to the instantiation of the general type of thing designated by the NP in which they occur. This was related to an underlying difference as to the kind of form-meaning correlate involved in framing adjectives, viz. a 'non-compositional' or 'scopal' one concerned with the expression of interpersonal rather than representational meanings. The versatility of framing adjectives in terms of the extent of their scope was argued to support this distinction.

In a next step, I compared *so-called* in section 3 to other framing adjectives such as *alleged* or *purported* in terms of the source of the framed designation, the propensity for dissociative uses, frequency, register, and collocation. Because *so-called* is both frequent and not particularly specialized in terms of collocates and register, it was argued to allow dissociative meaning developments more easily than less frequent framing adjectives like *purported* or adjectives like *alleged* with a more strictly delineated meaning and use.

The high incidence of dissociative uses of *so-called* served as a background to the exploratory qualitative study of 88 WebCorp observations of the pattern *Mister so-*

called X. The most frequent pattern, exemplified in *Mr. so-called "academic"*, is quite similar to the dissociative use of *so-called* outside of the *Mister so-called X* template, in that the referent of the NP is suggested not to be a real or a good *X* ("academic", for instance) because certain qualities usually associated with *Xes* ("academics") are missing. Occasionally, the headword in this ordinary dissociative pattern may be a (false) name which is unjustifiedly assumed by the referent of the NP. In a second prominent pattern, *Mister so-called* is combined with proper names or nicknames and no link can be made to any properties defining what it takes to be an X (e.g. *Mr Jagger* in *Mr so called Jagger*). This invective use was analyzed as subjectified compared to the ordinary dissociative use precisely because of the lack of any contentful criticism (viz. an accusation of wrongfully calling oneself X). In one infrequent pattern in the data, this purely invective attitude is explicitated in the part framed by *Mister so-called*. Thus, in *Mr. So-Called Conservative Who Wants to Censor the News Media*, the designation *Conservative Who Wants to Censor the News Media* is entirely the current speaker's. This pattern is the one that is the most strongly removed from the core meaning of framing adjectives, in which normally the framed designation is one used and subscribed to by some people, but *not* by the current speaker. At the same time, because this pattern is more explicit about the subjective attitude being expressed, it could be argued to be less subjective than the invective use with proper names and nicknames.

By closely studying internet data, it was possible to trace the meaning developments of *so-called* in the relatively new and productive pattern *Mister so-called X*. From its neutral use in stating the correct terminology (*tough so-called "lemon laws"*) to its seemingly bizarre applications in the pattern *Mister so-called X*, *so-called* displays an intriguing variety of interpersonal meanings of stance and affect which can be related in terms of subjectification.

Data sources

COBUILD *The Bank of English* corpus [http://www.cobuild.collins.co.uk]. London: HarperCollins Publishers.

SUBCORPORA:

npr	*US National Public Radio broadcasts*
today	*UK Today newspaper*
times	*UK Times newspaper*
usbooks	*US books; fiction & non-fiction*
oznews	*Australian newspapers*
bbc	*BBC World Service radio broadcasts*
ukmags	*UK magazines*
sunnow	*UK Sun newspaper*
ukspok	*UK transcribed informal speech*
ukbooks	*UK books; fiction & non-fiction*

| ukephem | UK ephemera (leaflets, adverts, etc.) |
| usephem | US ephemera (leaflets, adverts, etc.) |

Google [http://www.google.com].
Webcorp: The Web as corpus [http://www.webcorp.org.uk/].

References

Authier-Revuz, Jacqueline. 1995. *Ces mots qui ne vont pas de soi: boucles réflexives et non-coïncidences du dire.* Paris: Larousse. [Sciences du langage].

Bache, Carl and Niels Davidsen-Nielsen. 1997. *Mastering English: An advanced grammar for non-native and native speakers.* Berlin: Mouton de Gruyter.

Bakhtin, Mikhail M. 1984. *Problems of Dostoevsky's poetics* (Russian version translated by Caryl Emerson). Minneapolis: University of Minnesota Press. [Theory and history of literature 8].

Breban, Tine. 2006. "The grammaticalization of the English adjectives of comparison: A diachronic case study". *Corpus-based studies of diachronic English,* ed. by Roberta Facchinetti and Matti Rissanen, 253–288. Bern: Peter Lang. [Linguistic insights: Studies in language and communication 31].

Breban, Tine and Kristin Davidse. 2003. "Adjectives of comparison: The grammaticalization of their attribute uses into postdeterminer and classifier uses". *Folia Linguistica* XXXVII (3–4): 269–317.

Bybee, Joan and Paul J. Hopper (eds.). 2001. *Frequency and the emergence of linguistic structure.* Amsterdam: John Benjamins. [Typological Studies in Language 45].

Clear, Jeremy. 1993. "From Firth principles: Computational tools for the study of collocation". *Text and technology. In honour of John Sinclair,* ed. by Mona Baker, Gill Francis, and Elena Tognini-Bonelli, 271-292. Amsterdam: John Benjamins.

Davidse, Kristin. 2004. "The interaction of quantification and identification in English determiners". *Language, culture and mind,* ed. by Michel Achard and Suzanne Kemmer, 507–533. Stanford: CSLI Publications.

Fauconnier, Gilles. 1985. *Mental spaces: Aspects of meaning construction in natural language.* Cambridge (Mass.): MIT Press.

Halliday, Michael A.K. 1994 [1985]. *An introduction to functional grammar.* 2nd edn. [1st edn.] London: Arnold.

Hengeveld, Kees. 1989. "Layers and operators in Functional Grammar". *Journal of Linguistics* 25: 127–157.

Hoffmann, Sebastian. 2004. "Are low-frequency complex prepositions grammaticalized? On the limits of corpus data – and the importance of intuition". *Corpus approaches to grammaticalization in English,* ed. by Hans Lindquist and Christian Mair, 171–210. Amsterdam: John Benjamins.

Janda, Laura A. et al. 2003. "Linguists for the responsible use of internet data". Online publication at [http://www.unc.edu/~lajanda/responsible.html]. Accessed 3 May 2005.

Kehoe, Andrew and Antionette Renouf. 2002. "WebCorp: Applying the Web to linguistics and linguistics to the Web". Proceedings of the WWW2002 Conference, Honolulu, Hawaii. Online publication at [http://www2002.org/CDROM/poster/67/]. Accessed 3 May 2005.

Langacker, Ronald W. 1985. "Observations and speculations on subjectivity". *Iconicity in syntax,* ed. by John Haiman, 109-150. Amsterdam: John Benjamins. [Typological Studies in Language 6].

Langacker, Ronald W. 1991. *Foundations of Cognitive Grammar. Volume II: Descriptive application*. Stanford: Stanford University Press.

Langacker, Ronald W. 2002. "Discourse in Cognitive Grammar". *Cognitive Linguistics* 12(2): 143–188.

Leech, Geoffrey N. and Michael H. Short. 1981. *Style in fiction. A linguistic introduction to English fictional prose*. London: Longman. [English Language Series 13].

Louw, Bill. 1993. "Irony in the text or insincerity in the writer? The diagnostic potential of semantic prosodies". *Text and technology. In honour of John Sinclair*, ed. by Mona Baker, Gill Francis, and Elena Tognini-Bonelli, 157-176. Amsterdam: John Benjamins.

Mackintosh, Ellen. 2003. "Framing adjectives: 'so-called'". Unpublished term paper, University of Leuven.

McGregor, William B. 1997. *Semiotic Grammar*. Oxford: Clarendon Press.

Mey, Jacob L. 1999. *When voices clash: A study in literary pragmatics*. Berlin: Mouton de Gruyter. [Trends in linguistics 115].

Renouf, Antoinette. 2005. "Revisiting the 'corp' in WebCorp". Paper presented at the joint corpus conference ICAME 26 & AAACL 6, Ann Arbor, 12-15 May 2005.

Renouf, Antoinette, Andrew Kehoe, and David Mezquiriz. 2004. "The accidental corpus: Some issues in extracting linguistic information from the Web". *Advances in corpus linguistics: Papers from the 23rd International Conference on English Language Research on Computerized Corpora (ICAME 23)*, ed. by Karin Aijmer and Bengt Altenberg, 403–419. Amsterdam: Rodopi.

Resnik, Philip and Aaron Elkiss. 2004. "The Linguist's Search Engine: Getting started guide". Online publication at [http://lse.umiacs.umd.edu:8080/guide/lse_guide_techreport.html]. Accessed 3 May 2005.

Sinclair, John. 1991. *Corpus, concordance, collocation*. Oxford: Oxford University Press. [Describing English language].

Sinclair, John *et al.* 1990. *Collins COBUILD English grammar*. London: HarperCollins Publishers.

Stubbs, Michael. 1995. "Corpus evidence for norms of lexical collocation". *Principle and practice in applied linguistics. Studies in honour of H.G. Widdowson*, ed. by Guy Cook and Barbara Seidlhofer, 245-256. Oxford: Oxford University Press.

The Linguist's Search Engine [http://lse.umiacs.umd.edu:8080/].

Thompson, Geoff. 1996. "Voices in the text: Discourse perspectives on language reports". *Applied Linguistics* 17(4): 501–530.

Traugott, Elizabeth Closs. 1982. "From propositional to textual and expressive meanings: Some semantic-pragmatic aspects of grammaticalization". *Perspectives on historical linguistics*, ed. by Winfred P. Lehmann and Yakov Malkiel, 245–267. Amsterdam: John Benjamins. [Current issues in linguistic theory 24].

Traugott, Elizabeth Closs. 1989. "On the rise of epistemic meanings in English: An example of subjectification in semantic change". *Language* 65(1): 31–55.

Traugott, Elizabeth Closs. 1995. "Subjectification in grammaticalisation". *Subjectivity and subjectivisation. Linguistic perspectives*, ed. by Dieter Stein and Susan Wright, 37–54. Cambridge: Cambridge University Press.

Traugott, Elizabeth Closs. 2003. "From subjectification to intersubjectification". *Motives for language change*, ed. by Raymond Hickey, 124–139. Cambridge: Cambridge University Press.

Vanaelten, Babette and Stijn van Osch. 2003. "Framing adjectives: *alleged* and *purported*". Unpublished term paper, University of Leuven.

Vandelanotte, Lieven. 2002. "Prenominal adjectives in English: Structures and ordering". *Folia Linguistica* XXXVI (3-4): 219–259.

Vandelanotte, Lieven. 2005. "Types of speech and thought representation in English: Syntagmatic structure, deixis and expressivity, semantics". Ph.D. dissertation, University of Leuven.

Vandelanotte, Lieven. Forthcoming. "Dependency, framing, scope? The syntagmatic structure of sentences of speech or thought representation". *WORD*.

Van Langendonck, Willy. 1999. "Neurolinguistic and syntactic evidence for basic level meaning in proper names". *Functions of Language* 6(1): 95-138.

van Oostendorp, Marc and Ton van der Wouden. 1998. "DIGITAAL: Corpus Internet". *Nederlandse taalkunde* 4: 347-361. Also available online at [http://www.niederlandistik.fu-berlin.de/digitaal/digitaal-04.html]. Accessed 3 May 2005.

'Sorry to muddy the waters'

Accounting for speech act formulae and formulaic variation in a systemic functional model of language

Gordon Tucker
Cardiff University

In this paper I seek to provide a grammatical account of some aspects of the realisation of speech acts in spoken discourse that are considered formulaic and/or, in some sense elliptical, as described in Biber et al's (1999) description of the 'grammar of conversation'. Focusing on apologies involving *sorry*, I discuss the treatment of formulaic *sorry* in isolation, together with variants that include it. The discussion is set within the theoretical and descriptive framework of Systemic Functional Grammar (e.g. Halliday and Matthiessen 2004) and the solutions proposed are given in terms of (a) a functionally motivated grammatical structure associated with this framework and (b) system networks that represent the choices available to speakers in a given context.

1. Introduction

This chapter explores some of the problems that arise in the description of English when a range of well-observed phenomena associated with spoken interaction are taken into account. It focuses on one aspect of spoken interaction, namely speech act realisation, with particular attention to apologies based on the item *sorry*. It does not propose a dedicated 'grammar of speech', as such, in Brazil's sense (Brazil 1995), but examines how such phenomena can be accounted for in a systemic functional grammar (SFG) (e.g. Halliday and Matthiessen 2004, Fawcett 2000), both structurally and semantically, and how SFG can contribute to an understanding of the relationship between the pragmatic concerns and lexicogrammatical realisation[1]. Grammars, including systemic functional grammars, tend to be general, in the sense that they account for a general syntactic/se-

---

1. The term 'lexicogrammatical/lexicogrammar' reflects the integration of both the 'grammatical' and 'lexical' aspects of the realisation of meaning, increasingly accepted within functional linguistic paradigms at least, and proposed originally by Halliday (1961). Throughout this chapter, the more common term 'grammar' will be used, but always in the sense of an integral grammar.

mantic resource, rather than the resource that 'comes on line' in a given context. Grammars that are concerned with specifying and describing something like 'all and only all the sentences of a language' are, at the same time, not concerned with how the grammar is used, or the fact that choice is not equally distributed across the range of grammatical possibility. What such grammars may fail to capture, therefore, is the substantial differences noted between spoken and written instantiations. Grammatical variation across genres and registers is well documented, however, particularly in the corpus-based work of Biber and co-researchers (Biber 1988, Biber et al. 1999).

Significantly, spoken interaction, on a daily basis, typically involves a wide range of small social acts which arise from the nature of social interaction itself. Whether at work or at leisure, a human interactant is likely to engage in greetings and valedictions, thanking, offering and accepting, apologising, requesting and giving information. As Goffman (1971) points out, much of this behaviour is ritualistic. The high frequency of such a range of everyday acts has led to their performance through what have been described as 'conversational routines' (Coulmas 1981a, Aijmer 1996), marked by a high degree of formulaicity and fixedness of the language involved in the routines.

Even if one takes a systemic functional grammar as a general resource for realising meanings, from which a speaker may openly select, it is likely that with frequently occurring pragmatic demands in regular and familiar contexts, the speaker will make the same selection of meanings, leading to the same grammatical realisation. Over the course of time, the familiar regularity of the expression itself takes over, in terms of an increasing association with the act in question. The expression becomes an 'off the peg' solution to a given pragmatic demand. Over longer periods of time, this may also lead to the linguistic equivalent of geological erosion. One example is the transformation of the fully articulated valediction *God be with you* into *goodbye*. In other instances, the reduction appears to be brought about by the 'removal' of all but keywords in an expression, as with *sorry, thanks* and *congratulations*.

A linguistic solution that simply treated all such cases as reduced forms of some underlying fully clausal expression would miss the point. Any hypothesis of such reduction is phylogenetic in nature, not ontogenetic. Indeed, from an ontogenetic perspective, one might wish to see fuller clausal forms of minimal expressions such as *sorry* as secondary developments, rather than the converse[2]. As we have seen, other expressions are more recalcitrant in allowing a more fully clausal expression to be articulated. Such is the case of *thanks* and *help* (see Halliday and Matthiessen 2004: 154).

The grammarian is therefore forced to accept the observation that, with spoken language, there are expressions that are not easily describable in terms of a direct relationship with clause grammar. These are discussed in detail by Biber et al. (1999: 1038ff) under the general heading of a 'grammar of conversation'. Yet even where there is little or no relationship with the clause grammar, as might be the case with substan-

---

2.   In a similar vein, Mackenzie (1998), in his Incremental Functional Grammar, proposes that such full structures are in fact expansions of simple holophrastic utterances.

tial amounts of ellipsis in dialogic spoken interaction, the grammar must not only allow for it, but also account for it.

Furthermore, if linguistic expressions of the type we are considering here are not related to the clause grammar, to what extent might they be said to be 'grammar'? Again, their historical provenance is not a determining factor. The greeting *Good morning* exists for speakers outside the realm of the grammar. When there is a direct relationship between the utterance as single event and the socio-semantic (pragmatic?) option that is being realised, the symbolic organisation of a grammar may not be considered necessary. Halliday himself comments on this, suggesting that:

> In some instances the semantic network leads directly to the 'formal items' – to the actual words, phrases and clauses of the language. This is likely to happen only where there is a closed set of options in a clearly circumscribed social context [...] Systems of greetings would be of this kind. (Halliday 1973: 83)[3]

In Halliday's semantic network (1973: 83), there are options to realise greetings, for example, through 'time-bound' expressions such as *good morning, good afternoon* and 'time-free' expressions such as *hullo*, but these are seen as essentially semantic options, rather than those that depend on the potential of the grammatical resource.

Despite underlying grammatical phenomena, there would, indeed, seem to be no need to process such expressions grammatically either as speakers or hearers. This is the position taken within the study of formulaic language by authors such as Wray (2002). A learner of Italian, for example, can learn and use time-bound greetings/valedictions such as *buon giorno* (good morning), *buona sera* (good evening), *buona notte* (good night), without reference to grammatical gender that affects the modifying adjective, *buon* (masculine gender) versus *buona* (feminine gender).

The linguistic resource may then be perceived as divided between direct holistic expressions, whose potential grammatical properties are not activated, and expressions that arise from access to the full grammar. Taking a 'well-wishing' speech act as an example, the linguistic resource might be modelled as shown in the system network in Figure 1 below:

---

3. A 'network' or 'system network' is a central formalism in SFG. It represents linguistic organisation from a paradigmatic perspective, by setting out the choices (semantic or grammatical) that are available in the language as a set of related 'systems'. Each 'system' in the network has a given feature as an entry point and specifies the options that may be selected if the entry point condition is satisfied. System networks of various kinds are used through this chapter. For a discussion of the nature of system networks and their motivation see, for example, Martin (1987) and Fawcett (1988).

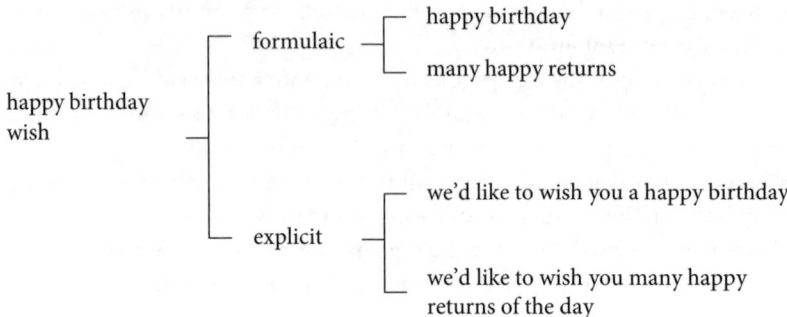

Figure 1. Some of the range of options available in wishing someone a happy birthday

The dichotomising of these two types of resource does not fully reflect the data. Halliday refers to systems of greetings as being of the 'closed set of options' type. Yet we find, in examples of spoken data, utterances that would appear to fall between the closed set of greetings and the set 'generated' by access to some kind of grammar, as the examples from the COBUILD Bank of English (Sinclair 1987a) below, show.

```
</dt> GOOD morning, ladies and gentlemen and welcome
aboard GOOD morning dear Queenslanders, you weird, gay-
bashing
A very good morning, Baron; how are you, sir.
And good morning to both of you. <p> VIN WEBER, Former
A very good morning to you -- it is days since we met.
```

In the corpus data above, two phenomena emerge: firstly, the elaboration of the nominal group in which *morning* is head, and secondly, the option of the vocative (e.g. *dear Queenslanders*), suggesting a grammatical unit that goes beyond the formulaic *good morning*. Furthermore, the presence of constituents such as *to you, to the both of you* indicates some kind of intermediacy of the expression between a clause (with *to you* as a participant role) and a nominal group, in which *to you* can only be explained as a qualifier (post-modifier).

There are clearly signs, however, that some kind of partial grammar is being accessed by speakers who produce expressions such as *a very good morning*. It would be possible to explain this away in terms of a closed set of expressions, e.g. *good morning, a good morning to you, a very good morning to you* etc., but as the members of the set increase, their treatment as independent, closed set realisations, not subject to underlying organisational principles, becomes less convincing and less tenable.

The kind of grammar that the variants of *good morning* exhibit is derived, at least in part, from the general grammatical resource, in terms of the grammar of nominal groups (e.g. Halliday and Matthiessen 2004: 311ff). We also find exploitation of the full clause with this kind of greeting, as example (1) from the British National Corpus (BNC) (Aston and Burnard 1998) shows.

(1)   *I wish you all a very good morning.* (BNC)

So although there may be considerable limitations on choice in such instances when drawing on the 'open' grammar, it would make little sense to set up entirely parallel grammatical systems to account for this partial grammatical behaviour.

This observation of the third kind of phenomenon (partial grammar) leads us towards a tripartite resource offering (a) a full open grammar, (b) access to parts of the full grammar (a kind of 'dipping-in' resource) and (c) a number of formulaic expressions which directly realise meanings without access to a grammar. These three resources are not discrete. However formulaic *good morning* may be considered to be, it also co-occurs in expressions which involve the other two parts of the resource, given examples such as *a very good morning* and *I wish you a very good morning.* In the interests of the single system (albeit containing different types of resource), there is an imperative at least to attempt some integration, rather than leave the relationship between the parts unexplained.

2.   The case of *sorry* and the speech act of apologising

Apologies as speech acts have been extensively studied from various perspectives (e.g. Coulmas 1981b, Edmondson 1981, Owen 1983, Blum Kulka et al. 1989, Holmes 1990, Aijmer 1996 and Deutschmann 2003), a number of these approaches involving corpus-derived data (e.g. Aijmer 1996 and Deutschmann 2003). The concerns addressed in this large body of 'apologies' research range from explication of the pragmatics, often within a speech act framework, to the nature of apologising as a social act (Holmes 1990) to strategies for apologising (Olshtein and Cohen 1983).

Naturally, given the relationship between the apologiser's social and pragmatic concerns and the linguistic mode of realisation, substantial attention has been given to the formal realisations of apologies. Furthermore, studies involving corpus data such as Aijmer (1996) (London-Lund Corpus of Spoken English) and Deutschmann (2003) (BNC), have also produced evidence of the distribution and variation of realisational tokens of apologising. Formal descriptions of the syntax have also been offered, at least in terms of constituents and elements, and specification of what is obligatory and optional (e.g. Aijmer 1996: 91, Deutschmann 2003: 53).

What accounts of apologies often omit however is (a) the relationship between the grammatical form and the underlying semantic/grammatical options, and (b) the explicit modelling of the formal resource, rather than a mere listing and description of formal types. These are the two central concerns of this present chapter. SFG, and specifically the Cardiff Grammar, aims to make explicit the relationship between semantic choice and formal realisation[4]. The Cardiff system networks have been pushed extensively in the direction of the underlying semantics, so that there is a claim that the systemic features in the network are in fact semantic features rather than grammatical ones.

This has important implications for the understanding of the choice of speech act realisation. Whilst claims can be made about the relationship between a speech act realisation and the speaker's concern in respect of politeness, face, etc., such claims need to explicate what it is in the nature of the grammar that corresponds, for example, to a more or less face-threatening utterance. Moreover, the grammar is not organised around the expression of a list of individual and different speech acts. So whilst there may be a 'grammar of apologising' and a 'grammar of thanking' etc., in terms of sets of potential utterances associated with each act respectively, speech acts draw, by and large, on the general resource and importantly share the general resource. The generalised systems of MOOD and MODALITY, in particular, are shared by all speech acts realized by clauses.

In this chapter, I shall mainly discuss *sorry* and its derivatives in respect of the linguistic resource associated with apologies. This decision is determined by available space and by the particular status that is attributed to *sorry* as a formulaic utterance.

As others have pointed out, and as the corpus evidence makes clear, speakers have a fairly conventional range of linguistic expression with which to perform their apologies. Summarising this resource in system network form, we have something like Figure 2.

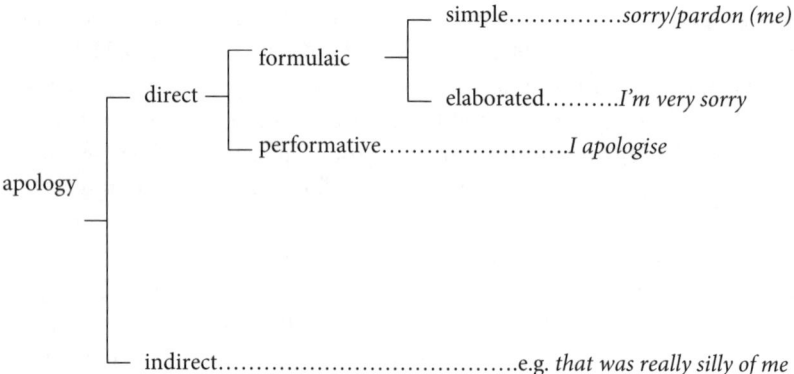

Figure 2. The range of options available for realising apologies

---

4.   The Cardiff Grammar is a computationally implemented SFG developed at Cardiff University, UK. Accounts of it, together with similarities and difference between Halliday's approach are found in Fawcett (2000) and Butler (2003). The grammatical analysis given in this chapter is based on the Cardiff Grammar.

Here we are concerned with the terminal features in the network that lead to apologies formulated on the basis of *sorry* and elaborations. Examples of the variations from the COBUILD Bank of English are given below.

```
I'm sorry mate. <tc
I'm sorry the bill's in the name of somebody
I'm sorry these slides are a bit grim at the front and
I'm sorry to keep you waiting. <ZZ1> <!--
I'm sorry about this. <p> Hoffert: It's been ex--
I'm sorry for the inconvenience," she said, `but I have
I'm sorry for what I did, but now I'm not afraid
I'm sorry if I was rude back there. But you were rude
I'm sorry. But you know. And I'm not against living in
I am most sorry, really I am. This is all my fault;
No, sorry, the restaurant is closed." `Anywhere in
oh, sorry, I'm getting emotional!" <p> There's times
I am really sorry for the unnecessary worry which has
I'm really so sorry about it. I really am." <pand says,
Ever so sorry, but no. Come and see the pigs here by
So sorry, everyone, I've been just beastly. This isn't
So terribly sorry. Don't know what got into me.
We're ever so terribly sorry: Newspapers and magazines never
```

3.   *Sorry* as formula

As a single lexical item, *sorry* is less evidently 'formulaic' than multi-word expressions, even though on corpus evidence it is by far the most frequently found realisation of an apology (Aijmer 1996: 85, Deutschmann 2003: 53). It is difficult to treat a single item in terms of a prefabricated expression, or an expression that is learnt and retrieved holistically. And although *sorry* can be treated as 'radically elliptical' or 'fragmentary' (see Aijmer 1996: 88), it may also be considered as a pragmatically complete isolate, an utterance which directly (and most commonly, as indicated above) realises an apology. In Aijmer's data from the LLC, *sorry*, as a single item expression, accounts for 107 out of 215 realisations of all direct apologies.

Furthermore, if we do not consider *sorry* to be an isolated formula, on the grounds that it can be accounted for as an elliptical form of *I'm sorry*, then some inconsistency may arise in the treatment of single item expressions in general, considering the difficulty of treating items such as *thanks*, *congratulations* etc. in a similar way. The item *sorry* need not therefore be seen as processed by the general grammar or even by a partial lexcogrammar.

If *sorry* is not generated by reference to the grammar, it has no grammatical status. It may be treated as a minor clause following Halliday and Matthiessen (2004: 153). Halliday does not include 'speech functions' performed with utterances such as *sorry* and *thanks* in his inventory of minor clauses, but it seems reasonable to suggest that they would fit here. Minor clauses are formally moodless, given that they precisely lack the Subject-Finite configuration that marks mood in its recognised sense (Halliday and Matthiessen 2004: 111ff.).

The treatment of such expressions as minor clauses creates some ambiguity as to their grammatical status, however. In Halliday's (1973: 83) discussion of salutations, expressions such as *Good morning* are considered direct realisations (albeit in terms of 'words, phrases, clauses') of choices in the semantic network, and not expressions that are produced by reference to the grammar. Yet Halliday and Matthiessen's 2004 treatment of speech functions such as greetings as minor clause suggests that they do have grammatical status. Indeed in Halliday and Matthiessen's (2004: 135) system network for MOOD, the feature [minor clause] is clearly a grammatical option.

Fawcett's approach to formulae within the Cardiff Grammar is to posit a 'formulaic element' (F), when 'a clause contains a segment that is not analyzable syntactically' (Fawcett 2000:305). It is thus a direct element of clause structure, as shown in Figure 3. Fawcett would appear, however, to be thinking primarily of fixed, ritualistic formulaic expressions, often single items, such as *thanks, sorry, hi*, rather than of more complex expressions which may be considered formulaic and which do have some form of syntactic constituency.

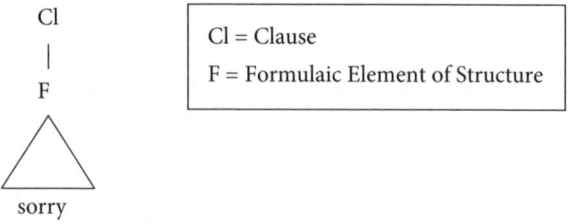

Figure 3. *Sorry* realizing a formulaic element of structure in a Clause

One advantage of Fawcett's approach, at least as far as single items are concerned, is that is lends itself to the treatment of expressions such as (2) and (3) below.

(2)   *do you intend to **say sorry**.* (BNC)

(3)   *Why should I **say sorry** when it's always my brother's fault?* (BNC)

This type of expression (e.g. *say sorry/thank you/hello/goodbye*) would appear to have a function in teaching children to perform speech acts and also how to perform them (Aijmer 1996: 84), but also in providing the language with additional lexical (verbal) resources for talking about speech acts (e.g. *apologise* versus *say sorry*). The Cardiff Grammar analysis of such verbs would be as in Figure 4.

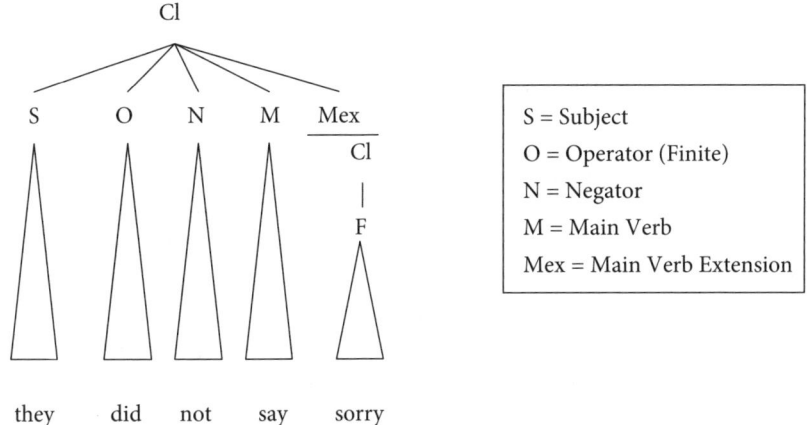

Figure 4. Cardiff Grammar analysis of the process *say sorry*

Note that *say sorry* is analysed above as a Main Verb (M) followed by a Main Verb Extension (Mex). This latter element of clause structure was introduced into the Cardiff Grammar to account for constituents within the clause that are better handled as part of a multi-word expression, rather than as a full complement or adjunct in a clause (Fawcett 2000: 259). Thus in the example above, the process, semantically an equivalent of *apologise*, is realised here by the combination of *say* and *sorry*, rather by a general verb *say*, which takes *sorry* as its Complement. A single choice, along the lines of Sinclair's idiom principle (Sinclair 1987b: 320), is therefore responsible for the realisation of a putative semantic feature [apologise] as *say sorry*, in parallel with the single choice leading to the verb *apologise*.

Both Halliday's and Fawcett's approaches, e.g. minor clause and formulaic element of structure in a clause, respectively, propose solutions within a grammatical context. Biber et al's approach, in the context of spoken English, to *sorry* and other speech acts such as *thanks* is twofold. Firstly, they are treated as 'inserts', as 'stand-alone words which are characterised in general, by their inability to enter into syntactic relations with other structures (Biber et al. 1999: 1082). Secondly, they are treated as 'syntactic non-clausal units' in that "they can be given a syntactic description in terms of the structures and categories of sentence grammar" (Biber et al. 1999: 1099). Biber et al. also clarify that, despite the fact that syntactic non-clausal units are not clause-based, "they may be classed as units which *are capable of* entering into syntactic relations with others for forming larger units such as clausal units." (Biber et al. 1999: 1082) (original emphasis). Furthermore, they also recognise that the boundary between inserts and syntactic non-clausal units is a gradual one (Biber et al. 1999: 1082).

In the case of *sorry* in isolation, much depends upon how such elements are viewed. Consider Wray's working definition of formulaic expressions, namely:

> a sequence, continuous or discontinuous, of words or other elements, which is, or appears to be, prefabricated: that is, stored or retrieved whole from memory at the time of use, rather than being subject to generation or analysis by the language grammar. (Wray 2002: 9)

Although Wray is concerned on the whole with sequences, rather than single words, she characterises such expressions as not being subject to generation or analysis by the language grammar. The isolate *sorry*, under this definition, would be stored and retrieved by users without reference to a clause grammar that categorises it as an adjective, specifies its grammatical potential in terms of intensification and complementation, and further specifies its relation, within an adjectival group, to a full clause. Thus, the utterances *sorry* and *sorry about that* reference different language production procedures. From the perspective of ontological language development in particular, this does not seem implausible. Learners of Italian, for example, in the author's personal experience at least, acquire the expression *scusi* (sorry) as a formulaic and conventional way of apologising long before the onset of any grammatical awareness that allows them to categorise it as a singular imperative form of the verb *scusare*, corresponding, moreover, to the polite V-form *Lei*, rather that to the intimate T-form *tu*, in which case the verbal morphology would be *scusa*.

The feature [formulaic] in Figure 2 above conceals a primary and important choice, namely that of processing *sorry* as a direct, non-grammatically referenced expression of an apology, [simple], or invoking the grammar associated with the adjective *sorry*, [elaborated]. But now, in the light of the discussion above, the question is raised of the formulaic status of elaborations such as *very sorry, I'm very sorry* etc. As we have observed, and in line with Wray's working definition, any elaboration of the kind *sorry about that* in order to be considered formulaic would again 'bypass' the grammar. And this would lead to a plethora of holistic expressions related solely by being variants on a theme, albeit reflecting different pragmatic concerns.

Indeed, this may be the case in the development of a speaker's language potential, a kind of protogrammatical stage, before the onset of a fuller adult, first language speaker grammar. It is, however, this fuller competence that we are addressing here, which does not remove the need to incorporate formulaicity, since this is clearly present in the language of adult speakers. We therefore assume the existence of a grammar of adjectives, both from an internal (adjectival group) perspective, and from an external (clausal) perspective. With this comes the assumption that, in producing variants of Biber et al's 'syntactic non-clausal units', speakers are accessing the whole or part of the full grammar of adjectives, and that they do so in order to exploit the semantic potential of such a grammar in order to fine-tune the expression of apologies involving *sorry*.

One further approach to the treatment of single, formulaic *sorry* in a systemic functional grammar remains to be considered, but given the discussion in Section 5 below, this remaining, alternative approach is more appropriately described there.

4. Variations

4.1 General considerations

The assignment of formulaic status to *sorry* does not preclude the availability of a fuller grammar with which to express apologies. Formulaic expressions tend to be the neutral manifestations of the speech act in question, as Aijmer observes, although she includes the clausal variation *I'm sorry* and focuses on the absence of intensifiers preceding *sorry* (Aijmer 1996: 82).

The relationship between the grammatical resource and the speech act to be expressed, as was suggested above, is one of fine-tuning. As we shall see, it is precisely the general semiotic resource of the grammar that is exploited, which makes it more important to examine the semantic and formal nature of the grammar itself.

A clearer understanding of the nature and range of the variation comes with an examination of the grammar of quality, as realised through the adjectival group (see Tucker 1998)[5]. The item *sorry* is a member of a class of adjectives that is susceptible of both tempering (intensification) and complementation. In terms of semantic classification it has the features [thing-oriented], [epithetic] and [typically human quality] (see Tucker 1998: 125), and from a perspective of appraisal theory within systemic functional linguisitics, its use is typically associated with 'affect' (Martin 2000: 148). It has two main related senses: (a) the 'apology' sense, under discussion here, and (b) the expression of sorrow, regret, compassion etc. where no responsibility is assumed by the speaker, as in (4).

(4)   *Well, I'm sorry for you, that's all.* (BNC)

The two senses above are rarely found with the adjective in its function as modifier in a nominal group. When it is used with this function, the nominal head is again rarely human and the sense of *sorry* might be glossed as 'unfortunate', 'wretched'.

---

5.   The term 'quality' is used in the Cardiff Grammar to refer to meanings realised by adjectives and their structure, compared with 'thing', for example, which refers to nouns and their structure. This is reflected in the term 'quality group' in Tucker (1998) and Fawcett (2000) which corresponds to 'adjectival group'.

An instance of the full potential of *sorry*-based clauses is given in the analysis in Figure 5.

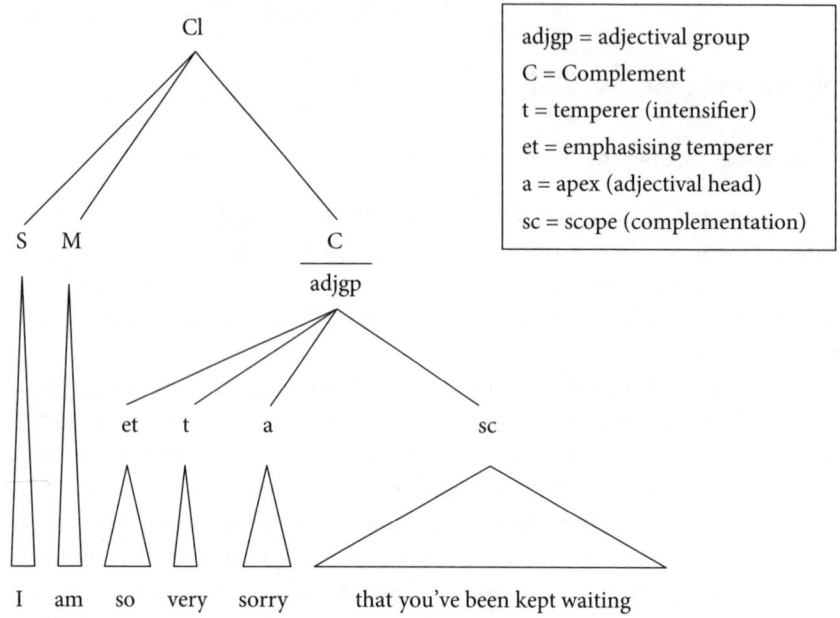

Figure 5. Analysis of a fairly fully elaborated apology based on *sorry*

4.2   The complementation of *sorry*

Where complementation of adjectives is found, the complement types are drawn from a general resource, yet the set of types that accompany a given adjective tend to be exclusive. Even if we take similar [human quality] adjectives such as *happy* and *pleased*, we find considerable overlap in types, particularly with expressions introduced with *about, for, that* and *to*, but, unlike *sorry*, *happy* and *pleased* may also be complemented by *with*. If we compare this complementation potential with that of the performative verb *apologise*, we find that the only clear overlap is with expressions introduced by *for*, as illustrated in (5) and (6).

(5)   *I'm sorry for any inconvenience caused.*

(6)   *I apologise for any inconvenience caused.*

We cannot, however, take the range of structures that may complement adjectives and verbs as purely formal attributes of the items in question. The complementation, in the case of *sorry*, is the location of the expression of the 'offence', and the grammatical variation available enables the speaker to select how to present the offence. The offences which give rise to apologies (see Deutschmann 2003: 64 for a categorisation)

are typically past, present or future actions or a failure to perform them. They are essentially events (or 'situations' within the Cardiff Grammar). Situations are congruently realised by clauses, but can be expressed as nominal groups, through the process
of nominalisation. Alternatively, the nominal group may represent some relevant
element(s) of the situation, as in (8) below. Speakers thus, in the first instance, have the
choice of specifying the offence situation congruently, expressing it as if it were a thing,
or focusing on some entity that participates in the situation, as shown in (7) and (8).

(7)   *Sorry about having to rush off like this.* (BNC)

(8)   *Sorry about the noise and the mosquitoes.* (BNC)

Secondly they have a (limited) choice in how the expression of sorrow (*I'm sorry*) is
logically related to the offence. This is achieved through the choice of preposition/con-
junction, where *sorry for* can be glossed as a more genuine expression of regret and
responsibility for it, and where *sorry about* can be glossed as providing the subject matter domain of the regret, namely the offence. Although *sorry for* and *sorry about* are
difficult to tease apart semantically, some indication of the possible sense of *sorry for* is
given by the fact the same preposition almost exclusively introduces the 'offence' with
the performative verb *apologise*.

Thirdly, the grammar provides for the expression of different perspectives on the
event, as congruently expressed, in term of finite or non-finite clauses, as shown in
Figure 6, where the original BNC example is shown alongside fabricated examples using alternative clausal forms.

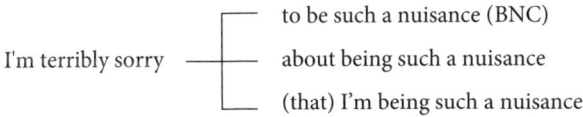

I'm terribly sorry
— to be such a nuisance (BNC)
— about being such a nuisance
— (that) I'm being such a nuisance

Figure 6. Variants in the clausal complementation potential of *sorry*

4.3   *Sorry but/sorry if*

Two sequences that occur significantly in corpus data are *sorry* followed by an *if*-clause
or by a co-ordinated clause introduced by *but*. Neither of these constructions after
sorry is a strict complementation of the adjective. Rather, the *if*-clause is either to be
treated as a dependent β clause in a clause complex (Halliday and Matthiessen 2004:
363ff) or as a dependent clause at Adjunct in the matrix clause (see Fawcett 2000: 271),
and the *but* clause is simply a paratactic, co-ordinated clause.

Again, it should be remembered that both types of clause, and the meanings they
realise, are part of the general resource, even though quite clearly the strong co-occurrence relationship between them and *sorry* gives them a particular significance in this
context and requires explanation.

4.4   Modification of *sorry*

Sorrow, or the expression of regret, is clearly susceptible of gradation. In traditional terms, *sorry* is a gradable adjective. As a term for the expression of regret, *sorry* may be seen to be minimally or maximally intensified, as shown in (9) – (11), although most attested examples of *quite sorry* seem to carry the interpretation of absoluteness, as in *quite right*, rather than a small degree, as in *quite good.*

> (9)   *I was quite sorry to have to say goodbye to some of my pupils.* (BNC)

> (10)   *I shall be extremely sorry to see it leave.* (BNC)

> (11)   *I felt a little sorry for the old fellow.* (BNC)

Whatever the interpretation of *quite*, however, it does not co-occur with *sorry* in the apology sense. Whilst a speaker may feel and express a modicum of regret for some event, as in (11), where he or she has no responsibility for it, the expression of a minimal feeling of regret in an apology presumably comes across to the addressee, to whom the apology is directed, as less than a whole-hearted one, to the extent that, thus expressed, no real apology will be deemed to have taken place.

A cautionary note is necessary here in respect of corpus data. As Deutschmann observes in his study of the spoken sub-corpus of the BNC, surprisingly few examples of intensifiers are found with apologies (Deutschmann 2003: 56).He also notes that previous studies by Aijmer (1996) and Owen (1983) claim higher percentages of intensification, and he hypothesises that this may be a result of changes in modern English, with 'hyperpolite forms' becoming less frequent. This would seem to be borne out to some extent by the increased number and range of intensifiers found in the BNC overall. Here we find not only the common degree temperers (intensifiers) *so* and *very*, but also a good number of examples of *terribly, dreadfully, awfully, really* and *tremendously*. Whilst it is clear that many of these are found in apologies, when the BNC source texts are examined, the most common context is dialogue in novels or imaginative writing.

What then do we conclude about the overall resource for tempering? Evidence based strictly on authentic spoken corpus data suggests that it is rare and limited, whereas in the novelist's conception, tempering is more common and more varied. One might be tempted to suggest that novelists, or at least the range of novelists represented in the BNC for example, are reflecting their intuitions of what is possible, perhaps in social contexts where 'hyperpolite forms' are required. Arguably a dedicated corpus of spoken English, based upon a given social milieu, perhaps with speakers of a given age, might well reveal a greater richness of 'hyperpolite' intensification. Exclusion of such forms (and meanings) might well reflect the general tendencies in spoken English, but would not at the same time reflect the overall potential. Further spoken data collection, across a wider range of social contexts, is likely to confirm the use of such intensifiers, although their inclusion in the overall grammatical resource will need to be accompanied by probabilistic statements, determined by the social contexts in question. The concept of probabilistic grammar is not new. Corpus-based research by Biber and collaborators reflects the relative probabilistic nature of grammatical constructions across genres (e.g. Biber et al. 1999) and systemic functional grammars – in particular the Cardiff Grammar – make use of probabilities on features within systems, both to reflect overall tendencies and those appertaining to given contexts (see Halliday 1991 and Fawcett et al. 1993). This issue will be further addressed in Section 5.

In systemic functional appraisal theory, intensification is explained in terms of 'amplification' (Martin 2000: 148) through which speakers raise or lower the interpersonal impact, force or volume of their utterances. Thus, *sorry* realises the speaker's affect which is then further graduated or amplified by the selection of an intensifier.

4.5 Presence of Subject + Finite with *sorry*

If we take *I'm/ I am sorry* as an elaboration of formulaic *sorry*, rather than taking the bare adjective as a reduction of the clausal form, then we must account for this elaboration. Formulaically and ritualistically, *sorry* is interpreted as an apology, whereby the apologiser is taken to be the performer (*I*). The utterance of the apology in terms of a finite clause containing an explicit Subject and the relational process in its present tense form (*am/are*) makes these two clausal elements salient. The presence of the performer pronominal form can be seen to provide clear self-identity on the part of the 'offender/apologiser', particularly as with bare *sorry* it is implicitly understood. The presence of the finite verbal form firstly gives a proposition "a point of reference in the here and now" (Halliday and Matthiessen 2004: 115), which makes explicit its immediacy. The non-reduced variant, *I am sorry*, further provides for constrastive emphasis, typically accompanied by tonic stress on *am*, thus signalling its positive rather than its negative polarity. Once again, these emphases are made explicit, rather than being left implicit in the formulaic utterance *sorry*.

4.6 Presence of the Vocative

Again, in the case of bare, formulaic *sorry*, the offended participant is left implicit. The assumption is that one addresses an apology to the recipient of the offence, namely, the addressee. The naming of the addressed, offended participant by means of a vocative can therefore be seen as an explicit, on-the-record recognition of his or her identity as such. Furthermore, it enables to speaker to mark the social status of the addressee, as in *sir, my friends, Mr Smith*, etc. The expression of a vocative is clearly not exclusive to apologies, and its selection draws on the general grammatical resource. The Cardiff Grammar allows for a Vocative element of structure (V) in various positions within the clause. However, the Vocative is also found with bare *sorry*, as in (12).

(12)   *Sorry, darling.* (BNC)

If we are not to consider all instances of bare *sorry* as elliptical, we must posit a partial grammar solution to the combination of *sorry* + vocative, or treat them as two independent co-occurring formulaic expressions, realised outside the domain of an organisational grammar.

4.7   The status of non-clausal expressions

With the exception of the choice of an explicit Subject + Finite Operator, as in *I'm sorry*, all realisations discussed above and represented in the system network in Figure 7 in Section 5 are non-clausal expressions, precisely in the sense that they have no Subject nor Finite Operator. They are all, including bare *sorry*, as will be made clear in Section 5, susceptible of treatment in terms of ellipsis, or better, non-realisation. We have already suggested that bare *sorry* may be treated as a formulaic element directly realising an apology, without reference to the grammar. Grammars, however, tend to be clause-based, in the sense that smaller units, such as nominal, adjectival and prepositional groups, are treated as constituents of clauses, rather than as independent, freestanding units. Yet, unless we are to posit full clausal ellipsis for all non-clausal expressions centred on *sorry*, it may be appropriate to recognise a degree of modularity in the grammar, in that language users may draw on the grammar of smaller units without reference to their constituency in the clause. This is also suggested by Halliday in his treatment of 'absolute' nominal groups found, for example in "headlines, labels, lists and suchlike", where their relationship to the clause in terms of Subject or Complement cannot be ascertained with certainty (Halliday and Matthiessen 2004: 154). This is the partial grammar referred to above, where the speaker 'dips into' the grammar of the adjectival group, in the case of *sorry*, as a self-standing grammar[6].

5.   The grammatical resource summarised

On the basis of the grammatical potential, we are able to model the variants of formulaic *sorry* as shown in Figure 7. The system network contains the four systems, the options in which were discussed above, namely PERFORMER, ADDRESSEE, SOURCE, REASON and DEGREE. Each system has an [unspecified] option which if selected, results in the bare formulaic realisation *sorry*. The selection of [specified] in each system would result in a realisation such as (13).

(13)   *I'm so terribly sorry to have to leave, Mary, but I'm needed back in London.*

---

6.   This proposal is made easier by the fact that English is not generally marked for case. The particular case that is assigned to 'absolutes' in languages such as Russian, German and Finnish, may weaken the claim.

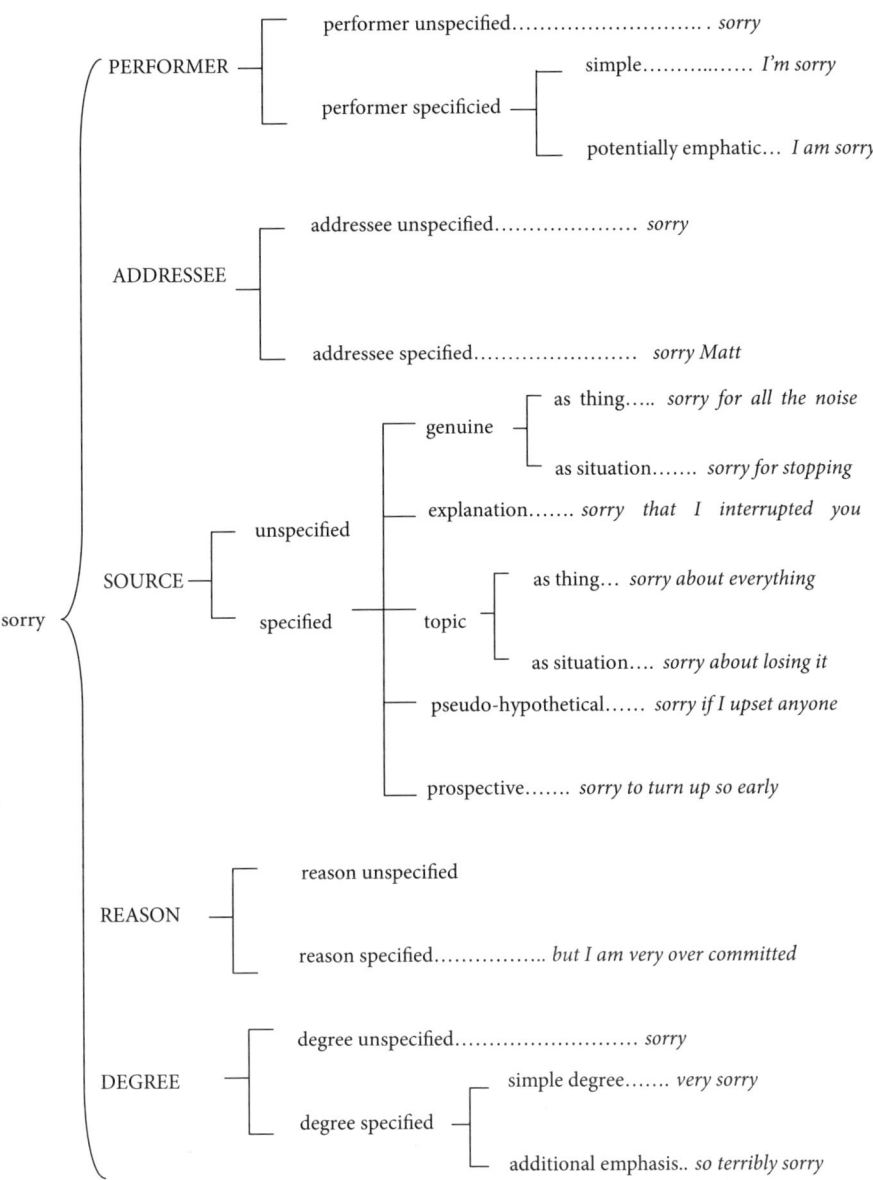

Figure 7. The overall resource for apologising with *sorry*

But what is the nature of the options represented in this network? As it stands, it is a specification of the potential centred around the lexical item *sorry*, and specifically in terms of its apology sense. The various systems are grammatically oriented, since the features specify options in meaning that are realised by elements of clause and group structure. Yet this is at odds with the system network approach within SFG, and particularly within the Cardiff Grammar, which incorporates lexically realised meanings into the grammar. In Tucker's (1998) discussion of the grammar of adjectivally realised meaning, the entry condition feature [sorry] results from selection within the system network for QUALITY, giving rise to realisations through the adjectival group. In this network, only the grammar directly dependent on the selection of the sense [sorry] is specified, which concerns its tempering (intensification) and the scope (complementation) potential. The only corresponding systems in the network in Figure 7 will be SOURCE and DEGREE, and even here the option [pseudo-hypothetical] is misplaced, since *if*-clauses are not generated in the QUALITY network, but in the SITUATION network in terms of a dependent clause realising the matrix clause element of Adjunct, as shown in Figure 8.

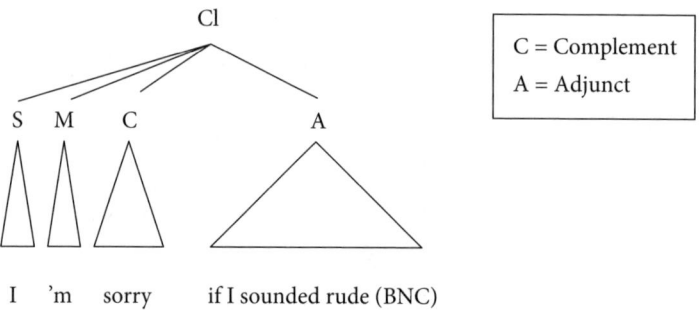

Figure 8. Cardiff Grammar analysis of an *if*-clause in an apology with *sorry*

The ADDRESSEE, PERFORMER and REASON systems also concern grammatical realisation at clause level. Subject and Main verb (*I am*) are clause elements, as is the vocative, and *but*-clauses involve co-ordination again at the clause level.

What is represented in Figure 7 is the grammatically realised semantic potential that is available in contexts where the speaker wishes to apologise with the item *sorry*. And this is only a part of the wider potential for apologising, as was shown schematically in Figure 2.

The fuller resource shown in Figure 7 is at least at one remove from the grammatical system network. And whilst it is organised on a grammatically oriented view of the options, the range of expressions that it covers are far from being closely related grammatically. To begin with, as we have seen, it includes the bare, formulaic single and multiple item utterances such as *sorry, I beg your pardon, pardon me, excuse me,* the grammatical status of which, in terms of their relationship to the clause, may be unclear. And whilst *I'm very sorry....* and *that was really silly of me* are both fully clausal in nature, they arise from the choice of very different options within the clause. The relationship between all realisations, formulaic or not, is that they are 'ways of doing' an apology, and as they exploit the general grammatical/semantic potential, they represent different 'ways of meaning'. They also tap into the lexical resource: the interpersonal construal of *sorry*, for example, exploits the lexical resource for expressing affect, as a category within appraisal theory (Martin 2000: 148ff). Similarly the choice of *silly* in the indirect apology *that was really silly of me* exploits the appraisal category of judgement in terms of social esteem (Martin 2000: 155ff). The verbal process *apologise*, on the other hand, exploits the lexis and grammar of performing the act of apology.

One question that arises, within SFG, is whether or not this kind of network can be considered to be a 'semantic network' as proposed primarily by Halliday (1973) and Hasan (1996). It might also seem to qualify as such under Halliday's (1973: 76) formulation, as given below.

> A semantic network is hypothesis about patterns of meaning, and in order to be valid it must satisfy three requirements. It has to account for the range of alternatives at the semantic stratum itself: and it has to relate these both 'upwards', in this instance to the categories of some general social theory or theory of behaviour, and 'downwards', to the categories of linguistic form at the stratum of grammar. (Halliday 1973: 76)

However, as Hasan points out:

> Halliday's semantic network is, thus, not an attempt to represent the meaning potential of a language in general terms; the meanings represented there may be described as crucial to a specific register; they are thus meanings that I have referred to as 'register specific meaning potential'. (Hasan 1996: 114)

The network for apologising does satisfy Halliday's formulation in that it accounts for the range of alternatives both downwards to grammatical realisation and upwards to part of a theory of behaviour, to the extent that apologising can be seen as a category of social behaviour within a context of culture. Yet, as it stands, it is not register-specific in Halliday's sense, but a '*contextually open* semantic system network' (original emphasis), that Hasan argues for, as the goal of semantic description (Hasan 1996:115). The options in the network in Figure 7 may correspond to different registers; we have already noted that instances of intensification such as *terribly sorry/dreadfully sorry* correspond, as Deutschmann puts it, to expressions associated with 'hyperpoliteness' (Deutschmann 2003: 56). Yet all such options are contained within the overall, generalised network. And, indeed, as has been pointed out, it is possible to relate the generality or universality of the various options to social contexts through the use of probabilities on options.

But let us return to the source of the network, that is, corpus data. If the locutionary acts which realise the illocutionary acts of apologising are potentially manifold, taking into account indirect acts, apologies exhibit strong tendencies to select the range of options represented in the network. In one sense, therefore, the network models the guidelines for conventional apologising.

Whilst contextually determined conditions or rules allow the hearer to interpret an utterance, however formulated, as a particular kind of speech act, at the same time, conventionality intervenes and provides speakers with generally acceptable, and importantly strongly formulaic, ways of performing the act in question. Put another way, speakers learn which options in the general meaning potential that the overall grammar represents are typically and conventionally drawn upon to perform a given speech act. And one of the consequences of this is strong formulaicity, as exemplified by *sorry* in the case of apologising.

In Halliday's terms, apologising is an option in the behaviour potential in the social context (Halliday 1973: 55). It is clearly not the only option when some form of offence has been perceived to have been committed, since the 'offender' may deem that no apology is necessary and can opt to remain silent or explain (away) the event that has given rise to the offence. If, however, the offender recognises the need to apologise, he or she will have to decide upon one of a number of possible strategies, as discussed by Aijmer (1996: 83) in terms of categories such as 'explicit' and 'implicit', both with subtypes 'emotional' and 'non-emotional'. The adoption of any given strategy will depend on a number of factors, including the nature of the offence, the degree of regret to be signalled, whether the apology involves an offence already committed or anticipates one that will be. Furthermore the degree to which the offence is face-threatening. All these factors are discussed in depth by Aijmer (1996).

As it stands, the network in Figure 7 represents only the expression potential in terms of *sorry* and the various options therein in terms of grammar-based categories. System networks, as formalisms representing choice, do not provide external, pragmatic motivation for one choice rather than another; they simply represent the options that are available. For example, the bottom-most system in Figure 7, the system for DEGREE, as we have seen, concerns the potential to amplify the degree of regret to be expressed. The motivation for choice here may be determined by such factors as the seriousness of the offence, the offender's need to show more or less contrition and also the degree to which, in certain social contexts, the 'hyperpolite' expression is conventionally required, as Deutschmann suggests. The system network in Figure 7 is therefore located somewhere between the speaker's goals and intentions and the grammatical resource that allows these goals and intentions to be reflected in the utterance.

Each option must correspond (a) to a set of socio-interactive and pragmatic considerations and (b) the general grammatical resource. What the system network does is limit the application of the general grammatical resource. As Deutschmann's corpus-based research shows, there is a strong likelihood of either no intensification of *sorry* or a limited set of intensifiers. The COBUILD Bank of English, for example, gives one citation of *sorry* intensified by *slightly,* as shown in (14).

(14)   *feeling irritated and slightly sorry for himself.* (COBUILD)

Whilst *slightly* is a possible intensifier of *sorry* in the sense intended above, it is clearly not available in terms of the expression of regret for an offence caused. It is therefore plausible to posit the kind of system network in Figure 7 as a constraining input into the grammatical resource. The consequence of choice in this network is a re-configuring of available options in the system network representing the general grammatical resource. This is achieved by the assignment of probabilities on the options available. Probabilities do not, of course, impose a particular option, unless this option is ruled out in a given context by the assignment of 0% (see [slightly] in Figure 9 below). If they can be translated into some aspect of the language user's mind, they represent the expectations that certain choices are more or less likely in a given context, which reflects the user's experience of and exposure to language in the course of his or her social interaction.

We can represent probabilities schematically as in Figure 9, where those assigned here are tentative and illustrative, and based loosely on corpus findings[7].

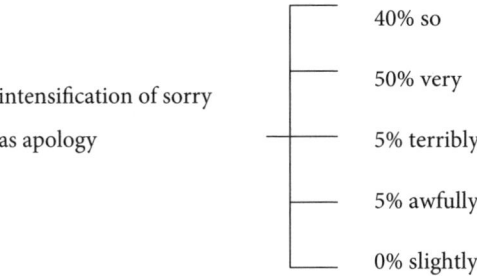

Figure 9. The assignment of probabilities to intensifiers of *sorry* as apology

We can now see a link between the kind of information modelled in Figure 7 and the various options available in the general grammar. Those original options, e.g. [performer specified], [purpose], [degree specified] etc. serve to guide the speaker into the relevant parts of the grammatical system network. The available set of options for intensifying *sorry*, for example, can now be presented as in Figure 9, rather than as they would be in respect of the intensifying potential for this kind of adjective in other contexts. In short, the Figure 7 features pre-determine or partially pre-determine grammatical selection, setting up particular pathways through the system network. Note that this also provides a solution for strongly formulaic and phraseological utterances of all kinds, in that all or most of the grammatical options can be pre-determined from the outset, as a single pathway through the network, thereby constituting a single choice, as claimed by Sinclair in his 'idiom principle' (Sinclair 1987b: 320). This approach to fixed and semi-fixed phraseological expressions is discussed in detail in Tucker (2005) and Tucker (in press).

---

7.   If the probabilities are assigned to features in systems, they must ultimately be established by reference to those tendencies that are attested in language use, which is why corpus evidence is extremely important.

What this approach also provides us with an alternative solution to single, formulaic *sorry* which was anticipated at the end of Section 3, albeit only in the case where a full grammar is available to the language user. Each of the systems in Figure 7 contains an [unspecified] option, which if chosen in each case results in the single item *sorry*. If the grammatical system network is to license the absence of all clause or group elements other than *sorry*, it too must provide options the selection of which result in what may be considered ellipsis. Let us therefore posit a feature [unrealised] in all relevant grammatical systems, in opposition to [realised]. The selection of [unrealised] would have the effect, through the application of the realisation rules that attach to certain features in the network and that are responsible for the structural output, of suppressing the realisation of any elements or constituents that were not required[8]. The selection of the complete set of [unspecified] options in Figure 7 would then pre-determine a corresponding set of obligatory [unrealised] options in the grammatical system network, and result in the sole realisation of *sorry*. The formulaicity of *sorry* is thus represented as a fully determined choice originating in the options in Figure 7.

It remains to be emphasised that such a solution constitutes a purely grammatical perspective on the issue that may or may not have any psycholinguistic validity.

6.   Conclusions

Given the narrow descriptive scope of this chapter, it can only be partially indicative of the range of issues that arise in dealing with speech act formulae and their variants. It has not dealt, for example, with some of the more impenetrable formulae such as *thanks*, *many thanks* and *thanks a lot*, and the extent to which these can be modelled by reference to the grammar. On the other hand, many of the phenomena that emerge in the case of *sorry* in terms of specification of the performer, addressee and intensification, also emerge elsewhere, in formulae such as *pleased to meet you* (Tucker 2005), and further research may indeed reveal a number of significant generalisations.

The discussion here has not touched specifically on the pragmatics of speech act realization, although there is a serious need to relate the various options to social context, in future work in this area. Yet in setting out the options that appear to be selected by language users in realising speech acts and relating these to the general grammatical potential, the kinds of solutions proposed do contribute to a more systematic and integrated approach.

---

8.   Realisation rules in the Cardiff Grammar relate the features in the network to structural and lexical realisation, by means of a set of operations. They place, for example, elements of structure in a unit and associate them with lexical items (exponence) or with other units that 'fill' them, such as an instruction to fill the Subject of a clause with a nominal group. See Fawcett (2000:175) for a full description of the rule types.

Naturally, they are solutions within the architecture of systemic functional grammar, both in structural terms and particularly in terms of the system network formalism for representing choice. Other grammatical theories will need to consider the structural aspects of such phenomena in their own terms, both from the perspective of the syntactic description and the restricted choice of realisation in a given context. It is clear, however, that, if grammatical theory and description is to account for such spoken phenomena, it must be prepared to attend to them.

References

Aijmer, Karin. 1996. *Conversational routines in English: convention and creativity.* London: Longman.

Aston, Guy and Lou Burnard. 1998. *The BNC handbook: Exploring the British National Corpus with SARA.* Edinburgh: Edinburgh University Press.

Biber, Douglas. 1988. *Variation across speech and writing.* Cambridge: Cambridge University Press.

Biber, Douglas, Stig Johansson, Geoffrey Leech, Susan Conrad and Edward Finegan. 1999. *Longman grammar of spoken and written English.* London: Longman.

Blum Kulka, Shoshana, Juliane House and Gabriele Kasper. 1989. *Cross cultural pragmatics: Requests and apologies.* Norwood (NJ): Ablex.

Brazil, David. 1995. *A grammar of speech.* Oxford: Oxford University Press.

Butler, Christopher S. 2003. *Structure and function: A guide to three major structural-functional theories.* Amsterdam: John Benjamins.

Coulmas, Florian (ed.). 1981a. *Conversational routine. Explorations in standardization communication situations and prepatterened speech.* The Hague: Mouton.

Coulmas, Florian. 1981b. "'Poison to your soul'. Thanks and apologies contrastively viewed". *Conversational routine. Explorations in standardization communication situations and prepatterened speech,* ed. by Florian Coulmas, 69–91. The Hague: Mouton.

Deutschmann, Mats. 2003. Apologising in British English. Doctoral dissertation. University of Umeå.

Edmondson, Willis J. 1981. "On saying you're sorry". *Conversational routine. Explorations in standardization communication situations and prepatterened speech,* ed. by Florian Coulmas, 273–288. The Hague: Mouton.

Fawcett, Robin P. 2000. *A theory of syntax for Systemic Functional Linguistics.* Amsterdam: John Benjamins.

Fawcett, Robin P. 1988. "What makes a good system network 'good'?: four pairs of concepts for such evaluations". *Systemic functional approaches to discourse; Selected papers from the 12th International Systemic Functional Workshop,* ed. by James D. Benson and William S. Greaves, 1–28. Norwood, NJ: Ablex.

Fawcett, Robin P., Gordon H. Tucker and Yuen Q. Lin. 1993. "The role of realization in realization: How a systemic grammar works". *From planning to realization in natural language generation,* ed. by Helmut Horacek and Michael Zock, 114–186. London: Pinter.

Goffman, Erving. 1971. *Relations in public: Microstudies of the public order.* London: Penguin.

Halliday, Michael A. K. 1961. "Categories of the theory of grammar". *WORD* 17: 241-292.

Halliday, Michael A. K. 1973. *Explorations in the functions of language.* London: Edward Arnold.

Halliday, Michael A. K. 1991. "Corpus studies and probabilistic grammar". *English corpus linguistics,* ed. by Karin Aijmer and Bengt Altenberg, 30–43. London: Longman.

Halliday, Michael A. K. and Christian M. I. M. Matthiessen. 2004. *An introduction to functional grammar*. 3rd edn. London: Arnold.

Hasan, Ruqaiya. 1996. *Ways of saying: Ways of meaning* (ed. by Carmel Cloran, David Butt and Geoffrey Williams). London: Cassell.

Holmes, Janet. 1990. "Apologies in New Zealand English". *Language and Society* 19(2): 155–199.

Mackenzie, J. Lachlan. 1998. "The basis of syntax in the holophrase". *Functional grammar and verbal interaction*. ed. by Mike Hannay and A. Machtelt Bolkenstein, 267–295. Amsterdam and Philadelphia: John Benjamins.

Martin, James R. 1987. "The meaning of features in systemic linguistics". *New developments in systemic linguistics. Volume 1: Theory and description*, ed. by Michael A. K. Halliday and Robin P. Fawcett, 14–40. London: Pinter.

Martin, James R. 2000. "Beyond exchange: Appraisal systems in English". *Evaluation in text: Authorial stance and the construction of discourse*, ed. by Susan Hunston and Geoff Thompson, 142–175. Oxford: Oxford University Press.

Olshtein, Elite and Andrew Cohen. 1983. "Apology: A speech act set". *Sociolinguistics and language acquisition*, ed. by Nessa Wolfson and Elliot Judd, 18–36. Rowley, MA: Newbury House.

Owen, Marion. 1983. *Apologies and remedial exchanges. A study of language use in social interaction*. Berlin: Mouton.

Sinclair, John McH. (1987a) *Looking up: An account of the COBUILD Project in lexical computing*. London: Collins.

Sinclair, John McH. 1987b. "Collocation: A progress report". *Language topics: Essays in honour of Michael Halliday*, ed. by Ross Steele and Terry Threadgold, 319–332. Amsterdam: John Benjamins.

Tucker, Gordon H. 1998. *The lexicogrammar of adjectives: A systemic functional approach to lexis*. London: Cassell Academic.

Tucker, Gordon H. 2005. "Extending the lexicogrammar: Towards a more comprehensive account of partially clausal and non-clausal expressions". *Language Sciences*, 27(6): 679–709.

Tucker, Gordon H. in press. "Between grammar and lexis: Towards a systemic functional account of phraseology". *Continuing discourse on language: A functional perspective, Volume 2*, ed. by Christian Matthiessen, Ruqaiaya Hasan and Jonathan Webster. London, Equinox.

Wray, Alison. 2002. *Formulaic language and the lexicon*. Cambridge: Cambridge University Press.

The discourse functionality of adjectival and adverbial epistemic expressions

Evidence from present-day English

Anne-Marie Simon-Vandenbergen and Karin Aijmer
Ghent University and Göteborg University

In this article we examine the adjectival and adverbial expressions *it is certain/ certainly, it is clear/clearly* and *it is obvious/obviously* in a corpus of present-day English, the *British National Corpus*. We aim to answer two questions. One is the question of how the constructional properties of the adjectival expressions create specific behavioural properties which are different from those of the adverbs. The second question is how the adjectival expressions are used rhetorically and how their discourse functionality differs from that of the corresponding adverbial expressions. Starting out from Nuyts' (2001) criteria, 'intersubjectivity', 'salience', 'performativity' and 'discourse strategy', we examine the extent to which the data confirm the relevance of these factors. We show that the reasons why speakers opt for adjectival or adverbial expressions are complex and that an explanation cannot limit itself to a single factor.

1. Introduction

The similarities and differences between adjectival and adverbial epistemic expressions have been discussed extensively by Nuyts (1993; 2001). By adjectival expressions we mean the impersonal constructions in which adjectives are used predicatively, such as *it is possible/probable/certain*, in contrast with *possibly/probably/certainly*. Starting from Nuyts' research and findings, which are based mainly on Dutch and German corpus data, this paper examines to what extent the behavioural properties of the adjectival construction as established by Nuyts apply to the English expressions as they occur in a corpus of present-day English, the *British National Corpus*. We shall limit ourselves to just three expressions of certainty, viz. *it is certain/certainly, it is clear/clearly, it is obvious/obviously*. We aim to answer two questions. One is the question of how the constructional properties of the adjectival expressions create specific behavioural possibilities which are different from those of adverbs, and how these determine their semantic properties. The second question is how these expressions are used rhetorically and how their discourse functionality differs from that of the corresponding adverbial expressions.

We shall first sketchily survey the behavioural properties of adjectival epistemic expressions as discussed in Nuyts (1993; 2001). We will then focus on the three expressions *it is certain/obvious/clear*, explain why these three have been selected for exploration, and study their usage in the corpus data. Finally a comparison with the adverbial counterparts is made.

2.   The behavioural properties of adjectival epistemic constructions

Nuyts (2001) critically examines previous accounts of the differences between adjectival and adverbial epistemic constructions (such as Bellert 1977; Lang 1979; Kiefer 1984; Perkins 1984; Hengeveld 1988), which have focused on syntactic properties and restrictions and have explained the semantic differences in terms of subjectivity and objectivity. As Nuyts gives a thorough and convincing analysis of the argumentation in the literature, we shall not repeat it here. We shall take Nuyts' conclusions as the starting point of our own analysis. These conclusions can be summed up as follows.

Firstly, the expressions differ from each other with regard to (inter)subjectivity. Nuyts distinguishes between what he calls 'subjective' and 'intersubjective' orientations. The former means that the epistemic expression signals the speaker's individual subjective evaluation of the state of affairs, while the latter involves an evaluation presented as shared with others. Nuyts demonstrates with corpus examples from Dutch and German that adverbs are neutral in this respect, i.e. that they occur in contexts in which there is "no suggestion whatsoever as to whether the epistemic evaluation is subjective or intersubjective" (2001: 66). In contrast, the adjectival constructions show a strong tendency towards intersubjectivity[1]. They tend to occur most frequently in contexts which favour such intersubjective evaluations, notably in scientific discourse.

Secondly, the factor performativity distinguishes adverbs from adjectival constructions. By 'performativity' Nuyts means the characteristic of "involving a personal commitment of the speaker" (2001: 62, note 5). Performative qualifications are to be distinguished from descriptive ones. Thus an utterance such as *They have probably run out of fuel* inherently implies the speaker's own commitment to the epistemic qualification, while *It was probable that they had run out of fuel* does not. Modal adverbs are said to be necessarily performative, while adjectival expressions can be descriptive.

---

1.   Nuyts uses the term 'evidentiality' in this context, claiming that modal adjectives "systematically involve an additional evidential meaning" (2001: 66). We prefer not to use the term 'evidentiality' here because of the confusion it may create. The relationship between modality and evidentiality in languages such as English which have no grammatical evidentials is complex and cannot be taken for granted. We feel that any position taken in this respect needs to be argued for in ways which are beyond the scope of the present paper.

Note, however, that even adjectives tend to be used in contexts where the speaker shares the evaluation "but does not consider this fact crucial for the ongoing discourse" (Nuyts 2001: 73).

Thirdly, the most important factor distinguishing between the expressions is salience. While adverbs cannot be focalized, adjectival expressions are used when the epistemic qualification receives strong focality in the discourse. They are hence more salient. A number of features which have been discussed in the literature as characterising the constructions can in Nuyts' view in fact be explained from this factor. These features include the possibility of being negated, of being used as 'reduced forms' of the type *that is probable*, the possibility of being in contrast with an alternative qualification, the possibility of being questioned. It appears that on all these features adjectives display focality, in contrast with adverbs, which tend to occupy non-central slots in the information structure.

The fourth factor which may be relevant for the distinction between the expressions is discourse strategy. However, Nuyts is very brief on this aspect, claiming that "[t]here are no occurrences in the corpus data" in which Dutch *waarschijnlijk* or German *wahrscheinlich* (both of which can be used as adverbs and as adjectives) "are manifestly used by the speaker to achieve any specific type of special effect in discourse" (2001: 101). This factor, Nuyts argues, is likely to be more strongly bound to individual lexical items than to the constructions themselves, and he concludes that "[a]ny further claims in this connection will therefore require additional investigation" (2001: 101). We shall pay attention to this factor in the present paper.

The factors '(inter)subjectivity', 'performativity', 'salience' and 'discourse strategy' will be examined in the following sections as they apply to the expressions of certainty.

3.   The data in this paper

A frequency count of adverbs which express a high degree of epistemic certainty reveals that of those adverbs which have an adjectival counterpart (thus excluding such adverbs as *of course* and *indeed*), the most frequent ones are *certainly, clearly, obviously,* and *surely*. Table 1 gives the rough frequencies in various corpora[2].

---

2.   The corpora excerpted are the *British National Corpus* (*BNC*), the *Bergen Corpus of London Teenage Language* (*COLT*), the *Lancaster Oslo/Bergen Corpus* (*LOB*), the *Wellington Spoken Corpus* (*WSC*) and the *Wellington Corpus* (*WC*). The versions used are those on the ICAME Collection of English Language Data. The *BNC* (100 million words in all) contains 10 million words of spoken English and 90% written data made up of informative and imaginative prose, the *COLT* Corpus (which is part of *BNC*) consists of conversations among teenagers in the London boroughs (see further www.hd.uib.no/colt/), *WSC* is a corpus of informal conversations representing New Zealand English, complementing the corpus of written New Zealand English and *LOB* consists of British English written texts. (For more information on the corpora see Kennedy 1998).

Table 1. Adverbs of certainty in corpora of English

Adverb	BNC (100m.)	COLT (500,000)	LOB (1m.)	WSC (1m.)	WC (1m.)
certainly	18,626	16	235	197	169
clearly	15,322 (8,274)	10	122	32	157
obviously	10,977	64	121	204	91
surely	6,340	7	123	38	73
definitely	3,121	43	22	137	26
inevitably	3,090	1	45	8	34
evidently	1,467	0	30	7	12
plainly	745	0	20	3	4

Table 2. Relative frequencies of the adverbs of certainty

Adverb	BNC	COLT	LOB	WSC	WC
certainly	31% (35%)	11%	33%	31%	30%
clearly	26 % (16%)	7%	17%	5%	28%
obviously	18 % (21%)	45%	17%	33%	16%
surely	11% (12%)	5%	17%	6%	13%
definitely	5% (6%)	30%	3%	22%	5%
inevitably	5% (6%)	1%	6%	1%	6%
evidently	2% (3%)		4%	1%	2%
plainly	2% (3%)		3%	0%	1%
Total	59,688 (52,640)	141	718	626	566
	100%	100%	100%	100%	100%

It should be noted that the frequencies represent all uses of the adverbs. In the case of *clearly* it is especially important, however, to separate the manner adverb from the modal one. In a *BNC* sample of 150 instances of *clearly*, 69 were manner adverb instances (i.e. 46%). If we take this as indicative of the proportion, the frequency of modal *clearly* is perhaps closer to 8,274 (the figure in brackets in Table 1) in the corpus as a whole.

Table 1 shows that the relative frequency of the adverbs differs considerably from corpus to corpus, and that it seems to correlate with speech vs. writing. *Clearly* is infrequent in spoken language (*COLT, WSC*), while *definitely* increases in speech. Teenagers seem to have a preference for *obviously*, which is four times as frequent as *certainly*. Table 2 gives the relative frequency of these eight adverbs in the same corpora. Percentages are rounded off to the nearest digit. In the *BNC* column the first percentages are based on the frequencies as given in Table 1. The figures in brackets give the percentages based on the extrapolated 8,274 instances of *clearly*. The figures in bold are the highest percentages within each of the corpora.

The differences in relative frequencies raise many questions about register, age-related as well as regional variation, which we cannot go into in this paper. What is interesting in the present context is how these frequencies compare with the adjectival structures. Table 3 gives an overview. Note that contracted and non-contracted forms are here taken together.

Table 3. Frequencies of the adjectival expressions in the corpora

Adjective	BNC	COLT	LOB	WSC	WC
it is/it's certain	112 (4%)	0	5 (12%)	1	1
it is/it's clear	1923 (**64%**)	1	16 (**39%**)	10 (**59%**)	19 (**59%**)
it is/it's obvious	457 (15%)	2	9 (22%)	4 (24%)	6 (19%)
it is/it's sure	23 (1%)	0	0	0	2
it is/it's definite	3	0	0	0	0
it is/it's inevitable	136 (5%)	0	3	1	2
it is/it's evident	243 (8%)	0	8 (20%)	0	1
it is/it's plain	89 (3%)	0	0	1	1
Total	2986	3	41	17	32

There are some striking differences between the relative frequencies of adverbs and corresponding adjectival expressions which emerge from Tables 2 and 3. In general, adverbs appear to be much more frequent than adjectival expressions. This is also what Nuyts found (1993: 937). Table 4 compares the figures.

Further, these relative frequencies appear to be different for the individual pairs. In the *BNC*, we get a proportion of 99% for *certainly*, 96% for *obviously* and 89% for *clearly*.[3] Further, while *certainly* is by far the most frequent adverb (except in teenage talk), *it is certain* is rather infrequent. The most frequent adjectival expression is *it is clear*, followed by *it is obvious*. This reversal of relative importance signals that adver-

---

3.   Note that in the case of the *surely/it is sure* pair, the adverb accounts for 99.63%. The specific functions that this adverb has developed, as described by Downing (2001) are responsible for this discrepancy. On the other hand it should be noted that the closest correspondence to *surely* is *I am sure* rather than *it is sure*.

bial and adjectival constructions are not just alternative ways of saying the same thing. If the difference were solely to be ascribed to the behavioural properties of the constructions as such, we would expect a parallel distribution in the corpora. What seems plausible, however, is that over and above the factors of (inter)subjectivity, salience, and performativity, which predictably apply in the same ways for the three item pairs, the factor discourse strategy accounts for rhetorical uses of the expressions which are specific to the individual lexical items. For example, we may expect the high frequency of *certainly* to be the result of certain uses of the adverb which are not shared by the adjectival expression. Further, there seems to be a scale of descending discrepancy between adverbial and adjectival frequencies, in the sense that the difference is greatest for *surely/it is sure* (i.e. the difference in frequency of adverb and adjective is largest), followed by the pair *certainly/it is certain,* while the difference in frequency is much smaller for the pair *obviously/it is obvious* and even fairly small in the case of the pair *clearly/it is clear*. This also needs to be accounted for.

Table 4. Relative frequencies of adverbs and adjectival expressions

	BNC	*COLT*	*LOB*	*WSC*	*WC*
Adverb					
n	59688	141	718	626	566
relative frequency	95%	98%	95%	97%	95%
Adjective					
n	2986	3	41	17	32
relative frequency	5%	2%	5%	3%	5%
Total (100%)	62674	144	759	643	598

In the following sections we shall first take a closer look at the adjectival expressions, and then compare their discourse uses with those of the corresponding adverbs. For the analysis, 100 instances of *it is certain, it is clear, it is obvious* were selected at random from the *BNC* data. The same number was taken for the contracted forms *it's obvious* and *it's clear*. Strikingly, only 13 occurrences were found of *it's certain*. These samples still contained some irrelevant instances, such as the following:

(1) The *general feel of this unintimidating textbook is that <u>it is certain to</u> inspire such a student with confidence. (CLL: written/ELT promotional leaflet)*: certain followed by a to-infinitive

(2) *This accounts for over 70 per cent of the combined reduction in annual surpluses, so if revenues fail to grow <u>it is obvious where</u> the axe will have to fall. (BN9: written/non-fiction)*: obvious followed by wh-interrogative clause

After weeding out the non-relevant cases this left us with the following numbers of examples which were studied in detail:

Table 5. Sub-sample from the *BNC* adjectival expressions

it is certain	92
it's certain	6
it is clear	94
it's clear	73
it is obvious	95
it's obvious	94

4. The factor (inter)subjectivity

Nuyts' finding (1993; 2001) was that adjectival expressions tend to convey an epistemic evaluation which is 'intersubjective', i.e. shared by others. Our data strongly support this view. The default case is that where the epistemic certainty is presented as based on indisputable evidence, either implicitly or explicitly. Example (3) is prototypical:

(3) I *don't think anyone is sure what happened to cause it, but **it is certain** that one aircraft loaded with incendiaries started to burn and the fire spread to the tow aircraft on either side. (B3F: written/non-fiction)*

The certainty in the second clause is not only in the speaker/writer's own mind but the result of evidence which is left unmentioned in this sentence. In the case of *certain* the evidence is typically 'reasoning' and is expressed in a clause of reason, which gives the warrant for the claim, as in (4–6):

(4) <u>As</u> *his reputation for making commemorative seats is well known in the area, **it is certain** he will quickly find a ready market for his work.(BM4: written/non-fiction/newspapers)*

(5) **It is certain** *that the Leapors would have been aware of the changes going on around them, <u>especially since</u> Philip Leapor would have been hired for landscaping projects. (AN4: written/non-fiction)*

(6) *However, for every successful adoption of a new crop or new variety of crop **it is certain** that there were many more failed attempts at innovation, <u>for</u> the African physical environment places many difficulties in the path of farmers. (A6M: written/non-fiction)*

The examples show, however, that the reasoning is added because the proposition qualified by *it is certain* is in fact the speaker's deduction, and is a kind of 'reasonable certainty' rather than one based on hard indisputable evidence. The use of the modals *will* and *would* in examples (4) and (5) expresses a hypothetical certainty rather than a factual one. In (6) also, the 'failed attempts' can only be deduced as a reasonable certainty based on the fact in the *for*-clause. In a few cases there is explicit concrete evidence with *certain*:

(7)   **It is certain** *from the size of some Chinese jade artefacts* that larger blocks were being quarried, probably in the region of Yarkand, from the sixteenth century. (FBA: written/non-fiction)

(8)   But **it is certain** *from several pieces of evidence* that they stayed on under the new management, as distinct ethnic groups, surviving until and beyond the Macedonian takeover in 331. (FBB: written/non-fiction)

What we see then is that the addition of the source of evidence has the dual effect of strengthening the speaker/writer's assessment of certainty and weakening it into a marker of 'reasonable certainty' which is in need of defence against alternative viewpoints.

In the case of *obvious* and *clear*, explicit mention of the evidential source is very frequent: in one third of the cases the evidence for the claim is mentioned. Some examples:

(9)   *These source rocks are the peridotites, and since geophysics tells us that the mantle consists of the same kind of material all over the world,* **it's clear** *that melting part of the mantle beneath Hawaii should produce the same kinds of rocks as those produced by melting part of the mantle beneath Iceland.* (ASR: written/ non-fiction)

(10)   *Nevertheless* **it is clear** *from the report* *that the committee took into account identified causes of indiscipline in schools in producing their recommendations.* (AN5: written/non-fiction)

(11)   *From the evidence presented above* **it is clear** *that there may be doubts about the designation of the term 'villa' for some of the buildings in the countryside.* (EB7: written/non-fiction)

(12)   *On the other hand,* **it is obvious** *from the appointments made* *that the strength of a candidate's convictions, including his political opinions, is not considered a disadvantage.* (FRT: written/non-fiction)

(13)   *Since two different groups of headlines appear in E (the last sheet but three)* **it is obvious** *that an interruption occurred while E was printing.* (GWM: written/ non-fiction)

(14)   **It is obvious,** *by the very nature of things,* *that the Scottish national party could win all 72 seats in Scotland and not have a majority in the House.* (HHX: written/non-fiction)

The inherent evidential nature of *it is clear* and *it is obvious* is thrown into focus when there is reference to empirical evidence or simply to visual perception:

(15) *From watching raindrops, bubbles and insects walking on ponds* **it is obvious** that water and other liquids have a surface tension. *(CEG: written/non-fiction)*

The perception may also be metaphorical, as in (16–19):

(16) But **it's obvious** *from a quick glance* that that plan that in fact a number of those settlements are already coalescing ...*(J9S: spoken/public meeting)*

(17) *If you look at what's happening to British cinema over the last 10 years or so,* then **it's clear** that it has tended to be production-led ... *(A4S: written/non-fiction/newspapers)*

(18) *Looking back,* **it's clear** that Cave has always been obsessed with this latent other within each individual, ...*(AB3: written/non-fiction)*

(19) And **it's clear,** *we're seeing already,* that Health Authorities haven't got the money to refer patients to the Trusts unless the Government steps in ... *(JJD: spoken/public/institutional/debate)*

In other cases the evidence is of a rational nature:

(20) **It's obvious** *when you come to think about it.* *(CGV: written/non-fiction)*

(21) *With the wisdom of hindsight* **it's obvious** that ... *(CHV: written/non-fiction)*

(22) And **it's obvious,** *once you've thought about it.* *(FMR: spoken/educational/informative/tutorial lesson)*

(23) **It's obvious,** *as soon as you start to think about it;* *(HJH: written/fiction)*

(24) *Given the anomalous circumstances of Germany,* **it is clear** that there needs to be some form of general realignment within the ERM. *(AKJ: written/non-fiction/newspapers)*

(25) In effect, *since socialisation is present as part of all social relationships* (...) **it is clear** that it is a much more subtle, complex and pervasive process than it might at first appear ...*(EDH: written/non-fiction)*

In some cases there is explicit mention of 'third persons', which has the effect of emphasising the intersubjective nature of the assessments *it is clear* and *it is obvious*. These 'third persons' are of two types: either specific or generic. Cases where a specific third person is mentioned are discussed in section 4 on performativity. In the case of generic reference, the effect is to present the evaluation as indisputable because it is shared. We shall come back to such instances in section 6 on rhetorical uses. Here are some examples:

(26) *The Profitboss doesn't need to throw a light on himself: he glows with profit achievement already – and* **it's obvious** *for all to see.* *(EW5: written/non-fiction)*

(27) **It's obvious** *to everyone not too blind to see* that such changes are vital to the mounting pressures on the existing system. *(J9J: spoken/public/institutional/meeting)*

(28)   *Because I've spent the last day or so watching you with other people, and frank-ly, Fran,* **it's obvious** <u>to anyone</u> *that when you're with me you act far differently. (JXV: written/fiction)*

There are also examples where the intersubjectivity is emphasised by mentioning that the speaker is only one of many people to whom something is 'obvious':

(29)   *However, if you take characters like Lysander and Demetrius in A Midsummer Night's Dream,* **it's obvious,** <u>even to me,</u> *that it would be ridiculous to try and look for complex psychology and motivation in them. (KRH: spoken/radio broadcast)*

(30)   *I don't think I have been fooled by artefacts, or overinterpreted my findings, though* **it is obvious** <u>even to me, let alone a critical outsider,</u> *that in fitting the data with a temporal cascade I have not formally proved all the necessary bio-chemical links. (G14: written/non-fiction)*

It appears then that the intersubjective reading is the default one for *it is certain/obvi-ous/clear.* It may be emphasised by the addition of the source of evidence (whether rational or empirical) as well as by explicit mention of 'others' whose evaluation is in-volved. However, the intersubjectivity can be overridden by the explicit mention of the speaker as sole evaluator. Such instances are infrequent, and even in such cases the adjectival expression suggests that what is clear/obvious to the speaker can in principle be clear/obvious to others, since the evidence is there for everyone to see:

(31)   **It is obvious** <u>to me</u> *that our branches are part of the main charity. (GXG: writ-ten/non-fiction)*

(32)   *'It's* **clear** <u>to me</u> *that they have to go well beyond the 25,000', said Paine Webber analyst Stephen Smith (CPJ: written/non-fiction)*

(33)   *It's a minefield; certainly Government agencies feel very uncomfortable about it but* <u>to us</u> *it's* **clear** <u>that</u> *TUPE will apply. (HC4: written/non-fiction)*

(34)   *The plethora of adjectives point, again, towards self-dramatisation and* **it is clear** <u>to me now</u> *that I used this device as a means of bearing depression in general. (CEE: written/non-fiction)*

5.   The factor performativity

As pointed out above (section 1), adverbs are necessarily performative, in the sense of expressing the speaker's commitment to the modal qualification, while the adjectival expressions can be used descriptively. It is clear that in some cases the descriptive na-ture is beyond dispute, such as references to past time or to someone else's evaluation (Nuyts 2001: 73). The question is whether the adjectival expressions are always descriptive or not, and Nuyts argues that in fact in most cases they are performative. As we only searched for present tense forms, we restrict the discussion to those cases.

First, there are certain behavioural syntactic properties of the adjectival expressions which correlate with descriptive usage. These include their occurrence in the protasis of conditional utterances (Nuyts 2001: 77). Examples from our data are the following:

(35) *If, by then, **it is obvious** that there is plenty of room to turn back into wind and land, this is the sensible thing to do. (A0H: written/non-fiction)*

(36) *The Code provides that the search should be discontinued if **it is clear** that the goods are not on the premises unless the police have the right to continue the search under different power. (EVK: written/non-fiction)*

Another context which requires a descriptive reading is a time clause in which it is the certainty itself which is temporally qualified. The following instance illustrates this:

(37) *Head-injured patients are normally admitted to hospital and kept there until **it is certain** that they are fully fit to return home. (AS0: written/non-fiction)*

Also in the following instance the adjunct *in two or three days* expresses the time 'when something becomes clear':

(38) *Thus a certain brinkmanship has gone on, with a hospital discharging an elderly person home, ostensibly on trial and then refusing to re-admit when in two or three days **it is clear** the person cannot cope. (CGD: written/non-fiction)*

A similar example is (39):

(39) *But already **it is certain** that the challenges ahead are at least as daunting as anything the Cold war produced. (A87: written/non-fiction/newspapers)*

Another indication of descriptive status is the nature of the question tags. Halliday and Matthiessen (2004: 613–614) point out that in the case of what they call 'metaphors of modality' such as *I think*, the modal status of the expressions is made clear by the fact that the question tags do not repeat the subject of the projecting clause (*I think*) but that of the projected clause (as *I think it can be done, can't it?*). In our data we found tags with *it's obvious* only, and they were of two types, as (40) and (41) illustrate:

(40) ***It's obvious** that you've always gone in for quite stylish displays of your fruit haven't you? (HF3: spoken/leisure/interview)*

(41) *What's a half plus a third? That's no problem, add the top two, add the bottom, its' going to be two fifths. **It's obvious,** isn't it? (KLG: spoken/educational/informative/tutoring session)*

In (40) the speaker asks for the addressee's agreement that he has 'always gone in for quite stylish displays', in (41) agreement is sought on the obviousness. Example (40) therefore qualifies as performative, while (41) is descriptive. If we replace the adjectival expression by the adverb *obviously*, only the tag *haven't you* is possible. Another way of putting this is that in (41) the construction *it's obvious* still has clausal status, while in (40) it has the status of a modal adverb (cf. Boye and Harder, forthcoming, on the status of complement-taking predicates).

Further, there are instances where a specific third person is mentioned who holds the view that something is clear or obvious, as well as cases where the contextual information necessitates a descriptive interpretation. Example (42) exemplifies the former type, example (43) the latter:

(42)   **It is obvious <u>to him</u>** *I am annoyed with myself. (HH0: written/fiction)*

(43)   <u>*From what I put in the papers*</u> **it's obvious** *that we're traders (KC1: spoken/conversation)*

In (43) the context indicates unambiguously that the fact 'that we're traders' should be obvious to the readers of the papers.

In actual fact, however, there are very few cases in which the assessment, even when it is ascribed to others, is not also shared by the speaker. This is also what Nuyts found, who claims that in most contexts "the (past or present) 'implicit agreement' reading is imminent" (2001: 73). Consider the following instances, in which the speaker clearly identifies with the third persons:

(44)   *However, <u>to the visitor in 1980</u>* **it is obvious** *that there have recently been big changes. (AL9: written/non-fiction)*

(45)   *Yasser Arafat sticks doggedly to the infinitely tortuous peace process, never saying 'no' to the Americans, even though* **it's obvious** <u>to him</u> *that what the Israelis want is surely unique in the history of peace negotiations: to both set their agenda and to appoint the other side's representatives. (A9J: written/non-fiction/newspapers)*

In conclusion, the adjectival expressions can be used descriptively, though in most cases they involve the speaker/writer as the evaluator, in agreement with 'others'.

6.   The factor salience

Adjectival expressions differ from adverbs in that they are salient in the discourse: the epistemic expression is given prominence in the information structure of the utterances. Nuyts points out that in the "overwhelming majority" of his instances of adjectival constructions "the epistemic qualification can indeed be considered very central information in the utterance" (2001: 79). One indicator of salience is thematic position: adjectival expressions are thematic in all but a few exceptional cases. A few exceptions to this overriding tendency are given in examples (46–48) below, in which there is some other element that competes for thematic prominence.

(46) *Some of these names* **it is certain** *were acquired at school but most when they began work and these nicknames completely took the place of their Christian names ... (H09:written/non-fiction)*

(47) *In contrast to Iacocca's blustery persona, Eaton is relatively reserved but, <u>beneath his calm demeanour,</u>* **it's clear** *that there lurks a tough and gritty leader. (BM5: written/non-fiction/magazines)*

(48) *And that <u>Sarah Miller is after him,</u>* **it's clear as daylight***. (FRP: written/fiction)*

Example (46) above is interesting in that *it is certain* is not followed by a *that*-clause but is as it were parenthetical, which turns it into a discourse marker of the type *I think*. In such cases it becomes non-prominent. Example (46) is the only example of this type in our data. Final position was found in two examples only, including (48). Second position is more frequent and occurs regularly when the type of evidence is made thematic, as in the following:

(49) *<u>With the wisdom of hindsight</u>* **it's obvious** *that...(CHV: written/non-fiction)*

(50) *<u>Thumbing through the trivia section of Number One Hits</u>* **it's obvious** *everything remains Beatle-oriented (CK5: written/non-fiction)*

(51) *Although <u>comparing them now with photographs taken in the 1930s</u>* **it's obvious** *that ...(EWB: written/non-fiction)*

(52) *<u>From the evidence presented above</u>* **it is clear** *that ...(EB7: written/non-fiction)*

(53) *<u>From the foregoing,</u>* **it is clear** *that ...(FBE: written/non-fiction)*

Salience is also enhanced by contrasting the evaluation explicitly with some other epistemic evaluation (cf. also Nuyts 2001: 84):

(54) *<u>While it remains unclear</u> what they were offering support about,* **it is certain** *they were helping the couple through their continuing marriage crisis (CEN: written/non-fiction/newspapers)*

(55) *<u>There is no certainty</u> that the House will hear them but* **it is certain** *that the Court of Appeal will not. (FBK: written/non-fiction)*

(56) *Precisely when these four additional kadiliks – or five, including mecca – became mevleviyts <u>is not clear</u> in every case, <u>though</u>* **it is certain** *in one case, <u>and entirely possible</u> in the others, that they were not made mevleviyts immediately on coming into Ottoman. (H7S: written/non-fiction)*

(57) *<u>While</u>* **it is certain** *that VAT will be added to domestic fuel from April next year, <u>what isn't known</u> is at what rate. (K26: written/non-fiction/television news script)*

(58) *Discounting such judgements of the moment,* **it is clear** *that Baldwin fought skilfully, and* **certain** *that he fought successfully. (EFN: written/non-fiction)*

Further, internal variation within the expressions is possible, which enhances their prominence. Consider:

(59) It *does seem* **clear** that ...*(GUJ: written/non-fiction)*

(60) It *might seem* **obvious** that ...*(BLX: written/non-fiction)*

(61) It is *blindingly* **obvious** that ...*(CEK: written/non-fiction/newspapers)*

(62) It is certain that at least some of your performances will be different from some others, but it is *also* **certain** that the technique ... *(K93: written/non-fiction)*

(63) It is *also quite* **clear** that... *(J7A: written/non-fiction)*

(64) And that Sarah Miller is after him, **it's clear** *as daylight*. *(FRP: written/fiction)*

While modal adverbs cannot be negated, adjectival expressions can. Table 6 gives the rough frequencies (before weeding) of positive and negated expressions as yielded by an automatic search:

Table 6. Relative proportion of positive and negative adjectival expressions

expression	positive	negative
it is (not) certain	99 (68%)	47 (32%)
it's/isn't certain	13 (93%)	1 (7%)
it is (not) obvious	302 (89%)	37 (11%)
it's/isn't obvious	155 (97%)	5 (3%)
it is (not) clear	1787 (81%)	412 (19%)
it's/isn't clear	136 (99%)	2 (1%)

Although the relative frequencies of negative expressions vary, they are fairly high in the case of non-contracted forms.[4] Their discourse function will be discussed in section 6. Here a few examples may suffice to show how the negation puts the expression into focus:

(65) Even if things go fairly badly **it is not certain** that voters would turn to labour as economic saviour. *(A44: written/non-fiction/newspapers)*

(66) Similarly, when we turn to care at home, **it is not clear** that if the costs of such support were to exceed those of residential care, they could or should be met. *(CFE: written/non-fiction/newspapers)*

(67) Yet **it is not obvious** that this was the case. *(A6G: written/non-fiction/newspapers)*

In conclusion, our data are in agreement with Nuyts that informational salience is an important feature of the adjectival expressions.

---

4.   Nuyts found 26.7% in his Dutch corpus and 48% in his German corpus, but his figures apply to all modal items (including weak possibility and probability). Our figures show that there is quite a lot of variation depending on the lexical item. Furthermore, the large majority of his examples involve negative incorporation of the type *onwaarschijnlijk, unwahrscheinlich* ('improbable').

7.   The factor discourse strategy

In this section we shall examine the apparent rhetorical functions which the adjectival expressions fulfil. It is predictable that some will be shared by all three, while others will be item-dependent. We found the following functions to be important: (i) presenting the evaluation as 'objective'; (ii) contrasting the evaluation with some other epistemic evaluation. These are not necessarily mutually exclusive, as examples will show.

(i)   Presenting the evaluation as objective

Presenting an epistemic assessment as objective is the rhetorical goal of what Halliday and Matthiessen (2004: 613ff.) call 'interpersonal metaphors of modality', which dress up a subjective proposition as if it were objective, and one way of doing this is by making the modal assessment into a proposition of its own. This is what the adjectival expressions do, in contrast with modal auxiliaries and adverbs. Through their impersonal nature they are useful expressions for giving one's claim more weight. The occurrence of such expressions in contexts such as scientific discourse and expository prose in general is to be expected. And there are indeed many instances of such use. What is tactically more interesting is the use of the expressions in contexts where there is little or no reason to assume that the evaluation is commonly shared by everyone. For example, in (68) below, the statement that 'she has relinquished her responsibility' is a subjective interpretation of the fact that hospitals have been closed:

(68)   *It's **clear** from all the hospital closures that she has relinquished her responsibility towards us. (CBC: written/non-fiction/newspapers)*

Consider also (69):

(69)   *It is **obvious** that there are some serious problems in Marx's account. (EDH: written/non-fiction)*

The claim that 'there are some serious problems in Marx's account' is disputable and unlikely to be agreed on by everyone.

The addition of generic third person referents to whom something is said to be clear or obvious is in principle superfluous since the default meaning is intersubjective. By the Gricean maxim of Quantity 'Do not make your contribution more informative than required' (Grice 1975) we can hence deduce that the speaker has some special reason for adding such information, and that reason is disputability of the claim. The rhetorical strategy employed then is attribution to a third person whose authority the speaker endorses (White 2003: 270). The expressions are dialogic in White's sense (White 2003) but contractive, as the speaker closes down the possibilities for disagreement. This type of expansion with a generic noun was found only with *obvious*. Examples (26–28) above illustrate this pattern. Another example is (70):

(70)   *Knowledge is required in that the person supplying knows, or **it is obvious** <u>to a reasonable man,</u> that those means are suitable for putting the invention into effect and that person so intends. (HXD: written/non-fiction)*

In none of these cases do we have a proposition which is based on 'hard facts', but rather an interpretation by the speaker which is presented as shared by all who have access to the 'evidence'.

The subjectivity may also be emphasised by the addition of reference to the speaker, as in examples (31–34) above and also the following:

(71)   ***It's clear** <u>to me</u> and <u>I think</u> it's clear to the majority in Congress that it's a matter for branches to decide who represents them in the various forums of the union. (HUD: spoken/congress/business)*

(72)   *Although he has been accused, of course, of social snobbery, <u>I think</u> **it's clear** that he observed the life around him closely and critically. (KRH: spoken/radio broadcast)*

Note that in the following instance there is an apparent paradox between the 'obviousness' and the speakers 'uncertainty':

(73)   *"Why, **it's obvious**", he said <u>uncertainly</u>. (HTH: written/fiction)*

However, even in those cases the expression conveys accessibility of evidence to everyone. In other words, the intersubjectivity is still part of the meaning. In general, we can say that the adjectival expressions are typically used in contexts where there are good grounds for assuming intersubjectivity. This is certainly the case for *certain* and *clear*. *It is obvious* does occur more frequently with the rhetorical function of conveying intersubjectivity to 'dress up' subjectivity but even there such clear cases are exceptional. More common are instances where the subjectivity is less 'tangible', i.e. cases which lie somewhere on the continuum from 'generally accepted statements' to 'purely subjective opinions'. For instance, if we compare (74) and (75) below, the former is close to the 'objective' end, as the 'clarity' is based on logic, while (75) is closer to the subjective end as the proposition qualified as 'clear' is one which contains subjective evaluations ("serious problems") and what the speaker considers as the necessary course of actions ("need to be tackled", "one major thing that's necessary"). In political rhetoric such uses are tactically useful. Compare:

(74)   ***It is clear** that the narrower a pulse becomes, the greater the bandwidth a system must possess in order to handle it properly. (K90: written/non-fiction)*

(75)   ***It's clear** that the majority of not only motorists but other road users, pedestrians, cyclists, bus passengers do feel that there are serious problems in urban areas, that they do need to be tackled and that one major thing that's necessary is better enforcement of existing regulations, particularly in two areas: one, drivers that drive badly and cause danger to others and secondly, the inconsiderate parker. (KRT: spoken/radio programme)*

(ii) Contrasting the evaluation with another epistemic evaluation

As Nuyts (2001: 97) points out, modal adjectives can be used "to contrast two qualifications". Rhetorically one good reason for qualifying a proposition as certain/obvious/clear is that other propositions are not. Table 7 gives an overview of the proportion of instances in which the expressions occurred in a contrastive context in our samples from the *BNC*. It should be noted that only those cases are included in which there is a contrast within the same sentence. It is therefore still possible that the actual number of contrastive contexts is higher if we look beyond sentence boundaries. Contexts which we regarded as contrastive include: *but*–clauses, concessive clauses, conditional-concessive clauses, contrastive clauses with *while, whereas.*

Table 7. Adjectival expressions in a contrastive context

expression	contrastive context no.	contrastive context %
it is/it's certain	49 (total 98)	50%
it is/it's obvious	26 (total 189)	14%
it is/it's clear	39 (total 167)	23%

In the case of *certain* the occurrence of one in two instances in a contrastive context is a striking discourse factor. It is, however, explicable from the nature of the lexical item: 'certainty', in contrast with 'obviousness' and 'clarity' is purely epistemic and therefore more 'superfluous' from the Gricean point of view than expressions which have an evidential meaning. Following the maxim of Quality 'Do not say that for which you lack adequate evidence' (Grice 1975), one only makes statements for which one has sufficient evidence. Hence, expressions of certainty are to be expected only in contexts where such certainty is not to be taken for granted for some reason or other. Contrastive contexts clearly favour the expression of modal certainty. For *it is certain*, the contrast with some other proposition seems to be an important motivating factor. This finding is in line with White's view of modality as a means by which speakers position themselves in a heteroglossic world in which differences in viewpoint are negotiated (White 2003). On the other hand, the large number of instances of *clear* and *obvious* with an explicit source of evidence (i.e. one third of all occurrences, cf. section 3 above) shows that reference to evidence for the claim is a good reason for using these two adjectival expressions. Contrastive contexts are therefore less 'crucial' as a motivating factor for them. Examples (76) to (81) illustrate the use of *it is certain* in contrast with what is not or less certain:

(76) *Whether or not in our time parents may be said to be justified by the sad statistics of the permissive society,* **it is certain** *that in the nineteenth century, parents had little option because of the sad statistics of mortality among children. (ACA: written/non-fiction)*

(77)   *Robert III <u>may</u> have been born in Dundonald Castle and **it is certain** that he spent much of his life there before he became king. (BM6: written/non-fiction)*

(78)   *<u>While it remains unclear</u> what they were offering support about, **it is certain** they were helping the couple through their continuing marriage crisis. (CEN: written/non-fiction/newspapers)*

(79)   *<u>There is no certainty</u> that the House will hear them but **it is certain** that the Court of Appeal will not. (FBK: written/non-fiction)*

(80)   *Who the other call was to, Jihan <u>has never revealed</u>, but **it is certain** that it must have been someone of the highest importance, and that her purpose was to obtain from the most authoritative source possible some outside indication of what was happening in Egypt. (FRL: written/non-fiction/coursebook on translation).*

(81)   *While **it is certain** that VAT will be added to domestic fuel from April next year, <u>what isn't known</u> is at what rate. (K26: written/news autocue data)*

Another type of indication of contrast is by means of negation. Table 6 above (section 5) shows the relative frequency of negated expressions. It is interesting to see that the relative frequencies follow the same trends as those displayed in Table 7 above: highest for *certain*, followed by *clear*, lowest for *obvious*. In other words, negation and contrastive context go hand in hand as motivating factors. This can be explained from the speakers' relative need to express that something is certain/clear/obvious to position themselves against alternative viewpoints. Saying that something is *not certain/not clear/not obvious* presupposes an alternative view, either real or imagined and as such motivates the use of the epistemic expression in the dialogic negotiation (White 2003 subsumes negation under the contractive heteroglossic options).

Another motivation for negated epistemic expressions is the contrast with rhetorically weaker items. Thus speakers may claim that 'p but it is not certain that q', where q is rhetorically stronger than p. This scale of rhetorical strength is invoked by Schwenter and Traugott (2000) to account for the use of *in fact* in certain contexts. Example (82) below clearly illustrates such a use of *it is not certain*, in that the word *reduced* in the first clause is weaker than the word *eliminated* in the second clause.

(82)   *Were all the surface repositories on Mars to be included then the depletions would be <u>reduced</u>, but **it is not certain** that they would be <u>eliminated</u>. (GW6: written/non-fiction)*

A third possible context is the contrast with something else which is 'certain/obvious/clear', as in example (83):

(83)   *That coins were minted in the name of bishops and churches is <u>clear</u>, but **it is not certain** that they mark an encroachment into a royal preserve. (HY0: written/non-fiction)*

While the negation simply means lack of epistemic certainty in the case of *it is not certain,* a frequent rhetorical meaning of *it is not obvious/clear* is that the speaker does not think it is the case. In other words, the negated form is an understatement for 'I do not think it is the case'. There is clear heteroglossic engagement (White's term 2003) going on in such cases. What the speaker means is much more than the literal sense that something 'is not obvious or clear'. The implicature is that, in contrast with some other voice which does believe that p, the speaker actually wishes to express disbelief that p. The 'other voice' may be mentioned explicitly in the sentence (as in example (84) below, or it may be in the context. Here are some examples:

(84) *First of all, **it is not obvious to me** that the speech strategies needed for typically male and female roles are so totally different and non-overlapping <u>as is often implied</u>. (CGF: written/non-fiction)*

(85) *<u>All the same</u>, **it is not obvious** that he differed much from his English predecessors in this sort of area, for the Anglo-Scandinavian background outlined in the Introduction again becomes relevant here. (HXX: written/non-fiction)*

(86) ***It is not clear to me** that new facilities are needed to enable the bank to address this problem of defence conversion. (AKL: written/non-fiction/newspapers)*

(87) *While Treitschke demonstrates how economic union in the Zollverein finally led to German unity under Prussian hegemony, **it is not clear** that there was necessarily any kind of secret agenda from the outset, rather, the natural pre-eminence of Prussia combined with other historical events beyond her control. (AMK: written/non-fiction)*

8. A brief comparison with the adverbs *certainly, obviously, clearly*

In this section we shall briefly compare the use of the adjectival expressions with the corresponding adverbs. It is not our intention to discuss the adverbs in detail, merely to point at some differences in discourse functions and rhetorical uses between the adjectival and the adverbial expressions as they were found in samples of 150 instances from the *BNC*. Of these, 69 had to be deducted for *clearly* because they expressed manner, and 13 had to be deducted for *obviously* for the same reason.

With regard to *it is certain* vs. *certainly*, the data show that the distinction between 'intersubjective' and 'subjective' epistemic evaluation is not a major factor in determining the choice. An important distinction must be made between instances where the adjective and the adverb can both be used, with or without a difference in subjectivity, and those where because of other factors the adjectival expression cannot substitute for the adverb. In (88) below, for instance, *it is certain* can replace the adverb without any (great) difference in meaning:

(88)   *It is now reckoned that 80 percent of laws enacted by Congress emanate from the executive – if one were to weight these laws in terms of importance, **almost certainly** that proportion would be higher. (GV5: written/non-fiction)*

(89)   *(…) **it is almost certain** that proportion would be higher (our own example).*

However, in many cases replacement is excluded because the adverb does not express epistemic certainty. Consider the following instances:

(90)   *I **certainly** join my hon. Friend in sending condolences to the bereaved family and wishing a speedy recovery to the injured. (HHW: spoken/Hansard)*

(91)   *That fund is set to increase by a further £1 million next year and I **certainly** expect motor projects to figure significantly within that increased expenditure. (HHX: spoken/Hansard)*

(92)   *Erm, so I would **certainly** be asking you to keep some contingency provision in that area, because we project some very expensive one-off demands on certain elements of children's services. (J3P: spoken/public/institutional/meeting)*

From an epistemic adverb *certainly* has developed in some contexts into a mere emphasiser. This means that it has lost lexical content in the process and no longer expresses the speaker's judgement in terms of probability (that would be absurd in examples (90–92) above) but the speaker's wish to assure the hearer of the truth of what he or she is saying. The process from 'I (speaker) believe that it is certain' to 'I (speaker) assure you (hearer) that it is certain' is one from subjectivity to 'inter-subjectivity' in the sense of Traugott and Dasher (2002:23): an orientation towards the hearer. In this view, intersubjective meanings "impact directly on the self-image or "face" needs" of speaker/writer or addressee/reader.[5] Traugott & Dasher point out that meaning development typically goes from subjective to inter-subjective in that sense, and this is what seems to have happened with *certainly*.

A second type of context in which substitution of the adverb by the adjectival expression is not possible is where the adverb has a focalising function: it has a restricted scope, which correlates with non-salience. Because adverbs are by nature much more versatile than adjectival expressions with their clause-like form, they can occur almost anywhere in the sentence. As a result they can serve the function of picking out any element as 'certain' in contrast with any other element. This has led to the development of the focalising function of *certainly*. Examples are the following, in which the scoped elements are underlined:

(93)   *The statue known in copies is of a long-haired youth, almost **certainly** <u>Apollo</u>. (FPW: written/non-fiction)*

---

5.   Note that the term *intersubjectivity* is used differently by Nuyts (2001) and Traugott and Dasher (2002), as explained.

(94)   *Bernie went up to the singer after the show and said, we thought you were called The Teenage Rebels, yet you're not teenagers and you're **certainly** not rebellious. (A6E: written/non-fiction/autobiography)*

(95)   *The percentage shareholding necessary to give control is problematical since as the degree of dispersal increases effective control can be exercised with a decreasing proportion of the votes, and **certainly** with considerably less than the 50 per cent required for a member or members to have the right to remove the board. (FP2: written/non-fiction)*

The very high frequency of the adverb *certainly* in contrast with the adjectival expression *it is certain* (see Tables 1 and 3 above) must be explained from the usefulness of the adverb in contexts where it has lost most of its epistemic meaning and has become an emphasiser and focaliser.

The sentence adverbs *obviously* and *clearly* both developed from manner adverbs (cf. *OED*). A comparison of the relative frequency as well as of the uses of *obviously* and *clearly* as manner adverbs in present-day English shows, however, that *obviously* has moved away further from its original meaning and uses than *clearly*. One indication of this is that as a manner adverb *obviously* is much more restricted in usage than *clearly*. Unambiguous instances of manner *obviously* are the following:

(96)   *The non-Roman, Eastern influence on the Celtic Church manifested itself **most obviously** in Irish monasticism. (EDY: written/non-fiction). (= 'manifested itself in the most obvious way')*

(97)   *Most often, related papers are easy to determine because of the specificity of titles in the field, and unrelated papers are **very obviously** unrelated. (HJ9: written/ non-fiction) (= 'are unrelated in a very obvious way')*

(98)   *Er, he **too obviously** is. (JJU: spoken/public/institutional/court case) (= 'he is in a too obvious way')*

(99)   *Still, if Brahms knew his Rheinberger, what this CD makes clear is how well Rheinberger knew his Brahms, who stands over these String Quartets, as Beethoven did over the young Brahms himself, only **much more obviously**: there are echoes of Brahms in the textures, the themes, the passage-work, the construction. (BMC: written/non-fiction/review) (= 'Brahms stands over these String Quartets in a much more obvious way')*

(100) *Maybe boys think we dress up to impress them, but they will only say something looks nice if it looks **obviously** sexy; other than that, they're hopeless. (ADG:written/non-fiction) (= 'if it looks sexy in an obvious way')*

In several of the examples above, the adverb is premodified by a degree adverb such as *most, more, very, too*. It is never in initial position but next to the verb or adjectival predicate which it qualifies. In such positions, however, it is not always possible to decide whether *obviously* expresses 'in an obvious way' (manner) or 'it is obvious' (modality). Such ambiguous or indeed ambivalent (as both meanings seem to be present) cases show how the process of grammaticalisation may have taken place. If something takes place 'in an obvious way' then the event can be presented as 'obvious to the speaker and to others'. Example (101) is an instance in which the manner interpretation is signalled by the premodifier *very*, but in which the modal interpretation is not far away:

(101)   *But in order to respond fully, our active participation as spectators is **very obviously** called into play – as well as called into question. (HRP: written/non-fiction).*

In example (102) *obviously* could mean both 'in an obvious way' and 'it was obvious':

(102)   *Legion was **obviously** intelligent, and deserved to be treated as such. (G1M: written/fiction).*

As a sentence adverb, *obviously* developed the meaning of 'it is easy for everyone to see or understand'. Examples are the following:

(103)   ***Obviously**, entering data can be done whenever there is more to add – and you can add columns as well as rows – but you will need to update the database definition accordingly. (HAC: written/non-fiction)*

(104)   ***Obviously** positive inflation may remain a feature of this hypothetical economy even if it is operating at the natural unemployment rate (i.e. owing to the persistence of inflationary expectations). (J0U: written/non-fiction)*

In cases such as (103) and (104) the adverb can be replaced by the adjectival expression without any difference in meaning. However, *obviously* has developed further rhetorical functions which are not shared by the adjectival expression. These are uses where the meaning 'it is easy for everyone to see or understand' has given rise to 'as everyone knows'. This meaning development entails a shift towards a rhetorical device for expressing common ground and hence for conveying concurrence. Its meaning in such contexts comes very close to that of *of course*, which is also used as a means of expressing that the information can be taken for granted and which as a result increases the interpersonal cost of disagreement (cf. Simon-Vandenbergen, White and Aijmer, forthcoming). Such uses of *obviously* are rhetorically very powerful and they contribute to the frequency of *obviously* in spoken interaction. Paradoxically at first sight, they can convey solidarity as well as superiority. The function of establishing common ground ('as we all know or expect') is useful in conversation to convey solidarity and lack of superiority:

(105)   *Cos you know, **obviously** nobody wants to talk to you at three o'clock in the morning, fast asleep aren't they, not much fun is it? (KPV: spoken/conversation)*

(106)   *Oh it's silly, it depends how many ca come, well **obviously** how common the car was. (KDA: spoken/conversation)*

(107)   *He finds the lessons boring so **obviously** they're gonna mess about. (KB7: spoken/ conversation)*

In (political) argumentation this type of *obviously* conveys superiority. In this type of context it is often used in a clause which expresses a concession, which is then contrasted with the main argument of the speaker. What is conceded is presented as 'obvious' and hence as known to everyone and hardly worth mentioning. The effect is to foreground the speaker's main point in the *but*-clause. Consider examples (108) and (109) below, in which the concession is made explicit in the processes *I recognize* and *I agree with you*, while the *but*-clause conveys the main argument:

(108)   *Can I just come back Chair, and I recognize **obviously** there is er, further work that's going on with this and support that it does, but there is a case with the Parliamentary Ombudsman in discipline on this at the moment, so on the way in which it's been handled by the Ministry. (J3S: spoken/public/institutional/meeting).*

(109)   ***Obviously** I agree with you that we should be putting the kids in challenging situations where they've gotta rise to the situation and use language in an effective way, but I don't know whether this is the best way (…) (F7F: spoken/educational/informative/teachers' conference)*

In conclusion, the rhetorical exploitation of *obviously* as a marker of common ground accounts for many of its uses, especially in spoken discourse. The adverb has developed in such contexts into a device for conveying shared expectations based on a shared world.

The adverb *clearly*, in contrast with *obviously*, has retained its sense as a manner adverb next to its sense as a modal adverb (see section 2 above). Instances in which the manner meaning is evident are about as frequent as those in which the modal meaning is expressed. Examples (110–112) illustrate the manner adverb:

(110)   *One of the only **clearly** identified causes of leukaemia in children is exposure to radiation. (AN9: written/non-fiction)*

(111)   *He had sat far back and to one side but the congregation was small for the early morning service and he had seen everything **clearly**. (ASN: written/fiction)*

(112)   *The political currency that underpinned the spread of UDCs is no longer **so clearly** in the government's control as it was a few years ago. (BN8: written/non-fiction)*

Like *obviously*, the adverb *clearly* also occurs in contexts where the meanings of manner and modality are not easily separated, and it is such contexts which provide an insight into how the grammaticalisation process may have taken place. Example (113) illustrates such ambivalent cases. Ross's external behaviour is a 'clear' signal of his inner state and warrants the claim that he was enjoying himself:

(113)   *Directing the building of what appeared to be a large fortification, Ross was **clearly** enjoying himself as he laughed and joked with the children, as perfectly*

> *at ease in these casual, unsophisticated surroundings as he was in the cosmo-*
> *politan offices of a smart City boardroom. (JXX: written/fiction)*

In the following examples *clearly* has the meaning of 'it is clear' and it is close to *obvi-*
ously in conveying 'it is easy to see or understand'

(114)   *Clearly, the orthopaedic resources in inner London are inadequate to meet cur-*
         rent needs. (EC7: written/non-fiction)

(115)   *But he added: 'Everybody recognises that the Government has to hold on to ex-*
         *isting policy until the replacement is ready to put in place, and **clearly** the Secre-*
         tary of State has to hold to his policy until an alternative has been agreed'. (A8X:
         written/non-fiction/newspapers)

(116)   *We can understand this by considering a person's reflection in a mirror which is*
         experienced as a re-figuring and deepening of the reflected image: the depth of
         the reflection, for example, shows that the reflection is not the mirror itself, al-
         *though, **clearly**, without the mirror there is no reflection. (B7M: written/non-*
         fiction/magazines)

On the other hand, *clearly* has not developed the 'common ground' reading to the extent
obviously has. It signals the speaker's evaluation of the state-of-affairs as 'easy to see or
understand', without making the further step towards the meaning 'as you know or may
expect'. This may explain its less frequent use in spoken discourse, as a comparison of the
frequencies of *obviously* and *clearly* in COLT and WSC in Table 1 shows. In contrast with
obviously, it has developed the meaning of subjective assessment but not the intersubjective meaning in the sense of Traugott and Dasher (2002: 22), i.e. the property of some
expressions of revealing "attention on the part of SP/W toward the image or other needs
of AD/R in that person's role as an interlocutor in the speech event". This may also explain why the difference in frequency between *it is clear* and *clearly* is less significant than
that between *it is obvious* and *obviously* (cf. Tables 1 and 3).

9.   Conclusions

In this paper we have aimed at contributing to the discussion of the differences, if any,
between adverbial and adjectival expressions of modal certainty. Starting out from
Nuyts' criteria we looked at the adjectival expressions *it is certain/obvious/clear* in a
sample of present-day English data. We found that Nuyts' characteristics of what he
calls 'intersubjectivity', 'salience' and 'performativity' are indeed relevant: adjectival
expressions mostly express intersubjective certainty, they tend to be salient, and they
can be descriptive. However, it is by no means always the case that they fulfil these
criteria. Firstly, with regard to intersubjectivity, we showed that even though the adjectival expressions convey that the assessment is shared or can be shared by others, the

speaker's own viewpoint is always part of the meaning. Further, there are some instances where the expressions are used as objectifying devices in the Hallidayan sense (Halliday and Matthiessen 2004: 615–616), i.e. to give an air of objectivity to what is in fact a subjective viewpoint. Secondly, with regard to salience, we found a few instances where the adjectival expressions were used in parenthetical ways. Even though they are exceptional, their occurrence in such non-focal positions is important and may signal a step towards loss of clausal status and increase of discourse marker status. In this respect they behave like expressions such as *I think* or *it seems to me*, which have developed further into discourse markers (see e.g. Thompson 2002, and Boye and Harder forthcoming for a critical discussion). Further, the possibility of having two types of question tags with the expressions, one repeating the *it* – subject of the 'main clause' and one repeating the subject of the 'subordinate' clause points to their dual nature. In cases where it is the subject of the subordinate clause which is picked up in the tag the clausal nature of *it is certain/clear/obvious* is being lost. What appears to be in the subclause is in fact the main clause (see Halliday and Matthiessen 2004: 614; Thompson 2002). Thirdly, the factor 'performativity' accounts for the fact that adjectival expressions can be descriptive instead of expressing the speaker's modal evaluation. However, while there are contexts which allow for a descriptive reading only, in most cases the adjectival expressions implicitly convey the speaker's modal assessment and are thus performative in that sense. In addition, it was found that the addition of nominals with generic reference (such as *anyone, all not too blind to see*) turns the expressions into rhetorical devices for conveying a subjective assessment disguised as a descriptive statement. In other words, although all three factors play a role, they cannot by themselves always account for the use of an adjectival rather than an adverbial expression. In the specific case of the three lexical items under investigation, we also felt it necessary to explain the differences in frequency of adjectives and adverbs.

The factor discourse strategy proved to be important. Two factors appeared to account for a large number of adjectival uses, viz. presenting the assessment as objective and contrasting the assessment with another modal evaluation. These factors directly correlate with the grammatical form of adjectival expressions: their clausal form with an *it*- subject makes them both impersonal and syntactically open to negation. A comparison with the adverbs has further shown that the latter are rhetorically exploited in different ways. Their positional versatility allows for great flexibility in scoping. This has led to the development of additional functions apart from epistemic certainty. In the case of *certainly* the use as emphasiser, with limited scope, accounts for a large number of instances. In the case of *obviously* the development of the heteroglossic meaning of concurrence with the alternative voice (expressing solidarity as well as superiority in argumentation) accounts for its usefulness in spoken discourse. In the case of *clearly* the development of such secondary rhetorical functions is not in evidence. It would seem that *clearly* has gone less far in its development from ideational to interpersonal meaning. *Certainly* has gone furthest, as it has lost much of its epistemic meaning in instances where it is a focaliser or emphasiser. This development accounts for the great gap between adjectival and adverbial frequencies in the case of *it is certain* and *certainly*.

In conclusion, this study has shown that the reasons why speakers opt for adjectival or adverbial modal expressions are complex and that an explanation cannot limit itself to a single factor. In this respect we are in complete agreement with Nuyts, who claims that the tendency to try and explain a particular linguistic phenomenon in terms of one single factor is "harmful" and leads to counter-intuitive assumptions (1993: 954). In addition, Nuyts mentions the possible role played by discursive strategies and claims that the latter may be dependent on the individual lexical items rather than on the constructions as grammatical units (2001: 101). We have shown that the rhetorical exploitation of epistemic certainty leads to different preferences which are dependent on the individual lexical items.

Further work in this area will need to look more closely at register variation and the sociolinguistic indexicality of the adjectival and adverbial expressions. The differences in relative frequencies in the corpora checked for this study suggest that the factor 'medium' (speech vs. writing) certainly plays a role. In addition, however, such factors as formality, type of activity, age, and power relations are potentially relevant in determining preferences. The distinction between constructions cannot be studied outside the context of their usefulness to speakers of the language, and such exploitation is creative and dynamic.

References

Bellert, Irena. 1977. "On semantic and distributional properties of sentential adverbs". *Linguistic Inquiry* 8: 337–351.

Boye, Kasper and Peter Harder. Forthcoming. "Complement-taking predicates: usage and linguistic structure".

Downing, Angela 2001. "'Surely you knew!' *Surely* as a marker of evidentiality and stance". *Functions of Language* 8(2): 251–282.

Grice, H. Paul. 1975. "Logic and conversation". In: Peter Cole and Jerry L. Morgan (eds.) *Syntax and semantics 3: Speech acts*, 41- 58. New York: Academic Press.

Lang, Ewald. 1979. "Zum Status der Satzadverbiale". *Slovo a Slovenost* 40: 200–213.

Kennedy, Graeme. 1998. *An introduction to corpus linguistics*. London: Longman.

Kiefer, Ferenc. 1984. "Focus and modality". *Groninger Arbeiten zur Germanistischen Linguistik* 24: 55–81.

Nuyts, Jan. 1993. "Epistemic modal adverbs and adjectives and the layered representation of conceptual and linguistic structure". *Linguistics* 31: 933–969.

Nuyts, Jan. 2001. *Epistemic modality, language, and conceptualization. A cognitive-pragmatic perspective*. Amsterdam: John Benjamins.

Perkins, Michael R. 1983. *Modal expressions in English*. London: Pinter.

Halliday, Michael A. K. and Christian M. I. M. Matthiessen. 2004. *An introduction to functional grammar*. 3rd edn. London. Arnold.

Hengeveld, Kees. 1988. "Illocution, mood and modality in a functional grammar of Spanish". *Journal of Semantics* 6: 227–269.

Schwenter, Scott A. and Elizabeth C. Traugott. 2000. "Invoking scalarity. The development of *in fact*". *Journal of Historical Pragmatics* 1(1): 7–25.

Simon-Vandenbergen, Anne-Marie, Peter R. R. White and Karin Aijmer. Forthcoming. "Presupposition and 'taking-for-granted' in mass communicated political argument. An illustration from British, Flemish and Swedish political colloquy". In: Gerda Lauerbach and Anita Fetzer (eds.) *Media discourse from an intercultural perspective.* Studies in Pragmatics. Amsterdam: Elsevier.

Thompson, Sandra A. 2002. "Object complements and conversation: Towards a realistic account". *Studies in Language* 26(1): 125–164.

Traugott, Elizabeth C. and Richard B. Dasher. 2002. *Regularity in semantic change.* Cambridge: Cambridge University Press.

White, Peter R. R. 2003. "Beyond modality and hedging: A dialogic view of the language of intersubjective stance". *Text* 23(2): 259–284.

Modality across World Englishes

The modals and semi-modals of prediction and volition

Peter C. Collins
University of New South Wales

This paper reports a corpus-based study which examined the uses of the modals and semi-modals which express meanings associated with prediction and volition (*will*, *shall*, *be going to/gonna*, *want to/wanna*, and *be about to*) in British, American and Australian English. Quantitative findings relating to regional and stylistic variation are presented, and consideration is given to the possible influence upon the relative popularity of modal uses of 'Americanization' and 'colloquialization'. It is suggested that these socially-driven dissemination processes provide possible explanations for, inter alia, the differing fortunes of the moribund *shall* on the one hand and on the other those of the popular semi-modals *be going to/gonna* and *want to/wanna*.

1. Introduction

This paper examines the uses and distribution of the modal expressions *will*, *shall*, *be going to/gonna*, *want to/wanna*, and *be about to*. Data are derived from two parallel (International Corpus of English) corpora of Australian English (AusE) and British English (BrE), plus a specially constructed, near-equivalent, corpus of spoken and written American English (AmE), which yielded 13,590 tokens.

It is intended that the use of parallel standard corpora will facilitate the exploration of both dialectal variation (across the three World Englishes examined) and of stylistic variation (across the dialogic/monologic and non-printed/printed subcategories of the corpora), and that it will provide the basis for a more detailed and comprehensive analysis of the modals and semi-modals of prediction and volition than that offered in previous quantitative studies on this topic. Coates' (1983) study of the modals in BrE is based on limited (and now somewhat dated) data from the British Survey of English Usage corpus. Collins' (1991) study of the modal forms presently under investigation is, like that of Coates, based on a small and now dated corpus (of 225,000 words of written and spoken AusE). Gotti (2003) examines the meanings of *will* and *shall* in the Middle English and Early Modern English subcomponents of the Helsinki Corpus of English texts, and draws comparisons with the findings reported in Coates (1983), Biber et al. (1999) and Mindt (1995), the latter two of whom fail to provide specific frequency figures. Berglund (1997) examines the frequency of *will, shall* and *be going to/gonna* as 'expressions of future' in various corpora of BrE (Lancaster-Oslo/ Bergen and London-Lund), AmE (Brown), and Indian English (Kolhapur), but she does not indicate the semantic basis for her screening (whether, for example, tokens expressing 'predictability', 'volition', 'obligation' and the like were excluded). Berglund (2000) uses the British National Corpus to examine the interrelationship between the use of *be going to/gonna* and such social variables as the age and social class of the speakers. Leech's (2003) diachronic study of the modals, based on a comparison of matching corpora of the 1960s (the LOB corpus of BrE and the Brown corpus of AmE) and the 1990s (the FLOB corpus of BrE and the Frown corpus of AmE), provides information on the frequencies of the forms under investigation here but not on the frequencies of their meanings/uses. Krug's (2000) study of grammaticalization with selected modals, likewise, contains relevant diachronic information, on *want to*, from a range of British and American corpora.

2.   The corpora

The International Corpus of English (ICE) is a collection (not yet complete) of million-word corpora representing national and regional varieties of English which provides a valuable resource for linguists pursuing comparative studies of English worldwide (see for example the ICE-based studies reported in a recent special issue of *World Englishes* 23:2, 2004). To ensure compatibility, each ICE corpus conforms to a common design, comprising 500 texts, each of 2,000 words, sampled in the early 1990s (300 spoken texts – 180 dialogic and 120 monologic; and 200 written texts – 50 non-printed and 150 printed). The present study is intended as a contribution to the growing body of ICE-based research[1]. All tokens of the modals *will* and *shall,* and of the semi-modals *be going to/gonna, want to/wanna,* and *be about to* were extracted from the ICE-AUS and ICE-GB corpora.

In addition, in order to fill the gap caused by the non-availability hitherto of an actual ICE-US corpus, tokens were extracted from a specially constructed American corpus (henceforth 'C-US'). The texts for C-US had two sources. For the spoken component the Santa Barbara corpus (SBC) was selected (which contains 116,458 words, this count determined by stripping out all but orthographic words from the transcripts). Insofar as the Santa Barbara texts are predominantly dialogic there is unfortunately some incom-

---

1.   The study whose findings are reported in this paper was supported by an Australian Research Council Discovery Grant.

parability with the ICE corpora, in which the spoken component is 60% dialogic and 40% monologic. For the written component of C-US 80,000 words were extracted from the Freiburg-Brown Corpus of Written American English (Frown), the selection of texts being made to match as closely as possible the ICE categories, as follows:

ICE	C-US
Non-printed (50 texts)	G1–3; P1–7 (10 texts)
Printed:informational (100 texts)	J1–8; F1–8; A1–4 (20 texts)
Printed:instructional (20 texts)	H1–2; E1–2 (4 texts)
Printed: persuasive (10 texts)	B1–2 (2 texts)
Printed: creative (20 texts)	K1–4 (4 texts)

All frequencies for C-US, which contains 196,458 words, were normalized to tokens per one million words, to match those for ICE-AUS and ICE-GB (by dividing the raw frequency count by the number of words in C-US and then multiplying by 1,000,000: see Biber, Conrad and Reppen (1998:263–4) for details of the methodology used). In addition frequencies for the spoken and written subcategories of ICE-AUS and ICE-GB were normalized to tokens per one million words. Frequencies are presented in Table 1 below.

Table 1. Frequencies of the modals/semi-modals of prediction and volition*

	ICE-AUS	ICE-GB	C-US	TOTAL
will	3868	3861	3950 (776)	(8505)
shall	100	223	102 (20)	(343)
be going to/gonna	1191	1056	2413 (474)	(2721)
want to/wanna	1039	578	1425 (280)	(1897)
about to	63	54	36 (7)	(124)
Total	6261	5772	7926 (1557)	(13590)

* For C-US figures are normalized to tokens per one million words; raw figures in parentheses.

A further source of data for AusE was provided by a questionnaire conducted in 2003 with 386 Australian respondents ranging in age from 10 to 65 and over[2]. Respondents were given sentences containing alternative modal expressions and asked to indicate which of two alternative modal expressions they would be more likely to use in: (a) a

---

2. The questionnaire was conducted under the auspices of the Macquarie University Dictionary Research Centre. Selected results were reported by the present author in the DRC's publication *Australian Style* 12:1 (2004) 11.

casual conversation with a friend; (b) a letter written on a serious matter to someone not known to them (the relevant item for the present study being *I'm sure it's/is going to be vs* will *be very entertaining*). The findings are discussed in Section 4 below.

3.   Meanings

In the present study the validity of the broad distinction between 'root' and 'epistemic' modality (as argued for by Coates 1983 and others) is accepted. Epistemic modality involves the speaker's inferences about the truth of a proposition, while root modality relates to the potential for an action to occur, as determined either deontically (via the imposition of an obligation, giving of a permission, etc., or intrinsically (via the will, ability, etc. of one of the parties, typically the subject-referent). The root category is admittedly somewhat semantically heterogeneous (leading a number of linguists to recognize more than one primary class here, most influentially Palmer 1990 with his distinction between 'deontic' and 'dynamic' modality). As we shall see, however, these meanings are not only related in various ways but also associated with similar syntactic patterns. There follows an account of the various uses associated with the basic meanings of the modal expressions under investigation, with exemplification from ICE-AUS, ICE-GB and C-US.

3.1   *Will*

As Table 1 above shows, *will* is by far the most frequently occurring of the modals and semi-modals examined and, we shall see, the primary exponent in English of its two basic meanings. In this study *will* is understood to subsume the three word forms: *will* (accounting for 57.43% of all tokens), *'ll* (36.32%) and *won't* (6.24%).

3.1.1   *Epistemic* will
Epistemic modality is concerned with the speaker's confidence in the truth of the proposition, based on evidence and knowledge (e.g. *John may/might/must/will be in his office*). The clearest cases of epistemic *will* are those involving reference to other-than-future situations (as noted by Palmer (1990:57) and Huddleston and Pullum (2002:188), as in:

(1)   a. *No and the level of acceleration ah at any point **will** be ah related to the ah instantaneous radius that it's turning.* [ICE-AUS S1B-064(B):261]
   b. *yeah like, every light switch **will** have its own computer or something you know.* [C-US SBC-017: 236–240]
   c. *Her father is a Welsh Labour M.P. so the election results **will** have been a disappointment for them.* [ICE-AUS W1B-008(noone):38]

In fact Palmer excludes from this category cases where *will* is used with reference to a future situation, while at the same time conceding that: "Where there is reference to future action, it is difficult, and sometimes impossible, to distinguish epistemic WILL from the WILL of futurity" (1990:57)[3]. Palmer's main argument for maintaining a distinction between futurity *will* and epistemic *will* rests on cases such as (2) which, in his view, do not involve an element of speaker judgement (Palmer 1990:163).

> (2) a. *'Cos she's she'll be seventeen after August so seventeen's normal but most people are seventeen turning eighteen and she's sixteen turning seventeen.* [ICE-AUS S1A-036(B):75]
> b. *Next Tuesday will be D day.* [ICE-AUS S2A-(K):107]
> c. *It'll be Christmas soon.* [ICE-GB W2F-016 #115:1]

While it is true that in such cases *will* comes close to being merely a marker of futurity, there is nevertheless an epistemic modal component, albeit minimal, relating to limitations to the speaker's knowledge (for example in (2a) the truth of the proposition is contingent upon the subject-referent's surviving until August). As Huddleston and Pullum (2002:190) observe, there is an inevitable and intimate connection between futurity and modality: "our knowledge about the future is inevitably much more limited than our knowledge about the past and the present, and what we say about the future will typically be perceived as having the character of a prediction rather than an unqualified factual assertion".

Examples such as (2), where the modal component is minimal, are rare. Typically the speaker is understood to be making a prediction rather than a factual statement about the future, with the modal component often being reinforced by an epistemic adjunct, such as *hopefully* in (3a), *possibly* in (3b), *probably* in (3c), and *most likely* in (3d):

> (3) a. *Hopefully the bridge will also be built at some stage.* [ICE-AUS W2A-035(noone):58]
> b. *We'll do it Wednesday or Thursday possibly.* [ICE-GB:S1A-038 #186:1:A]
> c. *I'm sitting here st- worrying about this one right here, and there probably won't even be l- one like this on the test.* [C-US SBC 09:1155–1160]
> d. *you'll most likely strengthen your defenses* [C-US Frown G03 118]

In the present study, then, as in Coates (1983) and Huddleston and Pullum (2002), the non-root, future-referring, use of the modal expressions under investigation (which is labelled 'prediction' by Coates) is treated as belonging to epistemic modality rather than futurity. The grounds for this decision are not merely the modal overlay that accompanies instances of this use, but also the co-occurrence patterns that it shares with the use of *will* to make comments about present time situations (Coates' 'predictability'). Con-

---

3. Like Palmer, Gotti (2003) treats futurity as non-epistemic, but he differs from Palmer in treating futurity – strangely, and without offering any explanation for his analysis – as a dynamic meaning.

sider the following pairs of examples, featuring in each case predictability *will* in (a), and prediction *will* in (b). In (4) both collocate with the epistemic adjunct *probably*; in (5) both are used with the perfect aspect; in (6) both are used with the progressive aspect; in (7) both are used with the passive voice; in (8) both are used with non-agentive verbs; in (9) both are used with stative verbs; in (10) both are used in the existential *there*-construction; and in (11) both are used in the *it*-extraposition construction.

(4) a. *We have a serial killer of backpackers in the state as you **will** probably know. The news has claimed headlines overseas I understand.* [ICE-AUS W1B-004(noone):62]

b. *or as my mother says you know I suppose this **will** probably turn her lesbian.* [ICE-GB:S1A-054 #43:1:B]

(5) a. *They **won't**'ve charged interest yet, have they?* [ICE-AUS S1A-083(A):272]

b. *The total Income Tax that the Association **will** have paid out by the end of 1990 will be in the vicinity of $33,000!!!* [ICE-AUS W1B-024:30]

(6) a. *Well you gotta sort of cos you're tryna do your homework and they'll be ringing you up and you gotta take them places.* [ICE-AUS S1A-060(B):189]

b. *I might do it this week-end because if I don't I'll be doing it while I'm trying to study.* [ICE-AUS S1A-087(B):307]

(7) a. *No and the level of acceleration ah at any point **will** be ah related to the ah instantaneous radius that it's turning.* [ICE-AUS S1B-064(B):261]

b. *And uh his hope is that sufficient employment **will** be found, for all the people at the different shrines who are in fact already Levites in Jerusalem.* [ICE-GB: S1B-001 #101:1:A]

(8) a. *Moisture **will** condense out of the air in a hot, muggy room onto the cold surfaces of a machine or box of floppy disks brought in from, say, the cold boot of a car in winter.* [ICE-GB W2B-033 #20:1]

b. *I'll bleed to death in the morning.* [ICE-AUS S1A-033(C):245]

(9) a. *Sometimes the importance of getting an officer to the destination quickly **will** outweigh the cost of transport.* [ICE-AUS W2D-003:238]

b. *It **will** fall for Shalimov who's just a little way out from goal but still, trying to persistently force the ball through.* [ICE-GB S2A-010 #220:1:A]

(10) a. *There **will** almost always be a discrepancy in the perception of the conduct between the parties to a complaint.* [ICE-AUS W2D-004(noone):74]

b. *Do you reckon there'll be the same questions in this test.* [ICE-AUS S1A-087(B):12]

(11) a. *In other words, if you look around the languages of the world, it **will** probably be true that if they have nouns and if they have verbs and if they have adjectives, the most common sorts of roles that these words play will be to refer to*

things in the case of nouns, to refer to actions in the case of verbs, to refer to descriptions in the case of adjectives [ICE-AUS S2A-022(noone):205]

b. *Next week with Julie it **will** be impossible to do anything at all.* [ICE-GB: W1B-007 #68:2]

Epistemic *will* is, by comparison with other epistemic modals that may be used with reference to future time situations (e.g *may, might, should, could*) semantically strong. Note the contrast beween epistemically weak *might* and semantically strong *will* in the following example:

(12) *You might be admired for your red tie, but you **will** be derided for your seventies attitudes.* [ICE-AUS S2A-044:34]

Predictability *will* is comparable in strength to epistemic *must*, as the possibility of substituting *must* for *will* without altering the strength of the speaker's claim in the following examples suggests:

(13) a. *they'll be familiar to you* [ICE-GB:S2A-021 #98:1:A]

b. *I think about the worst thing we could have at this party everyone is turns up thinking like I did when I went to Mike's oh there'll be an off-licence round the corner.* [ICE-GB:S1A-030 #192:1:A]

However *must* and *will* differ subtly in other respects, as explained by Huddleston and Pullum (2002:189): "*Must* conveys the idea of conclusion, and is often used in explanations: *Ed's late – he must have overslept.* With central-epistemic *will* it is more a matter of assumption or expectation, very often with a suggestion of future confirmation, as in: *I can't tell you what the word means but it will be in the dictionary.*" Epistemic *will* may also, as both Palmer (1990:138) and Huddleston and Pullum (2002:191–2) observe, convey a conditional meaning: more precisely, it may be used in the apodosis of conditional constructions, with past, present or future time situations, where it has a stronger sense than weak epistemic *may*. Examples follow:

(14) a. *"If you don't act you **won't** get any shares" is not quite true!* [ICE-AUS W1B-026:33]

b. *Because if you have fat in the system fat **will** slow down the rate of your digestion so that's the the key thing.* [ICE-AUS S2B-032(D):74]

c. *We need also to consider the local level where issues are also competing for attention, and some **will** struggle to rise up the agenda or never get onto the agenda at all if they challenge the position of dominant groups.* [ICE-GB W2A-014 #89:1]

3.1.2 *Root* will

Root *will* expresses a dynamic meaning, involving the potential for an activity or event deriving, characteristically, from the subject-referent's willingness or intention. In (15) note the contrast between the first instance of *won't*, which expresses this meaning ("I am unwilling/reluctant to take the case"), and the second, which occurs within a clausal complement to the noun *likelihood* with the non-agentive verb *come(up with)* and expresses epistemic prediction ("I can be predicted not to"):

(15)   *I'm not saying I **won't** take the case, but you've got to be prepared for the likelihood that I **won't** come up with anything.* [ICE-AUS W2F-008:73]

Dynamic *will* covers a range of uses: 'intention', where the focus is upon a future event that is planned, promised, threatened, etc., as in (16) below; and two uses in which the focus is upon the mind of a 'volitioner': 'willingness', where the volition is weak (comparable in strength to *want to*), as in (17) below, and 'insistence', where it is stronger, with the modal typically stressed and not contractible to *'ll*, as in (18) below.

(16)   a. *But it is the decision as to property rights on which I **will** concentrate.* [ICE-GB:S2B-046 #56:1:A]
       b. *In that case I **will** use a yellow pepper for this evening.* [C-US SBC-03: 9–12]

(17)   a. *But there's a lot of people you get who who **won't** accept that aren't willing to argue.* [ICE-GB:S1A-084 #117:1:B]
       b. *If you cannot agree **will** you please telephone this office before sending any further demands.* [ICE-GB W1B-023 #121:13]

(18)   a. *Something much better is, though: Bridge! I **will** certainly enrol, even the time is convenient: Tuesdays from 5.30pm – 7.30pm.* [ICE-AUS W1B-(noone):44]
       b. *I **will** most certainly bow to your ruling and I **will** state that I am I am a chartered surveyor and I **will** also state that I am the director of a property company from which I have from which I have drawn no remuneration since June nineteen eighty-seven.* [ICE-GB S1B-051 #152:1:A]

Huddleston and Pullum (2002:193) analyze volition as an implicature overlaid upon futurity, the implicature deriving from the assumption that the situation is under the control of the subject-referent. They note, furthermore, that with a 1st person subject (as in (16) and (18) above) volition tends to trigger a further implicature of commitment, such that the hearer might legitimately ask *Is that a promise?* However there is no doubt that dynamic and epistemic *will* are distinguishable. As we have already noted, epistemic *will* displays a number of co-occurrence patterns. The volitional component in dynamic *will* may moreover, as Huddleston and Pullum (2002:193) note, be heightened by such factors as negativeness (as in (17a) above and (19) below), by the selection of a closed interrogative – especially with a 2nd person subject, which questions the addressee's willingness and indirectly conveys a request – as in (17b) above and (20) below, or by occurrence in a conditional protasis, as in (21) below:

(19)   *On the other hand they're saying if you don't have an X-ray we **won't** give you your fee.* [ICE-GB S1A-088 #14:1:A]

(20) *Will you please explain to me the meaning of the phrase "Currently, NRMA's profits are 'locked up'" used in answer to L. G. Norman's letter?* [ICE-AUS W1B-026]

(21) *She paused, embarrassed but amused, being after all sure of her welcome. "That is, if you'll put up with me next week again, Ella."* [ICE-AUS W2F-020(noone):28]

Finally, consider the use of *will* exemplified in (22) below.

(22) *I'll withdraw that. Above your right eye. You'll say he headbutted you.* [ICE-AUS S1B 067(A):88]

Huddleston and Pullum (2002:194) identify this use as deriving via implicature from futurity: "if I predict your agentive actions (or someone else's) in a context where I have the authority to require them, I will be understood as tacitly invoking that authority". An alternative explanation proposed here is that in such cases *will* serves to express the speaker's will or insistence (such that the utterance would be most likely understood to have the illocutionary force of a directive).

3.1.3   *A second dynamic use of root* will?

Huddleston and Pullum (2002:194) propose a second dynamic use, 'propensity', which is said to be concerned with "characteristic or habitual behaviour of animates" (e.g. *She will sit there staring into space*) often with an attendant suggestion of the speaker's disapproval or resignation, or "general properties of inanimates" (e.g. *Oil will float on water*). A parallel analysis is found in Palmer (1990: 136–7), who distinguishes the two cases mentioned by Huddleston and Pullum as different subtypes which he calls respectively 'habit' ("concerned with habitual (or better, 'typical') behaviour") and 'power' ("volition applied to inanimate objects").

There is no doubt that 'habit' *will* belongs in the dynamic category when referring to a typical activity which the subject-referent insists upon engaging in. However examples of the following kind require a different analysis:

(23) a. *Almost every female can expect to mother her own young but most males* **will** *live a life of perpetual frustration.* [ICE-AUS S2B-034(A):113]
   b. *And often people in the street* **will** *come up to me and say "I yo yo".* [ICE-AUS S1B-035(B):256]
   c. *Sometimes the importance of getting an officer to the destination quickly* **will** *outweigh the cost of transport.* [ICE-AUS W2D-003:238]

Here the speaker makes an inference about the predictability of an activity based on its regular occurrence, and the disposition of the subject-referent is not salient. Such cases I have classified as epistemic rather than dynamic. Note, in this regard, that *used to* – excluded from this study on the grounds that it expresses aspectual rather than modal meaning – is used to express characteristic or habitual behaviour in the past, without any suggestion that the possibility of occurrence of the situation is attributable to properties of the subject-referent.

3.1.4   *Frequencies of* will

As Table 1 above shows, the most popular item by far of those under investigation was *will*, with well over twice as many tokens (11,679) as its closest rival *be going to* (4,660).

Table 2. Frequencies for *will/won't/'ll* in ICE-AUS, ICE-GB, and C-US. (Figures normalized to tokens per one million words; raw figures in parentheses.)

		ICE-AUS	ICE-GB	C-US	TOTAL
Root	Spoken	1403 (842)	1473 (884)	1752 (204)	(1930)
	Written	583 (233)	785 (314)	1575 (126)	(673)
	Total	1075 (1075)	1198 (1198)	1680 (330)	(2603)
Epistemic	Spoken	2867 (1720)	2345 (1407)	2421 (282)	(3409)
	Written	2683 (1073)	3140 (1256)	2052 (164)	(2493)
	Total	2793 (2793)	2663 (2663)	2270 (446)	(5902)
	TOTAL	3868 (3868)	3861 (3861)	3950 (776)	(8505)

As Table 2 indicates, *will* more commonly expresses epistemic than root modality in all three varieties. However the dominance of epistemic *will* is not as great in AmE (where epistemic tokens outnumber root by a ratio of 1.4:1) as it is in AusE (where the ratio is 2.6:1) or BrE (2.2:1).

When we compare the overall frequencies of *will* across the spoken-written dimension we find that it is only marginally more common in speech (by a ratio of 1.1:1). The totals for epistemic *will* are comparable across the three regional varieties, but for root *will* the picture is less uniform. While root *will* is equally popular in American speech and writing, in AusE and BrE it is approximately twice as popular in speech as it is in writing. This finding, viewed in conjunction with the greater popularity of *want to* in AmE than in AusE and BrE (see Section 3.5.2), may suggest that – at least in speech – root *will* is succumbing to the incursion of *want to* more rapidly in AmE than it is in the other two varieties.

Table 3. Raw frequencies for person of the subject with the modals/semi-modals of prediction and volition.

		1st person	2nd person	3rd person	Total
will	Root	1773 (68.1%)	200 (7.7%)	630 (24.2%)	2603 (100%)
	Epistemic	519 (8.8%)	660 (11.2%)	4723 (80.0%)	5902 (100%)
shall	Root	219 (68.0%)	1 (0.3%)	102 (31.7%)	322 (100%)
	Epistemic	15 (71.4%)	1 (4.8%)	5 (23.8%)	21 (100%)
be going to	Root	735 (63.7%)	178 (15.4%)	250 (21.7%)	1153 (100%)
	Epistemic	281 (18.0%)	183 (11.7%)	1094 (70.2%)	1558 (100%)
be about to	Root	3 (100%)	0	0	3 (100%)
	Epistemic	25 (20.7%)	5 (4.1%)	91 (75.2%)	121 (100%)
want to	Root	766 (40.5%)	538 (28.5%)	587 (31.0%)	1891 (100%)
	Epistemic	2 (33.3%)	3 (50.0%)	1 (16.7%)	6 (100%)

Finally, consider the relationship between uses of *will* and the person of its subject (see Table 3). Not surprisingly, insofar as we might expect speakers to find themselves more often in a position to describe their own volition than that of others, root *will* occurred most commonly with a 1st person subject (68.1%), and proportionately more so in AusE (74.2%) than in the other two varieties. By contrast, the results for epistemic *will* indicate that speakers far more commonly make predictions and predictabilty judgements about a third party (80.0%) than about either themselves or their addressee(s), a tendency that was stronger in BrE (84.0%) than in the other two varieties.

3.2   *Shall*

Though its frequency is strikingly lower than that of *will* (see Table 1 above), I have chosen to consider *shall* next on the grounds of its auxiliary status and traditional association with *will*. The figures for *shall* in Table 1 include *shan't* (of which there were only 4 tokens, 3 of them occurring in ICE-GB).

3.2.1   *Epistemic* shall

Epistemic *shall*, which may be used to express futurity or conditional consequence is, the present study shows, overwhelmingly outnumbered by epistemic *will*. There were only 21 tokens of epistemic *shall* in the three corpora, as against 5902 tokens of epistemic *will*. The findings of this study indicate that the traditional prescriptive rule, that in referring to the future *shall* should take a 1st person subject and *will* a 2nd or 3rd person subject, is out-of-step with the facts of contemporary usage: not only may epistemic *will* take a 1st person subject (8.8% of epistemic *will* tokens in the present study had a 1st person subject), but we also find examples of epistemic *shall* with a non-1st person subject (28.6% of all epistemic *shall*s in this study), as in:

(24) *my heart's desire is that my neighbour Ivan's donkey **shall** die tomorrow morning.* [ICE-GB S2B-047 #77:1:A]

According to Palmer (1990:162–3) *shall* is never epistemic in the narrow sense (i.e. with present or past reference), only in its futurity sense. Palmer presents this claim as supporting evidence for his treatment of future *will* and *shall* as non-epistemic. However examples do occur, as in (25):

(25) *Like those on the home front in earlier wars we **shall** often be imperfectly informed of what is happening, and this too puts our patience to the test.* [ICE-GB W2E-007 #22:1]

A number of the co-occurrence patterns that we find with epistemic *will* are also in evidence with *shall*. These include compatibility with an epistemic adjunct as in (26), use with the progressive aspect as in (27), use with a non-agentive verb as in (28), and use with a stative verb as in (29):

(26) *I **shall** probably look in at the College once or twice during the autumn, and hope to see you then.* [ICE-GB W1B-014 #69:4]

(27) *I understand that I **shall** be using this under my own responsibility.* [ICE-GB W1B-017 #115:14]

(28) *As we **shall** discover, the concept of child abuse is an extremely elusive one and means different things to different people.* [ICE-GB W2B-017 #26:1]

(29) *I **shall** have a fever by tonight, blood poisoning soon after.* [ICE-GB W2F-015 #131:1]

Like epistemic *will*, epistemic *shall* may occur in the apodosis of a conditional construction, as in:

(30) *if we cannot keep up with the competition then we **shall** uh have the kind of dire consequences which at the beginning of his talk uh David Baldwin uh was referring to.* [ICE-GB S2A-031 #53:2:A]

3.2.2   *Root* shall

Shall is sometimes volitional, more specifically intentional. It usually occurs with a 1st person subject (that with a 2nd or 3rd person subject more normally carrying a deontic implication). Examples follow:

(31) a. *We **shall** overcome.* [C-US Frown B02 79]
      b. *However as usual I **shall** begin with a review of the economic situation and prospects.* [ICE-GB S2B-041 #58:2:A]

The only truly deontic meaning found with the items under review is that which Huddleston and Pullum (2002:194) describe as 'constitutive/regulative', used with a 3rd person subject, and normally found in legal documents, regulations, and the like, as in (32):

(32) a. *Any time or place nominated for settlement* **shall** *merely be for convenience of the parties and their legal representatives.* [ICE-AUS W1B(noone):196]

b. *The Chairperson* **shall** *convene a meeting of the Council upon receipt of a written request for a meeting signed by at least four(4) Councillors (Subsection 128 (4) of the Act).* [ICE-AUS W2D-009(noone):44]

Further uses of *shall* which are identified by Huddleston and Pullum (2002:194) and Palmer (1990:74) as deontic might equally well be treated (and are as such in the present study) as volitional on the grounds that *shall* alternates readily with *will*. These include cases such as (33), where the speaker indicates a readiness to carry out the activity, and cases of the type *You shall have it tomorrow* (of which no corpus examples were found), where again the speaker indicates a readiness to carry out the activity but further, perhaps, undertakes an obligation or gives a guarantee to do so.

(33) a. **Shall** *I tell you what I did today and didn't do today.* [ICE-AUS S1A-100(M):2]

b. *What do you say, Mum?* **Shall** *I make an appointment with her?* [ICE-AUS W2F-020(noone):65]

3.2.3 *Frequencies of* shall

In Leech's (2003) study *shall* was found to have suffered the greatest decrease in frequency between 1961 and 1991/2 of all the modals in AmE writing, and the second largest in BrE (declining by 43.8% from Brown to Frown and 43.7% from LOB to FLOB). In the present study *shall* was outstripped by the only other modal auxiliary examined, *will*, by a ratio of 27.5:1. There were some striking differences between the dialects: the dispreference for *shall* was found to be less severe in the British corpus (with 223 tokens per million words) than in the Australian (100) and the American (102) corpora. The numbers for *shall* in C-US would have been even smaller had it not been for their high frequency in one, religious, text (SBC-020).

A comparison of the frequencies for *shall* across the spoken and written categories provides further insights into its relative unpopularity (see Table 4). If we focus on root *shall*, whose 322 tokens vastly outnumbered those of its epistemic counterpart (21 tokens), we find a major difference between speech and writing in the ICE-AUS results (the ratio for root *shall* being 1:3.5) suggestive of a decline in progress. Were it not for the skewing resulting from the presence of a religious text in C-US (SBC-020), as mentioned above, a similar ratio might have occurred for AmE: as it was, the ratio was 1:1.5)

Table 4. Frequencies for *shall/shan't* in ICE-AUS, ICE-GB, and C-US. (Figures normalized to tokens per one million words; raw figures in parentheses.)

		ICE-AUS	ICE-GB	C-US	TOTAL
Root	Spoken	50 (30)	213 (128)	59 (7)	(165)
	Written	173 (69)	203 (81)	88 (7)	(157)
	Total	99 (99)	209 (209)	71 (14)	(322)
Epistemic	Spoken	0 (0)	5 (3)	52 (6)	(9)
	Written	3 (1)	28 (11)	0 (0)	(12)
	Total	1 (1)	14 (14)	31 (6)	(21)
	TOTAL	100 (100)	223 (223)	102 (20)	(343)

As Table 3 above shows, *shall* prefers a 1st person subject in both its root and epistemic uses. In the case of root *shall* this preference is weaker in AusE (a finding possibly related to the finding, noted in Section 3.1.4 above, that root *will* more strongly prefers a 1st person subject in AusE).

3.3   *Be going to*

As Table 1 above indicates, *be going to* was the most frequent of the semi-modals. *Be going to* is an idiomatic expression which derives historically from the auxiliary *be* in construction with the lexical verb *go*, from which the meanings of motion and progressivity have been bleached in contemporary English. In some varieties the infinitival *to* is incorporated into a morphological compound that is typically represented in informal writing as *gonna*, sometimes *gunna*. There were 1689 tokens of *be going to* in the three corpora (as against 1032 tokens of *gonna/gunna*). The magnitude of the difference between the frequencies of the full form versus the compound in the three varieties (1047:9 in BrE, 574:617 in AusE, 68:406 in AmE) indicates that dissimilar transcription conventions were probably in operation for the various corpus compilation projects, but is undoubtedly also suggestive of dialectal variation, with AmE most tolerant of the compound.

3.3.1   *Epistemic* be going to

Epistemic *be going to* differs from *will* in always locating the situation in future time. When *be* is present tense it carries an implicature of immediacy, typically being used with situations that are about to occur or are already in train. This implicature is undoubtedly derived from the 'current orientation' (Palmer 1990:144) associated with present tense forms of *be*: the future is referred to from the standpoint of the present, thereby suggesting that there are features of the present time that are determining future events. In (34), for example, the game is understood to be in progress and nearing completion:

(34) *You're of course **gonna** win. Oh my God, here you go. We – oh you got him.* [C-US SBC-024 727–736]

Sometimes an adverb such as *just* or *now* is used to reinforce this sense of immediacy, as in:

(35) a. *OK Now I'm just **going to** put this into the folder.* [ICE-AUS S1A-081(A):409]
 b. *I'm just **going to** top up my tea again if you don't mind.* [ICE-GB S1A-067 #169:1:B]

(36) a. *So the convention clearly **is** now **going to** involve parties.* [ICE-GB S1B-011 #140:1:A]
 b. *Now you've been a scholar all your life and now suddenly you're **going to** be catapulted into public life as as Chief.* [ICE-GB S1B-047 #11:1:A]

A number of the familiar co-occurrence patterns that are associated with epistemic modality occur with *be going to*. These include compatibility with epistemic adjuncts as in (37), use with the progressive aspect as in (38), use with the passive voice as in (39), use with non-agentive verbs as in (40), use with stative verbs as in (41), use in the existential-*there* construction as in (42), and use in the *it*-extraposition construction as in (43):

(37) *Given the fact that most people see libraries as being to them as a user a relatively cost free if there's going to be a cost put on accessing electronic source material **is** this perhaps **going to** diminish the general usage of libraries.* [ICE-AUS S1B-043(A):199]

(38) *Um, the other thing I realize is,... uh,... think about how much of the time you're **gonna** be doing that.* [C-US SBC 016: 151–157]

(39) *Oh that's a big word. They're **going to** be impressed with that one.* [ICE-AUS S1A-043(B):270]

(40) *they're **gonna** die.* [C-US SBC 028: 470–471]

(41) *I want you to put that down.... cause it's **gonna** be important.* [C-US SBC 012: 1077–1082]

(42) *There's **going to** be dozens of celebrities twenty bands and in actual fact over two thousand five hundred people taking part in the parade.* [ICE-AUS S2A-010(A):8]

(43) *Another important aspect of speech-database collecting is the overall time it **is going to** take to mark-up a database of known size.* [ICE-AUS W2A-032(noone):18]

3.3.2   *Root* be going to

Like *shall*, *be going to* can be dynamic, but it tends to have the weaker sense of intention rather than willingness. Thus in (44) *I'm not going to talk about my credibility* would be appropriately paraphrased by "I don't intend to" whereas *I won't talk about my credibility* in the same context would be paraphraseable by "I refuse to".

(44)   *Well I'm not **going to** talk about my credibility.* [ICE-AUS S1B-046(B):176]

As Huddleston and Pullum (2002:212) observe, the difference illustrated here would be more pronounced in the preterite: in a situation where the speaker had planned to talk about his credibility but subsequently changed his mind it would be more appropriate for him to say *I wasn't going to talk about my credibility* than *I wouldn't talk about my credibility.*

The orientation towards intention is evident as well in cases where the matrix tense is past, as in (45), where *was going to* focuses on the intention that obtained previously, rather than on the intended tipping, and accordingly the sentence does not entail that the tipping actually occurred.

(45)   *I **was going to** tip them, but I wasn't prepared to b-.. buy the chair.* [C-US SBC 1168.41–1174.81]

3.3.3   *Frequencies of* be going to

As Table 1 above indicates, *be going to* was more than twice as frequent in the American corpus as in the Australian or British corpora. Leech's (2003) study confirms that *be going to* enjoyed a spectacular increase in popularity (51.6%) in American writing between 1961 and 1991/2 and suggests that it may be in the process of usurping some of the functions of *will* (see below). Leech's figures indicate that a significantly smaller increase has occurred in British writing over the same period (only18.5%). In a follow-up analysis of spoken British data (using a selection of texts from the Survey of English Usage corpus and ICE-GB) Leech noted a pronounced increase in the popularity of *be going to*, leading him to conclude: "The hypothesis that *be going to* has been increasing in frequency as a consequence of grammaticalization appears to be supported for spoken British English, though not for written British English" (p.232).

Of the items under review it is *be going to* that, as Table 5 shows, evidences by far the greatest preference for occurrence in speech over writing (by a ratio of 9.9:1). This finding suggests strongly that colloquialization is a relevant factor in the growing popularity of *be going to*. Another possible factor is 'Americanization', given that not only is *be going to* more frequent in AmE, but also the preference for speech over writing in the distribution of *be going to* is (slightly) stronger in AmE (10.5:1) than in the other two varieties (9.4:1 in AusE, and 9.2:1 in BrE).

The attractiveness of *be going to* for contemporary speakers may also be related to its syntactic flexibility. It can occur in a wider range of environments than *will* because *be* has the full set of inflectional forms apart from the present participle (*being going to).

Table 5. Frequencies for *be going to/gonna* in ICE-AUS, ICE-GB, and C-US. (Figures normalized to tokens per one million words; raw figures in parentheses.)

		ICE-AUS	ICE-GB	C-US	TOTAL
Root	Spoken	743 (446)	722 (433)	1743 (203)	(1082)
	Written	90 (36)	53 (21)	125 (10)	(67)
	Total	482 (482)	454 (454)	1084 (213)	(1149)
Epistemic	Spoken	1110 (666)	920 (552)	2078 (242)	(1460)
	Written	108 (43)	125 (50)	238 (19)	(112)
	Total	709 (709)	602 (602)	1329 (261)	(1572)
	TOTAL	1191 (1191)	1056 (1056)	2413 (474)	(2721)

The attractiveness of *be going to* for contemporary speakers may also be related to its syntactic flexibility. It can occur in a wider range of environments than *will* because *be* has the full set of inflectional forms apart from the present participle (*being going to).

Finally, is *be going to* as 'personal' as epistemic *will*? If we base our answer on that use of the two modal expressions which has by far the highest percentage of 1st person subjects (the root use), as Table 3 above indicates root *be going to* (for which 63.7% of tokens had a 1st person subject) was marginally less personal than root *will* (with 68.1%). By contrast, root *be going to* more strongly favoured a 2nd person subject (15.4%) than did root *will* (7.6%).

3.4 *Be about to*

3.4.1 *Meanings of* be about to

Be about to, which does not express root meaning, is like *be going to* in always locating the situation in future time when *be* is present tense, but the sense of immediacy that *be about to* carries is even stronger than is the case with *be going to*. For instance the use of *be about to* in (46a) suggests the imminence of the landing, and in (46b) the imminent appearance of the army detachments (which do in fact appear by the time the next few words have been uttered):

(46) a. I think I can hear the sound of an aircraft, uh in the distance, and I think they're *about to* come in to land. [ICE-GB S2A-008 #103:2:A]

b. And now following, *about to* come into our view coming into our view now, the detachments from the army. [ICE-GB S2A-019 #65:1:A]

Not surprisingly collocation with *just* is common, and more so than with *be going to*:

(47)   a.   *And so yeah I got home and um I put the garbage out and just just **about to** put the garbage out and the phone rang and I thought oh here we go.* [ICE-AUS S1A-007(B):204]

   b.   *I was just **about to** tuck into it and I noticed this great fly soaked in tomato sauce.* [ICE-GB S1A-055 #222:1:B]

While *be about to* is less grammaticalized than *be going to* (whose auxiliarization is in evidence phonologically in the appearance of *gonna* and semantically in the development of its volitional sense), there are several examples which suggest that *be about to* may have started to undergo a similar semantic development. In (48), for example, *am not about to* is paraphraseable as "refuse to":

(48)   *I wanted to tell you this because we were talking about it when I saw you and I wanted you to realise that I was **am** not **about to** be taken for a ride.* [ICE-GB W1B-005 #49:3]

3.4.2   *Frequencies of* be about to

In terms of its frequency *be about to* is a minor item (as Table 1 shows). Its popularity in speech and writing is comparable (being marginally preferred in the latter by a ratio of 1.1:1). Given the semantic similarities between *be about to* and (epistemic) *be going to* it is not surprising that they display similar behaviour in subject selection (as Table 3 above indicates, both strongly preferring a 3rd person subject and with 1st person preferred over 3rd person).

3.5   *Want to*

3.5.1   *Meanings of* want to

In Modern English *want to* is the item most consistently associated with the expression of volition, with a meaning comparable to that of willingness *will*. In the following examples *want to* is parahraseable by "be willing to".

(49)   a.   *when it comes to the the test before it you think oh I don't **want to** study again.* [ICE-AUS S1A-087(B):220]

   b.   *when you **want to** come and visit us give us a ring.* [ICE-AUS S1A-083(A):168]

   c.   *My brother **wanted to** live my life for me.* [C-US Frown P05 88]

According to Krug (2000:117ff) *want to* is undergoing modalization in its assumption of morphological and semantic features typical of modal auxiliaries. Morphologically, we find that in some varieties the infinitival *to* is incorporated into a compound that is often written in informal styles as *wanna*. There were 1577 tokens of *want to* in the three corpora (as against 320 tokens of *wanna*), indicating that as yet the level of acceptance for *wanna* is significantly less than that for *gonna*. As was the case with *be going to/gonna*, the magnitude of the difference between the frequencies of the full form versus the compound in the three varieties (575:3 in BrE, 841:198 in AusE, and 161:119 in AmE) again suggests that dissimilar transcription conventions were in operation for the various corpus compilation projects, but is undoubtedly also indicative of dialectal variation, with AmE once more the most tolerant of the compound.

Semantically, we find *want to* beginning to develop the same type of root/epistemic semantic duality that is characteristic of the modal class, as in (50), where the meaning of *wanna* is ambivalently dynamic ("he wouldn't be keen to get ….") and epistemic ("it would be unfortunate if he got …").

(50)   *Tough games for Agassi now. He wouldn't **wanna** get behind two sets to love against a big serve volleyer like Martin who's got some good groundies too.* [ICE-AUS S2A-004(B):138]

3.5.2   *Frequencies of* want to

The semi-modal *want to* was more than twice as popular in the American corpus than in the British (2.5:1), and almost 50% more popular than in the Australian corpus (1.4:1). These findings are compatible with those of two recent diachronic investigations that attest to the rising popularity of *want to*, particularly in AmE. Krug (2000) compared the frequencies of *want to* in samples of press and fictional writing in LOB/Brown and FLOB/Frown and concluded, on the basis of massive increases in the American corpora, that "while the rise of the new volitional modal probably did not originate in the US, the change obviously caught on more rapidly here than in Britain." (p.135). Leech's (2003) study found that *want to* enjoyed a spectacular increase in popularity (of 70%) in American writing between 1961 and 1991/2, but that a comparable increase did not occur in British writing (with *want to* in fact suffering a slight decline of 3.1%). Given these differences it is clearly important to examine the generic distribution of this and the other items under investigation (see below).

The findings of the present study confirm that *want to* is more strongly preferred in speech than in writing (by a ratio of 3.3:1), albeit less overwhelmingly than *be going to* (see Section 3.3.3. above). These findings confirm both the accuracy of Krug's (2000:136) claim that it is "approximately three times more common in spoken English". They furthermore confirm the validity of Krug's suggestion that "spoken performance data are influencing the written medium towards a greater use of this lexeme" (p.136); in other words, that colloquialization has had an important role to play in the frequency gains experienced by *want to* in contemporary English.

The findings for person (see Table 3 above) may hold the key to the relationship between *want to* and root *will*. *Want to* far more commonly takes a 2nd person subject (28.5%) than does root *will* (7.7%), while by contrast *want to* selects a 1st person subject less commonly (40.5%) than does root *will* (68.1%). This may suggest that *want to* is not invading the semantic territory of root *will* indiscriminately, but rather in a way that is bringing about a (partial) distributional complementarity.

Table 6. Frequencies for *want to/wanna* in ICE-AUS, ICE-GB, and C-US. (Figures normalized to tokens per one million words; raw figures in parentheses.)

		ICE-AUS	ICE-GB	C-US	TOTAL
Root	Spoken	1450 (870)	815 (489)	1958 (228)	(1587)
	Written	413 (165)	218 (87)	613 (49)	(301)
	Total	1035 (1035)	576 (576)	1410 (277)	(1888)
Epistemic	Spoken	6 (4)	3 (2)	9 (1)	(7)
	Written	0 (0)	0 (0)	25 (2)	(2)
	Total	4 (4)	2 (2)	15 (3)	(9)
	TOTAL	1039 (1039)	578 (578)	1425 (280)	(1897)

4. The Australian English questionnnaire

The data yielded by the Australian English questionnaire (see Table 7) served to reinforce some of the corpus findings. A sign of the vitality of *be going to* is its popularity amongst younger speakers in the questionnaire: *be going to* was tolerated comparatively more readily by younger respondents. A comparison of the youngest and oldest groups (10–24 vs 65+) reveals that both expressed a preference for *be going to* over *will* in speech but the preference was considerably stronger in the first group (2.1:1) than in the second (1.3:1). Even more striking was the tolerance towards *be going to* in writing shown by the youngest group (1:1.8) by comparison with the intolerance of the oldest group (1:9.7).

Table 7. *Will* and *be going to* in the Australian English Questionnaire

		Age 10–24	Age 25–44	Age 45–64	Age 65+	Total
Spoken	*Will*	16 (33%)	17 (41%)	41 (35%)	74 (44%)	148 (39%)
	Be going to	33 (67%)	24 (59%)	75 (65%)	96 (56%)	228 (61%)
Written	*Will*	32 (64%)	32 (78%)	100 (83%)	155 (91%)	319 (84%)
	Be going to	18 (36%)	9 (22%)	20 (17%)	16 (9%)	63 (16%)

5. Conclusion

We have found that each of the modal expressions studied has two basic meanings, root and epistemic, with a number of uses deriving via implicature from these basic meanings but not constituting separate meanings as such. While *will* is the primary exponent of both meanings, in all varieties, the supremacy of root *will* is under threat from *want to*, and that of epistemic *will* from *be going to*.

The study evidences a larger degree of colloquialization for *want to* in AmE (as reflected in its greater popularity in speech over writing in AmE than in the other varieties). This finding, combined with the finding that *want to* has a higher overall frequency in AmE suggests that it may be leading the way in the expansion of this semi-modal. It appears that colloquialization is even more strongly pushing the growth of *be going to*, whose preference for occurrence in speech by a ratio of almost ten to one is considerably greater than that for any of the other expressions examined. Frequencies for the remaining two items, *shall* and *be about to*, were small. The decline of *shall* has been less spectacular in BrE than in AusE and BrE, and in writing than speech. *Be about to* is available as an alternative to epistemic *be going to* for speakers who wish to express a strong sense of immediacy, but *be going to* has the advantage of having undergone a considerable degree of grammaticalization in the language.

References

Berglund, Ylva. 1997. "Future in Present-day English: corpus-based evidence on the rivalry of expressions". *ICAME Journal* 21: 7–19.

Berglund, Ylva. 2000. "*Gonna* and *going to* in the spoken component of the British National Corpus". *Corpus linguistics and linguistic theory*, ed. by Christian Mair and Marianne Hundt, 35–49. Amsterdam: Rodopi.

Biber, Douglas, Susan Conrad and Randi Reppen. 1998. *Corpus linguistics: Investigating language structure and use*. Cambridge: Cambridge University Press.

Biber, Douglas, Stig Johansson, Geoffrey Leech, Susan Conrad and Edward Finegan. 1999. *Longman grammar of spoken and written English*. London: Longman.

Coates, Jennifer. 1983. *The semantics of the modal auxiliaries*. London: Croom Helm.

Collins, Peter. 1991. "*Will* and *shall* in Australian English". *English computer corpora: Selected papers and research guide*, ed. by Stig Johansson and Anna-Brita Stenström, 181–199. Berlin: Mouton de Gruyter.

Gotti, Maurizio. 2003. "*Shall* and *will* in contemporary English: A comparison with past uses". *Modality in contemporary English*, ed. by Roberta Facchinetti, Manfred Krug and Frank Palmer, 267–300. Berlin: Mouton de Gruyter.

Huddleston, Rodney and Geoffrey Pullum. 2002. *The Cambridge grammar of the English language*. Cambridge: Cambridge University Press.

Krug, Manfred. 2000. *Emerging English modals. A corpus-based study of grammaticalization*. Berlin: Mouton de Gruyter.

Leech, Geoffrey. 2003. "Modality on the move: The English modal auxiliaries 1961–1992". *Modality in contemporary English*, ed. by Roberta Facchinetti, Manfred Krug and Frank Palmer, 223–240. Berlin: Mouton de Gruyter.

Mindt, Dieter. 1995. *An empirical grammar of the English verb: Modal verbs*. Berlin: Cornelsen Verlag.

Palmer, Frank. 1990. *Modality and the English modals*. London: Longman.

Name index

Subject index

Language index

Studies in Language Companion Series

A complete list of titles in this series can be found on the publishers' website, *www.benjamins.com*